Civil Liberties in Scotland
Cases & Materials

Civil Liberties in Scotland: Cases & Materials

Second Edition

K.D. EWING, LL.B. Ph.D.
Fellow of Trinity Hall, Cambridge,
Lecturer in Law in the University of Cambridge

&

W. FINNIE, LL. B.
Lecturer in Constitutional and Administrative Law,
University of Edinburgh

EDINBURGH
W. GREEN & SON LTD.
Law Publishers
St. Giles Street
1988

First Published in 1982
Second Edition 1988
Reprinted 1995

ISBN 0 414 00844 8

Printed in Great Britain
by Antony Rowe Ltd,
Chippenham, Wiltshire

Foreword to the First Edition

by
The Right Hon. Lord Murray

It is the mark of a mature, civilised society that its citizens enjoy and undertake rights and duties as persons which promote their integrity and freedom as individuals within the law. In a democratic society their essential equality as individuals is given fuller recognition. While these legal relations in no sense exhaust the law of persons, they form a central core of law which has special constitutional and social importance. This is the field of civil liberties and, on a wider and more abstract plane, of human rights. Civil liberties may be codified, as in many formal written constitutions, or they may be embedded mainly in the matrix of the ordinary law, as in countries of the common law style. Where there is no systematic codification, as in this country, there is the greater need for textbooks which make a critical and comprehensive study of these matters. The present book is an essay to that end, aiming at a concise yet reasonably comprehensive account of civil liberties in Scotland.

The authors of this slim but informative work are pioneers in a field which presents special problems in a small jurisdiction living in the shadow of a larger neighbour. At the same time proper note has to be taken of similar issues arising south of the Border, for example under United Kingdom statutes, which have been the subject of judicial determination there. The larger jurisdiction is likely to present more of these, especially in areas such as employment rights or discrimination on grounds of race or sex. These subjects are usefully covered. Inevitably it must be a matter of judgment what to include and what to omit, and the room for discussion is limited. Breach of the peace, for instance, is a topic which could well invite wider discussion; and petitions to the High Court for liberation might well have been mentioned. But space is precious. This well-packed volume will prove valuable, I am sure, to the ordinary legal practitioner as well as to students and citizens who wish to be well-informed about civil liberties in Scotland.

Edinburgh
July 1982   R.K.M.

PREFACE

In recent years, civil liberties have been a matter of acute concern. Debates about the scope of police powers; the purposes for and circumstances in which people may assemble, march and protest; and the effects of racial discrimination are all very familiar. This concern is reflected by the growing interest in civil liberties in law teaching throughout the country, with many institutions now offering a separate course in the subject, and with most constitutional law teachers devoting a considerable period of time to its exposition.

As we pointed out in the preface to the last edition, this is one of the first books on the subject in Scotland. It is perhaps surprising that the matter has lain dormant for so long: there is a clear need for a Scottish contribution because in many respects the law is distinctly Scottish, with the field being regulated by peculiarly Scottish statutes and by decisions of the Scottish courts. To a greater extent than was possible in the previous edition, we have sought on this occasion to emphasise this dimension while recognising, of course, that in many respects the law is the same as in England and Wales, with the process of convergence being only encouraged by the prominence assumed by the European Convention on Human Rights.

Our aim in this edition is to provide a compilation of materials mainly for the first-year student of civil liberties who may be taking the subject as part of a wider study of constitutional law. In so doing we are grateful to our publishers for having agreed to give us more space. This has enabled us not only to update and revise in order to take account of the major developments since the last edition: it has also enabled us to extend our treatment of the European Convention on Human Rights and to include new material on privacy (Chapter 4) and on official information (Chapter 7). The provision of extra space has also enabled us to respond to the very helpful reviews of the previous edition. As a result we hope that students and teachers will find this edition more useful than the last.

We wish to renew our gratitude to those people who helped in the completion of the first edition. To that list we should like to add by acknowledging the invaluable assistance provided by Val Chuter, Helen Dignan and Lisa White, who transformed chaotic scrawl into legible typescript, Conor Gearty for much helpful discussion of underlying issues of principle, and Andrew Mitchell for long tedious hours of proof-reading. We also wish to acknowledge again our great debt to Miss Iris Stewart who again responded with kindness and patience to the authors who on this occasion missed many publishing deadlines. Finally, we wish to record that the work is a joint work, that both authors/editors accept full responsibility for its contents; and that we alone are responsible for any errors.

We have endeavoured to state the law as at 31 December 1987, but have been able to take account of some later developments.

24 June 1988   KEITH EWING
                                                               WILSON FINNIE

TABLE OF CONTENTS

CHAPTER 7 — FREEDOM OF EXPRESSION

CHAPTER 8 — FREEDOM OF ASSEMBLY AND PUBLIC ORDER

TABLE OF CASES QUOTED

TABLE OF LEGISLATION QUOTED

CHAPTER 1

THE BACKGROUND TO CIVIL LIBERTIES LAW

I. INTRODUCTION

THE civil liberties of a people will depend upon a wide range of social, economic and political factors. The law merely reflects the interplay of non-legal forces. Important amongst the many considerations which will shape civil liberties law are institutional factors, including the structure and form of government within a nation, and the extent to which government is conducted according to law. In this chapter we examine the constitutional context of civil liberties in Scotland. First, we consider the extent to which the people of Scotland, as a part of the United Kingdom, have limited authority to determine the scope of their own freedom and liberty (whether political or economic). As in other areas of the law, civil liberties are determined in large measure by the Westminster Parliament, the composition of which may not reflect the political wishes of the people of Scotland. In this chapter we also consider the role of the courts in constraining the power of government. As we shall see, the judicial role in Scotland is limited compared with the judicial role in other western jurisdictions. Here the judges have no power to review the content of legislation, but may only review the manner of its enactment. But this is not to belittle the role of the courts. Apart from the pivotal role of the judges in the interpretation of legislation, the common law continues to play a significant part in the area of civil liberties.

II. THE CONSTITUTIONAL POSITION OF SCOTLAND

Until 1707 Scotland was a sovereign nation albeit that it had shared its monarch with another since 1603. Until 1707 Scotland had its own executive, legislature and judiciary. Since 1707, however, Scotland has been a member of a United Kingdom which was expanded in 1800 to include Ireland, and which was reduced in the twentieth century to exclude what is now the independent sovereign state of the Republic of Ireland. As a member of the United Kingdom, Scotland is dwarfed politically by England. For all practical purposes the destiny of the nation is determined in London. The Executive is based in London, though there is now a measure of administrative devolution. This may be, however, of rather limited legal significance, as the following case indicates.

1.   Agee v. Lord Advocate
1977 S.L.T. (Notes) 54

On 16 February 1977 the Home Secretary made a deportation order under s. 5(1) of the Immigration Act 1971. The order required the petitioner to leave the United Kingdom on the ground that the Home Secretary had deemed it to be conducive to the public good to deport the petitioner. The order was served in Edinburgh where Agee was residing. Thereupon he sought suspension of the order and a declarator that it was *ultra vires*. The petitioner also sought interdict and interim interdict against the Chief Constable of the Lothian and Borders Police from arresting him and enforcing his removal from the jurisdiction of the court. The motion for interim interdict was refused.

LORD KINCRAIG: "The sole ground advanced by counsel for the petitioner as justification for the motion was that there was a real question to try between the parties, namely, whether the deportation order, not having been made by the Secretary of State for Scotland, could effectively be enforced in Scotland, having regard to the provisions of s. 2 of the Secretary for Scotland Act 1887. Section 2(1) of the 1887 Act is in the following terms: 'All powers and duties vested in and imposed on one of Her Majesty's Principal Secretaries of State by any Act of Parliament, law, or custom, so far as such powers and duties relate to Scotland, and so far as they have not already been transferred to, vested in, and imposed on the Secretary for Scotland, shall, subject to the exceptions hereinafter mentioned, be transferred to, vested in, and imposed on the Secretary for Scotland.'

The office of Secretary for Scotland was initiated by the Secretary for Scotland Act 1885, to which Secretary certain powers and duties of Her Majesty's Principal Secretaries of State under certain enactments were transferred (see s. 5 of the 1885 Act). Counsel for the petitioner submitted that by virtue of s. 2(1) the exercise of any powers and the performance of any duties given by Acts of Parliament to a Principal Secretary of State, so far as they relate to Scotland, must be exercised and performed by the Secretary of State for Scotland, the successor to the Secretary for Scotland. He argued that as the Immigration Act 1971 applied to Scotland, and the power to enforce a deportation order was to be exercised in Scotland, that power could not be exercised by Mr Rees but by the Secretary of State for Scotland only, and the order not having been made by the Secretary of State for Scotland was not a valid warrant for requiring the petitioner to leave Scotland, or for any proceeding to enforce the order.

This is a question of law which is capable of being answered without further procedure. Unless counsel for the petitioner can show that his submission is correct in law interim interdict must be refused.

In my judgement the submission which was made to me is fallacious. The office of Secretary for Scotland remained in existence until 1926 when, by the Secretaries of State Act 1926, it was abolished. Section 1(1) of that Act provided that after the appointment of an additional principal Secretary of State: 'all the powers and duties of the Secretary for Scotland shall . . . become powers and duties of a Principal Secretary of State, and the office of Secretary for Scotland

and the office of Parliamentary Under Secretary for Health for Scotland shall be abolished.' The particular Secretary of State to whom the powers of the Secretary for Scotland were to pass is not stated in the section, and accordingly the section means that the powers and duties of the Secretary for Scotland shall become the powers and duties of any Principal Secretary of State. This is clear from the terms of s. 1(2), which provided that in the appointment of the additional Secretary of State, all property which at the time of the appointment was vested in the Secretary for Scotland as such, was to be transferred to and become vested in that additional Secretary of State. Further, s. 12 of the Interpretation Act 1889 provides in subs. (3) that in every Act whether passed before or after the commencement of the 1889 Act the expression 'Secretary of State' shall mean one of Her Majesty's Principal Secretaries of State for the time being. Thus the powers and duties of the Secretary for Scotland became vested in any one of Her Majesty's Principal Secretaries of State, including the Home Secretary.

The Immigration Act 1971 provides that powers of deporting persons under that Act shall be exercised by the Secretary of State, which means one of Her Majesty's Principal Secretaries of State. The Home Secretary is one of these. By virtue of s. 1(1) of the 1926 Act he is empowered to exercise the powers of the former Secretary for Scotland in so far as they relate to Scotland. For these reasons I hold that the attack on the validity of the deportation order, in so far as the enforcement of it in Scotland is concerned, fails, and that on that ground the petitioner's motion for interim interdict must be refused."

The Secretary of State sits in the Cabinet as the political head of the Scottish Office which is based in Edinburgh, with an office in London. There has been devolved to the Scottish Office responsibility for a range of administrative matters and as a result several of the principal departments of the Scottish Office will be engaged in work which will impinge in some way on civil liberties. These include the Scottish Development Department, the responsibilities of which include local government, roads and transport; the Scottish Education Department, responsible for schools and colleges (though not the universities); and the Scottish Home and Health Department. The responsibilities of the last include the police, prisons and the civil and criminal law. Matters not within the administrative jurisdiction of the Scottish Office will be the responsibility of the specialist "British" government department. So the Department of Employment, the Ministry of Defence and the Home Office may all sponsor legislation which will have an important bearing on the civil liberties of the people of Scotland. In the case of the Home Office, for example, the Home Secretary is responsible for broadcasting throughout the country. Kellas (1984: 33) points out that it is normally assumed that Scottish Office functions: "are determined by the degree to which Scotland differs from the rest of the country. For example, where Scots law, local government, or education are involved, it is appropriate to place these under the Scottish Office, but where there is no distinctly Scottish characteristic about a government function, it should be performed by a Great Britain . . . department." As Kellas points out, however: "This approach is sensible and convincing until one reflects that perhaps all administration in Scotland has to deal with 'distinctly Scottish characteristics', since these arise out of the separateness of Scottish society itself" (p. 33).

So far as the legislature is concerned, this too is based in London. Again, however, there are modifications of the Westminster system of government to accommodate Scotland. Scotland is over-represented in the House of Commons, in terms of the ratio of seats to population. There are now 72 Scottish seats in the Commons, which is 11.2 per cent of the Great Britain total, though Scotland accounts for only 9.4% of the Great Britain population. In a very real sense, however, the Scots are disenfranchised in that the people of Scotland are governed according to the political choice of the people of England. In 1983 for example, the Conservatives won the general election by a substantial majority (397 seats to Labour's 209). The people of Scotland, however, voted for a Labour government, returning 41 Labour members, 21 Conservatives, eight Alliance and two Scottish Nationalists. This is a difficulty which would have been alleviated had the Scotland Act 1978 been implemented. This proposed a measure of legislative devolution to Scotland. It was proposed to create a single-chamber Scottish Assembly based in Edinburgh. The Assembly would be popularly elected for a fixed term of four years. It was proposed that the Assembly would have wide-ranging powers in order to "give closer democratic control" and "help to foster the distinctive national tradition of Scotland." Although it was proposed that some key issues would be reserved for the Westminster Parliament, the proposed area of devolved power had important implications for the power of the people of Scotland to control their own destiny in civil liberties questions.

2. Our Changing Democracy. Devolution to Scotland and Wales
Cmnd. 6348 (1975)

"144. The separate character of Scots law and of the Scottish legal system was specially recognised in the Union between Scotland and England, and in this distinctively Scottish field the Government believe that extensive devolution is particularly appropriate.

145. The Scottish administration will have wide responsibilities in the range of subjects constituting Scots private law, such as the law of persons, delict, contract, property, trusts and succession. The Government recognise the importance of the development and reform of Scots law as a coherent and distinctive system. There is however a complex interaction between those subjects and areas such as company law, industrial relations and consumer protection where

consistency with the law in other parts of the United Kingdom is particularly important, for example in order to maintain a common framework for trade. Further study is proceeding to find the best way of reconciling maximum devolution in the field of private law with these wider United Kingdom interests.

146. The Scottish Law Commission will continue after devolution to have a major role in the coherent development of the whole of Scots law, whether in devolved or non-devolved matters. Because the Commission's functions will span both fields, legislative responsibility for its constitution and structure must remain with Parliament. The Scottish administration will however be responsible for appointing the Chairman and members of the Commission, for its running and for its general programme of work, though the Government will remain able to refer non-devolved matters to it.

147. The Scottish administration will also be given responsibility for the general criminal law, including the right to create new offences, to redefine or abolish existing offences, to determine penalties and to regulate the treatment of offenders (including prisons). There will however be certain exceptions. Firstly, there are those that may affect the security of the state, like the law on treason, espionage and measures against terrorism. Secondly, there are areas where the law can work efficiently only if it is uniform, such as explosives, firearms, and dangerous drugs and poisons. Finally, there are offences relating essentially to subject fields which will not be devolved, like taxation and road traffic law.

148. The enforcement of the criminal law through the police and the prosecution system—which in Scotland is not in any way under the control of the police— is part of the responsibility of the Government for the maintenance of law and order and the security of the state, and will extend to offences within both devolved and other fields. It would not be right that responsibility for law enforcement should rest with members of an administration not directly answerable to Parliament. The Secretary of State and the Lord Advocate will therefore retain their present responsibilities with regard to police and prosecution respectively. The police will retain their existing status and their relationship with local authorities, and the function of prosecution will continue to be exercised through the Crown Office and the procurator fiscal service.

149. The government have considered with special care where responsibility should lie for the main Scottish courts—the supreme courts (the High Court of Jurisdiciary and the Court of Session), the sheriff courts and the district courts. The Government are satisfied that responsibility for the different levels ought not to be split—separation would pose difficult problems over such matters as jurisdiction, procedure and administration. They believe that the supreme court judges should continue to be appointed by The Queen on the recommendation of the Government, and that responsibility for their tenure and conditions of office should not be devolved. The Government also believe that questions affecting the right of appeal from the Court of Session to the House of Lords—the court of final appeal in civil matters from the courts of every part of the United Kingdom—must remain a United Kingdom responsibility.

150. There remains however the question whether responsibility for the court system and its administration should remain with the Government and Parliament, or should be devolved subject to the qualifications noted in the previous paragraph. There are powerful arguments on both sides. The courts are a distinctive part of the Scottish legal heritage, and may therefore seem wholly suitable to be

entrusted to the care of Scotland's new Assembly, under Parliament's continuing ultimate sovereignty. The concept of the development of Scots law as a coherent system argues in favour of devolving the courts and the legal system along with the substantive law. It may be difficult, if responsibility is split, to decide the allocation of such borderline topics as court procedure and the law of evidence. On the other hand, it is arguable that the courts are essential elements in the core of constitutional unity of the United Kingdom and in the fabric of law and order; and that since they have to deal with disputes involving both devolved and non-devolved law, they should not be the responsibility of an Assembly which has no functions in the non-devolved fields. The same factors of public policy and national security which are relevant to the police and prosecution functions (paragraph 148 above) point towards maintaining United Kingdom responsibility for the courts and their jurisdiction, administration and procedure."

These proposals were never implemented. The implementation of the Scotland Act 1978 was conditional on a referendum being held in which 40 per cent of those entitled to vote did so in favour of its terms. Although a majority of those voting voted in favour of devolution, this fell short of the required 40 per cent. As a result the Scotland Act 1978 was repealed. So all legislative business for Scotland is conducted by Westminster. It is true that since 1894 there has been a Scottish Grand Committee which consists of all Scottish members of the House. Second Reading may be referred to this committee provided that the Speaker certifies that it relates exclusively to Scotland, and provided that the minister moves a motion to refer. But it is to be noted that while the debate takes place in committee, the vote on the Second Reading takes place on the floor of the House. This serves to ensure that votes are determined by the British members of the House, and not the Scottish members. It is also the case that since 1957 and 1962 respectively there are two Scottish Standing Committees. "These Committees take the clause-by-clause examination of Bills, and vote on such clauses and amendments to them. . . Important Bills go to the first committee, and minor ones to the second" (Kellas, 1984:87). The government will have a majority on these committees. Yet, although the Westminster system has been modified in response to the Scottish dimension (and modified still further by the fact that the Scottish Grand Committee now sits in Edinburgh), these modifications serve only to highlight the fragile nature of the legitimacy of the system under which Scotland is governed. Regardless of how the people of the country vote, Scotland is governed through Parliament by an executive drawn from a party which does not command the confidence of the Scottish people. It is this question of the legitimacy of Westminster to determine the political and other freedoms of the Scots which apparently lay behind the argument in the following case.

3.   Sillars v. Smith
1982 S.L.T. 539

Four accused persons were charged with vandalism, contrary to s. 78 (1) of the Criminal Justice (Scotland) Act 1980. Each of them argued before the sheriff that the 1980 Act had no legal validity. The argument was rejected by the sheriff who convicted each of the accused. They then appealed by stated case to the High Court.

SHERIFF MACVICAR: "The pleas and arguments stated by all four appellants were identical, as are the matters which it is desired by them to bring under review. I have therefore taken the liberty of stating a single case in respect of all the appellants.

The only matter which it is sought to bring under review is my decision to repel the plea to the competence of the proceedings. The first-named appellant presented the argument, on behalf of himself and the other appellants, in the form of a prepared statement which he read to the court, and which is annexed to the complaint. The attack on the competence of the proceedings was founded on the proposition that the Criminal Justice (Scotland) Act 1980 (s. 78 of which created the offence of vandalism with which the appellants were charged) has no constitutional validity and therefore no legal force. The argument in support of that proposition may be summarised as follows: 1. The Scotland Act 1978 (now repealed) provides for the creation of a Scottish Assembly (s. 1(1)). That Assembly was empowered to make laws, to be called Scottish Assembly Acts, but such an Act should be law only to the extent that it was within the legislative competence of the Assembly (ss. 17 and 18). A provision was to be within the legislative competence of the Assembly if, and only if, the matter to which it related was a devolved matter (Sched. 2, art. 1). A devolved matter was one of those included in the groups in Pt. I of Sched. 10 to the Act (s. 63(2)). Group 25 (crime) of Pt. I of Sched. 10 was to cover all criminal matters, including offences against property. Therefore if the Scotland Act 1978 had become law, the passing of the Criminal Justice (Scotland) Act 1980 (or any equivalent statute) would have been within the legislative competence of the Scottish Assembly, and not of the Parliament of the United Kingdom at Westminster. 2. Section 83 (1) of the 1978 Act provided: 'The preceding provisions of this Act (and the Schedules relating to them) shall not come into operation until such day as the Secretary of State may by order appoint.'

Section 83(4) provided: 'The first order under the section shall not be made unless a draft of it has been laid before Parliament and approved by a resolution of each House of Parliament.' Section 85 provided: (1) Before a draft of the first order to be made under section 83 of this Act is laid before Parliament a referendum shall be held in accordance with Schedule 17 to this Act on the question whether effect is to be given to the provisions of this Act. (2) If it appears to the Secretary of State that less than 40 per cent of the persons entitled to vote in the referendum have voted "Yes" in reply to the question posed in the Appendix to Schedule 17 to this Act or that a majority of the answers given in the referendum have been "No" he shall lay before Parliament the draft of an Order in Council for the repeal of this Act. (3) If a draft laid before Parliament under this section is approved by a resolution of each House Her Majesty in Council may make an Order in the terms of the draft.' The question to be asked in the referendum referred to in s. 85, in terms of Sched. 17 was: 'Do you want the provisions of the Scotland

Act 1978 to be put into effect?' 3. A referendum was duly held, in accordance with the provisions of s. 85, on 1 March 1979. Thereafter, the Secretary of State laid before Parliament the draft of an Order in Council for the repeal of the 1978 Act, proceeding upon the narrative that it appeared to him, on consideration of the result of the referendum, that he was required by s. 85(2) of the said Act, to lay before Parliament such an order. The said draft was approved by resolution of each House, and on 26 July 1979 the Scotland Act (Repeal) Order 1979 (S.I. 1979 No. 1978) was made and came into operation. The 1978 Act was thereby repealed. 4. The repeal of the 1978 Act was not in accordance with the wishes of the Scottish people, as may be deduced from the following considerations: (a) although the published figures of the voting in the referendum disclosed that less than 40 per cent of the persons entitled to vote had voted 'Yes' in reply to the question posed, a clear majority of about 77,000, of those who actually voted, voted 'Yes'; (b) at the general election in May 1979, a clear majority of electors voted against the Conservative (or Unionist) party, which was committed to the repeal of the 1978 Act. Conservative (or Unionist) Members of Parliament were returned in only 22 out of the 71 Scottish seats; (c) about two-thirds of the Scottish Members of Parliament voted against the resolution of the House of Commons which approved the said draft Order in Council. 5. In any event, the Secretary of State acted unlawfully in laying the draft order before Parliament. He stated publicly that he was not satisfied with the accuracy of the electoral register, and was not justified in stating in the order that it appeared to him that he was required by s. 85(2) to lay the draft order before Parliament. 6. The supremacy of Parliament is not unchallengeable in Scotland. There is good authority for the view that this has always been so (*MacCormick* v. *Lord Advocate*, 1953 S.L.T. 255; 1953 S.C. 396, per Lord President Cooper, Lord Carmont concurring). Further, Parliament itself has recognised that its will must on occasion yield to the authority of bodies other than itself, both by the introduction of referenda into the process of legislation, and by its acceptance of the principle that its sovereignty can be subjected to orders of the European Economic Community. 7. In these circumstances, Parliament acted unlawfully in resolving that the Scotland Act 1978 should be repealed. Accordingly, the passing of the Criminal Justice (Scotland) Act proceeded upon a pre-existing illegality, and was therefore itself tainted with illegality, which rendered the Act invalid. Quod erat demonstrandum.

I found it unnecessary to consider the argument in detail. I rejected the plea to the competence of the proceedings, upon the view that it is not competent for a court of summary criminal jurisdiction to question the validity of an Act of Parliament."

At the hearing of the appeal, the appellants repeated many of the arguments which had been raised before the sheriff. The High Court (Lord Justice-Clerk Wheatley, Lords Hunter and Dunpark) dismissed the appeal, and the following opinion was delivered:

"The appellants inter alios were charged on a summary complaint with a contravention of s. 78 of the Criminal Justice (Scotland) Act 1980. When the case was called in the sheriff court the appellants pled not guilty to the charge, and when they appeared at the trial diet they tabled a plea to the competency of the complaint before they were called on to plead. The sheriff allowed this plea to be tabled late, and thereafter heard parties on it but rejected it. The appellants then adhered to their pleas of not guilty and the case proceeded to trial. In the event the sheriff found all four appellants guilty and imposed fines on each of them. His entitlement to find them guilty on the facts is not challenged, the present appeal being taken only against his rejection of the plea to the competency of the complaint.

The submission of the appellants to the sheriff was in effect that Parliament acted unlawfully in resolving that the Scotland Act 1978 (which made provision for the setting up of a Scottish Assembly with certain legislative powers) should be repealed. The Scotland Act 1978 accordingly stood with legislative effect, and the provisions thereof in relation to the legislative powers of the Assembly precluded the passing by Parliament of the Criminal Justice (Scotland) Act 1980. The purported passing of that Act therefore constituted an illegality which rendered that Act, and consequently s. 78 thereof, invalid. The supremacy of Parliament was not unchallengeable in the Scottish courts, and accordingly it was competent for a Scottish court to determine that illegality and give effect to the consequences thereof by holding that a charge based on that illegal section of that illegal Act was in itself fundamentally illegal. In dismissing the plea to the competency the sheriff simply said that he rejected it upon the view that it is not competent for a court of summary criminal jurisdiction to question the validity of an Act of Parliament.

When the case came to this court on appeal the same basic arguments were presented, although they were enveloped in a variety of submissions which we do not find necessary to rehearse. As in the sheriff court the submissions were presented by the first-named appellant and adopted by the others. We go straight to the fundamental question whether the vires of an Act of Parliament which has gone through the whole parliamentary process, has received the Royal Assent and been brought into operation can be competently challenged in a Scottish court. That question has been definitively answered by two Scottish cases which span over a century in time. In *The Edinburgh and Dalkeith Railway Company* v. *Wauchope* (1842) 1 Bell's App. Cas. 252 in the House of Lords Lord Campbell said at p. 279: 'All that a court of justice can look to is the parliamentary roll; they see that an act has passed both Houses of Parliament, and that it has received the royal assent, and no court of justice can enquire into the manner in which it was introduced into parliament, what was done previously to its being introduced, or what passed in parliament during the various stages of its progress through both Houses of Parliament. I therefore trust that no such enquiry will hereafter be entered into in Scotland, and that due effect will be given to every act of Parliament, both private as well as public, upon the just construction which appears to arise upon it'. In *MacCormick* v. *Lord Advocate*, 1953 S.L.T. 255; 1953 S.C. 396 Lord President Cooper said: 'This at least is plain that there is neither precedent nor authority of any kind for the view that the domestic Courts of either Scotland or England have jurisdiction to determine whether a governmental act of the type here in controversy is or is not conform to the provisions of a Treaty'. While that was said in the context of the issue in that case it is a clear illustration on the principle enunciated by Lord Campbell (supra).

We are satisfied that there is sufficient in these passages alone to warrant the rebuttal of the appellants' plea to the competency, based as it is on a submission that the Act of 1980 which had gone though all the parliamentary processes and received the Royal Assent is invalid. In that situation we find it unnecessary to deal with the ancillary arguments which were adduced in purported support of that basic argument, since they fall within Lord Campbell's veto.

The question of law stated by the sheriff is: 'Did I err in law in repelling the plea to the competency of the proceedings?'. We answer that question in the negative and refuse the appeal."

So far as the judicial system is concerned, there is a greater measure of autonomy. Indeed, the legal system is safeguarded by the Treaty of Union which provides:

"XIX. That the Court of Session or Colledge of Justice do after the Union and notwithstanding thereof remain in all time coming within Scotland as it is now constituted by the Laws of that Kingdom and with the same Authority and Priviledges as before the Union subject nevertheless to such Regulations for the better Administration of Justice as shall be made by the Parliament of Great Britain. . . . And that the Court of Justiciary do also after the Union and notwithstanding thereof remain in all time coming within Scotland as it is now constituted by the Laws of that Kingdom and with the same Authority and Priviledges as before the Union subject nevertheless to such Regulations as shall be made by the Parliament of Great Britain and without prejudice of other Rights of Justiciary And that all Admiralty Jurisdictions be under the Lord High Admirall or Commissioners for the Admiralty of Great Britain for the time being And that the Court of Admiralty now Established in Scotland be continued. . . And that all other Courts now in being within the Kingdom of Scotland do remain but subject to Alterations by the Parliament of Great Britain And that all Inferior Courts within the said Limits do remain subordinate as they are now to the Supream Courts of Justice within the same in all time coming And that no Causes in Scotland be cognoscible by the Court of Chancery Queens-Bench Common-Pleas or any other Court in Westminster-hall And that the said Courts or any other of the like nature after the Union shall have no power to Cognosce Review or Alter the Acts or Sentences of the Judicatures within Scotland or stop the Execution of the same And that there be a Court of Exchequer in Scotland after the Union for deciding Questions concerning the Revenues of Customs and Excises there. . ."

It is to be noted, however, that the Scottish legal system does not enjoy complete autonomy. In civil cases, there is a right of appeal from the Court of Session to the House of Lords which is thus Scotland's Supreme court in non-criminal cases. Although by convention two Scots-trained lawyers will sit in Scottish appeals, the majority of members in the House will not be Scots lawyers. The criminal law, however, is regulated only from Edinburgh. Although a right of appeal in criminal cases on indictment was introduced in 1926 by the Criminal Appeal (Scotland) Act 1926, no provision was made for an appeal from the High Court of Justiciary to the House of Lords. This right of appeal in criminal cases is now to be found in the Criminal Procedure (Scotland) Act 1975, s. 228, which provides also that the decision of the appeal court is final and not subject to review. Appeals in summary cases have a much longer history, but there is no appeal beyond the High Court in these either.

The Scottish judges thus have an important role to play in developing the common law so far as it affects civil liberties and in interpreting statutes which impose criminal penalties. As we shall discover, much of the law relating to civil liberties occupies this territory. This is particularly significant in view of the declaratory power of the High Court: "the High Court of Justiciary still retains a power to create new crimes" (Gordon, 1978: 23), a power which tends to undermine the principle that "no one should be punished for an act which was not legally proscribed at the time he did it" *(ibid.)* and which tends "to constitute a usurpation by the court of the functions of Parliament" *(ibid.)*. It is also significant in view of the broad, flexible and malleable nature of the common law offences of Scotland. As Lord Avonside said in *Khaliq* v. *H.M. Advocate,* 1984 S.L.T. 137:

"The great strength of our common law in criminal matters is that it can be invoked to fill a need. It is not static. Over the centuries it has operated unless its jurisdiction is displaced by statute or by decision of the courts. It did not weaken by time or history. It is alive today in dealing with the present age as it was in dealing with questions raised in the past."

But what some might see as a strength, others will regard as a weakness in the sense that the broad nature of the principle allows the courts informally to declare what are in effect new crimes. This was done in *Khaliq,* where it was held to be an offence to sell glue-sniffing kits to children. Although it may well be that such conduct should be restrained by the criminal law, it may be questioned by what authority the judges may properly impose such restraints. Lord Avonside was of the view that: "It might seem that Parliament has found difficulty in dealing with [the] situation, but, if so, that is all the more reason for applying our common law." Others might argue that the alleged "difficulty" of Parliament was all the more reason for the judges exercising caution and restraint. but although it is true that the High Court thus has wide powers in criminal matters, this is subject always to the legislative supremacy of Parliament, and the problems we have already discussed.

III.   CIVIL LIBERTIES AND THE COURTS IN SCOTLAND

1.   PARLIAMENTARY SUPREMACY

In most western jurisdictions the power of the legislature is limited by a constitution. Usually the constitution will contain a Bill of Rights which guarantees fundamental liberties which the legislature may not violate. In the event of doubt the judges may be called upon in the final analysis to determine whether or not a piece of legislation is inconsistent with the guarantees in the Bill of Rights. If it is, the legislation may be declared invalid. Such is the position in the United States, Canada and the Republic of Ireland. New Zealand is about to impose such a restriction on the power of its Parliament. The traditional British position, in contrast, is that there are no legal limits on the power of Parliament."For us an Act of Parliament duly passed by Lords and Commons and assented to by the King, is supreme, and we are bound to give effect to its terms" *(Mortensen* v. *Peters* (1906) 8 F.(J.) 93, at pp. 100-101 *per* Lord Justice-General Dunedin). In practice this gives the *executive*(not the *legislature*) enormous political power. In our system of government the executive controls the legislature in the sense that the leading members of the executive (the Prime Minister and the Cabinet) are also members of the legislature, by the fact that almost all legislative proposals are initiated by the executive, and by the fact that for political reasons M.P.s are bound to vote for their party in the House. In a very real sense, and to a very large extent, the legislature simply gives legal authority to the wishes of the executive. As a result there is now no adequate parliamentary scrutiny (not to say control) over the content of legislation. And because of the doctrine of parliamentary sovereignty there is no judicial control over the content of legislation. The duty of the courts is to approve that which has been passed by Parliament.

But is Parliament sovereign? In the view of Lord Cooper in *MacCormick* v. *Lord Advocate,* 1953 S.L.T. 255, the "principle of the unlimited sovereignty of Parliament is a distinctively English principle which has no counterpart in Scottish constitutional law" (at p. 262). Lord Cooper continued in a passage of the first importance:

"Considering that the Union legislation extinguished the Parliaments of Scotland and England and replaced them by a new Parliament, I have difficulty in seeing why it should have been supposed that the new Parliament of Great Britain must inherit all the peculiar characteristics of the English Parliament but none of the Scottish Parliament, as if all that happened in 1707 was that Scottish representatives were admitted to the Parliament of England. That is not what was done. Further, the Treaty and the associated legislation, by which the Parliament of Great Britain was brought into being as the successor of the separate Parliaments of Scotland and England, contain some clauses which expressly reserve to the Parliament of Great Britain powers of subsequent modification, and other clauses which either contain no such power or emphatically exclude subsequent alteration by declarations that the provisions shall be fundamental and unalterable in all time coming, or declarations of a like effect. I have never been able to understand how it is possible to reconcile with elementary canons of construction the adoption by the English constitutional theorists of the same attitude to these markedly different types of provisions."

So Parliament is not sovereign. It is a Parliament with limited powers, limited at least by the Treaty of Union, and perhaps to an even greater extent unspecified by Lord Cooper. These are, however, legal limits with no practical implications. For as Lord Cooper also said:

"Accepting it that there are provisions in the Treaty of Union and associated legislation which are 'fundamental law,' and assuming for the moment that something is alleged to have been done—it matters not whether with legislative authority or not—in breach of that fundamental law, the question remains whether such a question is determinable as a justiciable issue in the Courts of either Scotland or England, in the same fashion as an issue of constitutional *vires* would be cognisable by the supreme Courts of the United States, or of South Africa or Australia. I reserve my opinion with regard to the provisions relating expressly to this Court and to the laws 'which concern private right' which are administered here. This is not such a question, but a matter of 'public right' (Articles XVIII and XIX). To put the matter in another way, it is of little avail to ask whether the Parliament of Great Britain 'can' do this thing or that, without going on to inquire who can stop them if they do. Any person 'can' repudiate his solemn engagement but he cannot normally do so with impunity. Only two answers have been suggested to this corollary to the main question. The first is the exceedingly cynical answer implied by Dicey (*Law of the Constitution* (9th ed.), p. 82) in the statement that 'it would be rash of the Imperial Parliament to abolish the Scotch Courts, and assimilate the law of Scotland to that of England. But no one can feel sure at what point Scottish resistance to such a change would become serious.' The other answer was that nowadays there may be room for the invocation of an 'advisory opinion' from the International Court of Justice. On these matters I express no view. This at least is plain, that there is neither precedent nor authority of any kind for the view that the domestic Courts of either Scotland or England have jurisdiction to determine whether a governmental act of the type here in controversy is or is not conform to the provisions of a Treaty, least of all when that Treaty is one under which both Scotland and England ceased to be independent states and merged their identity in an incorporating union. From the standpoint both of constitutional law and of international law the position appears to me to be unique, and I am constrained to hold that the action as laid is incompetent in respect that it has not been shown that the Court of Session has authority to entertain the issue sought to be raised."

Although the passage is equivocal, Lord Cooper does appear to suggest that although in principle the British Parliament is not supreme, it is so in practice because no court will grant a remedy in the event of "unlawful" conduct. But the question which arises is: how does this affect civil liberties? The Treaty deals with questions which are at best marginal to the present inquiry: trade between the two Kingdoms; the status of the Church of Scotland; and the position of Scots law in the new arrangements.

In one other respect, however, the Treaty does potentially contain a provision of central importance which in the hands of creative judges could have been a means of imposing significant practical limits on the power of Parliament. Indeed, Article XVIII of the Treaty offered the possibility that a Bill of Rights could have been introduced into Scots law indirectly. Article XVIII provides:

"That the laws concerning regulation of trade customs and such excises to which Scotland is by virtue of this treaty to be liable be the same in Scotland from and after the union as in England and that all other laws in use within the Kingdom of Scotland do after the union and notwithstanding thereof remain the same as before (except such as are contrary to or inconsistent with this treaty) but alterable by the Parliament of Great Britain with this difference betwixt the laws concerning public right policy and civil government and those which concern private right that the laws which concern public right policy and civil government may be made the same throughout the whole United Kingdom but that no alteration be made in laws which concern private right except for evident utility of the subjects within Scotland"

The Article is considered in the following case, which appears to foreclose the possibility of any judicial use of the Treaty as a limit to the power of Parliament.

4.   Gibson v. Lord Advocate
1975 S.L.T. 134

Gibson was a fisherman from Banff. Before the accession of the United Kingdom to the European Communities he was one of a small number of United Kingdom fishermen having exclusive rights to fish in United Kingdom territorial waters. Article 2 of EEC Regulation No. 2141/70, which however in terms of Articles 100 and 101 of the Treaty of Accession was not to come into effect until December 31, 1982, would give him only the same rights as all other EEC fishermen in United Kingdom waters. He contended that these provisions affected a matter of private right, were not for the evident utility of the subjects of Scotland, and that therefore s. 2(1) of the European Communities Act 1972, which gave them domestic effect, was contrary to Article XVIII of the Treaty of Union and null and void. He sought declarator to that effect, but was unsuccessful. On the question of the applicability of Article XVIII:

LORD KEITH: "In addition to the argument on relevancy there were addressed to me interesting arguments upon the question of jurisdiction and the competency of the action. These arguments raised constitutional issues of great potential importance, in particular whether the Court of Session has power to declare an Act of the United Kingdom Parliament to be void, whether an alleged discrepancy between an Act of Parliament and the Treaty or Act of Union is a justiciable issue in this court, and whether, with particular reference to article XVIII of the Act of Union, this court has power to decide whether an alteration of private law bearing to be effected by an Act of the United Kingdom Parliament is 'for the evident utility' of the subjects in Scotland. Having regard to my decision on relevancy, these are not live issues in the present case. The position was similar in *MacCormick* v. *Lord Advocate*. . . Like Lord President Cooper, I prefer to reserve my opinion on what the question would be if the United Kingdom Parliament passed an Act purporting to abolish the Court of Session or the Church of Scotland or to substitute English law for the whole body of Scots private law. I am, however, of opinion that the question whether a particular Act of the United Kingdom Parliament altering a particular aspect of Scots private law is or is not 'for the evident utility' of the subjects within Scotland is not a justiciable issue in this court. The making of decisions upon what must essentially be a political matter is not part of the function of the court, and it is highly undesirable that it should be. The function of the court is to adjudicate upon the particular rights and obligations of individual persons, natural or corporate, in relation to other persons or, in certain instances, to the state. A general inquiry into the utility of certain legislative measures as regards the population generally is quite outside its competence."

2. JUDICIAL REVIEW OF ADMINISTRATIVE ACTION

It is now clear that the Scottish courts have no authority to question Acts of Parliament. They do, however, have the authority to challenge the way in which statutory and other powers are exercised. In particular, they may intervene to ensure that any discretionary powers are exercised properly. This means that the discretion must be exercised reasonably and in accordance with the rules of natural justice. Although rather limited, these can be useful means for checking the activities of government, government departments and local authorities in circumstances where violations of civil liberties have taken place. It is in this way, for example, that the courts (in England and Wales) have been able to develop an expanding law on prisoners' rights. In the important *R.* v. *Hull Prison Visitors, ex p. St Germain (No.1)* [1978] Q.B. 678, it was held by the Court of Appeal that prison visitors act in a judicial capacity when dealing with prison discipline and that they must therefore apply the rules of natural justice in reaching their decision. In *R.* v. *Hull Prison Visitors (No.2)* [1979] 1 W.L.R. 1401 it was held that the prison visitors could not unreasonably exclude the right of an accused person to call witnesses in his defence; that in certain circumstances hearsay evidence should not be admitted against an accused person; and that generally there will be a right to cross-examine witnesses for the other side. More recently still, in *R.* v. *Home Secretary, ex p. Tarrant* [1985] Q.B. 251 it was held that a failure to permit legal representation by a prisoner on a disciplinary charge could amount to a breach of natural justice.

5. Council of Civil Service Unions v. Minister for
the Civil Service
[1984] 3 W.L.R. 1174

On December 22, 1983, the Minister for the Civil Service decided that new conditions of service would be introduced at Government Communications Headquarters (GCHQ). Staff would no longer be permitted to belong to national trade unions and would be free only to join a departmental staff association. This change was a response to the history of industrial action at GCHQ and was made under the authority of an Order-in-Council which empowers the Minister to give instructions for controlling the conduct of the home civil service. The instruction in this case was given without any prior consultation with the civil servants concerned or with the appropriate trade unions which they had been permitted and indeed encouraged to join.

The simple question before the courts was whether this instruction was bad on the ground of procedural impropriety. The unions succeeded at first instance before Glidewell J., but his decision was reversed by the Court of Appeal. A unanimous House of Lords upheld the Court of Appeal. It is to be noted, however, that the reasoning of their Lordships differed, with a minority (Lords Fraser and Templeman) deciding on a much narrower ground than the majority (Lords Diplock, Roskill and Scarman). Lord Diplock's is a seminal speech.

LORD FRASER OF TULLYBELTON "... The appeal raises a number of question. I shall consider first the question which I regard as the most important and also the most difficult. It concerns the royal prerogative.

The Royal Prerogative

The mechanism on which the Minister for the Civil Service relied to alter the terms and conditions of service at GCHQ was an 'instruction' issued by her under the Order in Council of 1982, article 4. That article so far as relevant provides as follows:

'As regards Her Majesty's Home Civil Service—(a) the Minister for the Civil Service may from time to time make regulations or give instructions— . . . (ii) for controlling the conduct of the service, and providing for the classification of all persons employed therein and . . . the conditions of service of all such persons;
. . .'

The Order in Council was not issued under powers conferred by any Act of Parliament. Like the previous Orders in Council on the same subject it was issued by the sovereign by virtue of her prerogative, but of course on the advice of the government of the day. In these circumstances Mr Alexander submitted that the instruction was not open to review by the courts because it was an emanation of the prerogative. This submission involves two propositions: (1) that prerogative powers are discretionary, that is to say they may be exercised at the discretion of the sovereign (acting on advice in accordance with modern constitutional practice) and the way in which they are exercised is not open to review by the courts; (2) that an instruction given in the exercise of a delegated power conferred by the sovereign under the prerogative enjoys the same immunity from review as if it were itself a direct exercise of prerogative power. Mr Blom-Cooper contested both of these propositions, but the main weight of his argument was directed against the second.

The first of these propositions is vouched by an impressive array of authority, which I do not propose to cite at all fully. Starting with *Blackstone's Commentaries*, 15th ed. (1809), p. 251 and *Chitty's Prerogatives of the Crown* (1820), pp. 6-7 they are at one in stating that, within the sphere of its prerogative powers, the Crown has an absolute discretion. In more recent times the best-known definition of the prerogative is that given in *Dicey, Law of the Constitution*, 8th ed. (1915), p. 421 which is as follows:

'The prerogative is the name for the remaining portion of the Crown's original authority, and is therefore, as already pointed out, the name for the residue of discretionary power left at any moment in the hands of the Crown, whether such power be in fact exercised by the King himself or by his ministers.'

Dicey's definition was quoted with approval in this House in *Attorney-General v. De Keyser's Royal Hotel Ltd.* [1920] A.C. 508 at p. 526 by Lord Dunedin and was impliedly accepted by the other Law Lords in that case. In *Burmah Oil Co. Ltd. v. Lord Advocate,* 1964 S.C. (H.L.) 117 Lord Reid, at p. 120, referred to Dicey's definition as being 'always quoted with approval' although he said it did not take him very far in that case. It was also referred to with apparent approval by Roskill L.J. (as my noble and learned friend then was) in *Laker Airways Ltd v.Department of Trade* [1977] Q.B. 643 at p. 719. As *De Keyser's* case shows the courts will inquire into whether a particular prerogative power exists or not, and if it does exist, into its extent. But once the existence and the extent of a power are established to the satisfaction of the court, the court cannot inquire into the propriety of its exercise. That is undoubtedly the position as laid down in the authorities to which I have briefly referred and it is plainly reasonable in relation to many of the most important prerogative powers which are concerned with control of the armed forces and with foreign policy and with other matters which are unsuitable for discussion or review in the law courts. In the present case the prerogative power involved was power to regulate the Home Civil Service, and I recognise there is no obvious reason why the mode of exercise of that power should be immune from review by the courts. Nevertheless to permit such review would run counter to the great weight of authority to which I have briefly referred. Having regard to the opinion I have reached on Mr Alexander's second proposition, it is unnecessary to decide whether his first proposition is sound or not and I prefer to leave that question open until it arises in a case where a decision upon it is necessary. I therefore assume, without deciding, that his first proposition is correct and that all powers exercised directly under the prerogative are immune from challenge in the courts. I pass to consider his second proposition.

The second proposition depends for its soundness upon whether the power conferred by article 4 of the Order in Council of 1982 on the Minister for the

Civil Service of 'providing for . . . the conditions of service' of the Civil Service is subject to an implied obligation to act fairly. (Such an obligation is sometimes referred to as an obligation to obey the rules of natural justice, but that is a less appropriate description, at least when applied, as in the present case, to a power which is executive and not judicial.) There is no doubt that, if the Order in Council of 1982 had been made under the authority of a statute, the power delegated to the Minister by article 4 would have been construed as being subject to an obligation to act fairly. I am unable to see why the words conferring the same powers should be construed differently merely because their source was an Order in Council made under the prerogative. It is all the more difficult in the face of article 6(4) of the Order in Council of 1982 which provides that the Interpretation Act 1978 shall apply to the Order; it would of course apply to a statutory order. There seems no sensible reason why the words should not bear the same meaning whatever the source of authority for the legislation in which they are contained. The Order in Council of 1982 was described by Sir Robert Armstrong in his first affidavit as primary legislation; that is, in my opinion, a correct description, subject to the qualification that the Order in Council, being made under the prerogative, derives its authority from the sovereign alone and not, as is more commonly the case with legislation, from the sovereign in Parliament. Legislation frequently delegates power from the legislating authority—the sovereign in one case, Parliament in the other—to some other person or body and, when that is done, the delegated powers are defined more or less closely by the legislation, in this case by article 4. But whatever their source, powers which are defined, either by reference to their object or by reference to procedure for their exercise, or in some other way, and whether the definition is expressed or implied, are in my opinion, normally subject to judicial control to ensure that they are not exceeded. By 'normally' I mean provided that considerations of national security do not require otherwise.

The courts have already shown themselves ready to control by way of judicial review the actions of a tribunal set up under the prerogative. *Reg.* v. *Criminal Injuries Compensation Board, ex p. Lain* [1967] 2 Q.B. 864 was such a case. In that case Lord Parker C.J. said, at p. 881:

'I can see no reason either in principle or in authority why a board set up as this board was set up is not a body of persons amenable to the jurisdiction of this court. True it is not set up by statute but the fact that it is set up by executive government, *i.e.* under the prerogative, does not render its acts any the less lawful. Indeed, the writ of certiorari has issued not only to courts set up by statute but to courts whose authority is derived, inter alia, from the prerogative. Once the jurisdiction is extended, as it clearly has been, to tribunals as opposed to courts, there is no reason why the remedy by way of certiorari cannot be invoked to a body of persons set up under the prerogative.'

That case was concerned with the actions of a board or tribunal exercising functions of a judicial character, but it is now established that certiorari is not limited to bodies performing judicial functions. In *R.* v. *Secretary of State for Home Affairs, ex p. Hosenball* [1977] 1 W.L.R. 766 which was concerned with the actions of the Secretary of State himself in refusing to give information about the reasons for making a deportation order against an alien, the Divisional Court and the Court of Appeal refused to make an order of certiorari because the refusal had been based on grounds of national security but, if it had been made in what Lord Denning M.R., at p. 778, called an 'ordinary case'—that is one in which national security was not involved—the position would have been different. Lord Denning M.R. said, at p. 781: 'if the body concerned, whether it be a minister or advisers, has acted unfairly, then the courts can review their proceedings so as to ensure, as far as may be, that justice is done.'

Accordingly I agree with the conclusion of Glidewell J. that there is no reason for treating the exercise of a power under article 4 any differently from the exercise of a statutory power merely because article 4 itself is found in an order issued under the prerogative.

It follows, in my opinion, that some of the reasoning in *Reg.* v. *Secretary of State for War* [1891] 2 Q.B. 326 and *Griffin* v. *Lord Advocate,* 1950 S.C. 448 is unsound, although the decisions themselves might perhaps be supported on the ground that they related to actions by the Crown connected with the armed forces. The former case was of course decided long before the modern development of judicial review and the latter, which was a decision of Lord Sorn in the Outer House, mainly followed it.

The duty to consult

Mr Blom-Cooper submitted that the Minister had a duty to consult the CCSU, on behalf of employees at GCHQ, before giving the instruction on December 22, 1983 for making an important change in their conditions of service. His main reason for so submitting was that the employees had a legitimate, or reasonable, expectation that there would be such prior consultation before any important change was made in their conditions.

It is clear that the employees did not have a legal right to prior consultation. The Order in Council confers no such right, and article 4 makes no reference at all to consultation. The Civil Service handbook (*Handbook for the new civil servant,* 1973 ed. as amended 1983) which explains the normal method of consultation through the departmental Whitley Council, does not suggest that there is any legal right to consultation; indeed it is careful to recognise that, in the operational field, considerations of urgency may make prior consultation impracticable. The Civil Service Pay and Conditions of Service Code expressly states:

'The following terms and conditions also apply to your appointment in the Civil Service. It should be understood, however, that in consequence of the constitutional position of the Crown, the Crown has the right to change its employees' conditions of service at any time, and that they hold their appointments at the pleasure of the Crown.'

But even where a person claiming some benefit or privilege has no legal right to it, as a matter or private law, he may have a legitimate expectation of receiving the benefit or privilege, and, if so, the courts will protect his expectation by judicial review as a matter of public law. This subject has been fully explained by my

noble and learned friend, Lord Diplock, in *O'Reilly* v. *Mackman* [1983] 2 A.C.
237 and I need not repeat what he has so recently said. Legitimate, or reasonable,
expectation may arise either from an express promise given on behalf of a public
authority or from the existence of a regular practice which the claimant can
reasonably expect to continue. Examples of the former type of expectation are
R. v. *Liverpool Corporation, ex p. Liverpool Taxi Fleet Operators' Association*
[1972] 2 Q.B. 299 and *Attorney-General of Hong Kong* v. *Ng Yuen Shiu* [1983]
2 A.C. 629. (I agree with Lord Diplock's view, expressed in the speech in this
appeal, that 'legitimate' is to be preferred to 'reasonable' in this context. I was
responsible for using the word 'reasonable' for the reason explained in *Ng Yuen
Shiu*, but it was intended only to be exegetical of 'legitimate.') An example of
the latter is *R.* v. *Board of Visitors of Hull Prison, ex p. St Germain* [1979] Q.B.
425 approved by this House in *O'Reilly*, at p. 274D. The submission on behalf
of the appellants is that the present case is of the latter type. The test of that is
whether the practice of prior consultation of the staff on significant changes in
their conditions of service was so well established by 1983 that it would be unfair
or inconsistent with good administration for the Government to depart from the
practice in this case. Legitimate expectations such as are now under consideration
will always relate to a benefit or privilege to which the claimant has no right
in private law, and it may even be to one which conflicts with his private law
rights. In the present case the evidence shows that, ever since GCHQ began in
1947, prior consultation has been the invariable rule when conditions of service
were to be significantly altered. Accordingly in my opinion if there had been
no question of national security involved, the appellants would have had a
legitimate expectation, that the minister would consult them before issuing the
instruction of December 22, 1983. The next question, therefore, is whether it has
been shown that consideration of national security supersedes the expectation.

National security

The issue here is not whether the minister's instruction was proper or fair or
justifiable on its merits. These matters are not for the courts to determine. The
sole issue is whether the decision on which the instruction was based was reached
by a process that was fair to the staff at GCHQ. As my noble and learned friend
Lord Brightman said in *Chief Constable of the North Wales Police* v. *Evans* [1982]
1 W.L.R. 1155 at p. 1173: 'Judicial review is concerned, not with the decision,
but with the decision-making process.'

I have already explained my reasons for holding that, if no question of national
security arose, the decision-making process in this case would have been unfair.
The respondent's case is that she deliberately made the decision without prior
consultation because prior consultation 'would involve a real risk that it would
occasion the very kind of disruption [at GCHQ] which was a threat to national
security and which it was intended to avoid.' I have quoted from paragraph 27(i)
of the respondent's printed case. Mr Blom-Cooper conceded that a reasonable
minister could reasonably have taken that view, but he argued strongly that the
respondent had failed to show that that was in fact the reason for her decision.
He supported his argument by saying, as I think was conceded by Mr Alexander,
that the reason given in paragraph 27(i) had not been mentioned to Glidewell
J. and that it had only emerged before the Court of Appeal. He described it as

an 'afterthought' and invited the House to hold that it had not been shown to have been the true reason.

The question is one of evidence. The decision on whether the requirements of national security outweigh the duty of fairness in any particular case is for the Government and not for the courts; the Government alone has access to the necessary information, and in any event the judicial process is unsuitable for reaching decisions on national security. But if the decision is successfully challenged, on the ground that it has been reached by a process which is unfair, then the Government is under an obligation to produce evidence that the decision was in fact based on grounds of national security. Authority for both these points is found in *The Zamora* [1916] 2 A.C. 77. The former point is dealt with in the well known passage from the advice of the Judicial Committee delivered by Lord Parker of Waddington, at p. 107:

'Those who are responsible for the national security must be the sole judges of what the national security requires. It would be obviously undesirable that such matters should be made the subject of evidence in a court of law or otherwise discussed in public.'

The second point, less often referred to, appears at p. 106 and more particularly at p. 108 where this passage occurs:

'In their Lordships' opinion the order appealed from was wrong, not because, as contended by the appellants, there is by international law no right at all to requisition ships or goods in the custody of the court, but because the judge had before him *no satisfactory evidence* that such a right was exercisable.' (Emphasis added.)

What was required was evidence that a cargo of copper in the custody of the Prize Court was urgently required for national purposes, but no evidence had been directed to that point. The claim on behalf of the Crown that it was entitled to requisition the copper therefore failed; considering that the decision was made in 1916 at a critical stage of the 1914-1918 war, it was a strong one. In *Chandler* v. *Director of Public Prosecutions* [1964] A.C. 763, which was an appeal by persons who had been convicted of a breach of the peace under section 1 of the Official Secrets Act 1911 by arranging a demonstration by the Campaign for Nuclear Disarmament on an operational air field at Wethersfield, Lord Reid said, at p. 790:

'The question more frequently arises as to what is or is not in the public interest. I do not subscribe to the view that the Government or a minister must always or even as a general rule have the last word about that. But here we are dealing with a very special matter—interfering with a prohibited place which Wethersfield was.'

But the court had had before it evidence from an air commodore that the airfield was of importance for national security. Both Lord Reid and Viscount Radcliffe, at p. 796, referred to the evidence as being relevant to their refusal of the appeal.

The evidence in support of this part of the respondent's case came from Sir Robert Armstrong in his first affidavit, especially at paragraph 16. Mr Blom-Cooper rightly pointed out that the affidavit does not in terms directly support paragraph 27(i). . . . But it does set out the respondent's view that to have entered into prior consultation would have served to bring out the vulnerability of areas of operation to those who had shown themselves ready to organise disruption. That must be read along with the earlier parts of the affidavit in which Sir Robert had dealt in some detail with the attitude of the trade unions which I have referred to earlier in this speech. The affidavit, read as a whole, does in my opinion undoubtedly constitute evidence that the Minister did indeed consider that prior consultation would have involved a risk of precipitating disruption at GCHQ. I am accordingly of opinion that the respondent has shown that her decision was one which not only could reasonably have been based, but was in fact based, on considerations of national security, which outweighed what would otherwise have been the reasonable expectation on the part of the appellants for prior consultation. In deciding that matter I must with respect differ from the decision of Glidewell J. but, as I have mentioned, I do so on a point that was not argued to him.

Minor matters

The judge held that had the prior consultations taken place they would not have been so limited that he could confidently say that they would have been futile. It is not necessary for me to reach a concluded view on this matter, but as present advised I am inclined to differ from the learned judge, especially because of the attitude of two of the trade union members of CCSU which declared that they were firmly against any no-strike agreement.

The Court of Appeal considered the proper construction of certain international labour conventions which they cite. I respectfully agree with Lord Lane C.J. who said that 'the correct meaning of the material articles of the Conventions is by no means clear,' but I do not propose to consider the matter as the Conventions are not part of the law in this country.

Mr Blom-Cooper submitted that the oral direction did not qualify as an 'instruction' within the meaning of article 4, and that for two reasons. First he said that there was no sufficient evidence of any instruction. In my opinion there is no substance in this ground. There is ample evidence in a letter dated February 7th, 1984 from Sir Robert Armstrong to the Director of GCHQ and also in the General Notice 100/84 and a covering letter issued by the Director to all employees at GCHQ. Secondly counsel said that the instruction did not sufficiently specify conditions that were being altered, but I agree with Glidewell J., and with the Court of Appeal, that the Minister's direction on December 22, 1983 did give 'instructions . . . providing for . . . the conditions of service' of employees at GCHQ in the sense of article 4 of the Order in Council of 1982. There was no obligation to put the instructions in writing, although that might perhaps have been expected in a matter so important as this. Nor was there any obligation to couch the instructions in any particular form. Accordingly I reject this submission.

For these reasons I would dismiss the appeal."

LORD DIPLOCK: "My Lords, the English law relating to judicial control of administrative actions has been developed upon a case to case basis which has virtually transformed it over the last three decades. The principles of public law that are applicable to the instant case are in my view well established by authorities that are sufficiently cited in the speech that will be delivered by my noble and learned friend, Lord Roskill. This obviates the necessity of my duplicating his citations: though I should put on record that after reading and rereading Lord Devlin's speech in *Chandler* v. *Director of Public Prosecutions* [1964] A.C. 763, I have gained no help from it, for I find some of his observations that are peripheral to what I understand to be the *ratio decidendi* difficult to reconcile with the actual decision that he felt able to reach and also with one another.

The only difficulty which the instant case has presented upon the facts as they have been summarised by my noble and learned friend, Lord Fraser of Tullybelton, and expanded in the judgment of Glidewell J. has been to identify what is, in my view, the one crucial point of law on which this appeal turns. It never was identified or even adumbrated in the respondent's argument at the hearing before Glidewell J. and so, excusably, finds no place in what otherwise I regard as an impeccable judgment. The consequence of this omission was that he found in favour of the applicants. Before the Court of Appeal the crucial point was advanced in argument by the Crown in terms that were unnecessarily and, in my view, unjustifiably wide. This stance was maintained in the appeal to this House, although, under your Lordships' encouragement, the narrower point of law that was really crucial was developed and relied on by the respondent in the alternative. Once that point has been accurately identified the evidence in the case in my view makes it inevitable that this appeal must be dismissed. I will attempt to state in summary form those principles of public law which lead me to this conclusion.

Judicial review, now regulated by R.S.C., Ord. 53, provides the means by which judicial control of administrative action is exercised. The subject-matter of every judicial review is a decision made by some person (or body of persons) whom I will call the 'decision-maker' or else a refusal by him to make a decision.

To qualify as a subject for judicial review the decision must have consequences which affect some person (or body of persons) other than the decision-maker, although it may affect him too. It must affect such other person either:

(a) by altering rights or obligations of that person which are enforceable by or against him in private law; or

(b) by depriving him of some benefit or advantage which either (i) he had in the past been permitted by the decision-maker to enjoy and which he can legitimately expect to be permitted to continue to do until there has been communicated to him some rational grounds for withdrawing it on which he has been given an opportunity to comment; or (ii) he has received assurance from the decision-maker will not be withdrawn without giving him first an opportunity of advancing reasons for contending that they should not be withdrawn. (I prefer to continue to call the kind of expectation that qualifies a decision for inclusion in class (b) a 'legitimate expectation' rather than a 'reasonable expectation,' in order thereby to indicate that it has consequences to which effect will be given in public law, whereas an expectation or hope that some benefit or advantage would continue to be enjoyed, although it might well be entertained by a 'reasonable' man, would not necessarily have such consequences. The recent decision of this House in *Re Findlay* [1984] 3 W.L.R. 1159 presents an example of the latter kind of expectation. 'Reasonable' furthermore bears different meanings according to whether the context in which it is being used is that of private law or of public law. To eliminate confusion it is best avoided in the latter.

For a decision to be susceptible to judicial review the decision-maker must be empowered by public law (and not merely, as in arbitration, by agreement between private parties) to make decisions that, if validly made, will lead to administrative action or abstention from action by an authority endowed by law with executive powers, which have one or other of the consequences mentioned in the preceding paragraph. The ultimate source of the decision-making power is nearly always nowadays a statute or subordinate legislation made under the statute; but in the absence of any statute regulating the subject-matter of the decision the source of the decision-making power may still be the common law itself, *i.e.* that part of the common law that is given by lawyers the label of 'the prerogative'. Where this is the source of decision-making power, the power is confined to executive officers of central as distinct from local government and in constitutional practice is generally exercised by those holding ministerial rank.

It was the prerogative that was relied on as the source of the power of the Minister for the Civil Service in reaching her decision of December 22, 1983 that membership of national trade unions should in future be barred to all members of the home civil service employed at GCHQ.

My Lords, I intend no discourtesy to counsel when I say that, intellectual interest apart, in answering the question of law raised in this appeal, I have derived little practical assistance from learned and esoteric analyses of the precise legal nature, boundaries and historical origin of 'the prerogative,' or of what powers exercisable by executive officers acting on behalf of central government that are not shared by private citizens qualify for inclusion under this particular label. It does not, for instance, seem to me to matter whether today the right of the executive government that happens to be in power to dismiss without notice any member of the home civil service upon which perforce it must rely for the administration of its policies, and the correlative disability of the executive government that is in power to agree with a civil servant that his service should be on terms that did not make him subject to instant dismissal, should be ascribed to 'the prerogative' or merely to a consequence of the survival, for entirely different reasons, of a rule of constitutional law whose origin is to be found in the theory that those by whom the administration of the realm is carried on do so as personal servants of the monarch who can dismiss them at will, because the King can do no wrong.

Nevertheless, whatever label may be attached to them there have unquestionably survived into the present day a residue of miscellaneous fields of law in which the executive government retains decision-making powers that are not dependent upon any statutory authority but nevertheless have consequences on the private rights or legitimate expectations of other persons which would render the decision subject to judicial review if the power of the decision-maker to make them were statutory in origin. From matters so relatively minor as the grant of pardons to condemned criminals, of honours to the good and great, of corporate personality to deserving bodies of persons, and of bounty from moneys made available to the executive government by Parliament, they extend to matters so vital to the survival and welfare of the nation as the conduct of relations with foreign states and—what lies at the heart of the present case—the defence of the realm against potential enemies. Adopting the phraseology used in the

European Convention on Human Rights 1953 (Convention for the Protection of Human Rights and Fundamental Freedoms (1953) (Cmd. 8969)) to which the United Kingdom is a party it has now become usual in statutes to refer to the latter as 'national security.'

My Lords, I see no reason why simply because a decision-making power is derived from a common law and not a statutory source, it should *for that reason only* be immune from judicial review. Judicial review has I think developed to a stage today when without reiterating any analysis of the steps by which the development has come about, one can conveniently classify under three heads the grounds upon which administrative action is subject to control by judicial review. The first ground I would call 'illegality,' the second 'irrationality' and the third 'procedural impropriety.' That is not to say that further developments on a case-by-case basis may not in course of time add further grounds. I have in mind particularly the possible adoption in the future of the principle of 'proportionality' which is recognised in the administrative law of several of our fellow members of the European Economic Community; but to dispose of the instant case the three already well-established heads that I have mentioned will suffice.

By 'illegality' as a ground for judicial review I mean that the decision-maker must understand correctly the law that regulates his decision-making power and must give effect to it. Whether he has or not is par excellence a justiciable question to be decided, in the event of dispute, by those persons, the judges, by whom the judicial power of the state is exercisable.

By 'irrationality' I mean what can by now be succinctly referred to as '*Wednesbury* unreasonableness' (*Associated Provincial Picture Houses Ltd.* v. *Wednesbury Corporation* [1948] 1 K. B. 223). It applies to a decision which is so outrageous in its defiance of logic or of accepted moral standards that no sensible person who had applied his mind to the question to be decided could have arrived at it. Whether a decision falls within this category is a question that judges by their training and experience should be well equipped to answer, or else there would be something badly wrong with our judicial system. To justify the court's exercise of this role, resort I think is today no longer needed to Viscount Radcliffe's ingenious explanation in *Edwards* v. *Bairstow* [1956] A.C. 14 of irrationality as a ground for a court's reversal of a decision by ascribing it to an inferred though unidentifiable mistake of law by the decision-maker. 'Irrationality' by now can stand upon its own feet as an accepted ground on which a decision may be attacked by judicial review.

I have described the third head as 'procedural impropriety' rather than failure to observe basic rules of natural justice or failure to act with procedural fairness towards the person who will be affected by the decision. This is because susceptibility to judicial review under this head covers also failure by an administrative tribunal to observe procedural rules that are expressly laid down in the legislative instrument by which its jurisdiction is conferred, even where such failure does not involve any denial of natural justice. But the instant case is not concerned with the proceedings of an administrative tribunal at all.

My Lords, that a decision of which the ultimate source of power to make it is not a statute but the common law (whether or not the common law is for this purpose given the label of 'the prerogative') may be the subject of judicial review on the ground of illegality is, I think, established by the cases cited by my noble and learned friend, Lord Roskill, and this extends to cases where the field of law to which the decision relates is national security, as the decision of this House itself in *Burmah Oil Co. Ltd.* v. *Lord Advocate*, 1964 S.C. (H.L.) 117 shows. While I see no *a priori* reason to rule out 'irrationality' as a ground for judicial review of a ministerial decision taken in the exercise of 'prerogative' powers, I find it difficult to envisage in any of the various fields in which the prerogative remains the only source of the relevant decision-making power a decision of a kind that would be open to attack through the judicial process upon this ground. Such decisions will generally involve the application of government policy. The reasons for the decision-maker taking one course rather than another do not normally involve questions to which, if disputed, the judicial process is adapted to provide the right answer, by which I mean that the kind of evidence that is admissible under judicial procedures and the way in which it has to be adduced tend to exclude from the attention of the court competing policy considerations which, if the executive discretion is to be wisely exercised, need to be weighed against one another—a balancing exercise which judges by their upbringing and experience are ill-qualified to perform. So I leave this as an open question to be dealt with on a case-to-case basis if, indeed, the case should ever arise.

As respects 'procedural propriety' I see no reason why it should not be a ground for judicial review of a decision made under powers of which the ultimate source is the prerogative. Such indeed was one of the grounds that formed the subject matter of judicial review in *R.* v. *Criminal Injuries Compensation Board. ex p. Lain* [1967] 2 Q.B. 864. Indeed, where the decision is one which does not alter rights or obligations enforceable in private law but only deprives a person of legitimate expectations, 'procedural impropriety' will normally provide the only ground on which the decision is open to judicial review. But in any event what procedure will satisfy the public law requirement of procedural propriety depends upon the subject-matter of the decision, the executive functions of the decision-maker (if the decision is not that of an administrative tribunal) and the particular circumstances in which the decision came to be made. My Lords, in the instant case the immediate subject-matter of the decision was a change in one of the terms of employment of civil servants employed at GCHQ. That the executive functions of the Minister for the Civil Service, in her capacity as such, included making a decision to change any of those terms, except in so far as they related to remuneration, expenses and allowances, is not disputed. It does not seem to me to be of any practical significance whether or not as a matter of strict legal analysis this power is based upon the rule of constitutional law to which I have already alluded that the employment of any civil servant may be terminated at any time without notice and that upon such termination the same civil servant may be re-engaged on different terms. The rule of terminability of employment in the civil service without notice, of which the existence is beyond doubt, must in any event have the consequence that the continued enjoyment by a civil servant in the *future* of a right under a particular term of his employment cannot be the subject of any right enforceable by him in private law; at most it can only be a legitimate expectation.

Prima facie, therefore, civil servants employed at GCHQ who were members of national trade unions had, at best, in December 1983, a legitimate expectation that they would continue to enjoy the benefits of such membership and of representation by those trade unions in any consultations and negotiations with representatives of the management of that government department as to changes in any term of their employment. So, but again prima facie only, they were entitled, as a matter of public law under the head of 'procedural propriety,' before administrative action was taken on a decision to withdraw that benefit, to have communicated to the national trade unions by which they had theretofore been represented the reason for such withdrawal, and for such unions to be given an opportunity to comment on it.

The reason why the Minister for the Civil Service decided on December 22, 1983 to withdraw this benefit was in the interests of national security. National security is the responsibility of the executive government; what action is needed to protect its interests is, as the cases cited by my learned friend, Lord Roskill, establish and common sense itself dictates, a matter upon which those upon whom the responsibility rests, and not the courts of justice, must have the last word. It is par excellence a non-justiciable question. The judicial process is totally inept to deal with the sort of problems which it involves.

The executive government likewise decided, and this would appear to be a collective decision of cabinet ministers involved, that the interests of national security required that no notice should be given of the decision before administrative action had been taken to give effect to it. The reason for this was the risk that advance notice to the national unions of the executive government's intention would attract the very disruptive action prejudicial to the national security the recurrence of which the decision barring membership of national trade unions to civil servants employed at GCHQ was designed to prevent.

There was ample evidence to which reference is made by others of your Lordships that this was indeed a real risk; so the crucial point of law in this case is whether procedural propriety must give way to national security when there is conflict between (1) on the one hand, the *prima facie* rule of 'procedural propriety' in public law, applicable to a case of legitimate expectations that a benefit ought not to be withdrawn until the reason for its proposed withdrawal has been communicated to the person who has theretofore enjoyed that benefit and that person has been given the opportunity to comment on the reason, and (2) on the other hand, action that is needed to be taken in the interests of national security, for which the executive government bears the responsibility and alone has access to sources of information that qualify it to judge what the necessary action is. To that there can, in my opinion, be only one sensible answer. That answer is 'Yes.'

I agree with your Lordships that this appeal must be dismissed."

There are a number of important points to note about this case. The first is that Lord Diplock's analysis of the grounds of review (illegality, irrationality and procedural impropriety) has been endorsed by the Court of Session in *City of Edinburgh D.C.* v. *Secretary of State for Scotland,* 1985 S.L.T 551. Secondly, it establishes common principles to be applied to all governmental power, regardless of its source. Thus, in the view of the majority, the exercise of prerogative and statutory powers are to be treated in the same way. Hitherto the courts could only review the exercise of statutory power. So far as the prerogative was concerned they could only determine whether a particular power existed, as in *Grieve v. Edinburgh and District Water Trustees,* 1918 2 S.L.T. 72; and if so what was its scope, as in *Burmah Oil Co. Ltd. v. Lord Advocate,* 1964 S.L.T. 218.

A third feature of the case is that it is not the exercise of all prerogative power which is subject to judicial review. In the view of their Lordships, the powers in question must be justiciable, and many, it seems, are not. Lord Roskill indicated that the list of non-justiciable powers is a long one which includes the making of treaties, the defence of the realm, the prerogative of mercy, the grant of honours, the dissolution of Parliament and the appointment of Ministers "as well as others" which he did not specify. It is to be pointed out that the requirement of justiciability is not confined to the royal prerogative. There are some statutory powers which are non-justiciable, with regard to some of the heads of review. One example of this is delegated legislation. In *City of Edinburgh D.C. v. Secretary of State for Scotland, supra,* Lord Jauncey concluded that :"the courts can only hold to be *ultra vires* a statutory instrument which has been laid before and considered by Parliament where that instrument is patently defective in that it purports to do what is not authorised by the enabling statute or where the procedure followed in making that instrument departed from the requirements of the enabling statute" (at p. 556).

A final feature of the case is perhaps the most disappointing. This is the willingness with which their Lordships are prepared to tolerate illegality by government where this is necessary for reasons of national security. It is to be noted that the unions would almost certainly have succeeded had this defence failed. The power in question was justiciable, and there had been a procedural impropriety in the making of the decision. Yet it is not clear that the House of Lords was compelled to accept the defence. Essentially, there are three options available to a court faced with such a plea.

1. A mere assertion by government that the decision was taken for reasons of national security will be enough to activate the defence.

2. A mere assertion that the decision was taken in the interests of national security is not enough. The government must lead evidence to show that the decision was in fact taken for reason of national security.

3. The provision of evidence is not enough. The government must go one stage further and show that the decision taken was reasonably necessary in the interests of national security.

The House of Lords adopted the second position, with only Lord Scarman prepared to take the third, more demanding, option. As a result, it does not matter how unreasonable the decision is, provided that there is evidence that it was taken for reasons of national security. Thus, what is in the interests of national security is a matter on which the government must have the last word, despite the recognition by Lord Devlin in *Chandler* v. *D.P.P.* [1964] A.C. 763 that:"Men can exaggerate the extent of their interests and so can the Crown" (at p. 811).

CHAPTER 2

THE EUROPEAN CONVENTION ON HUMAN RIGHTS

IN this chapter we move from the protection of civil liberties in domestic law to the standards set by the international community, and to remedies available under international law. By far the most important international document (simply in terms of its impact on domestic law) is the European Convention on Human Rights. The ECHR is a treaty under international law which was signed in Rome in 1950, ratified by the United Kingdom in 1951, coming into force in 1953. Like most human rights documents in the west, the Convention is confined to what might be referred to as "political" rights, and excludes matters of a social or economic nature. There is, for example, no protection of the right to employment, the right to housing, or the right to social security. It is to be noted, however, that these matters are the subject of a separate international treaty, the European Social Charter. Like the European Convention on Human rights, the Social Charter is a Treaty of the Council of Europe. The Council of Europe is not to be confused with the European Economic Community. The former is a quite distinct international association of nations, which is both older and larger than the EEC, though clearly it does not intrude so deeply into the economic life of Member States.

1. The European Convention on Human Rights

Article 1
"The High Contracting Parties shall secure to everyone within their jurisdiction the rights and freedoms defined in Section 1 of this Convention.

SECTION 1
Article 2
1. Everyone's right to life shall be protected by law. No one shall be deprived of his life intentionally save in the execution of a sentence of a court following his conviction of a crime for which this penalty is provided by law.
2. Deprivation of life shall not be regarded as inflicted in contravention of this Article when it results from the use of force which is no more than absolutely necessary:
(*a*) in defence of any person from unlawful violence;
(*b*) in order to effect a lawful arrest or to prevent the escape of a person lawfully detained;
(*c*) in action lawfully taken for the purpose of quelling a riot or insurrection.

Article 3
No one shall be subjected to torture or to inhuman or degrading treatment or punishment.

Article 4

1. No one shall be held in slavery or servitude.

2. No one shall be required to perform forced or compulsory labour.

3. For the purpose of this Article the term 'forced or compulsory' shall not include:

(a) any work required to be done in the ordinary course of detention imposed according to the provisions of Article 5 of this convention or during conditional release from such detention;

(b) any service of a military character or, in case of conscientious objectors in countries where they are recognised, service exacted instead of compulsory military service;

(c) any service exacted in case of an emergency or calamity threatening the life or well-being of the community;

(d) any work or service which forms part of normal civic obligations.

Article 5

1. Everyone has the right to liberty and security of person. No one shall be deprived of his liberty save in the following cases and in accordance with a procedure prescribed by law;

(a) the lawful detention of a person after conviction by a competent court;

(b) the lawful arrest or detention of a person for non-compliance with the lawful order of a court or in order to secure the fulfilment of any obligation prescribed by law;

(c) the lawful arrest or detention of a person effected for the purpose of bringing him before the competent legal authority on reasonable suspicion of having committed an offence or when it is reasonably considered necessary to prevent his committing an offence or fleeing after having done so;

(d) the detention of a minor by lawful order for the purpose of educational supervision or his lawful detention for the purpose of bringing him before the competent legal authority;

(e) the lawful detention of persons for the prevention of the spreading of infectious diseases, of persons of unsound mind, alcoholics or drug addicts or vagrants;

(f) the lawful arrest or detention of a person to prevent his effecting an unauthorised entry into the country or of a person against whom action is being taken with a view to deportation or extradition.

2. Everyone who is arrested shall be informed promptly, in a language which he understands, of the reasons for his arrest and of any charge against him.

3. Everyone arrested or detained in accordance with the provisions of paragraph 1(c) of this Article shall be brought promptly before a judge or other officer authorised by law to exercise judicial power and shall be entitled to trial within a reasonable time or to release pending trial. Release may be conditioned by guarantees to appear for trial.

4. Everyone who is deprived of his liberty by arrest or detention shall be entitled to take proceedings by which the lawfulness of his detention shall be decided speedily by a court and his release ordered if the detention is not lawful.

5. Everyone who has been the victim of arrest or detention in contravention of the provisions of this Article shall have an enforceable right to compensation.

Article 6

1. In the determination of his civil rights and obligations or of any criminal charge

against him, everyone is entitled to a fair and public hearing within a reasonable time by an independent and impartial tribunal established by law. Judgement shall be pronounced publicly but the press and public may be excluded from all or part of the trial in the interest of morals, public order or national security in a democratic society, where the interests of juveniles or the protection of the private life of the parties so require, or to the extent strictly necessary in the opinion of the court in special circumstances where publicity would prejudice the interests of justice.

2. Everyone charged with a criminal offence shall be presumed innocent until proved guilty according to law.

3. Everyone charged with a criminal offence has the following minimum rights;

(*a*) to be informed promptly, in a language which he understands and in detail, of the nature and cause of the accusation against him;

(*b*) to have adequate time and facilities for the preparation of his defence;

(*c*) to defend himself in person or through legal assistance of his own choosing or, if he has not sufficient means to pay for legal assistance, to be given it free when the interests of justice so require;

(*d*) to examine or have examined witnesses against him and to obtain the attendance and examination of witnesses on his behalf under the same conditions as witnesses against him;

(*e*) to have the free assistance of an interpreter if he cannot understand or speak the language used in court.

Article 7

1. No one shall be held guilty of any criminal offence on account of any act or omission which did not constitute a criminal offence under national or international law at the time when it was committed. Nor shall a heavier penalty be imposed than the one that was applicable at the time the criminal offence was committed.

2. This article shall not prejudice the trial and punishment of any person for any act or omission which at the time when it was committed, was criminal according to the general principles of law recognised by civilised nations.

Article 8

1. Everyone has the right to respect for his private and family life, his home and his correspondence.

2. There shall be no interference by a public authority with the exercise of this right except such as is in accordance with the law and is necessary in a democratic society in the interests of national security, public safety or the economic well-being of the country, for the prevention of disorder or crime, for the protection of health or morals, or for the protection of the rights and freedoms of others.

Article 9

1. Everyone has the right to freedom of thought, conscience and religion; this right includes freedom to change his religion or belief and freedom, either alone or in community with others and in public or private, to manifest his religion or belief, in worship, teaching, practice and observance.

2. Freedom to manifest one's religion or beliefs shall be subject only to such limitations as are prescribed by law and are necessary in a democratic society

in the interests of public safety, for the protection of public order, health or morals, or for the protection of the rights and freedoms of others.

Article 10

1. Everyone has the right to freedom of expression. This right shall include freedom to hold opinions and to receive and impart information and ideas without interference by public authority and regardless of frontiers. This Article shall not prevent States from requiring the licensing of broadcasting, television or cinema enterprises.

2. The exercise of these freedoms, since it carries with it duties and responsibilities, may be subject to such formalities, conditions, restrictions or penalties as are prescribed by law and are necessary in a democratic society, in the interests of national security, territorial integrity or public safety, for the prevention of disorder or crime, for the protection of health or morals, for the protection of the reputation or rights of others, for preventing the disclosure of information received in confidence, or for maintaining the authority and impartiality of the judiciary.

Article 11

1. Everyone has the right to freedom of peaceful assembly and to freedom of association with others, including the right to form and to join trade unions for the protection of his interests.

2. No restrictions shall be placed on the exercise of these rights other than such as are prescribed by law and are necessary in a democratic society in the interests of national security or public safety, for the prevention of disorder or crime, for the protection of health or morals or for the protection of the rights and freedoms of others. This Article shall not prevent the imposition of lawful restrictions on the exercise of these rights by members of the armed forces, of the police or of the administration of the State.

Article 12

Men and women of marriageable age have the right to marry and to found a family, according to the national laws governing the exercise of this right.

Article 13

Everyone whose rights and freedoms as set forth in this Convention are violated shall have an effective remedy before a national authority notwithstanding that the violation has been committed by persons acting in an official capacity.

Article 14

The enjoyment of the rights and freedoms set forth in this Convention shall be secured without discrimination on any ground such as sex, race, colour, language, religion, political or other opinion, national or social origin, association with a national minority, property, birth or other status.

Article 15

1. In time of war or other public emergency threatening the life of the nation any High Contracting Party may take measures derogating from its obligations under this Convention to the extent strictly required by the exigencies of the

situation, provided that such measures are not inconsistent with its other obligations under international law.

2. No derogation from Article 2, except in respect of deaths resulting from lawful acts of war, or from Articles 3, 4 (paragraph 1) and 7 shall be made under this provision.

3. Any High Contracting Party availing itself of this right of derogation shall keep the Secretary General of the Council of Europe fully informed of the measures which it has taken and the reasons therefor. It shall also inform the Secretary General of the Council of Europe when such measures have ceased to operate and the provisions of the Convention are again being fully executed.

Article 16

Nothing in Articles 10, 11 and 14 shall be regarded as preventing the High Contracting Parties from imposing restrictions on the political activities of aliens.

Article 17

Nothing in this Convention may be interpreted as implying for any State, group or person any right to engage in any activity or perform any act aimed at the destruction of any of the rights and freedoms set forth herein or at their limitation to a greater extent than is provided for in the Convention.

Article 18

The restrictions permitted under this Convention to the said rights and freedoms shall not be applied for any purpose other than those for which they have been prescribed. . .

Article 25

1. The commission may receive petitions addressed to the Secretary General of the Council of Europe from any person, non-governmental organisation or group of individuals claiming to be the victim of a violation by one of the High Contracting Parties of the rights set forth in this Convention, provided that the High Contracting Party against which the complaint has been lodged has declared that it recognises the competence of the commission to receive such petitions. Those of the High Contracting Parties who have made such a declaration undertake not to hinder in any way the effective exercise of this right.

2. Such declarations may be made for a specific period. . .

Article 46

1. Any of the High Contracting Parties may at any time declare that it recognises as compulsory *ipso facto* and without special agreement the jurisdiction of the Court in all matters concerning the interpretation and application of the present Convention.

2. The declarations referred to above may be made unconditionally or on condition of reciprocity on the part of several or certain other High Contracting Parties or for a specified period."

To the original text of the Convention have been annexed eight protocols, none of which has achieved the acceptance of all signatories to the original Convention. It is to be noted that under the Convention complaints may be brought either by one Member State against another, or by an individual citizen against a Member State, where the state so permits. Since 1966 Britain has for successive five-year periods recognised the individual right of petition under Article 25. The Convention sets up its own mechanism of enforcement via two organs: the European Commission of Human Rights and the European Court of Human Rights. Each has a number of members equal to the number of states which have ratified the Convention and no two members of either may be of the same nationality (although in theory nationals of non-Member States could be elected). The constitution and election of the two organs are governed by Articles 20-22, 33-37, 38-43. The Commission acts both as a filter and as a reconciling agent between the parties. Any person who feels that a state has violated his rights may write, saying why, to the European Commission of Human Rights, Strasbourg 67007, France.

At its next meeting the Commission then decides whether the application is "admissible." There are a number of grounds of inadmissibility; the most important being, first, that the applicant has not exhausted every remedy open to him in his own country; second, that the application has not been made within six months of exhaustion of domestic remedies; and third, that the application is "manifestly ill-founded" (Articles 26 and 27). If the Commission accepts the petition, it undertakes an investigation of it, and tries to effect a friendly settlement "on the basis of respect for Human Rights as defined in this Convention" (Article 28(b)). If it fails in this it draws up a report in which it expresses its views on the merits of the case. Within three months either the Commission, or the "defendant" state, or the state whose national the applicant is, or the applicant state where apposite, may refer the matter to the Court for judgment; an applicant under Article 25 cannot do so. The judgment of the Court is final and binding (Articles 52 and 53). If a commission report is not referred to the Court within three months, the Committee of Ministers of the Council of Europe may decide by a two-thirds majority that there has been a violation of the Convention and what remedial measures the "defendant" state must take. Its decision is binding (Article 32(4)).

Most of the cases which have been brought have been by individual petition. In fact, between 1955 and 1986 only nine inter-state cases had been considered by the Commission, in contrast with 11,659 decisions in cases which had come by way of individual petition. And of these 11,659 individual petitions only 492 were declared admissible by the Commission. So far as the source of complaints is concerned, this is shown in Table 1, for the years 1984 to 1986.

Table 1

Country	1984	1985	1986
Austria	36	42	61
Belgium	41	32	44
Denmark	5	12	13
France	59	70	86
Fed. Rep. Germany	115	104	106
Greece	—	—	1
Iceland	1	1	1
Ireland	8	5	4
Italy 21	53	63	
Liechtenstein	2	1	—
Luxembourg	1	1	2
Netherlands	45	34	50
Norway	4	3	3
Portugal	5	10	7
Spain	15	19	17
Sweden	51	64	68
Switzerland	49	33	50
United Kingdom	128	112	140

Source: European Commission of Human Rights: Survey of Activities and Statistics 1986

Although many applications have thus been brought against the United Kingdom, only one Scottish complaint has led to a decision of the Court.

2. Campbell and Cosans v. United Kingdom
[1982] 4 E.H.R.R.

This case concerned the use of corporal punishment in Scottish schools. Mrs Campbell complained that Strathclyde Regional Council had refused her requests for a guarantee that her son would not be punished in this way. He was in fact never so punished while he remained at the school. Mrs Cosan's son refused to accept corporal punishment, following the advice of his father. As a result he was suspended from school on September 23, 1976, and did not attend school again, ceasing to be of compulsory school age on May 31, 1977. In its decision, the Court considered claims that the use of corporal punishment as a disciplinary measure violated Article 3 of the Convention and Protocol 1, Article 2 (the text of which appears in the judgment).

"AS TO THE LAW

23. The court considers it preferable to begin by examining the issues arising under Article 3 of the Convention, this being the provision on which principal reliance was placed in the original applications to the Commission.

I. The alleged violation of Article 3 of the Convention

24. Mrs Campbell and Mrs Cosans claimed that, on account of the use of corporal punishment as a disciplinary measure in school, their sons Gordon and Jeffrey were victims of a violation of Article 3 which reads: 'No one shall be subjected to torture or to inhuman or degrading treatment or punishment.'

The Commission found no such violation. The Government agreed with this conclusion.

25. Neither Gordon Campbell nor Jeffrey Cosans was, in fact, strapped with the tawse. Accordingly, the Court does not in the present case have to consider under Article 3 an actual application of corporal punishment.

26. However, the Court is of the opinion that, provided it is sufficiently real and immediate, a mere threat of conduct prohibited by Article 3 may itself be in conflict with that provision. Thus, to threaten an individual with torture might in some circumstances constitute at least 'inhuman treatment.'

27. Although the system of corporal punishment can cause a certain degree of apprehension in those who may be subject to it, the Court nevertheless shares the Commission's view that the situation in which the applicants' sons found themselves did not amount to 'torture' or 'inhuman treatment,' within the meaning of Article 3: there is no evidence that they underwent suffering of the level inherent in these notions as they were interpreted and applied in the Court's *Ireland* v. *the United Kingdom* judgment of January 18, 1978.

28. The Court's judgment of April 25, 1978 in the Tyrer case does indicate certain criteria concerning the notion of 'degrading punishment'. In the present case no "punishment" has actually been inflicted. Nevertheless, it follows from that judgment that 'treatment' itself will not be 'degrading' unless the person concerned has undergone—either in the eyes of others or in his own eyes— humiliation or debasement attaining a minimum level of severity. That level has to be assessed with regard to the circumstances of the case (see the above-mentioned Ireland v. United Kingdom judgment).

29. Corporal chastisement is traditional in Scottish schools and, indeed, appears to be favoured by a large majority of parents. Of itself, this is not conclusive of the issue before the Court for the threat of a particular measure is not excluded from the category of "degrading," within the meaning of Article 3, simply because the measure has been in use for a long time or even meets with general approval (see, *mutatis mutandis,* the above-mentioned Tyrer judgment).

However, particularly in view of the above-mentioned circumstances obtaining in Scotland, it is not established that pupils at a school where such punishment is used are, solely by reason of the risk of being subjected thereto, humiliated or debased in the eyes of others to the requisite degree or at all.

30. As to whether the applicants' sons were humiliated or debased in their

own eyes, the Court observes first that a threat directed to an exceptionally insensitive person may have no significant effect on him but nevertheless be incontrovertibly degrading; and conversely, an exceptionally sensitive person might be deeply affected by a threat that could be described as degrading only by a distortion of the ordinary and usual meaning of the word. In any event, in the case of these two children, the Court, like the Commission, notes that it has not been shown by means of medical certificates or otherwise that they suffered any adverse psychological or other effects.

Jeffrey Cosans may well have experienced feelings of apprehension or disquiet when he came close to an infliction of the tawse, but such feelings are not sufficient to amount to degrading treatment, within the meaning of Article 3.

The same applies, *a fortiori,* to Gordon Campbell since he was never directly threatened with corporal punishment. It is true that counsel for his mother alleged at the hearings that group tension and a sense of alienation in the pupil are induced by the very existence of this practice but, even if this be so, these effects fall into a different category from humiliation or debasement.

31. To sum up, no violation of Article 3 is established. This conclusion renders it unnecessary for the Court to consider whether the applicants are entitled, under Article 25 of the Convention, to claim that their children were victims of such a violation, an issue that was examined by the Commission and was the subject of submissions by the Government.

II. The alleged violation of the second sentence of Article 2 of Protocol No. 1.

32. Article 2 of Protocol No. 1 reads as follows:

'No person shall be denied the right to education. In the exercise of any functions which it assumes in relation to education and to teaching, the State shall respect the right of parents to ensure such education and teaching in conformity with their own religious and philosophical convictions.'

Mrs Campbell and Mrs Cosans alleged that their rights under the second sentence of this Article were violated on account of the existence of corporal punishment as a disciplinary measure in the schools attended by their children.

The Government contested, on various grounds, the conclusion of the majority of the Commission that there had been such a violation.

33. The Government maintained in the first place that functions relating to the internal administration of a school, such as discipline, were ancillary and were not functions in relation to 'education' and to 'teaching,' within the meaning of Article 2, these terms denoting the provision of facilities and the imparting of information, respectively.

The Court would point out that the education of children is the whole process whereby, in any society, adults endeavour to transmit their beliefs, culture and other values to the young, whereas teaching or instruction refers in particular to the transmission of knowledge and to intellectual development.

It appears to the Court somewhat artificial to attempt to separate off matters relating to internal administration as if all such matters fell outside the scope of

Article 2. The use of corporal punishment may, in a sense, be said to belong to the internal administration of a school, but at the same time it is, when used, an integral part of the process whereby a school seeks to achieve the object for which it was established, including the development and moulding of the character and mental powers of its pupils. Moreover, as the Court pointed out in its Kjeldsen, Busk Madsen and Pedersen judgment of December 7, 1976, the second sentence of Article 2 is binding upon the Contracting States in the exercise of 'each and every' function that they undertake in the sphere of education and teaching, so that the fact that a given function may be considered to be ancillary is of no moment in this context.

34. The Government further argued that in Scotland the 'functions' assumed by central or local government in the educational field did not extend to matters of discipline.

It may be true that the day-to-day maintenance of discipline in the schools in question is left to the individual teacher; when he administers corporal punishment he is exercising not a power delegated to him by the State but a power vested in him by the common law by virtue of his status as a teacher, and the law in this respect can be changed only by Act of Parliament (see paragraphs 12, 15 and 17 above). Nevertheless, in regard to education in Scotland, the State has assumed responsibility for formulating general policy, and the schools attended by the applicants' children were State schools. Discipline is an integral, even indispensable, part of any educational system, with the result that the functions assumed by the State in Scotland must be taken to extend to questions of discipline in general, even if not to its everyday maintenance. Indeed, this is confirmed by the fact that central and local authorities participated in the preparation of the Code of Practice and that the Government themselves are committed to a policy aimed at abolishing corporal punishment.

35. Thirdly, in the submission of the Government, the obligation to respect philosophical convictions arises only in relation to the content of, and mode of conveying, information and knowledge and not in relation to all aspects of school administration.

As the Government pointed out, the Kjeldsen, Busk Madsen and Pedersen judgment states:

'The second sentence of Article 2 implies . . . that the State, in fulfilling the functions assumed by it in regard to education and teaching, must take care that information or knowledge included in the curriculum is conveyed in an objective, critical and pluralistic manner. The State is forbidden to pursue an aim of indoctrination that might be considered as not respecting parents' religious and philosophical convictions. That is the limit that must not be exceeded.'

However, that case concerned the content of instructions, whereas the second sentence of Article 2 has a broader scope, as is shown by the generality of its wording. This was confirmed by the Court in the same judgment when it held that the said sentence is binding upon the contracting States in the exercise, *inter alia,* of the function 'consisting of the organisation and financing of public education'. And in the present case the functions assumed by the respondent State in this area extend to the supervision of the Scottish educational system in general, which must include questions of discipline (see paragraph 34 above).

36. The Government also contested the conclusion of the majority of the Commission that the applicants' views on the use of corporal punishment amounted to 'philosophical convictions,' arguing, *inter alia,* that the expression did not extend to opinions on internal school administration, such as discipline, and that, if the majority were correct, there was no reason why objections to other methods of discipline, or simply to discipline in general, should not also amount to 'philosophical convictions.'

In its ordinary meaning the word 'convictions,' taken on its own, is not synonymous with the words 'opinions' and 'ideas', such as are utilised in Article 10 of the Convention, which guarantees freedom of expression; it is more akin to the term 'beliefs' (in the French text: *'convictions'*) appearing in Article 9— which guarantees freedom of thought, conscience and religion—and denotes views that attain a certain level of cogency, seriousness, cohesion and importance.

As regards the adjective 'philosophical,' it is not capable of exhaustive definition and little assistance as to its precise significance is to be gleaned from the *travaux préparatoires.* The Commission pointed out that the word 'philosophy' bears numerous meanings: it is used to allude to a fully-fledged system of thought or, rather loosely, to views on more or less trivial matters. The Court agrees with the Commission that neither of these two extremes can be adopted for the purposes of interpreting Article 2: the former would too narrowly restrict the scope of a right that is guaranteed to all parents and the latter might result in the inclusion of matters of insufficient weight or substance.

Having regard to the Convention as a whole, including Article 17, the expression 'philosophical convictions' in the present context denotes, in the court's opinion, such convictions as are worthy of respect in a 'democratic society' (see, most recently, the Young, James and Webster judgment of August 13, 1981), and are not incompatible with human dignity; in addition, they must not conflict with the fundamental right of the child to education, the whole of Article 2 being dominated by its first sentence (see the above-mentioned Kjeldsen, Busk Madsen and Pedersen judgment).

The applicants' views relate to a weighty and substantial aspect of human life and behaviour, namely the integrity of the person, the propriety or otherwise of the infliction of corporal punishment and the exclusion of the distress which the risk of such punishment entails. They are views which satisfy each of the various criteria listed above; it is this that distinguishes them from opinions that might be held on other methods of discipline or on discipline in general.

37. The Government pleaded, in the alternative, that the obligation to respect the applicants' convictions had been satisfied by the adoption of a policy of gradually eliminating corporal chastisement. They added that any other solution would be incompatible with the necessity of striking a balance between the opinions of supporters and opponents of this method of discipline and with the terms of the reservation to Article 2 made by the United Kingdom at the time of signing the Protocol, which reads:

'. . . in view of certain provisions of the Education Acts in force in the United Kingdom, the principle affirmed in the second sentence of Article 2 is accepted by the United Kingdom only so far as it is compatible with the provision of efficient instruction and training, and the avoidance of unreasonable public expenditure.'

The Court is unable to accept these submissions.

(a) Whilst the adoption of the policy referred to clearly foreshadows a move in the direction of the position taken by the applicants, it does not amount to 'respect' for their convictions. As it is confirmed by the fact that, in the course of the drafting of Article 2, the words 'have regard to' were replaced by the word 'respect', the latter word means more than 'acknowledge' or 'take into account'; in addition to a primarily negative undertaking, it implies some positive obligation on the part of the State (see, *mutatis mutandis,* the Marckx judgment of June 13, 1979). This being so, the duty to respect parental convictions in this sphere cannot be overridden by the alleged necessity of striking a balance between the conflicting views involved, nor is the Government's policy to move gradually towards the abolition of corporal punishment in itself sufficient to comply with this duty.

(b) As regards the United Kingdom reservation, the Court notes that the provision of domestic law cited in the present case by the Government is section 29(1) of the Education (Scotland) Act 1962 (see paragraph 14 above). Under Article 64 of the Convention, a reservation in respect of any provision is permitted only to the extent that any law in force in a State's territory at the time when the reservation is made is not in conformity with the provision. The Protocol was signed on behalf of the United Kingdom on March 20, 1952. However, section 29(1) was no more than a re-enactment of an identical provision in the Education (Scotland) Act 1946 and therefore goes no further than a law in force at the time when the reservation was made.

The Court accepts that certain solutions canvassed—such as the establishment of a dual system whereby in each sector there would be separate schools for the children of parents objecting to corporal punishment—would be incompatible, especially in the present economic situation, with the avoidance of unreasonable public expenditure. However, the Court does not regard it as established that other means of respecting the applicants' convictions, such as a system of exemption for individual pupils in a particular school, would necessarily be incompatible with 'the provision of efficient instruction and training, and the avoidance of unreasonable public expenditure.'

38. Mrs Campbell and Mrs Cosans have accordingly been victims of a violation of the second sentence of Article 2 of Protocol No. 1.

III. The alleged violation of the first sentence of Article 2 of Protocol No. 1.

39. Mrs Cosans alleged that, by reason of his suspension from school, her son Jeffrey had been denied the right to education, contrary to the first sentence of Article 2.

The Commission found it unnecessary to examine this issue, considering it to be absorbed by the finding of a violation of the second sentence. The Government, in an alternative plea, accepted this view but their principle submission was that the right of access to educational facilities which is guaranteed by the first sentence may be made subject to reasonable requirements and that, since Jeffrey's suspension was due to his and his parents' refusal to accept such a requirement, there had been no breach.

40. The Court considers that it is necessary to determine this issue. Of course, the existence of corporal punishment as a disciplinary measure in the school attended by her son Jeffrey underlay both of Mrs Cosans' allegations concerning Article 2, but there is a substantial difference between the factual basis of her two claims. In the case of the second sentence, the situation complained of was attendance at a school where recourse was had to a certain practice, whereas, in the case of the first sentence, it was the fact of being forbidden to attend; the consequences of the latter situation are more far-reaching than those of the former. Accordingly, a separate complaint, and not merely a further legal submission or argument, was involved (see, *mutatis mutandis*, the Le Compte, Van Leuven and De Meyere judgment of June 23, 1981).

Again, Article 2 constitutes a whole that is dominated by its first sentence, the right set out in the second sentence being an adjunct of the fundamental right to education (see the above-mentioned Kjeldsen, Busk Madsen and Pedersen judgment).

Finally, there is also a substantial difference between the legal basis of the two claims, for one concerns a right of a parent and the other a right of a child.

The issue arising under the first sentence is therefore not absorbed by the finding of a violation of the second.

41. The right to education guaranteed by the first sentence of Article 2 by its very nature calls for regulation by the State, but such regulation must never injure the substance of the right nor conflict with other rights enshrined in the Convention or its Protocols (see the judgment of July 23, 1968 on the merits of the "Belgian Linguistic" case).

The suspension of Jeffrey Cosans—which remained in force for nearly a whole school year—was motivated by his and his parents' refusal to accept that he receive or be liable to corporal chastisement. His return to school could have been secured only if his parents had acted contrary to their convictions, convictions which the United Kingdom is obliged to respect under the second sentence of Article 2 (see paragraphs 35-36 above). A condition of access to an educational establishment that conflicts in this way with another right enshrined in Protocol No. 1 cannot be described as reasonable and in any event falls outside the State's power of regulation under Article 2.

There has accordingly also been, as regards Jeffrey Cosans, breach of the first sentence of that Article.

IV. The application of Article 50 of the Convention

42. Counsel for Mrs Cosans stated that, should the Court find a violation of the Convention and/or Protocol No. 1, his client would seek just satisfaction under Article 50 in respect of moral damage and legal costs, but he did not quantify her claim. The Lord Advocate, for the Government, reserved his position, as did counsel for Mrs Campbell.

Accordingly, although it was raised under Rule 47 bis of the rules of Court, this question is not yet ready for decision. The Court must therefore reserve it and fix the further procedure, taking due account of the possibility of an agreement between the respondent State and the applicants."

Although *Campbell and Cosans* is the only decision of the court (so far) originating from Scotland, others may be in the pipeline. There have also been some 20 other decisions in cases from other parts of the United Kingdom, in most of which some violation of the Convention has been established, as a result of which changes to domestic law were implemented, many of these applying to Scotland in addition to England and Wales. We will encounter many of these cases at later stages in the book. In Chapter 4 (the right to privacy) we will consider how the Convention (particularly Article 8) has had an impact on prisoners' rights; on the legal position of homosexual behaviour; and the practice of State surveillance. In Chapter 6 we will consider the importance of the ECHR in shaping Scots law on freedom of expression, particularly the power of the press to publish prejudicial material while legal proceedings are active. In the meantime we may note here several landmark decisions which do not conveniently fall to be treated at length in later chapters, but which give an indication of the range of issues which fall within the jurisdiction of the Convention.

A.   Ireland v. United Kingdom (1978) 2 E.H.R.R 25

This was the first inter-state case against the United Kingdom to reach the European Court of Human Rights. It arose from the implementation of the policy of internment of suspected terrorists in Northern Ireland from 1971. The allegations of infringement of the Convention fell into two groups. First, it was alleged that a number of detainees had been severely beaten by the security forces. Second, it was alleged that the use of what were known as "the five techniques" of interrogation in depth constituted inhuman or degrading treatment. These five techniques included deprivation of sleep for long periods and forced standing spreadeagled against a wall for long periods. Their use was authorised by the authorities at high level, and two committees of inquiry in 1971-72 found their use acceptable, although following the second report the government ordered that they no longer be used. The European Court of Human Rights held that there had been a practice of inhuman treatment contrary to Article 3, ECHR, but that this did not amount to torture.

B.   Young, James and Webster v. United Kingdom (1981) 4 E.H.R.R. 38

Under the Trade Union and Labour Relations Act 1974, the institution of the "closed shop" was recognised as lawful. Individual employees in occupations subject to a closed shop agreement were entitled to refuse to join the union only on grounds of religious objection. Young, James and Webster were employees of British Rail, which in 1975 negotiated a closed shop agreement. They refused to join the union on the grounds that there should be individual freedom of choice on such matters, and that they objected to the policies of the unions concerned. They were dismissed, and argued that this was contrary to Article 11 of the Convention.

The complaint was upheld. The court found it unnecessary to decide whether the positive right to associate in Article 11 must necessarily imply the negative right not to associate. It did, however, hold that in certain circumstances the obligation to join a union on pain of dismissal could be a violation of Article 11(1). This would apply where the employees were given no choice as to which union to join and where membership of a particular organisation would violate other rights guaranteed by the Convention, such as Articles 9 (conscience) and 10 (expression).

C.   X v. United Kingdom (1981) 4 E.H.R.R. 188

In the law of each United Kingdom jurisdiction certain dangerous and mentally disordered criminal offenders may be ordered by the court of trial to be detained in a secure mental hospital, and in such cases an order restricting the discharge of the patient may be added to the order for committal. The effect of such an order, prior to X's case, was that neither the medical staff of the hospital nor the Mental Welfare Commission (in England, a mental health review tribunal) could discharge the patient. That responsibility lay exclusively with the appropriate Secretary of State, who also had a power to recall a discharged patient.

X had been committed to Broadmoor under these conditions, and had been conditionally discharged thus leaving him subject to recall. He was, in fact, so recalled with no detailed explanation for this being offered. He alleged that this was contrary to Article 5, ECHR in that he was being detained without having the right to challenge the substantive grounds of his detention as being "of unsound mind." The European Court of Human Rights ruled that a patient may only continue to be detained under Article 5(4) so long as his mental disorder persists and he must have access to a court which must be able to investigate the persistence of the disorder. So far as Scotland is concerned, this was implemented by the lengthy new sections inserted into the Mental Health (Scotland) Act 1960 by the Mental Health (Amendment) (Scotland) Act 1983 conferring on restricted patients rights of appeal to the sheriff against continued hospitalisation, against the conditions of conditional discharges, and against recalls to hospital.

3. Surjit Kaur v. Lord Advocate
[1980] 3 C.M.L.R. 79

Three children were born to two illegal immigrants in Scotland. The children therefore had the right to live in the United Kingdom. Their parents were deported and when the mother left she took the children with her. Founding on the inseparability of the family unit, the mother then raised an action for declarator that her deportation, and the consequent "constructive deportation" of the children, was a violation of their, and her, rights under Articles 3 and 8 of the Convention.

LORD ROSS: . . . "In my opinion the Convention cannot be regarded in any way as part of the Municipal law of Scotland. I accept that the Convention sets forth a number of very important principles relating to Human Rights, but the provisions of the Convention have never entered into the law of Scotland. As I understand it, the law of Scotland is to be found partly in enactments by a body with legislative power and partly in the common law. A Treaty or a Convention is not part of the law of Scotland unless and until Parliament has passed legislation giving effect to the Treaty provisions. . . .

I was also referred to various English cases. This is a field of law where it would be proper to seek assistance from reported decisions in the English Courts although these decisions are not binding in Scotland. . .

I now summarise the conclusions which I draw from these cases.

(1) In England, it is accepted that Conventions such as the European Convention on Human Rights are not part of the municipal law of England. [Here Lord Ross excerpted a number of comments.]

Although these English authorities are not binding on me, they appear to support my opinion that the Convention is not in any way part of the municipal law of Scotland.

(2) The second conclusion which may be drawn from the English authorities is that if there is any ambiguity in a United Kingdom statute, the Court in England may look at and have regard to the Convention as an aid to construction. Lord Denning M.R. said as much . . . in *R.* v. *Secretary of State for Home Affairs, ex p. Bhajan Singh* [1976] Q.B. 198:

'What is the position of the Convention in our English law? I would not depart in the least from what I said in the recent case of *Birdi* v. *Secretary of State for Home Affairs*. The Court can and should take the Convention into account. They should take it into account whenever interpreting a statute which affects the rights and liberties of the individual. It is to be assumed that the Crown, in taking its part in legislation, would do nothing which is in conflict with treaties. So the Court should now construe the Immigration Act 1971 as to be in conformity with a Convention and not against it.'

[Lord Ross then cited a number of other dicta to similar effect.]

With all respect to the distinguished judges in England who have said that the Courts should look to an International Convention such as the European Convention on Human Rights for the purpose of interpreting a United Kingdom Statute, I find such a concept extremely difficult to comprehend. If the Convention does not form part of the municipal law, I do not see why the Court should have regard to it at all. It was His Majesty's government in 1950 which was a High Contracting Party to the Convention. The Convention has been ratified by the United Kingdom, but, although this probably means, as counsel pointed out, that the Convention has been laid before both Houses of Parliament before it was ratified (the Ponsonby Rule), its provisions cannot be regarded as having the force of law. . . Under our constitution, it is the Queen in Parliament who legislates and not Her Majesty's government, and the Court does not require to have regard to Acts of Her Majesty's government when interpreting the law. It is significant that in Article 6 of the Condescendence the pursuers aver 'the Government of the United Kingdom is bound by the terms of the said Convention.' The government may be so bound, but I do not see how or why the Courts should be bound by the Convention. . .

So far as Scotland is concerned, I am of opinion that the Court is not entitled to have regard to the Convention either as an aid to construction or otherwise...

Counsel for the pursuers, however, contended further and in any event that the Convention was enforceable as part of Community law. Counsel referred to the European Communities Act 1972, and drew attention to the wide terms of section 2 (1) of the Act which deals *inter alia* with the enforceability of all rights 'created or arising by or under the treaties' . . . Counsel also submitted that the Court of Justice of the European Communities . . . had already expressed the view that the Convention was part of the law which has to be enforced under the Treaties and that this Court was obliged to follow that ruling and to enforce the Convention as part of Community law. Alternatively, if the matter was in doubt counsel for the pursuers submitted that I should refer the matter to the European Court.

Counsel for the pursuer relied in particular upon the judgment of the European Court in *Firma J. Nold KG* v. *E.C Commission* [1974] 2 C.M.L.R. 338. . .

Counsel contended that the present case fell directly under the decision in the case *Nold* and that the law of Scotland must be regarded as including those principles referred to in *Nold* because they were part of European law. Alternatively, if the matter were in doubt counsel contended that a reference should be made to the European Court. . . . It seems clear that for some purposes at least the European Court does enforce the principles contained in the Convention. There are a number of cases where the European Court has emphasised that it must ensure that the fundamental rights of individuals contained in the general principles of the law of the Community are enforced. . .

[In *Nold* it is stated at p. 354:]

'As this Court has already held, fundamental rights form an integral part of the general principles of law which it enforces. In assuring the protection of such rights, this Court is required to base itself on the constitutional traditions common to the member-States and therefore could not allow measures which are incompatible with the fundamental rights recognised and guaranteed by the constitutions of such States. The International Treaties on the protection of Human Rights in which the member-States have co-operated or to which they have adhered can also supply indications which may be taken into account within the framework of Community Law. . .'

. . . Having carefully considered the submissions made I have reached the conclusion that the argument on behalf of the pursuers is not well-founded. . . I agree with Lord McLuskey that the European Court does not deal with fundamental rights as such in the abstract; it only deals with them if they arise under Treaties and have a bearing on Community law questions. . .

In *The State* v. *Watson and Belmann* [1976] 2 C.M.L.R. 552, in the opinion of the Advocate General . . . at p. 563 . . . the Advocate General said:

'On the basis of this analogy between rules of Community Law and rules of International Law accepted by all member-States, some learned writers have felt justified in concluding that the provisions of the said Convention must be treated as forming an integral part of the Community Legal Order, whereas it seems clear to me that the spirit of the judgment did not involve any substantive reference to the provisions themselves, but merely a reference to the general principles of which, like the Community rules with which the judgment drew an analogy, they are a specific expression. . .

The extra-Community instruments under which those States have undertaken international obligations in order to ensure better protection for those rights can, without any question of their being incorporated as such in the Community order, be used to establish principles which are common to the States themselves. . .'

. . . In *Allgemeine Gold* v. *Commissioners of Customs and Excise* [1978] 2 C.M.L.R. 292, Donaldson J. (as he then was) observed that although fundamental rights enshrined in the Convention are relevant to a consideration of the rights and duties of the Community Institution *(sic)* and may be a background against which the express provisions of the EEC Treaty have to be interpreted, they do not form an implied, unexpressed part of the Treaty itself. . .

In concluding that the pursuers' argument is not well-founded, I am also influenced by the fact that the issue raised in the present case has no Community law content at all. The pursuers here are not seeking to protect some economic right, but merely to assert a right alleged to be conferred on them by the Convention...

For all these reasons, I am of opinion that the pursuers have not averred that they have any right under Community law. It follows that the pursuers' case is irrelevant and incompetent since they are seeking declarator of a right which they do not have either under the Municipal law of Scotland nor under Community law. The action therefore falls to be dismissed."

The approach taken by Lord Ross in *Surjit Kaur* was adopted by the Inner House in *Moore* v. *Secretary of State for Scotland*, 1985 S.L.T. 38, where a convicted prisoner raised an action for declarator that he had been wrongly convicted and for damages. One of the major issues in the case centred on section 263 of the Criminal Procedure (Scotland) Act 1975 which provides:

"Nothing in this Part of this Act shall affect the prerogative of mercy, but the Secretary of State on the consideration of any conviction of a person or the sentence (other than sentence of death) passed on a person who has been convicted, may, if he thinks fit, at any time, and whether or not an appeal against such conviction or sentence has previously been heard and determined by the High Court, refer the whole case to the High Court and the case shall be heard and determined, subject to any directions the High Court may make, as if it were an appeal under this Part of this Act. (2) The power of the Secretary of State under this section to refer to the High Court the case, or any point arising on the case, of a person convicted shall be exercisable whether or not that person has petitioned for the exercise of Her Majesty's mercy."

The question was whether the Secretary of State could be compelled to "activate" this provision. The Second Division took the view, however, that this discretion is unfettered, though in the course of so doing it referred to the Convention in the following terms:

"Finally, the pursuer put forward an argument which can only be interpreted as compelling the Secretary of State to 'activate' s. 263. It was based on the European Convention on Human Rights. Acknowledging that this Convention had not been brought into the law of Scotland by legislation, he submitted that nonetheless it had been accepted into European Community law by the European Communities Act 1972. As the United Kingdom is a member of the European Community then via the said Act this Convention had become part of the municipal law of Scotland. Faced with the decision of Lord Ross in *Kaur* v. *Lord Advocate* that the Convention had no effect on Scottish municipal law unless the legislature passed a law for that purpose, which the legislature had not done, the pursuer swept that decision aside by saying that he did not agree with it and that accordingly it was not binding upon him. As a layman, his summary dismissal of an authority in such a manner is understandable, however unsound it may be, but such a luxury cannot be afforded to the court. In our view Lord Ross was perfectly correct in holding that the Convention plays no part in our municipal law so long as it has not been introduced into it by legislation. Here again is a short answer to a submission by the pursuer. He seemed to think that to hold a decision in relation to an Indian national such as *Kaur* to be binding on him, a Scottish national, was discriminating against a Scotsman, and he considered that this offended against the EEC Treaty which forbids discrimination on nationality. To point out to him that it was the principle of law which was being invoked, irrespective of the nationality of the party to the case, was a fruitless exercise. In any event, the pursuer seemed to be unaware that if Community law is introduced into the municipal law, it is because the subject-matter has a Community content, and there is no such content here.

When regard is had to the purpose for which the pursuer wished to invoke the Articles of the European Convention on Human Rights the irrelevancy of the pursuer's submission becomes immediately apparent. Under reference to conds. 3 to 8 of his pleadings, which as already pointed out are hopelessly irrelevant, he maintains that his trial was conducted in a manner contrary to art. 6 (1), (3) (*b*) and (3) (*d*) of the said Convention. Article 6 (1) deals with the principle of everyone being entitled to a fair and public hearing by an independent and impartial tribunal established by law in the determination of a person's civil rights or obligations or of any criminal charge against him. Article 6 (3) (*b*) provides that everyone charged with a criminal offence has the right to have adequate time and facilities for the preparation of his defence. Article 6 (3) (*d*) gives the right to a person charged with a criminal offence to examine and cross-examine witnesses under the same conditions as are imposed on witnesses against him. The pursuer does not have to have recourse to these Articles under the Convention.

They are already part of our municipal law and can be dealt with under our own criminal code. This was just an illegitimate attempt to get round the difficulties presented by our municipal law by recourse to the provisions of a Convention which have not been incorporated into our municipal law, and that by a wholly unwarranted argument.

The pursuer also prayed in aid the provisions of Art. 13 of the Convention, and maintained that the Secretary of State's handling of his representations under s. 263 of the Act constituted a breach of that Article. The Article is in the following terms: 'Everyone whose rights and freedoms as set forth in this Convention are violated shall have an effective remedy before a national authority notwithstanding that the violation has been committed by persons acting in an official capacity.' Once again the pursuer proceeded on the basis that the fact that the Secretary of State had refused his application under s. 263 in itself established that there had been a violation of his rights. Insofar as he attempted to justify his assertion that his rights had been violated he relied on submissions with which we have already dealt and rejected. Insofar as there was an issue as to whether his rights had been violated, that had been tested in the first instance by the national authorities set up by Parliament to carry out his trial and resultant appeal, and his subsequent submissions were dealt with by the national authority appointed by Parliament to deal with them by s. 263 of the Act. Once again the court was presented by the pursuer with a submission which was simply an illegitimate stratagem to get round the insuperable obstacles which our municipal law presents to the success of his case."

Although the Court of Session thus appears clear in its view of the Convention, it is to be noted that the House of Lords is, at least in principle, much more equivocal. This is true of the House generally and of Scottish members in particular.

1. So far as the ECHR and statute law is concerned, it is clear that the terms of the Convention cannot displace the provisions of an otherwise inconsistent Act of Parliament. This is because of the doctrine of parliamentary sovereignty: the duty of the courts is to give effect to the will of Parliament, however inconsistent with international law that might be (*Mortensen* v. *Peters* (1906) 8 F.(J.)93). The House of Lords has, however, been willing to use the Convention as an aid to the construction of a statute. In *Waddington* v. *Miah* [1974] 1 W.L.R. 683 the defendant was charged as being an illegal immigrant, contrary to section 24 of the Immigration Act 1971. The section did not come into force until January 1973, but the charge related to events before that date. The defendant was nevertheless convicted and on appeal the conviction was quashed by the Court of Appeal, a decision which was upheld by the House of Lords. The speech of their Lordships was delivered by Lord Reid. The main question was whether section 24 was designed to be retrospective in its operation. In holding that it was not, Lord Reid had regard to Article 7 of the ECHR and said that: "it is hardly credible that any government department would promote or that Parliament would pass retrospective

criminal legislation" (at p. 694).

It may be, however, that not too much should be made of this decision. Their Lordships are not always willing to give so much weight to the Convention, and it is possible that they will use it as an aid only when it will facilitate the result they would in any event wish to reach. This is strongly suggested by *UKAPE* v. *ACAS* [1980] I.C.R. 201 which was concerned with the powers of ACAS under the Employment Protection Act 1975, ss. 11-16. Under the Act a trade union could refer a "recognition issue" to ACAS where an employer refused to enter into collective bargaining with the union. ACAS would then make inquiries of the workers concerned, and could in appropriate cases recommend the recognition of the union by the employer for the purposes of collective bargaining. In this case as employer who recognised other trade unions refused to recognise UKAPE. An ACAS inquiry found that there was strong support for UKAPE from the members of a particular section of the workforce, yet ACAS refused to recommend recognition because of hostility from the unions already established in the plant. The question which arose was whether ACAS had abused its discretion by failing to recommend recognition in these circumstances. The Court of Appeal replied in the affirmative, but this was overruled by the House of Lords.

In the Court of Appeal, Lord Denning drew inspiration from Article 11 of the Convention, and said:

"The European Convention has not yet been formally introduced into our statute law: see *R.* v. *Chief Immigration Officer, Heathrow Airport, ex p. Salamat Bibi* [1976] 1 W.L.R. 979. But the proposition in Article 11 accurately states the common law: and for myself, I think that when Parliament enacts legislation on trade unions, it must be taken not to intend to contravene that basic right.

Applying this proposition, it seems to me that these professional engineers have a right to form and join their own trade union. In this case they have exercised that right. They have formed UKAPE and they have joined it. The right is given to each one for a specific purpose—'for the protection of his interests.' What good is that right to him, I would ask? What good is it to him if UKAPE is disabled from protecting his interests—by being refused recognition—as a result of threats by the big battalions?

I would hold that this right of free association is part of English law. When the great majority of workers in a particular group wish to be represented by a union of their choice—and not to be represented by a rival union—ACAS should normally give effect to their wishes."

But a rather different approach was adopted in the House of Lords, where Lord Scarman said:

"Finally, the point on the European Convention. I agree with Lord Denning M.R. that Article 11 of the Convention and the common law recognise and protect the right of association, which in the present context includes the right to join a trade union. But it does not follow from the existence of the right that every trade union which can show it has members employed by a particular company or in a particular industry has a right to recognition for the purposes of collective bargaining. I would be surprised if either the Convention or the common law could be interpreted as compelling so chaotic a conclusion. If the common law is to be so understood (and I do not accept that it is), Parliament has averted the mischief by the statute. And, if it be a possible interpretation of the European Convention, I shall not adopt it, unless and until the European Court of Human Rights declares that it is correct. Suffice it to say that I understand why counsel for the respondents did not seek to support this ground of challenge in your Lordships' House. *Until such time as the statute is amended or the convention both becomes part of our law and is authoritatively interpreted in the way proposed by Lord Denning M.R., the point is a bad one"* (Emphasis added).

2. So far as the ECHR and the common law are concerned, there is authority for the view that in some circumstances the Convention is to be taken into account in applying and developing the legal principles. But the degree to which it will be taken into account appears to vary widely. *Broome* v. *Cassell & Co. Ltd.* [1972] A.C. 1027 is a case about the award of exemplary damages for a libel. Although the award of the lower court was upheld by the House, Lord Kilbrandon did say that:

"Counsel for the appellants pointed out, and I for one agree, that since all commercial publication is undertaken for profit, one must be watchful against holding the profit-motive to be sufficient to justify punitive damages: to do so would be seriously to hamper what must be regarded, at least since the European Convention was ratified, as a constitutional right to free speech. I can see that it could be in the public interest that publication should not be stopped merely because the publisher knows that his material is defamatory; it may well be in the public interest that matter injurious to others be disseminated. But if it were suggested that this freedom should also be enjoyed when the publisher either knows that, or does not care whether, his material is libellous—which means not only defamatory but also untrue—it would seem that the scale is being weighed too heavily against the protection of individuals from attacks by media of communication."

Lord Kilbrandon also said, however, that exemplary damages could be justified despite the "constitutional right to free speech":

"If a publisher knows, or has reason to believe, that the act of publication will subject him to compensatory damages, it must be that, since he is actuated by the profit-motive, he is confident that by that publication he will not be the loser. Some deterrent, over and above compensatory damages, may in these circumstances be called for."

So Lord Kilbrandon appears to be saying that the Convention is a factor to be considered, though he clearly implies that it is far from conclusive and may be displaced or discounted by other considerations.

A more significant case then is perhaps *Attorney-General* v. *BBC* [1981] A.C. 303, where the question was whether the Divisional Court could grant an injunction to restrain the BBC from broadcasting a programme which dealt with matters relating to an appeal pending before a local valuation court on the ground that the broadcast would be a contempt of court. The answer to the question depended on whether the local valuation court was part of the judicial power of the State. The House of Lords held that it was not, and in the course of his speech Lord Fraser of Tullybelton explained his position in terms which clearly gave a prominent role to the Convention:

"I agree that in deciding this appeal the House has to hold a balance between the principle of freedom of expression and the principle that the administration of justice must be kept free from outside interference. Neither principle is more important than the other, and where they come into conflict, as they do in this case, the boundary has to be drawn between the spheres in which they respectively operate. That is not the way in which the European Court of Human Rights would approach the question, as we see from the following passage in the report of *The Sunday Times* v. *United Kingdom* [1979] 2 E.H.R.R. 245 at p. 281:

'Whilst emphasising that it is not its function to pronounce itself on an interpretation of English law adopted in the House of Lords, the court points out that it has to take a different approach. The court is faced not with a choice between two conflicting principles, but with a principle of freedom of expression that is subject to a number of exceptions which must be narrowly interpreted.'

It is, therefore, not to be expected that a decision of this House on questions of this sort will invariably be consistent with those of the court. This House, and other courts in the United Kingdom, should have regard to the provisions of the Convention for the Protection of Human Rights and Fundamental Freedoms (1953) and to the decisions of the Court of Human Rights in cases, of which this in one, where our domestic law is not firmly settled. But the Convention does not form part of our law, and the decision on what that law is, is for our domestic courts and for this House.

R.S.C., Ord. 52, r. 1, provides that a Divisional Court of the Queen's Bench Division may punish contempt of court if it is committed in connection with 'proceedings in an inferior court' and the immediate question for decision is whether a local valuation court constituted in terms of the General Rate Act 1967 is an inferior court to which that rule applies. In order to answer the question satisfactorily it is necessary to find some way of ascertaining the class of tribunal which is protected by the law against contempt. The jurisdiction of the King's Bench division to afford protection to inferior courts has sometimes been regarded as the counterpart of its jurisdiction to correct them if they made an illegal exercise of arbitrary powers: see *R*. v. *Davies* [1906] 1 K.B. 32. But liability to correction by prerogative writs applies to bodies which are clearly not courts, and these are now so numerous that the fact that a body is liable to such correction is no indication that it is an inferior court. Another possibility might have been to define the class as consisting of all tribunals whose proceedings are protected by absolute privilege, but that also was (rightly) not suggested on behalf of the Attorney-General because it would unduly enlarge the class.

The contention on behalf of the Attorney-General was that the class of inferior courts to which Order 52 applied consisted of all bodies which possess certain characteristics, including having been created by the Crown or by Parliament, and administering justice in public, even though they were not courts of justice in the full sense. But that definition is open to two grave objections; it is too uncertain and it is probably too wide. Uncertainty is a serious objection because of the large number of tribunals set up by modern legislation, many of which might be on the borderline. It is undesirable that anyone intending to publish information in the newspapers or on radio or television relating to proceedings pending before a tribunal should have to examine in detail the functions and constitution of the tribunal in order to ascertain whether it is protected by the law against contempt. The second objection is even more serious, because, if protection is extended widely, the right to freedom of expression would be correspondingly reduced. That objection would have great weight with an English court without reference to the Convention, and it is reinforced by the Convention. The contention of the Attorney-General cannot therefore be accepted, and in my opinion, the class of inferior courts protected by the law against contempt should be limited to those which are truly courts of law, exercising the judicial power of the state. Not all bodies which are called courts will be included; for example, a court of referees under the Unemployment Insurance Act 1920 would not qualify—see *Collins* v. *Henry Whiteway & Co. Ltd.* [1927] 2 K.B. 378—nor, I think, would a court of inquiry under Part II of the Industrial Courts Act 1919. Both these courts perform administrative acts and are not courts of justice.

I recognise that limiting the protection against contempt in this way is difficult to justify in strict logic. It may well be that the need for protection against interference from newspaper articles or television programmes relating to pending proceedings before a tribunal is greater when the tribunal is not a court of law than when it is, because members of a tribunal which is not a court of law are often laymen who may find more difficulty in excluding irrelevant matter from their minds than the professional lawyers who constitute or preside over most courts of law. Nevertheless, strict logic must give way to the practical convenience of having a test which can be applied with reasonable certainty and of avoiding too great a curtailment of the right of freedom of expression.

For the reasons explained by others of your Lordships I agree that the local valuation court is not a court of law, but a body whose functions are of an administrative character. It is therefore not within the class of inferior courts to which the law of contempt applies."

But although the Convention may be used as a guide when the common law is unclear, it is unlikely that it will be used to alter the basis of the common law where the established principles are clear, even where they are thought to be no longer appropriate: *Gleaves* v. *Deakin* [1979] 2 All E.R. 497. In that case the House of Lords used the Convention to propose that the common law should be reformed. But the case provides no grounds to believe that the judges will assume the mantle of reformers themselves.

4.   European Convention on Human Rights Bill

"**1.**—(1) This Act may be cited as the European Human Rights Convention Act 1984.

(2) In this Act, except in so far as the context otherwise requires—

'the Convention' means the European Convention for the Protection of Human Rights and Fundamental Freedoms signed at Rome on 4th November 1950;

'the Protocols' means Protocol No. 1 to the Convention signed at Paris on 20th March 1952 and Protocol No. 4 to the Convention signed at Strasbourg on 16th September 1963;

'fundamental rights and freedoms' means the rights and freedoms guaranteed by the Convention and the Protocols as set out in Schedule 1 to this Act, subject to the restrictions thereto permitted by the Convention and the Protocols, and subject also to the reservations thereto made by the Government of the United Kingdom as set out in Schedule 2 to this Act;

'act' includes a deliberate omission;

'enactment' includes any Order in Council or instrument made under any enactment;

'statutory body' means a body established by or in pursuance of any enactment, and 'statutory office' means an office so established;

'public body' means a body of persons, whether corporate or unincorporate, carrying on a service or undertaking of a public nature and includes public authorities of all descriptions, and 'public office' shall be construed accordingly;

'the Crown' does not include Her Majesty in Her private capacity, or in right of her Duchy of Lancaster, or the Duchy of Cornwall.

2. Subject to the provisions of this Act, the fundamental rights and freedoms shall have the force of law in the United Kingdom.

3.—(1) Subject to the provisions of this Act, no person shall do any act to which this section applies and which infringes any of the fundamental rights and freedoms of any other person within the jurisdiction of the United Kingdom.

(2) This section applies—

(*a*) to an act done by or for the purposes of the Crown or of a Minister of the Crown,

(*b*) to an act done by or for the purposes of a statutory body, a person holding a statutory office, a public body, or a person holding public office.

(3) The obligation to comply with subsection (1) above is a duty owed to any person within the jurisdiction of the United Kingdom who may be adversely affected by a contravention of that subsection, and any breach of that duty is actionable in the United Kingdom accordingly.

4.—(1) Any enactment made or passed before the passing of this Act which authorises or requires any act to be done shall be taken to authorise or require that act to be done only in a manner and to the extent that it does not infringe any of the fundamental rights and freedoms of any person within the jurisdiction of the United Kingdom.

(2) Any enactment made or passed after the passing of this Act which authorises or requires any act to be done shall be taken to authorise or require that act to be done only in a manner and to the extent that it does not infringe any of the fundamental rights and freedoms of any person within the jurisdiction of the United Kingdom, save in so far as such enactment is an Act which expressly directs that this sub-section shall not apply to the doing of the act in question or is made pursuant to a power conferred by an Act which expressly so directs."

This measure, which is one of several such measures to have been introduced in Parliament, is interesting for several reasons. The first is clause 3, whereby it would bind acts of both the legislature and the executive. A similar impact has been made in Canada by the Charter of Rights and Freedoms 1982. This sets out a number of fundamental freedoms, democratic rights, mobility rights and equality rights. By section 32 it is provided:

"This Charter applies
(a) to the Parliament and government of Canada in respect of all matters within the authority of Parliament including all matters relating to the Yukon Territory and Northwest Territories; and
(b) to the legislature and government of each province in respect of all matters within the authority of the legislature of each province."

The operation of this measure was considered in *Operation Dismantle Inc.* v. *The Queen* [1985] 13 C.R.R. 287 where the Supreme Court of Canada was called upon to consider the application of the Charter to the decision of the federal cabinet to allow the testing of American Cruise missiles over Northern Canada. Although the action failed on its merits, it was nevertheless held that the courts had the power under the Charter to review Cabinet decisions, a power derived from the terms of section 32.

The second important feature of the Bill is the attempt at entrenchment (clause 4). Clearly, there would be little point in enacting the Convention into domestic law if it could be repealed expressly or impliedly by a subsequent enactment. Yet the attempt to entrench a provision, even as important as this one, gives rise to considerable legal and constitutional problems. The doctrine of parliamentary sovereignty is understood to mean the continuing sovereignty of Parliament. That is to say, each Parliament is sovereign and one parliament may not be bound by the wishes of its predecessors. Thus, in *Ellen Street Estates Ltd.* v. *Minister of Health* [1934] 1 K.B. 590, Scrutton L. J. expressed the view that: "the constitutional position [is] that Parliament can alter an Act previously passed, and it can do so by repealing in terms the previous Act . . . and it can do it also in another way—namely by enacting a provision which is clearly inconsistent with an earlier provision" (at pp. 595-596). On this basis a statutory measure like clause 4 of the Bill extracted above would be of little practical value. Parliament could state expressly that the safeguards in the Bill were to be qualified in a later statute. Alternatively, Parliament could impliedly qualify the safeguards by enacting a measure which is inconsistent with them. In both cases traditional doctrine would require the courts to give effect to the most recent expression of Parliament's will.

It is arguable perhaps that in appropriate cases the ground rules may be changed and that the courts will be willing to adapt to new constitutional arrangements. Some support for this view is provided by experience from Canada. In 1960 the federal legislature enacted a Bill of Rights. This provided in section 2:

"Every law of Canada shall, unless it is expressly declared by an Act of the Parliament of Canada that it shall operate notwithstanding the Canadian Bill of Rights, be so construed and applied as not to abrogate, abridge or infringe or to authorize the abrogation, abridgement or infringement of any of the rights or freedoms herein recognized and declared, and in particular, no law of Canada shall be construed or applied so as to. . ."

In determining what is meant by the phrase "law of Canada," it is necessary to refer to section 5(2). This provides:

"The expression 'law of Canada' in Part I means an Act of the Parliament of Canada enacted before or after the coming into force of this Act, any order, rule or regulation thereunder, and any law in force in Canada or in any part of Canada at the commencement of this Act that is subject to be repealed, abolished or altered by the Parliament of Canada."

In other words, an attempt was made not only to ensure that pre-Bill statutes were consistent with the document. An attempt was also made to ensure that post—Bill statutes were equally consistent with its terms. The legislature in 1960 thus sought to tie the hands of future Parliaments. And with this intention the judges were willing to comply. So in *Miller* v. *The Queen* [1977] S.C.R. 680, Laskin C. J. said *obiter* that the courts have acted upon section 5(2) to test the operative effect of future legislation in the face of the Bill of Rights (at p. 696).

But it should not be presumed that the House of Lords would be as willing as the Supreme Court of Canada to adapt to new constitutional settlements. The response of the courts in this country to the European Communities Act 1972 is an important reminder that the legal and constitutional problems of incorporation of a Bill of Rights are by no means formal or academic. Section 2(1) of the 1972 Act incorporated

Community law into domestic law, by enacting:

"All such rights, powers, liabilities, obligations and restrictions from time to time created or arising by or under the Treaties, and all such remedies and procedures from time to time provided for by or under the Treaties, as in accordance with the Treaties are without further enactment to be given legal effect or used in the United Kingdom shall be recognised and available in law, and be enforced, allowed and followed accordingly; and the expression "enforceable Community right" and similar expressions shall be read as referring to one to which this subsection applies."

Section 2(4) then purportedly attempts to give overriding supremacy to community law by providing that "*any enactment passed or to be passed . . . shall be construed and have effect* subject to the foregoing provisions of this Act" (emphasis added). The effect of this measure, which appears designed to entrench Community law (by giving it priority over domestic law) has yet to be considered by a Scottish court. The point arose only indirectly in *Prince* v. *Secretary of State for Scotland,* 1985 S.L.T. 74. In England, however, the question has been addressed, both by the Court of Appeal and by the House of Lords. The evidence which these cases provide suggests that there is little cause to be optimistic about the willingness of the judges to adapt.

Three quite different positions have been taken by the English judges in response to the 1972 Act, s.2. The first, by Lord Denning in *Felixstowe Dock and Railway Co.* v. *British Transport Docks Board* [1976] 2 C.M.L.R. 655 is what might be called the classic position. There he said:

"It seems to me that once the Bill is passed by Parliament and becomes a statute, that will dispose of all this discussion about the Treaty. These courts will then have to abide by the statute without regard."

Within three years, however, Lord Denning had appeared to reconsider this view. In *MacCarthys Ltd* v. *Smith* [1979] 3 All E.R. 325, he said:

"In construing our statute, we are entitled to look to the treaty as an aid to its construction; but not only as an aid but as an overriding force. If on close investigation it should appear that our legislation is deficient or is inconsistent with Community law by some oversight of our draftsmen then it is our bounden duty to give priority to Community law. Such is the result of s. 2(1) and (4) of the European Communities Act 1972."

Taking the most charitable view of this in favour of entrenchment, Lord Denning appears to be suggesting that in the event of conflict between Community law and domestic law, the former shall prevail. A triumph for entrenchment? The triumph is, however, limited. Lord Denning continued:

"if the time should come when our Parliament deliberately passes an Act with the intention of repudiating the Treaty or any provision in it or intentionally of acting inconsistently with it and says so in express terms then I should have thought that it would be the duty of our courts to follow the statute of our Parliament."

In effect, all this appears to be saying is that all that section 2 (4) does is to protect Community law from the operation of the doctrine of implied repeal. It does not protect it from express repeal. And indeed, the third major case on section 2(4) suggests that protection from implied repeal is not universal. In *Garland* v. *British Rail Engineering Ltd.* [1983] 2 A.C. 751, Lord Diplock raised the possibility that something:

"short of an express positive statement in an Act of Parliament passed after 1 January 1973 that a particular provision is intended to be made in breach of an obligation assumed by the United Kingdom under a Community treaty would justify an English court in construing that provision in a manner inconsistent with a Community treaty obligation of the United Kingdom however wide a departure from the prima facie meaning of the language of the provision might be needed in order to achieve consistency."

If similar reasoning was applied to clause 4 of the Bill above, the clause would have little effect. It would be open to Parliament to legislate in a manner which expressly or impliedly departs from the standards laid down in the Convention, provided in the latter case that it made its intention sufficiently clear.

CHAPTER 3

[Note: In this chapter the abbreviations CPSA and CJSA stand respectively for the Criminal Procedure (Scotland) Act 1975 and the Criminal Justice (Scotland) Act 1980]

LIBERTY AND POLICE POWERS

I. INTRODUCTION

THE role of the police and the extent of their powers are among the great perennial concerns of civil liberties lawyers. That this should be so is hardly surprising. Given its effects, the power of arrest is truly an awesome power. In a moment a man may be removed from the circle of his family and acquaintances, detained in spartan accommodation, denied access to his normal entertainments and rights of communication and subjected to constant supervision. Even if eventually found to be completely innocent, the long-term consequences may include the waste of up to 110 days (or, in rare cases, longer) of his life, the loss of employment and in the eyes of many people, a permanent loss of reputation—all without any right to compensation. Equally, the psychological shock of the exercise of powers of search (which at its most intrusive can include forcing entry with sledgehammers in the middle of the night) can be profound. Even if it is accepted that such powers are necessary, it is readily apparent that their ambit should be clearly and closely defined, and the manner of their exercise be anxiously scrutinised.

In this chapter, therefore, we begin the examination of police powers. The police have many functions; they are often the agency to which people with a problem instinctively turn when no other specialised social agency is relevant; indeed they have been called a "secret social service"(*Punch,* quoted in Bradley, Walker and Wilkie, (1986), p. 66). Nonetheless probably their prime functions, historically and in the eyes of most people, concern crime and the maintenance of public order. Broadly speaking they have a group of special powers concerned with each of those functions. In Chapter 8 we deal with the public order powers of the police, and in this chapter with powers for the suppression and detection of crime. The latter have most impact upon personal liberty and freedom of property. In addition, though not strictly police powers, we deal with two associated matters of criminal procedure which affect individual rights, namely the right not to be detained for more than a certain time while awaiting trial, and judicial examination which modifies the "right to silence."

In considering police powers in the investigation of crime, one point which helps explain some of the lack of clarity in the law should be borne in mind. This is that the role of the police is today much greater than it was 100 years ago. In the classical system, the lower judiciary (J.P.s and sheriffs) had an active role in criminal investigations, more like the modern continental judiciary than the modern Scottish. In criminal procedure the police acted very much as the agents of the judiciary rather than as independent investigators. Some of the old rules and assumptions (*e.g.* a general hostility to police questioning) can only be understood against this background.

II.   ARREST

We begin with an examination of the law of arrest, because the power to detain dates only from the Criminal Justice (Scotland) Act 1980, and can only be discussed adequately against the background of the pre-existing law of arrest and its difficulties. Three separate issues arise in connection with arrest: first, when and by whom it is competent; second, how it may be effected; and third, what are the rights of the person arrested?

A.   POWER TO ARREST

Arrests may be made initially on the order or warrant of a justice of the peace, sheriff or senior judge or without any warrant. However, at common law only the foregoing persons have the authority to *continue* a detention begun by arrest without warrant, and where an arrest is made without a warrant the person arrested must be taken before such a person to have the arrest retrospectively authorised. By statute (CPSA s. 321(4)) when a person is arrested without warrant he may be brought before a *summary* court without the police obtaining a warrant.

1.   WITH WARRANT

Although all J.P.s and members of the judiciary may issue warrants, in practice they are usually obtained by a petition (on printed forms) by the procurator fiscal to the local sheriff. A warrant to arrest was initially a means of arranging for the examination of a suspect, and certainly corroborated admissible evidence of complicity was not required to justify the issue of a warrant. Summary and solemn procedure forms differ only slightly.

1. Summary Procedure Form of Warrant

Under the Criminal Procedure (Scotland) Act, 1975
IN THE SHERIFF COURT OF

THE COMPLAINT OF THE PROCURATOR FISCAL AGAINST

Date of Birth:

The charge against you is that

Procurator-Fiscal Depute.

19 .—The Court grants Warrant to apprehend the said Accused and grants Warrant to search the person, dwellinghouse, and repositories of said Accused and any place where they may be found and to take possession of the property mentioned or referred to in the Complaint and all articles and documents likely to afford evidence of   guilt or of guilty participation.

Sheriff.

At common law a warrant can only be executed within the area of jurisdiction of the person who granted it (*e.g.* a sheriffdom if the warrant is granted by a sheriff). A Commissioner of Justiciary of course has jurisdiction throughout Scotland, and by statute (s. 15, CPSA) a sheriff's warrant may be executed anywhere in Scotland, by a constable who has authority for the area. By s. 17(4), CPSA all constables of any Scottish police force have authority to execute warrants anywhere in Scotland. An English warrant may be executed in Scotland by a Scottish constable and a Scottish warrant by an English constable in England (s. 17, CPSA and s. 39(1) (as amended), Criminal Law Act 1977). In addition English and Scottish constables have authority to execute warrants of either jurisdiction in the counties of Northumberland and Cumbria, and the Borders and Dumfries and Galloway Regions (s. 18, Police (Scotland) Act 1967).

Although the authority of a warrant is that of a sheriff, "the sheriff usually grants warrant to arrest an accused person as a matter of course. Such petitions being presented by responsible officials, are assumed to be well founded" (Renton and Brown (1983), para. 5.08). It follows from the absence at common law of a status of "detention on suspicion" (see Part III below) that everyone arrested, with or without a warrant, must be charged, and for that there must be evidence sufficient in law against him to warrant a charge. What exactly constitutes such evidence today is unclear. The Thomson Committee ((1975) paras. 3.07 and 3.08) considered, in the context of arrest without warrant, that evidence sufficient to charge means evidence sufficient to justify reporting a

particular person to the procurator fiscal as the offender. This would seem
to exclude the obtaining of a warrant on mere suspicion and such would
appear to be the committee's view (para. 3.13). A warrant may be used
to arrest someone solely to serve an indictment on him (*Lockhart* v. *Stokes,*
1981 S.L.T.(Sh.Ct.) 71).

When a person is arrested he is entitled to see the warrant so that he
knows of what he is accused (Hume, (1844) ii, 79). However, any police
officer may detain a person for whose arrest a warrant exists until the
warrant is fetched (*Farquharson* v. *Whyte* (1886) 1 White 26). In practice
this means that a person would be taken to the police station where the
warrant is. There are powers of entry in order to serve a warrant.

2.   Hume, "Commentaries on the Law of Scotland Respecting Crimes"
(4th ed., 1844)

"No officer shall in any case be justified for breaking open doors, to execute
his warrant, unless he have notified his errand to those within, and demanded
entrance. But, under that condition, he has a right by our law, though it may be
otherwise in England, to break open the doors of a house, to take the person
mentioned in his warrant; and this, whether he is certainly known to be the guilty
person, or is charged only on probable suspicion; and equally in his own house,
or that of another person, where he is, or is on probable suspicion believed to
be, at the time. For the officer is not obliged to trust the word of every one, perhaps
the friend or associate of the felon, in that matter; and why should any one refuse
liberty to an officer of the law, to search his house, which is no injury to him,
whether the person sought for be there at the time, or not? The officer has the
like privilege with us, on a warrant to search any house for stolen goods, and
to apprehend the possessors. If the officer duly observes these several precautions,
he certainly is not answerable, and neither may the magistrate be answerable,
though in truth the person accused be innocent of the charge, or even though
no such felony have been committed."

(Hume, ii, 80)

Hume (1844: ii, 75) and Alison (1833: ii, 117) both state, following
a case of 1694, that where a magistrate sees any offence committed and
the offender fleeing, or where he is credibly informed of the commission
of a serious violence by a person who saw the offence, he may give a
verbal warrant to apprehend the offender.

2.   WITHOUT WARRANT AT COMMON LAW

This is rather more complicated. It can be safely stated that, from being
something viewed as unusual and of restricted competence, arrest without
warrant at common law has become commonplace. At the same time the
rules as to when it is competent have become less strict, in favour of

a generalised "weighing up" of the situation. As we shall see, these common law powers have also been buttressed by a formidable array of statutory powers of arrest without warrant.

3. Hume, "Commentaries on the Law of Scotland Respecting Crimes"
(4th ed., 1844)

Hume discusses first magistrates' powers of arrest, then turns to constables':

> "In cases of breach of the peace, or violent threats of immediate mischief, as also in cases of felony which he has seen committed, or has information of from others who are sure of the fact, the like power of arresting belongs to a constable, or other officer of the law, proper to the execution of criminal warrants. But after taking the delinquent, the officer, in all such cases, has to carry him before a magistrate, to be dealt with according to law; for which purpose he may command the assistance of the neighbourhood. As to the breaking open of doors in such occasions, I have not found any authority, to warrant a constable in doing so, in his pursuit of one who flies after committing a breach of the peace; but rather a direction to him, in the act 1717, c. 8, to take notice of the master of the house, that he may be afterwards challenged for his contempt, in refusing admission. But it is not to be imagined, that a constable shall be subject to the like restraint in cases of murder, house-breaking, robbery, or the like, committed in his presence, or known to him by complaint of others who were present, or have been the sufferers on such occasions."

Here Hume, in using the word "felony," is probably using it in the sense of offences other than breach of the peace, thus differentiating between the two roles of the police. Hutcheson (1806) makes this distinction even more sharply, saying, first, that in cases of breach of the peace in his own view, a constable may arrest and put someone in prison or in the stocks "till the heat of their passion or intemperance is over" and then release them (p. 286); and, second, that "it is the proper business of a constable to keep the peace and not to punish breach of it. He has no power therefore to arrest a man for an affray, a breach of the peace out of his own view, without a warrant from a justice unless a felony were done" (p. 285).

4. Peggie v. Clark
(1868) 7 M. 89

Peggie was a carrier. He undertook to deliver some goods and hand over the price next day to the supplier, Gordon. He failed to do so and went away for three days. Meanwhile G. reported the matter to the police and the defender, a police constable, went to P's home to look for him, entered without a warrant and searched. On the next day, the defender found P., who had spent part of the money, and apprehended him. P. was released two hours later and sued successfully in the sheriff court on the grounds that the search and arrest were unlawful. The constable appealed.

LORD PRESIDENT (Inglis): "It appears to me that, if the superintendent had reasonable grounds for believing that the pursuer intended to appropriate the money, and for that purpose had absconded, it was right that he should take prompt measures for his apprehension; and the question therefore comes to be, whether he had reasonable grounds? Now, the event certainly goes far to justify him; for when the pursuer was apprehended on his return home, it appeared that he had spent a part of the money on his own account. Looking to all the circumstances, though it is a narrow case, I am inclined to agree with the Sheriff, that the defender had good ground for believing that the pursuer had committed a criminal breach of trust, and had thereupon absconded. . .

The ground on which the Sheriff puts his judgment is somewhat delicate and hazardous. He rests almost entirely on the 12th section of the County Police Act. . . I am not satisfied that that enactment introduced any new law, or extended the powers of police-officers to apprehend without warrant. But I am of the opinion that, under special circumstances, a police-officer is entitled to apprehend without warrant, and it will always be a question whether the circumstances justify the apprehension. There are some cases about which there can be no doubt,—thus, where a man is accused of murder, it would be a gross breach of duty on the part of a police-officer if, having an opportunity, he failed to apprehend the accused at once, and without a warrant. This is a different case, but, looking to the circumstances, I think they did justify the defender in proceeding without a warrant. But I rest my opinion on the common law, and not on the provision of the County Police Act. The Act, no doubt, fortifies a constable in the discharge of his duty, and defines it, but it gives him, in my opinion, no power beyond what he has at common law."

LORD DEAS: "I greatly doubt, with your Lordship, whether, according to the fair import of the Act, it materially extends in any way the power of apprehending without a written warrant . . . it does not say that the suspicion of the officer is to be enough, or that the persons are not to be accused in the ordinary way, and dealt with according to law. It would be a strong thing to suppose that a discretionary power was meant to be given to inferior officers, under all circumstances, to apprehend any person they chose, and for offences of whatever kind, on their own suspicion, without a warrant. There are many exceptional cases in which police-officers or constables are entitled to apprehend without a written warrant, and for such cases no statute was required. If a policeman or constable sees a crime committed, it is his duty to apprehend the criminal at once; or if the criminal is pointed out to him running off from the spot, the same rule would apply. If again, the criminal is hiding, or the officer is credibly informed, or has good reason to believe, that he is about to abscond, the officer may *de plano* apprehend him, to prevent justice from being defeated. The same thing would hold if the crime believed to have been committed was murder or the like, the very nature of the punishment of which would render absconding the probable and natural result of the crime itself. Still further, if a suspected individual belongs to a class of persons reputed to live by crime, or who have no fixed-residence or known means of honest livelihood, in all such cases a police-officer or constable has large powers of apprehending without a warrant. But I agree with your Lordship that the officer is not entitled to overstep the necessity or reasonable requirements of the particular case; and there ought, moreover, in no case, to be undue delay in following out such summary apprehension, by obtaining the appropriate formal warrant for the offender's detention. If an individual, even although expressly charged with crime by an aggrieved party, be a well-known householder,—a person of respectability—what, in our justiciary practice, we call a 'law abiding party,' and where there are no reasonable grounds for supposing that he means to abscond or flee from justice, I find nothing in this statute, any more than in the common law, to justify a police-officer or constable in apprehending him without a warrant.

I do not, therefore, rest my opinion in this case on any such construction of the statute as the Sheriff seems to have adopted, but on the special circumstances of this case; and the view I take of these circumstances entirely agrees with the view taken by your Lordship."

Lord Kinloch delivered a concurring opinion and Lord Ardmillan was absent.

There seems here to be a subtle shift from the fairly specific categories laid down by Hume. Those categories are still cited by the judges but particularly in the judgment of the Lord President there is an emphasis on a more general discretion on the part of constables ("under special circumstances, a police-officer is entitled to apprehend without a warrant, and it will always be a question whether the circumstances justify the apprehension"). In more recent textbooks (see e.g. Renton and Brown, (1983) paras. 5.18-5.26; Mill, (1944), Chap. 8; Angus, (1922), pp. 61-68), the old "rules" are restated but they are embedded in a cloud of qualifications and extensions, hints to constables about the evaluation of reliability of accusers and the like. Thus, for example, any rigid distinction between breach of the peace on the one hand and "felonies" on the other has been reduced to a sliding scale and the principle (Renton and Brown, (1983) para. 5.18) that "arrest is more easily justified the more serious the offence."

Nonetheless, all the examples suggested in the extracts above are examples "of persons caught more or less red-handed," as Lord Cooper put it in *Chalmers* v. *H.M. Advocate,* 1954 J.C. 66 at p. 78 (*cf. Bruce* v. *Adamson* (1899) 7 S.L.T. 77). This leaves open the question of whether persons merely suspected on circumstantial evidence and not seen by the constable or reported to him by a witness may be arrested without a warrant. The Thomson Committee (1975) based its recommendation for the introduction of detention on the impossibility of arrest in such circumstances by the police (paras. 3.10, 3.13), although earlier it had referred to two views (para. 3.06), one of which would accept police power extending "to the arrest of any suspected offender where this is necessary in the interests of justice." Certainly, as far as the police are concerned a person who is accused by a witness of an offence is only a suspect, and there may be insufficient evidence in law to convict. Surely then, the arrest of a person against whom there is a piece of incriminating real evidence, even if uncorroborated, is no greater infringement of his liberties and no less justifiable than his arrest on the basis of one uncorroborated accusation? Hume (1844: ii, 76) expresses doubts about the power of a private person to arrest on mere suspicion, thus implicitly accepting a constable's power to do so. Such also seems to be the view taken in *Pringle* v. *Bremner and Stirling* (1867) 5 M. (H.L.) 55. In that case police executing a search warrant for certain objects came across other evidence suggestive of complicity in the offence and arrested the pursuer, who was in possession of the evidence. In discussing what it would be necessary to prove in determining the wrongfulness or justifiability of the arrest, the Lord Chancellor said:

"Then again, with regard to the arrest and imprisonment of the pursuer,—as to that it is not alleged that there was any warrant at all; but then, it is said, the constable having discovered matters which, in his judgment, brought home to the pursuer complicity in the alleged crime, he was justified in exercising his discretion upon the subject, and in apprehending the pursuer and lodging him in prison. Again, I say, answering in the same way as I answered with regard to the searching for papers, the result will either justify him or will not justify him; if the papers he seized really proved or gave a fair and reasonable ground to believe that the pursuer was implicated in the grave crime which was charged, then, although the officer might have had no warrant for his apprehension (and he had no warrant upon this occasion), yet the event would justify him and he would protect himself by the circumstances afterwards discovered."

On the other hand, if arrest without warrant were competent on suspicion it is strange that this ground of lawfulness of arrest was not argued in *Wither* v. *Reid (see* Part II B of this chapter), although this can be explained on the alternative grounds suggested in Renton and Brown (1983: para. 5.22) citing *Lundie* v. *MacBrayne* (1894) 21 R. 1085, that where powers of arrest narrower than those at common law are conferred by statute, the statute must be complied with. Alternatively it might be that the evidence in *Wither* was thought to be insufficient. The Grampian Police (1980) and Renton and Brown (1983) both accept that such a power exists. If it does, it has been held in interpretating statutes giving such power that the arresting officer must honestly be suspicious and that there must not be a total absence of reasonable grounds for suspicion (*Shields* v. *Shearer*, 1914 S.C. (H.L.) 33; *McLeod* v. *Shaw*, 1981 S.L.T. (Notes) 93.

Pringle also appears to take this line).

It must be doubted whether the distinction drawn between powers to arrest respectable householders and "reputed" members of the criminal classes retains any validity. Even leaving aside modern notions of social equality, the remark smacks of the rejected Humeian notion of "general dole" as opposed to responsibility for particular offences. However, in so far as the distinction is based on the ease of tracing the person in the event of further proceedings it is still good law.

The existence of an objectively reasonable—or even a justified—suspicion is not by itself enough to justify arrest. Thus in *Wood* v. *N B Railway Co.* (1899) 1 F. 562, the pursuer was entitled to sue for wrongful arrest even though his trial for the offence for which he was arrested ended in his conviction. To justify arrest, there must also be an expectation of some frustration of the criminal process if an arrest is not made. Fear that the suspect will abscond is one justification. Others are that he is in an indecent state, or drunk or likely to repeat the offence. On the other hand, lapse of time from the commission of the offence argues against arrest. Other circumstances where arrest was held to be unlawful include: where a person who had just given evidence in court and whose address was known, was arrested on a charge of perjury when leaving the court (*Somerville* v. *Sutherland* (1899) 2 F. 185); where a person otherwise a respectable citizen and not caught red-handed was arrested on suspicion (*Bruce* v. *Adamson* (1899) 7 S.L.T. 77); and where a seaman whose identity was known and who was not likely to abscond was arrested six months after the date of the alleged offence (*Leask* v. *Burt* (1893) 21 R. 32).

It is commonly stated that there is a common law right to arrest someone found in suspicious circumstances in possession of goods he cannot account for. This rests upon a dictum in *Peggie,* but the other authorities cited in support of the proposition do not support it, and it is of no importance if there is a general power of arrest on suspicion.

The power of entry to effect arrest remains as stated by Hume, but the qualification of the power with respect to breaches of the peace may no longer be good law.

3.   WITHOUT WARRANT UNDER STATUTE

Scores of statutes confer powers to arrest without warrant. Some of these are very broad. This was particularly true of local legislation before the CGSA 1982 which often gave virtually plenary powers of arrest without warrant in large classes of offence. Other provisions, such as the following example, are very much more restricted.

5. Misuse of Drugs Act 1971

"Power of arrest

24.—(1) A constable may arrest without warrant a person who has committed, or whom the constable, with reasonable cause, suspects to have committed, an offence under this Act, if—

(a) he, with reasonable cause, believes that that person will abscond unless arrested; or

(b) the name and address of that person are unknown to, and cannot be ascertained by, him; or

(c) he is not satisfied that a name and address furnished by that person as his name and address are true.

(2) This section shall not prejudice any power of arrest conferred by law apart from this section."

Five matters require separate consideration as regards arrest without warrant.

First, it has been argued that there exists a principle that where a statute creates an offence and confers a power of arrest and even if there might be a broader common law power to arrest for the statutory offence, the narrower provisions of the statute must be complied with. Renton and Brown (1983: para. 5.22) derive this proposition from *Lundie* v. *MacBrayne* (1894) 21 R. 1085, where this was not argued but formed the tacit basis on which the court proceeded. This is true also of *Wither* v. *Reid,* 1979 S.L.T. 192, where otherwise a valid common law arrest on reasonable suspicion might have been pleaded.

Secondly it is not always clear whether statutes which confer a power of arrest without warrant impliedly also create a power of entry to effect arrest. The point was considered in the following case.

6. Shepherd v. Menzies
(1900) 37 S.L.R. 335

An inspector of the S.S.P.C.A. accompanied by a police constable on two occasions went on to a private farm upon receiving complaints of cruelty to horses. The conviction of a farmhand for cruelty followed and the farm owner sought interdict to prevent any future allegedly unlawful entry on his farm. The inspector of the S.S.P.C.A. pled in defence section 6 of the Cruelty to Animals (Scotland) Act 1850 which provided:

"When and so often as any of the offences against the provisions of this Act shall be committed, it shall be lawful for any constable, upon his own view thereof, or on the complaint and information of any other person who shall declare his name and place of abode to such constable, to seize and secure by the authority of this Act any offender, and forthwith, and without any other authority or warrant, to convey such offenders before a magistrate, to be dealt with for such offence according to law."

Refusing interdict the Lord Ordinary said:

"The question therefore is whether a police officer having reasonable grounds for believing that cruelty to animals is being practised on a farm within his district is not entitled, with or without warrant, to enter on the farm and take such steps as were taken here.

It has, of course, to be assumed that cruelty to animals is an offence, that is to say, a crime. It is not at common law, but it is made so by the statute . . . and accordingly I should at least greatly doubt whether, even apart from the procedure clauses of that statute, it could be held to be illegal for a police officer to do, and to do without a warrant, all that is here alleged. I rather imagine that at common law a police officer who has information that an offence is being committed may, if necessary, with or without a warrant, enter upon private property for the purpose of ascertaining the fact,—of stopping the commission of the offence, and if necessary of apprehending the wrong-doer.

But section 6 of the statute in question appears to me to place the matter beyond doubt. . . .

It cannot, I apprehend, be doubted that under this enactment, and in the circumstances of the present case, the police officer here was entitled to enter upon the complainer's farm for the purpose of finding and apprehending the person who was responsible for the alleged cruelty."

At reclaiming the Second Division also considered that the *words of the statute* authorised the entry. What is unclear is whether their Lordships understood that every right to arrest implies a right of entry, or whether—unlikely though it seems in this case—it is only the particular statute in question which did so. The trouble with the former view is that there are statutes (*e.g.* s. 50(2) of the Firearms Act 1968) which confer powers of arrest and, *separatim,* powers of entry to effect it. If *Shepherd* v. *Menzies* be considered to take the broader view, these powers are otiose. Partly in view of this conclusion the House of Lords in the English case *Finnigan* v. *Sandiford* [1981] 2 All E.R. 267 had no difficulty in coming to the unanimous view that: "It may confidently be stated as a matter of general principle that the mere conferment by statute of a power to arrest without warrant in given circumstances does not carry with it any power to enter private premises without the permission of the occupier, forcibly or otherwise" (*per* Lord Keith of Kinkel, but the statutory provision in question has been amended to obviate the particular result in *Finnigan;* see now *R.* v. *Fox* [1985] W.L.R. 1126).

Thirdly, statutory provisions for arrest without warrant are often restricted to situations where the constable fears that the suspect would otherwise abscond and does not know his name and address. This is now a general power, since section 1 of the CJSA creates the offence of refusing to give, or giving a false name and address, and adds a power of arrest without warrant.

Fourthly, one particularly drastic procedure involving arrest without warrant is that in section 12 of the Prevention of Terrorism (Temporary Provisions) Act 1984. This is normally referred to as "detention" under the Act and is accordingly dealt with in the part of this chapter concerned with detention, but it begins with an ordinary arrest without warrant. Even more drastic powers of arrest of terrorist suspects exist in Northern Ireland (see *McKee* v. *Chief Constable for Northern Ireland* [1985] 1 All E.R. 1).

The fifth point of note is a major extension of the jurisdiction of constables exercising statutory powers, which stems from the decision in *Binnie* v. *Donnelly*.

7. Binnie v. Donnelly
1981 S.L.T. 294

SHERIFF PATERSON: "[The] appellant was driving his car in Scotland when he was involved in an accident. After that accident, he drove on for a matter of yards and in doing so crossed from Scotland into England. A matter of yards into England the appellant was involved in another accident. Police arrived at the locus of the second accident; those police officers were serving members of the Lothian and Borders Police Force. Those officers required the appellant at the locus of the second accident to give a specimen of breath. He did so. The reading was positive. The appellant was arrested, taken to Kelso Police Station where a specimen for analysis was obtained. That analysis brought out a blood-alcohol level above that permitted by law. In addition to the admission of the facts, the respondent and counsel for the appellant were at one that if there had been a departure from the procedure laid down in the Road Traffic Act for obtaining a specimen for analysis such a departure would vitiate the analysis and the prosecution would fail. Parties were also at one on the problem which arises in this prosecution namely whether or not Scottish police officers acted within their powers in requiring a specimen of breath from a motorist who at the time the requirement was made was in England. If that requirement was within their powers then the appellant fell to be convicted. If, on the other hand, the police officers in making that requirement had acted ultra vires the appellant must be acquitted."

The sheriff convicted and Binnie appealed.

Refusing the appeal, Lord Cameron (with whom Lords Emslie and Stott agreed) said:

"In my opinion the solution to the problem of jurisdiction presented by this case is to be found in an examination of the language of the relevant statutory provisions which define and govern the powers and jurisdiction of police constables in Scotland and by reference to the precise wording of s. 8(2) of the Road Traffic Act 1972. The governing statute is the Police (Scotland) Act 1967, and in s. 17 it defines the general functions and jurisdiction of constables. By s. 51(1) of that Act 'functions' are defined to include 'powers and duties'. By s. 17(4) the geographical boundaries of a constable's jurisdiction are defined in these words: 'Any constable of a police force shall have all the powers and privileges of a constable throughout Scotland.' Subsection (8) provides: 'this section shall be without prejudice to section 18 of this Act, and to any other enactment conferring powers on a constable for particular purposes.' 'Enactment' also and necessarily includes Acts of Parliament, as is made clear by s. 82 of and Sched. 4 to the Act. Section 18, which repeats a provision of the earlier Act of 1857, provides a limited extension of the jurisdiction of constables of border counties of England or Scotland as respects the execution of warrants in such border counties. The language of s. 8(2) of the Road Traffic Act 1972 repeats precisely that of s. 2 of the Road Safety Act 1967 and provides: 'If an accident occurs owing to the presence of a motor vehicle on a road or other public place, a constable in uniform may require any person whom he has reasonable cause to believe was driving . . . the vehicle at the time of the accident to provide a specimen of breath for a breath test' and goes on in subss. (4) and (5) to give the constable power to arrest without warrant if the result of the test is positive or there is a failure to provide the requisite specimen of breath. Now the provisions of the statute are applicable to the whole United Kingdom and there is no limitative definition of a 'constable'. All that the statute prescribes in order to clothe the constable with the requisite power to require a breath test or without warrant to arrest is that he be in uniform. The police officers in the present case were constables and were in uniform and they had reasonable cause to believe that the appellant was the driver of the vehicle concerned in an accident on a road; and on a road in Scotland. The statute makes no reference to the border between England and Scotland or distinction between a Scottish or an English constable, though it is to be assumed that Parliament was fully aware of this fact in enacting legislation to be effectual throughout the United Kingdom. Now the powers conferred on a constable in uniform are powers conferred on him for a particular purpose, to operate the scheme of control over drivers of motor vehicles contained in the provisions of the Road Traffic Act 1972. It is also the case that s. 8 of the Act of 1972 repeats precisely the language of s. 2 of the Road Safety Act 1967, which received the Royal Assent prior to the passage of the Police (Scotland) Act of that year, so that the enactment of this particular extension of jurisdiction was on the statute book at the time the police legislation was before Parliament. Clearly therefore it was such an enactment as is covered by the language of s. 17(8) of the Police Act. The concept of trans-border jurisdiction was familiar to the legislature, as the provisions of s. 18 of the 1967 Act were a re-enactment of a provision which had been on the statute book since 1857. In my opinion the natural meaning to be given to the language of s. 8(2) is that no distinction is made between a constable according to whether he belongs to a police force raised and administered on one side of the border or the other, and that this conclusion is reinforced by consideration of the express wording of s. 17(8) of the 1967 Police Act where it clearly refers to an enactment which may for a particular purpose or particular purposes extend the jurisdiction and powers of a police officer beyond those normally possessed and exercisable by him. In my opinion the jurisdiction and power claimed in this case by the police officer are just such as the statute contemplates and the Road Traffic Act confers. For these reasons the learned sheriff in my view reached the right conclusion and his decision should be affirmed and the question in the case answered in the affirmative.''

B. HOW ARREST IS EFFECTED

We now turn to the second of the three aspects of the law of arrest which concern us, which is the procedure for arresting someone. At the outset let us point out that this is logically a completely separate question from whether there is a *power* to arrest. A constable may have a *power* to arrest in certain circumstances, but if he does not go through the prescribed procedure appropriate to making an arrest he cannot be said to have exercised the power and made an arrest, even if he wanted to. In the opposite case, if he lacks a *power* of arrest in certain circumstances, but goes through the correct *procedure* of arrest, then he has made an arrest. It will be an unlawful arrest, but an arrest all the same.

Potentially there are two possible ways of deciding whether an arrest has been made. Either a particular ritual form of words or procedure (*e.g.* touching a person on the shoulder with a truncheon) could be required or else the law could accept that any form of words or action which conveys the idea that a person has been deprived of his liberty would suffice. If we accept the second test, is it the subjective view of the person arrested, or of the constable, or is it a "neutral observer" test? Three cases are of relevance here. The first is *Wither* v. *Reid.*

8. Wither v. Reid
1979 S.L.T. 192

The Misuse of Drugs Act 1971, s. 24, made provision for an arrest without warrant where a constable did not know and could not find out the name and address of a suspect, or feared that, unless arrested, that suspect would abscond. Provision is also made under section 23(2) *(a)* for search without warrant on reasonable suspicion of possession of controlled drugs and for detention for that purpose.

Acting on a tip-off, which was in fact false, that Reid and a friend were bringing drugs from Aberdeen, constables met a train at Elgin. They informed Reid and her friend that they were under arrest and were to be searched. Reid resisted violently the attempts by women police officers to search her, and inflicted minimal injuries on the officers. No drugs were found. She was charged in consequence with assaulting a police officer in the execution of her duties. She was acquitted. On appeal:

LORD JUSTICE-CLERK (Wheatley): "The sheriff succinctly stated the issue which is the kernel of this appeal when he said in his note: 'If the search carried out by the two female police officers was lawful, there is in my view no question but that the accused is guilty of the offence charged; if, on the other hand, the search was unlawful, the accused in my view was entitled to use all necessary force—short of cruel excess—to resist the removal of her clothing and the indignity and humiliation of a body search'. . .

The Crown case was that on the findings-in-fact the police officers were lawfully acting under the authority of s. 23(2) *(a)* . . . despite the fact that Detective Sergeant Souden undoubtedly informed the respondent that he was arresting her and not just detaining her, because it was clear from the findings as a whole that he was purporting to act under s. 23(2) *(a)* procedure. Counsel for the respondent submitted that the fact that Detective Sergeant Souden unequivocally and undisputedly informed the respondent that he was arresting her established that she was in fact arrested at the railway station without any legal authority and that accordingly anything which followed thereafter at the hands of the police was illegal, and that this included the search of the respondent at the police station. This latter view was the one which commended itself to the sheriff and was the basis of his acquittal of the respondent. . .

There is, in my opinion, no doubt that Detective Sergeant Souden thought that he was acting under the s. 23(2) *(a)* procedure which provides the only statutory authority for a personal search. This, in my view, is borne out by the following facts. Detective Sergeant Souden informed the respondent (and her companion) at the railway station that they were being apprehended under the Misuse of Drugs Act 1971 on suspicion of being in possession of a controlled drug. Although he made it clear to the two suspects that they were under arrest, he informed them that they would be taken to Elgin police office and there searched for drugs, but that they would not be kept there any longer than necessary. In further explanation he informed the respondent that when the police had received information of a suspected drug offence they were bound to take suspects to a police station and search them for drugs and that she would be liberated as soon as possible. This explanation was repeated on at least two occasions in the police office. There was nothing in the evidence which would justify the invocation of s. 24(1) which authorises arrest. On the other hand the whole procedure followed the pattern of s. 23(2) *(a)* apart from the fact that Detective Sergeant Souden told the respondent that she was under arrest and not just being detained. . . Does the fact that Detective Sergeant Souden used the word 'arrest' when he should have used the word 'detention' vitiate the Crown case, albeit he and his colleagues followed the procedure relevant to detention under s. 23(2) *(a)*?. . . The issue may be put this way. Is the criterion what was said or what was done? Each case will have to be considered on its own facts, and in this case I have come to the conclusion that what was done had full statutory authority and was not vitiated by the fact that Detective Sergeant Souden informed the respondent that she was being arrested and taken to the police station to be searched for drugs when she should have been told that she was being detained and taken to the police station for that purpose. As she could have been detained and taken to the police station for that purpose under statutory authority I do not consider that the fact that Detective Sergeant Souden used the wrong word vitiates the procedure which was otherwise unimpeachable. I accept that a penal statute must be construed in favour of the subject when a doubt arises, but I do not consider this error in terminology should vitiate a conviction. The power of detention given under s. 23 (2) *(a)* connotes that the subject can in the given circumstances be taken to the police station even against his or her will, just as a power of arrest does. If the conditions of s. 23(2) *(a)* are satisfied and the procedure thereunder is followed, and the error in the use of the word did not result in the respondent being taken, even against her will, to the police station when if the correct word had been used she would not have been, I regard it as overstraining logic to say that such an error vitiated all that followed in this case. I have accordingly reached the conclusion that the sheriff erred in holding that it did."

LORD ROBERTSON: "In my opinion question 1 should be answered in the negative. It follows that question 2 should be answered in the affirmative. . . According to the sheriff, the police officers gave clear and unequivocal evidence that the respondent was arrested at the railway station under the Misuse of Drugs Act 1971.

If this is so, then the arrest in my opinion was unlawful. It was not an arrest under s. 24, but was a purported action under s. 23 (2) *(a)*. But that section does not give authority to arrest, only to 'detain' for a limited purpose. There is a vital distinction between 'arrest' and 'detention' *(Swankie* v. *Milne)*. It is true under s. 23 (2) *(a)* of the 1971 Act the police are entitled to detain the person suspected for the purpose of searching him, and for this purpose may be entitled to take him to a place where the search may take place. This place might conveniently be the nearest police station. But a penal statute must be construed strictly. In my opinion, in deference to the rights of the citizen, it must be made perfectly clear to the person against whom action is being taken under s. 23(2) *(a)* that that is what is being done and that he is not being arrested. If, as apparently happened in this case, the respondent was arrested and told that she was to be taken to the police station under arrest, then in my opinion that was an unlawful arrest. It will not do, in my opinion, to say that she was bound to know the law and so was bound to realise that, although the police officers used the word 'arrest,' they really meant 'detain,' and were proceeding under s. 23(2) *(a)*. The police also should know the law and if they were proceeding under s. 23 they should have done so explicitly.

I think the sheriff was right."

Lord Kissen delivered an opinion concurring with Lord Robertson.

Here there was a power to detain but no power of arrest. Yet the court, by accepting that there was an unlawful arrest rather than no arrest, was saying that the procedure sufficient to constitute an arrest was complied with. Moreover, the only police action which was consistent with an arrest but inconsistent with a detention was the use of words such as "under arrest." The court was therefore holding that the mere use of those words sufficed to turn a potentially lawful detention into an unlawful arrest.

The use of the word "arrest" may therefore not be a necessary, but it is a sufficient, procedure to effect an arrest. Two questions arise from this conclusion. First, is the use of other forms of words sufficient to constitute an arrest? Second, are there other means of executing an arrest, by restraint, actual or inferred? Two other cases shed some light on these issues.

9. Muir v. Magistrates of Hamilton
1910 1 S.L.T. 164

Muir was standing on a street corner with some friends one Sunday when, as he averred:

"Sergeant Smith of the Hamilton Burgh Constabulary, accompanied by a constable, both in uniform, approached the pursuer in an ostentatious and aggressive manner, and charged him with an offence against the licensing laws, in that he had gained access to the County Hotel, Hamilton, on the morning of that day, by falsely representing himself to be a *bona fide* traveller; that he had written his name in the book specially kept for *bona fide* travellers; and that he had thereafter ordered and been supplied with exciseable liquor. The pursuer strenuously denied the accusation, but Sergeant Smith insisted on the charge, and stated that the pursuer must go with him there and then to the said hotel to be identified. At first the pursuer thought that Sergeant Smith was merely joking, but when he realised that the sergeant had really apprehended him and intended to take him through the streets in custody, the pursuer became alarmed and offered to meet the police at the said hotel at half-past eight in the evening, when the pursuer was in the habit of passing the hotel on his way to work. . . Sergeant Smith refused to acquiesce in this proposal, and the pursuer was thereupon marched off through the crowded streets."

At the hotel the barmaid said definitely that Muir, whom she knew, had been nowhere near the hotel all day. Muir sued for wrongful arrest.

LORD ORDINARY (Salvesen): [His Lordship considered the question of vicarious liability of the magistrates and found against Muir.]

"If I am right so far, there is an end of the case; but, even on the merits, its seems to me very doubtful whether the pursuer has stated a relevant case. The only complaint against Sergeant Smith is that, having a suspicion that the pursuer had obtained exciseable liquor at the County Hotel, Hamilton, on the Sunday, by falsely representing himself to be a *bona fide* traveller, he 'insisted' that the pursuer should go with him to the hotel. . . There is no suggestion that any force was used, or that anything happened but that the pursuer went in the company of the police to the hotel. It is not said that the sergeant acted maliciously; and, on the pursuer's own statement, he appears to have had probable cause. The only possible ground of action is that Sergeant Smith had no warrant for the alleged apprehension.

In my opinion these facts do not disclose a case of apprehension at all. Had the pursuer refused to comply with Sergeant Smith's request, and had then been handcuffed and forcibly taken to the hotel for purposes of identification, the pursuer's case would have been stronger. All that happened, however, was that the sergeant asked the pursuer to accompany him to the County Hotel, and that the pursuer—fearing that if he did not comply with the request worse might happen—agreed to go. The pursuer being, in fact, innocent, I should have thought it in his interests to get himself cleared of suspicion by at once going down to the hotel. This makes it unnecessary to consider whether the bare fact that the sergeant had no warrant would have been a good ground of action, whether with or without an averment of malice and want of probable cause."

Despite its importance, the authority of this case is qualified by a number of factors. Strictly speaking the *ratio* turns on vicarious liability, not arrest. Moreover on that point its effect has been reversed by statute (Police

(Scotland) Act 1967, s. 39). Secondly, the fact that it is a case of reparation may have influenced the statements on arrest, given the general reluctance of the courts to subject the police to liability for honest, even if mistaken, attempts to do their duty (*Robertson* v. *Keith* 1936 S.L.T. 9, for which see Pt. II of Ch. 4 below). In addition, the fact that Muir had just spent a night in the cells after drinking too much seems to have been given some weight by Lord Salveson. With those *caveats,* this case seems to imply that the mere fact that a person seems to have been deprived of his liberty of action (we are not told whether Muir would have been physically compelled to accompany the sergeant had he tried to refuse, but it seems likely), and thinks that he has been arrested, is not sufficient to constitute an arrest.

10.   Swankie v. Milne
1973 J.C. 1

Swankie was convicted of driving with more than the permitted level of alcohol in his blood. He had nearly caused an accident with a police car, which had then given chase. The policemen, in plain clothes and therefore not entitled to administer a breath-test, took Swankie's keys and summoned uniformed colleagues, who then formed an opinion that Swankie was unfit to drive because of alcohol and tested his breath. It was found as a fact that, had Swankie attempted to leave, he would have been forcibly prevented. In these circumstances he unsuccessfully argued that he had been arrested and was not therefore driving or attempting to drive, and could not therefore be guilty of driving while unfit to do so because he had been drinking. On appeal:

Lord Cameron: "If there was no arrest then Mr Macaulay's first contention necessarily falls to the ground. Had the plain clothes officers in fact arrested or purported to arrest the appellant, then I can appreciate that a very difficult situation might arise with very different legal arguments. In such a situation it could be argued with force that once arrested a person is in the custody of the police and it would or might be difficult to maintain that he could at the same time be in the category of a person 'driving or attempting to drive a motor vehicle.' An arrest is something which in law differs from a detention by the police at their invitation or suggestion. In the latter case a person detained or invited to accompany police officers is, at that stage, under no legal compulsion to accept the invitation of detention. It may well be that in a particular case refusal to comply could lead to formal arrest, but until that stage is reached there is theoretical freedom to exercise a right to refuse to accept detention at the hands of police officers who are not armed with a warrant. I think it is important always to keep clear the distinction between arrest, which is a legal act taken by officers of the law duly authorised to do so and while acting in the course of their duty, carrying with it certain important legal consequences, and the mere detention of a person by a police officer. . . Once arrested not only is the freedom of action of the person arrested circumscribed but he is also placed in the protection of the law in respect, *e.g.* of questioning by a police officer. None of these consequences flows from a mere 'detention' for inquiry or to enable the officers or their colleagues to pursue investigation or put forward (as in this case) certain statutory requests. And a person is either arrested or he is not; there is no half-way house. In my opinion it is plain that there was no arrest of the appellant by the plain-clothes officers who stopped his van."

The Lord Justice-General (Emslie) delivered a concurring opinion and Lord Robertson concurred.

This is an extremely unsatisfactory case. In terms it supports the proposition that a person is either under arrest or free to go, but at the same time the police said they would have restrained Swankie if he had tried to leave; therefore by any normal use of the words Swankie was not free to go but he was not under arrest. The only way to reconcile the reasoning and the decision is to assign the phrase "not free to go" (and hence "under arrest") the meaning of "having attempted to leave, and been restrained" even if no attempt had been made precisely because of fore-knowledge of what would happen! Cynically we could probably conclude that it has more to do with judicial impatience with far-fetched technical defences to drink-driving offences than careful legal analysis. Nonetheless it remains an authority of weight until overruled.

From these cases in combination we may infer the following:

1. At common law a person is under arrest or at liberty. There is no half-way house.

2. A person is under arrest if that word, or probably some similar formal word, has been used to describe his position to him.

3. He is also under arrest if he has tried to leave and been physically restrained.

4. If neither 2 nor 3 apply, he has not been arrested

5. If there has been an arrest its lawfulness depends upon the existence of a power to arrest in the circumstances.

However we have not yet *quite* defined arrest. There is almost certainly an obligation on an arresting officer to tell a person *why* he is being arrested, and this obligation counts as part of the procedure necessary to make the arrest lawful. Article 5(2) of the European Convention on Human Rights says that: "Everyone who is arrested shall be informed promptly, in a language which he understands, of the reasons for his arrest and of any charge against him." However, as we have seen the Convention is not enforceable in Scottish courts, and in any case does not specify that failure to comply with article 5(2) renders the whole procedure of arrest unlawful. There is, in fact, no direct Scottish authority to that effect, but there is the highly persuasive House of Lords decision in the English case of *Christie* v. *Leachinsky.*

11. Christie v. Leachinsky
[1947] A.C. 573

Leachinsky was a rag-merchant in Liverpool, who bought bales of remnants in Leicester from a tailor. For reason not explained at the trial the police suspected Leachinsky of having dishonestly come by the bales. However, they purported to arrest him not for this but under a section of a Local Act which gave power to arrest only if the name and address of a suspect were unknown. In the instant case this was patently not true. For some reason the tailor in Leicester from whom he had bought the bales denied having sold them, and Leachinsky was sent to Leicester to stand trial for larceny. The tailor's evidence was, however, shown to be false, and Leachinsky was acquitted. He raised an action for false arrest and wrongful imprisonment against the Liverpool police. They initially pleaded justification under the Liverpool Local Act, but had to admit that it was not a good defence.

VISCOUNT SIMON: "If a policeman arrests without warrant when he entertains a reasonable suspicion of felony, is he under a duty to inform the suspect of the nature of the charge, and if he does not do so, is the detention a false imprisonment? In the Court of Appeal Scott L. J. strongly insisted that it was a false imprisonment. Arrest, he pointed out, was the first step in a criminal proceeding against a suspected person on a charge which was intended to be judicially investigated. If the arrest was authorised by a magisterial warrant, or if proceedings were instituted by the issue of a summons, it is clear law that the warrant or summons must specify the offence. . . Again, when an arrest is made on warrant, the warrant in normal cases has to be read to the person arrested. All this is for the obvious purpose of securing that a citizen who is *prima facie* entitled to personal freedom should know why for the time being his personal freedom is interfered with. Scott L. J. argued that if the law circumscribed the issue of warrants for arrest in this way it could hardly be that a policeman acting without a warrant was entitled to make an arrest without stating the charge on which the arrest was made. . . When the appeal came before your Lordships' House the arguments which had prevailed before the Court of Appeal were repeated, but it was not apparently realised by the counsel on either side that there is direct authority [here his Lordship reviewed the authorities].

The above citations, and others which are referred to by my noble and learned friend, Lord du Parcq, seem to me to establish the following propositions. (1) If a policeman arrests without warrant upon reasonable suspicion of felony, or of other crime of a sort which does not require a warrant, he must in ordinary circumstances inform the person arrested of the true ground of arrest. . . (2) If the citizen is not so informed but is nevertheless seized, the policeman, apart from certain exceptions, is liable for false imprisonment. (3) The requirement that the person arrested should be informed of the reason why he is seized naturally does not exist if the circumstances are such that he must know the general nature of the alleged offence for which he is detained. (4) The requirement that he should be so informed does not mean that technical or precise language need be used. The matter is a matter of substance, and turns on the elementary proposition that in this country a person is, *prima facie*, entitled to his freedom and is only required to submit to restraints on his freedom if he knows in substance the reason why it is claimed that this restraint should be imposed. (5) The person arrested cannot complain that he has not been supplied with the above information as and when he should be, if he himself produces the situation which makes it practically impossible to inform him, *e.g.* by immediate counter-attack or by running away. There may well be other exceptions to the general rule in addition to those I have indicated, and the above propositions are not intended to constitute a formal or complete code, but to indicate the general principles of our law on a very important matter. These principles equally apply to a private person who arrests on suspicion."

LORD SIMONDS: "These and similar considerations lead me to the view that it is not an essential condition of lawful arrest that the constable should at the time of arrest formulate any charge at all, much less the charge which may ultimately be found in the indictment. . .

The charge ultimately made will depend upon the view taken by the law of his act. In ninety-nine cases out of a hundred the same words may be used to define the charge or describe the act, nor is any technical precision necessary: for instance, if the act constituting the crime is the killing of another man, it will be immaterial that the arrest is for murder and at a later hour the charge of manslaughter is substituted. The arrested man is left in no doubt that the arrest is for that killing."

Lords Thankerton and du Parcq delivered concurring speeches.

Strictly defined, the *ratio* of this case is narrower than is usually alleged. It imposes no duty upon the police to inform someone why they are arrested, but only to tell the truth if they do so. However, the broader interpretation, that there is a duty to inform a person of the reason for the arrest, is now established.

The rule in *Christie* does not seem to have been discussed in any Scottish case. However, the relationship between arrest without and with a warrant (the latter being the desired model and the former a deviation to the extent required by the situation) is the same in Scotland and England, and the Scottish rules on showing a person the warrant in which he is arrested are the same. Accordingly the principles in *Christie* v. *Leachinsky* should apply in Scotland.

Even if they do, however, their operation is restricted in the case of an arrest under section 12 of the Prevention of Terrorism (Temporary Provisions) Act 1984 (see Pt. III of this chapter). Even where a person is suspected of involvement in a particular offence, such as terrorist murder, it has been held to satisfy the rule in *Christie* if he is told generally (echoing the words of the statute) that he is being arrested "on suspicion of involvement in terrorist activities." (*Ex p. Lynch* [1980] N.I.L.R. 126; for criticism of this case, see Finnie (1982)).

The rules on effecting an arrest are unclear and unsatisfactory. Their reform was considered by the Thomson Committee.

12. Second Report of the Committee on Scottish Criminal Procedure
(Chairman: Lord Thomson)
Cmnd. 6218 (1975)

"Police Custody
3.12   Since arrest and detention, which we describe in subsequent paragraphs, both involve taking a person into custody, we turn now to consider what test should be applied to determine whether or not a person is in police custody. In our view the crucial question is whether or not that person is free to go about his ordinary business. The test should not depend on any particular form of words used by police officers in addressing the person or on whether or not the person thinks that he is free to go. If the person would not in fact be allowed to go on his way should he attempt to do so, or even express a desire to do so, then he should be regarded as being no longer a free agent but as being in police custody. *We so recommend.*"

For discussion of this recommendation, which was not implemented by the CJSA, see Christie (1977) and Finnie (1980).

C.   RIGHTS OF PERSONS ARRESTED

It is sometimes loosely said (e,g, Thomson Committee (1975), para. 3.08), that on arrest a person gains rights such as communication with solicitors. As regards most of the rights of persons arrested, this is incorrect. Any person not detained or arrested can do anything he wishes, provided it is not illegal. In particular such persons may engage and talk to solicitors. This, be it noted, applies also in the case of persons who, following *Swankie* v. *Milne,* are not under arrest but are "helping the police with inquiries" at a police station. In general when a person is arrested he loses most of his rights, but by statute some rights of communication are expressly preserved. However, the right to use the police to convey messages to the outside world *is* a right gained on arrest.

The most basic rights of a person arrested are the right not to be ill-treated and the right not to be "locked up and forgotten about." In addition, statute expressly preserves or confers certain rights of communication with the outside world.

1. THE RIGHT NOT TO BE MALTREATED

13. The European Convention on Human Rights

"Article 3
No one shall be subjected to torture or to inhuman or degrading treatment."

This article may not be derogated from even under the emergency provisions of Article 15. A number of applications have alleged violation of the article, including *Ireland* v. *United Kingdom,* E.H.R.R. 25) where the United Kingdom was found guilty of violations. That case arose out of the mass internment of hundreds of suspected I.R.A. activists from 1971 onwards. It was alleged first that persons detained were subjected to assaults and secondly that the "five techniques" systematically used for interrogation constituted an infringement of the article, despite the endorsement of their use by two United Kingdom inquiries (Compton (1971); Parkes (1972)). The five techniques were: first, keeping a prisoner spreadeagled against a wall for hours at a time; second, deprivation of sleep; third, forcing a prisoner to wear a hood throughout the interrogation; fourth, deprivation of food and drink; and fifth, subjection to loud noise. The Court found the United Kingdom guilty of inhuman and degrading treatment on both counts.

The case is of importance for two reasons. In the first place, it decisively disposes of the complacent assumption that "it can't happen here," and that it is sufficient to trust to the innate decency of the police to ensure fair play. Allegations of violence on the part of the police are not uncommon, and the existence of examples like this has a direct bearing on the question of investigation of police complaints and the degree of supervision which ought to be exercised over them. Secondly, the case sets limits to the increasing tolerance shown by the Scottish judiciary to police interrogation (see Pt. VI of this chapter). Some at least of the five techniques are used by police forces in other countries.

The Convention cannot be directly relied on in Scottish courts (see Chap. 2) but the ordinary law of assault binds the police just as any other citizen. *Ireland* v. *United Kingdom,* however underlines the difficulty in setting agreed limits in any legal system as to what constitutes acceptable treatment for a lawful and necessary purpose.

2. RIGHTS AGAINST DELAY IN THE CRIMINAL PROCESS

Here two different rights are involved. First, there are rights to be brought before a judge rather than held in police custody. At a later stage there are rights not to be held too long awaiting trial (with the possibility of a not-guilty verdict and consequently of punishment though innocent).

14.   McDonald v. Lyon and Main
1851 J. Shaw 516

In the middle of the night constables Lyon and Main were awoken by the noise of McDonald forcing entry to a house where he assaulted the inhabitants. They arrested him and incarcerated him for some 60 hours before taking him to Dumbarton sheriff court, although on the day following his arrest a baillie court and a sheriff's small debt court had been held in the court house beneath which he was imprisoned. A bill of suspension and liberation was brought.

LORD JUSTICE-CLERK (Hope): "There can be no doubt in this case. . . Here the suspender was apprehended at an early hour on Monday morning, and confined, not in a prison, but in a room under it, during the whole of that day. It is said that one officer was obliged to go to Stirling; but if so, why did not the other insure his being taken before a magistrate? It is not pretended that the charge was one that would have been incompetent to have been preferred before the Baillies; but, even had it been, it was the duty of the other officer either to have taken him to Dumbarton himself, or obtained the assistance of special constables for that purpose. The idea of keeping him in jail from Monday morning to Wednesday afternoon is preposterous; and I would not have thought it possible that such a delay could have occurred. I think that twenty-four hours would have been too long, under the circumstances. I think therefore, that we must suspend, not on the ground that the constable had no warrant to apprehend—on the contrary, I hold a constable, called up in the night, in consequence of a brawl in the street, is entitled, without a warrant, to seize any person whom he shall find engaged therein; but then, for that very reason, he must, as soon as possible, bring his prisoner before a magistrate, in order that the magistrate may decide whether he will at once dispose of the case himself, or send the culprit to the Sheriff."

The other members of the court concurred.

There is thus a general right to be brought as soon as possible before a court. More specific limits are provided by statute. The modern "long-stop" provision in solemn procedure is s. 19(3), CPSA, which permits the sheriff to delay examination for up to 48 hours but even then only for the prisoner's benefit, to permit the attendance of his solicitor. So far as summary procedure is concerned, s. 321(3), CPSA provides:

"(3) A person apprehended under any such warrant as aforesaid or by virtue of the powers possessed at common law, or conferred by statute, shall wherever practicable be brought before a court competent to deal with the case either by way of trial or by way of remit to another court not later than in the course of the first lawful day after such person shall be taken into custody, such day not being a public or local holiday."

These provisions are designed to prevent the prisoner being detained at the hand of, and on the responsibility of, the *police* for longer than necessary. There are also provisions to prevent the prisoner lingering in prison by reason of dilatoriness on the part of the prosecutor.

15. Criminal Procedure (Scotland) Act 1975

"Prevention of delay in trials

101.—. . . (2) Subject to subsections (3), (4) and (5) below, an accused who is committed for any offence until liberated in due course of law shall not be detained by virtue of that committal for a total period of more than—

(*a*) 80 days, unless within that period the indictment is served on him, which failing he shall be liberated forthwith; or

(*b*) 110 days, unless the trial of the case is commenced within that period, which failing he shall be liberated forthwith and thereafter he shall be for ever free from all question or process for that offence.

(3) A single judge of the High Court may, on application made to him for the purpose, for any sufficient cause extend the period mentioned in subsection (2) (*a*) above:

Provided that he shall not extend the said period if he is satisfied that, but for some fault on the part of the prosecution, the indictment could have been served within that period.

(4) A single judge of the High Court may, on application made to him for the purpose, extend the period mentioned in subsection (2) (*b*) above where he is satisfied that delay in the commencement of the trial is due to—

(*a*) the illness of the accused or of a judge;

(*b*) the absence or illness of any necessary witness; or

(*c*) any other sufficient cause which is not attributable to any fault on the part of the prosecutor.

(5) The grant or refusal of any application to extend the periods mentioned in this section may be appealed against by note of appeal presented to the High Court; and that Court may affirm, reverse or amend the determination made on such application.

(6) For the purposes of this section, a trial shall be taken to commence when the oath is administered to the jury. . .

Prevention of delay in trials

331A.—(1) Subject to subsections (2) and (3) below, a person charged with a summary offence shall not be detained in that respect for a total of more than 40 days after the bringing of the complaint in court unless his trial is commenced within that period, failing which he shall be liberated forthwith and thereafter he shall be for ever free from all question or process for that offence.

(2) The sheriff may, on application made to him for the purpose, extend the period mentioned in subsection (1) above and order the accused to be detained awaiting trial for such period as he thinks fit where he is satisfied that delay in the commencement of the trial is due to—

(*a*) the illness of the accused or of a judge;

(*b*) the absence or illness of any necessary witness; or

(*c*) any other sufficient cause which is not attributable to any fault on the part of the prosecutor.

(3) The grant or refusal of any application to extend the period mentioned in subsection (1) above may be appealed against by note of appeal presented to the High Court; and that Court may affirm, reverse or amend the determination made on such application.

(4) For the purposes of this section, a trial shall be taken to commence when the first witness is sworn."

The principle embodied in these provisions dates back to the Criminal Procedure Act 1701, but the present version was inserted by section 14 CJSA. The major change made in the 1980 version is that the 110 days now run to the *commencement* of the trial, whereas previously the trial had to be *concluded* within 110 days. Elaborate procedure for requiring service of an indictment after 80 days was also abolished.

The sections only apply to a person who is in prison solely because of a committal warrant and not to a person who is also serving a sentence of imprisonment (*Wallace* v. *H.M. Advocate,* 1959 J.C. 71; *H.M. Advocate* v. *Park,* 1967 J.C. 70).

A further qualification of their effect (from the point of view of the accused) is that the extensions to the 80 days and 110 days limits may be granted *after* their expiry (*Farrell* v. *H.M. Advocate,* 1984 S.C.C.R. 301; *H.M. Advocate* v. *Bickerstaff,* 1926 J.C. 65, although in *Farrell* the court observed that it might well look for "very powerful reasons in support of the application" in such cases before granting it).

The real problem (from the accused's point of view) is the discretion granted by sections 101(4) and 331A(2) to extend these prescribed maximum periods in prison and the court's interpretation of that discretion. The most important and unsatisfactory case concerning the sections in recent times is that of *Gildea* v. *H.M. Advocate,* extracted below.

16.   Gildea v. H.M. Advocate
1983 S.L.T. 458

Gildea was accused of serious firearms offences and assault, and detained in custody. The 110-day period was due to expire on March 18, 1983. He was to be tried at a circuit court beginning on March 7, 1983. His case was fourth in the list and expected to begin on March 15, 1983. By that date, however, it was clear that the trial would not begin before March 18, and an application was made for an extension of the 110-day period and granted. The accused appealed to the High Court, unsuccessfully.

OPINION OF THE COURT (Lords Emslie, Cameron and Avonside): "It is accepted that the extension was granted because the judge was satisfied that the inability of the Crown to commence the trial of the appellant on or before 18 March 1983 was, under reference to the words of s. 101(4), due to a sufficient cause which was not attributable to the fault of the prosecutor. The submission for the appellant was that the judge erred in being so satisfied.

In approaching the question for our decision which is, we think, whether the judge was entitled to be so satisfied, it must be remembered that it was for the Crown to demonstrate that there was a sufficient cause for the difficulty in which they found themselves which was not attributable to any fault on the part of the Crown. As the Lord Justice-Clerk (Wheatley) pointed out in *H.M. Advocate* v. *McTavish*, 1974 S.L.T. 246; 1974 J.C. 19 (a case concerned with s. 43 of the Criminal Procedure (Scotland) Act 1887): 'That section was designed to give protection to the lieges, to ensure that they were not held in custody for an undue period of time before the case was finally disposed of. That is a very important right, and it can only be departed from when sufficient cause is shown to the court to justify that departure.'

These observations apply with full force to the provisions of s. 101 of the Act of 1975 which in its present form, was introduced by the Criminal Justice (Scotland) Act 1980. Equally apt are the words of the Lord Justice-Clerk (MacDonald), speaking again of s. 43 of the Act of 1887, in *H.M. Advocate* v. *Macaulay* (1892) 3 White 131 at p. 135: 'I remark first that this exception is framed to meet such difficulties as might happen without any failure in diligence upon the part of anyone at all, viz:—the illness or absence of a necessary witness or of a judge or juror. The words "or any other sufficient cause" must, therefore, relate to some other cause of a similar nature to those mentioned. But in addition to that, it must also be the fact that the prosecutor shall not be responsible for the failure.'

In this case the Crown sought to justify the grant of their application for extension in the following submission. It cannot be contended that in serving the indictment upon the appellant on 4 February 1983 there was any failure of due diligence, for it was then within reasonable contemplation that having regard to the business set down for disposal in Glasgow on the March circuit, the trial of the appellant would commence before 18 March 1983. The probabilities fall to be tested by consideration of the business set down for disposal in the south court, for it was known that the first trial for disposal on that circuit in the north court was quite unlikely to end before 18 March 1983. The first case for trial in the south court involved charges of injury to the danger of life, murder and contravention of s. 3(1) (b) of the Bail (Scotland) Act 1980. The accused was in custody and the 110-day period in his case was due to elapse on 20 March 1983. The wholly reasonable expectation that this trial would be concluded within two days was borne out in the result because it ended on 9 March. The second trial for south court disposal also involved an accused in custody and in his case the 110-day period was due to expire on 18 March 1983. This trial was reasonably estimated to require no more than two days to complete. In the event no trial took place because when the diet was called the accused pled guilty. The third trial was of a single accused charged with rape and there were only 23 witnesses on the Crown list. The entirely reasonable expectation was that this trial would be completed within two days and at worst on the third day. The fourth trial, that of the appellant, was accordingly expected to begin not later than 15 March and since it could not reasonably be expected to last more than two days it was confidently expected that the fifth trial of five accused, in the case of three of whom the 110-day period was due to expire on 18 March 1983, was likely to begin before that date. What in fact happened was unforeseen and was not reasonably foreseeable. The third trial on the south court list, contrary to all reasonable expectation, and for reasons difficult to understand, consumed not two days, not three days but five days of the time of the court. It was not suggested that this expenditure of time was due to any cause for which the Crown was or could be held responsible. In this situation the Crown had a difficult decision to make. The decision was to proceed at once with the fifth case on the list involving the five accused and to apply in the case of the appellant for the extension of time granted by the judge on 15 March 1983.

For the appellant the submission was that this explanation by the Crown did not satisfy the test which was prescribed by s. 101(4) (c). By delaying service of the indictment until 4 February 1983 the Crown failed to exercise due diligence and it was evident upon the explanation given by the advocate-depute that from that moment on they were at grave risk. Even if it be accepted that the forecasts of the time likely to be consumed by the first three south court trials were those mentioned by the advocate-depute the Crown was allowing itself a safety margin of only two days, at the most, if it were able to commence both the trial of the appellant and the fifth trial in the list before 18 March 1983. It is, it was said, notoriously difficult to predict the length of a trial on a charge of rape and it cannot be said that because the third trial in the list took five days to complete instead of two or three days this was not reasonably to be foreseen. The risk courted by the Crown was quite unacceptable, and by neglecting to requisition a special sitting for the disposal of the indictment against the appellant, or to release him from custody, the Crown cannot be held to have demonstrated that there was sufficient cause for which the Crown was not responsible, for their failure to be in a position to commence the trial of the appellant before 18 March 1983.

We do not pretend that the problem presented by this appeal is easy to resolve. With some hesitation, however, we have decided that the appeal should be refused. The Crown undoubtedly took a calculated risk in relation to the commencement of 110-day cases for disposal on the March circuit in the south court. The question is whether the decision to take that risk was unreasonable and whether the judge who heard the application and was himself the presiding judge in the south court was entitled to decide it was not. In our opinion he was so entitled and his decision was correct. The critical factor was the expected duration of the single accused rape trial, number three in the list. In our judgment it was wholly reasonable to predict, for that trial, a disposal time of one-and-a-half days to two days, and at the very worst three days. That it should take five days to complete, is, we think, almost impossible to understand, and it was not from what we know of the case reasonably to be anticipated. In the foregoing circumstances we are persuaded that the Crown was suddenly faced with such a difficulty as might happen without want of due diligence on the Crown's part, and that the judge who granted the extension sought, who, incidentally was the trial judge in the disposal of the single accused rape case which grossly overran its reasonably anticipated span, was well entitled to be satisfied that the Crown had established what required to be established in support of their application in terms of s. 101(4) (c) of the Act of 1975."

Appeal refused.

The objection to *Gildea* is that "fault" on the part of the prosecutor had previously been assumed to mean that matters *outwith his control* led to delay. In *Gildea,* however, the prosecution had taken a calculated risk on time-limits; they were responsible for scheduling cases and they (however unforseeably) got it wrong. The whole point of s. 101 is to protect prisoners from prosecution ill-will or indifference or mistake; *Gildea* jettisons that protection. The High Court took a similar line in *Dobbie* v. *H.M. Advocate,* 1986 S.L.T. 648.

3. RIGHTS OF COMMUNICATION

17. The Criminal Procedure (Scotland) Act 1975

"Prisoners before examination to have access to solicitor
19.—(1) Where any person has been arrested on any criminal charge, such person shall be entitled immediately upon such arrest:

(*a*) to have intimation sent to a solicitor that his professional assistance is required by such a person, and informing him of the place to which such person is to be taken for examination.

(*b*) to be told what rights there are under paragraph (*a*) above and subsections (2) and (3) below.

(2) Such solicitor shall be entitled to have a private interview with the person accused before he is examined on declaration, and to be present at such examination.

(3) It shall be in the power of the sheriff or justice to delay such examination for a period not exceeding 48 hours from and after the time of such person's arrest, in order to allow time for the attendance of such solicitor."

This substantive right to see a solicitor dates from 1887. The duty on the part of the police to inform a person arrested of these rights was added by the CJSA 1980, Sched. 7, para. 25. The police have no power to delay intimation. But no sanction is provided for refusal to do so or comply with any other provision of section 19. In *Cheyne* v. *McGregor,* 1941 J.C. 17 it was held, over an emphatic dissent by Lord Mackay, that refusal of a private interview is no bar to subsequent proceedings. Further, the right is to have intimation sent to a solicitor. Probably if that solicitor were for some reason not available the arrested person's right would be considered exhausted (see, *e.g. Law* v. *McNicol,* 1965 J.C. 32).

The person arrested may talk to the solicitor before examination. Examination is normally on the day following arrest, except possibly on Saturday or Sunday. Therefore a person arrested on a Friday evening may be lawfully kept in isolation in police hands for upwards of 70 hours. At a time when questioning by the police was frowned upon, and the judicial examination would have been the first attempt at ascertaining the accused's version of events, it might have been sufficient protection that the accused be forewarned by his solicitor of the perils of examination. Nowadays, though, the most important part of the questioning will normally have occurred, and any incriminating statements been made, before the examination, and often without legal assistance. In these circumstances section 19 smacks of "shutting the stable door after the horse has bolted."

18. The Criminal Justice (Scotland) Act 1980

"Right to have someone informed when arrested or detained
3.—(1) Without prejudice to section 19 or 305 of the 1975 Act (intimation to solicitor following arrest), a person who, not being a person in respect of whose custody or detention subsection (3) below applies—
    (a) has been arrested and is in custody in a police station or other premises, shall be entitled to have intimation of his custody and of the place where he is being held sent, to a person reasonably named by him. . .
without delay or, where some delay is necessary in the interest of the investigation or the prevention of crime or the apprehension of offenders, with no more delay than is so necessary; and the person shall be informed of such entitlement—
    (i) on arrival at the police station or other premises; or
    (ii) where he is not arrested, or as the case may be detained, until after such arrival, on such arrest or detention.
(2) Where the person mentioned in paragraph (*a*) of subsection (1) above requests such intimation to be sent as is specified in that paragraph there shall be recorded the time when such request is—
    (i) made;
    (ii) complied with.
(3) Without prejudice to the said section 19 or 305, a constable shall, where a person who has been arrested and is in such custody as is mentioned in paragraph (*a*) of subsection (1) above or who is being detained as is mentioned in paragraph (*b*) of that subsection appears to him to be a child, send without delay such intimation as is mentioned in the said paragraph (*a*), or as the case may be paragraph (*b*), to that person's parents if known; and the parent—
    (*a*) in a case where there is reasonable cause to suspect that he has been involved in the alleged offence in respect of which the person has been arrested or detained, may; and
    (*b*) in any other case shall be permitted access to the person.
(4) The nature and extent of any access permitted under subsection (3) above shall be subject to any restriction essential for the furtherance of the investigation or the well-being of the person.
(5) In subsection (3) above—
    (*a*) 'child' means a person under 16 years of age: and
    (*b*) 'parent' includes guardian."

These rights and their English equivalents (s. 56, Police and Criminal Evidence Act 1984) stem from a complaint to the European Commission on Human Rights about police denial of rights of access to persons under arrest.

The major weakness of these provisions is the same as those of the 1975 Act, namely, how are they to be enforced, especially since here the police are specifically granted a right to delay intimation? For detailed commentary see Gordon (1981) and Finnie (1981).

A final problem with these provisions for access is whether they apply to persons detained (for up to a week) under section 12 of the Prevention of Terrorism Act 1984. The problem has now been solved by the creation of parallel rights applying to such persons by section 35 of the Law Reform (Miscellaneous Provisions) (Scotland) Act 1985. These provisions are dealt with at the same time as section 12 of the 1984 Act in the following section of this chapter.

III.   DETENTION

19.   Chalmers v. H.M. Advocate
1954 S.L.T. 177

LORD JUSTICE-GENERAL (Cooper): "Putting aside the case of proper apprehension without a warrant of persons caught more or less red-handed, no person can be lawfully detained except after a charge has been made against him, and it is for this reason that I view with some uneasiness the situation disclosed in this case, and illustrated by the recent cases of *Rigg* and *Short,* in which a suspect is neither apprehended nor charged but is simply 'asked' to accompany two police officers to a police office to be there questioned. In former times such questioning, if undertaken, would be conducted by police officers visiting the home or place of business of the suspect and there precognoscing him, probably in the presence of a relation or friend. However convenient the modern practice may be, it must normally create a situation very unfavourable to the suspect. In the eyes of every ordinary citizen the venue is a sinister one. When he stands alone in such a place confronted by several police officers, usually some of high rank, the dice are loaded against him, especially as he knows that there is no one to corroborate him as to what exactly occurred during the interrogation, how it was conducted, and how long it lasted."

This is quoted as a particularly influential statement of the law. However, it has not always been clear that this was the position at common law (Lord Cooper himself accepted the existence of a status of "person detained on suspicion" in *Rigg,* 1946 J.C. 1) and indeed, as we have seen above, the existence of a power to arrest on suspicion is still not clearly or universally denied. *Chalmers* is the first in a series of cases emphasising the lack of a status of detention. Almost as striking as the emphatic assertion of the liberty of persons not arrested, however, is the judicial unwillingness to accept the logic of that position which led to the unsatisfactory judgment in *Swankie* v. *Milne.* This is not surprising in view of evidence to the effect that whatever the law might say the police routinely did detain (in the commonsense meaning of the word) on suspicion, and believed that the power to do so was necessary to their investigating role. Following the recommendation of the Thomson Committee (1975) a general power of detention was introduced by statute. Other important provisions for detention include section 12 of the Prevention of Terrorism (Temporary Provisions) Act 1984 and a group of powers to detain in order to search.

20.   Second Report of the Committee on Scottish Criminal Procedure
(Chairman: Lord Thomson)
Cmnd. 6218 (1975)

"Detention before arrest and charge
3.13   The policeman's real difficulty arises in investigations where he wants to interview a suspect or prevent him from interfering with evidence such as stolen property. At present the police are powerless to act without the consent of the very person who is likely to have most interest in refusing to give that consent. Clearly the police should not be entitled to arrest anyone they want to interview but it seems plainly wrong, for example, that a suspected violent criminal with significant evidence on his clothing has to be left at large while the police seek other evidence of his guilt sufficient to entitle them to charge.
3.14   We *recommend* that the practice of inviting persons to the police station should be regularised. We are convinced that it will continue if the law remains unchanged and that it can be controlled only by being recognised and made subject to clearly defined limits. We accept that certain people do and will continue to attend at police stations truly voluntarily, such as those who prefer to see the police there rather than have the police be seen to visit them, or those who call to confess to crime, but these are exceptional cases. Our recommendations will also cover the situation where the police stop in the street people who are suspected of committing or having recently committed an offence. At present, except where they act under Police Acts, which relate for the most part to stolen property, or under any other special statute such as the Road Traffic Act 1972, the police have no power to detain and question anyone in the street unless they are in a position to arrest him.
3.15   We *recommend,* therefore, a form of limited, or temporary arrest—arrest on suspicion. Since the rules governing this 'arrest' will differ from those governing arrest at the moment, we give it a separate name—detention. Detention will include power to take to and keep in a police station, but its duration will be limited by the following general rules:
a. it should not last longer than is necessary in the interests of justice;
b. it should be succeeded as soon as is reasonable by either release or arrest; and
c. it should not in any event exceed a fixed period of time at the end of which the detainee must be either released or arrested and charged."

21.   The Criminal Justice (Scotland) Act 1980

"Suspect or potential witness may be required by constable to identify himself.
1.—(1) Where a constable has reasonable grounds for suspecting that a person has committed or is committing an offence at any place, he may require—

(a)   that person, if the constable finds him at that place or at any place where the constable is entitled to be, to give his name and address and may ask him for an explanation of the circumstances which have given rise to the constable's suspicion;

(b)   any other person whom the constable finds at that place or at any place where the constable is entitled to be and who the constable believes has information relating to the offence, to give his name and address.

(2) The constable may require the person mentioned in paragraph (a) of subsection (1) above to remain with him while he (either or both)—

(a)   verifies any name and address given by the person:

Provided that the constable shall exercise his power under this paragraph only where it appears to him that such verification can be obtained quickly;

(b)   notes any explanation proffered by the person. . .

(4) A constable shall inform a person, when making a requirement of that person under—

(a)   paragraph (a) of subsection (1) above, of his suspicion and of the general nature of the offence which he suspects that the person has committed or is committing. . .

(c)   subsection (2) above, of why the person is being required to remain with him;

(d)   either of the said subsections, that failure to comply with the requirement may constitute an offence.

Detention and questioning at police station
2.—(1) Where a constable has reasonable grounds for suspecting that a person has committed or is committing an offence punishable by imprisonment, the constable may, for the purpose of facilitating the carrying out of investigations

(a)   into the offence; and

(b)   as to whether criminal proceedings should be instigated against the person, detain that person and take him as quickly as is reasonably practicable to a police station or other premises and, subject to the following provisions of this section, the detention may continue there.

(2) Detention under subsection (1) above shall be terminated not more than six hours after it begins or (if earlier)—

(a)   when the person is arrested; or

(b)   where there are no longer such grounds as are mentioned in the said subsection (1);

and when a person has been detained under subsection (1) above for a period of six hours, he shall be informed immediately upon expiry of this period that his detention has been terminated.

(3) Where a person has been released at the termination of a period of detention under subsection (1) above he shall not thereafter be detained, under that

subsection, on the same grounds or on any grounds arising out of the same circumstances.

(4) At the time when a constable detains a person under subsection (1) above, he shall inform the person of his suspicion, of the general nature of the offence which he suspects has been or is being committed and of the reason for the detention; and there shall be recorded—

> (a)   the place where detention begins and the police station or other premises to which the person is taken;
>
> (b)   the general nature of the suspected offence;
>
> (c)   the time when detention under subsection (1) above begins and the time of the person's arrival at the police station or other premises;
>
> (d)   the time when the person is informed of his rights in terms of subsection (7) below and of subsection (1) (b) of section 3 of this Act and the identity of the constable so informing him;
>
> (e)   where the person requests such intimation to be sent as is specified in section 3(1) (b) of this Act, the time when such request is—
>> (i) made;
>>
>> (ii) complied with; and
>
> (f)   the time of the person's departure from the police station or other premises or, where instead of being released he is arrested in respect of the alleged offence, the time of such arrest."

Almost identical powers of detention are given to customs officers by ss. 48 and 49 of the Criminal Justice (Scotland) Act 1987.

A person detained has the same rights to be treated humanely and to have his detention intimated to his solicitor and one other person reasonably named by him as does an arrested person (see Part II *C* of this chapter), save that the police may delay intimation to his solicitor as well as to the other person (s. 3, C.J.S.A. 1980).

These elaborate provisions and procedure involve a number of problems. One major problem raised by the introduction of detention, is that the government chose not to follow the Thomson Committee's views on arrest, and that therefore detention exists side by side with *Swankie* v. *Milne*. It is therefore possible for the police to continue to use the old practice of "inviting" people to the police station in the knowledge that the majority will feel that they are bound to comply. Such people are denied all the elaborate precautions built into detention, including, most importantly, the six-hour limit. It is doubly likely that this practice will continue in view of a second major problem with detention, which is that the Act provides little guidance as to when "detention" is to be considered as beginning. Is the test to be the use of the words "I detain you," or the exercise of restraint or the understanding of the parties, and if the last, of which party? In default of such guidance the judiciary will perhaps adopt the same indulgence to the police as *Muir* and *Swankie* evince and presume voluntary co-operation on the suspect's part. Although no cases have arisen from it, "voluntary attendance" is still practised on a large scale, though why, and whether it involves any abuse of the system, is debateable (Curran and Carnie (1986)).

A second problem stems from this and from the elaborate nature of the provisions. What happens if a provision or requirement is inadvertently not complied with? Does the whole process of detention become unlawful, and what is the status of the person "detained"? This question arose in *Cummings* v. *H.M. Advocate,* 1982 S.L.T. 487. Official forms are provided for use in detentions, leaving spaces for recording whether and at what time the various events provided for in sections 2 and 3 occur. In *Cummings* the form was not produced and the police witnesses sought to rely on their notebook entries as to compliance with the procedures laid down. Cummings argued that the failure to produce the official forms rendered the detention unlawful. The court held that the official forms in question were not prescribed by the Act and that the notebook entries were sufficient evidence of compliance with the statute. The court went further, however, and stressed that it did not necessarily accept the underlying submission that failure to comply with the statute would render the detention unlawful. This is probably not surprising if the submission were that any failure, whether or not inadvertant and no matter how trivial, would render the detention unlawful. On the other hand there must surely be hypothetical cases, such as deliberate non-compliance with the detainee's requests or failure to inform him of his rights, when the failures would render the detention unlawful.

What, in such a case, would be the status of the detainee? Presumably as the Act introduces a limited power in derogation of the suspect's common law rights, all the protection accorded to the police by the Act would fall if the limiting procedure is not complied with and the detainee's position would once again be governed by common law.

This does not entirely solve the problem, however, because of the tests adopted by the law for whether a person is at liberty or under arrest. There must be a risk that a person purportedly detained under what is then held to be an invalid detention is held not to have been under any compulsion whatsoever and is thus denied any redress for the unlawful and failed detention.

The second major statutory provision for detention is limited to the field of prevention and investigation of terrorism

22. Prevention of Terrorism (Temporary Provisions) Act 1984

"Powers of arrest and detention
12.—(1) Subject to subsection (2) below, a constable may arrest without warrant a person whom he has reasonable grounds for suspecting to be—
    (*a*) a person guilty of an offence under section 1, 9 or 10 above;
    (*b*) a person who is or has been concerned in the commission, preparation or instigation of acts of terrorism to which this Part of this Act applies;

(*c*)   a person subject to an exclusion order.

(2) The power of arrest conferred by subsection (1)(*c*) above is exercisable only—

  (*a*)   in Great Britain, if the exclusion order was made under section 4 above; and

  (*b*)   in Northern Ireland, if it was made under section 5 above.

(3) The acts of terrorism to which this Part of this Act applies are—

  (*a*)   acts of terrorism connected with the affairs of Northern Ireland; and

  (*b*)   acts of terrorism of any other description except acts connected solely with the affairs of the United Kingdom or any part of the United Kingdom other than Northern Ireland.

(4) A person arrested under this section shall not be detained in right of the arrest for more than 48 hours after his arrest; but the Secretary of State may, in any particular case, extend the period of 48 hours by a period or periods specified by him.

(5) Any such further period or periods shall not exceed five days in all.

(6) The following provisions (requirement to bring accused person before the court after his arrest) shall not apply to a person detained in right of the arrest

  (*a*)   section 43 of the Magistrates' Courts Act 1980;

  (*b*)   section 29 of the Children and Young Persons Act 1969;

  (*c*)   section 321(3) of the Criminal Procedure (Scotland) Act 1975;

  (*d*)   Article 131 of the Magistrates' Courts (Northern Ireland) Order 1981; and

  (*e*)   section 50(3) of the Children and Young Persons Act (Northern Ireland) 1968.

(7) Section 295(1) of the Criminal Procedure (Scotland) Act 1975 (interim liberation by officer in charge of police station) shall not apply to a person detained in right of an arrest under this section.

(8) The provisions of this section are without prejudice to any power of arrest exercisable apart from this section."

This Act is a descendant of the similarly named Act of 1974 which was passed in great haste in the wake of the Birmingham pub bombings of that year. The "temporary provisions" aspect of its nature stems from the fact that the Act has a maximum life of five years and within that period must be kept in force by an annual resolution of both Houses of Parliament. The Act is due to lapse in 1989 and during the annual debate on its renewal in 1988, the Home Secretary indicated that its successor would not be limited to a maximum life of five years. The Act applies only for the prevention of "terrorism." "Terrorism" is defined in section 14 as "the use of violence for political ends, and includes any use of violence for the purpose of putting the public or any section of the public in fear." The 1974 and 1976 Prevention of Terrorism Acts applied only to terrorism "connected with the affairs of Northern Ireland." Concern about the increasing violence in London connected with Middle East politics led to the inclusion of section 12(3)(*b*), so that terrorism connected with affairs abroad also falls within the scope of section 12. Curiously, terrorism connected with the affairs of the mainland of Great Britain does not fall within the section. Thus Scottish Nationalist or Cornish Nationalist terrorism does not fall within the scope of the Prevention of Terrorism Act. Lord Colville (1987) recommended that this anomaly should be rectified so that the Prevention of Terrorism Act applies to all kinds of terrorism.

Within this definition powers of arrest are given over a person guilty of an offence under section 1 or 9 or 10 of the Act: these refer respectively to giving assistance to a proscribed organisation (currently the IRA and the Irish National Liberation Army), to breach of, or assistance in the breach of, an exclusion order and to the assistance financially of acts of terrorism. Powers of arrest are also given under section 12(1)(b) of a person who is, or has been, concerned in the "commission, preparation or instigation" of acts of terrorism. Only one case has been reported under section 12, that is *Ex p. Lynch* [1980] N.I.L.R. 126. That case is important for establishing three points. Lynch was originally arrested under section 11 of the Northern Ireland (Emergency Provisions) Act 1978 on suspicion of "being a terrorist." He was detained without access to his wife, his solicitor or his doctor. Just before he was due to be released, information came to the attention of the police implicating him in a particular murder. Thereupon he was re-arrested under section 12(1)(b) of the Prevention of Terrorism Act. He applied for habeas corpus on three grounds—first, that suspicion of being involved in the same terrorist acts could not be used to detain him on two successive occasions under the different Acts; second, that he was not told when he was arrested the nature of the act or acts of terrorism which he was suspected of being involved in; finally, that even if the arrests had initially been lawful they ceased to be so by reason of his being denied access to his solicitor, family and doctor. The case was decided by the Lord Chief Justice (Lord Lowry).

As to the first ground, he decided that there was no impediment to Lynch's having been arrested first under one Act and then under the other *"or indeed twice in quick succession under the same provision"* (emphasis supplied). Despite the far-reaching consequences of this limb of the decision it would never seem to have been applied on the mainland to two successive arrests under section 12. In his second submission Lynch was relying upon the decision in *Christie* v. *Leachinsky* to the effect that when a person is arrested he must be told of the reasons for his arrest. Lord Lowry disposed of this submission, saying "the power conferred by section 12(1)(b) is wider and more general, being derived from a suspicion of the suspect's being concerned in the commission, preparation or instigation of acts of terrorism... The scope of this language is such that no specific crime need be suspected in order to ground a proper arrest under section 12."

Two objections to this decision spring to mind—first, even if no specific offence *need* be suspected, in Lynch's case he *was* suspected of a particular offence and surely in such circumstances the rule in *Christie* v. *Leachinsky* should apply. More generally, this interpretation of section 12 raises the question of its consonance with the European Convention on Human Rights. One of the major feature of the Prevention of Terrorism Act provisions for arrest over the years is the extremely low rate of prosecution and even lower rate of conviction arising from arrests under section 12. In Great Britain 6,246 people were detained between 1974 and 1986 under the three Prevention of Terrorism Acts (Colville (1987), para. 5. 2. 3), but only 575 of these detentions led to any charge at all. Almost inevitably this leads to the conclusion that the police view section 12 in the light as much of a provision for gathering intelligence as of one for enforcing the criminal law. Article 5 of the ECHR provides that everyone has the right to liberty and security of the person except in certain limited circumstances. The only one of those circumstances which could be relevant to section 12 of the Prevention of Terrorism Act is article 5(1)(c), that is "The lawful arrest or detention of a person effected for the purpose of bringing him before the competent legal authority on reasonable suspicion of having committed an offence or when it is reasonably considered necessary to prevent his committing an offence or fleeing after having done so." If section 12(1)(b) serves the purpose of intelligence gathering rather than prosecution of specific offences, then it would seem to be excluded by Article 5 of the European Convention. At one time an argument against this could have been made by virtue of the fact that the United Kingdom had availed itself of its right to derogate from certain articles of the Convention under article 15 of the Convention on the grounds of "emergency threatening the life of the nation." However, the United Kingdom has withdrawn its derogation under article 15 and therefore the full Convention applies throughout the United Kingdom again.

A second argument that section 12 breaches the ECHR rests on the fact that according to article 5(3) ECHR an arrested person must be "promptly brought before a judge." Can a delay of up to seven days be considered to conform to this requirement? In *Brogan and Others* v. *U.K.,* Application No. 11209/84, the European Commission of Human Rights decided in July 1987 that a detention of 5 days and 11 hours before going before a court violated the Convention, while one of 4 days 11 hours did not. The case has been referred to the Court.

The third of Lynch's arguments was that the conditions of his detention had rendered unlawful the original arrest by virtue of denial of access to the outside world. Lord Lowrie found no difficulty in deciding that, provided a detention were initially lawful, subsequent treatment could not render the detention itself unlawful, and that, as a matter of law the rights of a person *arrested* were not necessarily available to those *detained* under section 12. On this last point *Lynch* has been modified by according specific statutory rights to detainees.

23. Criminal Justice (Scotland) Act 1980
(as amended by Law Reform (Miscellaneous Provisions) (Scotland) Act 1985)

"Rights of persons arrested or detained in connection with terrorism

3A.—(1) A person who has been arrested or detained under the terrorism provisions and who is in detention in a police station or other premises shall be entitled to have intimation of his detention and of the place where he is being detained sent without delay to a solicitor and to another person reasonably named by him:

Provided that a police officer not below the rank of superintendent may authorise a delay (not extending longer than the period of 48 hours from the start of the detention) where, in his view, such delay is necessary on one of the grounds mentioned in section 3C(3) of this Act.

(2) Where a person arrested or detained under the terrorism provisions requests that the intimation be made, there shall be recorded the time when such request is—

(a) made; and

(b) complied with.

(3) A person arrested or detained under the terrorism provisions shall be entitled to consult a solicitor at any time, without delay:

Provided that a police officer not below the rank of superintendent may authorise a delay (not extending longer than the period of 48 hours from the start of the detention) where, in his view, such delay is necessary on one of the grounds mentioned in section 3C(3) of this Act.

(4) Subject to section 3C of this Act the consultation provided for in subsection (3) above shall be private.

Provision as to children detained in connection with terrorism

3B.—(1) Subject to the provisions of this section the provisions of section 3A of this Act apply to children as they apply to adults.

(2) Without prejudice to—

(a) subsection (3) of this section, or

(b) his entitlement, in terms of section 2A(1), to have intimation of his detention and of the place where he is being detained sent to a solicitor—

a person arrested or detained under the terrorism prevention provisions who appears to a constable to be a child shall not be entitled to have such intimation sent to any other person named by him.

(3) Where it appears to a constable that a person arrested or detained under the terrorism provisions is a child, he shall, subject to subsection (4), without delay—

(a) send intimation of the arrest or detention and of the place where the child is being held to his parent (if known); and

(b) allow such parent access to the child.

(4) A police officer not below the rank of superintendent may authorise

(a) a delay in compliance with the duty mentioned in subsection (3)(a) above;

(b) non-compliance with the duty mentioned in subsection (3)(b) above,

where such delay or, as the case may be, non-compliance is, in his view, necessary on one of the grounds mentioned in section 3C(3) of this Act:

Provided that any such delay in compliance with the duty mentioned in subsection (3)(*a*) shall not extend longer than the period of 48 hours from the start of the detention.

(5) There shall be recorded the time at which the intimation mentioned in subsection (3)(*a*) is made.

(6) Subject to section 3C of this Act the access mentioned in subsection (3)(*b*) above shall be private.

(7) Where a child is, by virtue of any enactment, in the care either of a local authority or of a voluntary organisation, the intimation shall be either to the authority or organisation or to the parent, and the right of access shall be exercisable both by an officer of the authority or organisation and by the parent; and subsections (4) and (6) above and section 3C of this Act shall apply in relation to intimation and access under this subsection as they apply to intimation and access under subsection (3) above.

Provisions relating to consultations and access in connection with terrorism

3C.—(1) An officer not below the rank of Assistant Chief Constable may direct that the consultation or access mentioned in sections 3A(3) and 3B(3) of this Act respectively be in the presence of a uniformed officer not below the rank of inspector if it appears to the officer giving the direction to be necessary on one of the grounds mentioned in subsection (3) below.

(2) A uniformed officer directed to be present during a consultation or, as the case may be, access shall be an officer who, in the opinion of the officer giving the direction, has no connection with the case.

(3) The grounds mentioned in sections 3A(1), 3A(3) and 3B(4) of this Act and in subsection (1) above are that it is in the interests of the investigation or prevention of crime, or of the apprehension, prosecution or conviction of offenders.

(4) Where delay or non-compliance is authorised in the exercising of any of the rights or, as the case may be, the carrying out of any of the duties, mentioned in sections 3A(1), 3A(3), and 3B(3) of this Act, there shall be recorded the reason for such delay or non-compliance.

Interpretation and effect of sections 3A to 3D

3D.—(1) In sections 3A to 3C and this section of this Act—

    (*a*) 'terrorism provisions' means—

        (i) section 12(1) of the Prevention of Terrorism (Temporary Provisions) Act 1984; or

        (ii) any provisions conferring a power of arrest or detention and contained in an order under section 13 of that Act; and

    (*b*) 'child' and 'parent' have the same meanings as in section 3 of this Act.

(2) The provisions of sections 3A to 3C and this section of this Act shall have effect, in relation to persons arrested or detained under the terrorism provisions, in place of any enactment or rule of law under or by virtue of which a person arrested or detained may be entitled to communicate or consult with any other person."

Numerous other statutes confer powers of detention for very limited purposes, most notably to search. An example follows.

24.   Criminal Justice (Scotland) Act 1980

"Search for offensive weapons
4.—(1) Where a constable has reasonable grounds for suspecting that any person is carrying an offensive weapon and has committed or is committing an offence under section 1 of the Prevention of Crime Act 1953 (prohibition of carrying of offensive weapons in public) the constable may search that person without warrant, and detain him for such time as is reasonably required to permit the search to be carried out; and he shall inform the person of the reason for such detention."

Statutes conferring powers of search commonly spell out the ancillary power to detain. Even where they did not, however, it would surely be implied as necessary. In some cases, where an intimate search is required (*e.g.* for suspected offences under the Misuse of Drugs Act 1971) it would also be reasonable to take the person to be searched to private premises such as a police station.

IV.   ADMISSIBILITY OF EVIDENCE

Before considering police powers of search and questioning, something must be said of their relationship to the admissibility of evidence thus obtained. Logically the definition of the powers of the police is a different thing from deciding whether to admit in court evidence obtained by exceeding those powers. If some real redress is available in other ways against police transgression of the limits of their powers and if evidence is equally convincing no matter how obtained, it may be that there is no objection to its being admitted in evidence. If so, a different view may be taken of real evidence on the one hand because however obtained it cannot lie, and of statements on the other, since the irregular means of obtaining them may render them less credible.

However, where, as in Scotland, no real redress is available against the police, inevitably the courts must consider whether, in admitting evidence improperly obtained, they are not in effect giving the police an incentive so to obtain it. In fact if there is no other effective remedy it is sophistry to draw any distinction between proper police action and actions which overstep the boundaries of legality but nonetheless produce admissible evidence (Godwin (1980)). If on the other hand the courts steadfastly refuse to admit such evidence they remove any advantage to be gained by the police in "stretching their powers." This is a choice which every legal system must make, and it is a constant battleground in Scotland in both courts and academic circles (see Gordon (1978), and Anon. (1979)

on statements, and for real evidence, Gray (1966) and J.T.C. (1969)).

As we shall see in Part VI below, admissibility as a separate limitation on police action is of little importance with regard to questioning, because the test of *admissibility* of statements obtained by questioning is now the same as the limits of police *powers* to question. An important exception is the problems posed by tape-recording of the questioning, which are problems caused by more general rules of evidence such as the "best evidence" rule and by the difficulty of severing parts of tapes. On the other hand, admissibility of *real* evidence is still a different matter from the lawfulness of its obtention, although it had been held by a Full Bench that real evidence is not necessarily to be excluded simply because improperly obtained.

25. Lawrie v. Muir
1950 J.C. 19

Acting on an honest misapprehension of their powers, two inspectors employed by a company which returned empty milk bottles to their owners searched Mrs Lawrie's dairy and found other people's milk bottles being used for the sale of L's milk, which was an offence under article 16(*a*) of the Milk (Control and Maximum Prices) (Great Britain) Order 1947. At her trial her objection to the admission of evidence of the bottles found was repelled and she was convicted. On appeal:

LORD JUSTICE-GENERAL (Cooper): "The matter has been remitted to a larger Court because of the importance and difficulty of the widest submission offered by the appellant, *viz:* that evidence obtained as a result of illegal entry, illegal search, illegal seizure or other like unlawful or irregular act, cannot be admitted in a criminal prosecution.

On this major issue there is little direct authority.

From the standpoint of principle it seems to me that the law must strive to reconcile two highly important interests which are liable to come into conflict— (*a*) the interest of the citizen to be protected from illegal or irregular invasions of his liberties by the authorities, and (*b*) the interest of the State to secure that evidence bearing upon the commission of crime and necessary to enable justice to be done shall not be withheld from Courts of law on any merely formal or technical ground. Neither of these objects can be insisted upon to the uttermost. The protection of the citizen is primarily protection for the innocent citizen against unwarranted, wrongful and perhaps highhanded interference, and the common sanction is an action of damages. The protection is not intended as a protection for the guilty citizen against the efforts of the public prosecutor to vindicate the law. On the other hand, the interest of the State cannot be magnified to the point of causing all the safeguards for the protection of the citizen to vanish, and of offering a positive inducement to the authorities to proceed by irregular methods. It is obvious that excessively rigid rules as to the exclusion of evidence bearing upon the commission of a crime might conceivably operate to the detriment and not the advantage of the accused, and might even lead to the conviction of the innocent; and extreme cases can easily be figured in which the exclusion of a vital piece of evidence from the knowledge of a jury because of some technical flaw in the conduct of the police would be an outrage upon common sense and a defiance of elementary justice. For these reasons, and in view of the expressions of judicial opinion to which I have referred, I find it quite impossible to affirm the appellant's extreme proposition. On the contrary, I adopt as a first approximation to the true rule the statement of Lord Justice-Clerk Aitchison that 'an irregularity in the obtaining of evidence does not *necessarily* make that evidence inadmissible.'

It remains to consider the implications of the word 'necessarily' which I have italicised. By using this word and by proceeding to the sentence which follows, Lord Aitchison seems to me to have indicated that there was, in his view, no absolute rule and that the question was one of circumstances. I respectfully agree. It would greatly facilitate the task of Judges were it possible to imprison the principle within the framework of a simple and unqualified maxim, but I do not think that it is feasible to do so. . . Irregularities require to be excused, and infringements of the formalities of the law in relation to these matters are not lightly to be condoned. Whether any given irregularity ought to be excused depends upon the nature of the irregularity and the circumstances under which it was committed. In particular, the case may bring into play the discretionary principle of fairness to the accused, which has been developed so fully in our law in relation to the admission in evidence of confessions or admissions by a person suspected or charged with crime. That principle would obviously require consideration in any case in which the departure from the strict procedure had been adopted deliberately with a view to securing the admission of evidence obtained by an unfair trick. Again, there are many statutory offences in relation to which Parliament has prescribed in detail in the interests of fairness a special procedure to be followed in obtaining evidence; and in such cases (of which the Sale of Food and Drugs Acts provide one example) it is very easy to see why a departure from the strict rules has often been held to be fatal to the prosecution's case. On the other hand, to take an extreme instance figured in argument, it would usually be wrong to exclude some highly incriminating production in a murder trial merely because it was found by a police officer in the course of a search authorised for a different purpose or before a proper warrant had been obtained."

The Lord Justice-Clerk (Thomson), Lords Mackay, Carmont, Jamieson, Russell and Keith concurred.

The court thereupon proceeded in the instant case to disallow the evidence and quashed the conviction. The test of admissibility is therefore one of how "excusable" the irregularity is. Beyond that vague formula it is difficult to be more specific, especially as cases often do not make absolutely clear whether in the circumstances evidence was properly obtained or whether it was improperly obtained but excusably so.

One commentator (J.T.C. (1969)) has suggested a two-part test. First, anything obtained by means themselves illegal (as opposed to simply "not authorised by a legal power") is inadmissable. Second, where the evidence is obtained in some other irregular way (*e.g.* by a trick) the test is the harm or affront caused to an innocent person by the means of obtaining the evidence. Though never judicially approved, or even discussed, this test seems to accord with all the reported cases.

There is even less distinction than in the case of real evidence between the lawfulness of interrogation techniques and the admissibility of statements thus obtained. Recent cases seem to establish that the test alike of lawfulness and admissibility is generally the same, namely "fairness."

One technical issue which has recently arisen, however, is that of admissibility of tape-recordings of interviews at police stations. The Thomson Committee (1975) was strongly in favour of compulsory recording of interrogations (paras. 7.13c and 7.21b). Throughout the Parliamentary history of the CJSA a connection was drawn between the introduction of detention for questioning and the safeguard of recording the questioning, but the government resisted all attempts to legislate for tape-recording. Instead a six-month "experiment" in tape-recording interviews in Falkirk and Dundee was set up. This was extended for successive periods and to police stations in Aberdeen and Glasgow. The Scottish Office working party supervising the experiment reported in 1985 (Scottish Home and Health Department (1985)) and recommended extension of the scheme throughout Scotland. The Government has accepted this. Probably one reason for delaying full-scale use of tape-recorders was difficulties about admissibility. (See (1981) SCOLAG Bul. 260 and 272.) The major difficulties have been resolved by *Lord Advocate's Reference (No. 1 of 1983)*, 1984 S.C.C.R. 62 and by s. 60 of the Criminal Justice (Scotland) Act 1987.

V.   SEARCH

In this section the word "search" is used loosely, to cover any means by which real evidence is obtained. No distinction is made between search of premises and search of the person, or removal of traces or taking of prints from the body. Instead consideration is given to what may be done without warrant, what may be done with a warrant and what may not be done at all.

A.   SEARCH WITHOUT WARRANT AT COMMON LAW

(i) *The police may not search a suspect in order to discover whether he has on him evidence justifying arrest, but an arrested suspect may be searched.*

26.   Jackson v. Stevenson
(1897) 2 Adam 255

Jackson was suspected by water bailiffs of poaching salmon and searched to see whether he was carrying the required implements. It was unclear whether this was before or after his arrest. He was convicted and appealed on two grounds, one being that the search was illegal because conducted before his apprehension.

LORD JUSTICE-GENERAL (Robertson): [His Lordship first considered the other ground of appeal and decided in Jackson's favour.] ". . . The Sheriff's statement of the facts does not make it quite clear whether the appellant had been apprehended before the bailiffs searched his person, or only after. . .

   The right of the bailiffs, be it observed, is to exercise the powers and authorities of constables in the same manner as if the statutory offences were breaches of the peace. Now, a constable is entitled to arrest, without a warrant, any person seen by him committing a breach of the peace, and he may arrest on the direct information of eye witnesses. Having arrested him, I make no doubt that the constable could search him. But it is a totally different matter to search a man in order to find evidence to determine whether you will apprehend him or not. If the search succeeds (such is the condition of the argument), you will apprehend him; but if the search does not succeed you will not apprehend him. Now, I have only to say that I know no authority for ascribing to constables the right to make such tentative searches, and they seem contrary to constitutional principle. If the constable requires to make such a search, it can only be because without it he is not justified in apprehending; and, without a warrant, to search a person not liable to apprehension seems palpably illegal. A constable or bailiff must make up his mind on what he sees (or hears on credible information) whether to arrest or not; and, if he does arrest in good faith, the law will protect him, whether his opinion at the time of the guilt of the person arrested prove accurate or not."

Lords Adam and Kinnear delivered concurring opinions on both grounds of appeal.

   In *Bell* v. *Leadbetter,* 1934 J.C. 74, the power of bailiffs to search a person after arrest was confirmed. The principle in *Jackson* is of course less important today, as on the basis of suspicion the police could detain him (provided the offence carried a possible sentence of imprisonment) and search him to see whether there was sufficient evidence to arrest. The key to the power to search is whether a person has been arrested. A person "helping the police with their inquiries" and who is eventually charged, but not arrested, may not be searched (*Adamson* v. *Martin,* 1916 S.C. 319 explained in *Adair* v. *McCarry,* 1933 S.L.T. 482).

(ii) *The right to "search" an arrested person extends to more than examining his clothes, and includes the taking of samples from the surface of the body, scraping from nails, examination of his body and taking his fingerprints.*

27. Adair v. McGarry
1933 S.L.T. 482

Some bottles stolen from a shop were discovered by the police. McGarry was arrested some days later on suspicion of the offence and, without a warrant or his consent, his fingerprints were taken, and proved to be identical to those on the bottles. On this evidence he was convicted. He appealed on the grounds that the prints were illegally obtained and inadmissible.

LORD JUSTICE-CLERK (Alness): " Viewed apart from authority, then, the problem presents itself to my mind thus—The police must be armed with all adequate and reasonable powers for the investigation and detection of crime. Is finger-printing a reasonable incident in that process, not forbidden by the common law, and not unduly invading the rights of the accused?

I say 'not forbidden by the common law,' because I think that phrase more correctly expounds the situation than the phrase 'authorised by the common law.' Let me explain what I mean by this. The system of detection of crime by means of finger prints is a modern scientific discovery, later in date than any of the statutes to which reference was made in the course of the debate, and it would not therefore be reasonable to look for, or to expect to find, institutional or common law authority for its practice.

As regards undue invasion of the personal rights of the accused, one must have a sense of proportion. Certain it is that in practice, hitherto unchallenged, a person who is suspected of crime may be brought—with reasonable violence in the event of his resistance—to the police station, that he may be paraded for purposes of identification, that he may be stripped, and that he may be searched for any incriminating natural or artificial mark upon his person. That mark may include a birth mark or natural deformity, a tattoo mark, or bloodstains, or the like. All these things are done with a view to establishing the identity of the suspect. And yet, it is argued that the comparatively innocuous process of taking a mould of the suspect's thumb is excluded from the rights of the police. I inquire—Why? To that question I have heard no adequate answer. The analogy of straining at a gnat and swallowing a camel suggests itself as apposite to the argument in question. The suggestion seems to be that the existence of a warrant . . . to which I shall subsequently advert, removes all objection to finger-printing. If I could see that any substantial protection is afforded to the accused by the existence of such a warrant, I could understand that view. But nothing is more certain than that such a warrant is a pure formality, is granted for the asking, is, so I am informed, never refused, and, moreover, is granted by a person who may know less about the matter than the police know. The suggested protection by way of warrant is quite illusory. If the accused is innocent, no harm is done by finger printing. He has not been subject to so great 'humiliation'—to use Mr Duffes's word— as he may admittedly be subjected to in accordance with time-honoured and unchallengeable practice. If, on the other hand, he is guilty, the process renders it more likely that his guilt may be established. That is, I apprehend, desirable."

The Lord Justice-General, Lord Sands and Lord Morison delivered concurring opinions, and Lord Hunter dissented.

In *Forrester* v. *H.M Advocate* 1952 J.C. 28, the competency of examination of body wounds of persons arrested was upheld. Powers of search without warrant of arrested persons do not however include a power to take blood-samples (*H.M. Advocate* v. *Milford,* below) or a power to take X-rays. In *Mackenzie* v. *Macaulay* (*The Scotsman,* September 23, 1981). Macaulay was accused of attempting to steal a truck and of stealing its ignition key. Evidence, in the form of a stomach X-ray, was produced to show that he had swallowed the key when arrested, but was ruled inadmissible because no search warrant had been obtained.

(iii) *In the case of urgency, when evidence might otherwise be lost, the police may search premises and person not arrested without warrant.*

28. H.M. Advocate v. McGuigan
1936 J.C. 16

At a trial for murder, rape and theft, counsel for the accused objected to the admission of evidence taken without warrant from the tent where McGuigan lived.

LORD JUSTICE-CLERK (Aitchison): "The ground of the objection is that this search was carried out, and I take it certain articles seized, without the warrant of a magistrate; and it is said, accordingly, that the search and the seizure of the articles were both illegal. Now, the facts are these: On the evening of 28th August the accused had been identified—or was alleged to have been identified—by Marjory Fenwick, and immediately thereafter he was apprehended and charged. . . Thereafter the accused was searched. Both the apprehension and the search of the accused were carried out without warrant. I have no doubt that, in the circumstances, this was quite regular. The police were amply justified in acting at their own hand . . . the same night Inspector Davidson went to the accused's tent. He found the tent occupied by the accused's mother and the accused's stepfather. He disclosed who he was, and what his purpose was. No objection was raised, as was natural enough. On the other hand, no consent was asked for, and the search proceeded. Now it must be obvious that, the accused having been arrested on so grave a charge as murder, it might be of the first importance to the ends of public justice that a search of the tent in which the accused had been living should be made forthwith. The police acted at their own hand, just as they acted at their own hand in apprehending and searching the person of the accused. In the circumstances, the matter being in the view of Inspector Davidson one of urgency, the police were entitled, in my view, to act without delay and without having obtained a warrant from a magistrate."

29. Bell v. Hogg
1967 J.C 49

Police investigating a theft of copper wire stopped a van, explained what they were doing to the occupants, and asked to see their hands, which bore traces of a substance which could be verdigris. They were taken to a police station and before arrest or charge, and without being told they could refuse, were asked to give a rubbing from their hands. This proved in fact to be verdigris, and they were convicted of the theft of the wire. A police witness deponed that, if the rubbings had not been taken, the accused might have asked to use the toilet and washed their hands. The accused appealed against the admission of the evidence of the rubbings.

LORD JUSTICE-GENERAL (Clyde): "In these circumstances, in my opinion, the sergeant took a perfectly proper and legitimate step in securing a record of what was on the appellants' hands before it was eliminated by washing or otherwise. The urgency of the matter is its justification. . . In the course of the argument in the present case the decision in *McGovern* v. *H.M. Advocate*, 1950 J.C. 33, was also referred to. In that case, which the Lord Justice-General described (at p. 34) as 'distinctly unusual,' the accused had not yet been charged nor apprehended in connection with a safe-blowing, but had been kept in the police station for some six hours, when 'as a further precaution' the police obtained the contents of his finger nails by scraping them with a view to subsequent chemical analysis of the scrapings. After carrying out this operation the police then 'deemed it advisable' to charge him. This incident was treated by the Court on the concession of the Crown as an irregular proceeding on the part of the police. There was no question of urgency and no knowledge by the police as to whether the scrapings would yield any evidence of the suspect's connection with the offence. This all makes it a highly special decision. In the present case there was on the contrary obvious urgency involved in the obtaining of the impressions; and the analysis of these impressions was necessary, not in the hope of connecting the appellants with the offences but in order to secure a reliable analysis of the grey-green marks on their hands which had been seen by the light of the torch at the railway station shortly beforehand, in order to confirm whether they were made by verdigris or not.

The test of the admissibility of the evidence of the analysis is whether what was done was done fairly. In this case there was no compulsion about what the police did. There is no trace or any suggestion of bullying or trickery on the part of the police, still less any element of third-degree treatment. I do not regard it as unfair that the accused were not specifically told that they need not consent to the impressions being taken. . .

In the situation in the present case, as disclosed by the findings of the Sheriff-substitute, in my opinion the police sergeant was well entitled to take the course which he did. It follows that the evidence regarding it and the analysis of the impressions on the blotting paper were competently admitted by the Sheriff-substitute."

Lords Migdale and Cameron delivered concurring opinions.

30.   McHugh v. H.M. Advocate
1978 J.C. 12

M. and another man were suspected of assault and the theft of a sum of money, some of it in banknotes of known numbers. Accordingly the police, without a warrant, went to the house of M.'s co-accused and, according to their evidence, which was disputed, cautioned, charged and arrested M. They then searched his person and found some of the numbered banknotes. At his trial evidence of the findings of these notes was admitted and he was convicted. He appealed on the grounds *inter alia* that this evidence should not have been admitted, because illegally obtained.

LORD JUSTICE-GENERAL (Emslie) delivering the opinion of the court (Lords Cameron and Avonside): "As we understood the argument, counsel began by saying that this was a cause in which the search was conducted without warrant. Although police who have lawfully arrested a person may quite properly search the arrested man without a warrant, it was not certain that an arrest had taken place in this case, or that if it had taken place, it had taken place legally. The only other circumstance in which a search of a citizen may be justified is where, although there is no warrant and no lawful arrest, the need to search is demanded as a matter of urgency to prevent the possible loss or destruction of important evidence. In this case, said Mr Taylor, it was by no means clear that the police were telling the truth when they said they arrested McHugh before they searched him. In any event, said Mr Taylor, it is by no means clear either that they had reasonable grounds for arresting McHugh, or that there were any considerations of urgency which could have justified the search which revealed the stolen property. . . The evidence bearing upon the circumstances of the search was all one way and remained unshaken in cross-examination. It was to the effect that the officers had set out with the primary purpose of arresting McHugh, for that was their allotted task. They carried out that task and the search was a sequel to the arrest. They did not arrest without reasonable cause, and in particular merely to provide an excuse for a search. In any event it is perfectly clear that the search of McHugh, a prime suspect, was according to the evidence, essential as a matter of urgency, to avoid any risk that any of the numbered notes which he might have in his possession would be lost, hidden or destroyed. In this state of matters and particularly having regard to the sufficient evidence of the urgent need to search, the criticism of the direction given by the trial Judge is without real substance."

These cases leave it uncertain whether the "urgency" doctrine is a rule of law (according powers of search to the police) or of evidence (rendering admissible what is irregularly obtained).

Whichever it is, the major question they raise is "how urgent is urgent?" The trend in these cases is towards the elimination of a need for search warrants in many situations (see also *Walsh* v. *MacPhail*, 1978 S.L.T. (Notes) 29 and *Hay* v. *H.M. Advocate*, 1968 J.C. 40). No one perhaps, would deny that there should be a power to act to save evidence of its nature perishable or in circumstances rendering likely its deliberate destruction. But *McHugh* stretches this concept to unnecessary lengths. Even if McHugh had not been arrested the court accepted that there were *grounds* for arrest and he was certainly physically detained. In these circumstances, and under the eyes of the police, how was he to destroy the banknotes? In any case, since he was unaware that they were numbered, and important evidence, he would be extremely loth to do so. There must remain a sharp suspicion that "urgency" has become a convenient way out of procedural mishaps, a second string to the prosecutor's bow.

However, *Leckie* v. *Milne*, 1982 S.L.T. 177 (below, p. 120, on which see Finnie, (1982a)) may, even if only by omission, herald a more restrictive judicial approach to the idea of "urgency."

B.   STATUTORY POWERS OF SEARCH WITHOUT A WARRANT

Dozens of statutes confer powers of search without warrant, mainly for very limited purposes. One example is the Misuse of Drugs Act 1971.

31.   Misuse of Drugs Act 1971

"23 . . . (2) If a constable has reasonable grounds to suspect that any person is in possession of a controlled drug in contravention of this Act or of any regulations made thereunder, the constable may—
   (a)   search that person, and detain him for the purpose of searching him;
   (b)   search any vehicle or vessel in which the constable suspects that the drug may be found, and for that purpose require the person in control of the vehicle or vessel to stop it;
   (c)   seize and detain, for the purposes of proceedings under this Act, anything found in the course of the search which appears to the constable to be evidence of an offence under this Act.
In this subsection 'vessel' includes a hovercraft within the meaning of the Hovercraft Act 1968; and nothing in this subsection shall prejudice any power of search or any power to seize or detain property which is exercisable by a constable apart from this subsection."

"Reasonable cause" in the context of drugs searches is discussed at length in Home Office (1970), summarised by the Thomson Committee (1975: paras. 3.19 and 3.20).

In a sense parallel with these specific powers of search without warrant are the general powers of search accompanying detention under the CJSA, which provide an equivalent to the general common law powers of search following arrest.

32.   The Criminal Justice (Scotland) Act 1980

"2 . . . (5) Where a person is detained under subsection (1) above, a constable may . . .

(b)   exercise the same powers of search as are available following an arrest; and

(c)   take fingerprints, palmprints and such other prints and impressions as the constable may, having regard to the circumstances of the suspected offence, reasonably consider appropriate:

Provided that the record of the prints and impressions so taken shall be destroyed immediately following a decision not to institute criminal proceedings against the person or on the conclusion of such proceedings otherwise than with a conviction or an order under section 182 or 383 (absolute discharge) or 183(1) or 384(1) (probation) of the 1975 Act.

(6) A constable may use reasonable force in exercising any power conferred by subsection (1), or by paragraph (b) or (c) of subsection (5), above."

C.   SEARCH WITH WARRANT

Search warrants, like arrest warrants, may in theory be issued by any magistrate, sheriff or Lord Commissioner of Justiciary at common law. Again like arrest warrants, they are usually in practice obtained by application on a printed form to the local sheriff. Some statutes, however, give powers of issuing warrants only to justices of the peace (e.g. Official Secrets Act 1911, s. 9). In such cases it is not clear whether only justices of the peace can issue warrants under such statutes or whether sheriffs and Lords Commissioners of Justiciary have inherently the limited powers of justices of the peace (see Black (1987)). A very few statutes (e.g. Prevention of Terrorism (Temporary Provisions) Act 1984, Sched. 3, para. 4(4)) give powers in limited cases to police officers to issue written orders equivalent to warrants to search (in the example given, an officer not below the rank of superintendent may authorise a search where the case is one of great emergency and in the interest of the State and immediate action is necessary).

Six points should be borne in mind about search warrants.

First, in Scotland a warrant may be obtained to search for evidence of any kind. In contrast, at common law in England warrants were competent only in the case of a few crimes, not including, for example, murder. This position was altered by the Police and Criminal Evidence Act 1984, but explains the relatively greater powers of search without warrant which the common law accorded the police in England in recent times.

Secondly, the categories of purposes for which warrants are competent are never closed. The kinds of evidence in which the law is reasonably interested expand with forensic science. The word "search" is in fact too narrow to cover the idea; rather the obtaining of real evidence of any kind may be competent under warrant, as the following case shows.

33.   Hay v. H.M. Advocate
1968 J.C. 40

The body of a murdered girl bearing impressions of teethmarks on the right breast was found near an approved school. Impressions were taken of the teeth of 29 inmates and staff, with their consent, in order to compare them with those on the body. All were eliminated as suspects except Hay. A warrant was sought, and granted, to take him to the Glasgow Dental Hospital for more detailed examination of his teeth. The evidence so obtained secured his conviction at his trial for the murder. He appealed.

The Lord Justice-General (Clyde) delivered the opinion of the court (Lords Guthrie, Migdale, Cameron and Johnston).

"As regards the first and main issue in the appeal—namely the legality of the warrant—it has been observed in more than one of the cases . . . that two conflicting considerations arise. On the one hand there is the need from the point of view of the public interest for promptitude and facility in the identification of accused persons and the discovery on their persons or on their premises of *indicia* either of guilt or innocence. On the other hand the liberty of the subject must be protected against any undue or unnecessary invasion of it.

In an endeavour as fairly as possible to hold the balance between these two considerations three general principles have been recognised and established by the Court. In the first place, once an accused has been apprehended, and therefore deprived of his liberty, the police have the right to search and examine him. In the second place, before the police have reached a stage in their investigations when they feel warranted in apprehending him, they have in general no right by the common law of Scotland to search or examine him or his premises without his consent. There may be circumstances, such as urgency or risk of evidence being lost, which would justify an immediate search or examination, but in the general case they cannot take this step at their own hand. But, in the third place, even before the apprehension of the accused they may be entitled to carry out a search of his premises or an examination of his person without his consent if they apply to a magistrate for a warrant for this purpose. Although the accused is not present nor legally represented at the hearing where the magistrate grants the warrant to examine or to search, the interposition of an independent judicial officer affords the basis for a fair reconciliation of the interest of the public in the suppression of crime and of the individual, who is entitled not to have the liberty of his person or his premises unduly jeopardised. A warrant of this limited kind will, however, only be granted in special circumstances. The hearing before the magistrate is by no means a formality, and he must be satisfied that the circumstances justify the taking of this unusual course, and that the warrant asked for is not too wide or oppressive. For he is the safeguard against the grant of too general a warrant. . .

In the circumstances of the present case the obtaining of the warrant prior to the examination in question in our opinion rendered the examination quite legal, and the evidence which resulted from it was therefore competent."

A second example is blood-testing. Advances in knowledge of blood-groups of independent systems and the statistical likelihood of their combining in one person's blood make it possible to state very precisely the chances of a bloodstain having come from a particular person. Accordingly in *H.M. Advocate* v. *Milford,* 1973 S.L.T. 12 a warrant was granted to take a blood sample. More recently still a technique has been discovered for genetic analysis of body-tissue, which is important in linking pieces of tissue with a particular person or in proving consanguinity. The relevance of these to criminal investigation is obvious.

The third point in connection with warrants is that in Scotland, unlike the system set up in England by the Police and Criminal Evidence Act, they grant plenary search powers. There are no classes of record exempt from search or subject to special safeguards, and the importance of confidentiality in the prized social roles of doctors, ministers of religion and the like do not confer special protection on materials accumulated in the course of that role.

Fourthly, the standard form of warrant is laid down by Act of Adjournal, but whether or not issued in that form, any warrant must contain certain formal details, which, if the warrant in question is a blank form, must appear in the correct place on the form. Normally, failure to comply with these requirements will render inadmissible evidence gathered under the defective warrant unless the missing or incorrect information is deemed unnecessary or the mistake immaterial.

34. H.M. Advocate v. Bell
1985 S.L.T. 349

Bell was accused of possession of controlled drugs contrary to the Misuse of Drugs Act 1971. The warrant under which evidence against him had been gathered was irregular in that the place of signing had been omitted and that the signature of the J.P. appeared in the middle of the text of the form and before the operative words "grant warrant as craved."

THE SHERIFF (J. S. Boyle): . . . "Now, I am firmly of the view that the omission is fatal to the validity of the purported warrant. I am unmoved by the Crown's submissions that, when s. 23(3) of the Misuse of Drugs Act 1971 authorises a justice to 'grant a warrant,' the statutory provision is fulfilled by the justice's assent, however expressed in writing, and, if it be necessary that the warrant be signed, that the writing by the justice of her name in gremio of the form of warrant constituted the adhibition of her 'signature.' From time immemorial, the law of Scotland has required that all deeds and writings of importance be authenticated to have any force or effect by subscription of the granter—the only recognised exceptions being those granted by the Sovereign who superscribes. The truly essential nature of this requirement is universally recognised in the practice of all branches of our law and finds expression, for example, in some of our earliest

Scots statutes still in force—the Subscription of Deeds Acts and the Interlocutors Acts of the 16th and 17th centuries.

In relation to warrants for apprehension and search in particular, one need only note the provisions of s. 309(2) of the Criminal Procedure (Scotland) Act 1975 which echoes similar sections in its predecessors throughout this century and emphasises the importance of such writings. I reject the suggestion made to me that the requirement in that section that such warrants should be signed did not necessarily mean that they must be subscribed. . .

I consider that any attempt that the Crown might make in the course of the trial of this case to prove by parole evidence that the justice 'granted' a search warrant in the absence of subscription, would be quite incompetent."

The procurator fiscal appealed to the High Court on the ground that the sheriff was not entitled in the whole circumstances to hold that a valid warrant had not been granted by the justice of the peace. The High Court refused the appeal. The following opinion was delivered by the Lord Justice-Clerk (Lord Wheatley), with whom Lords Stott and Brand concurred:

"In the result the sheriff, having heard arguments, decided that the warrant was invalid. The reason for that was that the warrant did not bear to be signed by the justice of the peace who was said to have issued the warrant. I do not require to go into the pros and cons of the argument because they are fully set out by the sheriff in the note appended to his interlocutor, and in my opinion, for the reasons which he so clearly sets out in that note, he was correct in the decision which he reached. Accordingly I am content simply to say that his reasoning was correct and the result which he reached was the right one.

In these circumstances I move your Lordships to refuse this appeal."

Similarly in *Bulloch* v. *H.M. Advocate,* 1980 S.L.T. (Notes) 5, the warrant was held defective. For excusable defects, see *H.M. Advocate* v. *Cumming,* 1983 S.C.C.R. 15.

A fifth point, bound up with the last, is that warrants which amount to a licence to the police to enter premises and look around generally for evidence of *any* crime, or which do not adequately specify what is being sought, are illegal.

35.   Bell v. Black and Morrison
(1865) 5 Irv. 57

In 1863 a campaign of opposition to the person named as minister to the parish of Dunbog in Fife went so far as the sending to him of threatening letters and an explosion outside his house. In executing one search warrant (itself the subject of litigation) the prosecutors came across evidence suggesting the complicity of five other persons. They petitioned for and received a search warrant in very wide terms, which was then sought to be suspended in the present case.

The petition in terms of which warrant was granted read as follows:

"That the petitioners are informed, and have reason to believe, that written documents and other articles referring to, and connected with, said conspiracy and threatening letters are in the possession of the said John Bell, &C . . . and as it is necessary, for the purpose of said precognition, to recover and take possession of the same, the present application for warrant to search becomes necessary. [The prayer was] to grant warrant to officers of Court, and their assistants, to search the dwelling-house, repositories, and premises, at Glenduckie, occupied by the said John Bell, &C . . . for the said written documents, and all other articles tending to establish guilt, or participation in said crimes, and to take possession thereof, to be produced before your Lordship, or otherwise to do in the premises as to your Lordship shall seem proper."

The Lord Justice-Clerk (Inglis) delivered the opinion of the court (Lords Ardmillan and Neaves).

"There are some marked and important peculiarities in this petition and warrant... In the first place, the warrant is granted against five different persons, none of whom is under a charge for any crime. It is stated in the petition that the persons against whom the warrant is asked are shown, by documents recovered in the course of the precognition against Pringle, to have been engaged in the same conspiracy, and in writing and sending threatening letters. But as no charge has yet been made against any of these five person, this amounts to no more than a statement of the suspicion or belief of the Procurator-fiscal that they are implicated in the same crimes as Pringle. In the second place, the leading object of the warrant is to obtain possession of the papers of the parties'against whom it is directed, without any limitation as to the kind of papers, for by the term 'written documents' nothing else can be meant than all writings of every description. The only limitation is to be found in the words which follow—'tending to establish guilt or participation in said crimes,' and in the words in the body of the petition—'referring to and connected with said conspiracy and threatening letters.' But these words, while they may be supposed in one sense to have a limiting effect, are in another view capable of a very elastic interpretation: for it is not proposed to limit the seizure of papers in each person's house to those which inculpate himself; but, on the contrary, the words of the warrant would justify the seizure of papers tending to inculpate anybody in the crimes charged against Pringle, or at least, and in the most favourable sense, would justify the seizure of any papers in the possession of the complainer Bell which would tend to inculpate any of the other four parties against whom the warrant is directed, in addition, of course, to Pringle, and so in regard to the papers of each of the four other persons against whom the warrant is issued. In the third place, the execution of the warrant is entrusted absolutely and without control to ordinary sheriff-officers and their assistants, who are thereby commanded, whether in the presence or absence of the parties, who are under no criminal charge, and who have no notice of the application for or granting of the warrant, to seize their whole papers *per aversionem,* and themselves to read and examine all these papers for the purpose of finding traces or proofs of guilt either against the owners and possessors of the papers, or against some other person or persons.

The question which is thus raised for our decision has been represented to us by the learned counsel as one of great importance, and no one can doubt that it is so. It involves considerations of such high constitutional principle, that if we had felt any hesitation as to the judgment we should pronounce, we should have asked the assistance and advice of other Judges of this Court. But entertaining no doubt at all, we consider it our duty at once to pronounce this warrant to be illegal. The seizure of papers, as distinguished from their recovery as articles of evidence, and also as distinguished from the seizure of other articles which are invested with no character of confidentiality or secrecy, is, under all circumstance, a matter of extreme delicacy. But the seizure of papers made in the circumstances with which we have to deal, is a proceeding quite unknown to the law of Scotland. Something was said of practice, though no example of such seizure as this was mentioned. We think it right to say that no mere official practice would, in our eyes, justify such a warrant. Nothing short of an Act of Parliament, or a rule of the common law founded on a usage known to and recognised by the Court, would at all affect our judgment on this question. If any such practice really exists, which we do not believe, the sooner it is put an end to the better. The Court are therefore of opinion that the warrant must be suspended."

In a later action for damages against the procurator fiscal the Lord Justice-Clerk delivered himself of the opinion that the above warrant was "as illegal as if it had been a warrant to bring up a party for examination under torture" (*Bell* v. *Black and Morrison* (1865) 3 M. 1026 at p. 1029). Not all of the judges seem to have taken quite such a strong view of the case. Lord Ardmillan, considering the same warrant in a second action for damages (*Nelson* v. *Black and Morrison* (1866) 4 M. 328 at p. 332) said:

"But, at the same time, a general warrant for a sweeping and indefinite search in the dwelling-house of a person not put under charge, for written documents, in regard to which there is this peculiarity that they must be read before it can be seen what they instruct, is a very strong and startling procedure; and if granted at all, such a warrant should have been accompanied by some security against oppression, and against the violation of private confidence. The most secret and sacred writings were, or might be, exposed to the perusal of a Sheriff Officer and his concurrents; and the personal attendance of the Sheriff, or some person of discretion and authority, to superintend the search, and to inspect and select the documents, was, in my opinion, necessary to secure the fair execution of the warrant, and to prevent its having oppressive consequences. The illegality of the warrant lay in the absence of such securities.

I am not prepared to say that a general search warrant for articles of evidence, and, among other articles, for written documents tending to instruct an occult conspiracy, could not, in any case, be granted to the public prosecutor against parties named in the petition, if accompanied by proper securities against oppressive execution. I agree with your Lordship that such a warrant might have been legally granted."

The ratio of this decision should not therefore be understood too widely, as the warrant was illegal by virtue of the conjunction of a number of factors. But see also *Webster* v. *Bethune* (1857) 2 Irv. 596.

A rare application of this principle in modern times occurred in 1987 in connection with the "Zircon Affair." As part of a series of programmes on government secrecy, BBC Scotland made a programme in which the existence of a previously unpublicised "spy-satellite" was made known.

The investigative journalist claimed that all his information was derived from public knowledge intelligently collated. Nonetheless, a breach of section 2 of the Official Secrets Act 1911 was suspected and Special Branch obtained a sheriff's search warrant. When officers presented themselves at the BBC studios it was noticed that the warrant authorised search for evidence of offences under "The Official Secrets Act" of which there are literally hundreds of various kinds and levels of seriousness. On presentation of a Bill of Suspension to Lord Clyde this warrant was suspended as illegal for lack of specificity and a warrant to search for evidence of offences under section 2 of the Act was subsequently obtained (*The Scotsman,* 2nd Feb 1987).

The final point to be made on the availability of warrants is that they are not restricted to cases where a person has been arrested. Indeed, even knowledge that an offence has been committed is not necessary. This was decided in the following case.

36. Stewart v. Roach
1950 S.C. 318

An inspector of police on the basis of an anonymous letter indicating that certain stolen goods were concealed in the houses of the pursuers applied to and obtained from a Justice of the Peace warrants in common form to search the pursuer's houses. No stolen goods were found. The pursuers raised an action to obtain damages for wrongous search.

LORD PRESIDENT (Cooper): "The consulted Judges, the Lord Justice-Clerk, Lord Jamieson and Lord Patrick, have returned the following opinion.

This case was sent to seven Judges on the question 'whether it is illegal to grant and execute a warrant to search for stolen goods the premises of a person who has not been apprehended nor charged with an offence'. . .

The sole point taken is that the searches were wrongous because the pursuers were neither charged nor apprehended before the warrants were applied for and obtained. Prior charge or apprehension is said to be an essential prerequisite. Otherwise, the warrants are admitted to be sufficiently specific and the procedure regular.

It is difficult to see on principle why the lesser invasion of the pursuers' rights involved in a search of their houses for stolen goods should be objectionable simply because the more extreme step of charging or apprehending them had not been taken. However that may be, it was argued to us that the matter was concluded by authority, and particularly by a decision of the High Court of Justiciary—*McLauchlan* v. *Renton*, 1911 J.C. 12 [that case was here outlined and the following general observation by Lord Salvesen, and concurred in by the Lord Justice-Clerk and Lord Ardwall, quoted]:

'There can be no doubt, at common law, it is illegal to grant a warrant to search the premises of any citizen who has not been charged with an offence, however much the Crown authorities may have reason for suspicion against him.' Lord Salvesen gives no authority for this pronouncement, but it is clear from the argument presented that the supposed basis of the doctrine is *Bell* v. *Black and Morrison*. . . The opinion of the Court was delivered by the Lord Justice-Clerk. Three grounds for the decision are stated: 'In the first place, the warrant is granted against five different persons, none of whom is under a charge for any crime.'

It will be observed that the first of these grounds is relevant to the present topic and indeed, as it turns out, is the only basis on which the argument for the pursuers rests. Had the Court regarded a charge as an essential prerequisite, we think that the opinion would have said so in terms and, indeed, that would have been decisive without further elaboration. It seems to us clear not only from the way in which the first ground is worded but also from the incidental reference to the absence of a criminal charge in the course of the formulation of the third ground, that they regarded the absence of charge as only one element for consideration in conjunction with the other circumstances of the case. The substance of the opinion is that, in the whole circumstances disclosed, what was sought was far too wide and not fenced with sufficient safeguards, especially having in view that no charge had been preferred.

That this is the true emphasis of the opinion appears from this later passage: 'The seizure of papers, as distinguished from their recovery as articles of evidence, and also as distinguished from the seizure of other articles which are invested with no character of confidentiality or secrecy, is, under all circumstances, a matter of extreme delicacy. But the seizure of papers made in the circumstances with which we have to deal, is a proceeding quite unknown to the law of Scotland.'

That this is the true view of this case is borne out by what was said by the Judges who took part in two subsequent cases in the Court of Session arising out of the same matter.

[The consulted judges here considered the opinions in the two actions for damages quoted in the last note.]

It is apparent that the First Division with both the previous cases before them give no countenance to the view that charge or apprehension is a prerequisite. Indeed, the opinion of Lord Deas goes far to negative it, while the opinion of Lord Ardmillan shows that he did not understand the opinion of the Court in the suspension as turning on that point.

In these circumstances we come without hesitation to the conclusion that charge or apprehension is not an essential prerequisite to the granting of a search warrant and that the proposition in *McLauchlan* v. *Renton* is too broadly stated."

The Lord President and Lords Carmont, Russell and Keith concurred in the opinion of the consulted judges.

D. LIMITS ON THE EXERCISE OF SEARCH POWERS

All powers of search, whether or not by warrant, presuppose the investigation of a particular offence or at least of a certain type of offence. However, once the police are lawfully on the premises, what if they find evidence which quite plainly shows that another offence has been committed, or more problematically which from their knowledge of the character and antecedents of the owner they think suspicious? Can they remove such evidence? Are they even, perhaps, entitled to search for evidence of *any* offence, or of any offence akin to that specified in the warrant? The objection to the law's taking such a direction is that it is potentially in conflict with the requirement of specificity of a warrant or of the suspicion of a particular offence on which common law powers are grounded. However, in keeping with the development of English law (compare *Entick* v. *Carrington* (1765) 19 St.Tr. 1030, 95 E.R. 807 and *Chic Fashions (West Wales) Ltd.* v. *Jones* [1968] 2 Q.B. 299) the law in Scotland has, within limits, tended to admit evidence of one offence discovered in the course of search for evidence of another. Two cases decided by Lord Guthrie in the 1950s highlight the difficulty of distinguishing between what is discovered without breaching the principle of limited search and what can only be discovered by such a breach.

37. H.M. Advocate v. Turnbull
1951 J.C. 96

Police investigating the affairs of an accountant and a client of his obtained a warrant on May 20, 1949, to search for evidence of fraudulent income tax returns made on behalf of the client. In executing this warrant they removed a large number of files relating to other clients and all clearly marked by the clients' names. Six months after investigation of these files, a retrospective warrant for their removal was obtained. At the accountant's trial on charges arising out of information in these files, objection was taken to their admissibility on the grounds that they were unlawfully removed.

LORD GUTHRIE: "The basis of the first submission was that the warrant granted on the first petition did not include the other documents, so that their retention and examination was without authority. They were the private papers of the accused and their unwarranted use for the purpose of obtaining evidence to enable further charges to be made against him was an infringement of the rights of the citizens. The files and the documents contained therein showed *ex facie* that they did not refer to the affairs of the client named in the first petition. When this was ascertained they should have been returned to the accused. Their continued retention and the examination of their contents were deliberate and inexcusable. The irregularity of their seizure and use could not be validated *ex post facto* by the warrant granted on the second petition. In these circumstances the documents so irregularly obtained should not be admitted in evidence.

The Advocate-depute argued in reply that, as the documents had been obtained under the first warrant, the police were entitled, when examination of them showed that other charges might lie, to retain and use them to assist inquiry into these charges. The objection was purely technical, he maintained, since a warrant was ultimately obtained under which these documents could have been secured. The evidence had not been obtained by any unfair trick and in these circumstances it was admissible. . .

The first matter argued, as to whether the retention and use of the documents was illegal, can be disposed of briefly. The general rule is that the search of private repositories by police officers is illegal unless a warrant has been obtained from a magistrate. Further, 'a wide and indefinite warrant to search for written documents' is illegal—*Nelson* v. *Black and Morrison,* referred to in *Stewart* v. *Roach.* Accordingly, as is shown by the form of the warrant ordinarily craved and granted, a warrant must be specific as to the purpose and limitations of the search. The warrant used in practice authorises the securing 'for the purpose of precognition and evidence, all writs tending to establish guilt or participation in the crime (or crimes) foresaid.' In the present case the warrant of 20th May 1949 was specifically limited to the recovery of writs relating to the crime specified in that petition. It contained no authorisation of a search for or seizure and retention of any other writs. Consequently the retention of files and their contents which obviously did not bear upon the affairs of the person mentioned in the first charge was not authorised by the warrant and was illegal. The initial illegality was not cured by the granting of the second warrant six months later after the contents of the writs had been examined and used to enable the subsequent charges to be brought. Possession and use of the documents was not obtained under that second warrant. It was not retroactive. It authorised future and not past actions of officers of law. The argument of the Advocate-depute that the objection taken by the defence is technical is without substance. To hold that the second warrant nullified the complaint of misuse of the first would be to utilise the results achieved by an illegal act to wipe out the illegality. Accordingly I am of the opinion that the warrant of 20th May 1949 only authorised the police officers to examine the documents in order to ascertain whether they fell within the scope of that warrant, and that the retention and examination of them in order to obtain evidence of other crimes was unauthorised and illegal. To reach the opposite conclusion would largely destroy the protection which the law affords to the citizen against invasion of his liberties by its requirements of the specific warrant of a magistrate for interference with these liberties.

[His Lordship then considered the general principles of admissibility.]

In the present case there were, firstly, no circumstances of urgency. Secondly, the retention and use over a period of six months of the documents bearing to relate to other matters than that mentioned in the petition show that the actions complained of were deliberate. The police officers did not accidentally stumble upon evidence of a plainly incriminating character in the course of a search for a different purpose. If the documents are incriminating, their incriminating character is only exposed by careful consideration of their contents. Thirdly, if information was in the hands of the criminal authorities implicating the accused in other crimes, these could have been mentioned in the petition containing the warrant under which the search was authorised. If they had no such information, the examination of private papers in the hope of finding incriminating material was interference with the rights of a citizen. Therefore to hold that evidence so obtained was admissible would, as I have said, tend to nullify the protection afforded to a citizen by the requirement of a magistrate's warrant, and would offer a positive inducement to the authorities to proceed by irregular methods. Fourthly, when I consider the matter in the light of the principle of fairness to the accused, it appears to me that the evidence so irregularly and deliberately obtained is intended to be the basis of a comparison between the figures actually submitted to the inspector of taxes and the information in the possession of the accused. If such important evidence upon a number of charges is tainted by the method by which it was deliberately secured, I am of the opinion that a fair trial upon these charges is rendered impossible.

Accordingly, when I apply the principles to be derived from the authorities to the facts of this case, I am driven to the conclusion that the objection taken to the admissibility of the documents is well founded. I shall therefore sustain the objection."

38. H.M. Advocate v. Hepper
1958 J.C. 39

Hepper was accused *inter alia* of the theft of an attaché case. The facts appear from Lord Guthrie's opinion.

LORD GUTHRIE: "On 19th November 1957 police officers called at the residence of the accused on business not connected with the present charge. The accused was at home and consented to the police searching his house. In the course of his examination in the witness-box, the detective superintendent who called at the accused's house was asked whether he had taken possession of anything, and objection was taken to the line of evidence. Counsel for the panel stated that the consent to a search was restricted to the business upon which the police had called at the accused's residence, and that, if the police in the course of that search discovered and removed an article which it was proposed to prove in evidence as relating to the present charge, such evidence should be excluded on the ground that it had been improperly obtained. . . In the present case I am of the opinion that the evidence is admissible. The police, in the course of their duty, when searching the accused's house with his consent in connexion with another matter, came upon the article which they removed. In *Turnbull* I distinguished that case, in which I excluded evidence as to documents taken possession of by police officers searching the accused's premises under a search warrant which clearly did not cover these documents, from a case in which police officers accidentally stumbled upon evidence of a plainly incriminating character in the course of a search for a different purpose. That distinction was based upon earlier authorities to which I was referred in *Turnbull's* case. It may be that the article which the police officers stumbled upon in their search of the accused's house was not an article of a plainly incriminating character, but it was at least an article of a very suspicious character, since it was an attaché case which contained within it the name and address of another person. In the circumstances, I do not think that the police officers acted in any way improperly in taking away that article in order to make further inquiries about it. If they had not done so, it might have disappeared. It appears to me that in the circumstances it was their duty, being officers charged with the protection of the public, to have acted as they did. But even if it cannot be put so highly, and if it be thought that their action was irregular, I am still of opinion that the evidence, even if irregularly obtained, is admissible in view of the interest of society in the detection of crime. I do not think that this is a case in which the evidence ought to be excluded because of a breach of the principle of fairness to the accused. I therefore hold that the evidence is admissible."

The Inland Revenue now has special and much wider powers of search in cases such as *Turnbull* (see *I.R.C.* v. *Rossminster* [1980] 1 All E.R. 80), but this does not affect the status of *Turnbull* as embodying a general principle.

In *Hepper,* it may be that the reference to the possibility of the disappearance of the articles in question if not taken away is a reference to the principle that urgency justifies search, and to see this as the distinction between *Hepper* and *Turnbull* (in which it was specifically stated that there was no urgency). However, the usual interpretation of the difference between the two is that in *Turnbull* the files, according to the names on the cover, had nothing to do with the warrant and should therefore not have been searched as they were not *ex facie* suspicious, whereas the briefcase in *Hepper* was. Unfortunately, neither report of *Hepper* discloses what was the business in connection with which Hepper gave the police permission to search his home, and, since only the name and address *inside* the case made it suspicious it is not clear whether opening the case was or was not within the scope of that permission, and on that hinges the alleged distinction.

Assuming, however, that the distinction is one between *ex facie* suspicious and *ex facie* innocent articles, it seems that this comes down to a distinction between documents and other articles. Most articles are suspicious, if at all, because of their appearance or where they are found, and are thus capable of being "stumbled upon." Documents on the other hand are capable of being suspicious if examined but incapable of examination by stumbling upon by reason of their innocuous appearance (this distinction between documents and other evidence obviously weighed heavily in the minds of the judges in *Bell* v. *Black and Morrison*).

However, the final case in this section does furnish an example of how even documents of a suspicious nature may be stumbled upon, as well as an interesting discussion of the limits of a search based upon various possible legal grounds.

39.   Leckie v. Miln
1982 S.L.T. 177

Leckie appealed against his conviction for theft on the grounds that the articles of theft of which he had been convicted had been unlawfully obtained and should not have been admitted in evidence.

OPINION OF THE HIGH COURT OF JUSTICIARY: "... The articles were in the first place certain business cards in the name of Mr Eisner and in the second place a library card in the name of the owner of the wallet taken from Harris Academy together with the receipt which had been in that wallet. The findings-in-fact which describe the search are findings 8, 9 and 10. According to finding 8 two police officers learned from their inspector that the appellant had been arrested on petition at Perth on a charge of sneak theft. That was all they were told. They were then instructed by the inspector to go to the appellant's house and search it. This they proceeded to do. But finding 8 tells us that the officers in question never saw the petition upon which the appellant had been arrested; that they were completely unaware of the nature of any charge in that petition except to the extent that it was a charge of theft of the sneak theft variety; that they did not know at all what articles had been stolen during that theft and did not, of course, in the circumstances, have the petition in their possession, containing the warrant to search, when they went to the appellant's house. On arrival at the house they met a lady called Miss Dailly (known as Mrs Leckie) and they informed her that they were police officers and that the appellant had been arrested by the police at Perth on a petition warrant. Having said that they informed Miss Dailly that they wished to search the house. No objection to the proposed search was made. Finding 10 then describes the search which took place and the discovery, in the course of that search, of the business cards to which we have referred in the top drawer of a chest of drawers in the only bedroom of the house, a top drawer which contained the clothing of Miss Dailly, and the discovery of the library ticket and the receipt which we have already mentioned inside a jacket hanging in the wardrobe of that bedroom. For the appellant the submission was that the search which was carried out in all the circumstances disclosed in findings 8, 9 and 10 was quite unlawful in respect that it was neither authorised by the warrant to search in the petition on which the appellant had been arrested in Perth nor was it authorised by any implied consent given by Miss Dailly. If that submission is sound, as counsel for the appellant urged us to accept, then it followed, according to counsel, that the evidence given by the police officers about their findings was inadmissible. This was not a case in which officers carrying out an active search within the scope of a lawful warrant came across articles unrelated to the particular crime with which they were concerned. In such a case the finding of other articles indicating guilt of other crimes may be perfectly admissible in evidence. The fundamental proposition here was that neither upon the warrant nor upon any implied consent was the active unlimited search carried out by the officers justified in law. The Crown position was simply this. There existed, no doubt, authority for a search of the appellant's premises and that authority was the warrant granted upon the petition on which the appellant had appeared in Perth. It is the case that the officers admittedly did not carry out an active search within the limitations of that warrant to search for they were wholly ignorant of the contents of the petition and the scope of the warrant to search granted upon its presentation. But given the authority for a lawful search of the premises, the search which was carried out was carried out by the officers in the manner in which they carried it out with the full consent given by Miss Dailly by plain implication. The question in the case therefore comes to be whether Miss Dailly did give consent for the unlimited search carried out by the officers, all as described in findings 8, 9 and 10. We are of opinion that by no stretch of the imagination can it be said that the consent given by Miss Dailly was consent for an active unlimited search regardless of the limitations in the warrant which admittedly existed. Finding 9 tells us that before Miss Dailly was informed that the officers wished to search the premises they told Miss Dailly that they were police officers and that the appellant had been arrested by the police at Perth on a petition warrant. It follows from that that any consent given by Miss Dailly must be assumed to have been given upon the footing that the officers intended to carry out a search within the authority contained in the warrant to which they referred, and that authority was, it is perfectly plain, an authority of a limited character. The search was nothing of the kind for, as we have already pointed out, the officers had no knowledge of the contents of the petition and what they did was to carry out a random search of the appellant's house in the hope of finding something which might conceivably have been the proceeds of a sneak theft anywhere. In those circumstances we are satisfied that the evidence of the finding of labels 2 and 4 should not have been admitted and if that is right then it follows that the conviction cannot stand for the evidence aliunde was insufficient to warrant the conviction of the appellant."

Note that the documents, evidence of which permitted Leckie's conviction, were of the same type as those which the police would have been looking for within the terms of the search warrant. But only their contents could have disclosed whether or not they were evidence of the offences in the warrant, so the police would have had to examine them. If, in doing so, they had found evidence of other offences then almost certainly the *Hepper* principle would have been applied by the court, and evidence of the findings of such documents admitted.

For more detailed commentary on this case see Finnie (1982a).

VI.   QUESTIONING

Until 1898 the accused was not usually a competent witness at his own trial. The only means of his bringing his explanation of events before the court was by way of the statements he volunteered in response to questions from the sheriff at the judicial examination held on the day following his arrest. Evidence might also be led as to statements he made to other persons, including the police, but at that time the police functioned principally as the executive arm of the prosecutor and magistrates and it was certainly no part of their function to question the persons they arrested to obtain statements. There was in fact some doubt as to the competence of police questions at all (*Millar* (1859) 3 Irv. 406).

Although the law was changed in 1898, the previous system left and in some respects still leaves its traces on the law. Even today there remains a right of silence on the part of the accused. In earlier law there was an insistence that statements must be not only voluntary but also spontaneous, coupled with an apparent presumption against the spontaneity of statements made in response to questions. Finally there was a persistence of a concept of admissibility separate from the question of the legality of obtention, which perhaps reached its most mechanical expression in *Chalmers* v. *H.M. Advocate,* 1954 S.L.T. 177, but which has since been progressively merged with the question of legality.

Side by side with these tendencies but also in a sense underlying them ran the principle that the conduct of the authorities must be "fair to the accused." The evolution of the law is largely the story of the principle of fairness occupying the centre of the stage to the exclusion of more mechanical rules, and accompanied by a greater tolerance of the activities of the police manifested in the counter principle of "fairness to the public" (although judicial reaction to the police questioning methods revealed by tape-recorders (see Pt. IV of this chapter) may be partially to reverse the latter development.

A.   RIGHT TO SILENCE AND STATUTORY MODIFICATIONS

The power to question and the right (or privilege) of silence are not, strictly speaking, opposites. Any one, including the police, has the right to ask questions of any other; the important point is whether they may detain them to do so, whether the person questioned is under a duty to reply, and whether the answers are admissible as evidence. It is also important to distinguish here between the absence of a duty to answer questions of any kind, and the absence of a duty to answer questions when to do so would incriminate the accused, which is more fundamental. The privilege against self-incrimination is an old one and almost universally recognised in Western legal systems (the most famous example being the Fifth Amendment to the U.S. Constitution). In Scotland it is a "sacred and inviolable principle" (*per* Lord Gillies in *Livingstone* v. *Murray* (1830) 9 S. 161) and is zealously protected by the common law, even in the face of an apparently contradictory statutory provision (*e.g. H.M. Advocate* v. *Von,* 1979 S.L.T. (Notes) 62).

At common law, there is no duty to answer police questions.

40.   Twycross v. Farrell
1973 S.L.T. (Notes) 85

"A police constable received a message from the headmaster of a local school that the headmaster had just seen some of his girl pupils being approached in the street by a young man selling a magazine which, from a previous incident in the district, the headmaster considered might be pornographic. The police constable drove to the school and saw the appellant holding a magazine and talking to girls from the school. The constable twice asked the appellant what he was doing and then asked for his name and address. The appellant made no answer to the constable, swore at him and then started to run away. The constable then seized hold of the appellant. The appellant then struggled and shouted and was only with difficulty detained until further police constables arrived. The appellant was convicted of resisting, obstructing, molesting and hindering the constable in the execution of his duty and of attempting to resist arrest. Counsel for the appellant contended that since the constable had no reasonable grounds for believing that the appellant had committed a crime he had no right to seize hold of the appellant and that accordingly by seizing hold of the appellant he was assaulting the appellant, against which assault the appellant was entitled to struggle in self defence. . . In allowing the appeal and quashing the conviction the court indicated that since there were no findings in the case to support the existence of a reasonable belief by the constable that the appellant had committed an offence, the constable had no right to attempt to stop the appellant from moving smartly away from the spot and that the appellant having been so stopped was entitled to struggle as he did."

To volunteer a false story to the police, thus setting in motion an investigation, is a crime (*Kerr* v. *Hill*, 1936 J.C. 71); apparently on the grounds of causing public expense. Yet to lie in the course of an investigation is equally likely to waste expensive police time, but it is not an offence (*Curlett* v. *McKechnie,* 1939 S.L.T. 11). Of course the same is true of failure to answer questions, but the latter can be justified on the grounds of lack of legal duty to assist the police, which is rather different from actively hindering them as in *Curlett*. In the English case of *Rice* v. *Connolly* [1966] 3 W.L.R. 17, Lord Parker C.J. said *obiter*: "In my judgement there is all the difference in the world between deliberately telling a false story—something which on no view a citizen has a right to do—and preserving silence or refusing to answer— something which he has every right to do." It may be, however, that the decision in *Curlett* is ripe for reconsideration (see *Carmichael* v. *Brannan,* 1985 S.C.C.R. 234 and *Skeen* v. *Shaw,* 1979 S.L.T. (Notes) 58).

Since *Twycross* was decided, section 1, CJSA has given to the police a power to require from a person an explanation of circumstances which make the police suspicious that he is guilty of the offence. The 1980 Act, however, refrains from making it an offence not to comply with such a "requirement," and therefore does not formally breach the right of silence. It *does* make it an offence for a person to refuse to give his name and address to a policeman in certain circumstances, which is a breach, albeit a trivial one, of the right of silence.

By contrast, section 2(7) of the Act specifically provides that a person detained under the Act "shall be under no obligation to answer any question other than to give his name and address, and a constable shall so inform him both on detaining him and on arrival at the police station or other premises where he is to be detained. This is a rough, but less extensive restatement in the context of detention of the common-law "caution" which traditionally has been given to a suspect by the police on arrest, on charge, and before making a statement. The common-law caution goes further by warning the suspect that any statement he *does* make may be used in evidence against him. The following case, concerning cautions under section 2(7) and at common law, signally reinforces the right of silence.

41. Tonge, Jack and Gray v. H.M. Advocate
1982 S.L.T. 506

Tonge and Gray were detained on suspicion of rape. Two policemen went to see each separately, intending to charge them. They gave to them a warning under section 2(7), CJSA but not a full common-law caution, then explained the investigation, and continued: "We believe that you, along with others, are responsible for this," or similar words. Both detainees then made incriminating statements. Jack was not detained but came voluntarily to the police station. The same officers interviewed him and cautioned him (though the nature of the caution was not clear in his case) and suggested that he had been involved in the offence. He too made an incriminating statement. At trial, all three were convicted of rape or attempted rape. They appealed successfully on the grounds that evidence of the incriminating statements was inadmissible.

LORD JUSTICE-GENERAL (Emslie): ". . . In the present case it is plain that on the relevant undisputed evidence no reasonable jury could have held that the alleged statements of Gray and Tonge had been voluntary and had not been extracted by unfair or improper means. It was, in the words of Lord Cameron, abundantly clear that the rules of fairness and fair dealing had been transgressed. A wholly new chapter began when Detective-Sergeant McMorran and Constable Jenkins approached these two appellants in detention. They had little or no evidence that the alleged crime had been committed or that either Gray or Tonge had been among its perpetrators. They hoped to get such evidence from Gray himself and it is an inescapable inference from the evidence that they hoped for the same response from Tonge. What they did was to accuse Gray and Tonge of participation in the alleged crime without first cautioning either. This was clearly calculated to provoke a response and the opening words of the response which the accusation elicited from each demonstrated that each was about to make a statement, possibly self-incriminating. Even then they did not caution either man and they did not caution either thereafter when it clearly began to appear that he was, in fact, about to incriminate himself. In these circumstances the unfairness of the police officers was manifest and it is clear from their own evidence that proper practice, prior to 1980, demanded the giving of a caution at least once to persons in the position of Gray and Tonge. Without their alleged statements there was no sufficient evidence to warrant their conviction and since the verdicts proceeded upon evidence which was inadmissible there has been a miscarriage of justice. . .

. . . I have come to be of the opinion that the alleged statements of Gray and Tonge were clearly inadmissible and should have been withheld from the jury. This was, in my opinion, one of those exceptional cases in which, upon the undisputed relevant evidence, it can be said that no reasonable jury could have held that the statements had been voluntary and had not been induced by unfair or improper means (vide *Balloch* v. *H.M. Advocate*). In my judgment upon a close scrutiny of the notes of evidence it is abundantly clear that the rules of fairness and fair dealing were flagrantly transgressed (vide *H.M. Advocate* v. *Whitelaw*). I do not say that in no circumstances will a statement by a detainee (a suspect within the meaning of s. 2(1)) be inadmissible merely because, when it was made, he had not received a full caution. What I do say is that the failure of the investigating officers to caution Gray and Tonge in the special circumstances of this case is fatal to the contention that the rules of fair dealing and fairness were properly observed.

In Gray's case the hope of the the two officers was that when they saw him he would provide what was conspicuously lacking, namely, self-incriminating evidence. He was already impressed with the character of a suspect within the meaning of s. 2(1) and they undoubtedly approached him with the hope in their hearts [*sic*], and with the intention of questioning him if necessary. It is of critical importance to notice what they did. They accused him of participation in the crime. Now, as is pointed out in Walkers' *Law of Evidence in Scotland*, p. 39, para. 45: 'It is proper practice that, when a person is charged with a crime, the caution should be given, since, without it, the reading of the charge may be interpreted by the accused as a question, or as an invitation to reply, in which case any statement then made is not spontaneous and voluntary.' I go further and say that the proper practice is now so long and so well entrenched that it may be taken that a full caution before a charge is made is a requirement of the law itself. The reading of a charge is calculated to provoke a response from the accused and it is quite essential that he should know, in advance, of his right to silence, and of the use which may be made of any response which he chooses to make. To charge an accused person without cautioning him is to put pressure upon him which may induce a response and I have no doubt that by accusing Gray, although not in the formal language of a charge, the accusation was clearly calculated, as a formal charge is calculated, to induce a response from the person accused. The accusation placed pressure upon Gray and I am persuaded that since no caution was administered before it was made, it is impossible to regard the statement made in response to it as spontaneous and voluntary. It was plainly induced by the accusation and in the circumstances was induced by unfair means. It cannot be left out of account either that no caution was administered when the first sentence uttered by Gray made it plain that he intended to make a statement, and that no caution was administered when it became obvious that he was about to incriminate himself. As the evidence of the police officers demonstrated it would have been proper practice to caution a suspect in Gray's position before he was allowed to proceed with a statement and, in my opinion, nothing in s. 2 of the Act of 1980 excuses compliance with that practice.

In Tonge's case I reach the same conclusion. Tonge, who had not received at any stage of the detention procedure a full caution in common law terms, was seen by the investigating officers with the single purpose of charging him. Had they carried out that purpose, they would have required to caution him. They did not do so. What they did, without cautioning him, was to accuse him of the crime, just as they had accused Gray of the crime. This, as Constable Jenkins agreed, was not a usual thing to do where the sole purpose of the encounter was to charge the suspect. Be that as it may the accusation was made without caution, no caution was administered when the first sentence of Tonge's response demonstrated that he was about to make a statement, and no caution was administered at any point while the alleged statement was being made. It is impossible to accept that the officers did not 'get a chance' to charge Tonge and the excuse for not cautioning him was the unfounded assumption that he had already received a full caution when he was detained under s. 2. For all the reasons which led me to hold that the alleged statement by Gray was inadmissible I also hold that the alleged statement by Tonge was inadmissible and should not have been left for consideration by the jury.

In light of what I have said, I would allow the appeals of Gray and Tonge and quash their conviction.

There remains for disposal the appeal of Jack. . .

The submission on behalf of Jack in all these circumstances was that the trial judge on the quoted passage misdirected the jury on a matter of great material importance and that there was in Jack's case a miscarriage of justice. The alleged statements by Jack were of critical importance in the Crown case. The jury had to decide whether they could accept the evidence of the two police officers as reliable to the effect that statements were made, and that they were in the terms which they alleged. They also had to consider the whole context in which the alleged statements were made and in particular, whether before Jack said anything at all, he had received, as Constable Jenkins deponed, a full caution at common law. The reliability of the evidence of the two police officers who were already at odds with one another as to their purpose in approaching Jack, fell to be tested sharply upon this question. The trial judge's charge was so framed as to divert the jury's attention from these important issues. What he did, perhaps upon a misapprehension of the evidence, was to instruct the jury that on the one hand the police witnesses maintained that Jack had received a full caution, that Jack on the other hand denied this, and that since Jack had not been detained no question arose in relation to any warning in terms of the 1980 Act. These instructions were accordingly to the effect that they had only to decide one question, namely whether to believe the two police officers or to believe Jack, and the quoted passage from the charge read as a whole was likely to be under-stood by the jury to contain a direction in law that they must not consider at all the possibility that Jack only received a warning under s. 2 of the Act of 1980. What he ought to have done and omitted to do was focus clearly for the jury the vital question of the reliability of the police officers and to instruct them how they should examine that question. In particular he should have drawn the jury's close attention to the evidence of Detective-Sergeant McMorran upon the matter of the warning allegedly given to Jack by Constable Jenkins. . .

For these reasons I am of opinion that in this difficult case . . . the misdirections on a matter of real importance were such as to lead me to conclude that they were likely to have led to a miscarriage of justice. I reach this conclusion with the less hesitation since it is likely, if the alleged statements by Gray and Tonge had not gone before the jury, the trial would have taken a different course. I would accordingly allow the appeal by Jack and quash his conviction.

Before leaving this case, which has illustrated the problems and confusion created by the provisions of s. 2 of the Act of 1980, I would strongly urge police officers throughout Scotland who proceed to accuse a detainee or to question him or to take from him a voluntary statement, to rely not at all on the efficacy of the warning described in s. 2(7), and to appreciate that if any use is to be made in evidence of anything said by a detainee in these circumstances the ordinary rules of fairness and fair dealing which have been developed by the common law should be strictly observed. The wise course will be, inter alia, to administer to the detainee in the events which I have mentioned a full caution in common law terms. The omission to give such a caution will, by itself, at the very least place the admissibility of anything said by the detainee in peril and the appeals by Gray and Tonge demonstrate circumstances in which the omission of the interviewing officer to caution these men in such terms was fatal."

LORD CAMERON: ". . . In expressing my concurrence with your Lordship in the chair I would only venture to add certain observations of my own on the provisions and operation of s. 2 of the Act of 1980. It is not a happily drafted section, and in particular it is not easy to understand the reason which induced the legislature to enact subs. (7). The section, by subs. (1), confers new powers on the police of detention for a limited period of a person suspected on reasonable grounds of having committed or of committing an offence punishable by imprisonment and, during that period, to interrogate a suspect, search and take finger print and other impressions, 'for the purpose of facilitating the carrying out of investigations—(a) into the offence; and (b) as to whether criminal proceedings should be instigated against the person.' The right to interrogate a suspect is contained in subs. (5) which provides that a constable 'may—(a) put questions to him in relation to the suspected offence.' The exercise of this power however is conditioned by the provisions of subs. (7), which provides that a person detained under subs. (1): 'shall be under no obligation to answer any question other than to give his name and address, and a constable shall so inform him both on so detaining him and on arrival at the police station or other premises'—to which he is to be taken 'as quickly as is reasonably practicable.' Now whatever else subs. (7) may mean, what it provides is neither an alternative to nor a substitute for the giving of a caution in the well-recognised and regular form in circumstances where the law and proper practice demands or requires. It is not indeed immediately apparent what useful purpose this innovative and possibly confusing provision is designed to serve, as the proviso to subs. (5) (a) states that: 'this paragraph [sic] shall be without prejudice to any existing rule of law as regards the admissibility in evidence of any answer given.' This, in my opinion means and can only mean that nothing in s. 2 alters the pre-existing rules of law or of safe and proper practice in the matters of cautioning persons who may be questioned in the course of police investigations of crimes or suspected crimes or at any time when a person is being charged with a crime or offence. It is of course well established that police officers are entitled to question a suspect as to his possible complicity in a crime which they are investigating, and that his replies will be admissible in evidence if they have not been extracted or compelled by unfair or improper means including threats, intimidations, offers of inducements, or cross-examination designed or intended to extract incriminating replies, but it is equally well recognised that in the case of one on whom suspicion of responsibility or complicity has centred, in order that his replies should be admissible in evidence, it is proper practice that any further questioning should be preceded by a caution in common form. The proviso to subs. 2(5) is of such wide generality that it leaves no doubt in my opinion that the warning specified in such limited terms which is required to be given in compliance with the provision of subs. (7), is not and cannot be in substitution for the cautions which the law and practice require to be given as a condition precedent to the admissibility of evidence obtained from questioning of a suspect or the replies to a charge made by an accused, but is of an entirely independent character which does not in any way determine the admissibility of evidence obtained by the questioning which the provisions of s. 2 permit.

It would appear to me to follow from this that in the case of a suspect of the kind figured in subs. (1) it would be wise and proper practice that he should receive a caution in recognised form before questions are put to him, in order that no conflict may arise as to the admissibility in evidence of any replies given by him, in the course of such questioning. This conclusion appears to me all the more necessary when it is kept in view that the whole basis on which the right to detain or to question rests on the very definite character of the police officer's suspicion as set out in subs. (1).

Apart however from the question as to what is required to make admissible in evidence any replies made by a suspect detained under the powers given by s. 2 to questions by a police officer in course of his authorised investigation, there are two other matters to which I would refer in relation to the actions of the police officers concerned in the investigations in this case. The first is as to the regular and well-known practice of police officers in taking a voluntary statement from one either suspected or actually charged with a crime, and the second is the rule of law which requires a caution to be given to an accused when a formal charge is made if his reply to the charge is to be admissible in evidence—either for or against him. The regular and proper practice when an accused or suspect indicates or intimates he wishes to make a voluntary statement is that the statement should be taken by officers unconnected with the particular investigation and authenticated by the signatures of the officers concerned and the maker of the statement himself. In the case of the appellants, although the detailed and incriminating statements ascribed to them are recorded in police notebooks, no attempt was made to have them given to or taken by independent officers, or even to have what is recorded in the officers' notebooks signed by the appellants themselves. The investigating officers in this case were fully aware of this proper practice and of the reasons for it, so that it cannot be argued that what is recorded in their notebooks and testified to in evidence were at the time regarded as 'voluntary statements' of the kind I have referred to.

As to the second, in my opinion it is a requirement, which goes beyond one of proper practice and is now a requirement of law, that when preferring a charge against an accused, police officers should caution him as to the possible use to be made of any reply made to that charge. Now the circumstances and manner in which the investigating officers proceeded in the case of all the appellants have already been fully set out by your Lordship, and I have no doubt that not only had the officers determined to prefer charges of rape even before they proceeded to interview the appellants, but also that their immediate intimation of their purpose and intention was in a form which, while lacking the precise formality of a charge, was no more and no less than the levelling, in words which were indistinguishable from those of the formal charge which immediately followed the 'voluntary statement,' a detailed accusation of rape—but one which in the case of the detainees Gray and Tonge was admittedly not preceded by a caution. At that stage of the inquiry there were at least serious grounds for doubt as to whether the police had sufficient evidence on which to justify making a charge, and it was thus a matter of the highest importance that the appellants should be induced to make some statements of an incriminatory character. In offering the explanation for their presence and the subject and purpose of their investigations the police officers concerned did so in a manner which was accusatorial in form and substance and, whether by design or inadvertence it matters not, would be likely to evoke from the person addressed some form of immediate response, explanatory or exculpatory or incriminating. That being so I am clearly of opinion that in the case of Gray and Tonge their statements, in the absence of a precedent caution, were inadmissible in evidence."

Lord Dunpark concurred.

This new rule was seen in operation in *Walkingshaw* v. *McIntyre,* 1985 S.C.C.R. 389. This was a prosecution for not having a TV licence. A post office inspector was furnished with a list of persons for whom there was no known licence and who were suspected of having a TV. The inspector went to the accused's door and asked whether he had a TV, then whether he had a licence, to which the accused said respectively "yes" and "no." Evidence of this was rejected on the grounds that, before asking the second question, the inspector should have cautioned the accused.

So the right of silence is fundamental. Two important modifications to it, which do not, however, require the suspect to incriminate himself, are section 11 of the Prevention of Terrorism (Temporary Provisions) Act 1984 and section 20A, CFSA (inserted by section 6(2), CJSA).

42.   Prevention of Terrorism (Temporary Provisions) Act 1984

"Information about acts of terrorism
11.—(1) If a person who has information which he knows or believes might be of material assistance—
   (*a*)   in preventing the commission by any other person of an act of terrorism to which this Part of this Act applies; or
   (*b*)   in securing the apprehension, prosecution or conviction of any other person for an offence involving the commission, preparation or instigation of an act of terrorism to which this Part of this Act applies,
fails without reasonable excuse to disclose that information as soon as reasonably practicable—

(i)   in England and Wales, to a constable;

(ii)   in Scotland, to a constable or the procurator fiscal; or

(iii)   in Northern Ireland, to a constable or a member of Her Majesty's forces,

he shall be guilty of an offence.

(2) A person guilty of an offence under subsection (1) above shall be liable—

(a)   on summary conviction to imprisonment for a term not exceeding six months, or to a fine not exceeding the statutory maximum, or both;

(b)   on conviction on indictment to imprisonment for a term not exceeding five years, or to a fine, or both."

The equivalent section in the Prevention of Terrorism (Temporary Provisions) Act 1976 made no reference to offences by "any other person" and could thus be read as requiring self-incrimination. However, in *Von v. H.M. Advocate*, 1979 S.L.T. (Notes) 62, Lord Ross excluded self-incriminating evidence by an accused who had not been notified of his right of silence. This decision was approved by Jellicoe (1983), which recommended that the statute explicitly incorporate it. Walker (1986), pp. 101-103) argues that self-incrimination may still be required if the information in question relates to acts of terrorism by a suspect which is inseparable from information about acts of terrorism by another person, but acknowledges that in Scotland the matter has been administratively resolved by police guidelines requiring that suspects be informed that they are not obliged to incriminate themselves. Even in the absence of such guidelines, Lord Ross's decision in *Von* fairly strongly excludes a duty to give *any* self-incriminatory evidence.

43.   The Criminal Procedure (Scotland) Act

"Accused at examination may be questioned by prosecutor

20A.—(1) Subject to the following provisions of this section, an accused on being brought before the sheriff for examination on any charge (whether that examination is the first examination or a further examination) may be questioned by the prosecutor in so far as such questioning is directed towards eliciting any denial, explanation, justification or comment which the accused may have as regards—

(a)   matters averred in the charge:

Provided that the particular aims of a line of questions under this paragraph shall be to determine—

(i) whether any account which the accused can give ostensibly discloses a category of defence (as for example alibi, incrimination, or the consent of an alleged victim); and

(ii) the nature and particulars of that defence;

(b)   the alleged making by the accused, to or in the hearing of an officer of police, of an extrajudicial confession (whether or not a full admission) relevant to the charge:

Provided that questions under this paragraph may only be put if the accused has, before the examination, received from the prosecutor or from an officer of police a written record of the confession allegedly made; or

(*c*) what is said in any declaration emitted in regard to the charge by the accused at the examination.

(2) The prosecutor shall, in framing questions in exercise of his power under subsection (1) above, have regard to the following principles—

(*a*) the questions should not be designed to challenge the truth of anything said by the accused;

(*b*) there should be no reiteration of a question which the accused has refused to answer at the examination; and

(*c*) there should be no leading questions; and the sheriff shall ensure that all questions are fairly put to, and understood by, the accused.

(3) The accused, where he is represented by a solicitor at the judicial examination, shall be told by the sheriff that he may consult that solicitor before answering any question.

(4) With the permission of the sheriff, the solicitor for the accused may ask the accused any question the purpose of which is to clarify any ambiguity in an answer given by the accused to the prosecutor at the examination or to give the accused an opportunity to answer any question which he has previously refused to answer.

(5) An accused may decline to answer a question under subsection (1) above; and, where he is subsequently tried on the charge mentioned in that subsection or on any other charge arising out of the circumstances which gave rise to the charge so mentioned, his having so declined may be commented upon by the prosecutor, the judge presiding at the trial, or any co-accused, only where and in so far as the accused (or any witness called on his behalf) in evidence avers something which could have been stated appropriately in answer to that question."

These provisions have been glossed by an eminent commentator (Gordon (1981: 21)) as follows:

"Judicial examination offers a way in which the conflict between the usefulness of obtaining from a suspect his account of the matter and some idea of his line of defence on the one hand, and the disadvantages of questioning in a police station on the other, can be reconciled by providing a judicial forum for such questioning in circumstances where there can be no dispute as to what was said, and where judicial supervision will ensure that any questioning is fair. The Thomson Committee saw the examination as providing the accused with an opportunity to state his position, and proffer his explanations, in a confidential judicial setting. They thought, too, that, while it would be wrong to draw any inferences from silence in a police station, such inferences could be drawn from silence at judicial examination, so that the reintroduction of the examination might make it more difficult for the accused to produce spurious defences at the trial. They also saw it as an important part of the whole procedure of police questioning itself. This was partly because it offered the accused an opportunity to complain about the police. But it was also linked to their recommendations for the recording of police 'interrogations,' and they hoped that the difficult problems which would be created if it were necessary to lead tapes in evidence at the trial might be avoided in many cases by putting to the accused at the examination any statements by him on which the prosecution wished to rely, since, if the accused admitted before the sheriff that he had made these statements, that admission would supersede and replace the tapes. The Committee went even further and recommended that no statements to the police should be admissible at the trial unless they had been put to the accused at examination.

The section does not follow the Thomson Committee report exactly, but the foregoing is a necessary prelude to understanding it.

Two particular deviations may be noted.

(1) Neither s. 2 nor this section makes any reference to tape recordings, but the Government have indicated that if tape recording is found to be practicable it will be introduced: H.C. Vol. 989, cols. 409, 410. In that event, the new s. 20A (1) (*b*) might enable the prosecutor to 'condense the tape,' so to speak, into a written record of such relevant matters as he proposed to rely on, as envisaged by Thomson II.

(2) The new provisions do not make it incompetent to lead a confession in evidence even where it has not been made the subject of judicial examination."

B. THE LIMITS OF INTERROGATION — THE OLDER VIEW

One important aspect of the right of silence is its effect on the questioning of suspects by the police and the admissibility in evidence of replies. May the police question suspects at all, or does the fact that a statement was made in reply to a question deprive it of its truly spontaneous and voluntary nature? The law on admissibility of statements is both complicated and continually shifting. One way of characterising its evolution is as a competition between two rules for primacy, one being a vague test of "fairness" or "fairness to the accused," the other being a more mechanical test based upon the stages of a criminal investigation.

Alternatively, Sheriff Gordon (1978) has characterised the law on statements in this century as arising "out of vagueness and judicial discretion" becoming formalised as rules in *Chalmers* and returning to "vagueness and discretion, this time jury discretion." But both the vagueness and the more precise rules run through the earlier cases; the change lies in the relative importance attached to each. Thus in *H.M. Advocate* v. *Aitken*, 1926 J.C. 83, Lord Anderson, disallowing evidence of a statement, said:

"The test of whether an alleged statement should or should not be admitted as evidence is to determine whether it would be fair in the circumstances of the accused person to admit the statement as evidence. Now, if that be, as I think it is, the test, it obviously involves consideration of the circumstances in which the statement was made. . .

I think there is a distinction to be drawn between a statement which is made by a person who has been accused of a crime, and a statement which is made by a person who has not been accused of a crime but who is merely suspected of having committed a crime. In the former case, that is to say, where a charge has been made, the prisoner is protected by several circumstances. . .

Now, it seems to me that the Court ought to be more jealous to safeguard the rights of a prisoner in a case where a charge has not yet been made, but where the prisoner has merely been detained by the police on suspicion."

Likewise in *Bell* v. *H.M. Advocate,* 1945 J.C. 61, dismissing an appeal founded on the allegedly wrongful admission of a statement, the Lord Justice-Clerk (Cooper), with whom Lords Mackay and Stevenson concurred, said:

"It seems to me, as has been pointed out in this Court before, that a clear distinction must be drawn between admission, confessions or other incriminating statements given or obtained from a person (1) who has been charged with a crime and is in custody awaiting trial, (2) who has been detained on suspicion, and (3) who has not been detained or charged, against whom perhaps there may be no evidence whatever justifying either detention or charge or even suspicion, but who is merely being questioned by the police in the exercise of their duties of investigating the commission of a crime . . . I have no wish . . . to weaken the insistence which the Court has always laid upon the necessity of fairness in investigation at all stages of a criminal inquiry or prosecution."

The pendulum swung most in favour of the more mechanical test in the Full Bench decision in *Chalmers.*

44.   Chalmers v. H.M. Advocate
1954 J.C. 66

Chalmers, aged 16, was convicted of robbery and murder. He appealed on the grounds that certain evidence admitted at his trial should not have been admitted. While investigating the murder the police obtained a non-incriminating statement from Chalmers. Later, other evidence cast doubt on its veracity, and the police began to suspect Chalmers. They took him to a police station, cautioned him and then, by their own admission, cross-examined him for five minutes until he burst into tears and made a confession, which was not put in evidence. Two hours later, after his father arrived, Chalmers was charged and was said to have stated: "I did it. He struck me." The appeal was allowed.

LORD JUSTICE-GENERAL (Cooper): "I have sympathy with the police in the difficult position in which they are often placed. We have no power to give instructions to the police, but we have the power and the duty to exclude from the cognisance of a jury evidence which, according to our practice and decisions, is inadmissible;

and the police have an interest to know why such decisions are taken. Were it possible to do so, I should like to be able to lay down comprehensive rules for the guidance of the police in all the situations which may arise in practice, but I am satisfied that this is impossible because in the borderline case so much turns upon the exact circumstances. . . This, however, it is possible to say with regard to Scots law. It is not the function of the police when investigating a crime to direct their endeavour to obtaining a confession from the suspect to be used as evidence against him at the trial. In some legal systems the inquisitorial method of investigation is allowed in different degrees and subject to various safeguards; but by our law self-incriminating statements when tendered in evidence at a criminal trial, are always jealously examined from the standpoint of being assured as to their spontaneity; and if, on a review of all the proved circumstances, that test is not satisfied, evidence of such statements will usually be excluded altogether. The theory of our law is that at the stage of initial investigation the police may question anyone with a view to acquiring information which may lead to the detection of the criminal; but that, when the stage has been reached at which suspicion, or more than suspicion, has in their view centred upon some person as the likely perpetrator of the crime, further interrogation of that person becomes very dangerous, and, if carried too far, *e.g.* to the point of extracting a confession by what amounts to cross-examination, the evidence of that confession will almost certainly be excluded. Once the accused has been apprehended and charged he has the statutory right to a private interview with a solicitor and to be brought before a magistrate with all convenient speed so that he may, if so advised, emit a declaration in presence of his solicitor under conditions which safeguard him against prejudice. . . In the eyes of every ordinary citizen the venue [*i.e.* a police station] is a sinister one. When he stands alone in such a place confronted by several police officers, usually, some of high rank, the dice are loaded against him, especially as he knows that there is no one to corroborate him as to what exactly occurred during the interrogation, how it was conducted, and how long it lasted. If under such circumstances cross examination is pursued with the result, though perhaps not with the deliberate object, of causing him to break down and to condemn himself out of his own mouth, the impropriety of the proceedings cannot be cured by the giving of any number of formal cautions or by the introduction of some officer other than the questioner to record the ultimate statement. In the ordinary case, as many decisions now demonstrate, that statement, if tendered in evidence at the trial, will not be treated as possessing that quality of spontaneity on which our law insists, and its rejection, when tendered in evidence, may, and sometimes does, wreck the prosecution. . ."

LORD JUSTICE-CLERK (Thomson): [On the question of admissibility] "The difficulty arises from the necessity of reconciling two principles:— (1) that no accused person is bound to incriminate himself, and (2) that what an accused person says—apart from what properly falls within the doctrine of *res gestae*—provided he says it freely and voluntarily, is admissible evidence against him. It is when the police, in the course of their duty as investigators of crime, interview someone in relation to some specific crime that the problem arises for decision whether something which has been said by an accused is admissible as evidence against him. Extreme cases are easy. At the one extreme, once the investigation has gone to the extent that somebody is specifically cautioned and charged thereafter nothing short of a voluntary statement is admissible against him. At the other extreme is the ordinary routine investigation of the police into the circumstances of the crime. In the course of such an investigation the man ultimately accused may be interviewed. It would unduly hamper the investigation of crime if the threat of inadmissibility were to tie the hands of the police in asking questions. It would help to defeat the ends of justice if what the person so questioned said in answer to ordinary and legitimate questions were not admissible in evidence against him. I am assuming throughout that the questioning is not tainted by bullying, pressure, third degree methods and so forth. Evidence obtained by such methods can never be admissible in our Courts, whatever stage the investigation has reached. But there comes a point of time in ordinary police investigation when the law intervenes to render inadmissible as evidence answers even to questions which are not tainted by such methods. After the point is reached, further interrogation is incompatible with the answers being regarded as a voluntary statement, and the law intervenes to safeguard the party questioned from possible self-incrimination. Just when that point of time is reached is in any particular case extremely difficult to define— or even for an experienced police official to realise its arrival. There does come a time, however, when a police officer, carrying out his duty honestly and conscientiously, ought to be in a position to appreciate that the man whom he is in process of questioning is under serious consideration as the perpetrator of the crime. Once that stage of suspicion is reached, the suspect is in the position that thereafter the only evidence admissible against him is his own voluntary statement. A voluntary statement is one which is given freely, not in response to pressure and inducement, and not elicited by cross-examination. This does not mean that, if a person elects to give a statement, it becomes inadmissible because he is asked some questions to clear up his account of the matter, but such questions as he is asked must not go beyond elucidation. It is important to keep in mind also that the point of time at which the axe falls is not necessarily related to the person being in custody or detention of some sort. The fact that he is detained may point to his being under suspicion but he may come under suspicion without having been detained."

Lords Carmont, Patrick and Mackintosh concurred.

The fourth edition of Renton and Brown (1972) gave the most extended consideration to this "classical" view of the permissibility of questioning, although it also recorded the beginnings of the "new approach" (below), and the logic of *Chalmers* and earlier cases should therefore be sought in that work.

The high-water mark of this classical view of the permissibility of questioning is probably *H.M. Advocate* v. *Campbell*, 1964 J.C. 80, in which after a murder a person claiming to be the murderer telephoned a reporter to arrange an appointment with him in order to "tell his story" and obtain money for his family. A policeman accompanied the reporter, disguised as a photographer, listened to the story and then cautioned the confessed murderer. It was held that he should have disclosed his identity and given the caution at the beginning of the interview and hence evidence of the statement was inadmissible.

LORD JUSTICE-CLERK (Grant): "On these agreed facts I am satisfied that the accused must be treated as being under suspicion at the time when this statement was made. Furthermore, although the statement was not made directly to the policeman, it is clear that the sole purpose of his presence was to hear that statement. In these circumstances there was a duty upon the policeman to warn and caution the accused before the statement was made. That not having been done, I rule that the evidence in regard to the statement is not admissible."

Although most of the cases on evidence of statements turn on techniques of questioning and the stages of investigation, it must not be forgotten that the underlying criterion at all times was that of "fairness to the accused" and that the application of that principle went and goes beyond those matters to other pressures brought to bear on the accused. Thus in *Law* v. *McNichol, 1965* J.C. 32, a suspect was arrested on December 24. His solicitor was notified but was otherwise engaged, time passed and he did not appear. A policeman pointed out to the suspect that the court was sitting that morning, but would not be on the 25th, and thus that if the matter were not disposed of that morning the suspect would be in prison over Christmas. A statement was then made, objection to the admissibility of which was taken at the trial, but dismissed. On appeal, however, the objection was upheld on the grounds of "unfairness to the accused".

There is a difference in emphasis between the opinions of Lord Cooper and Lord Thomson. The latter is much more categorical than that of Lord Cooper. At the time this distinction was not seized upon and Lord Thomson's opinion was widely accepted. The less firm expressions of Lord Cooper have proved more congenial to later, revisionist judges and been more widely quoted. Thus as Gordon (1978: 329) says, *Chalmers* "contained the seeds of its ineffectiveness."

C. THE LIMITS OF INTERROGATION—THE RECENT VIEW

For over a decade, Lord Thomson and Lord Cooper were taken to have laid down the same test. The shift in emphasis to Lord Cooper's view and the total displacement by development of that view of the "three-stage test" traced in the cases cited below probably derived from judicial unease that the law was making the job of the police and the prosecution too difficult, and probably reflected also a changing perception of the function of the police (police forces grew greatly in size and became much better trained and equipped in the decades following the Second World War). Even if these factors had not led to change it is difficult to see how the rules in *Chalmers* could have survived the introduction of detention in 1980. True, the spirit of *Chalmers could* have survived, but only in the form of a mechanical test with differing rules of admissibility for four or five categories of suspect, which would probably have been unworkably complicated (not least because of the uncertain relationship between arrest and detention).

45. Miln v. Cullen
1967 S.L.T. 35

After a car accident the police obtained a statement from one driver in which he stated his suspicion that the other was drunk and pointed out one man in a group some way off as the driver. It was conceded that at this point he fell under suspicion.

The police then went to the man and asked him whether he were the driver and he admitted he was. At his trial for drunken driving an objection was sustained to the admission of his reply to the police question, and he was acquitted. Allowing an appeal by the Crown, Lord Wheatley stated:

"The question for us, therefore, is whether the question was objectionable at common law in the circumstances which prevailed. The legal principles in this field of evidence were exhaustively canvassed in *Chalmers* v. *H.M. Advocate*, and it would appear from the arguments addressed to us by counsel for the respondent and other expressions of opinion voiced elsewhere that certain misconceptions have arisen from the decision and opinions in that case. If that be so, then the sooner these misconceptions are cleared up the better it is for all concerned. For instance, counsel for the respondent submitted that once a person came under suspicion no questions by a police officer and a fortioro no answers by the suspects were admissible in evidence. . . I need not rehearse all that was said by Lord Cooper in that context, but I deem it important to stress that in the variety of circumstances which might attend cases in each of these categories the basic ultimate test is fairness. While the law of Scotland has always very properly regarded fairness to an accused person as being an integral part of the administration of justice, fairness is not a unilateral consideration. Fairness to the public is also a legitimate consideration, and insofar as police officers in the exercise of their duties are prosecuting and protecting the public interest, it is the function of the Court to seek to provide a proper balance to secure that the rights of individuals are properly preserved while not hamstringing the police in their investigation of crime with a series of academic vetoes which ignore the realities and practicalities of the situation and discount completely the public interest. Even at the stage of routine investigations where much greater latitude is allowed, fairness is still the test, and that is always a question of circumstances. It is conceivable that even at that stage a question might be asked or some action might be perpetrated which produced an admission of guilt from the person being interviewed, and yet the evidence might be disallowed because the circumstances disclosed an unfairness to that person. At the other end of the scale, it is wrong to assume that after a person has been cautioned and charged questioning of that person is no longer admissible. All that was said in *Chalmers* and in the subsequent cases of *Manuel* v. *H.M. Advocate*, 1958 J.C. 58, 1958 S.L.T. (Notes) 44 and *Brown* v. *H.M. Advocate*, 1966 S.L.T. 105 was that at that stage questions or indeed actions which induced by some means or another self-incriminating statements by an accused which were not voluntary or spontaneous were liable to be ruled out as inadmissible. But once again the test is one of fairness. A question asked merely to clear up an ambiguity and not calculated to produce an incriminating answer might result in a self-induced incriminating answer by an accused person. Whether such evidence should be admitted or not will always be a question for the Court, having regard to all the circumstances and the basic touchstone of fairness. . . In each case the issue is—was the question in the circumstances a fair one?"

The Lord Justice-Clerk (Grant) and Lord Strachan delivered concurring opinions.

46. Jones v. Milne
1975 S.L.T. 2

In proceedings under the Fugitive Offenders Act 1967, Jones, accused of offences in Australia, was committed on a provisional warrant. He applied some two months later for a discharge from custody on the grounds that proceedings purportedly under the Act were a nullity. The High Court accepted this. However he also argued that because of the inadmissibility of certain statements to the police there was insufficient evidence before the sheriff to warrant his trial for some of the offences. Of this ground of appeal the court (Lord Justice-General, Lords Johnstone and Kissen) said:

"For the applicant, the argument was that the critical confessions were plainly inadmissible in evidence. In each case the confession was embodied in answers to police questioning. At the time the questions were put the applicant was suspected as the likely perpetrator of the offences concerned and had been cautioned. In each case it could be seen clearly at this stage that these confessions were extracted by what amounted to cross-examination designed to elicit an admission of guilt. In these circumstances, an application of the principles to be derived from the cases of *Chalmers* v. *H.M. Advocate* and *Miln* v. *Cullen* would require the exclusion of each of these confessions.

Had it been necessary to do so, we would have felt ourselves quite unable to sustain this argument. It is not our law that a suspect's answers to police questioning will never be admissible and in his opinion in the case of *Chalmers* the Lord Justice-General put the matter thus [here part of Lord Cooper's opinion was quoted].

As the opinions in the case of *Miln* show the objection is to interrogation in the proper sense of that word and to answers which can be seen to have been extracted from the suspect. In each case it is necessary to consider the whole circumstances to discover whether in these whole circumstances there has been unfairness on the part of the police. The mere fact that a suspected person is asked a question or questions by a police officer, before of after being cautioned, is not in itself unfairness, and if answers are to be excluded they must be seen to have been extracted by unfair means which place cross-examination, pressure and deception in close company. In our opinion, examination of the record of the circumstances in which each of the confessions was made makes it impossible to hold at this stage that they would not be admissible at any trial of the applicant in Scotland."

47. Hartley v. H.M. Advocate
1979 S.L.T. 26

In an appeal against Hartley's conviction for the murder of a five-year-old child, one ground of appeal was the admission by the trial judge of evidence of statements by Hartley who worked in the area where the body was found. He was interviewed, and was found to have been there at or around the time of the murder. An appointment was made for a further interview next day, which Hartley failed to keep. He was found elsewhere and voluntarily went to the police station and gave a statement which differed from the first. He then remained in the station for a number of hours more, and made incriminating statements.

The appeal was refused.

LORD AVONSIDE: "Detective Superintendent Samson, who was in charge of the case, and a constable, Turner, saw the appellant at 2.30 a.m. on Thursday morning. His purpose was to go over the statement of the appellant in detail. He cautioned the appellant. He considered him a suspect. The caution was in the usual proper form. The appellant said: 'It's okay, it wasn't me.' The officer went over the statement down to the part where the appellant was at the burn, and then showed him a photograph of the dead child and asked him, when he had been down there, had he seen this boy at the burn or in the vicinity of the swing park. The appellant answered: 'No.'

At this point senior counsel for the appellant intervened. . . Firstly, it was objected that the stage had now been reached when it was plain that the police were going to interrogate or cross-examine a suspect. Not only was that objectionable in itself, but it was rendered all the worse in the particular circumstances. The appellant had been in police custody for 12 hours. He was young. The nature of his confinement must have, and, it would be shown, did demoralise him, and render him particularly open to breakdown under prolonged cross-examination. The evidence about to be given should not be put before the jury.

Counsel first relied on the hardy perennial case of *Chalmers* v. *H.M. Advocate*, and particularly what was said by Lord Justice-General Cooper. Now I accept, and must accept, that once suspicion of crime has centred upon a person, that person is in some respects clearly under the protection of the law [Lord Avonside here quoted some dicta of Lord Cooper in *Chalmers*].

I make two observations on these dicta. Firstly, police officers may question a suspect so long as they do not stray into the field of interrogation. Secondly, and most importantly, cross-examination is just what it means. It consists in questioning an adverse witness in an effort to break down his evidence, to weaken or prejudice his evidence, or to elicit statements damaging to him and aiding the case of the cross-examiner.

Brown v. *H.M. Advocate*, 1966 S.L.T. 105 was also quoted. I should have thought that case unhelpful to counsel for the accused. I refer to what was said by Lord Justice-General Clyde at p. 107. He speaks of questioning and interrogation and concludes his remarks by saying: 'But the test in all of them is the simple and intelligible test which has worked well in practice—has what has taken place been fair or not?'

I pause to interject that that, in my understanding, is today in law the basic test and only test. There has been a steady move towards liberalisation so that justice must, of course, be done to the criminal , but equally justice must be done to the interest of the public and law and order. There have in recent years been many cases in which this has been stated. . .

The trial judge, very properly, in my opinion, was not at this stage prepared to exclude evidence. . .

Samson in due course resumed his evidence, explaining that a Detective Constable Turner took notes and correct notes, of what the appellant said. The appellant was asked general questions as to whether he had seen the dead boy or any other person at the locus, or whether he had heard any cry or shout. The answers were negative. He was asked if he was sure. The appellant became agitated and said: "I did see something. The wee boy was there and somebody else. He said he knew me. He said, 'Don't you say a word.' He was one of them from Job Creation. I think he'll come after me and get me too. I saw the wee boy. The guy had him over the edge. He was half in and half out of the burn, you know what I mean. The wee boy was squealing. I watched for about 10 minutes, then ran away frightened.' At this the appellant, after a pause, said: 'It was me.'

The appellant was then cautioned again. He made a clear confession which I will not repeat but which may be found in the notes of evidence. Samson tried to comfort the appellant, who had now broken down. The appellant said: 'I want to tell you everything.' Samson, very properly, said that if he, the appellant, wanted to make a further statement, an officer unconnected with the inquiry would have to be called in. The appellant said: 'No, the only person I'll tell is the fat policeman. I want to see him'; and 'Get him, I want to see him.'

This policeman was Detective Sergeant Hyslop, who had to be located and came to the station about 4 a.m. Hyslop reminded the appellant that he was still under caution and not obliged to say anything. The appellant said: 'I'm sorry. I wanted to tell you, but I told the other officers. I don't know why I did it. He was only a wee boy, but I was frightened. I pushed him in. I take these turns and I get violent, and I try not to remember about them. I'm sorry. What will happen now?' He was told he would be charged, and then said: 'Don't think bad of me, I wasn't myself.'. . .

In my opinion, the appellant made the clearest admission of murdering the boy McAllister. . .

I would refuse the appeal."

LORD GRIEVE: "The nearest Samson got to interrogating the appellant, in the sense of cross-examining him, was to ask him if he was sure of the correctness of the answers he had given to the few questions which he had been asked. In no way could that be described as cross-examination, the main purpose of which is to destroy the basis, or content, of the evidence of a witness. An advocate who limited his cross-examination of witnesses to the question: 'Are you sure of what you have just said?', would achieve little forensic success. It has been repeated over several years, with increasing emphasis . . . that the ultimate test is one of fairness—fairness not only to the accused but fairness also to those who investigate crime on behalf of the public. Statements made in answer to fair questions, such as: 'Are you sure?' could seldom be said to have been extracted by unfair means placing 'cross-examination, pressure and deception in close company.' Even when the person concerned is a suspect, it is not illegitimate to ask him questions. What is illegitimate is to use means to extract from a potential accused extra-judicial admissions which could not have been extracted from such a person in judicial proceedings against him, an accused person not being a compellable witness. In my opinion, the trial judge acted correctly. . ."

Lord Dunpark delivered a concurring opinion.

This case represents the final triumph of the fairness test (the "basic and the only test" *per* Lord Avonside) over the mechanical rules in *Chalmers* (see also *H.M. Advocate* v. *Whitelaw*, 1980 S.L.T. (Notes) 25 and *Lord Advocate's Reference (No. 1 of 1983)*, 1984 S.C.C.R. 62 in which the Lord Justice-General (Emslie) said that the "simple and intelligible test which has worked well in practice is whether what has taken place has been fair or not").

The major problem is that "fairness" is *not* simple and intelligible, but very much a question of individual interpretation (the trial judge in *Lord Advocate's Reference* found the interview unfair). Even allowing that unfairness places "cross-examination, pressure and deception in close company" (*Jones* v. *Milne, supra*) and that "cross-examination" and "interrogation" refer to "improper forms of questioning tainted with an element of bullying or pressure designed to break the will of the suspect or to force from him a confession against his will" (*Lord Advocate's Reference*) this still leaves wide scope for interpretation. In *Hartley*, for example, the appellant had been 12 hours in police custody, was young and had not slept or eaten when the crucial interview took place at the bizarre hour of 2.30 a.m. Can it really be said that he had not been "pressurised" or "softened-up" (remember that in *Eire* v. *United Kingdom* one of the condemned interrogation methods was deprivation of sleep).

Again, is the test a question of objective or subjective fairness. A given judge knows what he understands by cross-examination, but a given suspect may be particularly liable to intimidation. Does the test allow for this? When the test was "fairness to the accused" this presented no difficulty (*e.g. Rigg* (above)). Since *Hartley* the cases have seemed to demonstrate greater sympathy to, *e.g.* deaf-mutes (*H.M. Advocate* v. *Mair*, 1982 S.L.T. 471), the mentally handicapped (*H.M. Advocate* v. *Gilgannon*, 1983 S.C.C.R. 10) or persons whose personal relationships with a policeman's family may have been exploited (*H.M. Advocate* v.

Anderson, 1980 S.L.T. (Notes) 104). But what if the accused simply makes a mistake and believes there is a threat or makes a mistake about the consequences of a statement? Under the previous formula of "fairness to the accused" the law could take account of this. Thus in *H.M. Advocate* v. *McSwiggan,* 1937 S.L.T. 437, the appellant who was described as "a bit simple" was accused of incest. He believed the crime was incestuous impregnation and made an incriminating statement detailing his contraceptive techniques, which was excluded. Finally, if the test of fairness is a subjective one, does this logically allow more rigorous treatment of a particularly wily or legally-trained suspect or of a professional "hard man," veteran of many police interviews?

Side by side with these cases on the rules of admissibility runs a growing hostility to the procedure of the "trial within a trial." So long as the admissibility of evidence was not governed solely by the fairness of the means of obtaining it, admissibility was a different matter from veracity. It seemed logical, given that the jury cannot disregard completely credible but inadmissible evidence even if the professional judiciary can (though even that seems doubtful), that the question of admissibility should be decided first and outwith the hearing of the jury. This was warmly approved in *Chalmers.*

This so-called "trial within a trial" carries some disadvantages, however. It is time-consuming; even if evidence is held to be admissible it loses much of its effect on being led a second time for the jury's benefit; arguably if the test of admissibility is the factual one of "fairness to the accused" it risks a usurpation by the judge of a jury function; and witnesses may alter their testimony in the light of cross-examination. The procedure was thus criticised by the Lord Justice-General (Clyde) in *Thompson* v. *H.M. Advocate,* 1968 J.C. 61, and his criticisms were echoed in *H.M. Advocate* v. *Whitelaw (supra),* in *Hartley* itself, and in the *Lord Advocate's Reference.* This has been accompanied by an insistence that only if counsel's motion for a trial within a trial alleges a very clear case of unfairness should the procedure be used: otherwise the jury decides. There therefore seem to have emerged two kinds of unfairness, one legal form which goes to admissibility and a lesser, factual form which goes to veracity and which is for the jury to decide upon, the difference being principally one of the grossness of alleged police action.

Although all of these authorities are largely concerned with permissible types of questioning, there is no reason to doubt that other forms of pressure brought to bear to induce a statement may be impermissible, as in *Law* v. *McNicol (supra).*

CHAPTER 4

THE RIGHT TO PRIVACY

I. INTRODUCTION

1. Report of the Committee on Privacy
(Chairman: Kenneth Younger)
Cmnd. 5012 (1972)

"57. It might seem a prerequisite of our task that we should have agreed what privacy is and be able to say what we mean by it. The 'Justice' Committee on Privacy said:

'In the course of our work, we have become increasingly aware of the difficulties which seem to beset any attempt to find a precise or logical formula which could either circumscribe the meaning of the word "privacy" or define it exhaustively. We think that there are two underlying reasons for this. First and foremost, the notion of privacy has a substantial emotive content in that many of the things which we feel the need to preserve from the curiosity of our fellows are feelings, beliefs or matters of conduct which are themselves irrational. Secondly, the scope of privacy is governed to a considerable extent by the standards, fashions and mores of the society of which we form part, and these are subject to constant change, especially at the present time. We have therefore concluded that no purpose would be served by our making yet another attempt at developing an intellectually rigorous analysis. We prefer instead to leave the concept much as we have found it, that is as a notion about whose precise boundaries there will always be a variety of opinions, but about whose central area there will always be a large measure of agreement. At any given time, there will be certain things which almost everyone will agree ought to be part of the "private" area which people should be allowed to preserve from the intrusion of others, subject only to the overriding interest of the community as a whole where this plainly outweighs the private right. Surrounding this central area there will always be a "grey area" on which opinions will differ, and the extent of this grey area, as also that of the central one, is bound to vary from time to time.'

They concluded that this 'central area' should be given a general protection under the law, yet when they were obliged to select its ingredients in order to define it in clause 9 of their draft Right of Privacy Bill, they had to fall back on a list of examples of widely differing character.

58. The majority of us regard the 'Justice' Committee's conclusion as one more indication, and a highly significant one, that the concept of privacy cannot be satisfactorily defined. We have looked at many earlier attempts, and mention some below, and have noted that there are important differences between them all. Either they go very wide, equating the right to privacy with the right to be let alone, or they boil down to a catalogue of assorted values to which the adjective 'private' or 'personal' can reasonably, but not exclusively, be attached. We conclude from these manifold efforts that no useful purpose would be served by our also entering

the lists with yet another attempt to formulate a precise and comprehensive definition of privacy.

59. If one abandons the attempt to find a single and comprehensive definition of privacy, as we have done, the next task is to try to decide what are the values in which privacy is a major element, and then to decide which deserve protection. We agree with the 'Justice' Committee that there is an area of private matters about which there will always (if by that is meant: at any given time) be a large measure of agreement. We think that to describe this as a 'central area' is liable to be misleading, since it is in fact a grouping of distinct, if sometimes closely linked, areas. We agree also that there is a fringe or 'grey area' beyond this grouping on which opinions will differ. We agree further that opinions as to what are aspects of privacy will vary from time to time. Man, as the 'Justice' Committee point out, is a social animal; his society evolves; and this evolution will alter from time to time the public's view on what needs to be dealt with by the law. This brings us to the various concepts of privacy that have been advanced in other studies of the problem.

60. Professor Alan Westin first describes privacy as 'the state of solitude or small group intimacy.' The 'Justice' Bill speaks of a person's state of being 'protected from intrusion upon himself, his home, his family, his relationships and communications with others, his property and his business affairs, including intrusion by spying, prying, watching and besetting [and] the unauthorised overhearing . . . of spoken words. . .' The Nordic Conference, expanding on what they meant by the right of privacy (which they equated with the right to be let alone), spoke of a person's 'private, family or home life' as the first area to be protected, but they also singled out as activities against which a person should be protected: '(b) interference with his physical . . . integrity . . . (g) spying, prying, watching and besetting; [and] (h) interference with his correspondence. . .'

61. The second of Professor Westin's definitions is that 'Privacy is the claim of individuals, groups or institutions to determine for themselves when, how and to what extent information about them is communicated to others.' The 'Justice' Bill adds to a person's protection from the forms of intrusion mentioned above (paragraph 60): 'including intrusion by . . . the unauthorised use or disclosure of confidential information, or facts (including his name, identity or likeness) calculated to cause him distress, annoyance or embarrassment, or to place him in a false light.'

62. We consider first the broadest interpretation of privacy: the state of being left alone. We take this to mean freedom from human interference by any means. Privacy would be an element in it, but there are other elements of equal importance: protection from physical harm and restraint, freedom from direction, and peaceful enjoyment of one's surroundings. The threats to these could take the form of injurious acts by other private persons, of public impositions or of man-made disasters or nuisances, and any one of these might threaten several of the elements which constitute the state of being let alone. A badly maintained factory chimney which falls on your family in your private house causes physical harm and interferes with the peaceful enjoyment of your surroundings; it also invades your privacy, but most people would not spontaneously make that the reason for being angry about it. Arbitrary arrest at home interferes with peaceful enjoyment and involves direction; it is also an invasion of privacy, but is unlikely to be condemned primarily on that score.

63. If there were to be a right of privacy under the law it should not, in our opinion, be synonymous with a right to be let alone. An unqualified right of this kind would in any event be an unrealistic concept, incompatible with the concept of society, implying a willingness not to be let entirely alone and a recognition that other people may be interested and consequently concerned about us. If the concept were to be embodied into a right, its adaptation to the dominant pressures of life in society would require so many exceptions that it would lose all coherence and hence any valid meaning. We have concluded therefore that the type of conduct against which legal protection might be afforded on the ground of intrusion on privacy should be confined to injurious or annoying conduct deliberately aimed at a particular person or persons where the invasion of privacy is the principal wrong complained of.

64. The evidence we have received indicates that the main concern about what is termed invasion of privacy involves the treatment of personal information. The 'information' which we have been urged to protect is that in which a person should be regarded as having something in the nature of a proprietary interest, either, in most cases, because it relates personally to him or because he has been entrusted with it by the person to whom it relates, as in the case of a doctor, tutor, employer or friend of the family. If the information is passed to another recipient who is also acceptable, then that recipient in turn can be said to be entrusted with it.

65. It is not contended in all the evidence to us that the information concerned need be private, though if the information is also confidential its unauthorised handling is all the more objectionable. The unauthorised handling of information which may well be known or available through approved sources can also constitute a breach of privacy in certain circumstances. The most obvious example is where it is published at large to a far wider audience than would otherwise learn of it: the conduct of the mass information media is the main object of criticism under this heading. Another circumstance is where the information is directly used for commercial gain or other ulterior purpose without authority: use of a name or portrait in an advertisement is the most likely example, which shows how this circumstance may overlap with the first one of media publicity. A third circumstance is where the information is collated with other personal information so that a dossier is compiled on the individual concerned, which tells the compiler more than the isolated pieces could do—on the principle that the whole is greater than the sum of the parts.

66. The unauthorised use, by way of compilation, communication and dissemination, of personal information is not the whole extent of the concern about privacy and information. The means used to extract such information from its private domain may be at least equally offensive. This may involve none of the subsequent stages of handling the information, since it may have as its motive pure inquisitiveness or self-indulgence. A case in point would be the peeping Tom, who normally keeps the 'information' very much to himself. Usually, however, those who go to the trouble of prying to get information do so with the object of using it: by passing it on to particular recipients, storing it for future reference or disseminating it. The common factor in all these is intrusion into the domain in which the information has hitherto been kept private.

67. The concept of intrusion implies some geographically private area, and this is commonly conceived of as the home and garden, extending to other forms of accommodation, whether owned or merely occupied, such as a place of business

or a hotel room or lodging. But it goes further than that, involving also private, family or domestic activities away from owned or occupied property, which are not meant to be publicly observed though they may occur in what is legally a public place. It is possible that there could be deliberate intrusion without the object of acquiring information, but to provoke or inhibit a course of action. Ill-disposed neighbours might conduct a campaign of prying to induce people to move house, or otherwise annoy them. The law gives specific protection against this only in the cases of landlords harassing tenants and of the harassment of debtors.

68. Keeping strictly in mind that we are concerned only with injurious or annoying conduct deliberately aimed at a particular person or group of persons, we think it right to give the following activities our particular attention: intrusive gathering and dissemination of information by the publicity media, handling of credit information, unwarrantable intrusion into personal matters at work and in education and medicine, prying by neighbours and landlords, intrusive sales methods, investigations by private detectives, and industrial espionage. We have also given special attention to certain modern technical developments which affect privacy: the technical surveillance devices and computers."

II. PRIVACY AND SCOTS LAW

1. THE COMMON LAW ATTITUDE TO PRIVACY

In Scotland, as in England but unlike the USA, there is no general right to privacy. In the United States, the invasion of privacy may give rise to liability in tort (i.e. an actionable civil wrong, roughly equivalent to delict in Scotland). In Scotland, it is true that there is the latent possibility that the common law may be developed to offer protection. The reality, however, is that the judges seem reluctant:

"72. Both Professor T. B. Smith (a Scottish Law Commissioner) and Professor David M. Walker have suggested that under existing law the Scottish Court might entertain an action for invasion of privacy at least where *animus injuriandi* could be established. Professor Walker states: 'It is submitted that the principle of the *actio injuriarum* would justify a Scottish Court in giving a remedy for invasion of privacy; the kinds of conduct which amount to such infringement are certainly affronts to personality likely to cause hurt feelings, and if the person is aggrieved a remedy should be given.' This is no doubt true in theory, but it is much in doubt if the Court would give a remedy except perhaps in an extreme case. In 1957 a Sheriff Substitute who had himself been convicted a year before for the offence of careless driving wrote a letter to a newspaper advocating heavier fines for some motoring offences. Another newspaper then published an ironical comment on the situation. The Sheriff Substitute then sued the latter newspaper for damages for invasion of privacy. The Inner House of the Court of Session (the Appeal Court) agreed with the judge of first instance that the action was irrelevant, *i.e.* had no sound basis in law. In the course of his opinion, Lord Justice-Clerk Thomson said: 'The basis of this argument is that an unwarranted invasion of privacy by a newspaper is actionable. This Court is a Court of law. It is not a court of manners, taste or journalistic propriety and so far as newspaper articles are concerned its function is to administer the law of defamation. Defamation consists in the making of a false statement derogatory of the character or reputation of the person spoken of. If such a statement is made, then unless the statement is privileged the pursuer has his remedy. But I know of no authority to the effect that mere invasion of privacy however hurtful and whatever its purpose and however repugnant to good taste is itself actionable. Whether such an invasion might amount to an ingredient in malice in circumstances where it is incumbent on the pursuer to establish that the defender acted maliciously it is unnecessary to consider.' This decision may be regarded as a weighty authority against the proposition that the Scottish courts would entertain an action for damages for invasion of privacy. On the other hand, in Scotland it has been said that the remedy depends upon the right rather than the right upon the remedy as in England, and, the Scottish court might grant a remedy in an extreme case even though the remedy had never been granted before." (Younger, 1972: 306)

Although there is no general right to privacy, a limited degree of protection is offered both by common law and by statute. So far as the common law is concerned, a person's reputation may be protected by the law of defamation; a person's enjoyment of his or her property may be protected exceptionally by the law of trespass and nuisance; and a person's confidential information is protected in the sense that unauthorised disclosure "is actionable in Scotland under the principle of the *actio injuriarum*" (Younger, 1972: 305). In practice, however, not all of these grounds are likely to provide an effective remedy. With regard particularly to the protection of property by the law of trespass, it has been pointed out:

"Trespass: Land
59. Trespass is an infringement of an occupier's right of exclusive possession, constituted by any temporary intrusion into or entry on the lands and heritage of another, without his permission or legal justification. Trespass, however, is not often invoked in Scotland and it is doubtful if the remedies would be of much value in dealing with modern invasions of privacy. In Scotland, damages are not recoverable for a single trespass, particularly if innocent or unwitting, but only if some actual damage has been suffered. Interdict (*i.e.* injunction) is competent but will not be granted in the absence of any actual trespass or an explicit threat of trespass, or if there is no reasonable probability of a trespass being repeated. Also trespass will not justify interdict if done in good faith or if there has been no loss or apprehension of loss. Although in English Law any invasion of a legal right, however innocent, amounts to a legal wrong, that rule is no part of the law of Scotland, so care must be taken in seeking to apply English authorities on trespass to a Scottish case.

Trespass: Goods
60. 'Trespass as to a chattel in a Scottish lawyer's mouth is a perfectly unmeaning phrase.'" (Younger, 1972: 303-304)

The practical reality of the absence of any effective right to privacy (as opposed to a theoretical right) is amply demonstrated by the following case.

2. Robertson v. Keith
1936 S.L.T. 9

Mrs Margaret Robertson, a chemist in Rutherglen, brought this action against the Chief Constable of Lanarkshire. The Chief Constable had arranged, for a period of five days, a continuous watch to be placed on the pursuer's house in order to establish the whereabouts of a member of his force, Detective Inspector Anderson. He had taken leave of absence and had given a false address as to where he might be found during his absence. This was regarded as a serious breach of discipline.

The pursuer claimed damages "for loss suffered through the wrongful and illegal actings of the defender." She also claimed damages for defamation, averring that the presence of the police near her house gave rise to alarming rumours, and that her neighbours, acquaintances and customers were led to believe that she had committed serious criminal offences. As a result of these rumours, she claimed that she "suffered in her feelings" and that her "business was very seriously injured." The Lord Ordinary (Moncrieff) assoilzied the defender, and his decision was upheld by a unanimous bench of seven judges.

LORD PRESIDENT (NORMAND): "The pursuer maintained that the defender was liable in damages because the watch which he set for the purpose of discovering the whereabouts of Detective Inspector Anderson was an unwarranted and unlawful invasion of the pursuer's rights, and her counsel sought to equiparate the alleged wrong with a wrongful arrest by the police. It is not doubtful that any unwarranted and unlawful proceedings by a public officer resulting in injury to anyone will subject him to liability, and that in such a case proof of malice and want of probable cause is not required of the pursuer. The first question, therefore, is whether the action of the defender in ordering the watch to be set falls into this category. It was admitted and it is, I think, the law that if the watch had been set in the course of investigating a crime, and if it had led to some injury to the pursuer, she would have had no case unless she could prove malice and want of probable cause. The protection which is thus given to the police and other public officials acting in the exercise of their duty is a privilege founded on the public interest (*Beaton* v. *Ivory* (1887) 14 R. 1057), for it is of the highest importance that public officials should not be hindered in their duty by fears of incurring liability for damages if their conduct is subsequently impugned as indiscreet or imprudent or going beyond what the immediate necessities required. It was said, however, by pursuer's counsel that this privilege does not extend to the Chief Constable when he is acting under the powers vested in him for the maintenance of the discipline of the force. It would be strange if this distinction were valid, for the public interest is as deeply involved in the maintenance of the discipline of the police as it is in the investigation of any particular crime, though members of the public are not concerned in the actual maintenance of discipline in the way in which they may be concerned in the prevention or detection of crime. The Chief Constable is clearly acting in his public capacity whether he is exercising his disciplinary powers or his powers for the preservation of order and the prevention and detection of crime. In my opinion his privilege is the same in either case, and I think that the authorities are consistent with this principle (*McMurchy* v. *Campbell* (1887) 14 R. 725; *Innes* v. *Adamson* (1889) 17 R. 11). If, therefore, it was lawful for the defender to set a watch for Anderson at or about a place where he thought he might be found, he is entitled to the protection implied in requiring the pursuer to prove malice and want of probable cause. Nor does it seem doubtful that the setting of a watch was within the defender's legal power and an exercise of his powers and duties of discipline in relation to Anderson. There are averments that the police officers engaged on the watch committed trespass, and we were told that the watch amounted to an invasion of the pursuer's personal freedom and that it was an infringement of the law of the neighbourhood, by which I understood counsel to mean that it amounted to a nuisance. But there is no proof that the watch instructed by the defender involved any wrongous act of any kind, nor that any trespass, invasion of the pursuer's personal liberty, or nuisance was committed. I accept the Lord Ordinary's findings of fact on the nature and incidents of the watch which was kept, and I agree with him that nothing was done beyond what was necessary if the watch was to be effective. I accordingly hold that the defender is entitled to the protection that the pursuer must prove malice and want of probable cause.

An argument was presented that malice should be inferred from the circumstances under which the watch was set. It was said that there was no urgent necessity to find Anderson, and that the Chief Constable might have remained inactive till he returned to duty, as he did a few days later. It was further said that it was unreasonable to continue the watch from the Wednesday till the Monday morning when Anderson reported for duty, and that it could have been anticipated that a watch so long continued would cause annoyance to the pursuer and might give rise to public rumour hurtful to her reputation. The action of the defender was characterised as extravagant and unreasonable, and it was said that an inference of malice fell to be drawn from the circumstances to which I have referred. The reply made to this in law was that if what the defender did was an exercise of his disciplinary power and was unaccompanied by any unlawful act, the incidents of this lawful course of action could not be used to build up against him evidence of malice, and that if malice is to be established, extrinsic facts must be averred and proved. . .

In my view the question of malice is essentially a question of good faith. It has to be remembered that in order to succeed the pursuer has to prove both malice and want of probable cause. If there was proof of want of probable cause for any of the acts complained of, even though these acts were all of them singly within the lawful competence of the Chief Constable, it would be reasonable and possible to infer bad faith or malice either from extrinsic facts or from the manner in which the proceedings were carried out if, for example, they were accompanied by harshness, discourtesy, or inconsiderateness. But if there were probable cause, the presence or absence of malice matters not.

In the present case I hold that the watch and its incidents were in themselves lawful, and that there is no extrinsic evidence of malice. I may add that the evidence is that the police officers carried out their duty without discourtesy, and I consider that some of the comments made on the defender's conduct were exaggerated. I am also of opinion that the defender had probable cause for the action which he took."

LORD JUSTICE-CLERK (Aitchison): "Without entering upon further detailed examination of authority, the law, as I understand it, may be summarised in these propositions:

1. An act is *prima facie* within the competence of the public official doing or authorising it when it is the kind of act that is within his ordinary duty to discharge.

2. When a public official does an act that is *prima facie* within his ordinary duty, there is a presumption that he has acted within his authority.

3. This presumption is not absolute, but may be rebutted by shewing that the act was unrelated to any duty arising on the particular occasion, in which case the act ceases to be within the authority or competence of the public official and becomes unlawful.

4. Where an act is within the competence, no civil liability arises from the doing of the act unless it can be shewn that the act was done maliciously and without probable cause.

5. Want of probable cause and malice are not necessarily unrelated and independent. The absence of just cause may go to prove malice, and similarly the presence of oblique or dishonest motive may go to shew the absence of probable cause.

6. Malice may be inferred from recklessness, and the facts and circumstances from which it may be inferred need not be extrinsic to the circumstances in which the act is done or to the manner of doing it.

7. Circumstances may shew that an act was done with malice, or without probable cause, or that it was an act outwith the competence of the person doing or authorising it. In some cases, according to the angle from which the question is approached, the same facts may be habile to infer each of these conclusions.

8. The *onus probandi* is on the pursuer to shew that the act complained of is outwith the competence of the person doing or authorising it, or if, within the competence, that it was done maliciously and without probable cause.

There remains to consider the application of the law to the facts of this case. The questions are three: (1) Was what was done within the competence of the defender? (2) If so, was it done without probable cause? (3) Was it done maliciously? I will take these questions in the inverse order.

Where in this case is there evidence of malice or dishonest motive? There is no proved circumstance pointing to ill-will against the pursuer, or hostility, or even disagreement. It was said that the duration and severity of the watch disclosed an intention in the mind of the defender, reckless of consequences, to break Inspector Anderson at all costs, and that this, inferring a reckless disregard of the pursuer's interests, was proof of malice. It is, I think, a sufficient answer that when Anderson did report on the Monday he was allowed to tender his resignation. The defender might have chosen to arraign him on a grave charge of indiscipline, conviction upon which might have entailed a forfeiture of his pension rights. There is no evidence of antecedent ill-will against either Anderson or the pursuer.

Was there probable cause for the defender's action? Probable cause, as Sir John Salmond has pointed out (*Torts* (7th ed.), p.619), really means provable cause—that is, excusable or just cause. Can it be said in this case that the defender acted without just occasion or lawful excuse? Anderson had gone on leave without leaving his communications intact, which was in itself a breach of police regulations, although if done inadvertently, not of much moment; but what was a much graver matter, there was reason to think that Anderson was defying an order for his recall and that he was secreting himself in the pursuer's house. That being the position, I am unable to affirm that the Chief Constable was not entitled to take effective steps with a view to ascertaining the fact.

Was the setting and maintaining of the watch within the competence of the defender? This appears ultimately to be the real question in the case. I do not doubt that to set and maintain a police watch upon the house of a citizen, in circumstances that attract public attention and give rise to suspicion in the public mind, may, if done without just cause, amount to an invasion of the liberty of the citizen as truly and effectively as if the citizen were subjected to physical restraint. But whether in any case it is an unlawful invasion of liberty must depend upon the circumstances of the particular case. There are, and must be, many acts done by the police in the proper exercise of their functions that may affect injuriously innocent people and yet are acts done without legal wrong. It was conceded by counsel for the pursuer that if crime had been suspected as taking place in the pursuer's house it would have been a lawful exercise of police authority to watch the house. But it was argued that here there was no crime nor suspected crime, and that the indiscipline of Anderson was in truth a domestic matter that did not justify the steps that were taken. This argument is, in my view, unsound. Police discipline is primarily a domestic matter, a matter between the Chief Constable and his subordinates, but it is also a matter of vital public interest. No Chief Constable who had a proper sense of his responsibility could view with unconcern the deliberate defection of a superior officer committed within his jurisdiction in circumstances that pointed to wilful defiance. If the Chief Constable had reasonable ground for his suspicion (and this does not appear to be open to controversy) the conclusion is inevitable that he was entitled to set and maintain a watch so that he might have evidence of a grave dereliction of duty on the part of Anderson. The Lord Ordinary has held in fact that the actual watch was not made more onerous to the pursuer than was necessarily incidental to such a watch being maintained. This finding in fact has not been displaced.

A Chief Constable who is vested with high powers for the carrying out of his public office ought always to discharge his functions with a single eye to the public interest, and wherever possible in such a way as not to bring suspicion upon members of the community who have committed no breach of the law. In the present case I am not satisfied that the defender, as Chief Constable, acted imprudently or injudiciously, having regard to the difficult situation confronting him, although it may now appear, in the light of what has happened, that an alternative course might have been followed with advantage that would have been more in accord with caution and good sense."

2. STATUTORY PROTECTION OF PRIVACY

Although the common law thus offers no effective protection against the invasion of privacy, there is a wide range of statutory provisions which make up for this omission in well-defined discrete areas. First, there are measures which protect against unwanted publicity.

3. Judicial Proceedings (Regulation of Reports) Act 1926

"Restriction on publication of reports of judicial proceedings
1.—(1) It shall not be lawful to print or publish, or cause or procure to be printed or published—

(*a*) in relation to any judicial proceedings any indecent matter or indecent medical, surgical or physiological details being matter or details the publication of which would be calculated to injure public morals;

(*b*) in relaion to any judicial proceedings for dissolution of marriage, for nullity of marriage, or for judicial separation, or for restitution of conjugal rights, any particulars other than the following, that is to say:—

(i) the names, addresses and occupations of the parties and witnesses;

(ii) a concise statement of the charges, defences and countercharges in support of which evidence has been given;

(iii) submissions on any point of law arising in the course of the proceedings, and the decision of the courts thereon;

(iv) the summing-up of the judge and the finding of the jury (if any) and the judgment of the court and observations made by the judge in giving judgment:

Provided that nothing in this part of this subsection shall be held to permit the publication of anything contrary to the provisions of paragraph (*a*) of this subsection.

(2) If any person acts in contravention of the provisions of this Act, he shall in respect of each offence be liable, on summary conviction, to imprisonment for a term not exceeding four months, or to a fine not exceeding five hundred pounds, or to both such imprisonment and fine:

Provided that no person, other than a proprietor, editor, master printer or publisher, shall be liable to be convicted under this Act. . .

(4) Nothing in this section shall apply to the printing of any pleading, transcript of evidence or other document for use in connection with any judicial proceedings or the communication thereof to persons concerned in the proceedings, or to the printing or publishing of any notice or report in pursuance of the directions of the court; or to the printing or publishing of any matter in any separate volume or part of any bona fide series of law reports which does not form part of any other publication and consists solely of reports of proceedings in courts of law, or in any publication of a technical character bona fide intended for circulation among members of the legal or medical professions.

(5) In the application of this section to Scotland, for any reference to judicial proceedings for restitution of conjugal rights there shall be substituted a reference to an action of adherence or of adherence and aliment."

A second kind of intervention is protection against harassment. A good example here is the Conspiracy and Protection of Property Act 1875, designed to deal with picketing in trade disputes but with much wider implications.

4. Conspiracy and Protection of Property Act 1875
(as amended by Public Order Act 1986)

"7. *Penalty for intimidation or annoyance by violence or otherwise*
Every person who, with a view to compel any other person to abstain from doing or to do any act which such other person has a legal right to do or abstain from doing, wrongfully and without legal authority,—

1. Uses violence to or intimidates such other person or his wife or children, or injures his property; or,

2. Persistently follows such other person about from place to place; or,

3. Hides any tools, clothes, or other property owned or used by such other person, or deprives him of or hinders him in the use thereof; or,

4. Watches or besets the house or other place where such other person resides, or works, or carries on business, or happens to be, or the approach to such house or place; or,

5. Follows such other person with two or more other persons in a disorderly manner in or through any street or road,

[shall be liable on summary conviction to imprisonment for a term not exceeding six months or a fine not exceeding level 5 on the standard scale, or both]

[A constable may arrest without warrant anyone he reasonably suspects is committing an offence under this section.]"

The last provision (in parentheses) was added by the Public Order Act 1986. Lawful authority to picket is provided by the Trade Union and Labour Relations Act 1974, as amended by the Employment Act 1980. This permits people to attend outside their own place of work, in contemplation or furtherance of a trade dispute, for the limited purpose of peacefully obtaining or communicating information, or peacefully persuading people to work or abstain from working. This measure is discussed more fully in Chapter Eight.

A third form of intervention is the protection of all invasions of privacy (*i.e.* general rather than specific protections) by specific bodies or organisations. The two obvious targets of such intervention are the press and the broadcasting media. So far as the press are concerned, there is no statutory control of invasive journalism, though the self-regulatory Press Council has issued a *Declaration of Principle on Privacy* which provides:

"(i) The publication of information about the private life or concerns of individuals without their consent is only acceptable if there is a legitimate public interest overriding the right of privacy.
(ii) It is the responsibility of editors to ensure that enquiries into matters affecting the private life or concerns of individuals are only undertaken where in the Editor's opinion at the time a legitimate public interest in such matters may arise. The right to privacy is however not involved if the individuals concerned have freely consented to the pursuit of enquiries and publication.
(iii) The public interest relied on as the justification for publication or inquiries which conflict with a claim to privacy must be a legitimate and proper public interest and not only a prurient or morbid curiosity. 'Of interest to the public' is not

synonymous with 'in the public interest.' It should be recognised that entry into public life does not disqualify an individual from his right to privacy about his private affairs, save when the circumstances relating to the private life of an individual occupying a public position may be likely to affect the performance of his duties or public confidence in him or his office.

(iv) Invasion of privacy by deception, eavesdropping or technological methods which are not in themselves unlawful can however only be justified when it is in pursuit of information which ought to be published in the public interest and there is no other reasonably practicable method of obtaining or confirming it.

(v) The Council expects the obtaining of news or pictures to be carried out with sympathy and discretion. Reporters and photographers should do nothing to cause pain or humiliation to bereaved or distressed people unless it is clear that the publication of the news or pictures will serve a legitimate public interest and there is no other reasonably practical means of obtaining the material.

(vi) Editors are responsible for the actions of those employed by their newspapers and have a duty to ensure that all concerned are aware of the importance of respecting all legitimate claims to personal privacy."

(23rd Press Council Report (1976), p. 150.)

So far as the broadcasting authorities are concerned, the matter is now governed by the Broadcasting Act 1981. In Part III this provides for the continued existence of the Broadcasting Complaints Commission, appointed by the Home Secretary but independent of the BBC and the IBA. The functions of the Commission include a duty to consider and adjudicate upon complaints of "unwarranted infringement of privacy in, or in connection with the obtaining of material included in, sound or television programmes actually so broadcast" (1981 Act, s. 54(1) (*b*)). By section 55(4) the Commission shall not entertain, or proceed with the consideration of, a complaint if it appears to them—

"(*a*) that the complaint relates to the broadcasting of the relevant programme on an occasion more than five years after the death of the person affected; or

(*b*) that the unjust or unfair treatment or unwarranted infringement of privacy complained of is the subject of proceedings in a court of law in the United Kingdom; or

(*c*) that the unjust or unfair treatment or unwarranted infringement of privacy complained of is a matter in respect of which the person affected has a remedy by way of proceedings in a court of law in the United Kingdom, and that in the particular circumstances it is not appropriate for the Commission to consider a complaint about it; or

(*d*) that the complaint is frivolous;
or if it appears to them for any other reason inappropriate for them to entertain, or proceed with the consideration of, the complaint."

3. REFORM

5. Report of the Committee on Privacy
(Chairman: Kenneth Younger)
Cmnd. 5012 (1972)

"651. We are agreed, as we explained in Chapter 6, that the concept of privacy embodies values which are essential to the work of a free society. We do not regard respect for privacy as merely a question of taste which can be left to the interplay of free discussion and the restraints of social convention. We recognise also that under modern conditions the growing interdependence and organisation of individuals, together with technological developments, has subjected privacy to dangerous pressures. In the light of these pressures we are further agreed that privacy requires additional protection. The fundamental decision which we have had to make concerns the method by which protection is given. Should the law provide a remedy against invasions of privacy as such? Or is it sufficient to rely on the protection of privacy in each social situation where it is likely to come in issue—whether that protection takes the form of direct remedies, civil or criminal, or of other social forces operating under the pressure of public opinion—reinforced, we hope, by the publication of this Report?

652. Any general civil remedy would require hardly less general qualification in order to enable the courts (the judge or judge and jury) to achieve an acceptable balance between values implicit in respect for privacy and other values of at least equal importance to the well-being of society. We have particularly in mind the importance in a free society of the unimpeded circulation of true information and the occasions which would inevitably arise, if there were a general civil remedy for the protection of privacy, in which the courts would be called upon to balance, by reference to the 'public interest,' society's interest in the circulation of truth against the individual's claim for privacy.

653. We appreciate that there are countries (of which we give examples in Appendix J) in which it is precisely this balancing function which is left to the courts; and we point out in Appendix I that in English law the protection which is given to privacy by the action for breach of confidence may involve the courts in deciding whether the remedy should be refused on the grounds that the disclosure in question (as, for example, when it relates to the commission of a crime) was in the public interest. The vital difference, however, between decisions on what is in the public interest, taken by the courts in countries where a general remedy for invasions of privacy exists, and the decisions on the public interest taken by English courts in cases under existing laws which are relevant to the protection of specific aspects of privacy, is that the judicial function in the latter is much more circumscribed. Thus, in an action for breach of confidence the court is faced initially with a disclosure of information which has been given in confidence; similarly, in an action for defamation no question of the public interest arises until there is before the court a defamatory statement which is untrue. It is clear that the function of the courts in such circumstances is a less difficult one and one which is likely to give rise to less controversy than that which would face a court which was called upon to apply a much more general law to cases in which no relationship of confidence existed and no false statement had been made. In such cases a court

would in effect have to make an unguided choice, in the light of the public interest, between values which, in the abstract, might appear to have equal weight. We recognise that the courts could be given the task of considering, in the factual context of each case, whether a general right to privacy should be upheld against the claims of other values, in particular the value of the free circulation of true information. But we think that such a task might first make the law uncertain, at least for some time until the necessary range of precedents covering a wide range of situations had been established; and it might secondly extend the judicial role, as it is generally understood in our society, too far into the determination of controversial questions of a social and political character.

654. If privacy can be protected in no other way these disadvantages may have to be accepted, but we have thought it right rather to conduct our examination of privacy in the first instance with reference to the differing social contexts in which a claim for protection of privacy is, or could be, asserted.

655. We have now examined in Chapters 7 to 20 each of the specific areas in which substantial concern about intrusions into privacy has been brought to our attention. In some cases we have recommended that there should be legislation to create either a new offence in order to deal with new threats to privacy, for instance new technical surveillance devices; or a right of access by an individual to information held about him by a credit rating agency. In other cases we have thought it more effective to recommend that administrative controls should be established over a particular kind of activity, such as credit rating agencies and private detectives. In yet other cases where legal action has seemed too heavy an instrument and administrative control undesirable or unnecessary, we have preferred to rely on a measure of self-discipline being exercised by bodies whose activities involve a possible threat to privacy. Examples are the mass media, the universities, the medical profession and industrial employers.

656. Of these the mass media are by far the most important. On the one hand are the broadcasting authorities, which by virtue of Charter or Statute are already under extensive obligations to have regard to the interests of the public; on the other are the varied organs of the press, which are under no special legal restriction beyond the general law of the land, but have developed regulatory machinery of their own through the Press Council to handle complaints. As regards the broadcasting authorities and the press we have reached the conclusion that, in respect generally of their dissemination of information, it is best to rely for the protection of privacy upon improvements in the existing systems rather than upon new legislation. On the other hand we think that they should, along with ordinary citizens, be subject in their information-gathering activities to the restrictions on the use of technical surveillance devices which we have recommended. They are already bound by the law relating to the disclosure of information obtained in breach of confidence and would be subject to any restrictions in that branch of the law which might emerge as a result of the clarification recommended in Chapter 21.

657. Looking at the field as a whole, we have expressed the view that the existing law provides more effective relief from some kinds of intrusion into privacy than is generally appreciated. In particular it is our opinion that the law on breach of confidence, if some of its present ambiguities were to be authoritatively clarified (if necessary by legislation), would turn out to be a practical instrument for dealing with many complaints in the privacy field.

658. We have already referred to the need to balance the right of privacy against

other and countervailing rights, in particular freedom of information and the right to tell the truth freely unless compelling reasons for a legal limitation of this right can be adduced. We have often found this balance difficult to strike. At every stage we have been conscious of differing judgments about the precise area of privacy which should be protected under each heading and about the considerations of 'public interest' which might be held in each case to justify intrusion and so to override the right of privacy. These uncertainties are, no doubt, largely the consequence of the acknowledged lack of any clear and generally agreed definition of what privacy itself is; and of the only slightly less intractable problem of deciding precisely what is 'in the public interest' or, in a wider formulation, 'of public interest.'

659. Despite these difficulties we have reached broad agreement among ourselves about the practical approach which we wish to recommend under each of the headings dealt with in Chapters 7 to 21. We recognise that this piecemeal approach leaves some gaps. In the private sector (with which alone we are concerned) it is not difficult to think of some kinds of intrusion, most obviously by journalistic investigators or by prying neighbours, for which our recommendations provide no new legal remedy. In the second place, some of our proposals frankly rely, to an extent which some may find over-optimistic, upon the readiness of potentially intrusive agencies, such as the press, to respond not to legal sanctions but to the pressures of public and professional criticism and to the climate of our society. Yet other proposals rely upon codes of conduct or on negotiated conditions of employment as means of maintaining ethical standards.

660. Questions therefore arise whether the area which our recommendations would still leave legally unprotected is so important that it must somehow be covered; whether it is realistic to count upon the sense of responsibility of interested parties, or whether there is not a way of providing the additional support of legal sanctions, without at the same time requiring the courts to apply unduly vague criteria and to hammer out, without clear guidance from the statute book, the very definitions of privacy and of the public interest which have defied the best efforts of scholars and of successive draftsmen of parliamentary bills.

661. With these conflicting considerations in mind, we therefore turn to discuss the question whether a general right of privacy should be recognised by the law, on the lines proposed in Mr Walden's Right of Privacy Bill. In doing this we would emphasize our unanimous view that our various recommendations made in previous chapters should remain unaffected whatever the outcome of this argument. In particular the question whether the criminal law should be invoked in some cases has, in our view, been sufficiently dealt with under our specific headings and need not be considered in relation to a general right. Any civil remedy provided for infringement of a general right of privacy must, we feel sure, be considered as an addition to measures proposed under specific headings and not as an alternative to them.

662. The case for including a general right of privacy in the domestic law of the United Kingdom may reasonably start from the fact, to which attention was called in Chapter 2, that the Government of the United Kingdom is a party to the Universal Declaration of Human Rights, the United Nations Covenant on Civil and Political Rights and the European Convention for the Protection of Human Rights and Fundamental Freedoms, all of which in one form or another recognise the right of privacy in somewhat general terms. The principle therefore, is not in dispute, only

the nature of the domestic legislation which is needed to implement it.

663. A number of other countries in Europe, America and the Commonwealth, have adopted legislation in wide and general terms. While the effectiveness of these laws varies from country to country, there is evidence that some practical use is made of them and no evidence that the information media have complained that these laws unduly restrict their legitimate activities. It seems a natural deduction from this that similar action could usefully be undertaken in the United Kingdom without risk. We have naturally paid close attention to the experience of other countries, but we have noted that the methods of adjusting domestic legislation to the requirements of international agreements differ widely from one signatory state to another, and that this has been markedly true in the field of human rights. This is firstly because some legal systems are readier than others to declare a general right and then to leave to the courts the development of effective sanctions against violation of the right. The second relevant condition is the difference in the extent to which existing laws in particular countries are already believed to provide sufficiently for the protection of the new right. With regard to the first point we think that the best way to ensure regard for privacy is to provide specific and effective sanctions against clearly defined activities which unreasonably frustrate the individual in his search of privacy. As far as the second point is concerned, we have already described in detail the considerable extent to which privacy is already protected by existing English law. We have noted that in some countries, where the law of defamation is less developed than in England, new laws for the protection of privacy are being used in cases which in England would fall squarely under the heading of defamation. In Germany, we were told, the dividing line between privacy and defamation is already blurred. We do not ourselves favour a similar development here, believing that the law should continue to distinguish clearly in the sanctions which it provides between statements which are both defamatory and untrue and statements which, even if they may be offensive on other grounds, are neither of these things.

664. This raises the question whether the method which we have adopted is nevertheless inadequate because it leaves the citizen without a legal remedy for important kinds of intrusion upon his privacy; and whether a general right of privacy, which would fill in these gaps, would in practice carry with it serious dangers to the legitimate circulation of information, which is an important value in any democratic society. We have concluded that, so far as the principal areas of complaint are concerned, and especially those which arise from new technological developments, our specific recommendations are likely to be much more effective than any general declaration. Having covered these areas, we do not think that what remains uncovered is extensive; and our evidence does not suggest that the position in the uncovered area is deteriorating. We think moreover that to cover it by a blanket declaration of a right of privacy would introduce uncertainties into the law, the repercussions of which upon free circulation of information are difficult to foresee in detail but could be substantial.

665. We have found privacy to be a concept which means widely different things to different people and changes significantly over relatively short periods. In considering how the courts could handle so ill-defined and unstable a concept, we conclude that privacy is ill-suited to be the subject of a long process of definition through the building up of precedents over the years, since the judgments of the past would be an unreliable guide to any current evaluation of privacy. If, on the other

hand no body of judge-made precedent were built up, the law would remain, as it would certainly have to begin, highly uncertain and subject to the unguided judgments of juries from time to time. It is difficult to find any firm evidential base on which to assess the danger to the free circulation of information which might result from a legal situation of this kind. The press and broadcasting authorities have naturally expressed to us their concern about any extension into the field of truthful publication of the sort of restraints at present imposed on them by the law of defamation, especially if the practical limits of the extension are bound to remain somewhat indeterminable for a period of years. We do not think these fears can be discounted and we do not forget that others besides the mass media, for instance biographers, novelists or playwrights, might also be affected. We already have some experience of the uncertainties which result, for instance in obscenity cases, when courts of law are asked to make judgments on controversial matters, where statutory definitions are unsatisfactory, and social and moral opinion fluctuates rapidly.

666. It would, in our view, be unwise to extend this kind of uncertainty into a new branch of the law, unless there were compelling evidence of a substantial wrong, which must be righted even at some risk to other important values. Within the area covered by our terms of reference, evidence of this kind has been conspicuously lacking and we therefore see no reason to recommend that this risk should be taken.

667. Finally, we repeat what we said at the outset of this chapter. Privacy, however defined, embodies values which are essential to a free society. It requires the support of society as a whole. But the law is only one of the factors determining the climate of a democratic society and it is often only a minor factor. Education, professional standards and the free interplay of ideas and discussion through the mass media and the organs of political democracy can do at least as much as the law to establish and maintain standards of behaviour. We have explained in this report that we see risks in placing excessive reliance on the law in order to protect privacy. We believe that in our recommendations we have given to the law its due place in the protection of privacy and we see no need to extend it further."

III. PRIVACY AND THE EUROPEAN CONVENTION ON HUMAN RIGHTS

1. PRISONERS' RIGHTS

6. X v. United Kingdom (1986)
8 E.H.R.R. 274

"The Facts: The applicants are citizens of the United Kingdom. The first applicant was born in 1944 and at the time of lodging the application was detained in H.M. Prison, Saughton, Edinburgh. The second applicant was born in 1950 and is the first applicant's wife and a doctor by profession. She was residing in Glasgow when the application was lodged. The applicants originally complained to the Commission about restrictions on the first applicant's leave of absence from prison, the limitation on prisoners' visits to 12 per year and continually supervised visits on 'special escorted leave'. They also complained of restrictions on the first

applicant's telephone and typing facilities, sculpting activities, censorship of correspondence and an absence of effective remedies for their Convention claims. It is the latter two complaints which are the subject of the present decision. The applicant's correspondence complaints arise out of the fact that all the first applicant's incoming and outgoing mail was subject to control by the prison authorities and that the authorities only paid the postage of one outgoing, three-page letter per week. Further more in July 1981 one of the first applicant's letters to Mr Peter McDougall was stopped on the grounds that he was a 'media personality.' The government have acknowledged, however, that this decision was an error. While a prisoner in the 'Training for Freedom Hostel,' the first applicant was not allowed to have any contact with the media or to provide anyone with material intended for publication. Finally, the applicants allege that they had no effective domestic remedies at their disposal in respect of these complaints as well as their other original complaints to the Commission.

Complaints: The applicants complain that the restrictions on the first applicant's correspondence constituted an unjustified interference with their right to respect for correspondence, contrary to Art. 8 of the Convention. Moreover they complain they did not have an effective domestic remedy, either for this Convention claim or the other claims of breaches of the Convention submitted originally.

The Law:
    1. The applicants have complained of an unjustified interference with their right to respect for correspondence ensured by Art. 8 of the Convention and a lack of effective domestic remedies for their Convention complaints, contrary to Art. 13 of the Convention. The relevant part of Art. 8 of the Convention provides as follows:
    2. As regards the applicants' complaint of the screening of their correspondence by the prison censor, the Commission refers to its Report in the test case of *Silver and Others* v. *United Kingdom* (1983) 5 E.H.R.R. 347:
    'The Commission is of the opinion that, in principle, the mere supervision of prisoners' correspondence, even though it does constitute an interference with their right to respect for correspondence is nevertheless generally justified under the provisions of Art. 8(2). Such supervision is "in accordance with the law," prisoners being aware of the contents of the Prison Rules and, thus, that the prison authorities are authorised under Rule 33 of the Prison Rules 1964 to control, *i.e.* in the first instance, to screen their correspondence."
    The applicants contend that sometimes the verification procedure consisted in the prison censorship officer reading out loud the second applicant's letters in front of other prisoners and laughing or making comments about the contents. This is denied by the Government, who state that such officers have instructions to be discreet and to avoid embarrassment to prisoners. Moreover the first applicant had not complained of the prison censor's methods to the prison governor. The Commission concludes that, in the circumstances of the case, it has not been shown that the supervision of the applicants' correspondence was disrespectful of their rights under Art. 8 of the Convention. Accordingly the Commission finds no interference with the applicants' right to respect for correspondence and rejects this aspect of the case as being manifestly ill-

founded within the meaning of Art. 27(2) of the Convention.

3. The applicants have also complained of an interference with their right to respect for correspondence by virtue of the fact that the prison authorities only paid the postage of one of the first applicant's weekly letters, whereas his prison wages were insufficient to pay the postage of other letters because they were needed to buy special food for his vegetarian diet. The Commission considers that, as a general principle, Art. 8 of the Convention does not oblige a State Party to pay for all correspondence sent by prisoners. The financing of such correspondence must be examined in the light of the particular facts of each case, in the event that a prisoner's lack of private funds could constitute a severe limitation or denial of the possibility to correspond at all. However, the Commission finds that it has not been shown that the first applicant was severely restricted in his correspondence for financial reasons. In the circumstances of the case, therefore, the Commission concludes that the payment by the prison authorities of the postage of one of the first applicant's letters per week did not constitute an interference with the applicant's right to respect for correspondence ensured by Art. 8 of the Convention. Accordingly this aspect of the case must also be rejected as being manifestly ill-founded within the meaning of Art. 27(2) of the Convention.

4. In so far as one of the first applicant's letters was stopped by the prison authorities, albeit in error, the case resembles that of the aforementioned *Silver and Others* v. *United Kingdom.* It follows that this part of the application must be declared admissible, no grounds for declaring it inadmissible having been established.

5. Finally, the applicants have complained of a lack of effective domestic remedies in respect of their correspondence and other Convention claims. Art. 13 of the Convention provides as follows:. . .

The Commission notes that as regards the stopping of one of the first applicant's letters, there was apparently no effective remedy at his disposal and the Government has not submitted that there were any such remedies. In this respect, therefore, the application again resembles that of the test case of *Silver and Others* v. *United Kingdom* and must be declared admissible, no grounds for declaring it inadmissible having been established. As regards the applicants' complaint of an absence of remedies in respect of their other correspondence complaints and original complaints to the Commission, the Government has contended that an aggregate of domestic remedies was available and satisfied Art. 13 of the Convention. The Commission refers to the court's approach in the case of *Silver and Others* v. *United Kingdom:*

'The principles that emerge from the Court's jurisprudence on the interpretation of Art. 13 include the following:

(a) where an individual has an arguable claim to be the victim of a violation of the rights set forth in the Convention, he should have a remedy before a national authority in order both to have his claim decided and, if appropriate, to obtain redress (*Klass* v. *Germany* 2 E.H.R.R. 214 para. 64);

(b) the authority referred to in Art 13 may not necessarily be a judicial authority but, if it is not, its powers and the guarantees which it affords are relevant in determining whether the remedy before it is effective;

(c) although no single remedy may itself entirely satisfy the requirements of Art. 13, the aggregate of remedies provided for under domestic law may do so (see, *mutatis mutandis, X* v. *United Kingdom* 4 E.H.R.R. 188 para. 56 and *Van Droogenbroeck* v. *Belgium* 4 E.H.R.R. 443);

(d) neither Art. 13 nor the Convention in general lays down for the Contracting States any given manner for ensuring within their internal law the effective implementation of any of the provisions of the Convention—for example, by incorporating the Convention into domestic law (see *Swedish Engine Drivers' Union* v. *Sweden* 1 E.H.R.R. 617).

It follows from the last-mentioned principle that the application of Art .13 in a given case will depend upon the manner in which the Contracting State concerned has chosen to discharge its obligation under Art. 1 directly to secure to anyone within its jurisdiction the rights and freedoms set out in Section I.' (*Silver and Others* v. *United Kingdom* (1983) 5 E.H.R.R. 347 para. 113).

Of the four channels of complaint available under English law (an application to the Board of Visitors, the Parliamentary Commissioner for Administration or the Home Secretary and proceedings before the English courts) considered that only a petition to the Home Secretary, and possibly the courts, could provide an effective remedy as regards an alleged misapplication of directives but not as regards the compatibility of the directives with the Convention. It is to be noted that similar channels of complaint are available under Scottish law: applications to the prison Visiting Committees, the Parliamentary Commissioner for Administration or the Secretary of State for Scotland and the Scottish Courts. The Court continued in its *Silver and Others* v. *United Kingdom* (1983) 5 E.H.R.R. 347 para. 118 judgment as follows:

'The applicants made no allegation that the interferences with their correspondence were contrary to English law . . . Like the Commission, the Court has found that the majority of the measures complained of in the present proceedings were incompatible with the Convention . . . In most of the cases, the Government did not contest the Commission's findings. Neither did they maintain that the English courts could have found the measures to have been taken arbitrarily, in bad faith, for an improper motive or in an *ultra vires* manner.

In the Court's view, to the extent that the applicable norms, whether contained in the Rules or in the relevant Orders or Instructions, were incompatible with the Convention there could be no effective remedy as required by Art. 13 and consequently there has been a violation of that Art.

To the extent, however, that the said norms were compatible with Art. 8, the aggregate of the remedies available satisfied the requirements of Art. 13: . . . a petition to the Home Secretary was available to secure compliance with the directives issued by him and, as regards compliance with the Rules, the English courts had . . . supervisory jurisdiction. . . '

In the light of these considerations the Commission must proceed to examine whether the applicants' complaints concern a challenge to the validity of an order or instruction to the prison administration or a challenge to the method by which those directives had been executed. In the original application the applicants had complained of a breach of Art. 8 of the Convention regarding the restriction that prisoners are only allowed 12 visits per year. They also complained of the constant supervision of visits required whilst the first applicant was subject to the 'Special Escorted Leave' system. It seems that in respect of these complaints the applicants are challenging the compatibility of actual administrative directives with the Convention. Similarly complaints about discriminatory prison régimes and restrictions on the applicant's correspondence appear to challenge the administrative directives. In these instances complex issues, therefore, arise as to whether the applicants had an effective domestic remedy as required by Art. 13 of the Convention. Accordingly this aspect of the case should be declared admissible, no reason for declaring it inadmissible having been established. However, the applicants' complaints concerning the first applicant's lack of typing, sculpting and telephone facilities appear to have been matters within the prison governor's general, administrative discretion, subject to material resources, and which were not the subject of specific instructions. It would, therefore, appear that a petition to the Secretary of State for Scotland constituted, on an institutional level, an effective remedy for the purposes of Art. 13 of the Convention even if the result was actually negative in the first applicant's case. The Commission concludes, therefore, that this aspect of the case must be rejected as being manifestly ill-founded within the meaning of Art. 27(2) of the Convention.

Held: Art. 8 complaint of stopping of letter and Art. 13 in same respect and Art. 8 complaints regarding restrictions on correspondence and visits: admissible; remainder of application: inadmissible."

On 27th April 1988, the European Court of Human Rights *held* that interference with correspondence with Mr. McDougall was a violation of the Convention. On every other issue they found for the U.K. Government..

2. SEXUAL FREEDOM

Until 1980 homosexual conduct was a criminal offence, even if it took place in private. As late as the Sexual Offences (Scotland) Act 1976, Parliament provided that:

"Any male person who, in public or private, commits, or is party to the commission of, or procures or attempts to procure the commission by any male person of, any acts of gross indecency with another male person shall be liable on conviction on indictment to imprisonment for a term not exceeding two years or on summary conviction to imprisonment for a term not exceeding three months."

The position is now governed by the Criminal Justice (Scotland) Act 1980, which relaxes the offence, but falls far short of equality of treatment between homosexual and heterosexual conduct.

7. Criminal Justice (Scotland) Act 1980

"Homosexual offences

80.—(1) Subject to the provisions of this section, a homosexual act in private shall not be an offence provided that the parties consent thereto and have attained the age of 21 years.

(2) An act which would otherwise be treated for the purposes of this Act as being done in private shall not be so treated if done—

(a)   when more than two person take part or are present or

(b)   in a lavatory to which the public have, or are permitted to have access whether on payment or otherwise.

(3) a male person who is suffering from mental deficiency which is of such a nature or degree that he is incapable of living an independent life or of guarding himself against serious exploitation cannot in law give any consent which, by virtue of subsection (1) above, would prevent a homosexual act from being an offence; but a person shall not be convicted on account of the incapacity of such a male person to consent, of an offence consisting of such an act if he proves that he did not know and had no reason to suspect that male person to be suffering from such mental deficiency.

(4) . . .

(5) Subsection (1) above shall not prevent a homosexual act from being an offence under any provision of the Army Act 1955, the Air Force Act 1955 or the Naval Discipline Act 1957.

(6) In this section 'a homosexual act' means sodomy or an act of gross indecency by one male person with another male person.

(7) Subject to the provisions of subsection (3) above, it shall be an offence to commit or to be party to the commission of, or to procure or attempt to procure the commission of a homosexual act—

(a)   otherwise than in private;

(b)   without the consent of both parties to the act;

(c)   with a person under the age of 21 years; or

(d)   where the act is committed on board a United Kingdom merchant ship, wherever it may be, by a male person who is a member of the crew of that ship with another male person who is a member of the crew of that ship or any other United Kingdom merchant ship.

(8) In this section—

'member of the crew' in relation to a ship, includes the master of the ship;

'United Kingdom merchant ship' means a ship registered in the United Kingdom habitually used or used at the time of the alleged offence for the purposes of carrying passengers or goods for reward.

(9) It shall be an offence to procure or attempt to procure the commission of a homosexual act between two other male persons.

(10) From the commencement of this section a person who commits or is party to the commission of an offence under subsection (7) or subsection (9) above shall be liable on conviction on indictment to imprisonment for a term not exceeding two years or to a fine or to both and on summary conviction to imprisonment for a term not exceeding three months, or to a fine not exceeding the prescribed sum (within the meaning of section 289B of the 1975 Act).

(11) It shall be a defence to a charge of committing a homosexual act under

subsection (7) (*c*) above that the person so charged being under the age of 24 years who had not previously been charged with like offence, had reasonable cause to believe that the other person was of or above the age of 21 years.

(12) A person who knowingly lives wholly or in part on the earnings of another from male prostitution or who solicits or importunes any male person for the purpose of procuring the commission of a homosexual act within the meaning of subsection (6) above shall be liable:

> (*a*) on summary conviction to imprisonment for a term not exceeding six months; or
>
> (*b*) on conviction on indictment to imprisonment for a term not exceeding two years.

(13) Premises shall be treated for the purposes of sections 13 and 14 of the Sexual Offences (Scotland) Act 1976 as a brothel if people resort to it for the purpose of homosexual acts within the meaning of subsection (6) above in circumstances in which resort thereto for heterosexual practices would have led to its being treated as a brothel for the purposes of those sections.

(14) No proceedings for an offence to which this subsection applies shall be commenced after the expiration of 12 months from the date on which that offence was committed. This subsection applies to:

> (a) the offences mentioned in subsections (7) and (9) above; and
>
> (b) any offence under subsection (12) above which consists of soliciting or

importuning any male person for the purpose of procuring the commission of a homosexual act."

Subsection (4) was repealed by the Mental Health (Scotland) Act 1984, s. 107 of which now makes similar provision. It is an offence under that section for a man on the staff of, or who manages or carries on a hospital or nursing home to indulge in homosexual acts with a patient on the premises. It is likewise an offence for a man to have such relations with a man suffering from mental disorder who is in his guardianship or custody or care under the Act.

It will be seen that under section 80 a homosexual act (as defined by section 80(6)) will not be an offence provided that it is done in private; that it does not involve a person known to suffer "from mental disorder" (that is, "mental illness or mental handicap however caused or manifested"); that it is not an offence against military regulations; that it does not involve a person under the age of 21; and that it is not committed between the members of a crew on a merchant ship. It is far from clear from these restrictions whether section 80 is a sufficient compliance with the demands of Article 8 of the ECHR. It is to be pointed out, however, that the European court has accepted that certain limits on homosexual freedom may be justified. *Dudgeon* v. *United Kingdom* [1981] 3 E.H.R.R. 40 was concerned with whether the Offences against the Person Act 1861 and the Criminal Law Amendment Act 1885 violated Article 8. The Act in question provided that both buggery and gross indecency were offences in Northern Ireland. Although the Court held that the legislation did amount to a breach, in doing so it also said the there "can be no denial that some degree of regulation of male homosexual conduct, as indeed of other forms of sexual conduct, by means of the criminal law, can be justified as necessary in a democratic society'" as provided by Article 8(2). In particular the Court acknowledged "the legitimate necessity in a democratic society for some degree of control over homosexual conduct notably in order to provide safeguards against the exploitation and corruption of those who are specially vulnerable by reason, for example, of their youth." The law of Northern Ireland was subsequently changed to give effect to the decision. It is also to be noted that the military regulations which prohibit homosexual conduct have been upheld by the Commission: see (1984) 6 E.H.R.R. 354.

It is to be emphasised that section 80 gives only a minimal protection to homosexual conduct. It makes it an offence to commit an act of sodomy or "gross indecency" in public (including a public lavatory). It is to be pointed out, however, that other manifestations of affection between homosexual men may attract criminal penalties on other grounds. In *Masterson* v. *Holden* [1986] 3 All E.R. 39, for example, two men standing at a bus stop were cuddling and kissing each other on the lips. One then placed his hand on the bottom of the other and squeezed his buttocks. Two young women pedestrians took exception to this conduct, police officers approached, and the men were arrested and charged under the Metropolitan Police Act 1839 with using insulting behaviour, whereby a breach of the peace may be occasioned. They were convicted and their appeal was dismissed, with Glidewell L.J. saying that:

"Overt homosexual conduct in a public street . . . may well be considered by many persons to be objectionable, to be conduct which ought to be confined to a private place. The fact it is objectionable does not constitute an offence. But the display of such objectionable conduct in a public street may well be regarded by another person, particularly by a young woman, as conduct which insults her by suggesting that she is somebody who would find such conduct in public acceptable herself" (at p. 44).

Although the offence is not one known to Scots law, it is quite clear that its functional equivalent, breach of the peace, would be available to the police if they wished to prosecute conduct similar to that revealed by the facts in *Masterson* v. *Holden*.

3. STATE SURVEILLANCE

A third area where privacy issues have been raised in Britain relates to the practice of telephone tapping. This is something which gives rise to a dilemma in a democratic society, for on the one hand the interception of communications taking place between private citizens is a major invasion of privacy, yet on the other hand it is an important weapon available to the police and security services whose business it is to maintain law and order and protect national security (Diplock, (1981: 3)). Before 1985 the practice was not regulated by law but on the basis of administrative guidelines operated by the Home Office and the Scottish Office. According to official information, interceptions were made only on the authority of a warrant issued by the Home Secretary, the Secretary of State for Scotland or the Secretary of State for Northern Ireland. A warrant would be issued for the detection of serious crime or for gathering intelligence about subversive, terrorist and espionage activities which are capable of constituting a threat to the peace or safety of the realm. (Diplock (1981: 6)). In 1985 it was revealed (Cmnd. 9438 p.5) that the Foreign Secretary also issues warrants for the gathering of intelligence to support the Government's foreign and defence policies. In the years 1980-85 the Home Secretary issued 1920 warrants, the Foreign Secretary 553 and the Scottish Secretary 302 (Home Office (1985: Annex 2)).

The legality of these arrangements was challenged in *Malone* v. *Metropolitan Police Commissioner* [1979] Ch 344. During Malone's trial for handling stolen goods, the prosecution had said that the accused's telephone had been tapped with the authority of a warrant. Malone then unsuccessfully sought a declaration that the tapping was unlawful as a violation of his right to privacy, his right to property, and his right to confidentiality in conversation on the telephone. In the absence of any unlawful conduct on any of these grounds, the court was unable to grant a remedy, for although there was no express authorisation of the practice, nor was there any express prohibition, and in the view of Sir Robert Megarry, England is not a country where everything is forbidden unless it is expressly permitted. So, if the tapping of telephones could be carried out without breaking the law it did not require any statutory or common law powers to justify it. At this point, Malone made an application to Strasbourg (Sir Robert Megarry having held that the ECHR could not form the basis of an action in the domestic courts). The essence of the complaint was that the practice of telephone tapping in Britain violated the right to privacy safeguarded by Article 8 of the Convention. The main question for the Court was whether the practice could be justified under Article 8(2), on the ground that the practice was in accordance with law, and that it was necessary in a democratic society in the interests of national security, etc. In upholding the complaint, the Court held that the practice was not in accordance with law (despite Sir Robert Megarry's decision that it was not unlawful). In the view of the Court, the phrase "in accordance with law" means that the law "must be sufficiently clear in its terms to give citizens an adequate indication as to the circumstances in which and the conditions on which public authorities are empowered to resort to this secret and potentially dangerous interference with the right to respect for private life and correspondence." The British government lost simply because domestic law did not regulate the circumstances in which the power to intercept could be exercised with sufficient clarity. Having so decided the Court felt it unnecessary to decide whether the practice was unlawful on the additional ground that it exceeded what was necessary in a democratic society for the protection of national security. As a result, the government was compelled to legislate, though no guidance was given by the Court as to what should be the content of the legislation.

8. Interception of Communications Act 1985

"Prohibition on interception
1.—(1) Subject to the following provisions of this section, a person who intentionally intercepts a communication in the course of its transmission by post or by means of a public telecommunication system shall be guilty of an offence and liable—

(a) on summary conviction, to a fine not exceeding the statutory maximum;

(b) on conviction on indictment, to imprisonment for a term not exceeding two years or to a fine or to both.

(2) A person shall not be guilty of an offence under this section if—

(a) the communication is intercepted in obedience to a warrant issued by the Secretary of State under section 2 below; or

(b) that person has reasonable grounds for believing that the person to whom, or the person by whom, the communication is sent has consented to the interception.

(3) A person shall be not guilty of an offence under this section if—

(a) the communication is intercepted for purposes connected with the provision of postal or public telecommunication services or with the enforcement of any enactment relating to the use of those services; or

(b) the communication is being transmitted by wireless telegraphy and is intercepted, with the authority of the Secretary of State, for purposes connected with the issue of licences under the Wireless Telegraphy Act 1949 or the prevention or detection of interference with wireless telegraphy.

(4) No proceedings in respect of an offence under this section shall be instituted—

(a) In England and Wales, except by or with the consent of the Director of Public Prosecutions;

(b) in Northern Ireland, except by or with the consent of the Director of Public Prosecutions for Northern Ireland.

Warrants for interception
2.—(1) Subject to the provisions of this section and section 3 below, the Secretary of State may issue a warrant requiring the person to whom it is addressed to intercept, in the course of their transmission by post or by means of a public telecommunication system, such communications as are described in the warrant; and such a warrant may also require the person to whom it is addressed to disclose the intercepted material to such persons and in such manner as are described in the warrant.

(2) The Secretary of State shall not issue a warrant under this section unless he considers that the warrant is necessary—

(*a*)   in the interests of national security;

(*b*)   for the purpose of preventing or detecting serious crime; or

(*c*)   for the purpose of safeguarding the economic well-being of the United Kingdom.

(3) The matters to be taken into account in considering whether a warrant is necessary as mentioned in subsection (2) above shall include whether the information which it is considered necessary to acquire could reasonably be acquired by other means.

(4) A warrant shall not be considered necessary as mentioned in subsection (2) (*c*) above unless the information which it is considered necessary to acquire is information relating to the acts or intentions of persons outside the British Islands.

(5) References in the following provisions of this Act to a warrant are references to a warrant under this section.

Scope of warrants

3.—(1) subject to subsection (2) below, the interception required by a warrant shall be the interception of—

(*a*)   such communications as are sent to or from one or more addresses specified in the warrant, being an address or addresses likely to be used for the transmission of communications to or from—

(i) one particular person specified or described in the warrant; or

(ii) one particular set of premises so specified or described; and

(*b*)   such other communications (if any) as it is necessary to intercept in order to intercept communications falling within paragraph (*a*) above.

(2) Subsection (1) above shall not apply to a warrant if—

(*a*)   the interception required by the warrant is the interception, in the course of their transmission by means of a public telecommunications system, of—

(i) such external communications as are described in the warrant; and

(ii) such other communications (if any) as it is necessary to intercept in order to intercept such external communications as are so described; and

(*b*)   at the time when the warrant is issued, the Secretary of State issues a certificate certifying the descriptions of intercepted material the examination of which he considers necessary as mentioned in section 2(2) above.

(3) A certificate such as is mentioned in subsection (2) above shall not specify an address in the British Islands for the purpose of including communications sent to or from that address in the certified material unless—

(*a*)   the Secretary of State considers that the examination of communications sent to or from that address is necessary for the purpose of preventing or detecting acts of terrorism; and

(*b*)   communications sent to or from that address are included in the certified material only in so far as they are sent within such a period, not exceeding three months, as is specified in the certificate.

(4) A certificate such as is mentioned in subsection (2) above shall not be issued except under the hand of the Secretary of State.

(5) References in the following provisions of this Act to a certificate are references to a certificate such as is mentioned in subsection (2) above.

Issue and duration of warrants

4.—(1) A warrant shall not be issued except—

(*a*) under the hand of the Secretary of State; or

(*b*) in an urgent case where the Secretary of State has expressly authorised its issue and a statement of that fact is endorsed thereon, under the hand of an official of his department of or above the rank of Assistant Under Secretary of State.

(2) A warrant shall, unless renewed under subsection (3) below, cease to have effect at the end of the relevant period.

(3) The Secretary of State may, at any time before the end of the relevant period, renew a warrant if he considers that the warrant continues to be necessary as mentioned in section 2(2) above.

(4) If, at any time before the end of the relevant period, the Secretary of State considers that a warrant is no longer necessary as mentioned in section 2(2) above, he shall cancel the warrant.

(5) A warrant shall not be renewed except by an instrument under the hand of the Secretary of State.

(6) In this section 'the relevant period'

(*a*) in relation to a warrant which has not been renewed, means—

(i) if the warrant was issued under subsection (1)(*a*) above, the period of two months beginning with the day on which it was issued; and

(ii) if the warrant was issued under subsection (1)(*b*) above, the period ending with the second working day following that day;

(*b*) in relation to a warrant which was last renewed within the period mentioned in paragraph (*a*)(ii) above, means the period of two months beginning with the day on which it was so renewed; and

(*c*) in relation to a warrant which was last renewed at any other time, means—

(i) if the instrument by which it was so renewed is endorsed with a statement that the renewal is considered necessary as mentioned in section 2(2)(*a*) or (*c*) above, the period of six months beginning with the day on which it was so renewed; and

(ii) if that instrument is not so endorsed, the period of one month beginning with that day.

Modification of Warrants, etc.

5.—(1) The Secretary of State may at any time—

(*a*) modify a warrant by the insertion of any address which he considers likely to be used as mentioned in section 3(1)(*a*) above; or

(*b*) modify a certificate so as to include in the certified material any material the examination of which he considers necessary as mentioned in section 2(2) above

(2) If at any time the Secretary of State considers that any address specified in a warrant is no longer likely to be used as mentioned in section 3(1)(*a*) above, he shall modify the warrant by the deletion of that address.

(3) If at any time the Secretary of State considers that the material certified by a certificate includes any material the examination of which is no longer necessary as mentioned in section 2(2) above, he shall modify the certificate so as to exclude that material from the certified material.

(4) A warrant or certificate shall not be modified under subsection (1) above

except by an instrument under the hand of the Secretary of State or, in an urgent case—

(a) under the hand of a person holding office under the Crown who is expressly authorised by the warrant or certificate to modify it on the Secretary of State's behalf; or

(b) where the Secretary of State has expressly authorised the modification and a statement of that fact is endorsed on the instrument, under the hand of such an officer as is mentioned in section 4(1)(b) above.

(5) An instrument made under subsection (4)(a) or (b) above shall cease to have effect at the end of the fifth working day following the day on which it was issued.

Safeguards

6.—(1) Where the Secretary of State issues a warrant he shall, unless such arrangements have already been made, make such arrangements as he considers necessary for the purpose of securing—

(a) that the requirements of subsections (2) and (3) below are satisfied in relation to the intercepted material; and

(b) where a certificate is issued in relation to the warrant, that so much of the intercepted material as is not certified by the certificate is not read, looked at or listened to by any person.

(2) The requirements of this subsection are satisfied in relation to any intercepted material if each of the following, namely—

(a) the extent to which the material is disclosed;

(b) the number of persons to whom any of the material is disclosed;

(c) the extent to which the material is copied; and

(d) the number of copies made of any of the material,

is limited to the minimum that is necessary as mentioned in section 2(2) above.

(3) The requirements of this subsection are satisfied in relation to any intercepted material if each copy made of any of that material is destroyed as soon as its retention is no longer necessary as mentioned in section 2(2) above.

The Tribunal

7.—(1) There shall be a tribunal (in this Act referred to as 'the Tribunal') in relation to which the provisions of Schedule 1 to this Act shall apply.

(2) Any person who believes that communications sent to or by him have been intercepted in the course of their transmission by post or by means of a public telecommunication system may apply to the Tribunal for an investigation under this section.

(3) On such an application (other than one appearing to the Tribunal to be frivolous or vexatious), the Tribunal shall investigate—

(a) whether there is or has been a relevant warrant or a relevant certificate; and

(b) where there is or has been such a warrant or certificate, whether there has been any contravention of sections 2 to 5 above in relation to that warrant or certificate.

(4) If, on an investigation, the Tribunal, applying the principles applicable by a court on an application for judicial review, conclude that there has been a contravention of sections 2 to 5 above in relation to a relevant warrant or a relevant certificate, they shall—

(a) give notice to the applicant stating that conclusion;

(b) make a report of their findings to the Prime Minister; and

(c) if they think fit, make an order under subsection (5) below.

(5) An order under this subsection may do one or more of the following, namely—

(a) quash the relevant warrant or the relevant certificate;

(b) direct the destruction of copies of the intercepted material or, as the case may be, so much of it as is certified by the relevant certificate;

(c) direct the Secretary of State to pay to the applicant such sum by way of compensation as may be specified in the order.

(6) A notice given or report made under subsection (4) above shall state the effect of any order under subsection (5) above made in the case in question.

(7) If, on an investigation, the Tribunal come to any conclusion other than that mentioned in subsection (4) above, they shall give notice to the applicant stating that there has been no contravention of sections 2 to 5 above in relation to a relevant warrant or a relevant certificate.

(8) The decisions of the Tribunal (including any decisions as to their jurisdiction) shall not be subject to appeal or liable to be questioned in any court.

(9) For the purposes of this section—

(a) a warrant is a relevant warrant in relation to an applicant if—

(i) the applicant is specified or described in the warrant; or

(ii) an address used for the transmission of communications to or from a set of premises in the British Islands where the applicant resides or works is so specified;

(b) a certificate is a relevant certificate in relation to an applicant if and to the extent that an address used as mentioned in paragraph (a)(ii) above is specified in the certificate for the purpose of including communications sent to or from that address in the certified material.

The Commissioner

8.—(1) The Prime Minister shall appoint a person who holds or has held a high judicial office (in this section referred to as 'the Commissioner') to carry out the following functions, namely—

(a) to keep under review the carrying out by the Secretary of State of the functions conferred on him by sections 2 to 5 above and the adequacy of any arrangements made to the purposes of section 6 above; and

(b) to give to the Tribunal all such assistance as the Tribunal may require for the purpose of enabling them to carry out their functions under this Act.

(2) The Commissioner shall hold office in accordance with the terms of his appointment and there shall be paid to him out of money provided by Parliament such allowances as the Treasury may determine.

(3) It shall be the duty of every person holding office under the Crown or engaged in the business of the Post Office or in the running of a public telecommunication system to disclose or give to the Commissioner such documents or information as he may require for the purpose of enabling him to carry out his functions under this section.

(4) It shall be the duty of the Tribunal to send to the Commissioner a copy of every report made by them under section 7(4) above.

(5) If at any time it appears to the Commissioner—

(a)   that there has been a contravention of sections 2 to 5 above which has not been the subject of a report made by the Tribunal under section 7(4) above; or

(b)   that any arrangements made for the purposes of section 6 above have proved inadequate, he shall make a report to the Prime Minister with respect to that contravention or those arrangements.

(6) As soon as practicable after the end of each calendar year, the Commissioner shall make a report to the Prime Minister with respect to the carrying out of his functions under this section.

(7) The Prime Minister shall lay before each House of Parliament a copy of every annual report made by the Commissioner under subsection (6) above together with a statement as to whether any matter has been excluded from that copy in pursuance of subsection (8) below.

(8) If it appears to the Prime Minister, after consultation with the Commissioner, that the publication of any matter in an annual report would be prejudicial to national security, to the prevention or detection of serious crime or to the economic wellbeing of the United Kingdom, the Prime Minister may exclude that matter from the copy of the report as laid before each House of Parliament.

Exclusion of evidence

9.—(1) In any proceedings before any court or tribunal no evidence shall be adduced and no question in cross-examination shall be asked which (in either case) tends to suggest—

(a)   that an offence under section 1 above has been or is to be committed by any of the persons mentioned in subsection (2) below; or

(b)   that a warrant has been or is to be issued to any of those persons.

(2) The persons referred to in subsection(1) above are—

(a)   any person holding office under the Crown;

(b)   the Post Office and any person engaged in the business of the Post Office; and

(c)   any public telecommunications operator and any person engaged in the running of a public telecommunication system.

(3) Subsection (1) above does not apply—

(a)   in relation to proceedings for a relevant offence or proceedings before the Tribunal; or

(b)   where the evidence is adduced or the question in cross-examination is asked for the purpose of establishing the fairness or unfairness of a dismissal on grounds of an offence under section 1 above or of conduct from which such an offence might be inferred;

and paragraph (a) of that subsection does not apply where a person has been convicted of the offence under that section.

(4) In this section 'relevant offence' means—

(a)   an offence under section 1 above or under section 45 of the Telegraph Act 1863 section 20 of the Telegraph Act 1868, section 58 of the Post Office Act 1953 or section 45 of the 1984 Act;

(b)   an offence under section 1 or 2 of the Official Secrets Act 1911 relating to any sketch, plan, model, article, note, document or information which tends to suggest as mentioned in subsection (1) above;

(c) perjury committed in the course of proceedings for a relevant offence;

(d) attempting or conspiring to commit, or aiding, abetting, counselling or procuring the commission of, an offence falling within any of the preceding paragraphs; and

(e) contempt of court committed in the course of, or in relation to, proceedings for a relevant offence.

Interpretation

10.—(1) In this Act, unless the context otherwise requires—

'the 1984 Act, means the Telecommunications Act 1984;

'address' means any postal or telecommunication address;

'copy,' in relation to intercepted material, means any of the following, whether or not in document form—

(a) any copy, extract or summary of the material; and

(b) any record of the identities of the persons to or by whom the material was sent,

and cognate expressions shall be construed accordingly;

'external communication' means a communication sent or received outside the British Islands;

'high judicial office' has the same meaning as in the Appellate Jurisdiction Act 1876;

'intercepted material,' in relation to a warrant, means the communications intercepted in obedience to that warrant;

'person' includes any organisation and any association or combination of persons;

'public telecommunications operator' and 'public telecommunications system' have the same meanings as in the 1984 Act;

'public telecommunication service' means a telecommunication service provided by means of a public telecommunication system;

'statutory maximum' has the meaning given by section 74 of the Criminal Justice Act 1982;

'telecommunication service' has the same meaning as in the 1984 Act;

'the Tribunal' means the tribunal established under section 7 above;

'wireless telegraphy' has the same meaning as in the Wireless Telegraphy Act 1949;

'working day' means any day other than a Saturday, a Sunday, Christmas Day, Good Friday or a day which is a bank holiday under the Banking and Financial Dealings Act 1971 in any part of the United Kingdom.

(2) For the purposes of this Act a communication which is in the course of its transmission otherwise than by means of a public telecommunication system shall be deemed to be in the course of its transmission by the means of such a system if its mode of transmission identifies it as a communication which—

(a) is to be or has been transmitted by means of such a system; and

(b) has been sent from, or is to be sent to, a country or territory outside the British Islands.

(3) For the purposes of this Act conduct which constitutes or, if it took place in the United Kingdom, would constitute one or more offences shall be regarded as serious crime if, and only if—

(*a*)   it involves the use of violence, results in substantial financial gain or is conduct by a large number of persons in pursuit of a common purpose; or

(*b*)   the offence or one of the offences is an offence for which a person who has attained the age of twenty-one and has no previous convictions could reasonably be expected to be sentenced to imprisonment for a term of three years or more.

*   *   *

SCHEDULE 1

THE TRIBUNAL

Constitution of Tribunal

1.—(1) The Tribunal shall consist of five members each of whom shall be a barrister, advocate or solicitor of not less than 10 years' standing.

(2) The members of the Tribunal shall be such persons as Her Majesty may by Letters Patent appoint and shall, subject to the following sub-paragraphs, hold office during good behaviour.

(3) A member of the Tribunal shall vacate office at the end of the period of five years beginning with the day of his appointment but shall be eligible for reappointment.

(4) A member of the Tribunal may be relieved of office by Her Majesty at his own request.

(5) A member of the Tribunal may be removed from office by Her Majesty on an Address presented to Her by both Houses of Parliament.

President and Vice-President

2.—(1) Her Majesty may by Letters Patent appoint as President or Vice-President of the Tribunal a person who is, or by virtue of those Letters will be, a member of the Tribunal.

(2) If at any time the President of the Tribunal is temporarily unable to carry out the functions of the President under this Schedule, the Vice-President shall carry out those functions.

(3) A person shall cease to be President or Vice-President of the Tribunal if he ceases to be a member of the Tribunal.

Procedure of Tribunal

3. The functions of the Tribunal in relation to any application made to them shall be capable of being carried out, in any place in the United Kingdom, by any two or more members of the Tribunal designated for the purpose by their President; and different members of the Tribunal may carry out functions in relation to different applications at the same time.

4.—(1) It shall be the duty of every person holding office under the Crown or engaged in the business of the Post Office or in the running of a public telecommunications system to disclose or give to the Tribunal such documents or information as they may require for the purpose of enabling them to carry out their functions under this Act.

(2) Subject to paragraph 6(2) below, the Tribunal shall carry out their functions under this Act (except their functions in relation to reports under section 7(4) of this Act) in such a way as to secure that no document or information which is disclosed or given to the Tribunal is disclosed or given to any person (including an applicant to the Tribunal or a person holding office under the Crown) without the consent of the person who disclosed or gave it to the Tribunal; and accordingly the Tribunal shall not, except in reports under section 7(4) of this Act, give reasons for any decision made by them.

(3) Subject to sub-paragraph (2) above, the Tribunal may determine their own procedure."

CHAPTER 5

[Note: In this chapter the abbreviations R.R.A., S.D.A., E.O.C. and C.R.E. stand respectively for Race Relations Act, Sex Discrimination Act, Equal Opportunities Commission and Commission for Racial Equality.]

THE RIGHT TO EQUAL TREATMENT

In this chapter we examine the law relating to discrimination. In British law, comprehensive protection is extended only to discrimination on the grounds of sex and race, though in many other jurisdictions anti-discrimination laws apply to such matters as religion, age and social origin. The main concern of policy makers in this country has been with racial discrimination, and the demand for legislation to combat it arose partly because of the inability of the common law to adapt to the needs of a multi-racial society. It was lawful to discriminate on racial grounds on such matters as the offer of employment, the provision of housing, and the provision of a host of other goods, services and facilities. Where the common law did provide some scope for development, the judges failed to respond. For example, innkeepers are under a duty not to refuse unreasonably to accept any traveller, yet in *Rothfield* v. *North British Railway Company,* 1920 2 S.L.T. 269, the Inner House refused to provide the pursuer with a remedy after he had been excluded from a famous Edinburgh hotel on what appeared to be overtly racist grounds.

In the 1960s racial discrimination was commonplace and the absence of any controls did little to resolve growing racial tension, particularly in English cities. Yet Parliament's initial response was feeble and half-hearted. Following a number of unsuccessful Private Member's Bills stretching back to the early 1950s and racial disturbances in London in the late 1950s, the new Labour government implemented an election pledge to deal with racial discrimination by enacting the Race Relations Act 1965. But this only applied to discrimination in places of public resort, such as hotels, theatres and transport, and could only be enforced in Scotland by the Lord Advocate who would act on a reference made by the Race Relations Board following a complaint to the Board by an aggrieved individual. Such a measure was wholly inadequate to deal with the problem of racism, and continuing pressure, both inside and outside Parliament, and a growing awareness of a deep-rooted and extensive pattern of racial discrimination in many fields, led to the repeal of the 1965 Act and its replacement with the more comprehensive Race Relations Act 1968.

The 1968 Act applied to racial discrimination in the provision of goods, services and facilities, in the employment field, and in the disposal of housing accommodation. However, the Act continued the pattern set in 1965 by denying the individual any direct access to the courts or tribunals. Enforcement was by means of a complaint by an individual to the Race Relations Board, which if it was unable to arrange a settlement, could bring proceedings for a remedy by way of declarator, interdict or damages. This pattern of administrative enforcement only was not departed from until the third and final stage of the development of British discrimination law, the Race Relations Act 1976. This Act repealed the 1968 Act and introduced several important changes and improvements to the law. One was the extension of the meaning of discrimination, which had hitherto applied only to direct discrimination (*i.e.* to less favourable treatment), to cover indirect discrimination (*i.e.* conduct fair in form but discriminatory in practice). A second change was the introduction of individual enforcement machinery. Although administrative enforcement has been retained, individuals may now take action under the statute either in industrial tribunals or the sheriff court, whichever is appropriate in the circumstances.

By the time this third stage in the development of race relations legislation had been reached, Parliament had already taken steps to deal with the problem of sex discrimination. Certain forms of sex discrimination had been declared unlawful as early as 1919 by the Sex Disqualification (Removal) Act. However, this was limited to entry to offices, professions and vocations and was in any event narrowly construed by the courts (see Creighton (1979): 67-76). In 1970 these measures were added to by the Equal Pay Act which provides for the equal treatment of men and women in the application of terms and conditions of employment. In 1975, the concept of equal treatment was extended to a wide range of other fields by the Sex Discrimination Act, which proved to be the model for the subsequent Race Relations Act. The enactment of these measures to deal with sex discrimination met with remarkably little resistance. Although the direct social consequences of sex discrimination are perhaps not quite so dramatic as those of racism, once legislation against racial discrimination was introduced, the case for its extension to sex discrimination, in the face of mounting pressure for reform, appeared unanswerable. It is also true that such legislation was necessary in order to meet this country's international obligations, and in particular the 1970 and 1975 Acts anticipated requirements arising under Article 119 of the Treaty of Rome and EEC Directive 76/207.

Advances continue to be made in discrimination law, though because this arises as a result of Britain's membership of the EEC, the advances tend to be mainly in the area of sex discrimination. EEC law continues to have an impact in two ways. First, domestic legislation has had to be amended to bring it up to Community standards. An example of this is the introduction of the Equal Pay (Amendment) Regulations 1983 (S.I. 1983 No. 1794), giving women the right to equal pay not only with men doing like work but also with those engaged on work of equal value. Another example is the Sex Discrimination Act 1986 which introduced a number of changes following decisions of the European Court of Justice. The most significant was the provision introducing the same retirement age for men and women for the purposes of unfair dismissal. The second way in which EEC law has had an impact relates to the fact that the domestic courts are now entertaining actions directly to enforce Community standards. This may arise where existing domestic law does not confer rights as extensive as those provided for by Community law, so that it becomes necessary to rely on the latter rather than the former, or where a public body is relying on the authority of a statute or regulation which conflicts with or is inconsistent with Community law, as in *R.* v. *Secretary of State for Education, ex p. Schaffter* [1987] I.R.L.R. 53.

1. THE MEANING OF DISCRIMINATION

1. The Sex Discrimination Act 1975

"Sex discrimination against women
    1.—(1) A person discriminates against a woman in any circumstances relevant for the purposes of any provision of this Act if—
    (*a*) on the ground of her sex he treats her less favourably than he treats or would treat a man, or
    (*b*) he applies to her a requirement or condition which he applies or would apply equally to a man but—
        (i) which is such that the proportion of women who can comply with it is considerably smaller than the proportion of men who can comply with it, and
        (ii) which he cannot show to be justifiable irrespective of the sex of the person to whom it is applied, and
        (iii) which is to her detriment because she cannot comply with it.
    (2) If a person treats or would treat a man differently according to the man's marital status, his treatment of a woman is for the purposes of subsection (1)(a) to be compared to his treatment of a man having the like marital status.

Sex discrimination against men
    2.—(1) Section 1, and the provisions of Parts II and III relating to sex discrimination against women, are to be read as applying equally to the treatment of men, and for that purpose shall have effect with such modifications as are requisite.
    (2) In the application of subsection (1) no account shall be taken of special treatment afforded to women in connection with pregnancy or childbirth.

Discrimination against married persons in employment field
    3.—(1) A person discriminates against a married person of either sex in any

circumstances relevant for the purposes of any provision of Part II if—

(a)   on the ground of his or her marital status he treats that person less favourably than he treats or would treat an unmarried person of the same sex, or

(b)   he applies to that person a requirement or condition which he applies or would apply equally to an unmarried person but—

(i) which is such that the proportion of married persons who can comply with it is considerably smaller than the proportion of unmarried persons of the same sex who can comply with it, and

(ii) which he cannot show to be justifiable irrespective of the marital status of the person to whom it is applied, and

(iii) which is to that person's detriment because he cannot comply with it.

(2) For the purposes of subsection (1), a provision of Part II framed with references to discrimination against women shall be treated as applying equally to the treatment of men, and for that purpose shall have effect with such modifications as are requisite."

2.   The Race Relations Act 1976

"Racial discrimination

1.—(1) A person discriminates against another in any circumstances relevant for the purposes of any provision of this Act if—

(a)   on racial grounds he treats that other less favourably than he treats or would treat other persons; or

(b)   he applies to that other a requirement or condition which he applies or would apply equally to persons not of the same racial group as that other but—

(i) which is such that the proportion of persons of the same racial group as that other who can comply with it is considerably smaller than the proportion of persons not of that racial group who can comply with it; and

(ii) which he cannot show to be justifiable irrespective of the colour, race, nationality or ethnic or national origins of the person to whom it is applied; and

(iii) which is to the detriment of that other because he cannot comply with it.

(2) It is hereby declared that, for the purposes of this Act, segregating a person from other persons on racial grounds is treating him less favourably than they are treated.

Meaning of 'racial grounds,' 'racial group,' etc.

3.—(1) In this Act, unless the context otherwise requires—

'racial grounds' means any of the following grounds, namely colour, race, nationality or ethnic or national origins;

'racial group' means a group of persons defined by reference to colour, race, nationality or ethnic or national origins, and references to a person's racial group refer to any racial group into which he falls.

(2) The fact that a racial group comprises two or more distinct racial groups does

not prevent it from constituting a particular racial group for the purposes of this Act.

(3) In this Act—

(a) references to discrimination refer to any discrimination falling within section 1 or 2; and

(b) references to racial discrimination refer to any discrimination falling within section 1,

and related expressions shall be construed accordingly.

(4) A comparison of the case of a person of a particular racial group with that of a person not of that group under section 1(1) must be such that the relevant circumstances in the one case are the same, or not materially different, in the other."

Section 2 of the R.R.A. makes it unlawful to victimise (that is, to treat less favourably) anyone who has brought proceedings under the Act or has otherwise supported such proceedings or drawn attention to an alleged act of discrimination. By section 4, the S.D.A. applies a similar protection for people involved in proceedings under that Act and the Equal Pay Act 1970. In practice, however, victimisation is very difficult to establish. See *Kirby* v. *Manpower Services Commission* [1980] 1 W.L.R. 725, and *Cornelius* v. *University College of Swansea* [1987] I.R.L.R. 142.

Sections 1(1)(a) of both of these Acts regulate direct discrimination while sections 1(1)(b) regulate indirect discrimination. The latter concept was unknown to the Race Relations Acts 1965 and 1968, and its purpose is explained by the Home Office (1975) in the following terms:

"One important weakness in the existing legislation is the narrowness of the definition of unlawful discrimination upon which it is based: the less favourable treatment of one person than of another on the ground of colour, race or ethnic or national origins. What matters under this definition is the reason or reasons for the discrimination. An unlawful motive may be inferred from the fact that a black person is treated less favourably than a white person; but, in the absence of discriminatory motive, the present law does not cover practices and procedures which have a discriminatory effect upon members of a racial minority and which are not justifiable. While it is right that motive should be relevant in determining whether an alleged discriminator should compensate his victim, it is insufficient for the law to deal only with overt discrimination. It should also prohibit practices which are fair in a formal sense but discriminatory in their operation and effect. For example, employers and trade unions should be required to dismantle unjustifiable barriers to employment opportunities when the barriers operate to discriminate against racial minorities. Such barriers are against the public interest irrespective of motive and whether or not they operate against an identifiable individual victim."

The concept of indirect discrimination was modelled on judicial developments in the United States, particularly the landmark Supreme Court decision in *Griggs* v. *Duke Power Co.*, 401 U.S. 424 (1971), where it was said:

"The Act [*sc.* Federal Civil Rights Act 1964] proscribes not only overt discrimination but also practices that are fair in form but discriminatory in operation. The touchstone is business necessity. If an employment practice which operates to exclude Negroes cannot be shown to be related to job performance, the practice is prohibited.'

This regulation of indirect discrimination was taken at the initiative of the Supreme Court; no such concept was embraced in the legislation. Although it might have been possible for British courts to have taken a similar initiative on the basis of section 1(1)(*a*), this could not be guaranteed, and the inclusion of section 1(1)(*b*) was a wise precaution against judicial conservatism.

Positive discrimination is deliberately impermissible (see Home Office (1975: para 57)). To discriminate in favour of one racial group would be to discriminate against another, and this would be unlawful in terms of section 1. Nevertheless, the R.R.A. does allow for some positive action, it being provided by section 35 that: "Nothing in Parts II to IV shall render unlawful any act done in affording persons of a particular racial group access to facilities or services to meet the special needs of persons of that group in regard to their education, training or welfare, or any ancillary benefits." See also sections 36 and 38, and S.D.A., sections 47 and 48. For positive discrimination in the United States, see *University of California Regents* v. *Bakke,* 438 U.S. 265 (1978). See further, Edwards (1987), Lustgarten (1980: 14-25), and Creighton (1979: 158-159). On the meaning of discrimination in the R.R.A. see Lustgarten (1978). On segregation (R.R.A., s. 1(2)), see *Pel Ltd* v. *Modgill* [1980] I.R.L.R. 142.

A. THE SCOPE OF THE LEGISLATION

3. Mandla v. Dowell-Lee
[1983] 2 A.C. 548

A parent wanted to enrol his son in a private school in Birmingham, called Park Grove School. He was told by the headmaster that the boy (a Sikh) could be admitted only if he wore the school uniform and that the wearing of a turban would not be permitted. The father (also a Sikh) then complained to the Commission for Racial Equality, which took up the case. The county court, before which the case was heard, dismissed the complaint on the ground that Sikhs were not a racial group and that the R.R.A. therefore did not apply. The Court of Appeal agreed, but the House of Lords reversed.

LORD FRASER OF TULLYBELTON: "It is not suggested that Sikhs are a group defined by reference to colour, race, nationality or *national* origins. In none of these respects are they distinguishable from many other groups, especially those living, like most Sikhs, in the Punjab. The argument turns entirely upon whether they are a group defined by '*ethnic* origins.' It is therefore necessary to ascertain the sense in which the word 'ethnic' is used in the Act of 1976. We were referred to various dictionary definitions. The *Oxford English Dictionary* (1897 ed.) gives two meanings of 'ethnic' The first is 'Pertaining to nations not Christian or Jewish, gentile, heathen, pagan.' That clearly cannot be its meaning in the Act of 1976, because it is inconceivable that Parliament would have legislated against racial discrimination intending that the protection should not apply either to Christians or (above all) to Jews. Neither party contended that that was the relevant meaning for the present purpose. The second meaning given in the *Oxford English Dictionary* (1897 ed.) was 'Pertaining to race; peculiar to a race or nation; ethnological.' A slightly shorter form of that meaning (omitting 'peculiar to a race or nation') was given by the *Concise Oxford Dictionary* in 1934 and was expressly accepted by Lord Denning M.R. as the correct meaning for the present purpose. Oliver and Kerr L.JJ. also accepted that meaning as being substantially correct, and Oliver L.J. [1983] Q.B. 1, H said that the word 'ethnic' in its popular meaning involved 'essentially a racial concept—the concept of something with which the members of the group are born; some fixed or inherited characteristic.' The respondent, who appeared on his own behalf, submitted that that was the relevant meaning of 'ethnic' in the Act of 1976, and that it did not apply to Sikhs because they were essentially a religious group, and they shared their racial characteristics with other religious groups, including Hindus and Muslims, living in the Punjab.

My Lords, I recognise that 'ethnic' conveys a flavour of race but it cannot, in my opinion, have been used in the Act of 1976 in a strictly racial or biological sense. For one thing, it would be absurd to suppose that Parliament can have intended that membership of a particular racial group should depend upon scientific proof that a person possessed the relevant distinctive biological characteristics (assuming that such characteristics exist). The practical difficulties of such proof would be prohibitive, and it is clear that Parliament must have used the word in some more popular sense. For another thing, the briefest glance at the evidence in this case is enough to show that, within the human race, there are very few, if any, distinctions which are scientifically recognised as racial. I respectfully agree with the view of Lord Simon of Glaisdale in *Ealing London Borough Council* v. *Race Relations Board* [1972] A.C. 342, 362, referring to the long title of the Race Relations Act 1968 (which was in terms identical with part of the long title of the Act of 1976) when he said: 'Moreover, "racial" is not a term of art, either legal or, I surmise, scientific. I apprehend that anthropologists would dispute how far the word "race" is biologically at all relevant to the species amusingly called homo sapiens.' A few lines lower down, after quoting part of section 1(1) of the Act, the noble and learned Lord said: 'This is rubbery and elusive language—understandably when the draftsman is dealing with so unprecise a concept as "race" in its popular sense and endeavouring to leave no loophole for evasion.'

I turn, therefore, to the third and wider meaning which is given in the *Supplement to the Oxford English Dictionary* (1972). It is as follows: 'pertaining to or having common racial, cultural, religious, or linguistic characteristics, esp. designating a racial or other group within a larger system; ...' Mr Irvine, for the appellants, while not accepting the third (1972) meaning as directly applicable for the present purpose, relied on it to this extent, that it introduces a reference to cultural and other characteristics, and is not limited to racial characteristics. The 1972 meaning is, in my opinion, too loose and vague to be accepted as it stands. It is capable of being read as implying that any one of the adjectives, 'racial, cultural, religious, *or* linguistic' would be enough to constitute an ethnic group. That cannot be the sense in which 'ethnic' is used in the Act of 1976, as that Act is not concerned at all with discrimination on religious grounds. Similarly, it cannot have ben used to mean simply any 'racial *or other* group.' If that were the meaning of 'ethnic,' it would add nothing to the word group, and would lead to a result which would be unnacceptably wide. But in seeking for the true meaning of 'ethnic,' in the statute, we are not tied to the precise definition in any dictionary. The value of the 1972 definition is, in my view, that it shows that ethnic has come to be commonly used in a sense appreciably wider than the strictly racial or biological. That appears to me to be consistent with the ordinary experience of those who read newspapers at the present day. In my opinion, the word 'ethnic' still retains a racial flavour but it is used nowadays in an extended sense to include other characteristics which may be commonly thought of as being associated with common racial origin.

For a group to constitute an ethnic group in the sense of the Act of 1976, it must, in my opinion, regard itself, and be regarded by others, as a distinct community by virtue of certain characteristics. Some of these characteristics are essential; others are not essential but one or more of them will commonly be found and will help to distinguish the group from the surrounding community. The conditions which appear to me to be essential are these: (1) a long shared history, of which the group is conscious as distinguishing it from other groups, and the memory of which it keeps alive; (2) a cultural tradition of its own, including family and social customs and manners, often but not necessarily associated with religious observance. In addition to those two essential characteristics the following characteristics are, in my opinion, relevant; (3) either a common geographical origin, or descent from a small number of common ancestors; (4) a common language, not necessarily peculiar to the group; (5) a common literature peculiar to the group; (6) a common religion different from that of neighbouring groups or from the general community surrounding it; (7) being a minority or being an oppressed or a dominant group within a larger community, for example a conquered people (say, the inhabitants of England shortly after the Norman conquest) and their conquerors might both be ethnic groups.

A group defined by reference to enough of these characteristics would be capable of including converts, for example, persons who marry into the group, and of excluding apostates. Provided a person who joins the group feels himself or herself to be a member of it, and is accepted by other members, then he is, for the purposes of the Act, a member. That appears to be consistent with the words at the end of section 3(1): 'references to a person's racial group refer to any racial group into which he falls.' In my opinion, it is possible for a person to fall into a particular racial group either by birth or by adherence, and it makes no difference, so far as the Act of 1976 is concerned, by which route he finds his way into the group. This view does not involve creating any inconsistency between direct discrimination under paragraph (*a*) and indirect discrimination under paragraph (*b*). A person may treat another relatively unfavourably 'on racial grounds' because he regards that other as being of a particular race, or belonging to a particular racial group, even if his belief is, from a scientific point of view, completely erroneous.

Finally on this part of the argument, I think it is proper to mention that the word 'ethnic' is of Greek origin, being derived from the Greek word 'ethnos,' the basic meaning of which appears to have been simply 'a group' not limited by reference to racial or any other distinguishing characteristics: see *Liddell and Scott's Greek English Lexicon,* 8th ed. (Oxford 1897). I do not suggest that the meaning of the English word in a modern statute ought to be governed by the meaning of the Greek word from which it is derived, but the fact that the meaning of the latter was wide avoids one possible limitation on the meaning of the English word.

My Lords, I have attempted so far to explain the reasons why, in my opinion, the word 'ethnic' in the Act of 1976 should be construed relatively widely, in what was referred to by Mr Irvine as a broad, cultural/historic sense. The conclusion at which I have arrived by construction of the Act itself is greatly strengthened by consideration of the decision of the Court of Appeal in New Zealand (Richmond P., Woodhouse and Richardson JJ.) in *King-Ansell* v. *Police* [1979] 2 N.Z.L.R. 531. That case was discovered by the industry of the appellants' counsel, but unfortunately not until after the Court of Appeal in England had decided the case now under appeal. If it had been before the Court of Appeal it might well have affected their decision. In that case the appellant had been convicted by a magistrate of an offence under the New Zealand Race Relations Act 1971, the offence consisting of publishing a pamphlet with intent to incite ill-will against Jews, 'on the ground of their ethnic origins.' The question of law arising on the appeal concerned the meaning to be given to the words 'ethnic . . . origins of that group of persons' in section 25(1) of the Act. The decision of the Court of Appeal was that Jews in New Zealand did form a group with common ethnic origins within the meaning of the Act. The structure of the New Zealand Act differs considerably from that of the Act of 1976, but the offence created by section 25 of the New Zealand Act (*viz.* inciting ill-will against any group of persons on the ground of their 'colour, race, or ethnic or national origins') raises the same question of construction as the present appeal, in a context which is identical except that the New Zealand Act does not mention 'nationality,' and the Act of 1976 does. The reasoning of all members of the New Zealand court was substantially similar, and it can, I think, be sufficiently indicated by quoting the following short passages. The first is from the judgment of Woodhouse J. at p. 538 where, after referring to the meaning given by the *Supplement to the Oxford English Dictionary* (1972), which I have already quoted, he says:

'The distinguishing features of an ethnic group or of the ethnic origins of a group would usually depend upon a combination, present together, of characteristics of the kind indicated in the *Supplement.* In any case it would be a mistake to regard this or any other dictionary meaning as though it had to be imported word for word into a statutory definition and construed accordingly. However, subject to those qualifications, I think that for purposes of construing the expression "ethnic origins" the 1972 *Supplement* is a helpful guide and I accept it.'

Richardson J. said, at p.542: 'The real test is whether the individuals or the group regard themselves and are regarded by others in the community as having a particular historical identity in terms of their colour or their racial, national or ethnic origins. That must be based on a belief shared by members of the group.' And the same learned judge said, at p. 543: 'a group is identifiable in terms of its ethnic origins if it is a segment of the population distinguished from others by a sufficient combination of shared customs, beliefs, traditions and characteristics derived from a common or presumed common past, even if not drawn from what in biological terms is a common racial stock. It is that combination which gives them an historically determined social identity in their own eyes and in the eyes of those outside the group. They have a distinct social identity based not simply on group cohesion and solidarity but also on their belief as to their historical antecedents.'

My Lords, that last passage sums up in a way upon which I could not hope to improve the views which I have been endeavouring to express. It is important that courts in English-speaking countries should, if possible construe the words which we are considering in the same way where they occur in the same context, and I am happy to say that I find no difficulty at all in agreeing with the construction favoured by the New Zealand Court of Appeal.

There is only one respect in which that decision rests upon a basis that is not fully applicable to the instant appeal. That appears from the long title of the New Zealand Act which is as follows: 'An Act to affirm and promote racial equality in New Zealand and to implement the International Convention on the Elimination of All Forms of Racial Discrimination.' Neither the Act of 1976 nor its predecessors in the United Kingdom, the Race Relations Acts 1965 and 1968, refer to the International Convention on the Elimination of All Forms of Racial Discrimination (1969) (Cmnd. 4108). The Convention was adopted on March 7, 1966, and was signed by the United Kingdom on October 11, 1966, subject to reservations which are not now material. It was not ratified by the United Kingdom until March 7, 1969. Under the Convention the States Parties undertook, inter alia, to prohibit racial discrimination in all its forms, and to guarantee the rights of everyone 'without distinction as to race, colour, or national or ethnic origin' of equality before the law, notably in certain rights which were specified including education (article 5(e)(v)). The words which I have quoted are very close to the words found in the Act of 1976 and in its predecessors in this country, and they are certainly quite consistent with these United Kingdom Acts having been passed in implementation of the obligation imposed by the Convention. But it is unnecessary to rely in this case upon any special rules of construction applicable to legislation which gives effect to international conventions, because for the reasons already explained, a strict or legalistic construction of the words would not, in any event, be appropriate.

The respondent admitted, rightly in my opinion, that, if the proper construction of the word 'ethnic' in section 3 of the Act of 1976 is a wide one, on lines such as I have suggested, the Sikhs would qualify as a group defined by ethnic origins for the purposes of the Act. It is, therefore, unnecessary to consider in any detail the relevant characteristics of the Sikhs. They were originally a religious community founded about the end of the 15th century in the Punjab by Guru Nanak, who was born in 1469. But the community is no longer purely religious in character. Their present position is summarised sufficiently for present purposes in the opinion of the learned judge in the county court in the following passage:

'The evidence in my judgment shows that Sikhs are a distinctive and self-conscious community. They have a history going back to the 15th century. They have a written language which a small proportion of Sikhs can read but which can be read by a much higher proportion of Sikhs than of Hindus. They were at one time politically supreme in the Punjab.'

The result is, in my opinion, that Sikhs are a group defined by a reference to ethnic origins for the purpose of the Act of 1976, although they are not biologically distinguishable from the other peoples living in the Punjab. That is true whether one is considering the position before the partition of 1947, when the Sikhs lived mainly in that part of the Punjab which is now Pakistan, or after 1947, since when most of them have moved into India."

Lord Templeman delivered a concurring speech. Lords Edmund-Davies, Roskill and Brandon concurred with both speeches.

B. DIRECT DISCRIMINATION

The application of the concept of direct discrimination got off to a bad start with the decision of the Court of Appeal in *Peake* v. *Automotive Products Ltd.* [1978] Q.B. 233 where the respondent company operated a rule whereby women were permitted to leave work five minutes before male employees. The rule allegedly existed for safety reasons, to protect women from a crush if employees left together. The E.A.T. held that this practice unlawfully discriminated against men. The decision was overturned by the Court of Appeal. Lord Denning took the view that: "arrangements which are made in the interests of safety or in the interests of good administration are not infringements of the law even though they may be more favourable to women than to men; or conversely more favourable to men than to women." He continued by holding that if this was wrong, the discrimination was perfectly harmless and he would apply the maxim *De minimis non curat lex.* For his part, Shaw L.J. said:

"The Sex Discrimination Act 1975 was not, in my judgment, designed to provide a basis for capricious and empty complaints of differentiation between the sexes. Nor was it intended to operate as a statutory abolition of every instinct of chivalry and consideration on the part of men for the opposite sex. The phrase used in all the prohibitions imposed by the Act is 'discrimination against' one sex or the other. This, to my mind, involves an element of something which is inherently adverse or hostile to the interests of the persons of the sex which is said to be discriminated against.

No doubt differentiation which appears to confer some benefit on one sex may by implication be said to impose a detriment on the opposite sex. In the present case the union unreservedly approved the arrangements which were made in the interests of safety and which have existed for 30 years. The union thought them desirable and sensible and not in the least discriminatory, and I entirely agree."

4. Ministry of Defence v. Jeremiah
[1980] Q.B. 87

Men who volunteered for overtime at an ordnance factory in Wales were required to work in a colour bursting shop for some of the time. Women who volunteered for overtime were not required to do such work, because it was dusty and dirty and was not regarded as women's work. In upholding the E.A.T., the Court of Appeal held that the practice was unlawful. One of the questions which arose in the case was whether the employer's practice discriminated against men within terms of section 1(1)(a) of the S.D.A.

LORD DENNING M.R.: "Next, the Ministry relies on *Peake* v. *Automotive Products Ltd.* . . . Turning to that case again, I think we were under a disadvantage, because Mr Peake appeared in person: and we were not referred to some of the relevant parts of the statute. There were two grounds for the decision. Now on reconsideration, I think the only sound ground was that the discrimination was de minimis. Mr Lester told us that, on a petition to the Appeal Committee of the House of Lords, they refused leave to appeal for that very reason. They thought that the decision was correct on the de minimis ground. In these circumstances, the other ground (about chivalry and administrative practice) should no longer be relied upon."

BRANDON L.J.: "The third main ground of appeal was that the case was governed by the principle said to have been laid down by this court in *Peake* v. *Automotive Products Ltd*. In that case it was held that a difference between the treatment of men and women with regard to time of ceasing work (a difference which was of five minutes only) did not constitute unlawful discrimination against the men. There were two grounds for the decision. The first ground was that arrangements made in the interest of safety and good administration did not constitute unlawful discrimination even if they were more favourable to workers of one sex than to those of the other. The second ground was that the difference of treatment was in any case de minimis.

It was argued for the applicant that, in so far as that case was decided on the first ground as distinct from the second, it was decided per incuriam and should not be followed. I do not find it necessary to express any opinion one way or the other on this contention, because it seems to me that, even assuming that the first ground of decision was correct and is binding on this court, it has no application to the facts of this case. There is no finding by the industrial tribunal that the difference in treatment here in question arose out of arrangements made in the interests of safety or good administration; nor, so far as I can see, was there any evidence on which such a finding could possibly have been made.

The fourth main ground of appeal was that there was no evidence that the employers, in treating men and woman examiners differently as regards working in the colour bursting shops, were acting in any way inherently adverse or hostile to the interests of the men. This ground is based on the language used by Shaw L.J., in his judgement in *Peake* v. *Automotive Products Ltd*. With respect to Shaw L. J. who was the only member of the court to express himself in that way, I am not persuaded that it is right to interpret the concept of unlawful discrimination under the Act of 1975 in quite as forceful a way as he did in that judgment. I think, as I indicated earlier, that the sole question to be answered in this case was whether the men examiners were put under a disadvantage by comparison with the women examiners. That was a question of fact; it was answered by the industrial tribunal in the affirmative; and I can see nothing wrong in law with that answer.

For the reasons which I have given, subject to a variation in the terms of the declaration made which may have to be considered further, I would dismiss the appeal."

BRIGHTMAN L.J.: "I do not say that the mere deprivation of choice for one sex, or some other differentiation in their treatment, is necessarily unlawful discrimination. The deprivation of choice, or differentiation, in the sort of case we are considering, must be associated with a detriment. It is possible to imagine a case where one sex has a choice but the other does not, yet there is nevertheless no detriment to the latter sex, that is to say, no unlawful discrimination. Railway carriages used to have compartments marked 'Ladies Only.' A lady had a choice of travelling in an ordinary compartment or in a 'Ladies Only' compartment. A man had no such choice. In such a case a court would conclude that there was no sensible detriment to the men flowing from the absence of choice. A similar case might arise on factory premises where there might be two canteens with equal amenities, one canteen for men and women and the other for women only. A court would conclude, other things being equal, that there was no unlawful discrimination, though the ladies had a choice where they ate, and the men did not."

5.   Coleman v. Skyrail Oceanic Ltd.
[1981] I.R.L.R. 398

Mrs Coleman was dismissed from her job as a booking clerk in the respondents' travel agency. She had married an employee of a rival firm, and both employers were concerned about the possible leakage of confidential information. The respondents decided to dismiss, on the assumption that the husband was probably the breadwinner and that it would be fairer if they dismissed Mrs Coleman rather than have Mr Coleman dismissed by the other employer. The question arose whether the respondents had thereby discriminated against Mrs Coleman.

LAWTON L.J.: "The foundation of Mr Lester's submission that there had been unlawful discrimination against Mrs Coleman because of her sex was the evidence provided by the respondents' answer in the relevant point (b), to which I have already referred, and Mr Mozes' evidence when he said: 'We came to that decision (that is to dismiss Mrs Coleman) on the assumption that the husband was the breadwinner.' The respondents made no enquiries about the financial position of the husband. Had they done so they would have discovered that he was earning a modest wage of £46 per week net, which in 1978 would have provided a poor standard of living for himself and his wife if she did not make any contribution to the family income. General assumptions of this kind, said Mr Lester, did discriminate against women because they took no account of individual circumstances and all too often were without any factual basis. This was so with regard to the assumption which Mr Mozes made. The statistics set out in the Fifth Annual Report of the Equal Opportunities Commission, 1980 show that in 56.2% of all households married women contribute to the income. The courts, both in the United Kingdom and the United States, have adjudged that general assumptions, or, as they are called in the United States stereotyped assumptions, do amount to discrimination against women. That this has been accepted by the Supreme Court of the United States seems clear: see *Weinberger* v. *Wiesenfeld*, 95 S.Ct. 1225 (1975) and *City of Los Angeles, Department of Water and Power* v. *Manhart*, 98 S.Ct. 1370 (1978). The authorities in this country are not so clear. In *Noble* v. *David Gold and Son (Holdings) Ltd.*, which was concerned with the reasons why a number of women had been made redundant, discrimination on grounds of sex being alleged on their behalf, this court found for the employers; but the reason which the Master of the Rolls gave was different from that which I gave. Lord Justice Ackner agreed with both of us. The reason I gave was that 'Employers when offering jobs must not assume that women are less capable of doing them than men and vice versa... Much will depend upon the applicant's personal attributes'... I adjudged that on the evidence in that case the employers had had regard to personal qualities...

Mr Burke-Gaffney also submitted that the evidence did not establish that the respondents discriminated against Mrs Coleman on the ground of her sex. The assumption which they made had no sexual connotation because a breadwinner can be of either sex. This is so; but, in the circumstances of this case, the assumption was that husbands are breadwinners and wives are not. Such an assumption is, in my judgment, based on sex. On the issue of liability I would allow the appeal...

Mr Lester submitted that I was right to decide as I did and Mr Burke-Gaffney on behalf of the respondents did not submit otherwise. Having considered this matter again I am satisfied that the dismissal of a woman based upon an assumption that men are more likely than women to be the primary supporters of their spouses and children can amount to discrimination under the Sex Discrimination Act 1975."

Sir David Cairns delivered a concurring judgment. Shaw L.J. dissented.

These cases indicate that there is much confusion of thought in the Court of Appeal in the application of the S.D.A., and that there is much substance in the view of the E.O.C. that the court is still unable to see women otherwise than as "delicate blooms to be carefully nurtured." Only Lawton L.J. has seriously attempted to construe the Act in a manner consistent with the intention of Parliament. Almost without exception, the other judges have employed various methods of obstruction and have displayed some remarkably crude prejudices in so doing (see esp. the dissenting judgment by Shaw L.J. in *Coleman*).

One interesting uncertainty which the post-*Peake* developments have spawned is whether that case can now be regarded as having been overruled on all but the *de minimis* question (on which see *Gill* v. *El Vino Co. Ltd.* [1983] 1 All E.R. 398). In particular, it is uncertain whether Shaw L.J.'s motive requirement retains any authority. Only Brandon L.J. in *Jeremiah* expressly rejected this construction, and it cannot be assumed that its rejection is implicit in the other judgments delivered in that case. However, the E.A.T. under Slynn J. has shown no desire to follow Shaw L.J. In *Grieg* v. *Community Industry* [1979] I.C.R. 356, the E.A.T. said in a discussion of *Peake*:

"Moreover, Shaw L.J. said that there had to be an element of something which is inherently adverse or hostile to the interest of the person of the sex which is said to be discriminated against. We do not read that as in any sense meaning that the hostility has to be either intentional or expressed. What has to be considered is whether what has been done is in itself inherently adverse or hostile to the interests of the person of the sex which is said to be discriminated against. It seems to us that a refusal of employment simply on the ground that a girl is a girl is in itself inherently adverse or hostile in the sense intended by Shaw L.J., and his definition, of course, is to be read against the words of s. 1(1)(a) which refer to less favourable treatment on the ground of sex."

See also *Page* v. *Freight Hire (Tank Haulage) Ltd.* [1981] I.C.R. 299 and *Seide* v. *Gillette Industries Ltd.* [1980] I.R.L.R. 427.

6. Porcelli v. Strathclyde Regional Council
[1985] I.C.R. 177

The applicant was a science laboratory technician employed by the council. Between August 1980 and September 19, 1983 she was employed at Bellahouston Academy. She was transferred at her own request to another school on the latter date. The evidence shows that two male employees (Coles and Reid) had pursued a policy of vindictive unpleasantness towards Porcelli for the deliberate purpose of forcing her to apply to another school. On one occasion they threw out personal belongings of the applicant, shortly after which her evidence avers that:

"Mr Coles began subjecting me to sexual harassment. During morning and afternoon teabreaks in the technicians' room I became aware of him deliberately staring at me and following me with his eyes when I moved about the room. He also began to make suggestive remarks. He would, for example, pick up a screw nail and ask me if I would like a screw. Another example was when he picked up a glass rod holder—which is shaped like a penis—and asked if I had any use for it. On several occasions he opened the *Daily Record* at page 3 and commented on my physical appearance in comparison with that of the nude female depicted in the newspaper. The atmosphere in the technicians' room became so unpleasant for me that I stopped using it during break times when Mr Coles and Mr Reid were there. After I stopped using the technicians' room Mr Coles began to harass me in the preparation room. It was his practice to come behind me and take me unawares so that when I turned round he would brush against me. In addition to sexually harassing me Mr Coles began to behave in an intimidating way towards me. On several occasions he deliberately allowed swing doors to slam back in my face when I was carrying apparatus and could not protect myself."

The claim was rejected by an industrial tribunal, but upheld by the E.A.T. On appeal to the Court of Session:

LORD PRESIDENT: "Although it is necessary for a woman seeking to found a claim upon section 6(2)(*b*) of the Act to establish that her employer had discriminated against her by dismissing her or subjecting her to some other detriment it is accepted by the employers for the purposes of this appeal, that if the applicant who was not dismissed, was discriminated against within the meaning of section 1(1)(*a*) she was subjected to a detriment within the meaning of section 6(2)(*b*). The employers, in my opinion, were well advised to make that concession on the facts of this case for, as was pointed out by Brandon L.J. in *Ministry of Defence* v. *Jeremiah* [1980] I.C.R. 13, 26, 'detriment,' simply means 'disadvantage' in its statutory context. I have to say also that for the purpose of this appeal the employers did not seek to maintain that if the applicant was discriminated against by Coles and Reid within the meaning of section 1(1)(*a*) they would not be responsible for their actings. In the result, accordingly, the critical issues in the appeal required attention to be concentrated upon the decision of the industrial tribunal in so far as it bore to deal with the matter of discrimination within the meaning of section 1(1)(*a*). Upon these issues no assistance whatever is to be found in any decided case in the United Kingdom or elsewhere and I am happy to record that we at least begin our task with the advantage that the parties to the appeal were at one in submitting, correctly in my opinion, that, as it applies to the facts of this case, section 1(1)(*a*) gives rise to two questions: (first) was the applicant subjected by Coles and Reid to treatment on the ground of her sex (*i.e.* because she was a woman) and (second) if so, was she treated less favourably than the man with whom she falls to be compared would have been treated by these men?

For the employers the submission was that in the proved circumstances of this case the industrial tribunal was clearly of opinion that the episodes of 'sexual harassment' of the applicant by Coles were merely part of a single campaign against her founded upon dislike for her as a colleague. Such treatment of the applicant was not, accordingly, to be seen as having been meted out to her because she was a woman but because she was heartily disliked by Coles and Reid as a person and as a colleague. In any event, said counsel for the employers, the industrial tribunal correctly understood and applied section 1(1)(*a*) in that they went on to decide upon the evidence that Coles and Reid would have treated an equally disliked male colleague just as unfavourably as they had treated the applicant. In these circumstances the appeal tribunal was not entitled to interfere with their decision to dismiss the applicant's application because it cannot be seen to be flawed by an error of approach in law.

After some initial hesitation which I freely confess I have come to be of opinion that for the reasons advanced by the Dean of Faculty for the applicant the submissions for the employers fall to be rejected. Section 1(1)(*a*) is concerned with 'treatment' and not with the motive or objective of the person responsible for it. Although in some cases it will be obvious that there is a sex-related purpose in the mind of a person who indulges in unwanted and objectionable sexual overtures to a woman or exposes her to offensive sexual jokes or observations that is not this case. But it does not follow that because the campaign pursued against the applicant as a whole had no sex-related motive or objective, the treatment of the applicant by Coles, which was of the nature of 'sexual harassment' is not to be regarded as having been 'on the ground of her sex' within the meaning of section 1(1)(*a*). In my opinion this particular part of the campaign was plainly adopted against the applicant because she was a woman. It was a particular kind of weapon, based upon the sex of the victim, which, as the industrial tribunal recognised would not have been used against an equally disliked man. Indeed, I do not understand from the reasons of the industrial tribunal that they were not entirely satisfied upon that matter, and they were in my opinion well entitled to be so satisfied upon a proper interpretation of section 1(1)(*a*). As I read their reasons the decision against the applicant, which they reached with evident regret, proceeded only upon their view that Coles and Reid would have treated an equally disliked male colleague just as unfavourably as they had treated the applicant. It is at this point, in my opinion, that their decision is vulnerable.

The industrial tribunal reached their decision by finding that Coles' and Reid's treatment of an equally disliked male colleague would have been just as unpleasant. Where they went wrong, however, was in failing to notice that a material part of the campaign against the applicant consisted of sexual harassment, a particularly degrading and unacceptable form of treatment which it must be taken to have been the intention of Parliament to restrain. From their reasons it is to be understood that they were satisfied that this form of treatment—sexual harassment in any form— would not have figured in a campaign by Coles and Reid directed against a man. In this situation the treatment of the applicant fell to be seen as very different in a material respect from that which would have been inflicted on a male colleague, regardless of equality of overall unpleasantness, and that being so it appears to me that upon a proper application of section 1(1)(*a*) the industrial tribunal ought to have asked themselves whether in that respect the applicant had been treated by Coles (on the ground of her sex) 'less favourably' than he would have treated a man with whom her position fell to be compared. Had they asked themselves that question it is impossible to believe that they would not have answered it in the affirmative. In the result it has not been shown that the appeal tribunal were not entitled to substitute their own decision in the applicant's favour for that of the industrial tribunal and I am of opinion that the appeal by the employers should be refused."

Lords Grieve and Brand delivered concurring opinions.

This is an important decision on an important issue. It is to be noted that an employer is liable for the unlawful discriminatory conduct of a person in the course of his employment (S.D.A. s. 41(1)). This liability attaches even where the acts were done without the employer's knowledge or approval. It is, however, a defence (s. 41(3)) in proceedings under the Act that the employer took "such steps as were reasonably practical to prevent the employee from doing the unlawful act, or from doing in the course of his employment acts of that description." There are indications that the Employment Appeal Tribunal will readily permit this to be used as a safe haven for employers: see *Balgobin* v. *Tower Hamlets L.B.C.* [1987] I.R.L.R. 401. There is also authority for the view that sexual harassment may amount to a breach of the contract of employment by the employer (*Western Excavation Ltd.* v. *Sharp* [1978] I.C.R. 221).

C. INDIRECT DISCRIMINATION

The definition of indirect discrimination in both the S.D.A. and the R.R.A.

contains at least three central provisions:
- —the applicant must show that the respondent has applied a *requirement or condition;*
- —with which the proportion of members of one sex or racial group who *can comply* is considerably smaller than the proportion of members of another sex or racial group;
- —and the respondent is unable to show that the requirement or condition is *justifiable* irrespective of sex or race.

We examine each of these provisions in turn.

1. "REQUIREMENT OR CONDITION"

7. Perera v. Civil Service Commission
[1983] I.R.L.R. 166

Perera, a civil servant, tried for promotion to the grade of legal assistant. The only requirement was that the successful candidate should be a barrister, though the selection board took into account four other factors. These were the applicant's command of English, degree of experience in the United Kingdom, nationality and age. Perera complained *inter alia,* that he had been the victim of indirect discrimination. Both the Employment Appeal Tribunal and the Court of Appeal rejected his claim.

STEPHENSON L.J.: " The matters which have to be established by an applicant who claims that he has been discriminated against indirectly are, first of all, that there has been a requirement or condition, as Mr Perera put it, a 'must', something which has to be complied with. Here there was a requirement or condition for candidates for the post of legal assistant in the Civil Service: it was that the candidate should be either a qualified member of the English Bar or a qualified Solicitor of the Supreme Court of this country—an admitted man or a barrister; and those conditions or requirements—those 'musts'—were fulfilled by Mr Perera. But, as he admitted in his argument before the Appeal Tribunal and before this court, there is no other express requirement or condition, and he has to find a requirement or condition in the general combination of factors which he says the Interviewing Board took into account. He cannot formulate, as in my judgment he has to, what the particular requirement or condition is which he says has been applied to him and to his attempt to obtain a post of legal assistant. That is the hurdle which as it seems to me, he is unable to get over. If he were able to prove a particular requirement or condition, he would then have to prove that it had been applied by the Commission's Interviewing Board. Then he would have to prove one further thing, namely, that a substantially smaller proportion of persons of his racial group would be able to comply with that requirement than the proportion of similarly qualified persons in a different racial group: similarly qualified because, as Miss Caws has pointed out, like must be compared with like. . . But in my opinion none of those factors could possibly be regarded as a requirement or a condition in the sense that the lack of it, whether of British nationality or even of the ability to communicate well in English, would be an absolute bar. The whole of the evidence indicates that a brilliant man whose personal qualities made him suitable as a legal assistant might well have been sent forward on a short list by the Interviewing Board in spite of being, perhaps, below standard on his knowledge of English and his ability to communicate in that language.

That is only an illustration, but once it appears clear from the evidence that the Industrial Tribunal were entitled to conclude that it was personal qualities for which the Interviewing Board were mainly looking, and it was personal qualities, as stated in the chairman's report and as was made clear by the markings of all the members of the Tribunal, which, in the opinion of the Board, Mr Perera lacked, and that that was the reason for not sending him forward on the short list, the case of indirect discrimination which Mr Perera seeks to make in my opinion falls to the ground.

As I have said, I think the Appeal Tribunal correctly stated the law as to indirect discrimination. I agree with them that there was no application here of any requirement or condition, and no evidence of it. In my judgment Mr Perera has failed to prove what he has to prove in order to show a case of indirect discrimination."

O'Connor L.J. delivered a concurring judgment. Sir George Baker concurred.

It is perhaps unsatisfactory that the legislation can be out-manoeuvred by this simple device; and there may be much to commend in the proposal of the C.R.E. that the term "requirement or condition" be replaced with "any practice, policy or situation." For similar problems under the S.D.A., see *Watches of Switzerland Ltd.* v. *Savell* [1983] I.R.L.R. 141.

2. "CAN COMPLY"

8. Price v. Civil Service Commission
[1977] 1 W.L.R. 1417

The question in this case was whether an advertisement for candidates between the ages of 17 and 28 indirectly discriminated against women on the ground that considerably fewer women than men could comply with the age requirement.

PHILLIPS J.: "Section 1(1)(*b*) deals with indirect discrimination. The scheme is to define in sub-paragraph (i) in fairly wide terms activities which are *prima facie* discriminatory, and in effect to provide that they are to constitute discrimination unless the person acting can within sub-paragraph (ii) show that they are justifiable irrespective of the sex of the person discriminated against. Thus sub-paragraph (i) proscribes a wide range of activity but permits the party acting to justify it. The test is whether the condition is such that the proportion of women who can comply with it is considerably smaller than the proportion of men who can comply with it. Examples usually given are of physical attributes such as height or strength or weight. But the sub-paragraph goes much further than that, and would extend to educational or professional qualifications, if they are of a kind which few women but many men possess. Thus an advertisement which required as a condition for appointment to a post a degree in engineering, or the status of a barrister-at-law, would seem to be *prima facie* discriminatory in that the proportion of women who can comply with the condition is considerably smaller than the proportion of men who can comply with it. No doubt in those and other similar cases the advertiser would have no difficulty in showing the condition to be justifiable. Accordingly such cases are not brought in practice because it is known that though they might pass the test of sub-paragraph (i) they will fail at that of sub-paragraph (ii). Thus it by no means follows that because a claimant can satisfy sub-paragraph (i) he or she will eventually be able to establish an act of discrimination. The applicant failed to persuade the industrial tribunal that she could satisfy sub-paragraph (i). Thus the case has not yet been determined upon the merits, and we have not had the benefit of hearing the evidence and arguments relevant to the question whether the conditions can be shown to be justifiable. The case has not got beyond the preliminary point...

Experience shows that when considering section 1(1)(*b*) it is necessary to define with some precision the requirement or condition which is called in question. Even when the facts are not in dispute it is possible to formulate the requirement or condition, usually at all events, in more than one way: the precise formulation is important when considering sub-paragraphs (i), (ii) and (iii). A fair way of putting it in the present case seems to be that candidates for the post of executive officer must not be over 28 years of age. We do not accept the submission of counsel for the Civil Service Commission that the words 'can comply' must be construed narrowly, and we think that the industrial tribunal were wrong to accept this submission. In one sense it can be said that any female applicant can comply with the condition. She is not obliged to marry, or to have children, or to mind children; she may find somebody to look after them, and as a last resort she may put them into care. In this sense no doubt counsel for the Civil Service Commission is right in saying that any female applicant can comply with the condition. Such a construction appears to us to be wholly out of sympathy with the spirit and intent of the Act. Further, it should be repeated that compliance with sub-paragraph (i) is only a preliminary step, which does not lead to a finding that an act is one of discrimination unless the person acting fails to show that it is justifiable. 'Can' is defined (*The Shorter Oxford English Dictionary*, 3rd. ed. (1944) p. 255) 'To be able; to have the power or capacity.' It is a word with many shades of meaning, and we are satisfied that it should not be too narrowly—nor too broadly—construed in its context in section 1(1)(*b*)(i). It should not be said that a person 'can' do something merely because it is theoretically possible for him to do so; it is necessary to see whether he can do so in practice. Applying this approach to the circumstances of this case, it is relevant in determining whether women can comply with the condition to take into account the current usual behaviour of women in this respect, as observed in practice, putting on one side behaviour and responses which are unusual or extreme.

Knowledge and experience suggest that a considerable number of women between the mid-twenties and the mid-thirties are engaged in bearing children and in minding children, and that while many find it possible to take up employment many others, while desiring to do so, find it impossible, and that many of the latter as their children get older find that they can follow their wish and seek employment.

This knowledge and experience is confirmed by some of the statistical evidence produced to the industrial tribunal (and by certain additional statistical evidence put in by consent of the parties on the hearing of the appeal). This demonstrates clearly that the economic activity of a woman with at least one Advanced Level falls off markedly about the age of 23, reaching a bottom at about the age of 33 when it climbs gradually to a plateau at about 45.

Basing ourselves on this and other evidence, we should have no hesitation in concluding that our own knowledge and experience is confirmed, and that it is safe to say that the condition is one which it is in practice harder for women to comply with than it is for men. We should be inclined to go further and say that there are undoubtedly women of whom it may be properly said in the terms of section 1(1)(b)(i) that they 'cannot' comply with the condition, because they are women; that is to say because of their involvement with their children. But this is not enough to enable the applicant to satisfy the requirements of sub-paragraph (i). The difficulty we have is in saying whether the proportion of women who can comply with the condition is *considerably smaller* than the proportion of men who can comply with it. It follows from what we have said earlier that we do not agree with the approach of the industrial tribunal to this question, and it follows that there has never been a finding of fact based upon the evidence correctly approached and interpreted.

At one stage of the hearing we thought that it might be in order for us to make a finding ourselves on the basis of the evidence given to the industrial tribunal, together with that put in by consent on the hearing of the appeal. At the end of the day we have come to the conclusion that we ought not to do so. The difficulty is that most of the evidence is statistical, and is of a kind which needs to be analysed and interpreted, since it is designed for other purposes, and it is not entirely easy to draw relevant conclusions. We think it *does* confirm the likelihood that women are put into difficulties by the condition, and that there are women who would wish to apply to be an executive officer and could do so in, say their thirties, but cannot do so in their late twenties. The difficulty is to quantify this in the terms of a 'considerably smaller' result. We find that it would be unsafe for us to reach a conclusion without having had the benefit of hearing the statistician give evidence and be subjected to cross-examination upon the proper analysis and inferences to be drawn from the statistics.

Accordingly we propose to allow the appeal and to remit the case to be heard afresh, bearing in mind the terms of this judgment and such guidance as we have been unable to give."

This decision was endorsed by the House of Lords in *Mandla* v. *Dowell Lee* [1983] 2 A.C. 548, where Lord Fraser of Tullybelton said, in the context of the Race Relations Act (at pp. 565-566):

"It is obvious that Sikhs, like anyone else 'can' refrain from wearing a turban, if 'can' is construed literally. But if the broad cultural/historic meaning of ethnic is the appropriate meaning of the word in the Act of 1976, then a literal reading of the word 'can' would deprive Sikhs and members of other groups defined by reference to their ethnic origins of much of the protection which Parliament evidently intended the Act to afford to them. They 'can' comply with almost any requirement or condition if they are willing to give up their distinctive customs and cultural rules. On the other hand, if ethnic means inherited or unalterable, as the Court of Appeal thought it did, then 'can' ought logically to be read literally. The word 'can' is used with many shades of meaning. In the context of section 1(1)(*b*)(i) of the Act of 1976 it must, in my opinion, have been intended by Parliament to be read not as meaning 'can physically,' so as to indicate a theoretical possibility, but as meaning 'can in practice' or 'can consistently with the customs and cultural conditions of the racial group.' The latter meaning was attributed to the word by the Employment Appeal Tribunal in *Price* v. *Civil Service Commission* [1978] I.C.R. 27, on a construction of the parallel provision in the Sex Discrimination Act 1975. I agree with their construction of the word in that context. Accordingly I am of the opinion that the 'No turban' rule was not one with which the second appellant could, in the relevant sense, comply."

3. "JUSTIFIABLE"

9. Steel v. Union of Post Office Workers
[1978] 1 W.L.R. 64

Before 1975 postwomen were regarded as temporary full-time employees whereas men engaged in similar work were regarded as permanent full-time employees. Shortly before the S.D.A. came into force, women were admitted into this last category, with their seniority running from their date of admission. Seniority as a permanent full-time employee was important for several reasons, one of these being the allocation of walks. In March 1976, Mrs Steel applied for an advertised walk but was unsuccessful, the successful candidate being a man much younger than herself who had been employed only since 1973 whereas she had been employed since 1961. Did the seniority requirement contravene section 1(1)(*b*)(ii) of the S.D.A.? In the E.A.T. it was conceded that the requirement of seniority was one which a considerably smaller proportion of women than men could comply with and it was held that the requirement was to the detriment of Mrs Steel within the terms of section 1(1)(*b*)(iii).

PHILLIPS J.: "The purpose of (ii) is clear enough. There may be discrimination by indirect means by requiring a condition equally of men and women, but one which few women but most men can satisfy. A requirement that a candidate should be six-foot high, or capable of lifting 200 pounds, or have a degree in engineering in practice would rule out more female applicants than male. It is discriminatory unless the employer (in this case) can show it to be justifiable irrespective of sex. There is no doubt that the onus of proof here lies upon the employer, and that it is a heavy onus in the sense that before it is discharged the industrial tribunal will need to be satisfied that the case is a genuine one; somewhat in the way that it must when a not dissimilar case is made by an employer under section 1(3) of the Equal Pay Act (as amended). The question is what considerations are relevant and proper to be taken into account when determining whether the requirement or condition was justifiable; in particular, is it sufficient merely to take into account the needs of the enterprise for the purpose of which the requirement or condition has been imposed, or is it necessary to look at all the circumstances including the discriminatory effect of the requirement or condition? We are satisfied that the latter is the case and that the industrial tribunal has to weigh up the needs of the enterprise against the discriminatory effect of the requirement or condition. Were it not so, many acts *prima facie* discriminatory would be allowed when there was no overriding need...

Owing to the way in which the case went before the industrial tribunal, this is a matter upon which they have made no finding, and upon which the parties may wish to call further evidence. In these circumstances we have reluctantly come to the conclusion that it would be wrong for us to decide the question for ourselves; accordingly we shall remit the case for further hearing upon this point. To summarise the position so as to avoid any doubt, we are satisfied that the complainant is entitled to succeed in her claim against the Post Office under section 1(1)(*b*) and section 6(2)(*a*) unless the Post Office can show that the seniority rule was justifiable irrespective of the sex of the person to whom it is applied.

It may be helpful if we add a word of detail about what we consider to be the right approach to this question. First, the onus of proof lies upon the party asserting this proposition, in this case the Post Office. Secondly, it is a heavy onus in the sense that at the end of the day the industrial tribunal must be satisfied that the case is a genuine one where it can be said that the requirement or condition is necessary. Thirdly, in deciding whether the employer has discharged the onus the industrial tribunal should take into account all the circumstances, including the discriminatory effect of the requirement or condition if it is permitted to continue. Fourthly, it is necessary to weigh the need for the requirement or condition against that effect. Fifthly, it is right to distinguish between a requirement or condition which is necessary and one which is merely convenient, and for this purpose it is relevant to consider whether the employer can find some other and non-discriminatory method of achieving his object.

Turning to the facts of this case, it will be right to inquire whether it is necessary to allot walks by seniority or whether some other method is feasible, to consider whether the seniority rule could not be revised so as to give the women some credit for their temporary service, and to consider the extent of the disadvantage which the women suffer under the present system in terms of numbers and likely duration. Assistance may be obtained from the judgments in the Supreme Court of the United States in *Griggs* v. *Duke Power Co.* Although the terms of the Act there in question are different from those of the Sex Discrimination Act 1975, it seems to us that the approach adopted by the court is relevant."

The effectiveness of the provisions relating to indirect discrimination depends to a large extent on the way in which the defence of justification is construed. *Steel* suggests that the respondent would have a difficult task at this hurdle. Since that decision, however, the burden on respondents has eased considerably. In *Singh* v. *Rowntree MacIntosh Ltd.* [1979] I.C.R. 554 Mr Singh was offered employment by the respondent company on the condition that he shaved his beard. He complained that this condition was indirectly discriminatory, on the ground that the number of Sikhs who could comply with the requirement of no facial hair was considerably smaller than the number of non-Sikhs who could comply. The principal question before the Employment Appeal Tribunal was whether the requirement was justifiable. In holding that it was, Lord MacDonald said:

"The onus of proving that a requirement is justifiable is on the party who discriminates but it is not accurate to describe it as a heavy onus. It is the ordinary burden of proof applicable to a civil case, *viz* a balance of the probabilities: *National Vulcan Engineering Insurance Group Ltd.* v. *Wade* [1978]I.C.R. 800.

Finally in *Steel* v. *Union of Post Office Workers* Phillips J. said, at p. 188:

'It is right to distinguish between a requirement or condition which is necessary and one which is merely convenient, and for this purpose it is relevant to consider whether the employer can find some other and non-discriminatory method of achieving his object.'

This is the passage which counsel for the complainant primarily relied on before us. He argued that the company had not shown a genuine necessity for their requirement that employees should not wear beards and that it was at best a convenience. He pointed to the fact that in their other factories they did not insist on the requirement and that even in Edinburgh they tolerated lesser forms of facial adornment such as moustaches and side-whiskers.

These, however, were all matters before the industrial tribunal and carefully considered by them and unless the word 'necessity' is to be rigidly construed in this context as meaning something absolutely essential we do not consider that they can be said to have reached a wrong conclusion.

We have no doubt that a requirement which is merely convenient will not suffice. Something more is required and it may be that it is proper to describe it as necessary provided that term is applied reasonably and with common sense. In *Steel* v. *Union of Post Office Workers* and *Price* v. *Civil Service Commission* (No. 2) [1978] I.R.L.R. 3 (decided by an industrial tribunal on remit from the appeal tribunal) we can well see the argument that the requirements were not in the circumstances necessary even in the broadest sense of that word. They were at best convenient, even if that. Here, however, we are dealing with an employer who is a manufacturer of foodstuffs, who is in competition with other manufacturers, and who considers it important that the highest standards of hygiene are seen to apply to his products. In this context at least we feel that consideration has to be given to what is reasonable and that the industrial tribunal did not err in approaching their task on that basis.

Moreover in this industry at least an employer must be allowed some independence of judgment as to what he deems to be commercially expedient in the conduct of his business. Standards of hygiene may vary between manufacturers and indeed between sections of the consuming public. We do not consider that a employer can be said to have acted unjustifiably if he adopts a standard in one of his factories which is supported by medical advice and which has the approval of a local food and drugs officer. He cannot reasonably be said to have adopted such a standard as a matter of convenience. It could more properly be described as a commercial necessity for the purposes of his business. In assessing it it is proper to consider it in the light of any discriminatory effect its application may have, and that, in the present case, the industrial tribunal have done."

A similar decision was reached by the Court of Appeal in England and

Wales (*Panesar* v. *Nestlé Co. Ltd.* [1980] I.C.R. 144). And in *Kingston Area Health Authority* v. *Kaur* [1981] I.R.L.R. 337 it was held to be justifiable to insist that nurses wore uniforms even though there was an express statutory provision which said that the wearing of the uniform was not compulsory, and even though the requirement to wear the uniform excluded Sikh women who could not wear the uniform because of their religious obligation to wear trousers. This trend away from *Steel* is evident also in the decision of the Court of Appeal in *Ojutiku* v. *Manpower Services Commission* [1982] I.R.L.R. 418 where Eveleigh L.J. held that a person justifies his or her conduct by producing "reasons for doing something which would be acceptable to right-thinking people as sound and tolerable reasons for so doing." In the same case Kerr L.J. said that "justifiable" is a perfectly easily understandable ordinary word and that it clearly implies a lower standard than "necessary." This trend away from the principled position in *Steel* is continued by the House of Lords in *Mandla* v. *Dowell Lee* where Lord Fraser, although not going perhaps as far as the Court of Appeal in *Ojutiku*, said (at pp. 566-567):

"The word 'justifiable' occurs in section 1(1)(*b*)(ii). It raises a problem which is, in my opinion, more difficult than the problem of the word 'can.' But in the end I have reached a firm opinion that the respondent has not been able to show that the 'No turban' rule was justifiable in the relevant sense. Regarded purely from the point of view of the respondent, it was no doubt perfectly justifiable. He explained that he had no intention of discriminating against Sikhs. In 1978 the school had about 300 pupils (about 75 per cent boys and 25 per cent girls) of whom over 200 were English, five were Sikhs, 34 Hindus, 16 Persians, six negroes, seven Chinese and 15 from European countries. The reasons for having a school uniform were largely reasons of practical convenience—to minimise external differences between races and social classes, to discourage the 'competitive fashions' which he said tend to exist in a teenage community, and to present a Christian image of the school to outsiders, including prospective parents. The respondent explained the difficulty for a headmaster of explaining to a non-Sikh pupil why the rules about wearing correct school uniform were enforced against him if they were relaxed in favour of a Sikh. In my view these reasons could not, either individually or collectively, provide a sufficient justification for the respondent to apply a condition that is *prima facie* discriminatory under the Act.

An attempted justification of the 'No turban' rule, which requires more serious consideration, was that the respondent sought to run a Christian school, accepting pupils of all religions and races, and that he objected to the turban on the ground that it was an outward manifestation of a non-Christian faith. Indeed, he regarded it as a challenge to that faith. I have much sympathy with the respondent on this part of the case and I would have been glad to find that the rule was justifiable within the meaning of the statute, if I could have done so. But in my opinion that is impossible. The onus under paragraph (ii) is on the respondent to show that the condition which he seeks to apply is not indeed a necessary condition, but that it is in all circumstances justifiable 'irrespective of the colour, race, nationality or ethnic or national origins of the person to whom it is applied'; that is to say that it is justifiable without regard to the ethnic origin of that person. But in this case the principal justification on which the respondent relies is that the turban is objectionable just because it is a manifestation of the second appellant's ethnic origins. That is not, in my view, a justification which is admissible under paragraph (ii). The kind of justification that might fall within that provision would be one based on public health, as in *Panesar* v. *Nestlé Co. Ltd. (Note)* [1980] I.C.R. 144, where the Court of Appeal held that a rule forbidding the wearing of beards in the respondent's chocolate factory was justifiable within the meaning of section 1(1)(*b*)(ii) on hygienic grounds, notwithstanding that the proportion of Sikhs who could [*sc.* conscientiously] comply with it was considerably smaller than the proportion of non-Sikhs who could comply with it. Again, it might be possible for the school to show that a rule insisting upon a fixed diet, which included some dish (for example, pork) which some racial groups could not conscientiously eat was justifiable if the school proved that the cost of providing special meals for the particular group would be prohibitive. Questions of that sort would be questions of fact for the tribunal of fact, and if there was evidence on which it could find the condition to be justifiable its finding would not be liable to be disturbed on appeal.

But in the present case I am of opinion that the respondents have not been able to show that the 'No turban' rule was justifiable."

Although the complainant thus eventually succeeded at this hurdle in *Mandla*, the law as it stands on justification is nevertheless unsatisfactory. The C.R.E. has proposed that the defence be amended so that it is not enough that respondents show the discriminatory practice to be justifiable. Rather they should be required to show that it is necessary.

II. SCOPE OF THE LEGISLATION

A. EMPLOYMENT

10. The Race Relations Act 1976

"Discrimination against applicants and employees
4.—(1) It is unlawful for a person, in relation to employment by him at an establishment in Great Britain, to discriminate against another—
    (*a*) in the arrangements he makes for the purpose of determining who should be offered that employment; or
    (*b*) in the terms on which he offers him that employment; or
    (*c*) by refusing or deliberately omitting to offer him that employment.
(2) It is unlawful for a person, in the case of a person employed by him at an establishment in Great Britain, to discriminate against that employee—
    (*a*) in the terms of employment which he affords him; or
    (*b*) in the way he affords him access to opportunities for promotion, transfer or training, or to any other benefits, facilities or services, or by refusing or deliberately omitting to afford him access to them; or
    (*c*) by dismissing him, or subjecting him to any other detriment.
(3) Except in relation to discrimination falling within section 2, subsections (1)

and (2) do not apply to employment for the purposes of a private household.

(4) Subsection (2) does not apply to benefits, facilities or services of any description if the employer is concerned with the provision (for payment or not) of benefits, facilities or services of that description to the public, or to a section of the public comprising the employee in question, unless—

(a) that provision differs in a material respect from the provision of the benefits, facilities or services by the employer to his employees; or

(b) the provision of the benefits, facilities or services to the employee in question is regulated by his contract of employment; or

(c) the benefits, facilities or services relate to training."

"Employment" is defined in section 78 as meaning "employment under a contract of service or of apprenticeship or a contract personally to execute any work or labour." See *Hugh Jones* v. *St. John's College, Cambridge* [1979] I.C.R. 848. The Act specifically provides that its provisions extend to Crown employment: see section 75. See also *Department of the Environment* v. *Fox* [1979] I.C.R. 736. Special provision is made in section 7 for discrimination against contract workers. Measures similar to section 4 of the Race Relations Act are found in section 6 of the S.D.A. (with the same definition of employment in section 82, with the application to Crown employment in section 85, and with the special provisions regarding contract workers in section 9). However, it may be noted that there are several important differences between sections 4 and 6. Perhaps the most important is that the equivalent of section 4(2) in the 1975 Act does not apply to benefits consisting of the payment of money when the provision of these benefits is regulated by the woman's contract of employment (s. 6(6)): see also the related provisions in section 6(5). In the last case, the woman will be entitled to equal treatment with men in certain circumstances by virtue of the Equal Pay Act 1970.

11. Noble v. David Gold and Son (Holdings) Ltd.
[1980] I.C.R. 543

A redundancy situation arose as a result of which women packers employed in a warehouse were dismissed while male colleagues were retained. The company made this decision on the basis that the women's work was light work and was of a different kind altogether from that of the men. The men were engaged in the heavier tasks of unloading, carrying and lifting which the women could not do because they were not physically capable of carrying the weights. It was the light work which had diminished, causing the redundancies. The Court of Appeal held that there had been no unlawful discrimination.

LORD DENNING M.R.: "I find it helpful to consider this case as if there were two establishments—one establishment in which there were men doing heavy work, and another establishment in which there were women doing lighter work. I suggested a parallel in the course of argument yesterday: in the Inns of Court the heavy work is done by outside porters. They do the lifting and carrying, and so forth. Inside, at the tables, the waiting and serving of the meals is done by the women. It is the men who are engaged in the establishment which does the heavier work: and the women who are engaged in the establishment which does the lighter work. There is no sex discrimination at all. It is a natural division which comes about because of the different physical qualities of the two sexes.

That is the way in which the industrial tribunal viewed this warehouse. Although it was one warehouse, there were these two establishments within it: one of which was staffed by men, and the other by women. The question is: was there unlawful discrimination here? It seems to me that, if it was not like work, and if there was a falling off of work calling for redundancies in the women's 'establishment,' there was no unlawful discrimination against the women. It was not on the grounds of sex that they were dismissed but on the ground that these redundancies were only in that establishment."

Lawton L.J. delivered a concurring judgment. Ackner L.J. concurred.

12. Ministry of Defence v. Jeremiah
[1980] Q.B. 87

(The facts are stated above at pp. 188-189)

LORD DENNING M.R.: "On this section the critical word is 'detriment.' Now I must say that I think it is a detriment for Mr Jeremiah to be required to work in the colour bursting shop—when women are not. Test it by the converse. If a woman were so required, it would obviously be a detriment to her—to have to work in dirty and dusty conditions when she did not wish to do so. Likewise with a man. What is sauce for the goose is sauce for the gander—nowadays.

But it is said that any 'detriment' is removed by the payment of 4p an hour for working in the colour bursting shop. By that money, Mr Jeremiah is compensated for the dirty and dusty work. So, it is then said, he is not subjected to any detriment. I do not accept this argument. The 'obnoxious pay' of 4p an hour is made solely because it is compensation for the dirty work. If the women were required to do the work, they would get it just the same. It is not paid because of the difference in the sexes. It is, therefore, quite irrelevant. If it were paid because of the differences in the sexes, it would be unlawful under section 77(1) of the Act. An employer cannot buy a right to discriminate by making an extra payment to the man. If he could, it would drive a gaping hole in the statute. All the men would pass through it."

BRIGHTMAN L.J.: "In deciding whether or not there is a detriment to a worker who complains, the court must in my opinion take all the circumstances into account. To take an example from the facts of the present case, if (a) a male worker is under a duty to work in the colour bursting shop one day a fortnight and is compensated with a dirty work payment of 4p an hour and consequential pay-related pension benefits, and (b) a female worker has no such duty, and (c) a male worker complains, there is clearly discrimination based on sex. The question before the tribunal in my view would be whether a reasonable male worker would or might take the view that there was a detriment. I say, 'would or might,' because tastes differ. Some male workers might take the view that the 4p an hour bonus, with consequent increase in pension rights, made the dirty work well worth while, and not therefore detrimental to their interests. Other male workers might take the view that it was not worth while, that it was to their detriment. It would be unrealistic to expect a tribunal to decide which group of workers were correct in their assessment. I think a detriment exists if a reasonable worker would or might take the view that the duty was in all circumstances to his detriment. It may be said that, on this interpretation of the Act, both a male worker and a female worker might complain about the same discrimination and that both might be right. I see no anomaly in such a result. The purpose of the legislation is to secure equal treatment of the sexes so far as appropriate."

Brandon L.J. concurred.

13. De Souza v. Automobile Association
[1985] I.R.L.R. 87

Mrs de Souza, a coloured woman was engaged as a secretary/personal assistant to a manager. She alleged that one employee (Boud) told another (Kincaid) to "go and get his typing done by the wog." She was then told by Kincaid that Boud had referred to her as "a wog." The question before the E.A.T. was whether Mrs de Souza had been subjected to a detriment. The E.A.T. held that she had not.

POPPLEWELL J.: "Mr Allen, in the course of a well developed and attractive argument, has submitted that the use of abusive language which causes upset is subjecting someone to a detriment within s. 4(2)(c); that if you offend someone at work it must amount to a detriment; and that because this applicant had to work where there was express racial prejudice she was subjected to a situation which amounted to a detriment. What 'detriment' means, it is said, is causing loss or damage to somebody; that to upset a person's feelings gives rise to a loss or damage which is capable of being evaluated and which is properly recoverable in law. Mr Allen says that the use of that phrase would be naturally offensive to a coloured person and was in fact highly offensive to this particular applicant. It is argued that it would be quite wrong, in an Act designed to prevent discrimination and to control racial prejudice, that an employee can be racially abused albeit not to her face and yet have no remedy.

The phrase 'other detriment' has received surprisingly little judicial consideration. The researches of counsel have only provided few relevant authorities, one of which is *Ministry of Defence* v. *Jeremiah* [1979] I.R.L.R. 436…

It is important to recognise that s. 4 is dealing with discrimination in the field of employment. It is not dealing with racial prejudice. They may, and often do, go hand-in-hand, but behaviour which can be characterised as racially obnoxious may not necessarily result in discrimination. It is important too, to look at the actual wording of s. 4(2)(c): 'by dismissing him or subjecting him to any other detriment.'' If the *ejusdem generis* rule applies and is given its very widest interpretation, it is still difficult to relate the mere use of offensive language to a third party with any form of dismissal.

On behalf of the respondents it was pointed out that s. 32, which imposes vicarious liability on employers for acts of their employees, refers to *'anything done,'* by a person in the course of his employment. It is argued that anything done is different from anything said. We do not accept that argument. Additionally, say the respondents, there is a distinction between prejudice and discrimination. Before s. 4 can bite on expressions of racial prejudice it must have an effect in relation to the applicant's employment either by causing dismissal or by causing a detriment. However deplorable it may be to describe a coloured person as a 'wog' to a third person, it is not and cannot be construed as putting her under a present or future disadvantage in relation to her employment.

. . . It is, in our judgment, impossible to say that the use of the phrase by one manager to another (even though overheard by the applicant), deplorable though it is, can properly be described as a detriment. The absence of any reported cases supporting the applicant's contention merely fortifies us in our conclusion.

Finally may we say (because there is no greater area for misunderstanding than in the field of race relations) that we are concerned here only with whether the applicant's complaint constitutes discrimination within the Act. We find that it does not. We repeat that we do not approve, and indeed utterly deplore, the use of this sort of language in the field of employment or indeed elsewhere.

Accordingly the appeal is dismissed.

Leave to appeal to Court of Appeal, refused."

Genuine occupational qualification (G.O.Q.)

Section 4 of the R.R.A. does not apply where being a member of a particular racial group is a genuine occupational qualification (s. 5(1)). This is defined as arising where for reasons of authenticity, it is necessary to have someone of a particular race for dramatic performances, modelling, or engaged in an establishment where food and drink are provided. The latter category thus makes it lawful to advertise for Chinese waiters. Significantly, however, section 5(1) does not apply where the employer already has employees of the racial group, (a) who are able to carry out the required duties; (b) whom it would be reasonable to employ on those duties; and (c) whose numbers are sufficient to meet the employer's likely requirements in respect of those duties without undue inconvenience. Similar provisions are to be found in the S.D.A. (s. 7). Here, however, the G.O.Q. is more extensive.

14. The Sex Discrimination Act 1975

"7 . . . (2) Being a man is a genuine occupational qualification for a job only where—

(*a*)   the essential nature of the job calls for a man for reasons of physiology (excluding physical strength or stamina) or, in dramatic performances or other entertainment, for reasons of authenticity, so that the essential nature of the job would be materially different if carried out by a woman; or

(*b*)   the job needs to be held by a man to preserve decency or privacy because—

(i) it is likely to involve physical contact with men in circumstances where they might reasonably object to it being carried out by a woman, or

(ii) the holder of the job is likely to do his work in circumstances where men might reasonably object to the presence of a woman because they are in a state of undress or are using sanitary facilities; or

(*ba*) the job is likely to involve the holder of the job doing his work, or living, in a private home and needs to be held by a man because objection might reasonably be taken to allowing to a woman—

(i) the degree of physical or social contact with a person living in the home, or

(ii) the knowledge of intimate details of such a person's life, which is likely, because of the nature or circumstances of the job or of the home, to be allowed to, or available to, the holder of the job; or

(*c*)   the nature or location of the establishment makes it impracticable for the holder of the job to live elsewhere than in premises provided by the employer, and—

(i) the only such premises which are available for persons holding that kind of job are lived in, or normally lived in, by men and are not equipped with separate sleeping accommodation for women and sanitary facilities which could be used by women in privacy from men, and

(ii) it is not reasonable to expect the employer either to equip those premises with such accommodation and facilities or to provide other premises for women; or

(*d*)   the nature of the establishment, or of the part of it within which the work is done, requires the job to be held by a man because—

(i) it is, or is part of, a hospital, prison or other establishment for persons requiring special care, supervision or attention, and

(ii) those persons are all men (disregarding any woman whose presence is exceptional), and

(iii) it is reasonable, having regard to the essential character of the establishment or that part, that the job should not be held by a woman; or

(*e*)   the holder of the job provides individuals with personal services promoting their welfare or education, or similar personal services, and those services can most effectively be provided by a man, or

(*f*)   the job needs to be held by a man because of restrictions imposed by the laws regulating the employment of women, or

(*g*)   the job needs to be held by a man because it is likely to involve the performance of duties outside the United Kingdom in a country whose laws or customs are such that the duties could not, or could not effectively, be performed by a woman, or

(*h*)   the job is one of two to be held by a married couple."

In *Wylie* v. *Dee & Co (Menswear) Ltd.* [1978] I.R.L.R. 103, it was held by a Glasgow industrial tribunal that section 7(2)(*b*) did not operate to justify discrimination against a woman who was refused a job in a men's clothing shop on the ground that it was not appropriate that a woman should take the men's inside leg measurements. In its judgment, the tribunal said:

"Accordingly, the Tribunal were far from satisfied on the evidence that the requirement to measure inside legs arose on very many occasions. Many men know their measurements. An assistant also can make an estimate of the size through experience by looking at the man. The applicant, in fact, did have considerable experience. Furthermore, as pointed out, there are other methods of arriving at the correct measurement short of taking a direct measurement. One factor was that there were seven male assistants employed. The Tribunal, on the evidence, did not think there was much difficulty in asking one of these men to take the measurement of an inside leg on occasions where it appeared necessary to do so, and where a man seemed hesitant about allowing a woman to do so. It is within the knowledge of the Tribunal that in some stores notices are put up stating that male assistants, if available, will take the measurements if required."

A similar refusal to consider a man for employment in a ladies' clothing shop in Glasgow has also been held to be unlawful discrimination: *Rowan* v. *Etams plc, The Scotsman*, 27.4.88. See also *Sisley* v. *Britannia Security Systems Ltd.* [1983] I.R.L.R. 404.

Discrimination by other bodies in employment field

Sections 10-16 of the R.R.A. regulate discrimination by bodies other than employers in the employment field. These are partnerships with more than six partners (s. 10); trade unions (s. 11); qualifying bodies (s. 12); vocational training bodies (s. 13); employment agencies (s. 14); the Manpower Services Commission (s. 15); and the police (s. 16). With the exception of the last-mentioned category, similar provision is made in the S.D.A., though unlike the R.R.A., the S.D.A. now applies to partnerships, regardless of size. However, the S.D.A. also makes provision for special classes of employment or office in relation to which the Act is excluded in whole or in part. These exclusions apply to the police, prison officers, ministers of religion and mineworkers (see ss. 17-21).

B. EDUCATION

15. The Race Relations Act 1976

"Discrimination by bodies in charge of educational establishments

17. It is unlawful, in relation to an educational establishment falling within column 1 of the following table, for a person indicated in relation to the establishment in column 2 (the 'responsible body') to discriminate against a person—

    (*a*) in the terms on which it offers to admit him to the establishment as a pupil; or (*b*) by refusing or deliberately omitting to accept an application for his admission to the establishment as a pupil; or

(*c*) where he is a pupil of the establishment—

(i) in the way it affords him access to any benefits, facilities or services, or by refusing or deliberately omitting to afford him access to them; or

(ii) by excluding him from the establishment or subjecting him to any other detriment.

TABLE

SCOTLAND

Establishment	Responsible body
6. Educational establishment managed by an education authority	Education authority.
7. Educational establishment in respect of which the managers are for the time being receiving grants und er section 73(*c*) or (*d*) of the Education (Scotland) Act 1980.	Managers of the educational establishment.
8. University.	Governing body.
9. Independent school.	Proprietor.
10. Any other educational establishment (not falling within paragraphs 6, 7 and 9) providing full or part-time school education or further education.	Managers of the educational establishment.

Other discrimination by local education authorities
18 . . . (2) It is unlawful for an education authority, in carrying out such of its functions under the Education (Scotland) Act 1980 as do not fall under section 17, to do any act which constitutes racial discrimination."

In practice, section 17 gives rise to only a small number of complaints. Corresponding provisions in the S.D.A. are to be found in sections 22 and 23. One issue which has caused some difficulty here relates to the secondary school curriculum. In its report for 1980, the E.O.C. pointed out that: "In some schools, girls are still denied access to the craft subjects which may lead them to further education, vocational training, day-release and a wide range of employment opportunities" (p. 15). It may be noted that there are exceptions in the S.D.A. for single-sex schools (s. 26), and for further education courses in physical training (s. 28).

C. PROVISION OF GOODS, FACILITIES OR SERVICES

16. The Race Relations Act 1976

"Discrimination in provision of goods, facilities or services
20.—(1) It is unlawful for any person concerned with the provision (for payment or not) of goods, facilities or services to the public or a section of the public to discriminate against a person who seeks to obtain or use those goods, facilities or services—

  (a) by refusing or deliberately omitting to provide him with any of them; or
  (b) by refusing or deliberately omitting to provide him with goods, facilities or services of the like quality, in the like manner and on the like terms as are normal in the first-mentioned person's case in relation to other members of the public or (where the person so seeking belongs to a section of the public) to other members of that section."

Subsection (2) provides examples of the facilities and services mentioned in subs. (1). These are—(a) access to and use of any place which members of the public are permitted to enter; (b) accommodation in a hotel, boarding house or similar establishment; (c) facilities by way of banking or insurance or for grants, loans, credit or finance; (d) facilities for education; (e) facilities for entertainment, recreation or refreshment; (f) facilities for transport or travel; (g) the services of any profession or trade, or any local or other public authority. Identical provisions are to be found in section 29 of the S.D.A.

17. Charter v. Race Relations Board
[1973] A.C. 868

Mr Slick was denied membership of the East Ham South Conservative Club on racial grounds. The House of Lords held by a majority (Lord Morris dissenting) that the club did not provide services to the public or a section of the public.

LORD REID: "Now let me come to clubs. I leave out of account various societies or associations which call themselves clubs but have no premises where members meet for social intercourse. No doubt social clubs vary in character. Some are small, some large. Some are very exclusive, some less so. It is suggested in the judgment of the Court of Appeal that a distinction can be drawn between those which restrict membership to persons who have certain qualifications and those which do not. This is linked to a distinction between personal and impersonal qualities which I must confess I do not understand. If the truth is that there is a careful selection of candidates for membership so that only those who are thought to be acceptable to other members are admitted, then I do not see how it can matter that candidates for membership of certain clubs must be Conservatives or members of particular universities or travellers or reformers whereas other similar clubs make no such restrictions. Members are not admitted because they have these qualifications, but because on personal grounds they are thought to be acceptable. No doubt Conservatives or graduates of a particular university are a section of the public but it does not at all follow that a number of Conservatives or graduates selected for personal reasons must also be a section of the public. I would regard with the greatest suspicion any interpretation of the Act which required us to hold that of two apparently similar clubs one is within the Act because it restricts membership in this way but the other is not because it does not. The result would be absurd. . .

The Act of 1968 was preceded by an Act of 1965 which forbade discrimination in relation to various places of public resort. The scope of the Act of 1968 is obviously much wider but it still appears to me to be confined to situations in which there can be said to be some public element. I have already said that the words 'the public or a section of the public' in section 2 must have been intended to have some limiting effect. And the provisions in the Act which limit its scope in various particular contexts appear to me to flow from this general conception. I would infer from the Act as a whole that the legislature thought all discrimination on racial grounds to be deplorable but thought it unwise or impracticable to attempt to apply legal sanctions in situations of a purely private character.

Some clubs have a very domestic appearance and atmosphere, others less so. Suppose a club begins by meeting in members' houses and then acquires small premises of its own but preserves its former character. The mere move to its own premises does not seem to me to introduce any public element. I cannot see any reasonable or workable dividing line so long as there is operated a genuine system of personal selection of members. There is no public element where a personally selected group of people meet in private premises and the club which they constitute does not provide facilities or services to the public or any section of the public. So section 2 does not apply.

But a clear dividing line does emerge if entry to a club is no more than a formality. This may be because the club rules do not provide for any true selection or because in practice the rules are disregarded. There are, or at least have been, clubs which are in fact no more difficult to enter than a restaurant. There may be some delay, and there may be entry money and a subscription but that makes no difference. In fact the club services and facilities are provided to any one of the public who wishes to come in, provided that he does not have such obvious disqualification as might cause the manager of, say, a good restaurant to exclude him. And it would make no difference if entry were confined to a particular section of the public—Conservatives or graduates or any other."

This decision was followed and extended by the House of Lords in *Dockers' Labour Club and Institute* v. *Race Relations Board* [1976] A.C. 285 where it was held that *Charter* applied to associate club members. This meant that the member of one club could be lawfully excluded on racial grounds from a neighbouring club of which he would otherwise be entitled to associate membership because of his membership of the first club.

These decisions have been overturned in so far as they relate to private clubs which fall within the scope of section 25 of the R.R.A. However, the cases are still important for the interpretation they place on the phrase, "a section of the public." Moreover, the decisions relating to clubs are still

significant in the area of sex discrimination, in view of the fact that the
S.D.A. does not apply to clubs. In its Annual Report for 1979, the E.O.C.
said at p. 24:

"A continuing cause of dissatisfaction has been the unequal treatment of women
club members who, in many cases, although full subscribers, are denied voting
rights or equal access to club facilities. Since private clubs are not covered by the
provisions of the Sex Discrimination Act, there is little that the Commission can do
other than to encourage complainants to persist in raising, or causing to be raised,
at the annual general meetings and other suitable occasions, the absurdity of
discriminatory rules in clubs where membership is in any event open to both sexes."

The E.O.C. has proposed that section 29 of the S.D.A. be amended to deal
with this problem: E.O.C. (1980: 39).

Section 2 of the 1968 Act generated a third important House of Lords
case, *Applin* v. *Race Relations Board* [1975] A.C. 259 where it was held
that the fostering of children in care constituted the provision of facilities
or services to a section of the public, namely the children in care. Any racial
discrimination by foster parents as to whom they would accept for fostering
was therefore held unlawful. However, this decision has been reversed by
section 23(2) of the R.R.A. which provides that section 20(1) does not
apply to anything done by a person as a participant in arrangements by
which he takes into his home and treats as if they were members of his
family, children, elderly persons, or persons requiring a special degree of
care and attention.

18. R. v. Immigration Appeal Tribunal, ex p. Kassam
[1980] 1 W.L.R. 1037

Kassam had been admitted to this country as a visitor. During his stay here,
he married a woman who had been admitted as a student. The Secretary of
State decided to deport him, despite the fact that his wife remained here.
Kassam complained that there had been a breach of the S.D.A. because the
immigration rules allowed a wife to remain in this country during the
period of her husband's stay, but not vice versa. One of the issues in the case
was whether the immigration procedure came under section 29 of the
S.D.A.

STEPHENSON L.J.: "In giving leave to immigrants to enter or remain here, is not the
Secretary of State a person concerned with the provision of facilities to a section
of the public and discriminating against a man who seeks to obtain or use those
facilities—the facilities which resemble facilities for travel, which the statute gives
as an example? The Immigration Act 1971 itself speaks of a person obtaining leave:
for instance in section 3(3)(*b*) and section 3(4) and the language of the Immigration
Rules points also to an affirmative answer. Is not 'a passenger seeking entry as a
visitor' or 'to study in the United Kingdom' (paragraphs 15 and 18 of H.C. 79) a

man or woman 'who seeks to obtain' a facility from such a person?

Mr Latham concedes that immigrants applying for leave are a section of the public, but he submits that the Secretary of State does not provide facilities and the immigrant does not obtain or use them when he or she obtains leave from him or his immigration officers. Section 29 is concerned with what he called 'market-place activities.' The Secretary of State is exercising statutory powers to control immigration and any facilities he may be said in the course of their exercise to provide or to be concerned in providing are not within the aim or purview of the section.

I am of the opinion that the Secretary of State is not a person concerned with the provisions [sic] of facilities to a section of the public. Section 29(1) and (2) repeat, *mutatis mutandis,* section 2(1) and (2) of the Race Relations Act 1968 (now repealed and re-enacted in section 20(1) and (2) of the Act of 1976) and so are not free from judicial interpretation. But read in their natural and ordinary meaning they are not aimed at, and do not hit, the Secretary of State concerned with giving leave to enter or remain in the exercise of his powers under the Immigration Act 1971. The kind of facilities with which the sections of the Acts of 1975 and 1976 are concerned is of the same order as goods and services, and though it may not always be easy to say whether a particular person (or body of persons) is a person concerned with the provision of any of those three things to the public or a section of the public and although a Minister of the Crown or a government department might be such a person (for instance, in former days the Postmaster General, as Sir David Cairns suggested in argument), I am clearly of the opinion that the Secretary of State in acting under the Immigration Act and Rules is not such a person, and he cannot be held to have unlawfully discriminated against the applicant by refusing to give him leave to remain here while his wife was a student, or by refusing to interpret or alter the immigration rule, paragraph 22 of H.C. 79, which is relevant to this appeal. He is operating in a field outside the fields in which Parliament has forbidden sex discrimination.

I therefore find it unnecessary to consider Mr Latham's submission that if the Secretary of State comes within section 29, any discrimination on his part is saved from being unlawful by section 51(1) of the Act of 1975."

ACKNER L.J.: "In my judgment, when the Secretary of State is exercising his discretion in relation to powers granted to him by the Immigration Act 1971, he is not providing a facility within the meaning of section 29 of the Act. The word 'facilities' in that section is flanked on one side by the word 'goods' and on the other by the word 'services.' This suggests to my mind that the word 'facilities' is not to be given a wholly unrestricted meaning but must be limited or confined to facilities that are akin to goods or services. Section 29(2) provides examples of the facilities and services mentioned in section 29(1). These examples support the view which I have expressed above.

In my judgment when the Secretary of State allows an immigrant to enter and stay in this country, he is granting a permission, he is not providing a facility. It could, of course, be said that he is conferring a benefit. Significantly, the word benefit is used in section 34 as additional to facilities or services: see section 34(2)(b), 'the provision of benefits, facilities or services. . .' and section 34(4) 'conferring benefits. . . .'"

Sir David Cairns agreed.

19. Re Amin
[1983] 2 A.C. 818

In 1976 the applicant, a United Kingdom passport holder resident in Bombay, applied to an entry clearance officer for a special voucher to enable her to settle in the United Kingdom. The officer refused to entertain her application on the ground that, not being a head of household, she was not eligible to apply for a special voucher. She was granted leave to apply to the Divisional Court for judicial review of the officer's decision and sought an order of mandamus requiring him to entertain her application for a voucher. The Divisional Court refused her application. She appealed to the Court of Appeal, contending that, on refusal of a special voucher, she ought to have been granted a right of an appeal to an adjudicator under section 13(2) of the Immigration Act 1971 and that she had been discriminated against under the S.D.A. The Court of Appeal held that she had no right of appeal to the adjudicator under section 13(2) of the Act of 1971 and dismissed her appeal. By a majority (3:2) the House of Lords also dismissed her appeal. One of the issues for consideration was whether the special voucher scheme violated the S.D.A.

LORD FRASER OF TULLYBELTON: "In my opinion the entry clearance officer who dealt with the appellant's application for a special voucher did discriminate against the appellant on the grounds of her sex. He had to do so because the special voucher scheme is in its nature discriminatory against women. The evidence in the case includes an affidavit from a principal in the Immigration and Nationality Department of the Home Office. Paragraph 4 of the affidavit is in these terms:

'4. There is no discrimination on the ground of sex. A woman holding a United Kingdom passport is eligible for consideration for the grant of a special voucher if she is widowed or single and a head of household or if she is married and obliged to take on all the responsibilities of the head of household owing to her husband's long term medical disability. In 1977 over 24 per cent of the special voucher holders arriving in the United Kingdom were women.'

The assertion in the first sentence of that paragraph that there is no discrimination on the ground of sex is in my opinion shown by the later part of the paragraph to be erroneous. The special voucher scheme proceeds upon the assumption that in a household which consists of, or includes, a married couple the husband is normally head of household. Only in exceptional circumstances, where the husband suffers from long-term medical disability, is the wife regarded as the head of household. That may be perfectly reasonable, in accordance with the general understanding in the United Kingdom and elsewhere, but it seems to me plainly discriminatory against women. Test it in this way. If the applicant for a special voucher had been, not the appellant in this case, but a brother of hers, who had married an Indian woman and gone to live in India, he would have been treated as head of his household (assuming that he was not disabled) and, as such, entitled to apply for a special voucher. I see no answer to the argument that he would have been treated in that respect more favourably than the appellant, and that the only reason for his more favourable treatment would have been his sex. I do not accept the suggestion that, for the purposes of the special voucher scheme, headship of a household is a fact which is independent of sex. That might be correct if inquiry were made in each case into such matters as whether the husband or the wife is the financial provider of the household or whether he or she makes the most important decisions; but such inquiries would be impracticable. The practice therefore is that the husband is assumed to be the head of household in a normal case. Accordingly I consider that there was sex discrimination in this case.

But not all sex discrimination is unlawful. Part I of the Act merely defines discrimination and it contains no provision for making it unlawful. Discrimination is only unlawful if it occurs in one of the fields in which it is prohibited by Parts II, III or IV of the Act. The decision of the Court of Appeal to that effect in *R. v. Immigration Appeal Tribunal, ex p. Kassam* [1980] 1 W.L.R. 1037 was in my opinion correct, and I reject the argument by the appellant's counsel that that case was wrongly decided. The alternative contention by counsel for the appellant, if *Kassam* was rightly decided, was that the discrimination involved in the special voucher scheme was rendered unlawful because it fell within the provisions of section 29... [Here Lord Fraser quoted s. 29, identical to s. 20 R.R.A.: see extract 16 above].

It was said that the granting of special vouchers for entry into the United Kingdom was provision of facilities or services to a section of the public, and that the wide general words of subsection (1) of section 29 were not cut down by the examples given in subsection (2) which are only 'examples' and are not an exhaustive list of the circumstances in which the section applies. Reliance was also placed on paragraph (*g*) of section 29(2) which expressly refers to services of a public authority and which has been held to apply to the Inland Revenue: see *Savjani* v. *Inland Revenue Commissioners* [1981] Q.B. 458.

My Lords, I accept that the examples in section 29(2) are not exhaustive, but they are, in my opinion, useful pointers to aid in the construction of subsection (1). Section 29 as a whole seems to me to apply to the direct provision of facilities or services, and not to the mere grant of permission to use facilities. That is in accordance with the words of subsection (1), and it is reinforced by some of the examples in subsection (2). Example (*a*) is 'access to *and use of* any place' and the words that I have emphasised indicate that the paragraph contemplates actual provision of facilities which the person will use. Example (*d*) refers, in my view, to the actual provision of schools and other facilities for education, but not to the mere grant of an entry certificate or a special voucher to enable a student to enter the United Kingdom in order to study here. Example (*g*) seems to me to be contemplating things such as medical services, or library facilities, which can be directly provided by local or other public authorities. So in *Savjani,* Templeman L.J. took the view that the Inland Revenue performed two separate functions—first a duty of collecting revenue and secondly a service of providing taxpayers with information. He said, at p. 467:

'As [counsel] on behalf of the revenue submitted, the board and the inspector are performing duties—those duties laid upon them by the Act which I have mentioned—but, in my judgment, it does not necessarily follow that the board and the inspector are not voluntarily, or in order to carry out their duty, also performing services for the taxpayer. The duty is to collect the right amount of revenue; but, in my judgment, there is a service to the taxpayer provided by the board and the inspector by the provision, dissemination and implementation of regulations which will enable the taxpayer to know that he is entitled to a deduction or a repayment, which will [enable] him to know how he is to satisfy the inspector or the board if he is so entitled, and which will enable him to obtain the actual deduction or repayment which Parliament said he is to have.'

In so far as that passage states the ground of the Court of Appeal's decision in that case I agree with it. If Lord Denning M.R., at pp. 465-466, intended to base his decision on wider grounds, I would respectfully disagree with him. In the present case the entry clearance officer in Bombay was in my opinion not providing a service for would-be immigrants; rather he was performing his duty of controlling them.

Counsel for the appellant sought to draw support for his contention from section 85(1) of the Act of 1975 which provides:

'This Act applies—(a) to an act done by or for purposes of a Minister of the Crown or government department, or (b) to an act done on behalf of the Crown by a statutory body, or a person holding a statutory office, as it applies to an act done by a private person.'

That section puts an act done on behalf of the Crown on a par with an act done by a private person, and it does not in terms restrict the comparison to an act *of the same kind* done by a private person. But in my opinion it applies only to acts done on behalf of the Crown which are of a kind similar to acts that might be done by a private person. It does not mean that the Act is to apply to any act of any kind done on behalf of the Crown by a person holding statutory office. There must be acts (which include deliberate omissions—see section 82(1)), done in the course of formulating or carrying out government policy, which are quite different in kind from any act that would ever be done by a private person, and to which the Act does not apply. I would respectfully agree with the observations on the corresponding provision of the Race Relations Act 1976 made by Woolf, J. in *Home Office* v. *Commission for Racial Equality* [1982] Q.B. 385, 395B-C. Part V of the Act of 1975 makes exceptions for certain acts including acts done for the purpose of national security (section 52) and for acts which are 'necessary' in order to comply with certain statutory requirements: section 51. These exceptions will no doubt be effective to protect acts which are of a kind that would otherwise be unlawful under the Act. But they do not in my view obviate the necessity for construing section 29 as applying only to acts which are at least similar to acts that could be done by private persons.

For these reasons I would dismiss the appeal on both grounds. The appellant must pay the respondent's costs of the appeal."

Lords Keith and Brightman concurred. Lords Scarman and Brandon dissented.

D. HOUSING

20. The Race Relations Act 1976

"Discrimination in disposal or management of premises
21.—(1) It is unlawful for a person, in relation to premises in Great Britain of which he has power to dispose, to discriminate against another—

  (a) in the terms on which he offers him those premises; or
  (b) by refusing his application for those premises; or
  (c) in his treatment of him in relation to any list of persons in need of premises of that description.

(2) It is unlawful for a person, in relation to premises managed by him, to discriminate against a person occupying the premises—

  (a) in the way he affords him access to any benefits or facilities, or by refusing or deliberately omitting to afford him access to them; or
  (b) by evicting him, or subjecting him to any other detriment.

(3) Subsection (1) does not apply to a person who owns an estate or interest in the premises and wholly occupies them unless he uses the services of an estate agent for the purposes of the disposal of the premises, or publishes or causes to be published an advertisement in connection with the disposal."

Identical provisions are to be found in the S.D.A., s. 30. It may be noted that an exception is made in both Acts for discrimination in the disposal of certain small dwellings (R.R.A., s. 22; S.D.A., s. 32).

E. ADVERTISEMENTS

21. The Race Relations Act 1976

"Discriminatory advertisements
29.—(1) It is unlawful to publish or to cause to be published an advertisement which indicates, or might reasonably be understood as indicating, an intention by a person to do an act of discrimination, whether the doing of that act by him would be lawful or, by virtue of Part II or III, unlawful.

(2) Subsection (1) does not apply to an advertisement—

  (a) if the intended act would be lawful by virtue of any of sections 5, 6, 7(3) and (4), 10(3), 26, 34(2)(b), 35 to 39 and 41; or
  (b) if the advertisement relates to the services of an employment agency (within the meaning of section 14(1)) and the intended act only concerns employment which the employer could by virtue of section 5, 6 or 7(3) or (4) lawfully refuse to offer to persons against whom the advertisement indicates an intention to discriminate.

(3) Subsection (1) does not apply to an advertisement which indicates that persons of any class defined otherwise than by reference to colour, race or ethnic or national origins are required for employment outside Great Britain.

(4) The publisher of an advertisement made unlawful by subsection (1) shall not be subject to any liability under that subsection in respect of the publication of the

advertisement if he proves—

(a) that the advertisement was published in reliance on a statement made to him by the person who caused it to be published to the effect that, by reason of the operation of subsection (2) or (3), the publication would not be unlawful; and

(b) that it was reasonable for him to rely on the statement.

(5) A person who knowingly or recklessly makes a statement such as is mentioned in subsection (4)(a) which in a material respect is false or misleading commits an offence. . ."

"Advertisement" is defined in section 78 as including every form of advertisement or notice, whether to the public or not, and whether in a newspaper or other publication, by television or radio, by display of notices, signs, labels, showcards or goods, by distribution of samples, circulars, catalogues, price lists or other material, by exhibition of pictures, models or films, or in any other way, and references to the publishing of advertisements are to be construed accordingly.

22. Commission for Racial Equality v. Associated Newspapers Group Ltd.
[1978] 1 W.L.R. 905

This was an action brought under section 6(1) of the R.R.A. 1968 which was similar in terms to section 29(1) above. The question which arose was whether an advertisement for nurses for South Africa which included the words "All White Patients" indicated or could reasonably be understood as indicating an intention to do an act of discrimination. The county court held that it did not.

LORD DENNING M.R.: "Those words seem to me to import a test similar to that which is applied in libel cases where there is no true innuendo pleaded and the question is: what is the natural and ordinary meaning of the words? Upon this question, no evidence is admissible to show what was intended by the words by the person who inserted the advertisement or published it: nor is evidence admissible to show what the readers of the advertisement understood by them: see *Hough* v. *London Express Newspapers Ltd.* [1940] 2 K.B. 507, 515. The question is one for the tribunal of fact: what would an ordinary reasonable man or woman understand by the words? Not an unreasonably suspicious person; not one who is apt to look for hidden meanings; not one who is of this racial group or that; not one who knows South Africa well; not one who knows nothing of it; not even a member of the Race Relations Board. But just an ordinary reasonable person; see *Lewis* v. *Daily Telegraph Ltd.* [1964] A.C. 234, 259, 260 *per* Lord Reid. Applying such a test, it is very much a matter of impression for the tribunal of fact. So much so that one person or set of persons may get one impression and another person or set of persons another impression. When the balance is even, no superior court can say that the first tribunal is wrong.

So, coming to this advertisement, these were the arguments on each side: Mr Dehn said that 'all white patients' was just part of the description of the job, like 'all the year sunshine.' An ordinary reader would not draw the inference that coloured nurses were excluded. After all, an ordinary person in this country knows that, in our hospitals where most of the patients are white, many of the nurses are black or coloured. So also it might be in South Africa. Even a specialist reader who knew South Africa well would know (as was said in a letter written by the Race Relations Board) that 'some hospitals have been granted temporary exemption from job-reservation provisions, to allow them to cope with the shortage of nurses.'

Mr Lester urged the contrary. He said that an ordinary man would know that in South Africa there was 'apartheid'—the separation of black from white races—and that by saying 'all white patients' an ordinary reader would understand that there were to be white nurses only, and not coloured nurses.

It is a nicely balanced question. There is much to be said on each side as to what a reasonable person would or would not understand the meaning of this advertisement to be. . . We should not reverse it unless satisfied that it was wrong. I am by no means satisfied that it was wrong, and, therefore, I would dismiss the appeal."

SHAW L.J.: "I agree. It seems to me that the ultimate question is whether, in the context of all the circumstances prevailing at the time of publication, it is reasonable to understand the text of the advertisement complained of as indicating an intention to do an act of discrimination. This is a question narrower than that which asks whether a possible meaning which can reasonably be attributed to the text of the advertisement is that it indicates an intention to do an act of discrimination. The answer to this question may well be in the affirmative when the answer to the first one is in the negative.

As to whether in the present case a contravention of section 6 was established, I see no compelling reason to differ from the decision of the court below. I would dismiss the appeal."

Waller L.J. agreed.

Similar provisions are to be found in the S.D.A., s. 38. However, the 1975 provisions are narrower and do not apply to all acts of discrimination, but only to those specifically unlawful in terms of that Act. Unlike most of the other provisions of the Acts which may be enforced both by individual complainants and by the Commissions (see *infra*, pp. 223-241), the provisions dealing with advertisements may only be enforced by the Commissions (ss. 63 and 72 respectively). However, it may be possible for an individual to bring a complaint about a discriminatory advertisement under section 4 of the R.R.A. and section 6 of the S.D.A. See *Brindley* v. *Tayside Health Board* [1976] I.R.L.R. 364.

F. INSTRUCTIONS AND PRESSURE TO DISCRIMINATE

23. The Race Relations Act 1976

"*Instructions to discriminate*
30. It is unlawful for a person—
    (*a*) who has authority over another person; or
    (*b*) in accordance with whose wishes that other person is accustomed to act,

to instruct him to do any act which is unlawful by virtue of Part II or III, or procure or attempt to procure the doing by him of any such act.

Pressure to discriminate
31.—(1) It is unlawful to induce, or attempt to induce, a person to do any act which contravenes Part II or III.

(2) An attempted inducement is not prevented from falling within subsection (1) because it is not made directly to the person in question, if it is made in such a way that he is likely to hear of it."

Similar provisions may be found in sections 39 and 40 of the S.D.A. In both cases, however, as with discriminatory advertisements, enforcement is normally only at the hands of the Commissions (sections 63 and 72 respectively). However, the E.A.T. has developed an individual remedy for application in cases of instructions to discriminate on racial grounds.

24. Showboat Entertainment Centre Ltd. v. Owens
[1984] 1 All E.R. 836

The applicant, who was white, was dismissed from his job as manager of an amusement centre. He was dismissed for failing to comply with an instruction to exclude young blacks from the centre. Following the dismissal, Mr Owens complained that he had been dismissed contrary to section 4 of the 1976 Act. The principal question before the E.A.T., however, was whether he had been discriminated against within the meaning of section 1(1)(a).

BROWNE-WILKINSON J.: "We have not found this an easy case to decide and our minds have changed from time to time during the course of the argument. But in the end we accept that the argument of counsel for Mr Owens is correct. In our judgment the words of s. 1(1)(a) are capable of two possible meanings, the one reflecting the broad approach of counsel for Mr Owens and the other the narrower approach of counsel for Showboat. It is plain that the person 'against' whom there has been discrimination is the person who is being treated less favourably by the discriminator, *i.e.* the words 'that other' in para. (a) refer back to 'another' in the phrase 'a person discriminates against another' at the beginning of the subsection. Therefore the only question is whether Mr Owens was treated less favourably 'on racial grounds'. Certainly the main thrust of the legislation is to give protection to those discriminated against on the grounds of their own racial characteristics. But the words 'on racial grounds' are perfectly capable in their ordinary sense of covering any reason for an action based on race, whether it be the race of the person affected by the action or of others.

We do not find that any of the arguments of counsel for Showboat compel us to give the words a narrow meaning. The fact that the giving of racialist instructions is dealt with separately in s. 30 in a part of the Act headed 'Other Unlawful Acts' is in our judgment explicable without requiring the words 'on racial grounds' to be given a narrow meaning. The mere giving of racialist instructions is not, on any view, rendered unlawful by the earlier provisions of the Act. Parts II and III of the 1976 Act only render discrimination unlawful to the extent that such discrimination has been manifested in the various ways specifically mentioned in Pts. II and III. Therefore, apart from s. 30, the mere giving of the instruction unaccompanied by any action pursuant to such an instruction which falls within Pt. II or Pt. III would not be rendered unlawful by Pt. II or Pt. III of the Act. Therefore, s. 30 by making unlawful the giving of the instruction itself is creating another unlawful act, namely the mere giving of the instruction. Moreover, there is nothing manifestly absurd in giving the Commission for Racial Equality the right to take proceedings to stop the giving of such instructions (if necessary by means of an application for an injunction under s. 63(4)) at the same time as giving a right of individual redress to someone who has actually suffered as a result of such instruction.

We do not accept the submission of counsel for Showboat that Pt. IV (including s. 30) is dealing only with matters which are preparatory to (and predate) any actual act of discrimination. Although s. 29 (dealing with advertisements) and s. 31 (dealing with inducement to commit unlawful acts) relate to acts predating any discrimination rendered unlawful by Pts. II and III, s. 28 is dealing with discriminatory practices which may concurrently give rise to individual claims under Pts. II and III. Moreover, ss. 32 and 33 create vicarious liability concurrent with the liability of the prime wrongdoer. We can see no pattern indicating that Pt. IV as a whole deals only with matters which predate discrimination rendered unlawful by Pts. II and III.

At this stage we should note a point not relied on by counsel for Showboat but which has caused us some hesitation. Section 1 of the 1976 Act deals with direct discrimination in subs. (1)(a) and indirect discrimination in subs. (1)(b). It seems to us clear that in relation to indirect discrimination under subs. (1)(b) the discrimination must relate to the race of the person against whom it is exercised. Thus the requirement or condition is applied to 'that other'; it is the racial group of 'that other' whose ability to comply with the requirement has to be considered; it is detriment to 'that other' which has to be shown. Throughout the section, the words 'that other' relate back to the person who at the beginning of the section is the person against whom there has been discrimination. It seemed to us that if, for the purposes of indirect discrimination, the racial characteristics of the complainant were the only relevant ones, it might be argued that the same must also be true in relation to direct discrimination under s. 1(1)(a). However, counsel for Showboat did not take up the suggestion, and in relation to this case, counsel for Mr Owens provided the answer. He said that if, for example, an employee refused to carry out an indirectly discriminatory recruitment policy on the grounds that it was racially discriminatory and was dismissed for such refusal, his dismissal would be 'on racial grounds' within s. 1(1)(a), notwithstanding that his refusal was a refusal to be a party to indirect discrimination within s. 1(1)(b).

We can therefore see nothing in the wording of the 1976 Act which makes it clear that the words 'on racial grounds' cover only the race of the complainant. As we have said, it seems to us that on the words of the Act alone it is open to give the words either a narrow or a broad construction. In *Race Relations Board* v. *Charter* [1973] 1 All E.R. 512 at 516, [1973] A.C. 868 at 887 Lord Reid said (of the 1968 Act): 'I would infer from the {1968] Act as a whole that the legislature thought all discrimination on racial grounds to be deplorable but thought it unwise or impracticable to attempt to apply legal sanctions in situations of a purely private character.' We are not here dealing with matters of a purely private character. Moreover Parliament, by s. 30 has shown that the giving of instructions to discriminate on racial grounds was conduct of a kind within its intendment. The only question is whether Parliament's intentions stopped short of giving a remedy to somebody to whom such instructions were given. We find it impossible to believe that Parliament intended that a person dismissed for refusing to obey an unlawful discriminatory instruction should be without a remedy. It places any employee in an impossible position if he has to choose between being party to an illegality and losing his job. It seems to us that Parliament must have intended such an employee to be protected so far as possible from the consequences of doing his lawful duty by refusing to obey such an instruction. We do not consider that the 52-week qualifying period thought by Parliament to be appropriate in relation to other cases of unfair dismissal would be thought to be appropriate in cases of racial discrimination to which no such time limit is attached. Nor do we think that the existence of the Commission for Racial Equality's right to enforce s. 30 affects our view: there is no reason why the individual's right to complain of the wrong done to him and the Commission for Racial Equality's right to stop unlawful action generally by injunction should not coexist.

We therefore conclude that s. 1(1)(a) covers all cases of discrimination on racial grounds whether the racial characteristics in question are those of the person treated less favourably or of some other person. The only question in each case is whether the unfavourable treatment afforded to the claimant was caused by racial considerations."

III. ENFORCEMENT OF THE LEGISLATION

A. ENFORCEMENT BY INDIVIDUALS

The provisions of the Acts may be enforced in two different ways. The first is by individuals who have suffered discrimination. Complaints in the employment field may be presented to industrial tribunals, while complaints in other fields may be made to sheriff courts (S.D.A., ss. 63, 66; R.R.A., ss. 54, 57). Where a complaint in the employment field is upheld, the tribunal is empowered to make any of the following awards that it considers just and equitable: (a) an order declaring the rights of the parties; (b) an order of compensation; and (c) a recommendation to take steps to obviate or reduce the effect of discrimination on the complainant (S.D.A., s. 65; R.R.A., s. 56). Complaints in the other areas to which the Acts apply are to be treated in the same way as any other claim for breach of statutory duty. This means that damages will be available as in the law of delict. The Acts specifically provide that damages may be awarded for injury to feelings, and also state that no damages are to be available where the claim is based on indirect discrimination and the respondent can show that he had no intention to discriminate (see S.D.A., s. 66, R.R.A., s. 57).

1. Burden of Proof

25. Humphreys v. Board of Managers of St George's School
[1978] I.C.R. 546

Mrs Humphreys unsuccessfully applied for a teaching post with the respondents. She was not appointed, although she was much better qualified than the man who was. She complained to an industrial tribunal claiming a breach of the S.D.A., but the tribunal dismissed the case after hearing her argument, and without hearing a representative of the school. Mrs Humphreys successfully appealed to the E.A.T.

Phillips J.: "To go on to the next important matter, it is this. As between the complainant on the one hand, and Mr Gilbert on the other hand, the complainant was better qualified educationally. She was a Bachelor of Education, whereas Mr Gilbert was not a graduate but held the minimum qualification which it was necessary for him to have in order to be able to teach. Furthermore, the complainant had been qualified and had experience since sometime in 1970 or shortly thereafter, whereas Mr Gilbert, at the date when the vacancies were first announced, was still in his probationary period as a teacher, and had only just come out of the probationary period at the date of the interviews for appointment. The complainant's case, put quite simply, was that this was a situation where the less well qualified, and markedly the less well qualified, person was appointed and where the person with markedly the less teaching experience was appointed. She says, but says no more than, that at least indicates a case which needs looking into and which demands an explanation. It is fair to say of the employers that they were there present, ready and willing to give an explanation; and very likely—we do not know—they had a perfectly good explanation to give. So this case does raise an important question as to the proper approach by industrial tribunals in situations of this kind.

It is a question about which we have already said something in *Oxford* v. *Department of Health and Social Security* [1977] I.C.R. 884. All we need do for present purposes is to repeat what was said then by a different division of the appeal tribunal. We pointed out that the burden of proof, formally at least, was upon the applicant; that it is a burden which may move very easily to the respondent as a result of the evidence by the applicant. In that case the industrial tribunal had expressed themselves in this way, at p. 886:

'At the conclusion of the [complainant's] case, we were inclined to reject his claim on the basis that no case against the [employers] had been established. Nevertheless, bearing in mind the difficulties the [complainant] faced, we decided to hear evidence from the [employers] and to give the [complainant] every opportunity to examine their witnesses and question them on matters he considered relevant.'

Then the judgment of the appeal tribunal continued, at p. 887:

'It seems to us that that was a very proper course to have adopted, and we would recommend it as being the course which in most circumstances is the right course to adopt. It further seems to us that, while the burden of proof lies upon the applicant, it would only be in exceptional or frivolous cases that it would be right for the industrial tribunal to find at the end of the applicant's case that there was no case to answer and that it was not necessary to hear what the respondents had to say about it.'

We repeat and endorse those observations. In truth an application of this kind, and the nature of the hearing before an industrial tribunal if justice is to be done, must partake of something at all events of the nature of an inquiry into what has gone on. We do not say, we cannot say, that in no circumstances at all can the industrial tribunal, having heard the applicant, say: 'That is enough: we wish to hear no more.' But such a course should be reserved, we think, for what we described as exceptional or frivolous cases. It does not seem to us that this case falls within that category. Here was a lady against whom nothing had been said, who was far and away the better qualified educationally, and who had by far and away the longer relevant service. In those circumstances we think that the industrial tribunal would have been wiser, and it could have been expected that they would have thought it better, to hear what the employers or the representatives present had to say about it.

Mr Hand, without conceding, does not really dissent from the view that in the case of a straight competition between two applicants for one post, of different sexes, where one is much better qualified technically or educationally than the other, and has had considerably longer relevant service, ordinarily one would expect, that having been established, and that candidate having been rejected in favour of the less well-qualified, that what the industrial tribunal would do would be to proceed to hear the respondents to the appeal. But what he says distinguishes this case is that his cross-examination demonstrated clearly what were the reasons which led the appointing body to appoint the less-qualified candidate. We do not agree about that, as we have already indicated. The cross-examination was helpful, the answers were frank, but it does not seem to us to establish clearly—indeed we are left in considerable doubt—what was the policy or approach of the appointing body as to the distribution of vacancies, or as to the method upon which they proceeded."

The Northern Ireland Court of Appeal adopted a somewhat similar approach in *Wallace* v. *South Eastern Education and Library Board* [1980] I.R.L.R. 193 and *Conway* v. *Queen's University of Belfast* [1981] I.R.L.R. 137. In the first case, the court endorsed an observation by Kilner Brown J. in *Moberly* v. *Commonwealth Hall* [1977] I.C.R. 791 to the effect that, where there has been established an act of discrimination, *prima facie* that raises a case which calls for an answer. In the second case this was explained as meaning that a case is to be answered where there appears to be a *prima facie* unfair preference. See also *Khanna* v. *M.O.D.* [1981] I.C.R. 653.

For reasons outlined by Lord Fraser in the following extract, overcoming the burden of proof is a major obstacle in complaints under either the S.D.A. or R.R.A. For this reason the E.O.C. has recommended that the burden be switched to defendants, and the C.R.E. is currently examining the position. But despite the difficulties facing complainants, the E.A.T. has displayed a certain insensitivity in insisting that:

"It does not seem to us to be sufficient merely to consider whether the fact that the person is of a particular racial group within the definition of the statute is any part of the background, or is (as is said in other cases) a *causa sine qua non* of what happens. It seems to us that the question which has to be asked is whether the activating cause of what happens is that the employer has treated a person less favourably than others on racial grounds."

(*Seide* v. *Gillette Industries Ltd.* [1980] I.R.L.R. 427, Slynn J. presiding.) In view of the well-known practical problems facing complainants under this legislation, it may have been thought sufficient and appropriate that racial grounds existed as a contributing factor in the defendant's action. More recently, the E.A.T., Slynn J. again presiding, has suggested that where there are several grounds for the defendant's action, the complainant should establish that racial grounds constituted a substantial reason for the action before he would succeed under the R.R.A. (*Owen & Briggs* v. *James* [1981] I.C.R. 337). So the complainant must not only overcome the burden of proof, he must also show that the discrimination was a substantial reason for, and an activating cause of, the action.

2. RECOVERY OF DOCUMENTS

26. Science Research Council v. Nassé
Leyland Cars (B.L. Cars Ltd.) v. Vyas
[1979] I.C.R. 921

In these consolidated appeals, the appellants alleged that they had been discriminated against, one on grounds of race, the other on grounds of sex, in their respective applications for transfer and promotion. The appellants sought the production and inspection (corresponding to "recovery and inspection" in Scots law) of records and reports relating to the qualification of themselves and of their fellow-employees who applied for the posts. Two issues arose in the case: the first was whether such documents were protected from disclosure by public interest immunity, and the second was the circumstances in which confidential documents should be disclosed in such proceedings.

LORD FRASER OF TULLYBELTON: "My Lords, these appeals raise questions of much practical importance about the powers of industrial tribunals and county courts to order discovery and inspection of confidential documents in proceedings by persons complaining of discrimination on the grounds of sex, race, or trade union activities, contrary to the recent Acts making such discrimination unlawful. . .
    Both respondents rightly accepted that the reports were not entitled to immunity

from disclosure merely because they were confidential. . .

The argument based on the need for candour in reporting echoes the argument which was presented in *Conway* v. *Rimmer* [1968] A.C. 910 and I do not think that it has any greater weight now than it had then. The objections by and on behalf of employees other than the complainers to having their confidential reports disclosed, readily understandable as they are, do not create a public interest against disclosure. They are based on a private interest which must yield, in accordance with well-established principles, to the greater public interest that is deemed to exist in ascertaining the truth in order to do justice between the parties to litigation. I am not satisfied that disclosure of the contents of confidential reports of the kind in question here would have serious consequences upon the efficiency of British industry. In any event, the possibility of industrial unrest is not a sufficient reason for the courts to fail to give full effect to the intentions of Parliament; the courts cannot refuse to apply the law between litigants because of threats by third parties...

Two other considerations point against immunity. One is that in some cases immunity would make it impossible for an employee to enforce his rights under the Acts. The confidential information is almost always in the possession of the employer, and, in cases where discrimination cannot be inferred from the bare fact that someone other than the complainer has been selected for preferment, it may be of vital importance to the complainer to have access to the reports on the preferred individual. This is particularly true where the complaint is based on discrimination on grounds of race or sex, because in those cases the onus of proof is on the complainer. But even where the complaint is of discrimination for trade union activities, and the onus is on the employer, disclosure may be essential in order to do justice between the parties.

The second consideration is that, if public interest immunity applied, it could not be waived either by the employer alone, or by the employer with the consent of the individual who is the subject of a report and on the person who made it. That would be inconvenient, and, in my opinion, quite unnecessarily restrictive.

For these reasons I think that the confidential reports in question here are not protected by public interest immunity. I pass now to consider the circumstances in which production ought to be ordered by a tribunal."

Lord Fraser then considered the Industrial Tribunals (Labour Relations) Regulations 1974 which provide that industrial tribunals may grant such discovery or inspection of documents as might be granted by a county court. A county court may grant discovery or inspection only if this is necessary for disposing fairly of the proceedings or for saving costs.

"Are there then special reasons why the ordinary rules should be applied in a way different from that in which they are applied by the county court? Some reasons were suggested. . .

Another suggested reason why discovery in proceedings under the statutes should be more restricted than in ordinary civil proceedings was that disclosure of personal particulars about an employee (such as the successful candidate for promotion) would be more objectionable when made to a colleague beside whom he would have to continue working than it would be when made by a party to an ordinary litigation who would not usually have a continuing relationship with the opposing party. A hearing in private (which may be ordered by a tribunal for the purpose of hearing evidence of information communicated to the witness in confidence—rule 6(1)(*b*) in the Schedule to the 1974 Regulations)—provides no solution of this difficulty, because it does not avoid disclosure to the complainer, who is a fellow employee. There is force in this argument, but it should be possible, by the use of the ordinary rules of discovery, to protect an employee from any embarrassing disclosure which is not absolutely necessary for disposal of the case. Discovery of confidential reports sought by one party and objected to by the other should not be ordered when the same information can be obtained from other sources which are not confidential or which do not contain sensitive material. The court or tribunal always has a discretion to refuse to order discovery where it would operate oppressively; oppression could occur if the quantity of documents involved is large or if the information is private and could be obtained in another way without infringing privacy; . . . Where discovery of confidential reports has to be ordered in spite of objections, every effort should be made to avoid disclosing sensitive information by covering up any parts of the documents disclosure of which is not essential. But where disclosure is necessary then in my opinion it must be made and personal privacy must be sacrificed in the interest of justice.

Where the holder of reports or other documents objects to producing them on the ground that they have been written on the basis that they will be confidential or when they contain sensitive private particulars about third parties, it will be the duty of the judge or of an appropriate officer of the court to read them and decide whether disclosure of the contents is necessary for the fair disposal of the case, or for saving expense. On a procedural level, we heard some argument about the stage at which discovery ought to be ordered in proceedings before an industrial tribunal. The respondents contended that discovery and inspection should not normally be made until the hearing. The appellants contended that it should normally be made at the interlocutory stage. Rule 4(1) certainly contemplates disclosure at the interlocutory stage as a possibility; but it does not seem to indicate that it is to be the normal practice. I can see arguments tending in both directions. In favour of early disclosure, there is the fact that there will be cases where discovery should satisfy a complainer that his complaint is unfounded and that proceedings ought to be dropped at once without further expenditure of time and money. Moreover if the number of documents to be discovered is large, then discovery at the hearing will almost certainly cause delay. On the other hand the procedure before an industrial tribunal is less formal than in court, the pleadings are exiguous; and hearings often take place very shortly after proceedings have been instituted. These are all factors tending to suggest that interlocutory procedure relating to discovery should be avoided if possible. . . The solution seems to me very much a matter for the industrial tribunals and the Employment Appeal Tribunal to work out in the light of experience; the practice probably ought to be flexible and to have a high regard to such matters as the nature of the case and the volume of documents involved. I agree entirely with the observations on this matter of Arnold J. in *British Railways Board* v. *Natarjan* [1979] I.C.R. 326, 333.

We were reminded during the argument that the statutes under which these appeals arise apply not only to England but also to Scotland (though not to Northern Ireland) and our attention was called to S.I. 1974 No. 1387 which regulates the procedure of tribunals in Scotland by rules which are almost exactly the same *mutatis mutandis* as the rules for tribunals in England. The effect is to apply the sheriff court rules as to granting commission and diligence for recovery of documents. If there had been anything in Scots law or practice on this matter which seemed to make the kind of approach that I have suggested unsuitable for application in Scotland, I would have reconsidered my view. But I do not think there is. It seems that confidentiality (in the sense of immunity) is rather more extensive in Scotland where it applies to a private diary—see *Duke of Argyll* v. *Duchess of Argyll,* 1962 S.C.(H.L.) 88—than in England, but I do not think that there is any difference in the extent of immunity relevant to the question raised here. The court in Scotland will exercise its discretion to refuse to order a third party to produce private documents containing relevant information if the information has been (or I think can be) obtained from other sources which do not involve disclosing private information: see *North British Railway Co.* v. *Garroway* (1893) 20 R. 397. The Scottish system of having excerpts taken from books and records by a commissioner, appointed as an officer of the court, would make it easy in a case where disclosure is to be dealt with at the interlocutory stage, to avoid disclosing personal particulars about third parties, unless their disclosure is essential. Accordingly I do not see any reason why the views I have expressed in these appeals should not be conveniently applicable by a tribunal sitting in Scotland.

The result is that I agree substantially with the principle stated in the Court of Appeal by Lord Denning M.R.... except that I would omit from it the words 'in the very rare cases.' I doubt whether the cases in which the chairman of an industrial tribunal will decide that disclosure of confidential reports is necessary will be very rare, and I do not think it would be right to suggest that the chairman should approach consideration of any particular case with a presumption against disclosure."

Lords Wilberforce, Salmon, Edmund-Davies and Scarman delivered concurring speeches.

In the Court of Appeal, Lord Denning had said ([1978] I.C.R. 1124 at p. 1139):

"the industrial tribunals should not order or permit the disclosure of reports or references that have been given and received in confidence except in the very rare cases where, after inspection of a particular document, the chairman decides that it is essential in the interests of justice that the confidence should be overridden; and then only subject to such conditions as to the divulging of it as he shall think fit to impose—both for the protection of the maker of the document and the subject of it."

3. REMEDIES

27. Orphanos v. Queen Mary College
[1985] 2 W.L.R. 703

The plaintiff, a citizen of Cyprus, had been resident in Britain for the purposes of education since 1978. In October 1982 he was accepted by

Queen Mary College for enrolment in a three-year degree programme. As a foreign student he was charged more than British and EEC students, having been informed that to be classified as a home student he would have to be resident in the EEC for the three years prior to September 1, 1982. In December 1982 a House of Lords decision concluded that a person who had been in Britain for the purpose of receiving education could be treated as ordinarily resident here for the purposes of paying fees at the same rate as home students. Thereupon the college decided that the plaintiff would be liable to pay reduced rates for the second and third years of his course, but refused to give a refund of the first year's fees, to the extent that the overseas fees exceeded the home fees. He complained successfully that the obligation that he pay the overseas rate for 1982-1983 was contrary to the R.R.A. The requirement in that year that he be ordinarily resident in the EEC before being eligible to pay at the reduced rate only was held to be indirectly discriminatory. Having succeeded this far, one question was whether Mr Orphanos could get restitution of his money.

LORD FRASER OF TULLYBELTON: 'On behalf of Mr Orphanos it is claimed that, if he has established a breach by the college of section 1(1)(b) and section 17 of the Act of 1976, as I hold that he has, he is entitled either to restitution of the excess of £1,320 which he paid for the first half-year's fees, or to damages. The claim for restitution is founded on section 72, which, so far as relevant, provides:

'(1) A term of a contract is void where—(a) its inclusion renders the making of the contract unlawful by virtue of this Act; ... (2) Subsection (1) does not apply to a term the inclusion of which constitutes, or is in furtherance of, or provides for, unlawful discrimination against a party to the contract, but the term shall be unenforceable against that party.'

Subsection (2) applies to this case as the objectionable term constitutes unlawful discrimination against Mr Orphanos who is a party to the contract. So the term is unenforceable against him, but that is not itself enough to entitle him to restitution of the amount overpaid. For that he relies on section 72(6) which has to be read along with subsection (5). These subsections provide:

'(5) On the application of any person interested in a contract to which subsection (2) applies, a designated county court ... may make such order as it thinks just for removing or modifying any term made unenforceable by that subsection; ... (6) An order under subsection (5) may include provision as respects any period before the making of the order.'

The argument for Mr Orphanos is that the word 'provision' in section 72(6) is wide enough to include an order, or a term in an order, for repayment of a sum overpaid. Mr Beloff invited us to remit the matter to the county court for the judge to make such order for repayment as, in his discretion, he might think just. In my opinion this argument involves reading into the word 'provision' in section 72(6) far more than it can properly stand. Section 72(5) empowers the court to make an order for removing or modifying an unenforceable term, and the power given by section 72(6) to include a retrospective provision must in my opinion be limited to provisions which are ancillary to or consequential upon the main part of the order. An order for repayment would not be of that character. Moreover, claims by a person against whom discrimination has been committed have as a rule to be made under section 57 of the Act of 1976, and are subject to short limitation periods fixed by section 68(1) and (2). But if a claim for restitution could be pursued under section 72(6) it would not be subject to those limitation periods, and it seems very unlikely that that can have been intended.

Accordingly I reject the argument based on section 72(6).

Damages

A claim for damages would be made on the basis that Mr Orphanos has suffered damage to the extent to which he has been overcharged for the first year's fees, namely £1,320, perhaps with the addition of a further sum for loss of interest on that sum or for the cost of borrowing it. I shall assume, without deciding, that a claim for damages could be properly mounted on that basis. The question then arises whether it would be excluded by section 57(3) of the Act of 1976.

Before turning to the terms of that subsection I draw attention to the fact that it occurs in Part VIII of the Act of 1976 which deals with enforcement. The first section in Part VIII is section 53 which provides, so far as relevant:

'(1) Except as provided by this Act no proceedings, whether civil or criminal, shall lie against any person in respect of an act by reason that the act is unlawful by virtue of a provision of this Act. (2) Subsection (1) does not preclude the making of an order of certiorari, mandamus or prohibition.'

The effect of that section is that, apart from judicial review and the equivalent procedure in Scotland under subsection (3), any proceedings to enforce the Act are prohibited except such as fall within the separate code, authorised by the Act itself. Section 54, 55 and 56 provide an elaborate code for enforcement of remedies in the field of employment. Section 57 makes provision for enforcement of claims under Part III of the Act which is the part that includes section 17 relating to discrimination in the field of education, being the field to which this appeal relates. Section 57(1) so far as relevant provides:

'A claim by any person ("the claimant") that another person ("the respondent")—(c) has committed an act of discrimination against the claimant which is unlawful by virtue of Part III; . . . may be made the subject of civil proceedings in like manner as any *other* claim in tort or (in Scotland) in reparation for breach of statutory duty.' (Emphasis added).

The reference to any 'other' claim in tort or in reparation shows that it is only claims of those types which are permitted under the Act of 1976. Consequently a claim for money had and received in England, or under the *condictio indebiti* in Scotland, is not admissible. Subsection 57(3) provides:

'as respects an unlawful act of discrimination falling within section 1(1)(b), no award of damages shall be made if the respondent proves that the requirement or condition in question was not applied with the intention of treating the claimant unfavourably on racial grounds.'

May L.J. in the Court of Appeal had no difficulty in holding that although the college had, in his view, discriminated against Mr Orphanos on racial grounds, it had done so unintentionally. I have reached the same conclusion, though with rather more difficulty. I approach the consideration of section 57(3) with two points in mind. First, the subsection applies only to an unlawful act of discrimination under section 1(1)(*b*), that is to acts of indirect discrimination, and it does not apply to acts of direct discrimination under section 1(1)(*a*). No doubt the reason is that an act of direct discrimination falling within section 1(1)(*a*) would necessarily be done with the intention of treating the claimant unfairly on racial grounds. Secondly, the subsection evidently assumes that not all acts of indirect discrimination falling within section 1(1)(*b*) need be done with that intent; without that assumption the subsection would be useless. So it is not right to say that any discrimination on racial grounds which (like the college's residence requirement) cannot be justified under section 1(1)(*b*)(ii) irrespective of the nationality of the claimant, must necessarily have been applied with the intention of treating him unfairly on racial grounds. Section 57(3) is looking at the subjective intention of the discriminator. Subsection 1(1)(*b*)(ii), on the other hand, is looking at the objective possibility of justifying the discrimination without reference to any of the racial grounds. When the college applied the residence test to Mr Orphanos their intention was to discriminate against persons who did not reside in the EEC area but there is, in my opinion, no ground for suggesting that they were intending to discriminate against them on the ground of their nationality or on any other racial grounds. Unfortunately, the discrimination on the grounds of residence cannot be justified irrespective of nationality, and it is therefore unlawful under the Act of 1976, but its unlawfulness is unintentional and accidental. I would therefore hold that, the requirement in question not having been applied with the intention of treating Mr Orphanos unfavourably on racial grounds, he is precluded by the provisions of section 57(3) from obtaining an award of damages."

Lords Diplock, Keith, Roskill and Bridge concurred.

Orphanos highlights important gaps in the legislation so far as financial recompense is concerned. But even where damages or compensation are available, in practice compensation has been very small. As we have seen, the legislation expressly permits compensation for injury to feelings. Yet in 1983 the average sum was only £200, and sometimes amounts well below this have been awarded, such as in a case in 1984 referred to by the C.R.E. where £30 was awarded to a youth who had lost a Y.T.S. place because of discrimination and was said by the tribunal to have been "shattered." The C.R.E. continued by pointing out:

"Save for one exceptional award of £5,000 made in 1985 to a medical consultant not appointed because of discrimination, the highest sum previously awarded so far as we are aware was £750 in 1982 to each of three white applicants who had been discriminated against by a Nigerian-owned company. The compensation is generally regarded as too low by complainants, as a survey of our own shows. The Commission shares that view. The level of compensation for injury to feelings in racial discrimination cases has trivialised the whole matter and enabled people to make light of a serious hurt."

(C.R.E. (1985: para. 27))

The problem was hardly helped by *North West Thames R.H.A.* v. *Noone* [1987] I.R.L.R. 357 where the E.A.T. commented on a decision of an industrial tribunal to award £5,000 for injury to feelings. This was described as being "way out of line," the E.A.T. referring to other cases where sums had been awarded "in terms of hundreds of pounds rather than thousands of pounds."

28. Irvine v. Prestcold Ltd.
[1981] I.R.L.R. 281

An industrial tribunal found that Mrs Irvine had been the victim of unlawful sex discrimination in her unsuccessful application for promotion. Apart from awarding compensation, the tribunal made the following recommendation:

"That the applicant be seriously considered as the most suitable candidate for the position of service administration manager as soon as it falls vacant, and that she be given opportunities for career development meanwhile, and that in the alternative she should continue to receive the difference in salary referred to above until she has been promoted either to that job or to a job of equivalent status."

The Employment Appeal Tribunal found the recommendation unsatisfactory, as did the Court of Appeal:

Fox L.J.: "I will deal first with the form of the recommendation of the Industrial Tribunal. I do not think that it is satisfactorily expressed. First the ambit of the words 'in the alternative' is obscure. In the alternative to what? Is it to all the preceding matters referred to in the recommendation or only to the recommendation that Mrs Irvine be given opportunities for career development? Secondly, it is not clear from what point of time the salary payment referred to is to be made. Was Mrs Irvine to receive the higher salary only in the event and from the time of non-compliance with one or other of the recommendations previously set forth? Or was she to get it in any event from the end of the four months' period until she was appointed service administration manager or to a job of equivalent status? The words 'in the alternative' suggest the former, but the words 'continue to receive' suggest the latter. And it is not easy to spell out of the recommendation a 'specified period' within which action is to be taken. But whatever may be the correct answers to these problems, it seems to me that the Industrial Tribunal had no power to make the recommendation which it did as to payment of an increased salary to Mrs Irvine.

In approaching the construction of s. 65(1)(c) it is to be borne in mind that it is not necessary for the protection of the complainant that the power conferred by para. (*c*) to make recommendations should extend to the remuneration to be paid to an employee. Para (*b*) confers upon the Tribunal power to order the employer to pay compensation for the discrimination complained of. It seems to me, therefore, that monetary compensation for the loss of remuneration is fully provided for by para. (*b*).

If para. (*c*) authorises recommendations as to wages, the amount might exceed the limit on compensation provided by s. 65(2) as amended. While it is true that the employer would not be obliged to pay the wages and that, if he did not, the employee could only return to the Tribunal and ask for compensation under (*b*) which is subject to the limits, I do not think that such a position was contemplated by Parliament at all. I think that monetary compensation is dealt with by (*b*).

When one comes to the language of para. (*c*) itself, I do not think that it is at all apt to cover recommendations as to payment of remuneration. The paragraph authorises the making of 'a recommendation that the respondent take within a specific period action appearing to the Tribunal to be practicable.' The paragraph is, therefore, concerned with the taking of some action 'within a specified period.' It is I think concerned with the taking of action without undue delay: an example is that given by the Appeals Tribunal, namely the provision of training facilities within a specified period. It seems to me that the words '*within*' a specified period are inapt to cover a recommendation *during* a period which might well extend over several years and even (if, for example, the position in question did not become vacant) over the whole of the employee's future period of employment by the employer. I am not saying that the taking of action may not extend over a substantial period but only that the payment of remuneration for employment does not, as a matter of the ordinary use of English, fit the description 'take within a specified period action, etc'. Accordingly, I think that the Appeal Tribunal reached the correct conclusion as to the ambit of para. (*c*) in s. 65(1). It is not necessary for me to express a view as to the opinion of the Appeal Tribunal as to the precise meaning of 'a specified period'."

Ormrod L.J. and Bush J. agreed.

B. ENFORCEMENT BY ADMINISTRATIVE AGENCY

The second method of enforcement is by the C.R.E. and E.O.C. Although it is crucial that individuals have direct access to the courts and tribunals to pursue their rights, it is equally important that an administrative agency should retain some enforcement function. Discrimination is a matter of public as well as private concern and the private remedies may not always be sufficient:

"Most victims do not complain. Many do not know that they have suffered discrimination. Others are reluctant to complain because they do not want to relive the humiliation which they suffered, or because they have no confidence in the effectiveness of the complaints procedure and the redress which it is likely to provide for them. Some complaints are trivial; others are misconceived. Although it is necessary for the law to provide effective remedies for the individual victim, it is also essential that the application of the law should not depend upon the making of an individual complaint."

Home Office (1975)). Moreover enforcement by an administrative agency may be the only effective method of dealing with an insidious and deep-rooted policy of discrimination being conducted by an individual or an organisation.

29. The Race Relations Act 1976

"Establishment and duties of Commission
43.—(1) There shall be a body of Commissioners named the Commission for Racial Equality consisting of at least eight but not more than fifteen individuals each appointed by the Secretary of State on a full-time or part-time basis, which shall have the following duties—

(*a*) to work towards the elimination of discrimination;

(*b*) to promote equality of opportunity, and good relations, between persons of different racial groups generally; and

(*c*) to keep under review the working of this Act and, when they are so required by the Secretary of State or otherwise think it necessary, draw up and submit to the Secretary of State proposals for amending it.

Power to conduct formal investigation
48.—(1) Without prejudice to their general power to do anything requisite for the performance of their duties under section 43(1), the Commission may if they think fit, and shall if required by the Secretary of State, conduct a formal investigation for any purpose connected with the carrying out of those duties. . .

Terms of reference
49. . . (2) Terms of reference for the investigation shall be drawn up by the Commission or, if the Commission were required by the Secretary of State to conduct the investigation, after consulting the Commission.

(3) It shall be the duty of the Commission to give general notice of the holding of the investigation unless the terms of reference confine it to activities of persons named in them, but in such a case the Commission shall in the prescribed manner give those persons notice of the holding of the investigation.

(4) Where the terms of reference of the investigation confine it to activities of persons named in them and the Commission in the course of it propose to investigate any act made unlawful by this Act which they believe that a person so named may have done, the Commission shall—

(*a*) inform that person of their belief and of their proposal to investigate the act in question; and

(*b*) offer him an opportunity of making oral or written representations with regard to it (or both oral and written representations if he thinks fit);

and a person so named who avails himself of an opportunity under this subsection of making oral representations may be represented—

(i)   by counsel or a solicitor; or

(ii)   by some other person of his choice, not being a person to whom the Commission object on the ground that he is unsuitable. . .

Power to obtain information

50.—(1) For the purposes of a formal investigation the Commission, by a notice in the prescribed form served on him in the prescribed manner—

(a)   may require any person to furnish such written informationas may be described in the notice, and may specify the time at which, and the manner and form in which, the information is to be furnished;

(b)   may require any person to attend at such time and place as is specified in the notice and give oral information about, and produce all documents in his possession or control relating to, any matter specified in the notice.

(2) Except as provided by section 60, a notice shall be served under subsection (1) only where—

(a)   service of the notice was authorised by an order made by the Secretary of State; or

(b)   the terms of reference of the investigation state that the Commission believe that a person named in them may have done or may be doing acts of all or any of the following descriptions—

(i) unlawful discriminatory acts;

(ii) contraventions of section 28; and

(iii) contraventions of sections 29, 30 or 31, and confine the investigation to those acts.

(3) A notice under subsection (1) shall not require a person—

(a)   to give information, or produce any documents, which he could not be compelled to give in evidence, or produce, in civil proceedings before the High Court or the Court of Session; or

(b)   to attend at any place unless the necessary expenses of his journey to and from that place are paid or tendered to him.

(4) If a person fails to comply with a notice served on him under subsection (1) or the Commission have reasonable cause to believe that he intends not to comply with it, the commission may apply to a county court or, in Scotland, a sheriff court for an order requiring him to comply with it or with such directions for the like purpose as may be contained in the order. . .

Recommendations and reports on formal investigations

51.—(1) If in the light of any of their findings in a formal investigation it appears to the Commission necessary or expedient, whether during the course of the investigation or after its conclusion—

(a)   to make to any person, with a view to promoting equality of opportunity between persons of different racial groups who are affected by any of his activities, recommendations for changes in his policies or procedures, or as to any other matters; or

(b)   to make to the Secretary of State any recommendations, whether for changes in the law or otherwise,

the Commission shall make those recommendations accordingly.

(2) The Commission shall prepare a report of their findings in any formal investigation conducted by them."

Section 53 of the S.D.A. establishes the Equal Opportunities Commission which is charged with the same function as the C.R.E. in the field of sex discrimination. Provisions similar to sections 46 and 48-51 above may be found in sections 57-60 of the S.D.A. The area over which formal investigations may be conducted is fairly extensive. The effect of section 43(1)(b) of the R.R.A. (and section 53(1)(b) of the S.D.A.) is such that it enables the C.R.E. (and the E.O.C.) to conduct investigations in areas to which the Act does not extend to make discrimination unlawful. So in *Home Office* v. *C.R.E.* [1981] 1 All E.R. 1042, it was held that section 43(1)(b) was sufficient to enable the C.R.E. to conduct an investigation into immigration policy. However, this may prove to be of little benefit where the Commission's investigation involves the activities of a government department, for under section 50 the Commission may need the authority of the Home Secretary before it can issue a notice requiring anyone to provide information for the purposes of the investigation.

Where in the course of a formal investigation either Commission is satisfied that a person is committing or has committed unlawful discriminatory acts, the Commission may serve on him a non-discrimination notice which will require him not to commit any such unlawful acts (S.D.A, sections 67-70; R.R.A., sections 58-61). Before the notice is issued, the Commission must give the party on whom it is to be served advance warning that it is minded to issue such a notice. The party then has an opportunity to make representation to the Commission. If, nevertheless, the Commission proceeds, there is a right of appeal (on which see *C.R.E.* v. *Amari Plastics Ltd.* [1982] 2 W.L.R. 972) against any requirement of the notice to either an industrial tribunal (if the requirement relates to acts which are within the jurisdiction of the tribunal), or to a sheriff court. There is also the possibility of judicial review of a non-discrimination notice: see *R.* v. *Commission for Racial Equality, ex p. Westminster City Council* [1985] I.C.R. 827. If within five years of a non-discrimination notice being served, it appears that the person on whom the notice was served will commit an unlawful discriminatory act unless restrained, the Commission may apply for an interdict to stop any such unlawful act being committed (S.D.A., s. 71; R.R.A. s. 62).

30. R. v. Commission for Racial Equality, ex p. Hillingdon London Borough Council
[1982] A.C. 779

The respondent council's area included Heathrow Airport, and in consequence the council had the responsibility under the Housing (Homeless Persons) Act 1977 of providing accommodation for immigrant families arriving at the airport who had made no prior arrangements for living accommodation. The council felt that that responsibility should be borne nationally rather than locally, and in November 1978, in order to attract publicity to their view, a member of the council collected an Asian family from the overnight accommodation with which they had been provided by the council and took them to the Foreign and Commonwealth Office, where he left them. At about the same time, a white family who had emigrated from Rhodesia were held by the council not to be intentionally homeless and provided with temporary accommodation. The two cases, together with an earlier one, led the C.R.E. to believe that the council might be discriminating on racial grounds in the provision by them of housing for homeless persons arriving at the airport from other countries. By resolutions of December 6, 1978, and November 7, 1979, the Commission drew up terms of reference under section 49 of the R.R.A. 1976 with a view to a formal investigation under sections 48 to 52, stating that they believed that the council might have done or might be doing acts in contravention of the R.R.A. including discrimination in the provision of facilities and services and the disposal of premises "to the public or such sections thereof as are or were in need of housing through homelessness." By letter of November 13, 1979, the Commission informed the council of their determination to embark on a formal investigation with those terms of reference. Woolf J. granted an application by the council for judicial review in the form of an order of certiorari to quash the Commission's determination, and the Court of Appeal dismissed an appeal by the Commission.

The Commission appealed.

LORD DIPLOCK: "It is a condition precedent to every formal investigation embarked upon by the commission on their own initiative that terms of reference for the investigation should have been drawn up by them, and where the terms of reference are confined to the activities of named persons it is also, in my view, a condition precedent to the drawing up of any terms of reference for an investigation of this kind (which like Griffiths L.J. I shall refer to as a 'belief investigation') that the commission should have formed the belief, and should so state in the terms of reference, that the named persons may have done or may be doing discriminatory acts made unlawful by the Act of a kind specified in the terms of reference. Although the draftsmanship of the two sections lacks self-consistency, this is I think the necessary meaning of section 49(4) when read in conjunction with section 50(2)(b). The draftsman appears to use the expressions 'activities,' 'acts' and 'act' in the singular interchangeably. Section 49(3) and (4) are clearly intended to refer to the same kind of investigation as section 50(2) (b), i.e. a belief investigation. The wording of this paragraph makes it plain that in order to entitle the commission to exercise the power to obtain oral and written information and documents granted by subsection (1) of section 50 and supported by the sanctions for which subsections (4), (5) and (6) provide, the terms of reference must state that the commission believe that a person whose 'activities' (vide section 49(3)) it is proposed to investigate may have done or may be doing acts of a kind made unlawful by the Act, and must also 'confine the investigation to those acts.' These last words of the paragraph are important; for the commission's belief *as stated in the terms of reference* defines and limits the scope of the full investigation and thus of the information that the commission may lawfully demand under section 50(1). Having regard to the wide variety of acts that are made unlawful by the Act, particularly section 20, fairness requires that the statement in the terms of reference as to the kind of acts which the commission believe the persons named may have done or may be doing should not be expressed in any wider language than is justified by the genuine extent of the commission's belief.

I turn back now to section 49(4), which provides for the preliminary inquiry that must be undertaken by the commission after the terms of reference have been drawn up but before the commission can embark upon the full investigation. In the context of this subsection 'any act' must mean the same 'acts' in section 50(2)(b), *i.e.* the kind of unlawful acts specified in the terms of reference which the commissioners believe the persons named may have done or may be doing. The requirement at this preliminary inquiry stage to inform the persons named of any act which the commission propose to investigate applies to every such act and serves to inform such persons what the commission proposes shall be the kinds of acts to which the full investigation should be limited. To give to the expression 'act' in this subsection a meaning narrower than that which I have ascribed to it and to limit it to individual acts rather than kinds of acts would impose upon the investigatory powers of the commission fetters that Parliament could never have intended. Racial discrimination is generally covert, easy to dissemble, difficult to expose. If the commission discover what they believe to be *prima facie* evidence of even one or two instances of racial discrimination by a particular person the circumstances may be such that they may not unreasonably suspect that these are but instances of a more widespread discrimination of a similar kind that has not yet been uncovered.

The purpose of the preliminary inquiry stage is to give the persons named in the term of reference an opportunity of making written or oral representations or both, with regard to the proposal to embark upon a full investigation of unlawful discriminatory acts of the kinds specified in the terms of reference. The purpose of such representations is not expressly stated in the subsection but it would in my view plainly cover representations by any person named that the proposed full investigation should not be proceeded with at all, or that its terms of reference should be made narrower in the exercise of the commissioners' powers under subsection (5), or as to the manner in which the full investigation should be conducted.

The Act lays down no detailed rules for the conduct of the preliminary inquiry. It refers only to the reception by the commission of representations by or on behalf of persons named to which the commission must give proper consideration. It is not an occasion for adducing evidence to the commission; this would involve the commission in embarking upon the full investigation to which the completion of the preliminary enquiry is expressly made a condition precedent by subsection (1). It is, however, the sort of enquiry at which in the event of oral representations being proffered Parliament considered it appropriate that a person named should, if he wished, be represented by counsel or a solicitor, which suggests that in conducting it the commission are exercising a quasi-judicial function; but I do not think that in administrative law as it has developed over the last 20 years attaching the label 'quasi-judicial' to it is of any significance. Where an Act of Parliament confers upon an administrative body functions which involve its making decisions which affect to their detriment the rights of other persons or curtail their liberty to do as they please, there is a presumption that Parliament intended that the administrative body should act fairly towards those persons who will be affected by their decision.

So far as the preliminary inquiry under section 49(4) is concerned, the manifest purpose of the subsection is that before deciding to embark upon a full investigation the commission should hear what any person whom it suspects of unlawful discriminatory acts has got to say as to why and to what extent the commission's suspicions are unjustified: *audi alteram partem*, the first rule of natural justice, is expressly required to be observed by the commission at this stage.

The right of a person to be heard in support of his objection to a proposal to embark upon an investigation of his activities cannot be exercised effectively unless that person is informed with reasonable specificity what are the kinds of acts to which the proposed investigation is to be directed and confined. The commission cannot 'throw the book at him'; they cannot, without further particularisation of the kinds of acts of which he is suspected, tell him no more than that they believe that he may have done or may be doing *some* acts that are capable of amounting to unlawful discrimination under the Act of 1976 or under some very broadly drafted sections of it, such as section 20, if their real belief (which is a condition precedent to embarking upon a belief investigation at all) is confined to a belief that he may have done or may be doing only acts of one of more particular kinds that fall within the general definition of unlawful acts contained in some broadly drafted section.

My Lords, the importance of confining the terms of reference of a belief investigation to the particular kinds of acts which the commission genuinely believe the persons named may have done or may be doing does not end at the preliminary inquiry stage. I have already drawn attention to the limits that the terms of reference impose upon the commission's coercive powers for obtaining information. They also impose limits on the kinds of acts that may be made the subject of a non-discrimination notice under section 58 served by the commission on persons named in the course of a belief investigation, which sets in train the cumbrous and unsatisfactory procedure for which sections 58 and 59 provide. This procedure is the subject of a recent judgment of the Court of Appeal in *Commission for Racial Equality* v. *Amari Plastics Ltd.* [1982] Q.B. 1194, to which reference may conveniently be made since the commission, although given leave to appeal from it, do not dispute that the reasons for judgment correctly state the legal effect of those sections. Finally, it is to be observed that when the procedure laid down in sections 58 and 59 is completed a non-discrimination notice may attract the final sanction of an injunction by a county court or a restraining order by a sheriff court to secure its observance.

I turn now to the terms of reference in the instant case. Those drawn up by the commission by their resolution of December 6, 1978 were in the following terms, in which I have placed square brackets round those words that were omitted in the subsequent resolution of November 7, 1979:

'The Commission for Racial Equality believe that Hillingdon Borough Council ('the council'), by themselves, their officers and servants may have done or may be doing acts of the following description in contravention of the Race Relations Act 1976. (a) Unlawful discriminatory acts in breach of section 20(1)(*a*) and/or

20(1)(*b*) read together with section 1(1)(*a*) and 1(1)(*b*) (direct [and indirect] discrimination in the provision of facilities or services to the public or such sections thereof as are or were in need of housing through homelessness). (b) Giving instructions to officers and servants of the council in breach of section 30 to do acts which are unlawful by virtue of section 20(1)(*a*) and 20(1)(*b*) read together with section 1(1)(*a*) and 1(1)(*b*) (instructing others to discriminate directly [and/or indirectly] in the provision of facilities or services to the public or such sections thereof as are or were in need of housing through homelessness), or procuring the doing of any such acts by servants of the council. (c) Unlawful discriminatory acts in breach of section 21(1)(*a*) and/or 21(1)(*b*) read together with section 1(1)(*a*) and 1(1)(*b*) (direct [and indirect] discrimination in the disposal of premises and/or the terms on which premises are offered to persons in need of housing through homelessness). (d) Giving instructions to officers and servants of the council in breach of section 30 to do acts which are unlawful by virtue of section 21(1)(*a*) and/ or 21(1)(*b*) read together with section 1(1)(*a*) and 1(1)(*b*) (instructing others to discriminate directly [and/or indirectly] in the disposal of premises and/or the terms on which premises are offered to persons in need of housing through homelessness, or procuring the doing of any such acts by servants of the council). [(e) The application of unlawful discriminatory practices in breach of section 28 (the application of requirements or conditions to the provision of facilities or services and the disposal of premises to a member of any particular racial group in need of housing through homelessness which results in or would be likely to result in an act of indirect discrimination, whether or not there has been any occasion for applying them to such a person).] The investigation shall be confined to these acts.'

It is to be observed that the section of the public in relation to which it is stated that the commission believe that the council may have been or may be discriminating upon racial grounds is *all* members of the public who are in need of housing through homelessness. (I assume that the commission meant the word 'or' in the phrase 'public or such sections thereof' which appears in paragraphs (*a*) and (*b*) to be treated as if it were not used disjunctively but was intended to cut down the wide meaning of the word 'public' that precedes it.) The terms of reference, however, do not confine the belief investigation to that much smaller section of the public who have newly arrived in this country as immigrants and are for that reason in need of housing through homelessness.

These terms of reference were communicated by the commission to the council by letter of March 9, 1979, which also set out at considerable length what were said to be the best particulars that the commission at that stage could give of the facts and matters which formed the basis of their belief that was stated in the terms of reference. The fact that those particulars did relate to immigrant families newly arrived at Heathrow Airport would not confine the terms of reference to this particular subsection of the wider section of the public who were in need of housing through homelessness. It is consistent with a belief by the commission that if the council practised racial discrimination against newly arrived immigrants, they also did so against members of ethnic minority groups already living in this country.

At the council's request the preliminary inquiry under section 49(1) included an oral hearing in August 1979 which lasted 2/: days. Whether as a result of this or not, the terms of reference were revised by the commission by resolution of November 7, 1979; but this revision, as can be seen by the square brackets that I have caused to be inserted in citing the resolution of December 6, 1978, consisted of eliminating paragraph (e) of the earlier resolution. The wide terms in which what the commission believed had been stated in paragraphs (a) to (d) remained unaltered except that the references in those paragraphs to 'indirect' as distinct from 'direct' discrimination were deleted.

In communicating this resolution to the council the commission stated their intention to 'exercise their power to embark on a formal investigation with the terms of references set out above.' Enclosed with the letter was a draft statement to the press which the commission proposed to issue, which was in the following terms:

'DRAFT PRESS RELEASE
'FORMAL INVESTIGATION INTO HILLINGDON BOROUGH COUNCIL.
'The Commission for Racial Equality have decided to embark upon a formal investigation into certain activities of Hillingdon Borough Council.

'The investigation will be concerned with the treatment by the council of ethnic minority families arriving in Hillingdon from abroad and applying as homeless to the council for accommodation. The commission will be examining whether some of these families have been treated less favourably than others on racial grounds.

The commission wish to emphasise that at this stage they have not formed any view as to whether or not unlawful discrimination has occurred.'

The description in this press notice of what the formal investigation would be concerned with is much narrower than the terms of reference, but it is the terms of reference, not any press notice, that determines the kinds of unlawful discriminatory acts on the part of the council and its officers in respect of which the commission are entitled to exercise under section 50 coercive investigatory powers. The relevance of the press notice is that it suggests, as the commission have now candidly conceded to be the fact, that while in November 1979 they did believe that the council might have discriminated on special grounds in the provision of accommodation for a section of the public consisting of immigrant families arriving at Heathrow Airport and claiming on arrival to be homeless, they had not then formed any belief that the council's discriminatory treatment on racial grounds of persons claiming to be homeless might have extended to any wider section of the public than that. Towards the end of his judgment delivered on April 15, 1981, on the proceedings for judicial review and quashing of the commission's resolution to embark on a formal investigation with those wide terms of reference, Woolf J. stated, as I think correctly, in two sentences, the way in which the commission had gone wrong in law. He said:

'What the commission, in my view, have clearly done is to announce that they have decided to embark upon a general and unlimited form of investigation because they have a basis for believing that there may have been a limited category of acts which would justify an investigation confined to those acts. This, in my view, is quite contrary to the intent manifest by section 49 and section 50.'

I agree, however, with Griffiths L.J. [1982] Q.B. 276, 293 that earlier in his judgment at first instance the learned judge had put the strength with which the commission must hold the relevant belief too high when he said that 'there must be something which causes them to believe that it is more likely than not that there may have been an act of discrimination.' This state of mind, which corresponds with the civil burden of proof, is one which must be reached by the commission in the course of the full investigation in order to justify the service of a non-discriminatory notice under section 58. To entitle the commission to embark upon the full investigation it is enough that there should be material before the commission sufficient to raise in the minds of reasonable men, possessed of the experience of covert racial discrimination that has been acquired by the commission, a suspicion that there may have been acts by the person named of racial discrimination of the kind which it is proposed to investigate.

I also agree with Griffiths L.J., at p.302, that Woolf J. put the scope of the permitted terms of reference too narrowly when he said that they were 'to be confined, with reasonable precision, to the same period, scope and persons as [those to which] the material, on which the commission base their belief, relates.' So to confine the terms of reference would emasculate the commission's investigatory powers. If they are of opinion that from individual acts which raise a suspicion that they may have been influenced by racial discrimination an inference can be drawn that the persons doing those acts were also following a more general policy of racial discrimination, the commission are entitled to draw up terms of reference wide enough to enable them to ascertain whether such inference is justified or not. But such is not the instant case; the commission never did draw any inference of this kind nor did they suspect the council of doing any acts of discrimination upon racial grounds except in relation to that particular section of the public which consisted of immigrant families newly arrived at Heathrow Airport who claimed to be homeless.

My Lords, at the conclusion of Woolf J.'s judgment at first instance quashing the commission's decision to embark upon a formal investigation with the wide terms of reference set out in the resolution, counsel for the commission invited the learned judge to make a declaration that the commission were entitled to proceed with a formal investigation with revised terms of reference drawn up to comply with the terms of the judgment. Woolf J. pointed out that there was nothing in the quashing order that he was making which would prevent the commission from reconsidering their resolution of November 7, 1979, and deciding to embark upon an investigation with different terms of reference.

If the commission thought, in April 1981, that a full investigation into events that they suspected had occurred what was by then some 2 1/2 years ago and which the council had throughout steadfastly denied justified the expenditure in manpower and in public money that such an investigation would involve, it is a pity that they did not take the learned judge's hint. Instead they appealed to the Court of Appeal against his judgment.

It does not appear that before the Court of Appeal the commission acknowledged, in terms, that they had no belief that the council's discriminatory treatment on racial grounds of persons claiming to be homeless might also have extended to any wider section of the public than immigrant families newly arrived at Heathrow airport. The commission's primary submission in the Court of Appeal was that, in the absence of bad faith on the part of the commission, the court had no jurisdiction to undertake any judicial review of the terms of reference for a formal investigation drawn up by the commission. This submission, which was repeated in this House, was rejected by the Court of Appeal, in my view obviously rightly. I am content, without repeating them, to adopt the reasons given by

Griffiths L.J. in his judgment, at pp. 298D—300G, for not accepting this submission.

What the commission did in the Court of Appeal appears to have been to disavow any *intention* to extend the full investigation to discriminatory treatment by the council of any wider section of the public than immigrant families newly arrived at Heathrow and claiming to be homeless, and on the strength of this disavowal as evidenced contemporaneously by the press release to submit that notwithstanding the much wider terms of reference that the commission had drawn up the court ought, as a matter of discretion, to decline to quash the commission's resolution to embark on the full investigation under those terms of reference.

My Lords, if the trial judge was satisfied that because of the breadth of terms of reference the decision to embark upon the full investigation was ultra vires, any discretion whether or not to quash it was vested in him. Even assuming that what the Court of Appeal, as I think rightly, regarded as the too narrow view taken by Woolf J. of what would be lawful terms of reference had the effect of vesting in that court a fresh discretion of its own, the Court of Appeal also exercised its substituted discretion in favour of quashing the commission's decision. Faced with concurrent decisions of the trial judge and of the Court of Appeal as to the way the discretion should be exercised, it would be contrary to your Lordships' oft-stated practice to interfere, unless a very powerful case could be made out for doing so. So far from this being so in the instant appeal, the current intention of the commission at the time when it embarks upon the full investigation appears to me to be irrelevant, whether they do or do not choose to express it in a press release. If in the course of investigating the council's treatment of immigrant families arriving at Heathrow Airport the commission were to uncover evidence which caused them to believe that the council might have carried out a more general policy of discriminating on racial grounds against persons claiming to be homeless, it would, in my view, be the duty of the commission under the terms of reference as actually drawn up to extend their investigation into this wider field.

My Lords, as I have already mentioned, in this House the commission, both in their written case and at the oral hearing, expressly admitted that at no time did they have any real belief that the council might have done or might be doing unlawful discriminatory acts in the provision of facilities or services to any persons who were in need of housing through homelessness other than members of immigrant families arriving at Heathrow Airport and claiming to be homeless. This admission makes this House's task in disposing of the appeal a very simple one. The existence of such a belief on the part of the commission was a condition precedent to their embarking on a belief investigation with the wide terms of reference that they drew up. The condition precedent was not complied with. This in itself is sufficient reason for holding the commission's decision of December 6, 1978, and November 7, 1979, to be ultra vires and void. Even without that admission, which does not appear to have been made expressly in the Court of Appeal, I would have dismissed the appeal for the reasons given in the judgment of Griffiths L.J. with which Waterhouse J. concurred.

In the Court of Appeal Griffiths L.J. and Waterhouse J., at the invitation of the commission, went on to express obiter their views as to whether the material relied upon by the commission as the foundation of their belief that the council discriminated upon racial grounds in their treatment of that section of the public that consisted of immigrant families newly arrived in the country at Heathrow and claiming to be homeless would have justified the commission in embarking upon a belief investigation with narrower terms of reference limited to that particular section of the public.

My Lords, this is a purely hypothetical question into which I do not think it proper that this House should enter. For this reason no argument has been heard upon it and, for my part, I must not be taken as expressing either approval or disapproval of the views that were expressed obiter by Griffiths L.J. and Waterhouse J., but only after what the former described as much fluctuation in his mind. After the great expenditure of public money that has already resulted from the commission's insistence on pursuing this matter right up to your Lordships' House despite the trial judge's intimation that there was nothing in his order to prevent the commission from embarking upon a formal investigation with terms of reference confined to the only matters which they in fact intended to investigate, I find it difficult to believe that the commission will persist in trying afresh to embark upon a formal investigation into incidents that they believe may have happened no less than 3½ years ago. The responsibility for deciding whether or not to do so, however, lies with the commission, not with your Lordships' House.

I would dismiss this appeal.

Lords Fraser of Tullybelton, Scarman, Roskill and Brightman concurred. See also *Re Prestige Group* [1984] 1 W.L.R. 335.

CHAPTER 6

FREEDOM OF RELIGION

I. INTRODUCTION

In this chapter we examine the nature and the limits of religious freedom
in Scots law. We begin by briefly sketching the special legal status of the
Church of Scotland and the Protestant religion. We then proceed to
examine how the courts and Parliament have taken steps to reinforce
religious values and religious observance. Historically, the full panoply of
the criminal law was used for this purpose, with blasphemy laws protecting
the Christian religion from vilification, and the Sunday observance laws
ensuring that there was nothing to distract the lieges from their holy duties.
These provisions survive in some form as anachronisms of the modern law,
and indeed are reinforced by a number of important facilities and privileges
which have been extended to promote the spread of religious ideology and
to assist the churches.

Chief amongst these measures are the statutory provisions relating to the
education of children, which effectively provide a framework of
compulsory religious education in Scottish schools. Other examples of this
type of facility or assistance are the provision of time for religious
broadcasting (on which see Annan (1977)), and the exemption of religious
bodies from rates and taxation (on which see the Valuation and Rating
(Scotland) Act 1956, s. 22, and Robilliard (1984)). Our third purpose in this
chapter is to examine how far the state tolerates the practice of minority
religions, given its commitment to the church. We pursue this enquiry by
looking at how religious beliefs and practices may present difficulties in a
number of fields and by examining how, if at all, the law responds to any
problems or conflicts which arise. Scotland, of course has a much smaller
immigrant population than England, and these problems loom less large.
Useful English comparison can be found in Poulter (1986: ch. 7 and 8).

II. THE CHURCH OF SCOTLAND

The status of the Church of Scotland as the national church was confirmed
and preserved by the Treaty of Union. The Treaty states that as it is
"reasonable and necessary that the True Protestant Religion, as presently
professed within this Kingdom . . . should be effectually and unalterably
secured; Therefore Her Majesty with advice and consent of the . . . Estates
of Parliament Doth hereby Establish and Confirm the said True Protestant
Religion . . . to continue without any alteration . . . in all succeeding
generations." The Treaty further provides that presbyterian government

shall be the only mode of government of the Church of Scotland. But although the Treaty established the supremacy of the presbyterian church in Scotland, the relationship between church and state was not always a happy one. In fact it was not until 1921 that it was satisfactorily settled. The Church of Scotland Act 1921 establishes the independence of the church from state control and, in so doing, permits a remarkable degree of internal freedom to the church in matters of doctrine, worship and discipline.

1. The Church of Scotland Act 1921

"Effect of Declaratory Articles

1. The Declaratory Articles are lawful articles, and the constitution of the Church of Scotland in matters spiritual is as therein set forth, and no limitation of the liberty, rights, and powers in matters spiritual therein set forth shall be derived from any statute or law affecting the Church of Scotland in matters spiritual at present in force, it being hereby declared that in all questions of construction the Declaratory Articles shall prevail, and that all such statutes and laws shall be construed in conformity therewith and in subordination thereto, and all such statutes and laws in so far as they are inconsistent with the Declaratory Articles are hereby repealed and declared to be of no effect.

Other Churches not to be prejudiced

2. Nothing contained in this Act or in any other Act affecting the Church of Scotland shall prejudice the recognition of any other Church in Scotland as a Christian Church protected by law in the exercise of its spiritual functions.

Jurisdiction of Civil Courts

3. Subject to the recognition of the matters dealt with in the Declaratory Articles as matters spiritual, nothing in this Act contained shall affect or prejudice the jurisdiction of the civil courts in relation to any matter of a civil nature.

SCHEDULE

ARTICLES DECLARATORY OF THE CONSTITUTION OF THE CHURCH OF SCOTLAND IN MATTERS SPIRITUAL

*   *   *

II. The principal subordinate standard of the Church of Scotland is the Westminster Confession of Faith approved by the General Assembly of 1647, containing the sum and substance of the Faith of the Reformed Church. Its government is Presbyterian, and is exercised through Kirk Sessions, Presbyteries, Provincial Synods, and General Assemblies.

*   *   *

III. This Church is in historical continuity with the Church of Scotland which was reformed in 1560, whose liberties were ratified in 1592, and for whose security provision was made in the Treaty of Union of 1707. The continuity and identity of the Church of Scotland are not prejudiced by the adoption of these Articles. As a national Church representative of the Christian Faith of the Scottish people it acknowledges its distinctive call and duty to bring the ordinances of religion to the people in every parish of Scotland through a territorial ministry.

IV. This Church, as part of the Universal Church wherein the Lord Jesus Christ has appointed a government in the hands of Church office-bearers, receives from Him, its Divine King and Head, and from Him alone, the right and power subject to no civil authority to legislate, and to adjudicate finally, in all matters of doctrine, worship, government, and discipline in the Church, including the right to determine all questions concerning membership and office in the Church, the constitution and membership of its Courts, and the mode of election of its office-bearers, and to define the boundaries of the spheres of labour of its ministers and other office-bearers. . .

V. This Church has the inherent right, free from interference by civil authority, but under the safeguards for deliberate action and legislation provided by the Church itself, to frame or adopt its subordinate standards, to declare the sense in which it understands its Confession of Faith, to modify the forms of expression therein, or to formulate other doctrinal statements, and to define the relation thereto of its office-bearers and members, but always in agreement with the Word of God and the fundamental doctrines of the Christian Faith contained in the said Confession, of which agreement the Church shall be sole judge, and with due regard to liberty of opinion in points which do not enter into the substance of the Faith.

VI. This church acknowledges the divine appointment and authority of the civil magistrate within his own sphere.

*   *   *

VII. The Church has the right to interpret these Articles, and, subject to the safeguards for deliberate action and legislation provided by the Church itself, to modify or add to them."

An important feature of the 1921 Act is the fact that the civil courts cannot review matters properly within the jurisdiction of the judicatories of the church. The assemblies of other churches have no exclusive jurisdiction and are subject to judicial review. In the eyes of the law, these other churches are voluntary associations whose members are bound together by contract. But although a relationship based on contract could give the courts considerable scope for involvement in the domestic affairs of the churches, they have wisely refrained from such involvement. In *McDonald* v. *Burns,* 1940 S.L.T. 325, Lord Justice-Clerk Aitchison said that the courts would only exceptionally interfere with the proceedings of a body of a non-established church, as in a case of *ultra vires,* or a breach of natural justice. This approach was recently confirmed in *Brentnall* v *Free Presbyterian Church of Scotland,* 1986 S.L.T. 471. For a detailed account of the effects of establishment, see Taylor (1957). For a full and interesting analysis of the development of the Church of Scotland, see Lyall (1980).

III.   STATE SUPPORT FOR RELIGION AND PUBLIC WORSHIP

A.   BLASPHEMY

2.   Bowman v. Secular Society Ltd.
[1917] A.C. 406

This case concerned the validity of a bequest to the Secular Society, a body which sought to promote the principle that human conduct should be based upon natural knowledge and not upon supernatural belief. The action was by a relative of the testator who challenged the bequest partly on the ground that any attack on Christian religion was illegal, however decent and temperate the form of attack. The House of Lords held the bequest valid.

LORD FINLAY, L.C.: "In my opinion the appellants have failed to establish that all attacks upon religion are at common law punishable as blasphemous. There are no doubt to be found in the cases many expressions to the effect that Christianity is part of the law of England, but no decision has been brought to our notice in which a conviction took place for the advocacy of principles at variance with Christianity, apart from circumstances of scurrility or intemperance of language. . .

We have been referred by Lord Dunedin to the law of Scotland on this subject as stated in Hume's Criminal Law (vol. 1, p. 568), and it appears to be the case that in Scotland scurrility or indecency is an essential element of the crime of blasphemy at common law. Certain Scotch [sic.] statutes which made it a crime to contravene certain doctrines have been repealed. The consequences of the view put forward on behalf of the appellants would be somewhat startling, and in the absence of any actual decision to the contrary I think we must hold that the law of England on this point is the same as that of Scotland, and that the crime of blasphemy is not constituted by a temperate attack on religion in which the decencies of controversy are maintained."

(Lord Finlay dissented on another ground.)

The last reported prosecution for blasphemy in Scotland is *Henry Robinson* (1843) 1 Broun 643, where it was held that anything which vilified the Holy Scriptures and Christian religion was an offence. It was also said (by Lord Justice-Clerk Hope) that a mere denial of the truth and authority of the scriptures and the Christian religion was blasphemous. The passages in the *Bowman* case suggest that this no longer reflects the modern law, and indeed it has been argued that blasphemy is no longer a crime in Scotland (Gordon, (1978a: 998)). But whatever the legal status of blasphemy, it is unlikely that a prosecution would now be brought, it being more probable that the Crown would proceed on some other ground, such as breach of the peace if the circumstances justified such a charge. Although it is true that a conviction for blasphemy was recently upheld by the House of Lords in *R. v. Lemon* [1979] A.C. 617, that was initiated as a private prosecution, and it is only in exceptional circumstances that such a prosecution will be permitted in Scotland (see *H.* v. *Sweeney* 1983 S.L.T. 48). For an interesting review of blasphemy in Scotland, see Maher (1977).

In principle, the crime of blasphemy seems difficult to justify. In a multiracial and increasingly secular society, there is no reason why Christian values should enjoy any special status in the eyes of the criminal law. During the Second Reading debate of an unsuccessful Blasphemy Laws (Amendment) Bill in January 1930, the following point was forcefully made:

"If language is used by anyone which is genuinely indecent, or which so hurts the feelings of people that it tends to cause public disturbance, these offences can be adequately dealt with under the existing law. The offenders can be prosecuted either for indecent language or for language calculated to cause a breach of the peace. There will still be ample resources for the preservation of decency and public order."

(234 H.C. Debs. 500). *Cf.* Law Commission (1981).

B.   SUNDAY OBSERVANCE

3.   The Sunday Act 1661

"Act for the due observation of the Sabbath day

Our Soverane Lord with advice and consent of his Estates of Parliament . . . Inhibites and discharges. . . keeping of mercats or using any sorts of Merchandise on the [sabbath day] under the pains and penalties following, viz. ten pounds."

Between 1503 and 1706 the Scots Parliament passed at least 13 statutes dealing with Sunday observance. The 1661 Act and the Sunday Trading Act 1579, which also prohibits the keeping of markets or fairs on Sundays, are almost all that survive (if, indeed, they are not in desuetude: *Middleton* v. *Tough,* 1908 S.C. (J) 32). In practice, the courts have shown a marked reluctance to enforce these measures, and in any event the penalty of £10 Scots is unlikely to be an effective deterrent. It is difficult to see what useful purpose these provisions serve, and little would be lost if they were repealed by the next Statute Law (Revision) Act.

Unlike in England and Wales (Shops Act 1950, Pt. IV), there is in Scotland no general prohibition against the opening of shops on Sundays, though it is possible for a local authority to require shops in its area to close early on Sundays (Shops Act 1950, s. 8). The statutory provisions which do apply in Scotland tend to deal with marginal areas of social and economic activity, including herring fishing, hairdressing and betting. Indeed, changing social values would make it extremely difficult to justify any serious control over what may now be lawfully done on Sundays. It is important to note that these changing values have informed the policies of both licensing authorities and legislators. Thus many licensing authorities permit theatres and cinemas to open on Sundays, and since 1976 it has been possible for public houses to obtain licenses for Sunday opening.

4. Report of the Departmental Committee on Scottish Licensing Laws

(Chairman: Dr Christopher Clayson)
Cmnd. 5354 (1973)

"9.58 To take first the principle of Sunday observance we, like the Guest Committee before us, fully recognise that some people sincerely hold the view that only works of necessity and mercy should be carried out on Sundays. As our predecessors pointed out, however, for many years there has been an increasing tendency towards a less strict attitude towards Sunday observance and this is a fact which it would be wrong to ignore. There is no doubt that this trend has continued in the last ten years or so, and perhaps more quickly in that period than previously. Like the Guest Committee, therefore, we feel we would not be justified in recommending against Sunday opening of public houses on Sabbatarian grounds alone. Similarly, the change which our predecessors noted in the traditional Scottish attitude to Sunday has continued in the last decade, although the tradition clings more strongly in some parts of the country than in others. The Guest Committee formed the view in their day that Sunday opening would not necessarily be repugnant to Scottish sentiment. We share that view. On the question of the need for a rest day for publicans and those employed in public houses, we fully accept this point. We do not see, however, that if public houses were allowed to open on Sundays this would mean a seven-day working week for the publican and his staff. We would expect that those involved would ensure that if they worked on a Sunday they would have an equivalent rest day on some other day during the week. So far as the social benefits of the traditional day of rest for the population at large are concerned, it could be argued that the fact that public houses are closed on Sundays does in fact detract from these benefits. (In this connection the proposals which we make in a later chapter to facilitate access by families are relevant.) As to the point of an increase in crime, drunken driving and rowdyism on Sundays, we think it is significant that the Association of Chief Police Officers (Scotland) was among the organisations in favour of Sunday opening."

Sunday opening was permitted under the Licensing (Scotland) Act 1976. Applications for Sunday opening must be made to the licensing authorities within the terms of Schedule 4 to the Act. Under section 16 of the Act, objections may be lodged by neighbouring residents, by a community council, by an organised church, or by the Chief Constable, and the application may be refused if the licensing authorities are "satisfied that the opening and use on a Sunday of the premises to which the application

relates would cause undue disturbance or public nuisance in the locality"
(para. 7). An appeal lies from a decision of the licensing authorities to the
sheriff, either by an objector or by the applicant. (See *Freeland* v. *City of
Glasgow District Licensing Board,* 1980 S.L.T. (Sh.Ct.) 125.) Apart from
the power to reject particular applications for Sunday opening, the
licensing authorities have the further power under Schedule 4 to impose a
Sunday restriction order:

"19. Where on a complaint being made to a licensing board by any person
mentioned in section 16(1) of this Act, the board is satisfied that the use of licensed
premises is the cause of undue disturbance or public nuisance having regard to the
way of life in the community in the locality on a Sunday, the board may make an
order (in this Part of this Schedule referred to as a 'Sunday restriction order'), and
the effect of the Sunday restriction order is that there shall be no permitted hours
on Sunday for such period as may be specified in the order or that the permitted
hours on Sunday shall be reduced by such a time and for such a period as may be
so specified."

C.   EDUCATION

5.   The Education (Scotland) Act 1980

"Religious instruction
8.—(1) Whereas it has been the custom in the public schools of Scotland for
religious observance to be practised and for instruction in religion to be given to
pupils whose parents did not object to such observance of instruction, but with
liberty to parents, without forfeiting any of the other advantages of the schools, to
elect that their children should not take part in such observance or receive such
instruction, be it enacted that education authorities shall be at liberty to continue the
said custom, subject to the provisions of section 9 of this Act.
(2) It shall not be lawful for an education authority to discontinue religious
observance or the provision of instruction in religion in terms of subsection (1)
above, unless and until a resolution in favour of such discontinuance duly passed
by the authority has been submitted to a poll of the local government electors for
the education area taken for the purpose, and has been approved by a majority of
electors voting thereat.

Conscience clause
9. Every public school and every grant-aided school shall be open to pupils of
all denominations, and any pupil may be withdrawn by his parents from any
instruction in religious subjects and from any religious observance in any such
school; and no pupil shall in any such school be placed at any disadvantage with
respect to the secular instruction given therein by reason of the denomination to
which such pupil or his parents belong, or by reason of his being withdrawn from
any instruction in religious subjects."

In 1968 the Secretary of State appointed a committee under the chairmanship of Professor W.M. Millar to review the practice regarding moral and religious education in non-denominational schools. The committee, which reported in 1972, with a number of suggestions for improving the quality of religious education, found no evidence of any move in any local educational authority's area to have a poll taken to discontinue religious education in terms of what is now section 8(2).

Very few parents exercise the right available to them in section 9 of the 1980 Act. The Millar Committee found that in 96 per cent of primary schools no parents, or less than 1 per cent of parents, exercised this right. In the remaining 4 per cent of primary schools, between 1 per cent and 10 per cent of parents elected to withdraw their children. In 93 per cent of secondary schools, no parents or less than 1 per cent exercised their right, and of the remaining 7 per cent, again between 1 per cent and 10 per cent of the parents sought the exemption of their children. The continuing relevance and future of the conscience clause was considered by the Millar Committee.

6. Report of a Committee on Moral and Religious Education in Scottish Schools
Scottish Office (1972)

"(a) Primary School

We have recommended . . . that in the primary school religious education should largely avoid the kind of formal instruction in religion for which the 'conscience clause' was designed, and should be part of the children's exploration of their world and their relations with each other which the various activities in the classroom are designed to further. In this context it is particularly difficult—and indeed futile—to try to draw a line between what is religious and what is not, and the more a teacher has succeeded in removing the barriers between 'subjects' in the primary school the more difficult it will be for her to tell at which points a child who is to be withdrawn from religious education should be asked to do something else. The development of the integrated day and the use of project methods is likely to make withdrawal from 'instruction in religious subjects' less and less meaningful and may well create problems in the few cases where the parents insist on having their children withdrawn. It would be possible to simplify the problems by dealing with religious education in a fairly isolated way, but this would be to damage the real value of religious education, and we think it would be quite wrong to do this simply in order to make it easier to organise withdrawal of a child when it is requested. We recommend that when parents send a request to a primary school for withdrawal of their child or children the headteacher and the class teacher should discuss this with the parents to ensure that the parents understand the nature of the religious education being given in the school, the dislocation of the child's education that may be caused, and the problems that can result from a child being obviously isolated from his own group in certain circumstances. There should, of course, be no attempt to persuade the parents against their wishes to give up their right to have their children withdrawn, and if they insist the teacher should try to see that this is carried out with the minimum of disturbance both to the child concerned and the rest of the class. But we hope that if our general recommendations are followed parents will see religious education as an essential part of their children's education as a whole.

(b) *Secondary School*

From the section we have written on the secondary school in the previous chapter it will be clear that we regard religious education as an important element in every child's education at the secondary stage, and that we want it to move away completely from any attempt at indoctrination or conversion. So we expect that few parents will wish to have their children withdrawn from the kind of religious education in the secondary school that we have proposed. There will not be the same difficulties in identifying 'religious education' as there is likely to be in the primary school, since even in a situation where a team of teachers is dealing with the group of related subjects . . . it should generally be possible to mark out that time that could be described as religious education. But again we think the headteacher or an appropriate senior teacher should discuss with parents any request for withdrawal of children to make sure that the request is not based on a misconception of what religious education means in the school.

The right of withdrawal guaranteed by law belongs to the parent, but problems arise in the later years of secondary school when pupils themselves ask to be excused religious education, and particularly services of worship. Our view is that for pupils below the statutory school leaving age the question of withdrawal should be entirely a matter between the parent and the school. But the young people who remain at school for a fifth and a sixth year are beginning to be faced much more clearly with a range of situations where personal and moral choice is called for and are frequently exhorted to be responsible in using their freedom of choice; and they tend to feel—to some extent rightly—that the fact that they are at school through choice and not by compulsion should have implications for their freedom to be involved in or stay away from particular activities of the school. Requests from pupils in the fifth and sixth years of secondary school to withdraw from religious education should be treated seriously by the head teacher, and he or an appropriate deputy should discuss such a request with the pupil. If he is fairly certain that the pupil objects on grounds of genuine personal belief to being involved in religious education (even of the kind we propose) or services of worship, and if the parents raise no objection, we think such requests should be granted."

IV. RELIGIOUS TOLERANCE

A. EMPLOYMENT

7. Ahmad v. Inner London Education Authority
[1976] I.C.R. 461; [1977] I.C.R. 490

Mr Ahmad was employed as a schoolteacher. He was a practising Muslim and insisted on taking time off work every Friday to attend a nearby mosque for prayers. The lunch break at school was between 12.30 and 1.30 p.m., whereas the prayers were held between 1.00 and 2.00 p.m., and Mr Ahmad did not return to the school until 2.15 or 2.20 p.m. Following some protest from fellow employees, the I.L.E.A. eventually sought to deal with the issue by offering Mr Ahmad a new contract as a part-time teacher engaged for four and one-half days per week. His original contract was a full-time one. On receiving this offer, Mr Ahmad resigned, claiming that he had been unfairly dismissed. An industrial tribunal dismissed his claim and his appeals to both the Employment Appeal Tribunal and the Court of Appeal (by a majority) were unsuccessful.

PHILLIPS J. (E.A.T.): "The cause of the trouble lies in the employee's religious convictions: he is a devout Moslem. . . The employee wished to attend the mosque on Fridays. This is, unless there is good reason to be excused, a matter of obligation for practising Moslems. It is said in the reasons given by the industrial tribunal that: 'The only acceptable excuses are to be a woman, a child, a traveller, a slave or to be sick.' At his previous schools, where there was no mosque within easy reach, it had sufficed for him to say his prayers in a room set aside for that purpose. When he was in the school where these matters came to a head there was a mosque nearer at hand.

The conflict arose from the fact that his absence to go to the mosque meant that he would not be available to take classes which otherwise it would have been his duty to take. So, on the one hand, the education authority required him to be present because he was a full-time primary teacher, and, on the other hand, he desired leave of absence so as to carry out his religious obligations. Those two requirements—his, to go to the mosque; the educational authority's, to have him present to teach—were irreconcilable. There was a long process of negotiation and discussion, but eventually the employee was informed that he could not be granted permission to be absent every Friday and, if he insisted, he must accept appointment as a four-and-half day temporary teacher. . . He found that unacceptable and so he parted company with the employers. . .

There is no doubt at all that, as the industrial tribunal found, under his contract with the employers, the employee was duty bound to be in the school on Friday afternoons. It is equally clear that he was required to work full-time. Further, it found that under that contract, freely entered into, he had worked satisfactorily for something like five years, and that no mention had been made before he was employed of his requirement to attend a mosque. The industrial tribunal found, rightly, in our judgment, that there was no question of there having been any variation of the terms of his employment, though at various times, when employed in different schools, ad *hoc* arrangements had been made with individual headmasters, sometimes to pray in a room set aside for that purpose, on one or two occasions actually to attend a mosque. Accordingly, had the employee done what he wanted to do, that is, to absent himself for part of Friday afternoons, contrary to the wishes of his employers, he would have been acting in breach of his contract.

Reliance was placed by him on clause 9 of the staff code. That clause is set out in the tribunal's reasons and makes provision for absence of a full day's duration for religious observance on particular days. The tribunal found, in our judgment, correctly, that that did not extend to cover a case such as this, where a teacher desired to be absent every week, as here, on part of Friday. It is quite clear from the concluding words of that clause that the leave is to be 'restricted to days which are generally recognised in their religion as days when no work may be done.' No doubt what was in mind there was a day such as Good Friday, the Day of Atonement or something of that kind. Clearly it does not apply to a day every week during some part of which the member of that religion is required to attend his place of worship; so we are satisfied that the clause affords the employee no assistance.

The industrial tribunal concluded by looking at the matter quite generally and coming to the conclusion that in all the circumstances the employers had behaved quite reasonably in the course which they took in this difficult situation. They pointed out (and with this we would agree) that matters of this kind are better resolved by agreement at national level. The difficulties are obvious. We have now in this country persons of many different religions, and to accommodate them all in a workable time-table cannot be easy. Matters of this sort are far better dealt with by general agreement."

In order to bring a successful unfair dismissal case, an employee must not be within the categories of workers excluded from the legislation (now to be found in the Employment Protection (Consolidation) Act 1978, Part V). Those excluded include people engaged by the employer for less than two years, and some part-time workers (which thus excludes many women). If the employee is not excluded, he or she must show that there had been a dismissal. This means a termination by the employer; the expiry of a fixed-term contract; or what is known as constructive dismissal—that is to say, resignation by the employee in response to a breach of a fundamental term of the employment contract by the employer. If there has been a dismissal of an eligible employee, the merits may then be considered. In order to succeed, the applicant must satisfy an industrial tribunal first that the dismissal was for one of the five general reasons permitted by the Act, and secondly, that the employer acted reasonably in accordance with equity and the substantial merits of the case in treating that reason as a ground for dismissal.

A dismissal on the ground of religious belief or practice alone would almost certainly be unfair, being unlikely to cross the first of these two hurdles. Where, however, the dismissal is caused by a conflict between the employee's practice or observance of his religion and the demands of his job, much will depend on the circumstances of the case. Particularly in large enterprises (and where the employee's presence is not indispensable), an employer may be expected to accommodate the needs of his employee and to make some adjustment for them provided that the employee's demands are not unreasonable. However, employers will not always be required to go as far as the I.L.E.A. in the *Ahmad* case, where the employee was offered a fresh contract for a four and one-half day week. Dismissals have been held to be fair in one case where the employee on joining the Seventh-Day Adventists refused to work compulsory Saturday overtime, and in another case where the employee, a Sikh, refused to shave his beard on religious grounds. This was required by his employer for reasons of hygiene: see respectively *Esson* v. *London Transport Executive* [1975] I.R.L.R. 48, and *Singh* v. *Lyons Maid Ltd.* [1975] I.R.L.R. 328.

B. MARRIAGE

8. The Marriage (Scotland) Act 1977

"Persons who may solemnise marriage
 8.—(1) A marriage may be solemnised by and only by—
 (*a*) a person who is—
   (i) a minister of the Church of Scotland; or
   (ii) a minister, clergyman, pastor, or priest of a religious body prescribed by regulations made by the Secretary of State, or who, not being one of the foregoing, is recognised by a religious body so prescribed as entitled to solemnise marriage on its behalf; or
   (iii) registered under section 9 of this Act; or
   (iv) temporarily authorised under section 12 of this Act; or
 (*b*) a person who is a district registrar or assistant registrar appointed under section 17 of this Act.
 (2) In this Act—
 (*a*) any such person as is mentioned in subsection (1)(*a*) above is referred to as an 'approved celebrant,' and a marriage solemnised by an approved celebrant is referred to as a 'religious marriage';
 (b) any such person as is mentioned in subsection (1)(*b*) above is referred to as an 'authorised registrar,' and a marriage solemnised by an authorised registrar is referred to as a 'civil marriage.'

Registration of nominated persons as celebrants
 9.—(1) A religious body, not being—
 (*a*) the Church of Scotland; or
 (*b*) prescribed by virtue of section 8(1)(*a*)(ii) of this Act,
may nominate to the Registrar General any of its members who it desires should be registered under this section as empowered to solemnise marriages:
 Provided that any such nominee must, at the date of his nomination, be 21 years of age or over.
 (2) The Registrar General shall reject a nomination made under subsection (1) above if in his opinion—
 (*a*) the nominating body is not a religious body; or
 (*b*) the marriage ceremony used by that body is not of an appropriate form; or
 (c) the nominee is not a fit and proper person to solemnise a marriage; or
 (*d*) there are already registered under this section sufficient members of the same religious body as the nominee to meet the needs of that body."

Section 10 of the 1977 Act makes provision for the removal of a celebrant's name from the authorised list by the Registrar General, generally on the grounds relating to unfitness for office. Section 11 enables the religious body to change its celebrant or to cancel the registration of any such celebrant. Section 12 enables the Registrar General to grant a temporary authorisation to solemnise marriages. A marriage solemnised by an approved celebrant must be one in which both parties to the marriage are present and at which two witnesses purporting to be over 16 are present (s. 13).

Regulations made under section 8(1)(ii) have prescribed the following religious bodies: the Baptist Union of Scotland; the Congregational Church of Scotland; the Episcopal Church in Scotland and other churches of the Anglican Communion; the Free Church of Scotland; the Free Presbyterian Church of Scotland; the Hebrew Congregation; the Methodist Church in Scotland; the Religious Society of Friends; the Roman Catholic Church; the Salvation Army; the Scottish Unitarian Association; and the United Free Church of Scotland (Marriage (Prescription of Religious Bodies) (Scotland) Regulations S.I. 1977/1670).

These provisions give effect to the recommendations of Kilbrandon (1969). Under the pre-1977 law a marriage could be registered only if it was celebrated by a clergyman of a Christian denomination or according to Jewish or Quaker usages (Registration of Births, Deaths and Marriages (Scotland) Act 1965, s. 29). This gave rise to two problems: first, it presented the Registrar of Births, Deaths and Marriages, who had the duty to issue marriage schedules to appropriate celebrants, with the difficult task of determining who was a "clergyman" of a "Christian denomination," a not inconsiderable problem in marginal cases. Second, the law discriminated against non-Christian ecclesiastical marriages. The 1977 Act removes the latter impediment and goes some way towards dealing with the first problem, though the Registrar General may now have to determine what is a religious body, just as he was required before 1977 to determine what was a Christian denomination.

9. The Matrimonial Proceedings (Polygamous Marriages) Act 1972

"Matrimonial relief and declarations as to validity in respect of polygamous marriages: Scotland

2.—(1) A court in Scotland shall not be precluded from entertaining proceedings for, or granting, any such decree as is mentioned in subsection (2) below by reason only that the marriage to which the proceedings relate was entered into under a law which permits polygamy.

(2) The decrees referred to in subsection (1) above are—

(*a*)   a decree of divorce;

(*b*)   a decree of nullity of marriage; . . .

.   .   .   .   .   .

(*d*)   a decree of judicial separation;

(e) a decree of separation and aliment, adherence and aliment, or interim aliment;

(f) a decree of declarator that a marriage is valid or invalid;

(g) any other decree involving a determination as to the validity of a marriage; and the reference in subsection (1) above to granting such a decree as aforesaid includes a reference to making any ancillary order which the court has power to make in proceedings for such a decree.

(3) This section has effect whether or not either party to the marriage in question has for the time being any spouse additional to the other party; and provision may be made by rules of court—

(a) for requiring notice of proceedings brought by virtue of this section to be served on any such other spouse; and

(b) for conferring on any such other spouse the right to be heard in any such proceedings;

in such cases as may be specified in the rules."

At common law the courts, in both England and Scotland, refused to recognise a marriage which was merely potentially polygamous. The marriage law of this country is based on Christian values, and so marriages must be monogamous. A spouse in a polygamous marriage was thus unable to obtain a matrimonial remedy where, say, his partner was guilty of adultery (*Muhammad* v. *Suna*. 1956 S.C. 366). The 1972 Act was passed following criticism of the common law position by the Law Commission (1971). Polygamous marriages are also recognised for social security purposes and for limited purposes at common law (see Clive (1982: 128-135)). It should be emphasised, however, that the recognition of polygamous marriages is a limited one. In particular, it may be noted that a marriage contracted in this country while an earlier marriage survived would almost certainly be bigamous and therefore a crime, regardless of any claims that the parties' religion permitted such marriage: *cf. R.* v. *Sarwan Singh* [1962] 3 All E.R. 612 and Leslie (1972).

C. EDUCATION

10. The Education (Scotland) Act 1980

"Transference of denominational schools to education authorities
16.—(1) It shall be lawful for the person or persons vested with the titles of any school established after 21st November 1918, to which section 18 of the Act of 1918 would have applied had the school been in existence at that date, with the consent of the trustees of any trust upon which the school is held and of the Secretary of State, to transfer the school together with the site thereof and any land or buildings and furniture held and used in connection therewith, by sale, lease or otherwise, to the education authority, who shall be bound to accept such transfer, upon such terms as to price, rent, or other consideration as may be agreed, or as may be determined,

failing agreement, by an arbiter appointed by the Secretary of State upon the application of either party.

Provision, maintenance and equipment of schools and other buildings

17.—. . .

(2) In any case where an education authority are satisfied, whether upon representations made to them by any church or denominational body acting on behalf of the parents of children belonging to such church or body or otherwise, that a new school is required for the accommodation of children whose parents are resident within the area of the authority, regard being had to the religious belief of such parents, it shall be lawful for the education authority to provide a new school...

Management of denominational schools

21.—(1) Any school transferred to an educational authority under section 16(1) of this Act shall be held, maintained and managed by the educational authority as a public school.

(2) In any such school the education authority shall have the sole power of regulating the curriculum and of appointing teachers:

Provided that—

 (i) all teachers appointed to the staff of any such school by the education authority shall in every case be teachers who satisfy the Secretary of State as to qualification, and are approved as regards their religious belief and character by representatives of the church or denominational body in whose interest the school has been conducted;

 (ii) subject to the provisions of section 9 of this Act, the time set apart for religious instruction or observance in any such school shall not be less than that so set apart according to the use and wont of the former management of the school.

(3) For each school the education authority shall appoint as supervisor of religious instruction, without remuneration, a person approved as regards religious belief and character as aforesaid, and the supervisor so appointed shall report to the education authority as to the efficiency of the religious instruction given in such school, and shall be entitled to enter the school at all times set apart for religious instruction or observance.

(4) In every such school the education authority shall give facilities for the holding of religious examinations.

(5) Subsections (1) to (4) above, so far as applicable, shall have effect in relation to any school provided by an education authority under section 17(2) of this Act as they have effect in relation to schools transferred to an education authority as mentioned in subsection (1) above, subject to the modification that the time set apart for religious instruction in any school so provided shall be not less than that so set apart in schools in the same education area which have been transferred as mentioned in subsection (1) above.

(6) Any question which may arise as to the due fulfilment or observance of any provision or requirement of the foregoing provisions of this section shall be determined by the Secretary of State."

Compulsory education was introduced in 1872, but, in the belief that public education meant presbyterian education, the Roman Catholic community maintained its own voluntary schools independent of the state system. However, the financial burden of this system was a heavy one, and Roman Catholic schools were characterised by their inferior buildings and equipment and by their poorly-paid teachers. Partly in the belief that the inadequate education provided by these schools was contrary to the "national interest," the Education (Scotland) Act 1918 was passed to enable the schools to be brought within the state system and to be maintained at public expense, while retaining their distinctive religious flavour. Sections 16, 17 and 21 of the 1980 Act contain provisions almost identical in terms to those to be found in section 18 of the 1918 Act. For an account of the enactment of the 1918 Act, see Brother Kenneth (1965).

The transfer of schools under the 1918 Act appears to have taken place smoothly, and few difficulties were encountered (see Scottish Education Department (1943)). At September 1980, there were 457 denominational schools in Scotland, of which 450 were Roman Catholic, six Episcopalian, and one Jewish. In contrast, there were 2,418 state-run non-denominational primary and secondary schools. The existence of denominational schools has given rise to some controversy in recent years. Both the major political parties have flirted with appeals for an end to segregation, and the S.T.U.C. passed resolutions to this effect in 1970 and 1974. The view of the teaching unions in Scotland has long been that the agreement of the Roman Catholic community is an essential prerequisite to any movement towards desegregation. In the case of one such union, the E.I.S., this stance was adopted in the belief that any other commitment would profoundly divide its membership.

The arguments for desegregation have been mainly two. The first was that Roman Catholic education was inferior to that provided by the non-denominational schools. Research indicated, however, that although this may have been true even up to the early 1970s, it is so no longer. There is now no appreciable difference in pupil/teacher ratios in the two different types of school; and although there are indications of inferior academic performance by children of Roman Catholic schools, this can be explained largely on socio-economic grounds. See Payne and Ford, (1977). The second argument for desegregation is based on social and political grounds. The S.T.U.C. claim that denominational schools are divisive (S.T.U.C. (1974: 289)), while elements within the Labour party have noted the existence of religious bigotry and hatred, together with the emergence of youth gangs organised on religious grounds. Because of this, there was some pressure in the Labour party to work towards educational integration as a step in the direction of a united society free from religious intolerance. (The Labour Party Scottish Council, (1972).

As pupil numbers have fallen dramatically in recent years and school closures have been necessitated in the interests of economy, extra pressure has been felt upon the denominational schools and litigation has ensued:

Deane v. *Lothian Regional Council*, 1986 S.L.T. 22; *Scottish Hierarchy of the Roman Catholic Church* v. *Highland Regional Council*, 1987 S.L.T. 708.

V. THE LIMITS OF TOLERANCE

In those and in other ways the state has by legislation taken steps to accommodate the non-Presbyterian minorities. There are, however, limits to the willingness of the state to accommodate. These arise particularly in the field of the criminal law.

11.   R. v. Senior
[1899] 1 Q.B. 283

The Prevention of Cruelty to Children Act 1894 provided by section 1 that if any person with custody, charge, or care of any child wilfully neglected the child in a manner likely to cause injury to the child's health, that person was guilty of a misdemeanour. In this case the prisoner was convicted of the manslaughter of his infant child for deliberately refusing to call in medical aid which would probably have saved the child's life. The prisoner was a member of a sect called the Peculiar People, who objected on religious grounds to medical treatment.

LORD RUSSELL C.J.: "Neglect is the want of reasonable care—that is, the omission of such steps as a reasonable parent would take, such as are usually taken in the ordinary experience of mankind—that is, in such a case as the present, provided the parent had such means as would enable him to take the necessary steps. I agree with the statement in the summing-up, that the standard of neglect varied as time went on, and that many things might be legitimately looked upon as evidence of neglect in one generation, which would not have been thought so in a preceding generation, and that regard must be had to the habits and thoughts of the time. At the present day, when medical aid is within the reach of the humblest and poorest members of the community, it cannot reasonably be suggested that the omission to provide medical aid for a dying child does not amount to neglect. Mr Sutton contended that because the prisoner was proved to be an affectionate parent, and was willing to do all things for the benefit of his child, except the one thing which was necessary in the present case, he ought not to be found guilty of the offence of manslaughter, on the ground that he abstained from providing medical aid for his child in consequence of his peculiar views in the matter; but we cannot shut our eyes to the danger which might arise if we were to accede to that argument, for where is the line to be drawn? In the present case the prisoner is shewn to have had an objection to the use of medicine; but other cases might arise, such, for instance, as the case of a child with a broken thigh, where a surgical operation was necessary, which had to be performed with the aid of an anaesthetic; could the father refuse to allow the anaesthetic to be administered? Or take the case of a child that was in danger of suffocation, so that the operation of tracheotomy was necessary in order to save its life, and an anaesthetic was required to be administered.

I think it cannot be doubted that, if this case had arisen under the Act of 1868, there would have been ample evidence to warrant a conviction, and in my opinion there is also ample evidence where the case arises under the Act of 1894. I am of opinion that . . . the conviction ought to be affirmed."

GRANTHAM J.: "Taking the last of the two words, 'wilfully neglects,' first, was the omission of what was left undone by the prisoner neglect? The jury say it was. Then was what was left undone wilfully left undone— that is, was the neglect to provide medical aid the wilful act of the prisoner? Mr Sutton can only rely upon the fact that the prisoner was one of the sect called the 'Peculiar People'; but that fact of itself goes to shew that what he omitted he left undone with intent—that is, wilfully. Can it be said that this is not wilful neglect? I am clearly of the opinion that the prisoner's conduct amounted to wilful neglect, and that the summing-up of the learned judge was right."

The Scottish provisions corresponding to section 1 of the 1894 Act are to be found in the Children and Young Persons (Scotland) Act 1937, s. 12. *Senior* was cited with apparent approval in *Clark* v. *H.M. Advocate*, 1968 J.C. 53. The case is particularly relevant to the modern practice of Jehovah's Witnesses to refuse blood transfusions for themselves and their children. Following *Senior*, the refusal to consent would almost certainly be an offence. But this will be of no assistance to the child who may die if denied treatment. Where the child's illness is known to the local authority, it may be possible for the child to be taken into care either under section 15 or Part III of the Social Work (Scotland) Act 1968, and for the local authority to assume parental rights under section 16 of that Act. In either case, however, this procedure will take some time to operate and will clearly be inappropriate in any emergency. Where, however, the doctor proceeds with treatment contrary to the wishes of the parent, it seems highly unlikely that he would be prosecuted for assault or that an action for damages against him would succeed. Although it may be true that parental consent is normally necessary for an operation on a child (see *Whitehall* v. *Whitehall*, 1958 S.C. 252), it would be difficult to resist the conclusion in a civil action that the doctor's assault was justified.

12.   R. v. John
[1974] 1 W.L.R. 624

The appellant refused to provide a specimen of blood when required to do so under the Road Safety Act 1967, s. 3(3), because as a Mesmerist he considered this to be contrary to his religion. Section 3 provided that it was an offence to fail to provide a specimen without reasonable excuse. Did the appellant's religious beliefs provide him with a reasonable excuse for failing to provide the specimen?

ROSKILL L.J.: "It is right to say of course that any state of affairs which involves persons committing criminal offences because of beliefs sincerely held by them, is, to put it at its lowest, highly distasteful for any court. Ever since the early or middle part of the 18th century, the courts of this country have prided themselves on the liberality of their approach to matters of conscience. That attitude has continued for the last 200 years at least. Accordingly, any argument such as that to which this court has listened on behalf of the appellant is entitled to and must receive respect. For a man to be punished for an offence which is committed by reason only of his adherence to his own religion or belief can only be justified if the court is satisfied that the clear intention of the statute creating the offence was in the interests of the community as a whole to override the privileges otherwise attaching to freedom of conscience and belief, which it must always be the duty of the courts to protect and defend. There are examples mentioned in argument where this has happened. One is the National Service legislation before, during and after the war. Persons holding sincere objection to military service were nonetheless compelled to serve in one or other of various spheres of activity subject to due safeguards. Another is the recent case in the Divisional Court, *Hunter* v. *Mann* [1974] 2 W.L.R. 742, where a doctor whose professional etiquette precluded him from giving certain information which the statute required him to give was prosecuted and fined. Other examples can be found in the law of evidence. There is no privilege attaching to the confessional. There is no privilege attaching to communications between doctor and patient. In these matters Parliament and the courts have found it necessary, in the interests of the community as a whole, to override the personal right of the individual to maintain his own belief. The position is by no means uncommon.

It is against that background that one turns to consider the position under the road traffic legislation. Anyone recollecting the introduction of these provisions in 1967 will recall that they were bitterly opposed, on the ground that they restricted individual liberty. They rendered persons liable to arrest on the road if a breath test proved to be positive. That was an infringement of personal liberty, albeit only for a limited period, by enabling the alleged offender to be taken to a police station. Nonetheless Parliament found it necessary, because of the difficulty of enforcing the former law in relation to driving when ability to drive was allegedly impaired through drink or drugs, to introduce the code which first found its place on the statute book in 1967. It was in many respects a drastic code which infringed the personal liberty of individuals. But Parliament found it necessary to introduce that code in the interests of the public as a whole, to prevent the public as a whole being victimised by those who were persistently driving after consuming an excessive quantity of alcohol but who all too often were not brought to justice because of the difficulty of bringing home a charge in the courts. The very introduction of the limit of 80 milligrammes of alcohol in 100 millilitres of blood was itself an infringement of individual rights.

It is therefore against the background of a statute which by its very terms does restrict individual rights that one has to construe the crucial words that are now in section 9 of the Act of 1972 'without reasonable excuse.' It is suggested that any excuse will do, if based upon belief sincerely held. But that, with great respect to the skill with which the argument has been advanced, involves making the person seeking to set up that excuse as reasonable being the judge in his own cause. He becomes entitled to say 'Because I believe a certain thing, that belief of my own, personal to myself, affords me a reasonable excuse for not complying with what other people would have to comply with.' In other words the person concerned is really seeking to say not 'I cannot,' but 'I ought not.'

In the view of this court, that is not well founded. As I said a few moments ago, the Road Traffic Act 1972 provides rules for the safety of the public. It provides rules in order to protect the public from certain classes of users of the road. The securing of that protection involves restriction on the liberty of individuals.

It is against that background that one returns to consider the language used in *R. v. Lennard* [1973] 1 W.L.R. 483 It may be—and we say this with the utmost respect to Lawton and Scarman L.JJ.— that the language used, if construed too strictly, might involve an over-rigid approach to the language of the section. Certainly, in the view of this court and in the light of what was said by Scarman L.J. in *R. v. Reid (Philip)* [1973] 1 W.L.R. 1283, 1289, the court did not intend to lay down something rigid and exhaustive. In truth what the court was saying was that for an excuse to be capable of being a reasonable excuse, it must be an excuse which is related to the capacity of the person concerned to supply a sample, be it of urine or be it of blood. It is not related to his belief whether or not he ought, because of his personal faith or belief, to be required to supply a sample of urine or blood. There is, in the view of this court, this very marked difference between the two positions. One depends on whether or not, for example, he is in a mental or physical condition which enables him physically to give the sample. It may be in some cases that he will not be in that condition. Such facts, if proved, may at least be capable of affording a reasonable excuse for not giving the sample. But it is not enough for someone to come along and say 'True others are obliged to comply with the law, but my personal faith or belief frees me from the obligations which rest upon others.'

That, with all respect to the appellant and to the sincerity of his beliefs, is what he is seeking to say in this court. This court must reject that argument. This conclusion does involve to some extent a restriction on the liberty of the individual, but it is a consequence that flows from what Parliament found necessary when these provisions were first introduced in 1967 for the benefit of the public as a whole."

Both *Senior* and *John* show clearly that religious belief will not normally be a good defence to a criminal charge. It is, of course, open to Parliament to provide otherwise. One example of this is the Motor-cycle Crash Helmets (Religious Exemption) Act 1976 which provides that the duty to wear a helmet does not apply to followers of the Sikh religion. However, that exception applies to an offence of little substance (albeit that the duty is controversial) which is designed mainly for the protection of the cyclist rather than his victim. If it were otherwise any such exemption would be extremely difficult to justify. And it is to be noted that just as the accused may not plead his or her own religious belief as a defence, nor may he plead the religious belief of his or her victim which may have led to more serious injury of the victim than might otherwise have been sustained. This is illustrated by *R. v. Blaue* [1975] 1 W.L.R. 1411, where the accused was convicted of the manslaughter of a girl whom he had attacked with a knife and who had died after refusing a blood transfusion. She was a Jehovah's Witness. Blaue unsuccessfully appealed against his conviction arguing that unreasonable behaviour by the victim broke the chain of causation. In dismissing the appeal, Lawton L.J. said:

"The physical cause of death in this case was the bleeding into the pleural cavity arising from the penetration of the lung. This had not been brought about by any decision made by the deceased but by the stab wound.

Mr Comyn tried to overcome this line of reasoning by submitting that the jury should have been directed that if they thought the deceased's decision not to have a blood transfusion was an unreasonable one, then the chain of causation would have been broken. At once the question arises—reasonable by whose standards? Those of Jehovah's Witnesses? Humanists? Roman Catholics? Protestants of Anglo-Saxon descent? The man on the Clapham omnibus? But he might well be an admirer of Eleazar who suffered death rather than eat the flesh of swine (2 Maccabees, ch.6, vv. 18-31) or of Sir Thomas More who, unlike nearly all his contemporaries, was unwilling to accept Henry VIII as Head of the Church of England. Those brought up in the Hebraic and Christian traditions would probably be reluctant to accept that these martyrs caused their own deaths.

As was pointed out to Mr Comyn in the course of argument, two cases, each raising the same issue of reasonableness because of religious beliefs, could produce different verdicts depending on where the cases were tried. It has long been the policy of the law that those who use violence on other people must take their victims as they find them. This in our judgment means the whole man, not just the physical man. It does not lie in the mouth of the assailant to say that his victim's religious beliefs which inhibited him from accepting certain kinds of treatment were unreasonable."

CHAPTER 7

FREEDOM OF EXPRESSION

I. INTRODUCTION

THE recognition of freedom of expression is fundamental to any society which lays claim to being democratic. As J. S. Mill observed: "The time . . . is gone by, when any defence would be necessary of the 'liberty of the press' as one of the securities against corrupt or tyrannical government" (*On Liberty,* Chap. 2). In a similar vein, the United States Supreme Court remarked in *Stromberg* v. *California,* 283 U.S. 359 (1931):

"The maintenance of the opportunity for free political discussion to the end that government may be responsive to the will of the people and that changes may be obtained by lawful means, an opportunity essential to the security of the Republic, is a fundamental principle of our constitutional system." (at p. 369).

These remarks apply with equal force to our own constitutional system, notwithstanding the substantial differences between it and the American constitution.

Yet, while freedom of expression is thus essential for the circulation of political ideas and the effective accountability of government, this is not the only function it serves. Other considerations are discussed in the following extract.

1. Report of the Committee on Obscenity and Film Censorship
(Chairman: Bernard Williams)
Cmnd. 7772 (1979)

"5.15. The freedom of expression is not for [J.S. Mill] just one more example of freedom from coercion but is a very special and fundamental form of freedom. It is clear that many of our witnesses share this view, some of them for Mill's own reasons, and we think it important to give those reasons some attention. Some of Mill's reasons we believe to be still very relevant today. Some of his arguments, however, were always flimsy and are yet more so in modern conditions. His basic thought was that human beings have no infallible source of knowledge about human nature or how human affairs may develop, and do not know in advance what arrangements or forms of life may make people happy or enable them to be, as Mill impassionately wanted them to be, original, tolerant and uncowed individuals. Since we do not know in advance, we do not know what new proposals, ideas or forms of expression may contribute to the development of man and society.

5.16. From this Mill drew the conclusion that we have no basis for suppressing or censoring any of them. He did so, in particular, because he thought (and many others have shared this view) that the only way the truth could emerge was by a form of natural selection in a 'free market' of ideas: if all ideas were allowed expression, good ideas would multiply, bad ideas would die out. This conception, if sound, would have very powerful consequences. It is important, for instance, that it would tell almost as much against restricting a publication as against suppressing it, since any constraint on a work's availability will reduce the chance of its message being heard. However, we do not find Mill's conception entirely convincing. . .

5.19. Even in the area of ideas, the notion of a 'free market' has to be regarded with some scepticism, and the faith in *laissez-faire* shown by the nineteenth century and earlier does not altogether meet modern conditions. If everyone talks at once, truth will not prevail, since no one can be heard and nothing will prevail: and falsehood indeed may prevail, if powerful agencies can gain an undue hold on the market. Even in natural science, which Mill regarded as the paradigm, he neglected the importance of scientific institutions and the filter against cranks which is operated, and necessarily operated, by expert opinion, excluding from serious consideration what it sees as incompetence. Against the principle that truth is strong and (given the chance) will prevail, must be set Gresham's Law, that bad money drives out good, which has some application in matters of culture and which predicts that it will not necessarily be the most interesting ideas or the most valuable works of art that survive in competition—above all, in commercial competition.

5.20. Thus we cannot entirely agree that 'the Truth certainly would do well enough if she were left to fend for herself'; she may need more of a chance than that. This point can surely justify intervention. Intervention, however, need not be and should not be negative intervention: it can take the form of such things as state subventions for the arts, or policies of refusing to design television programmes solely on the basis of ratings, or subsidising institutions of critical enquiry. This is not just a point about the rights of minorities; it involves Mill's own basic idea (though differently applied) that progress involves a belief or a value being first a minority belief or value, which must be preserved if it is ever to reach further.

5.21. The fact that the market-place model is an inadequate basis for the value of free expression does not mean that one replaces the market with monopoly, and institutes a censorship by the State or by worthy citizens. There is certainly no reason to think that that would do better in the detection of error or the advance of enlightenment. The more basic idea, to which Mill attached the market-place model, remains a correct and profound idea: that we do not know in advance what social, moral or intellectual developments will turn out to be possible, necessary or desirable for human beings and for their future, and free expression, intellectual and artistic—something which may need to be fostered and protected as well as merely permitted—is essential to human development, as a process which does not merely happen (in some form or another, it will happen anyway), but so far as possible is rationally understood. It is essential to it, moreover, not just as a means to it, but as part of it. Since human beings are not just subject to their history but aspire to be conscious of it, the development of human individuals, of society and of humanity in general, is a process itself properly constituted in part by free expression and the exchange of human communication.

5.22. We realise that some may disagree with this basic idea because they think that fundamental human moral truths have been laid down unchangeably for all time, for instance in religious terms. Mill, certainly, thought that there was no such revealed truth, and his arguments for freedom of expression and those of people who think like him are to that extent an expression of religious scepticism. We would suggest, however, that even those who believe that there are revealed truths of morality and religion should attend very anxiously to the argument for freedom of expression. First, the barest facts of cultural history show that any set of supposed revealed truths which have survived have received constantly new applications and interpretations, to which new moral perceptions have contributed. Second, every believer in some set of moral certainties has to share the world with other believers in some different set of moral certainties. If they share the same society, at least, and even if they could come to do so, they have some common interest in not accepting principles which would allow someone else's certainty to persecute their own. Third, many religious believers in moral certainties also believe that human beings have been created not just to obey or mirror those certainties, but freely to live by them, and that institutions of free expression can be in fact a more developed representation of the religious consciousness itself than authoritarian institutions. We have thus not been surprised, though we have been impressed, by the constructive concern for freedom of expression which has been shown by many of the submissions we have received from religious bodies, disturbed though most of them have been by the present situation.

5.23. Because we believe that the value of the freedom of expression is connected with the open future of human development, we do find a difficulty with certain proposals for obscenity law we have received, which both admit the fact of changing standards, and also invoke present standards to justify the actual suppression of certain publications. The Nationwide Festival of Light and others, following a formulation of Lord Longford's Committee, have recommended the suppression of what grossly affronts 'contemporary standards of decency or humanity accepted by the public at large.' But while some such provision might ground, as we shall ourselves suggest, a *restriction* of some material, to prevent its offending the public at large, the position of trying to justify suppression—which, if successful, is permanent—on the basis of what are acknowledged to be contemporary standards, seems to us to make, more than is justified, present views the determinant of the future."

But although the freedom of expression is recognised and cherished in most civilised societies, this will almost invariably be subject to exceptions. In the first place, it is normal to justify restrictions to protect individuals from harm. A question of some importance is, for whose benefit should the the freedom be restricted: other people who will be affected, or the citizen who may be harmed by his own exercise of the freedom?

"5.26. The presumption in favour of freedom of expression is strong, but it is a presumption, and it can be overruled by considerations of harms which the speech or publication in question may cause. The first question that arises is, harms to whom? . . . In particular, in the case of publications, there is the question whether supposed harm to consumers—i.e. those who voluntarily choose to read the material—is, just in itself, to count. Mill and many others who advance what we have called the 'harm condition' for coercing behaviour would say that it did not. They say this because they accept the principle that, if one is dealing with adult persons, it is best to assume that each person is the best judge of whether he or she is being harmed. This additional principle makes an important difference. The harm condition by itself would not necessarily produce very liberal results. One might agree that laws should only suppress what does harm but think that disgusting books should be suppressed by law because their readers (though those readers would not themselves agree) are in fact harmed by them. With this other principle added, however, such paternalist laws would be ruled out."

(Williams (1979))

The harm conditions would justify a number of controls. First, it would justify some control of pornographic speech, if it could be established not that this caused harm to those who read it, but that those who read it might thereby cause harm to other people. Secondly, it would justify control to protect the integrity of the judicial process, and in particular the right of an accused person to be given a fair trial. Control might be justified if it could be shown that media publicity would undermine the right of the accused. And thirdly, control could be justified to prevent harm to national security. There is clearly a case for some limits on the right to publish confidential information relating to national security. On this issue, however, it is important to strike a balance which is sufficient to protect the security of the nation without extending to meet the convenience of the government. In this chapter we consider how Scots law restricts freedom of expression in response to each of these considerations. But before we do so, we deal first with the question of prior restraints of theatrical productions, the cinema, and television.

II. PRIOR RESTRAINTS IN SCOTS LAW

1. THE THEATRE

The Theatres Act 1843 provided that every new play or any new part of a play to be acted in any theatre in Great Britain was to be sent to the Lord Chamberlain who had power to disallow the presentation of the play or any part thereof (s. 12). The Lord Chamberlain could forbid the presentation of a play or part thereof if he was of the "opinion that it is fitting for the Preservation of good Manners, Decorum, or of the public Peace so to do." There is evidence that the Lord Chamberlain sometimes used this power to exercise a political censorship, disallowing, for example, plays critical of the leadership of the U.S.A.

In 1967 a Joint Committee on Censorship of the Theatre (H.C. 503, 1967) recommended that censorship of plays should cease and that there should be freedom of speech in the theatre, subject to overriding requirements of the criminal law. The Joint Committee seemed especially concerned that political censorship should be ended, on the ground that the existence of such powers was inappropriate in a modern democratic society. The position is now governed by the Theatres Act 1968, section 1 of which repeals the Theatres Act 1843. In abolishing pre-censorship, the 1968 Act did not, however, give *carte-blanche* to directors to do as they please. A number of statutory offences were introduced in order to prevent the presentation of obscene performances (s. 2); to prevent the incitement of racial hatred by means of a public performance (s. 5, now repealed and substituted by s. 20, Public Order Act 1986); and to prevent the provocation of a breach of the peace by means of a public performance (s. 6). A number of exceptions to these restraints are contained in section 7. Those responsible for theatrical production may also be subjected to criminal liability on several grounds discussed in the following sections of this chapter.

2. The Cinema

2. The Cinemas Act 1985

"Licence required for exhibitions
1.—(1) Subject to sections 5 to 8 below, no premises shall be used for a film exhibition unless they are licensed for the purpose under this section.

(2) A licensing authority may grant a licence under this section to such a person as they think fit to use any premises specified in the licence for the purpose of film exhibitions on such terms and conditions and subject to such restrictions as, subject to regulations under section 4 below, they may determine.

(3) Without prejudice to the generality of subsection (2) above, it shall be the duty of a licensing authority, in granting a licence under this section as respects any premises,—

   (a) to impose conditions or restrictions prohibiting the admission of children to film exhibitions involving the showing of works designated, by the authority or by such other body as may be specified in the licence, as works unsuitable for children; and

   (b) to consider what (if any) conditions or restrictions should be imposed as to the admission of children to other film exhibitions involving the showing of works designated, by the authority or by such other body as may be specified in the licence, as works of such other description as may be so specified.

*   *   *

Regulations by Secretary of State
4.—(1) Subject to sections 5 and 6 below, no film exhibition shall be given unless regulations made by the Secretary of State under this section are complied with.

(2) The matters for which provision may be made by regulations under this section are—

   (a) safety in connection with the giving of film exhibitions (including the keeping and handling, in premises where other entertainments are being given or meetings held, of cinematograph film used or to be used for the purposes of film exhibitions or other articles or equipment so used or to be used);

(b) the health and welfare of children in relation to attendance at film exhibitions.

(3) Regulations under this section shall be made by statutory instrument which shall be subject to annulment in pursuance of a resolution of either House of Parliament.

*   *   *

Appeals against decisions of licensing authority

16.—(1) Any person aggrieved—

(a)   by the refusal or revocation of a licence,

(b)   by any terms, conditions or restrictions on or subject to which a licence is granted, or

(c)   by the refusal of a renewal or transfer of a licence,

may appeal to the Crown court or, in Scotland, to the sheriff."

The Cinemas Act 1985 is merely a consolidating measure. The law on film censorship has its origins in the Cinematograph Act 1909. The crucial provisions were sections 1 and 2 which corresponded with sections 1(1) and 1 (2) of the 1985 Act. Sections 1 (3), 4 and 16 have their origins in the Cinematograph Act 1952. In commenting on these provisions, the Williams Committee said: "Parliament has never legislated for the censorship of films: it is purely a matter of accident that the film censorship system was able to find some statutory support when it first struggled into existence just before the First World War" (Williams (1979: para. 3.1)). Thus, as the historical account in Appendix 2 of the Williams Report demonstrates, the exclusive purpose of the 1909 Act was to protect the public from the risk of fire and there is no evidence that the government anticipated that it might be used for censorship. However, it was soon realised that section 2 contained wide terms which enabled authorities to impose conditions other than those relating to public safety. In *L.C.C.* v. *Bermondsey Bioscope Co. Ltd.* [1911] 1 K.B. 445 a prohibition on Sunday opening of cinemas was upheld, with Alverstone L.C.J. adding the crucially important point that section 2 "is intended to confer on the [local authority] a discretion as to the conditions which they will impose, so long as these conditions are not unreasonable." It was feared that this dictum would permit local authorities to censor films. So, faced with the prospect of different local authorities adopting different approaches to the showing of films, which would thereby frustrate any system of national film distribution, the film industry established the British Board of Film Censors. The purpose of the board was to approve films before they were released, in the hope that the certificates issued by the board would be accepted by the licensing authorities throughout the country. In practice this is what happened, though it is important to note that licensing authorities retain the right not to show a film which has a B.B.F.C. certificate; or to show a film which has been denied such a certificate; or to vary the age restriction attached by the board to a film. The following case traces the development of the B.B.F.C. and reviews the practice relating to the issuing of certificates by it. The case is also important for highlighting the scope for judicial supervision of licensing authority decisions.

3. Classic Cinema Ltd. v. Motherwell D.C.
1977 S.L.T. (Sh. Ct.) 69

The licensing authority granted a licence under section 2 of the 1909 Act on the condition that no "X" films would be shown on Sundays. The licensee successfully contested this condition, though another condition imposed by the authority was upheld.

THE SHERIFF PRINCIPAL (R. Reid, Q.C.): "Section 6 (1)(b) and (5) of the Cinematograph Act 1952 provides that: 'Any person aggrieved . . . by any terms, conditions and restrictions on or subject to which such a license or consent is granted, may appeal to the sheriff.' It will be seen that the statute gives no indication of the approach to be adopted or the test to be applied by the sheriff in disposing of the appeal . . . I do not think that licensing decisions should have the privileged status accorded to bye-laws, but should be treated in much the same way as decisions relating to licences granted under the Gaming Act 1968. This approach requires that weight should be given to the decisions of the local authority, particularly in matters in which it represents local opinion, so that a judge should only differ on appeal when, having regard to the whole of the material before him, he is satisfied that the local authority's decision cannot be supported. . .

There was evidence in the appeal to the effect that the wide discretion granted to local authorities by section 2(1) of the 1909 Act had originally resulted in differences of opinion between local authorities as to films which might be exhibited in their areas. These differences caused serious difficulty to exhibitors and a typical British compromise came into being to avoid the worse results of the wide discretion Parliament had conferred. The film industry set up the British Board of Film Censors with the function of classifying films for the purpose of assisting local authorities to carry out their duties under the Act. Local authorities were not, of course, entitled to delegate their powers to the British Board of Censors or bind themselves to follow blindly the rulings of the Board, but classification by the Board became accepted and enabled a substantial measure of uniformity to be introduced into the licensing of films for public exhibition. Films were originally classified as suitable for universal exhibition ('U') or suitable for exhibition to adults only ('A'). In England, local authorities commonly imposed a condition that children could not attend an 'A' film unless accompanied by an adult. According to the evidence, in Scotland the general practice was to publicise the 'A' classification and to leave it to their parents to decide whether or not their children should see the film. As scenes of sex and violence became more common in films, it was felt that the classification was inadequate, and an 'AA' classification was introduced to designate films unsuitable for viewing by children under 14, and an 'X' classification to designate films unsuitable for viewing by persons under 18. When the new classifications were introduced the question arose between exhibitors and local authorities whether the latter should treat the 'AA' classification as advisory only and permit children under the age of 14, if accompanied by a responsible adult, to view such films, or whether children under 14 should be excluded from films so classified. In an attempt to resolve differences of approach the Cinematograph Exhibitors' Association attempted to agree a model licence with local authorities. The licence could not bind local authorities, but was a further attempt to introduce a measure of uniformity into film licensing. In the first draft of the model licence there were alternative clauses embodying both interpretations of the condition appropriate to the 'AA' classification. Finally, the association and local authorities agreed a condition which permitted children to see such films if accompanied by a responsible adult. The local authority in the present case have taken the other view. This refusal to follow the terms of the model licence, and the fact that the 'A' classification has been treated in Scotland as an advisory classification, provide the slender grounds on which the decision of a local authority embodied in condition 5 has been challenged.

The witness for the local authority explained that its licensing committee thought that 'AA' films were unsuitable viewing for children under 14 and that to permit children to see such films if accompanied by their parents, was misleading to parents in that it raised expectations that these films were suitable for viewing by children and put parents in a difficult position when scenes unsuitable for children were depicted. In these circumstances, the local authority preferred clear-cut prohibition. It appears to me that this is just the kind of decisions which a local authority is entitled to take. It is in no way unreasonable and I do not think I am entitled to interfere with it.

I turn to condition 11. This condition provides 'No "X" certificate films shall be shown on Sundays.' The local authority's witness explained that the condition had been imposed for moral reasons because members of the licensing committee considered that too many "X" films were being shown, because it was distasteful to many members of the community that such films should be shown on Sundays. There was also a fear that, owing to the lack of other entertainment on Sundays, there would be an unusually strong temptation for persons under 18 to seek admission to the cinema on Sunday evenings and there was, at the same time, a desire to provide wholesome entertainment for young persons on Sunday evenings. If matters had rested there, I would have felt it as difficult to interfere as in the case of condition 5, but there was abundant and unchallenged evidence of matters which did not appear to have been taken into consideration by the local authority which put a very different complexion on the matter. In the first place, there was evidence that young people rarely attended cinemas on Sunday even when 'U' or 'A' films were exhibited. A typical Sunday evening audience, according to the evidence, consisted of young adults and older single people, particularly those who lived alone and felt a need to seek entertainment on Sunday evenings. This audience will not come to see 'U' and 'A' films unless they are new showings of good quality. Second, and more important, the evidence showed that it was, in practice, impossible to obtain a sufficient number of 'U' and 'A' films with reasonable power to draw audiences for viewing on Sunday evenings. It appears that the number of

'X' films made each year exceeds the total of films in all other classifications. Moreover, such non-'X' films as are made are not freely available. Some of the cinema chains have preferential rights to the showing of films produced by particular film companies, and this inevitably restricts exhibitors in their choice of new films. There are other factors which restrict choice in the system adopted for distribution of films. All films are distributed through film distributors under contracts providing for payment to the distributor of a proportion of the takings at the box office. Because the distributor has an interest in the size of an audience he is concerned to see that films are shown which will attract the largest audiences. Copies of films are fairly expensive—they were said to cost about £600 each—and the distributor is also naturally anxious to maximise his return on the capital invested in the copy of a film. For these reasons, the choice of films offered by distributors to exhibitors is restricted. Moreover, because the distributor bears part of the cost of transporting films between distribution centres and cinemas, it is generally difficult to book a film for a one-day showing. Distributors much prefer bookings for three to seven days. The exhibitor's booking manager is not entirely without influence. There is some expertise in choosing films which will prove attractive in particular cinemas, but his choice is restricted by these various factors. Further, commercial considerations may restrict drastically the showing of 'U' and 'A' films which are offered by the distributor. Any 'U' and 'A' films more than five years old will probably have been shown on television and have no ability to attract an audience if screened in a cinema. . . On this evidence I have come to accept the conclusion of a number of witnesses who gave evidence for the appellants that the consequence of allowing condition 11 to remain in force would be that the cinema would require to close on many Sundays, either because no non-'X' film was available or because such non-'X' films as were available were quite unprofitable to show. . . The members of the licensing committee . . . could not reasonably have imposed this condition. It is, in my view, so onerous that it comes near to endangering the continuance of the licensed activity. For this reason, I have decided that it should be deleted from the license."

The most detailed review of film censorship in modern times is to be found in Williams (1979). Some of those who submitted evidence to the Williams Committee argued that pre-censorship of films should be abolished. Some of these witnesses placed great emphasis on artistic freedom; others argued that the cinema should be treated in the same way as the theatre; and still others simply stressed the right of adults to freedom of choice and the unacceptability of the notion that certain people were qualified to judge what was right and wrong for everyone else to see (para. 12. 4). In rejecting these arguments, the Committee said:

"12.8. . . We are taken further towards accepting [pre-censorship of films] by the facts that the major part of our evidence supported the continuation of film censorship, that the present system has in the main worked effectively and well and that most other countries appear to regard film censorship as acceptable and desirable. What clinched the argument for some of us at least was the sight of some of the films with which the censorship presently interferes. We feel it necessary to say to many people who express liberal sentiments about the principle of adult freedom to choose that we were totally unprepared for the sadistic material that some film makers are prepared to produce. We are not here referring to the explicit portrayal of sexual activity or to anything which simply attracts charges of offensiveness. Films that exploit a taste for torture and sadistic violence do raise further, and disturbing, questions. . .

12.11 Some people told us that if there is material which we were satisfied should not be made available to the public, the proper way to suppress it is by way of making it the subject of determination by the courts, rather than by prior restraint. Prior restraint, it is commonly recognised, is a more effective means for suppressing material than is offered by the subsequent punishment approach. Its advantages are that it provides certainty, consistency and speed of decision and the possibility of continuous review by the same group of people; it avoids the delays of criminal trials and decisions by courts who know nothing of films and are not representative of the film-going public; it provides a more refined control, capable of identifying which elements of a film are objectionable and therefore allowing the distributor the opportunity of reacting; and it prevents objectionable material from becoming available at all rather than trying to retrieve it after publication and thereby giving it more publicity. We freely admit, and have already made clear, that we are in part encouraged to favour pre-censorship by the fact that it is what already exists. What we have to consider is, realistically, not whether we would institute a system of censorship if it were a novelty but whether we should abandon a functioning system; or rather, to put it more exactly, whether we should continue to use the system for the protection of young audiences (as almost all our witnesses considered necessary), but at the same time refuse to use the system to control films for adult viewing. We were very much impressed, moreover, by a different kind of argument. The impact of a film can depend on very subtle factors, which will not at all be caught by simple statements of what is being shown on the screen, and because of this the law is too inflexible an instrument through which to impose a control. An *ad hoc* judgment, grounded on certain guidelines, is a more efficient and sensitive way of controlling this medium. All these considerations together led us to the conclusion that films, even those shown to adults only, should continue to be censored."

But having accepted the case for some continued censorship, Williams also recommended reform of the arrangements then in force. First, it was proposed that local licensing, which featured so prominently in the *Classic Cinema* case, should be abolished: the committee concluded that the existence of such power could not "be justified by any local variation in taste and opinion" (para. 12.19). Secondly, the committee recommended the creation of a new statutory body, the Film Examining Board, to replace the British Board of Film Censors. The F.E.B. would establish policy and principles for the censorship of films and would appoint film examiners who would perform this task, with a right of appeal to the F.E.B. against a decision of an examiner. Although the committee levelled no criticism at the B.B.F.C., it was felt that it should be replaced. This was because the public esteem of the B.B.F.C. suffered from its close connections with the film industry and because it had no legal authority, and no power to ensure that its decisions were implemented. The third major change recommended by Williams was for new categories of certificate. New classifications have in fact been introduced: U (suitable for all); PG (some scenes unsuitable for children); 15 (passed only for persons age 15 and over); R18 (restricted distribution and only for people age 18 or over).

3. BROADCASTING

4. Lynch v. BBC
[1983] N.I.L.R. 193

The plaintiff was the Chairman of the Northern Ireland Executive of the Workers' Party. At the general election in 1983 the party nominated candidates in 14 of the 17 Northern Ireland constituencies. The BBC decided during the election to broadcast special forum programmes on television and special phone-in programmes on radio, each of which programmes would relate to a specific political party. In order to participate, a party had to nominate candidates in at least five of the Northern Ireland constituencies and to have polled at least 5 per cent of the first preference votes in the Northern Ireland Assembly election in 1982. The Workers' Party failed to qualify because although it satisfied the first condition, it did not satisfy the second. The plaintiff contended that the exclusion of his party was a breach of the BBC's duty to be impartial, and he sought an interlocutory injunction restraining the BBC: "from excluding from taking part in special items to be broadcast concerning the elections for the United Kingdom Parliament at Westminster to be held on the 9th June 1983 and from broadcasting any special item relating to the said elections without the participation of the plaintiff."

HUTTON J.: "Counsel for the plaintiff, Mr Harvey, accepted that there was no statute which imposed a duty on the B.B.C. to be impartial, but he submitted that there was a legal duty resting on the B.B.C. to be impartial which was to be implied from certain provisions of the B.B.C.'s Royal Charter and Licence and from undertakings given by the B.B.C. to the Government. In support of his submission Mr Harvey relied on the following passages in documents emanating from the B.B.C. and on passages in the Royal Charter and Licence. The B.B.C. Annual Report and Handbook 1983 at page 139 contains the following account of the foundation of the B.B.C.:

'The constitutional position of the B.B.C., which has remained broadly unaltered since the granting of the first Charter in 1927, was determined largely by the policy adopted by the British Broadcasting Company from 1922 (when the broadcasting service in this country began) to 1926, after which the new-formed Corporation took over.

The Company was formed, at the invitation of the then Postmaster General, by the principal manufacturers of wireless apparatus, who appointed as their

General Manager Mr J.C.W. Reith (the late Lord Reith). The Company soon became widely known as "the B.B.C.". It was required under Licence, to provide a service to the reasonable satisfaction of the Postmaster General'. The Postmaster General was the final arbiter as to what kind of matter might or might not be broadcast. The company had no Charter.

The B.B.C.'s policy during those years was based on Reith's conviction, that broadcasting had great potential, as being in the future a source, not only of entertainment, but also of information and enlightenment available to all. Its motive should be that of public service, and he stressed the need for high standards and a strong sense of responsibility. The Company established a policy of absolute impartiality in broadcasting talks and speeches. On the basis of its record and rapid progress the Company sought constantly to establish its claim to a greater measure of independence in dealing with news, events and opinions—the broadcasting of which had been subject to many restrictions. It was on the basis of approval of what had been done, and of a recognition of the further possibilities, that Lord Crawford's Committee of 1925, which had been appointed by the Government to advise on future management and control, recommended that the broadcasting service should be conducted in the future by a public corporation "acting as trustee for the national interest".

In accordance with the Crawford Committee's recommendations, the entire property and undertaking of the British Broadcasting Company "as a going concern", together with its existing contracts and staff, were taken over by the British Broadcasting Corporation on 1st January 1927.'

By a letter dated 13 June 1964 the Chairman of the B.B.C., Lord Normanbrook, informed the Postmaster General:

'For the standards of programmes broadcast by the B.B.C., the responsibility rests with the Board of Governors. The Board recognise their duty to ensure that programmes maintain a high general standard in all respects (and in particular in respect of their content and quality), and a proper balance and wide range in their subject matter. They accept that the planning of particular broadcasts at appropriate times is a significant factor in the achievement of a programme pattern designed to fulfil these requirements. They will continue to follow their established practice of the so-called watershed, the object of which is to exclude from the earlier part of the evening programmes which might be unsuitable for children. The board recall that the Postmaster-General has relied on them to maintain the Corporation's policy of treating controversial subjects with due impartiality, and they intend to continue this policy both in the Corporation's news services and in the more general field of programmes dealing with matters of public policy.'

By a Resolution of the Board of Governors of the B.B.C. dated 8th January 1981 the Board formally resolved:

'. . . to renew their public assurances concerning programme standards in the knowledge that Governments of all Parties have always recognised that responsibility for the programmes broadcast by the Corporation rests on the Board of Governors.

In so doing the Board recalled those many statements (in Annual Reports to Parliament and in speeches and policy documents) which have served over the years to reassure Parliament and the public that the Corporation's adherence to high standards remains unchanged and that it seeks to improve them wherever possible.

In particular the Board noted that the late Lord Normanbrook, as their Chairman, had given assurances to the Postmaster General (The Rt. Hon. Reginald Bevins, M.P.) in a letter dated 13th June 1964, and resolved to renew them.

Accordingly, the Board reaffirm their recognition of a duty to ensure that programmes maintain a high general standard in all respects (and in particular in respect of content and quality), and to provide a properly balanced service which displays a wide range of subject matter. They accept that in order to serve the tastes and needs of different audiences and, in particular, to show concern for the young, programmes must be placed at appropriate times.

The Board recall that it has always been their object to treat controversial subjects with due impartiality, and they intend to continue this policy both in the Corporation's news services and in the more general field of programmes dealing with matters of public policy.'

By a Licence dated 2 April 1981 the Home Secretary, pursuant to the powers conferred by section 1 of the Wireless and Telegraphy Act 1949, granted a new Licence to the B.B.C. This Licence recited the resolution dated 8 January 1981 as follows:

'AND WHEREAS by a resolution dated the 8th January 1981 and annexed hereto the Corporation has renewed the assurances previously given in respect of the general standards of programmes broadcast by the Corporation.'

Clause 13(4) of the Licence provides:

'(4)   The Secretary of State may from time to time by notice in writing require the Corporation to refrain at any specified time or at all times from sending any matter or matter of any class specified in such notice; and the Secretary of State may at any time or times vary or revoke any such notice. The Corporation may at its discretion announce or refrain from announcing that such a notice has been given or has been varied or revoked.'

The Royal Charter for the continuation of the B.B.C. was granted on 7 July 1981. The Royal Charter contains the following recital:

'AND WHEREAS in view of the widespread interest which is taken by Our Peoples in broadcasting services and of the great value of such services as means of disseminating information, education and entertainment, We believe it to be in the interests of Our Peoples in Our United Kingdom and elsewhere within the Commonwealth that the Corporation should continue to provide broadcasting services pursuant to such licences and agreements in that behalf as Our Secretary of State may from time to time grant to and make with the Corporation.'

Article 3 of the Royal Charter provides:

"The objects of the Corporation are as follows:
(a) To provide, as public services, broadcasting services or wireless telegraphy by the method of telephony for general reception in sound, by the method of television for general reception in visual images and by the methods of television and telephony in combination for general reception in visual images with sound, in our United Kingdom of Great Britain and Northern Ireland. . ."

Counsel for the plaintiff submitted that the passages set out above gave rise to an implied legal duty on the B.B.C. to act impartially between political parties. He submitted that the reason why the Home Secretary had not given a notice in writing to the B.B.C. under clause 13(4) of the Licence requiring the Corporation to refrain from broadcasting a political programme on behalf of a political party which would be in breach of the principle of impartiality was because an implied legal duty of impartiality already rested on the B.B.C. Counsel further referred to section 4(1) of the Broadcasting Act 1981 which provides in relation to the Independent Broadcasting Authority:

'4.(1)   It shall be the duty of the Authority to satisfy themselves that, so far as possible, the programmes broadcast by the Authority comply with the following requirements, that is to say— . . .
(b)   that a sufficient amount of time in the programmes is given to news and news features and that all news given in the programmes (in whatever form) is presented with due accuracy and impartiality; ...
(f)   that due impartiality is preserved on the part of the persons providing the programmes as respects matters of political or industrial controversy or relating to current public policy.'

Counsel submitted that the reason why a similar duty was not expressly imposed on the B.B.C. by the royal Charter or by the Licence or by statute was because the B.B.C. was subject to an implied legal duty to preserve due impartiality in respect of matters of political controversy.

I do not accept the submissions advanced by Counsel for the plaintiff. In my judgment the B.B.C. is under no legal duty enforceable by the courts to act with impartiality as between different political parties. It appears that the B.B.C., as a matter of policy, seeks to act with impartiality as respects matters of political controversy, but I consider that the discharge of this policy by the B.B.C. is not subject to the control of the courts. There is no statute which imposes a duty on the B.B.C. to act with impartiality. There is no provision in the Royal Charter or in the Licence which expressly imposes a duty on the B.B.C. to act with impartiality, although the Licence does contain a number of provisions expressly stating that the Corporation shall refrain from sending certain broadcast matters. Thus Clause 13(6) provides:

The Corporation shall at all times refrain from sending any broadcast matter which includes any technical device which, by using images of very brief duration or by any other means, exploits the possibility of conveying a message to, or otherwise influencing the minds of, members of an audience without their being aware, or fully aware, of what has been done.'

And Clause 13(7) provides:

'The Corporation shall at all times refrain from sending any broadcast matter expressing the opinion of the Corporation on current affairs or on matters of public policy, other than broadcasting and matter contained in programmes which consist only of proceedings in either House of Parliament or proceedings of a local authority, a committee of a local authority or a committee of two or more local authorities.'

In my judgment the Royal Charter and the Licence do not impose by implication a duty on the B.B.C. to act with impartiality in political matters (but I express no opinion on the question whether a duty expressly imposed by the Licence would constitute a legal duty enforceable by the courts; it may be that the only remedy for the breach of such a duty would be the revocation by the Home Secretary of the Licence under section 1(4) of the Wireless Telegraphy Act 1949). The letter of Lord Normanbrook dated 13 June 1964 refers to 'the Corporation's *policy* of treating controversial subjects with due impartiality' and states that the board 'intend to continue this *policy*'. And the Resolution of the Board of Governors dated 8 January 1981 states that:

'The Board recall that it has always been their *object* to treat controversial subjects with due impartiality, and they intend to continue this *policy* both in the Corporation's news services and in the more general field of programmes dealing with matters of public policy.' (The italics are mine.)

Therefore I consider that there is no valid basis for holding that the letter and the Resolution give rise to a legal duty resting on the Corporation to be impartial or that the recital of the Resolution in the Licence imposes a legal duty on the Corporation."

Hutton J. concluded by saying that if the view was taken that the BBC had failed to act impartially, the remedy lay in the Home Secretary imposing a requirement in the licence granted to the Corporation or in Parliament imposing a duty by statute. He also said that even if the BBC had been under a legal duty, he would not have granted the remedy sought on the ground that it had not exercised its discretion unreasonably.

As with the BBC, the IBA also operates under constraints, though these are imposed by statute, and as such are subject to judicial review. The principal statute is the Broadcasting Act 1981 which provides for the continued existence of the IBA and which by section 2(2) provides:

"It shall be the duty of the Authority—
    (*a*) to provide the television and local sound broadcasting services as a public service for disseminating information, education and entertainment;

(*b*)   to ensure that the programmes broadcast by the Authority in each area maintain a high general standard in all respects (and in particular in respect of their content and quality), and a proper balance and wide range in their subject matter, having regard both to the programmes as a whole and also to the days of the week on which, and the times of the day at which, the programmes are broadcast; and

(*c*)   to secure a wide showing or (as the case may be) hearing for programmes of merit."

So far as programme content is concerned, this is governed by section 4 which provides in turn:

"(1) It shall be the duty of the Authority to satisfy themselves that, so far as possible, the programmes broadcast by the Authority comply with the following requirements, that is to say—

(*a*)   that nothing is included in the programmes which offends against good taste or decency or is likely to encourage or incite to crime or to lead to disorder or to be offensive to public feeling;

(*b*)   that a sufficient amount of time in the programmes is given to news and news features and that all news given in the programmes (in whatever form) is presented with due accuracy and impartiality;

(*c*)   that proper proportions of the recorded and other matter included in the programmes are of British origin and of British performance;

(*d*)   that the programmes broadcast from any station or stations contain a suitable proportion of matter calculated to appeal specially to the tastes and outlook of persons served by the station or stations and, where another language as well as English is in common use and among those so served, a suitable proportion of matter in that language;

(*e*)   in the case of local sound broadcasting services, that the programmes broadcast from different stations for reception in different localities do not consist of identical or similar material to an extent inconsistent with the character of the services as local sound broadcasting services; and

(*f*)   that due impartiality is preserved on the part of the persons providing the programmes as respects matters of political or industrial controversy or relating to current public policy.

In applying paragraph (*f*), a series of programmes may be considered as a whole."

The 1981 Act also provides that the programmes broadcast by the IBA may contain advertisements. These advertisements must comply with the rules in Schedule 2 to the 1981 Act. The rules provide, *e.g.* that the advertisements must be recognisable and distinguishable from programmes and from each other; they must not be excessively noisy or strident; and they must not be given so much time as to detract from the value of the programmes as a medium of information, education and entertainment. Moreover, no advertisement shall be permitted on behalf of a religious or political body or which is directed towards any religious or political end or has any relation to any industrial dispute.

Of these controls on content the ones which, in Scotland at least, have led to litigation are those concerning the treatment of politics and political parties in an impartial way. This is a particularly acute problem in Scotland, since it forms not only a distinct political forum, but also a distinct broadcasting forum, in the sense that programme schedules in Scotland are not the same as in England. Theoretically there is scope to treat Scotland, for broadcasting purposes, as a political entity, and to apply different rules to attain "impartiality" in the allocation of time to political parties and views. These issues are at the heart of the following two cases.

5. Wilson v. Independent Broadcasting Authority
1979 S.L.T. 279

This was a petition for an interim interdict to restrain the IBA from proceeding with broadcasts on the Scottish devolution referendum in 1979. The petitioners claimed that the schedule proposed by the IBA was in breach of sections 2(2)(*b*) and 4(1)(*f*) of the Independent Broadcasting Authority Act 1973 (identical to ss. 2(2)(*b*) and 4(1)(*f*) of the 1981 Act) because more broadcasting time would be given to the side campaigning for a "No" vote; section 2(2)(*b*) of the 1973 Act imposed a duty on the IBA to ensure that the programmes broadcast by it maintain a proper balance and wide range in their subject-matter

LORD ROSS: "In Scotland, I see no reason in principle why an individual should not sue in order to prevent a breach by a public body of a duty owed by that public body to the public. It may well be that the Lord Advocate could be a petitioner if the interests of the public as a whole were affected (see *Magistrates of Buckhaven and Methil* v. *Wemyss Coal Company,* 1932 S.L.T. 79, per Lord Sands), but I see no reason why an individual should not sue provided always that the individual can qualify an interest. . .

Having considered the petitioners' averments, I am of the opinion that the petitioners have averred sufficient interest. (1) They are voters and the referendum gives them the choice to say 'Yes' or 'No'. (2) They belong to an organisation or group who apparently believe that the question should be answered 'No'. (3) It is implicit in the name of the organisation or group, that the petitioners wish to persuade other voters to vote 'No'. It is plain from the petition and the answers that the petitioners and the political parties believe that the programmes are likely to be influential upon the electorate in Scotland, and if that is so the petitioners have an interest to see that the respondents do not act in breach of any statutory duties in relation to such programmes. . .

The petitioners' complaint is that the arrangements for party political broadcasts which the respondents have made, if implemented, would constitute a breach by the respondents of a statutory duty to ensure that programmes broadcast by them maintained a proper balance.

Counsel for the respondents argued with great persuasiveness that s. 2(2)(*b*) was not concerned with ensuring a balanced viewpoint, but related only to the subject-matter in its quantitative and qualitative sense. If that were so, and if the petitioners were correct, counsel submitted that there would be no need for s. 4(1)(*f*) which would have no content.

Although I feel that there is considerable force in respondent's counsel's submission I have come to be of opinion that the construction which he seeks to place on s. 2(2)(*b*) is unduly restrictive. It may well be that the duty in question would require the respondents to maintain a proper balance between programmes containing different subject-matters. For example, a balance would require to be maintained between religious programmes, sport, current affairs and so on. But I do not consider that that is the only balance that s. 2(2)(*b*) requires the respondents to ensure is maintained. The statute does not state that programmes should maintain a proper balance between different subject-matters but that the programmes should maintain a proper balance in their subject-matter. In my opinion the subsection would also require inter alia a proper balance to be maintained in relation to programmes on any particular subject-matter. The Scottish referendum is in itself a subject-matter and in my opinion, s. 2(2)(*b*) places on the respondents a duty to ensure that programmes broadcast by them on the subject of the referendum maintain a proper balance.

I accept that when arranging party political broadcasts in connection with a general election, all possible political viewpoints cannot be covered, and, for example, some participants in a general election and some minor parties may be excluded (see *Grieve* v. *Douglas-Home,* 1965 S.L.T. at p. 193 per Lord Kilbrandon). But the situation is different with a referendum where the electorate is being invited to answer a question 'Yes' or 'No'. Where the subject matter of programmes being broadcast is the referendum, I am of the opinion that a proper balance must be maintained between programmes favouring 'Yes' and programmes favouring 'No'. It is plain from both the petition and the answers that the party political broadcasts with which the petitioners are concerned are not normal party political broadcasts but are to be devoted specifically to the issue to be put to the electorate in the referendum. This puts them in a special category and they cannot be treated as if they were ordinary political broadcasts...

Being satisfied that a prima facie case of breach has been averred, the question then arises as to whether the court has power to pronounce interdict in such a situation.

Where such a breach has been averred, I am of the opinion that the court is entitled to grant the remedy sought. It is important that the Act does not provide any specific method of enforcing the duty. It creates no offence and imposes no sanctions. It provides no remedy for the breach. In that situation I am of the opinion that the court does have power to interdict the continuance of the breach of duty. Indeed, if the court does not have power, how is the duty imposed on the respondents to be enforced?"

6. Wilson v. Independent Broadcasting Authority (No.2)
1988 S.L.T. 276

LORD PROSSER: "This is a petition for judicial review. The petitioners are the Scottish National Party. The respondents are the Independent Broadcasting Authority. The review which is sought relates to the respondents' proposed allocation of party election broadcasts to be transmitted in Scotland during the forthcoming general election campaign. The petitioners asked me to grant a declarator that in proposing to allocate to the petitioners a number of broadcasts less than that allocated to respectively the Conservative party (which I shall refer to as 'the Conservatives'), the Labour party ('Labour'), and the SDP/Liberal Alliance ('the Alliance'), the respondents are failing to act in accordance with their duties under ss. 2(2)(b) and 4(i)(f) of the Broadcasting Act 1981; and a further declarator that in order to comply with these statutory duties, if any party election broadcasts are to be transmitted to any part of Scotland during the general election campaign, the respondents are bound to secure that an equal number of broadcasts, of equal duration, be allocated to each of the Conservatives, Labour, the Alliance and the petitioners. . .

Section 2(2)(b) of the 1981 Act provides: [his Lordship quoted the terms of the provision and continued:] It was submitted for the petitioners that in reading the words 'in each area' I should regard Scotland as an area; and while I am not satisfied that this is necessarily correct I am prepared to do so in the absence of any contrary submission. . .

During a general election campaign, it is the practice of the respondents to carry a certain number of broadcasts on behalf of each of the principal political parties. In deciding which parties should be allocated broadcasts, and how many broadcasts should be allocated to each, the respondents take account of recommendations made by a body known as the Party Political Broadcasting Committee, which includes representatives of the main political parties, and also of the respondents and the B.B.C. The respondents are however the body responsible for the actual allocation and transmission of party election broadcasts, and for securing that in any allocation they comply with their duties under the 1981 Act. In the past it appears that the committee normally took the initiative in making such recommendations, and that these were accepted by the respondents. In 1983 however the committee did not reach an agreed recommendation, and the respondents accordingly had to make an allocation without the benefit of such agreement. In 1987 the respondents made certain proposals to the committee, according to which the Conservatives, Labour and the Alliance would be offered five broadcasts of up to 10 minutes each (on I.T.V. and Channel 4), the petitioners two such broadcasts in Scotland, Plaid Cymru one such broadcast in Wales, and other parties who nominate at least 50 candidates, one broadcast of five minutes' duration. The committee has produced no agreed response to these proposals, and I was informed that as no such response would now be considered and given, the proposals put to the committee had in effect become the respondents' actual intended allocation. . .

Before turning to the issues in the present application, it is convenient to say something about the background. Between 1955 and 1965, no regional variations were permitted in the allocation of election broadcasts. Since 1965 the petitioners have been given an allocation, with their broadcasts being transmitted in Scotland only. I was given to understand that they would not want to broadcast to the rest of the United Kingdom. In relation to what the petitioners' counsel called "the United Kingdom parties", I was given to understand that this 'regionalisation' takes the form of their total allocation being divided between certain broadcasts which are transmitted to the whole of the United Kingdom, and others which are not. Of the five 10 minute broadcasts allocated to each of the Conservatives, Labour and the Alliance under the respondents' present proposals, three would be transmitted throughout the United Kingdom. Two would be transmitted only within Scotland could thus be expected to have a specifically 'Scottish' content. Corresponding to these two 'Scottish' broadcasts, there would be two transmissions excluding Scotland. There would not be any variation between transmissions in, for example, different regions of England.

Historically there have, of course, been quite substantial variations, since the advent of television, in the number of candidates put up by different parties, and in the number of votes cast for, and seats won by, such parties. There has in addition been the creation of the Social Democratic Party and the Alliance. The petitioners lodged in process a schedule showing details of votes case at general elections and numbers of seats contested and won by the various parties over the years since 1970 in Scotland. The schedule also gives certain details in relation to the European elections of 1984, the Scottish regional elections of 1986, and local government by-elections in 1986 in Scotland. . .

Since 1983, in by-elections in Great Britain, I was informed that the Alliance had gained 39 per cent of the votes cast, the Conservatives 30.4 per cent and Labour 28.4 per cent—but there have been no by-elections in Scotland, and the petitioners have accordingly not been involved. In the European elections of 1984 the Scottish figures show the petitioners obtaining more of the vote than the Alliance; and in the regional elections of 1986 they obtained rather more votes than either the Conservatives or the Alliance. In Scottish local by-elections in 1986, the petitioners' share of the vote exceeds that of both the Conservatives and the Alliance combined, and in those by-elections which were not on the same day as the 1986 regional elections, they came close (with 33.4 per cent) to the Labour share at 36.5 per cent. These shares are thus comparable to their October 1974 general election share of the vote, not far short of the Labour vote, and are very substantially different from their 11.8 per cent share in the 1983 general election. In the absence of any Scottish parliamentary by-elections these recent results are the only available indication of the petitioners' voting strength.

I turn to the issue between the parties. . .

Taking questions of statutory construction first I consider an argument advanced by counsel for the respondents to the effect that s. 2(2)(b) imposed no requirement relevant to the present circumstances. What had to be ensured was a proper balance in the subject matter of programmes. This, it was contended, meant a proper balance between various categories of subject matter, such as sport on the one hand or politics on the other. There was no requirement of balance within any one such category: if coverage of sport were wholly devoted to football or indeed to the exploits of a single football club, then that would constitute no imbalance with which this subsection at least was concerned. So, too, any imbalance between the treatment of one political party and another would be untouched by this section. Politics was one 'subject matter' and the proper balance required by the subsection was not a balance within that subject matter but between it and other subject matters.

Reference was made to the opinion of Lord Robertson in *Wolfe* v. *I.B.A.* [unreported] which it was submitted I should prefer on this point to the opinion of Lord Ross in *Wilson* v. *I.B.A.* The words of the subsection and its predecessors are not perhaps very happily drafted; and I am not at all sure how a 'proper' balance between such broad topics as sport and politics would be judged. I am not however persuaded that a statute which provides for that imponderable question to be put in the balance would be likely to ignore the need for balance within what might be called one particular subject matter. The words of the subsection appear to me to be equally referable to such internal balance or to the balance between subjects. In particular they appear to me to be referable to a balance between various programmes in a field such as politics, even if there is a problem in relation to the balancing of viewpoints within a single programme. I concur with Lord Ross's opinion in *Wilson*, and consider that in the rather different area now in issue, s. 2(2)(*b*) requires the respondents to ensure a proper balance in the presentation of party politics through election broadcasts.

So far as s. 4(1)(*f*) is concerned it was contended for the respondents that the subsection was not in point. At first sight, with its reference to matters of political controversy, this is the provision which one might expect to be most in point. I have however come to the view that its purpose is the maintenance of impartiality on the part of any one individual programme provider, rather than the creation of overall balance between several such programme providers by a mix of programmes any one of which may be partial. Even the provision for considering a series as a whole does not seem to me to move away from the single programme provider. The inherent partiality of party election broadcasts in my view renders it impossible for this particular subsection's requirement to be met. Having regard to the words 'so far as possible' which qualify the requirement, I find no breach. The fact that this subsection is not in my view a mechanism for balance in party election broadcasts confirms my opinion that if such balance has not been ignored in the statute, s. 2(2)(*b*) is the provision designed to deal with it.

What then of s. 2(2)(*b*)? On behalf of the petitioners it was contended that television is now a major element in any election as a means of communication with the electorate. To allow the United Kingdom parties five broadcasts against the petitioners' two was to give a significant advantage to each of these parties' candidates, and to put the petitioners' candidate in any constituency in Scotland at a serious disadvantage.

It was contended for the petitioners that the 'Scottish dimension' was something distinct from the United Kingdom dimension. This was recognised in many aspects of the constitution: the Union itself, the law, the Scottish Office, and other examples were cited. The reference of the Scotland Act 1978 to a referendum in Scotland alone was stressed. In the particular field of broadcasting, the structure of the broadcasting authorities in general and their practice of having 'Scottish' election broadcasts in particular were identified as illustrating the existence of a Scottish dimension, separate from and requiring consideration separately from, the ordinary United Kingdom dimension. That United Kingdom dimension justified an initial allocation of election broadcasts; but in final allocation, one could not ignore the Scottish dimension and give the petitioners a share which would merely reflect their share of United Kingdom votes or seats or candidates. One must consider the petitioners, in Scotland, on the basis of a comparison with United Kingdom parties in Scotland. In that context, which it was maintained the respondents had failed properly to consider, the petitioners were to be regarded as of equivalent significance with the other parties, and should receive an equivalent share of election broadcasts. More specifically the respondents had failed in their duty under s. 2(2)(*b*), by having regard to by-elections as a reason for giving the Alliance parity with the Conservatives and Labour (in itself an acceptable consideration) but treating the absence of by-elections in Scotland as a reason for holding the petitioners' allocation at its old level. Other criteria were available, and had been ignored: the European and local election results gave an indication (comparable, as I understood the contention, to the Alliance's by-election successes in England and Wales) that the petitioners were a force comparable to the other parties in Scotland, warranting an equal allocation of election broadcasts.

In any event, the weight traditionally given to the number of candidates rather than the election results should be maintained. If all four parties were fighting all (or virtually all) seats, proper balance could only be maintained by equal allocation. This proposition was not based merely on the fact of an equal number of candidates, which might be produced by a 'party' with no background or substance. However, with a vote at the last election of over 10 per cent, the petitioners were entitled to equal treatment with others who (while gaining more last time) had in recent times obtained only that level of success, and who in other elections in 1986 were significantly less successful than the petitioners. The number of seats won was the least significant factor having regard to the electoral system; but the pattern of seats won over the years was a relevant factor, when coupled with the voting pattern, as showing a party's 'strength' and its right to equal campaigning rights. It was essential that this comparison should be made within the Scottish dimension. The respondents had failed in this respect, and the result, in that dimension, was a lack of proper balance. The respondents had expressly stated that in reaching their decision, they had taken into account a number of factors, including the strength of parties in the outgoing Parliament, the results of by-elections, and the numbers of candidates likely to be nominated. But they had failed to adapt this approach to the Scottish dimension, and to the evidence available as to strengths in that dimension. The result was a failure to achieve the balance which it was their duty to ensure.

In a number of respects, the approach of the respondents, as spoken to by counsel, coincided with that demanded of them by the petitioners. It was accepted that the percentage of votes received should be given more weight than the number of seats won, in any assessment of a party's 'strength'. It was acknowledged that this approach, with the Alliance not far behind Labour in their 1983 share of votes, was the starting point in granting parity to the Alliance. The Alliance's results in by-elections, both in percentage terms and in terms of seats gained, had been a further consideration, as had their intention to contest all seats in Great Britain. Research had also shown that the Alliance were regarded as having been unfairly treated by the 5:5:4 allocation in 1983. I did not understand the petitioners to dispute either the grant of such parity or the considerations which had led to it on a United Kingdom basis. Moreover counsel for the petitioners accepted that the petitioners could succeed in establishing breach of duty under s. 2(2)(b) only if no reasonable authority could have concluded that a proper balance was ensured by the proposed allocations. It is only in more limited respects, and perhaps especially in the assessment of the 'Scottish dimension' that the parties are truly at odds.

The absence of Scottish by-election evidence was not regarded by the respondents as justifying recourse to the local or European election figures as a test of strength. Their view was that in such elections voters had a different basis of voting, and they thought it right to disregard these results. In my view this may or may not be 'right'—but I see nothing inherently irrational or untenable in such a view, and I see no breach of duty in the decision to leave this material out of account in an assessment of relative strengths. ...

The respondents' approach, taking the last general election percentages as a starting point or basis, regardless of previous results, may seem to give too much emphasis to one result, and to pay too little respect to earlier and very different results which showed greater 'strength'. Cutting the share of election broadcast time in consequence of a fall in votes won might be seen as helping to increase a trend, when more help in reversing that trend might be seen as fairer. But again I see nothing illogical or untenable in the approach adopted, with the last general trial of strength, being treated as the best test of strength unless or until other material, regarded as relevant, comes to hand. . .

Even taking the 1983 voting shares (with some credit to the Alliance for by-election successes) as the evidence of relative strength, I am not satisfied that the respondents' proposals need to be seen as in conflict with the petitioners' contention that parties with roughly 10 per cent or more should be treated as having sufficient strength to deserve parity of broadcast time if 'proper balance' is to be achieved.

It is clear that the so called 'Scottish dimension' has been acknowledged (whether adequately or not) in the respondents' proposals. Allocations are not based simply on proportions of the total number of United Kingdom votes, or seats, or candidates. The petitioners' allocation of two election broadcasts flows from an acknowledgement of their position in Scotland, since in United Kingdom terms they would, under the respondents' general proposals, receive only one broadcast, and that of half the length.

The word 'dimension' is not perhaps an adequate one. A Scottish or United Kingdom dimension might take many forms. There are no doubt certain topics of 'purely' Scottish concern in the election, and many of predominantly Scottish concern. There will be other topics of concern throughout the United Kingdom, but which in Scotland take a different form, requiring special policies or special treatment. There will be other topics which are not thus special to Scotland, but which in their general form may nonetheless be seen from a peculiarly Scottish viewpoint. There are no doubt many other ways of seeing and describing this Scottish element or dimension in the matters which the political parties may wish to raise in their broadcasts. The need to raise them is acknowledged not merely in the allocation of four times as much broadcasting time to the petitioners as they would otherwise receive, but also in the division of the United Kingdom parties' time into three 'United Kingdom' broadcasts and two which can be devoted to such Scottish treatment without being transmitted to an audience outside Scotland. The broadcasts which can be expected to deal with the Scottish dimension in this sense are thus indeed on a basis of parity, at two each for all four contenders.

The Scottish dimension is, however, to be observed also in the parties' own functions and aims. The petitioners do not, as the other political parties do, aspire to United Kingdom office. Correspondingly, the petitioners do not in general, as I understand matters, seek to present policies which meet specifically non-Scottish problems, or non-Scottish aspects of general problems, or non-Scottish view points on matters which are otherwise common to all United Kingdom voters. Correspondingly, the petitioners do not seek to present candidates outside Scotland, or to persuade non-Scottish voters to support them. Counsel for the respondents submitted that it was not they who were ignoring the Scottish dimension, but the petitioners who were under estimating this United Kingdom dimension. It was necessary to give the United Kingdom parties broadcasting time, not only through the two non-Scottish transmissions (which could be used for material which at least need not be presented to Scottish voters) but through additional broadcasts—the three United Kingdom broadcasts allocated to each—which would allow them to present to all the electorate, including the electorate in Scotland, the party policies upon which they sought election to Parliament and indeed government, as a United Kingdom party.

It is contended for the petitioners that by having these three 'extra' broadcasts, which are denied to the petitioners, the other parties have an advantage in 'persuasion time' over the petitioners. It would however surprise many Scots, I think—and not least the petitioners—if any of the other parties were to use their United Kingdom platform on these occasions to concentrate on Scottish concerns or to respond to specifically Scottish viewpoints. If they were to do so, no doubt they might have an advantage over the petitioners in that respect. But having regard to the United Kingdom dimension of their aims and interests, I can see no improper balance in an allocation of time to the United Kingdom parties to deal with that dimension and broadcast on that plane. Whether the allocation is the best, or is right, is not for me to judge. But there would be at least a problem, if parity were granted to the petitioners, in the availability to them of five programmes devoted to Scottish policies and viewpoints, while the other parties would be forced to cover much else in the same time, or to split their transmissions so that Scottish voters would see only Scottish angled material. The rejection of such an approach, and the adoption of an allocation which gives extra time to the United Kingdom parties for United Kingdom transmissions, must in my opinion be regarded as a tenable decision, reflecting United Kingdom dimensions as well as a Scottish dimension, and consistent with the respondents' duty to ensure a proper balance.

In these circumstances I do not consider that on the pleadings or the factual material before me the petitioners have shown that they are entitled to the remedy they seek. That being so, I refuse the declarators sought."

These cases served as a reminder to the IBA of the limits imposed by the Act. But their effect should not be exaggerated. For, while the courts may police the margins of the statutory powers of the Authority, they have wisely shown a marked reluctance to interfere with programme content. Apart from *Wilson (No. 2)*, the leading case is *Attorney-General* v. *Independent Broadcasting Authority (ex rel. McWhirter)* [1975] 1 Q.B. 629. McWhirter sought an injunction to restrain the IBA from showing a film about Andy Warhol on the ground that it offended against good taste and decency and was likely to be offensive. His complaint was based on Sunday newspaper reports. In the *News of the World*, it was said: "This TV shocker is the worst ever. A programme which goes further than anything I have ever seen on TV is to be screened on Tuesday night. Millions of viewers will find its frankness offensive." According to the *Sunday Mirror:*

"Andy Warhol film shocker for ITV. Television viewers are about to see what many will consider to be the most permissive shocker to be shown on British screens. . . I have been shown a preview of this remarkable documentary. It includes: A FAT GIRL, stripping to the waist, daubing her breasts with paint and then painting a canvas with them. She also throws paint down a lavatory pan to form weird patterns. This one she calls Flush Art."

"A discussion between a young girl and a man dressed as a Hell's Angel on how they can have sex. She says she will only do it at 60 m.p.h. on his motor cycle."

"Conversations are laced with four-letter words. . . It's all there all right. Especially transvestites, lesbianism and the whole freaky scene which surrounds Warhol."

The application for the interlocutory injunction came before the court on the day the film was due to be shown. It was granted on January 16, 1973, but discharged on February 5, 1973, when Lord Denning said:

"In section 3 of the Television Act 1964, Parliament specified several requirements with which programmes should comply. The first is: '. . . that nothing is included in the programmes which offends against good taste or decency or is likely to . . . be offensive to public feeling.' I would stress the words 'nothing is included.' Those words show that the programme is to be judged, not as a whole, but in its several parts, piece by piece. If a documentary dealt with life in the underworld on a restrained level, but then included by way of illustration 30 seconds of pornographic photographs, it would be a breach of the statutory requirements. It would not be cured by words being said at the beginning that 'some part of this programme may be offensive to some people.' Viewers may switch on in the middle of the programme, and, in any case, the statute does not permit of a warning being an excuse for non-compliance.

Such being the statutory requirements, Parliament puts a duty on the Independent Broadcasting Authority to 'satisfy themselves' that they are complied with 'so far as possible.'

This does not mean, of course, that the members of the authority are themselves to see every programme or go through it. They can and must leave a great deal to the staff. They are entitled in the ordinary way to accept the advice of their staff on the programmes in general, and on any programme in particular: see *Lewisham Metropolitan Borough and Town Clerk* v. *Roberts* [1949] 2 K.B. 608, 621 and 629. It is only in a most exceptional case that they may be expected to see a programme for themselves in order to be 'satisfied.' But there are such exceptional cases, just as there are exceptional cases when a Minister must satisfy himself personally. It depends how serious is the case: see *Liversidge* v. *Anderson* [1942] A.C. 206, 223-224.

Was this film a programme which they ought to have seen for themselves? Let me state the circumstances. (i) The programme was prepared by one of the programme companies called A.T.V. Network Ltd. In its original form, the staff of Independent Broadcasting Authority were so unhappy about it that they thought that the programme should be seen by the authority itself. (ii) A.T.V. Network Ltd. thereupon deleted some of the material and introduced the film with a warning that 'some people may find Warhol's views unusual and possibly offensive.' (iii) In the light of those modifications, the Director-General and staff of the Independent Broadcasting Authority felt able to recommend that the programme be transmitted as the usual network documentary on Tuesday, January 16, 1973, at 10.30 p.m. They made an intervention report to that effect. The Independent Broadcasting Authority accepted that recommendation but did not see the film themselves. (iv)

On January 12 or 13, journalists were invited to a preview of the film. (v) On Sunday, January 14, 1973, and Monday, January 15, some of the journalists in their papers made severe criticisms of the film. If their accounts were correct, it included incidents which were indecent and likely to be offensive to public feeling. The 'News of the World,' in particular said that 'millions of viewers will find its frankness offensive.' (vi) On reading those newspaper reports, the chairman and directors of one of the channels, Anglia Television, determined to have the film screened privately for them to see. They came to the unanimous conclusion that the programme, if broadcast, was likely to be offensive to public feeling. They announced that they were not going to supply it for broadcasting. (vii) The Independent Broadcasting Authority, however, did not see it. Some of them had an informal discussion with the senior staff, and, on their assurance, were prepared to let it be broadcast.

The question is: did the Independent Broadcasting Authority do what was sufficient, or ought they not to have seen the film for themselves, as the chairman of Anglia Television and their directors did? When the matter was brought before this court on Tuesday, January 16, it appeared that there was a prima facie case for saying that they had not done what was reasonably sufficient to satisfy themselves that 'so far as possible' there was nothing indecent or offensive in the programme. It was better to postpone its showing for a little while, using a substitute film, rather than let it go out that evening. Meanwhile, the matter could be properly considered in all its aspects, both as to the locus standi of Mr McWhirter and as to the fulfilment of the statutory requirements.

In the circumstances I think that the Independent Broadcasting Authority ought to have seen the film for themselves on the Monday or Tuesday before passing it. Since that time they have done so. So have the General Advisory Council. The members of the general council are drawn from a broad cross section of the people, and are as representative and responsible a body as you could find anywhere. The general council, by a majority of 17 to one, passed this resolution: 'The council felt that the staff were right to advise the authority that the film which they had seen was suitable to be shown at the suggested time.' The members of the Independent Broadcasting Authority are likewise most representative and responsible. Ten out off the 11 saw the film and unanimously reaffirmed the decisions 'that the programme is suitable for transmission in the 10.30 slot, and that it is satisfied that the programme complies with the requirements of section 3(1)(a) of the Television Act 1964.'

If those decisions are to be accepted as valid, they are decisive. The Independent Broadcasting Authority are the people who matter. They are the censors. The courts have no right whatever—and I may add no desire whatever—to interfere with their decisions so long as they reach them in accordance with law: see *Secretary of State for Employment* v. *ASLEF* (No. 2) [1972] 2 Q.B. 455. Mr Le Quesne submitted, however, that the Independent Broadcasting Authority had misdirected themselves. He said that they had regarded the film as a whole, and not piece by piece as the statute required. Alternatively, he said that their decision was one to which they could not reasonably have come.

To test these submissions we ourselves saw the film. I hesitate to express my own views upon it, but it is part of the evidence before us and I feel I should do so. I can understand that some people would think it entertaining, but I must speak as

I find. Viewing it as a whole, the film struck me as dreary and dull. It shows the sort of people—the perverts and homosexuals—who surround Mr Warhol and whom he portrays in his work. But, taken as a whole, it is not offensive. Viewing it piece by piece, there are some incidents which seemed to me to be inserted in an attempt to liven up the dullness—an attempt which did not succeed, at least so far as I was concerned. These are the incidents which struck the newspaper reporters and were described by them, and which, no doubt, struck the chairman of Anglia Television and his colleagues. They only form about one-tenth of the whole. Speaking for myself, I would take the same view as the newspaper reporters and the chairman and directors of Anglia Television. I should have thought that those individual incidents could be regarded as indecent and likely to be offensive to many. But my views do not matter, unless they go to show that the Independent Broadcasting Authority misdirected themselves or came to a conclusion to which they could not reasonably come. I am certainly not prepared to say that. Quite the contrary. On seeing the film, they came to a decision to which they might reasonably come, and this court has no right whatever to interfere with it.

I would therefore lift the injunction. The programme can be shown as soon as can be arranged. No doubt many will wish to see it to form their own view. Some will write to the Independent Broadcasting Authority and tell them. It should give the Independent Broadcasting Authority a good guide to public feeling, and so help them in the difficult decisions which they have to make in the future. But they should always remember that there is a silent majority of good people who say little but view a lot. Their feelings are to be respected as well as those of the vociferous minority who, in the name of freedom, shout for ugliness in all its forms.

So let the programme be shown. We will not stop it."

III. OBSCENITY

1. THE BACKGROUND

The modern law on obscenity is to be found in the Civic Government (Scotland) Act 1982, s. 51. Before the coming into force of this measure, the position was governed by a range of statutory provisions, and more recently by the common law.

7. The Burgh Police (Scotland) Act 1892

"380. Every person who is guilty of any of the following acts or omissions within the burgh shall, in respect thereof, be liable to a penalty not exceeding the respective amounts, or to imprisonment for a period not exceeding the respective periods herein after mentioned; videlicet,—

To a penalty of twenty-five pounds, or alternatively without penalty, to imprisonment for sixty days, every person who. . .

(3) Publishes, prints, or offers for sale or distribution, or sells, distributes, or exhibits to view, or causes to be published, printed, exhibited to view, or distributed, any indecent, or obscene book, paper, print, photograph, drawing, painting, representation, model or figure, or publicly exhibits any disgusting or

indecent object, or writes or draws any indecent or obscene word, figure, or representation in or on any place where it can be seen by the public, or sings or recites in public any obscene song or ballad."

Local statutes in Dundee and Aberdeen made substantially similar provision. The Glasgow Corporation Consolidation (General Powers) Order Confirmation Act 1960 was slightly different. By section 162 a magistrate could, on a complaint by the procurator fiscal, grant a warrant to a police officer, not under the rank of inspector, to enter and search a shop or other place in which the magistrate had reasonable grounds for believing that any profane, indecent or obscene article, book, paper, print, photograph, drawing, painting, or representation was kept for sale, or lending, or hire, or for publication for purposes of gain. The police might seize and remove any relevant material found in the shop and the occupier who kept such material would if convicted be liable to a fine or to 60 days' imprisonment.

8. Galletly v. Laird
1953 S.L.T. 67

William Galletly was charged in the police court at Paisley on a complaint that within his premises as a bookseller's shop he did "exhibit to view" books which were indecent or obscene, contrary to section 380(3) of the 1892 Act. He was convicted and the magistrate ordered the materials to be destroyed. Galletly appealed to the High Court.

LORD JUSTICE-GENERAL (Cooper): "To justify a conviction in a case of this type the Court ought to be satisfied of two elements, *viz.*: (1) That the book or picture is of such a nature as to be calculated to produce a pernicious effect in depraving and corrupting those who are open to such influences; and (2) that such book or picture is being indiscriminately exhibited or circulated or offered for sale in such circumstances as to justify the inference that it is likely to fall (and perhaps intended to fall) into the hands of persons liable to be so corrupted.

The second of these elements seems to me the more important, for this reason that a book or picture, however indecent or obscene, will create no social evil of the type sought to be suppressed so long as it is kept in proper custody and under responsible control. The mischief resides not so much in the book or picture *per se* as in the use to which it is put, usually deliberately and for gain by the trafficker in pornography, who makes a business of inspiring and catering for depraved and perverted tastes. Such cases are usually not difficult to recognise, and it is easy to understand why Parliament should have confided to local officers of police and magistrates the recognition and detection of what is in a real sense a local public nuisance. These penal provisions are not aimed at setting up in each locality a *censor morum* with the duty of compiling on the principles of Mrs Grundy an *index expurgatorius* of the literary and artistic productions of all the ages, and with the power of imprisoning reputable dealers who justifiably stock literary, scientific, artistic and philosophic works which, however unsuitable for indiscriminate distribution to the curious adolescents, are perfectly appropriate for study by the serious scholar. I am quite unmoved by the suggestion that these prosecutions reveal a grave threat to the liberty of respectable booksellers, librarians and others, who were said to be afraid lest there might be discovered in their possession some work—perhaps a celebrated classic—which might offend the susceptibilities of the type of magistrate whom Lord Sands described as 'the morose Puritan'. It is impossible to read these provisions and the immediate context in which they occur without being convinced that their purpose is quite different, and that their use for the object suggested would be unjustifiable. I note, for example, that the other branches of the fasciculus in the Burgh Police Act are concerned *inter alia*, with penalising indecent exposure, the harbouring of prostitutes, and the allowance by the occupier of any building of 'riotous or disorderly conduct within the same'. Equally I am not dismayed by the idea that the opinion of the magistrate before whom the case is brought is virtually determinative of the question whether the books or pictures libelled are or are not indecent or obscene. Once it is understood that the emphasis falls to be laid upon the second of the elements defined above, it seems to me to be not only intelligible but inevitable that the character of the offending books or pictures should be ascertained by the only method by which such a fact can be ascertained, *viz.:* by reading the books or looking at the pictures. The book or picture itself provides the best evidence of its own indecency or obscenity or of the absence of such qualities; and if in any case the magistrate's decision is challenged, the only method by which an appellate tribunal could determine whether the magistrate was entitled to reach the conclusion which he did would be by examining the book or picture, not with a view to re-trying the case but solely with a view to discovering whether they revealed evidence on which a reasonable magistrate would be entitled to condemn them as indecent or obscene...

The magistrate [in this case] disallowed cross-examination by the complainer's solicitor and positive evidence tendered for the defence designed to show that books other than those referred to in the complaint circulated freely in Paisley and were available in the local public library, the suggestion apparently being that these other books were not materially different in character from those complained of. I consider that the magistrate's ruling was right. The character of other books is a collateral issue, the exploration of which would be endless and futile. If the books produced by the prosecution are indecent or obscene, their quality in that respect cannot be made any better by examining other books, or listening to the opinions of other people with regard to these other books. . .

The statute uses the expression 'indecent or obscene', the complaint echoes the statute, and the magistrate found the accused guilty as libelled as regards certain of the books. It was maintained that this was to return a general conviction on an alternative charge, and reference was made to the opinion of Lord Sands in *McGowan* v. *Langmuir*, 1931 S.L.T. 94 where his Lordship engaged in a philological analysis of the vocabulary of indecency. I am willing to accept it that in general parlance 'obscene' is a stronger epithet than 'indecent', and even to adopt Lord Sands' suggestion that the former is the superlative and the latter is the comparative of the positive 'immodest'. But I do not believe, and I do not read the judgment in *McGowan* (*supra*) as deciding, that these subtleties played any part when this section was drafted in 1892. As applied in a penal provision to books or representations of the type in question the adjectives 'indecent or obscene' are, in my view, employed tautologically to convey a single idea and perfectly clear idea at that, and it would be palpably absurd to ask courts to wade through such a collection as has been produced in these cases for the purpose of uselessly classifying the condemned material into different grades of indecency.

In the result I consider that the attacks upon this conviction fail and that the bill should be refused."

Lords Carmont and Russell concurred.

There is an obvious difference in the approach adopted by Lord Cooper in *Galletly* v. *Laird* and that adopted by Lord Sands in the earlier case, *McGowan* v. *Langmuir*, 1931 S.L.T. 94. In *McGowan*, Lord Sands said at p.96:

"I do not think that the two words 'indecent' and 'obscene' are synonymous. The one may shade into the other, but there is a difference of meaning. It is easier to illustrate than define, and I illustrate thus. For a male bather to enter the water nude in the presence of ladies would be indecent, but it would not necessarily be obscene. But if he directed the attention of a lady to a certain member of his body his conduct would certainly be obscene. The matter might be roughly expressed thus in the ascending scale: Positive—Immodest; Comparative—Indecent; Superlative—Obscene. These, however, are not rigid categories. The same conduct which in certain circumstances may merit only the milder description, may in other circumstances deserve a harder one. 'Indecent' is a milder term than 'obscene', and as it satisfied the purposes of this case if the prints in question are indecent, I shall apply that test."

It appears, however, that Lord Cooper's approach is the one which was subsequently applied in practice. It is similar to the statutory test in English law (Obscene Publications Act 1959, s. 1) and to the test adopted by the Edinburgh Corporation Order Confirmation Act 1967 which provided:

"451.—(1) In this head of this Part of this Order:—
    (a) 'indecent or obscene article' means an article of such nature as to be calculated to deprave or corrupt persons open to depraving or corrupting influences, and includes:—
        (i) any description of article containing or embodying matter to be read or looked at, or both;
        (ii) any sound record;
        (iii) any film, slide, transparency or other record of pictures or any other optical projection; and
        (iv) any set of articles which are intended to be read, looked at, displayed, listened to, shown or projected in combination; and
    (b) 'publication' means publication indiscriminately, or in such circumstances as to justify the inference that the indecent or obscene article is likely to fall into the hands of, or be seen or heard by, persons open to depraving or

corrupting influences, and includes:—
(i) exhibiting, distributing, circulating, selling, letting for hire, lending, or offering for sale or for hire; and
(ii) showing, playing, or projecting (in the case of an article containing, or embodying matter to be looked at, or a record);
and 'publish' shall be construed accordingly:
Provided that paragraph (b)(ii) of this subsection shall not apply to anything done in the course of a cinematograph exhibition (within the meaning of the Cinematograph Act, 1952), other than one excluded from the Cinematograph Act, 1909, by section 7(4) of that Act (which relates to exhibitions in private houses to which the public is not admitted), or to anything done in the course of television or sound broadcasting."

2. RE-ENTER THE COMMON LAW

9. Watt v. Annan
1978 S.L.T. 198

Watt was charged and convicted on a summary complaint as follows:

"you did on 2nd October 1976 at the premises known as the Grapes Hotel, East Calder, conduct yourself in a shamelessly indecent manner and did exhibit or cause to be exhibited to a number of persons a film of an obscene or indecent nature, which depicted *inter alia* sexual intercourse, involving a number of male and female persons, acts of masturbation, oral sex and unnatural acts and practices, including the drinking of urine and inserting a candle into the private parts of female persons appearing in said film, and said film was liable to create depraved, inordinate and lustful desires in those watching said film and to corrupt the morals of the lieges."

The film was shown behind locked doors in the lounge bar of the hotel. Watt was the supplier and owner of the film and a member of a social club of which all others present were also members.

LORD CAMERON: "The statement that 'all shamelessly indecent conduct is criminal' makes its first appearance in the first edition of MacDonald's *Criminal Law* and is repeated in all subsequent editions without comment or criticism in any decided case. It was approved by Lord Clyde in *MacLaughlan* v. *Boyd,* 1933 S.L.T. at p. 631 when he declared it to be sound and correctly expressing the law of Scotland. It is true that this observation was obiter but it was concurred in by the other members of the court and has not been since subjected to criticism or doubt. It is clear however that, as the Crown maintained, it is not the indencency of the conduct itself which makes it criminal but it is the quality of 'shamelessness', and the question is what is the content of this qualification? It was accepted, and rightly so, in the submission for the Crown that for the conduct to be criminal, in such circumstances as the facts in the present case disclose, it must be directed towards some person or persons with an intention or knowledge that it should corrupt or be calculated or liable to corrupt or deprave those towards whom the indecent or obscene conduct was directed. Whether or not conduct which is admittedly indecent or obscene is to be held criminal will depend on the proof of the necessary mens rea and upon the facts and circumstances of the particular case. It would be impracticable as well as undesirable to attempt to define precisely the limits and ambit of this particular offence, far less to decide that the nature of the premises or place in which the conduct charged has occurred should alone be decisive in transforming conduct which would otherwise be the proper subject of prosecution into conduct which may do no more than offend the canons of personal propriety or standards of contemporary morals. If it were considered desirable or necessary that this was a chapter of the criminal law in which precise boundaries or limits were to be set then it might be thought that the task is one which is more appropriate for the hand of the legislator.

In the present case there is no dispute that the film displayed amply deserved the description of indecent or obscene or that its display was calculated or liable to corrupt or deprave the morals of those who viewed it, whether they were consenters or otherwise. The question is then narrowed to this, whether the circumstances of the display as found by the sheriff in this case were such as to render the conduct of the appellant shamelessly indecent. . . Neither the publicity nor the privacy of the locus of the conduct charged necessarily affects far less determines the criminal quality of indecent conduct libelled as shameless. That this is so can be readily inferred from the context in which this statement of the law appears, particularly in MacDonald's first edition and in those subsequent editions which were revised by the Lord Justice-Clerk himself. In my opinion therefore it is not essential to the relevancy of a charge of shamelessly indecent conduct that it must be libelled that the conduct in question occurred in a public place or was a matter of public exhibition. . .

The criminal character of the act of indecency must therefore depend on proof of the necessary criminal intent as well as proof of the nature of the conduct itself and of the circumstances in which it takes place. Conduct that may be legitimate and innocent in the laboratory of the anthropologist may well be shamelessly indecent if carried on or exhibited in other places or circumstances, and whether these can be characterised as private or public may be no matter. In any event, it may well be asked what should be the criterion of 'publicity' as opposed to 'privacy' which is to determine the critical issue of deciding that conduct which might otherwise be regarded only as in conflict with accepted morals becomes in breach of the criminal law. To this question the submissions for the appellant provide no answer and the obscene publication cases are no guide. In these circumstances and for these reasons I am of opinion that the appellant's attack on the relevancy of this complaint fails. . ."

The Lord Justice-General (Emslie) and Lord Johnston agreed.

Before *Watt* v. *Annan,* the last reported prosecution at common law was *Henry Robinson* (1843) 1 Broun 590, where the accused was charged with exposing for sale obscene work "intended to vitiate and corrupt the morals of the lieges . . . and to raise and create in their minds inordinate and lustful desires." Although Lord Justice-General Clyde alluded to the existence of common law liability in *McGowan* v. *Langmuir,* the common law lay dormant, perhaps appropriate only in those areas where the statutory offences did not apply (on which see Finnie, (1981a)). Yet to the prosecutor the re-introduction of some form of common law liability must have appeared desirable on several counts, not the least of these being that the statutes controlled only a limited range of activity and did not extend, *e.g.* to the conduct which led to the prosecution in *Watt* v. *Annan*. A second and perhaps more important advantage of the common law to the prosecutor is that the penalties which may be exacted are substantially greater than the £25 fine (or 60 days' imprisonment) then permitted by the statutes. It seems that for this reason the Crown resorted to the common law as a basis for prosecution even in those areas where the statutes applied. In *Robertson* v. *Smith*, 1979 S.L.T. (Notes) 51, the accused was convicted at Dundee sheriff court on a complaint which libelled *inter alia* that he conducted himself "in a shamelessly indecent manner, that he did sell, expose for sale and have for sale 1,060 indecent and obscene books and magazines . . . five indecent and obscene films . . . and a pack of indecent and obscene playing cards, which books, magazines, films and playing cards were likely to deprave and corrupt the morals of the lieges and to create in their minds inordinate and lustful desires." The evidence was broadly that following a search of the accused's shop premises the police found the offending articles, some on display in the front shop and some in the back room. The shop was constructed so that it was impossible to see inside the shop from outside, but there was a sign outside indicating that it was a bookseller's shop and that no one under 18 would be admitted. The accused appealed by stated case. The appeal was dismissed. In delivering the opinion of the court, Lord Cameron said:

"I would, as at present advised, be disposed to regard the offence of exposure of obscene material for sale as one which may competently be comprehended within the general category of shameless and indecent conduct according to the common law of Scotland. If indecent exposure of the person falls within the generic of 'shameless indecent conduct' at common law, exposure for sale of obscene publications or reproductions would not appear to me to differ in quality but only in species. . .

Counsel for the appellant's second principal argument was founded upon the assertion that the sheriff did not apply his mind to the issue of mens rea or to the facts and circumstances of the particular case, in respect that he made no finding that the appellant's conduct as occupier of the premises was indecent or shameless. There was, in particular, no finding as to the mode of display of the publications libelled within the front shop. There was thus no finding indicative of mens rea, more especially that there was no specific finding that the appellant owned or ran the business. In the absence of any such necessary findings the material for conviction was insufficient. In my opinion there is no substance in this argument. The appellant is found to be occupier of the premises, the stock of material in the back shop is found to be *his* 'reserve' stock, the premises advertise a bookselling business with access denied to persons under 18. There is no window display, but on the contrary the contents of the shop are screened effectively from outside view and it is impossible to see into the shop from outside. All this appears to me more than ample to demonstrate that the appellant was fully aware of the type of custom he was seeking to cultivate and of the nature of the wares that he was offering to the adult public for sale. The care taken to conceal the wares from outward view was both an invitation and an indication of the character and quality of the goods inside."

Having thus established that the exposure of obscene material for sale was an offence at common law, three questions arose as to the scope of the offence. The first relates to the essence of the offence, a matter considered in *Ingram* v. *Macari*, 1984 S.L.T. 92 where remarkable similarities with the statutory offences were revealed. The respondent had been charged in the following terms: "that . . . in the shop premises occupied by you at 90 East High Street, Forfar . . . you did conduct yourself in a shamelessly indecent manner, and sell one magazine of an indecent and obscene nature, namely 'Rustler, Vol.5, No. 8', and did further expose for sale and have for sale 262 indecent and obscene books and magazines." The sheriff held that the charge was irrelevant and he dismissed the complaint on the ground that the charge did not aver that the indecent and obscene material was liable or likely to deprave and corrupt the morals of the lieges and to create in their minds inordinate and lustful desires. The Crown appealed successfully against the dismissal, with the High Court writing:

"In our opinion the submission for the Crown is sound and must receive effect. As the Crown concedes, the substance of offences of the kind with which this complaint is concerned is sale or exposure for sale of indecent and obscene material (*Robertson* v. *Smith*, 1979 S.L.T. (Notes) 51 at p. 52). The question is whether for the purposes of pure relevancy of a charge at common law that charge must libel expressly that the allegedly indecent and obscene articles are liable to corrupt and deprave those likely to be exposed to their influence. There can be no doubt that the answer to that question is no. It is to be found in the opinion of the court delivered by the Lord Justice-General (Cooper) in *Galletly*. That case establishes that under the statutory provisions such as those with which the case was concerned, which make it an offence to sell or expose for sale 'indecent or obscene' articles of publications, the words 'indecent or obscene' imply the liability of the articles or publications concerned to corrupt and deprave. As the Lord Justice-General said in his opinion (1953 S.L.T. at p. 71): 'different as these and other like provisions are in detail, there seems to me to run through all the provisions on the subject, and also through the rules of our own common law as exemplified by such cases as *Robinson* (1843) 1 Broun 590, 643, a common policy aimed at providing a remedy for an undoubted social evil; and in view of the argument to which we listened it will be simplest to begin with certain general observations, derived from a survey of the statutes and of a series of decisions both in Scotland and in England. To justify a conviction in a case of this type the Court ought to be satisfied of two elements, viz. (1) that the book or picture is of such a nature as to be calculated to produce a pernicious effect in depraving and corrupting those who are open to such influences; and (2) that such book or picture is being indiscriminately exhibited or circulated or offered for sale in such circumstances as to justify the inference that it is likely to fall (and perhaps intended to fall) into the hands of persons liable to be so corrupted.'

If, therefore, for the purposes of statutory offences the words 'indecent or obscene' convey a single idea involving the liability of articles so described to corrupt and deprave, there is no reason whatever for supposing that at common law the words 'indecent and obscene' do not carry the same implication. In the result the liability of the allegedly indecent and obscene publications to corrupt and deprave is of the essence of the common law offence just as it is of the statutory offences and must be established. This liability, however, is implied in the words 'indecent or obscene' in their statutory context or 'indecent and obscene' in the context of a common law charge. They do not therefore require to be expressly libelled for the purposes of relevancy."

The second question raised by the offence admitted in *Robertson* v. *Smith, supra* is to establish what is meant by "exposure for sale." This was subsequently considered in *Scott* v. *Smith,* 1981 S.L.T. (Notes) 22, where the accused did not openly display the articles in question but produced a selection of materials from a drawer when asked by a customer whether he had any adult magazines for sale. In his opinion, Lord Cameron said:

"What in fact he did was, at the request of a customer, to lay before the customer a number of magazines which have been found to be obscene publications, and that finding is not challenged. In respect of these articles they were certainly displayed for one purpose alone—to attract the customer and for sale. They were taken from a drawer in the shop which contained other obscene magazines. . . Other similar magazines were found, not in a drawer but (1) on a shelf behind the counter, and (2) on the shop floor behind the counter. Even though they were 'not visible to the casual visitor' equally they were not concealed. All were of the same character according to the sheriff's findings, and these are not challenged.

It is not open to dispute that all the magazines found were held by the appellant for sale to members of the public and formed part of his stock held in immediate readiness to meet the desires or requests of any member of the public who came to the shop as a prospective customer for 'adult books' as indicative of the type and character of the literary works desired. The appellant at once recognised the nature and purpose of his customer's request and consequently offered and displayed a selection of his wares in this particular line of literature.

There must be many bookshops—both new and second-hand—where significant parts of the books on sale are not visible to the casual visitor, but because of this fact it could scarcely be argued that the books in question were not being exposed for sale. It seems to me that decision of the issue of what is 'exposure for sale' in any given case is largely one of fact and circumstance. I do not think it would be practicable or profitable to attempt to define within rigid limits or boundaries what is comprised within the words 'exposed for sale'.

In the present case the sheriff had before him facts which made it clear that a substantial stock of obscene magazines was kept in immediate readiness for sale in drawers and on shelves and even on the floor adjacent to the counter over which sales took place. Further , there was undoubted display of a selection of the stock when the general request was made 'whether he [the appellant] had any adult books'. This was not the case of a sale of a particularly requested item, but a display of a representative selection of stock in response to a general question as to whether a particular type of periodical or book was kept in stock by the shopkeeper. It was in reference to this general request that there was what may fairly enough be described as an 'exposure' of stock—for the purpose of securing a sale. I think that on the facts found by the sheriff in this case he was entitled to hold established that the appellant had 'exposed for sale' the magazines and periodicals specified in the schedules annexed to the complaint."

The third issue raised by the cases after *Robertson* v. *Smith* is whether there were any limitations on the scope of the offence. In *Tudhope* v. *Sommerville*, 1981 S.L.T. 117 the High Court held that the crime did not extend to wholesalers of indecent material. In delivering the opinion of the court, Lord Cameron said:

"No doubt it is a crime at common law to expose for sale in premises to which the public are invited to resort or to which they are given access for the purpose of being invited to purchase or be supplied with obscene or indecent literature, but that is a very different matter from warehousing literature of that type. It has not as yet been suggested that to do so constitutes a common law offence according to the law of Scotland. While disclaiming an intention to describe what is charged here as falling within the category of shameless and indecent conduct, the advocate-depute sought to formulate the offence as falling within the category of 'trafficking in obscene material' by analogy with 'trafficking' by actual exposure for sale. In effect, the argument for the Crown was that what is libelled in this complaint was an 'aspect' of what had already and for long been held to be criminal conduct. In my opinion this will not do: the criminal element in charges of exposure for sale of obscene or indecent material lies in the exposure to the public. The mere possession of such material is not by that fact alone rendered criminal at common law; here there is no affront to public decency or morals nor any action which of itself is designed or calculated to corrupt the morals of the lieges. The lieges are in no sense brought in actual contact or potential contact with the (assumedly) corrupting influence so long as it remains passively in the accused's warehouse. On the other hand, possession in retail shop premises in circumstances indicative that such material is part of that retailer' s stock in trade and is kept in such manner and in such place as to yield the conclusion that that stock is being offered for sale, may well however provide the necessary basis for conviction of the offence of shameless and indecent conduct. . . The Crown in the present appeal seek to push the boundaries of criminal responsibility further than has been recognised in the past, by contending that it is the purpose for which the possession exists which constitutes its criminal character, as it is an 'aspect' of what has already been held criminal, namely the exposure for sale. But at what point is the line to be drawn? At the wholesaler? But if he is to be held liable at common law and the offence is not 'shameless and indecent conduct,' on what ground should the publisher or printer escape? The argument for the Crown—and in a case in which neither conspiracy nor concert is alleged (and I reserve my opinion on the relevancy of such a charge affecting the retailer, wholesaler or publisher or printer)—went beyond the bounds of conduct which directly affected or might affect members of the public."

The other limitation had emerged earlier in *Dean* v. *John Menzies (Holdings) Ltd.*, 1981 S.L.T. 50 where it was held that the offence cannot be committed by a limited liability company on the ground that shamelessness is an attribute of which human beings alone are capable and is not something which can be imputed to a company. The case is also important for the indications of dissent by Lords Stott and Maxwell about developments of shameless indecency generally. In his opinion, Lord Stott said this was "an area of law in which (as is perhaps indicated by the archaic and faintly ludicrous wording of the complaint) commonsense is not noticeably at a premium" (p. 60). But notwithstanding this decision, the Crown seemed undaunted and continued to fish for small fry, with prosecutions being brought against the proprietors of small business, and remarkably, against junior employees (including shop assistants) of the corporate bodies which could not be prosecuted.

Sensibly, however, sheriffs appeared reluctant to convict such people, who after all will bear no responsibility for the policy of their employer: see *Tudhope* v. *Barlow*, 1981 S.L.T. (Sh.Ct) 94. This was a clear abuse of power by the Crown Office which ought to have been firmly dealt with by the courts. However, following the reform of the statutory offences, it is likely that shameless indecency will now play a marginal role in the control of so-called indecent or obscene publications. Many would argue that it should have had no such role in the first place. Even if it is conceded that the Executive needed more powers than those contained in the Burgh Police (Scotland) Act 1892, it is a constitutional impropriety to take an initiative which by-passes Parliament by seeking the endorsement of a compliant court. Certainly reports of shameless indecency cases have declined, and in one which *has* recently been reported (*Lockhart* v. *Stephen*, 1987 S.C.C.R. 642) the sheriff (Stewart) emphasised that the standard, as said in *Tudhope* v. *Barlow*, is the current standards of ordinary decent people, that those standards have changed enormously since the offence of shameless indecency was revived, and that a live performance in a pub which, though perhaps vulgar, disgusting and offensive, gave no encouragement to violent sadistic practices, but only encouraged normal sexual activity among adults according to the general standards of today is not likely to deprave and corrupt and so is not shamelessly indecent. The interested reader should compare the facts alleged in the complaint, as compared with that in *Watt* v. *Annan*, to appreciate just how much the current standards of ordinary decent people have changed!

3. The New Legal Regime

10. Report of the Committee on Obscenity and Film Censorship
(Chairman: Bernard Williams)
Cmnd. 7772 (1979)

"SUMMARY OF PROPOSALS

General

1. The existing variety of laws in this field should be scrapped and a comprehensive new statute should start afresh (see paragraph 2.29).

2. Terms such as 'obscene', 'indecent' and 'deprave and corrupt' should be abandoned as having outlived their usefulness (paragraph 9.21).

3. The law should rest partly on the basis of harms caused by or involved in the existence of the material: these alone can justify prohibitions; and partly on the basis of the public's legitimate interests in not being offended by the display and availability of the material: this can justify no more than the imposition of restrictions designed to protect the ordinary citizen from unreasonable offence (paragraphs 9.7 and 10.2).

4. The principle object of the law should be to prevent certain kinds of material causing offence to reasonable people or being made available to young people (paragraph 9.7).

5. Only a small class of material should be forbidden to those who want it, because an objective assessment of likely harm does not support a wider prohibition (paragraph 10.8)

6. The printed word should be neither restricted nor prohibited since its nature makes it neither immediately offensive nor capable of involving the harms we identify, and because of its importance in conveying ideas (paragraph 7.22).

Restriction

7. Restrictions should apply to matter (other than the printed word) and to a performance whose unrestricted availability is offensive to reasonable people by reason of the manner in which it portrays, deals with or relates to violence, cruelty or horror, or sexual, faecal or urinary functions or genital organs (paragraphs 9.36 and 11.8).

8. Restriction is to consist in a ban
 (i) on the display, sale, hire etc. of restricted material other than by way of postal or other delivery and
 (ii) on the presentation of any restricted performance
  other than in premises (or part of premises having a separate access from the street)
  (a) to which persons under the age of eighteen are not admitted, and
  (b) to which access is possible only by passing a prominent warning notice in specified terms, and
  (c) which make no display to persons not passing beyond the warning notice, other than the name of the business and an indication of its nature (paragraphs 9.15 and 11.8). . .

13. It should not be an offence for a person under the age of eighteen to seek to gain entry to premises in which restricted material is being displayed, sold or hired or in which a restricted performance is being presented, or to order restricted material to be sent to him or her (paragraph 9.44)...

Prohibition

19. Prohibited material should consist of photographs and films whose production appears to the court to have involved the exploitation for sexual purposes of any person where either

(a) that person appears from the evidence as a whole to have been at the relevant time under the age of sixteen, or

(b) the material gives reason to believe that actual physical harm was inflicted on that person (paragraph 10.6).

20. It should be an offence to take any prohibited photograph or film, to distribute or show it, to have it with a view to its being distributed or shown, or to advertise it as being available for distribution or showing (paragraph 10.13)...

24. A live performance should be prohibited if

(a) it involves actual sexual activity of a kind which, in the circumstances in which it was given, would be offensive to reasonable people (sexual activity including the act of masturbation and forms of genital, anal or oral connection between humans and animals as well as between humans), or

(b) it involves the sexual exploitation of any person under the age of sixteen (paragraph 11.15)."

No action has yet been taken to implement the proposals of the Williams Committee. There have, however, been two major statutory initiatives since Williams. The first was the enactment of the Indecent Displays (Control) Act 1981, sponsored by a backbencher, Mr Tim Sainsbury. The Act (which repealed the provisions of s. 380(3) of the Burgh Police (Scotland) Act 1892 which made it an offence to exhibit to view indecent or obscene materials) gives substantial effect to the recommendations in para. 8 above. However, the major departure is that the Act applies to "indecent" material whereas Williams had recommended the abolition of the old legal standards and their replacement with a provision based on offence to reasonable people.

The Act provides that it is an offence to display indecent material in a public place. A public place is defined as a place to which the public have or are permitted to have access (whether on payment or otherwise) while the matter is displayed. The Act does not apply where:

(i) the place is one to which the public are permitted to have access only on payment which is or includes payment for the display; or

(ii) the place is a shop or any part of a shop to which the public can only gain access by passing beyond an adequate warning notice. The notice must state that persons passing beyond it will find material on display which they may consider indecent. Persons under 18 must not be permitted entry and this must be stated on the notice.

The Act specifically adopts a number of exclusions which deal with the theatre, television, the cinema, art galleries and museums. Prosecution under the Act may lead to imprisonment or a fine, or both.

11. The Civic Government (Scotland) Act 1982

"*Obscene material*

51.—(1) Subject to subsection (4) below, any person who displays any obscene material in any public place or in any other place where it can be seen by the public shall be guilty of an offence under this section.

(2) Subject to subsection (4) below, any person who publishes, sells or distributes or, with a view to its eventual sale or distribution, makes, prints, has or keeps any obscene material shall be guilty of an offence under this section.

(3) A person guilty of an offence under this section shall be liable, on summary conviction, to a fine not exceeding the prescribed sum or to imprisonment for a period not exceeding 3 months or to both or, on conviction on indictment, to a fine or to imprisonment for a period not exceeding two years or to both.

(4) A person shall not be convicted of an offence under this section if he proves that he had used all due diligence to avoid committing the offence.

(5) Under an indictment for or on a complaint of a breach of subsection (1) above, the court may, if satisfied that the person accused is guilty of an offence under section 1(1) of the Indecent Displays (Control) Act 1981 (offence of public display of indecent matter), convict him of a breach of the said section 1(1).

(6) Nothing in this section applies in relation to any matter—

(*a*) included in a television or sound broadcast by the British Broadcasting Corporation or the Independent Broadcasting Authority or a programme transmitted to the premises of subscribers to a diffusion service licensed by the Secretary of State; or

(*b*) included in a performance of a play (within the meaning of the Theatres Act 1968).

*   *   *

(8) In this section—

'material' includes any book, magazine, bill, paper, print, film, tape, disc or other kind of recording (whether of sound or visual images or both), photograph, drawing, painting, representation, model or figure;

'photograph' includes the negative as well as the positive version;

'public place' has the same meaning as in section 133 of this Act except that it includes any place to which at the material time the public are permitted to have access, whether on payment or otherwise;

'prescribed sum' has the same meaning as in section 289B of the Criminal Procedure (Scotland) Act 1975;

and the reference to publishing includes a reference to playing, projecting or otherwise reproducing."

A major feature of section 51 is that it applies only to obscene material, whereas the 1892 Act applied to both indecent and obscene material. The reason was explained in the House of Lords in the following terms:

"The one major difference between Clause 51 and the existing law on obscenity in the 1892 Act, is that, unlike the provision in the 1892 Act, which covers indecent and obscene material. Clause 51 is restricted to obscene material. This has been done primarily in order to remove an inconsistency which now arises under Scottish law as a result of the passing of the Indecent Displays (Control) Act 1981. The 1981 Act implicitly permits the display of indecent material in certain clearly defined circumstances—for instance, behind a warning notice. Under the present law on obscenity in Scotland, however, a shopkeeper who complies with the 1981 Act and withdraws behind such a notice material which could be regarded as indecent could still find himself falling foul of the criminal law on the grounds that he is offering indecent material for sale. This difficulty does not arise in England and Wales because the prohibition on offering for sale under the Obscene Publications Act 1959 applies only to obscene material. The restriction of Clause 51 to obscene material only thus not only removes this inconsistency but secures a greater measure of uniformity in relation to the law on obscenity throughout Great Britain. The clause does not attempt a definition of 'obscene' but leaves it, as at present, to the courts to interpret that term in light of the prevailing moral consensus." (425 H.L. Debs col. 673).

One consequence of this change is that the courts will have to embark upon the inquiry disapproved by Lord Cooper in *Galletly* v. *Laird,* 1953 S.L.T. 67; that is to say, "it will now be the task of the Scottish courts to draw [a] distinction between 'indecent' and 'obscene'" (Solicitor-General for Scotland, First Scottish Standing Committee, June 22, 1982, 16th sitting, col. 552). Thus, it will not be unlawful to sell indecent material, provided that a warning notice is put up. But even if a warning notice is put up, it will be unlawful to sell obscene material.

A second major feature of section 51 is that it does not define "obscene." This is a point which was raised in Standing Committee where the Solicitor-General for Scotland asserted that: "Obscenity is a relative concept which may vary according to the circumstances and locality, and it would be difficult if not impossible to produce a workable and generally acceptable definition" (*ibid.,* col. 551). It was therefore thought that the term "should be left to the interpretation of the courts in the light of the prevailing moral consensus" (*ibid.*), albeit that "the courts are unlikely to welcome this burden" (*ibid.,* col. 552). It was anticipated, however (on the basis of a dictum in *Ingram* v. *Macari,* 1982 S.L.T. 92), that "the words 'deprave and corrupt' [will be] read into the legislation automatically as a definition of obscenity. The courts already apply the test [under the previous statutes and the common law]." The Solicitor-General continued by expressing the view that this would be a reasonable qualification to attach to the statute (*ibid.,* col. 552). It remains to be seen whether the statute will displace completely the much-criticised use of the common law. By extending the scope of the statutory offence and by increasing the penalties there ought now to be no need to use the common law.

The continuing application of this test would thus appear to expose Scots law to the range of difficulties which the similar test in English law has presented to the courts. One question which has arisen is whether the offence is limited to sexual matters. The English courts have been prepared to hold that the glorification of drug-taking is obscene because of the tendency to deprave and corrupt (*John Calder (Publications) Ltd.* v. *Powell* [1965] 1 Q.B. 509). A second question is whether it is unlawful to offer for sale material which has an adverse effect in the sense that it is likely to repel people rather than cause them to behave in a depraved or corrupted fashion. In *R.* v. *Anderson* [1972] 1 Q.B. 304, it was held that failure by a trial judge to deal with this in his direction to the jury amounted to "a substantial and serious misdirection." A third question is whether it is unlawful to offer for sale material to a likely audience which is already corrupted. In *D.P.P.* v. *Whyte* [1972] A.C. 849 the House of Lords divided three to two in replying in the affirmative. In the course of his speech, Lord Wilberforce said at pp. 862-863:

"Let us see what they have done. Having confined the class of likely readers to males of middle age and upwards they have held that they were not satisfied that the books would have a tendency to deprave and corrupt a significant proportion of them. They reached this result by a process of inference: none of the readers was called to the witness box. The process was:

(i) 'the significant proportion of future recipients of the . . . articles were going to be the hard core'—note the conclusory words—'of regular customers of the . . . said shop'; (ii) the regular customers they saw as 'inadequate, pathetic, dirty minded men, seeking cheap thrills—addicts to this type of material, whose morals were already in a state of depravity and corruption'; (iii) there was grave doubt 'whether such minds could be said to be open to any immoral influences which the . . . articles were capable of exerting.'

My Lords, I appreciate genuinely the efforts which the justices made to administer this legislation; it is obvious that they gave the case a great deal of attention and thought. It is no reflection on their ability that in this very difficult task they fell into error. But, in my opinion, the process I have just stated was erroneous in itself and the facts to which it was applied lead clearly to the conclusion that the respondents should have been convicted. Putting aside the considerable deficiencies in the factual basis of the process (is it really to be supposed that every, or with minor exceptions, every male of forty and upwards who has visited or may visit this shop is of the character described—what is meant by 'significant proportion'?), to state as a proposition that all these men are incapable of being depraved and corrupted because they are addicts is not a finding of fact, but an assumption contrary to the whole basis of the Act. The Act's purpose is to prevent the depraving and corrupting of men's minds by certain types of writing: it could never have been intended to except from the legislative protection a large body of citizens merely because, in different degrees, they had previously been exposed, or exposed themselves, to the 'obscene' material. The Act is not merely concerned with the once and for all corruption of the wholly innocent; it equally protects the less innocent from further corruption, the addict from feeding or increasing his addiction. To say this is not to negate the principle of relative 'obscenity': certainly the tendency to deprave and corrupt is not to be estimated in relation to some assumed standard of purity of some reasonable man. It is the likely reader. And to apply different tests to teenagers, members of men's clubs or men in various occupations or localities would be a matter of common sense. But the argument here is not: 'Well, nobody reads this until he is over forty and by then he won't come to any harm': it is quite different. It assumes the possibility of corruption by the articles in question, indeed the fact of it is found, and argues from that to an absence of corrupting tendency. The passage contains its own refutation. These very men, it states, are depraved and corrupted by these very articles. In itself it proves the case: it should have led to conviction."

English statutes contain two important defences to a charge of obscenity. The first is the defence of public good whereby a conviction will not lie if it is proved that the publication of the article in question was justified in the interests of science, literature, art or learning, or of other subjects of general concern. The existence of this defence in Scotland appears to have been conceded by Lord Cooper in *Galletly* and was certainly anticipated by Lord Sands in *McGowan* v. *Langmuir*. As was made clear in the parliamentary debates these cases will continue to be authoritative under the new statutory régime. The second defence recognised by English law is that of innocent publication whereby a conviction will not lie if the accused proves that he had not examined the article in question and had no reasonable cause to suspect that by having it he risked prosecution. Although this defence is perhaps limited in scope, it would not be difficult to establish its existence from Lord Cooper's remarks that what the law is aiming to control is the deliberate trafficking in pornography by those who make a business of catering for depraved and perverted tastes. It may be noted that this defence was explicitly recognised by the Edinburgh Corporation Order Confirmation Act 1967 (s. 453(2)), but by no other. And it may well be, of course, that the activity covered by this defence will also be covered by the only explicit defence in section 51, that is to say, the provision in subsection (4). It was pointed out in Standing Committee that section 51(4) would operate to protect employees from being prosecuted. In view of the fact that corporations may now be convicted (thus dealing with the *John Menzies* problem), it is unlikely that the Crown would in any event move against employees.

Before leaving this subject, it is to be noted that many will regret that the Scottish Office did not act more adventurously. The "deprave and corrupt" test has been widely criticised, and it is a pity perhaps that the opportunity was not taken to meet these criticisms. Thus, in *Whyte's* case Lord Wilberforce said (at p. 862):

"It can only have been the pressure of Parliamentary compromise which can have produced a test so difficult for the courts. No definition of 'deprave and corrupt' is offered—no guideline as to what kind of influence is meant. Is it criminal conduct, general or sexual, that is feared (and we may note that the articles here treated of sadistic and violent behaviour), or departure from some mode of morality, sexual or otherwise, and if so whose code, or from accepted or other beliefs, or the arousing of erotic desires 'normal' or 'abnormal,' or, as the justices have said, 'private fantasies.' Some, perhaps most, of these alternatives involve deep questions of psychology and ethics: how are the courts to deal with them? Well might they have said that such words provide a formula which cannot in practice be applied. What they have said is, first, that no definition of deprave and corrupt can be provided (*R. v. Calder & Boyars Ltd.* [1969] 1 Q.B. 151), though the words are meant to be strong and emphatic (see *R. v. Knuller (Publishing, Printing and Promotions) Ltd.* [1972] 3 W.L.R. 143, 148, 180, *per* Lord Reid and Lord Simon of Glaisdale); secondly, that judges or juries must decide for or against a tendency to deprave and corrupt as a question of fact and must do so without expert, that is psychological or sociological or medical, advice (*R. v. Anderson*). I simply state this attitude as a fact; it is not appropriate to endorse or to disapprove it on this present occasion. I have serious doubts whether the Act will continue to be workable in this way, or whether it will produce tolerable results. The present is, or in any rational system ought to be, a simple case, yet the illogical and unscientific character of the Act has forced the justices into untenable positions."

IV. CONTEMPT OF COURT

1. The Nature of Contempt

Contempt of court covers a multitude of sins. In *Johnson* v. *Grant,* 1923 S.C. 789, the Lord Justice-General (Clyde) expressed the following view:

"The phrase 'contempt of Court' does not in the least describe the true nature of the class of offence with which we are here concerned, and which is prosecuted in the civil Court by petition and complaint with the concurrence of the Lord Advocate. The offence consists in interfering with the administration of the law; in impeding and perverting the course of justice. The malversation of an officer of Court is an example of it. Another, and often venial, example is the publication in the press of references to a pending litigation calculated to prejudice one of the parties or to bias the jury. A third, and a much more serious, instance is where people take upon themselves to break the law and then to defy its administration—in short directly to impede and to pervert the course of justice. The currency of the phrase is particularly regrettable, inasmuch as it seems to have encouraged the idea that all that has to be done by a person who has, however deliberately, committed this class of offence, and then wishes to avoid the consequences of his conduct, is to present an apology, as for an offence against the dignity of the Court. It is not the dignity of the Court which is offended—a petty and misleading view of the issues involved—it is the fundamental supremacy of the law which is challenged. That is why conduct of this kind is properly treated as deserving of criminal punishment; it is intolerable in any civilised and well-ordered society. Further, not only has no one the power to purge himself of a deliberate offence by saying he is sorry, but the mere circumstance that he presents a belated expression of contrition has, with regard to the public aspect of the matter, almost no importance at all."

For our purposes, we are concerned only with how the law of contempt restricts free expression in the press and elsewhere. We look first at how the law protects judges from criticism and secondly at how it is used to ensure that accused persons are given a fair trial.

2. "Murmuring" Judges

"Slandering judges, which is sometimes called 'murmuring judges' is a crime at common law" (Gordon 1978a: 1089). Gordon continues by asserting that it is not contempt of court "merely to criticise a judge's decision or to urge that the law as decided by him is unjust or immoral and in need of amendment. Generally speaking, the courts are unwilling to treat criticisms of judges or courts as contempt unless they are clearly disrespectful in their terms or are likely to interfere with the proper administration of justice" (*ibid*). In *Glasgow Corporation* v. *Hedderwick & Sons Ltd.*, 1918 S.C. 639 Lord Skerrington said: "anyone is entitled to criticise the law, provided that he does so in a manner not calculated to interfere with the administration of justice." The First Division rejected as contemptuous a newspaper article which urged an appeal against a sheriff's decision on the ground that the decision struck at the root of the purity of civic administration.

12. Milburn
1946 S.L.T. 219

Milburn was fined by the chairman of the Land Court for contempt. He had written a letter to the clerk of the court which included the following passage:

"I do not know what powers the Land Court has with regard to march fences, but possibly a word from yourself to the grazing constable might do more than anything which I or my factor could say. In past days a word from the landlord or from his ground officer might have gone a long way, but the landlord has, it seems, lost his prestige with the Crofters—a loss which has hardly been lessened by the Scottish Land Court in connection with affairs at Melness during the last few years. The landlord as a matter of fact notified the Scottish Home Department by letters dated 28th July 1943 and 10th June 1944 that he had reserved the right to bring complaint before Parliament."

When called before the Land Court, Milburn explained that the letter was intended as an intimation of dislike of the legislation which operated in the field. However, the chairman construed the letter as (i) a request for action by the Land Court in the interests of Milburn; (ii) a complaint about previous decisions affecting Milburn; and (iii) an intimation of a continuing threat to bring pressure on the Land Court. Milburn successfully petitioned the Court of Session where it was held that the chairman had put an unreasonable construction on the letter.

LORD PRESIDENT (Normand): " It is always of the highest importance, and especially in a process of contempt of Court, that the Court should be most careful to exclude not only everything which might create prejudice, but everything which might be thought to prejudice the Court. It has been said over and over again that the greatest restraint and discretion should be used by the Court in dealing with contempt of Court, lest a process, the purpose of which is to prevent interference with the administration of justice, should degenerate into an oppressive or vindictive abuse of the Court's powers. In the present case I regret to say that, in my view, a perverse interpretation was put upon a letter which may have been indiscreet and regrettable, but which was not directed towards interference with the administration of justice. The Court should never forget that disappointed litigants sometimes feel aggrieved and that some of them are ill-tempered, and that they may say or write things which are foolish and reprehensible. The Court should be on its guard against putting an overstrained construction upon such utterances, and above all it should not be too ready to find in them an attempt to interfere with the administration of justice and to visit them with the penal consequences of contempt of Court."

3. PREJUDICING A FAIR TRIAL

A second function of the law of contempt is to regulate a conflict between two fundamental civil liberties: freedom of expression on the one hand, and the right to a fair trial on the other. Unlimited press freedom may lead to excessive pre-trial publicity (with accusations of guilt against the accused) which may make it impossible to guarantee a fair trial before a jury which has not already prejudged the issues. It is a function of the law of contempt to strike a balance between these competing claims. In Scotland, the balance has been struck clearly in favour of the right of the accused, and the law seeks to prohibit expression to the extent that it conflicts with this basic right. In *Stirling* v. *Associated Newspapers Ltd.,* 1960 S.L.T. 5, the Lord Justice-General (Clyde) said:

". . . the Press in this country is free, free in particular fairly to report anything that occurs in open Court, when a trial takes place, free to publicise anything that is said or done by a Judge, or a counsel, or a witness, or by the jury at that trial. For, in doing so, the Press is performing a genuine public service in enabling the public to see for themselves whether justice is being done. The high standard of discrimination and fairness with which this work has been done by responsible Scottish newspapers has made it unnecessary for our Courts to lay down rules in this matter. We have been content to rely on their honour, their good sense and their discrimination. But freedom does not mean license, and the freedom which the Press rightly enjoys carries its own responsibilities. If that freedom is abused, and if the content of a newspaper is such as to be likely to endanger the prospects of a fair and impartial trial in Scotland, then, it is the duty of this Court, and it has always been recognised to be the duty of this Court, to take cognisance of it, and to punish the wrong that such conduct involves.

We are not concerned with the motive for which the wrong is done, whether it is to pander to sensationalism, to increase the circulation of the newspaper, or whatever else it may be. Our duty is always to present any violation of those principles of fair play which it is the pride of this country to extend even to the worst of criminals."

The legal position is now governed by the Contempt of Court Act 1981, which was passed for two reasons. The first was to implement the major recommendations of the Phillimore Committee on Contempt of Court (Phillimore, 1974). The second was to bring English law into line with the European Convention on Human Rights following the decision in *Sunday Times* v. *United Kingdom* (1979) 2 E.H.R.R. 245.

The background to the *Sunday Times* case was the decision of the House of Lords in *Attorney-General* v. *Times Newspapers Ltd.* [1974] A.C. 273. In that case the *Sunday Times* was prohibited from publishing an article claiming that Distillers Ltd. were negligent in their marketing of Thalidomide, a drug for pregnant women. Although writs had been issued against the company, the litigation had been dormant for several years, with the parties trying to reach a settlement. Nevertheless, the House of Lords prohibited publication on the ground that "anything in the nature of prejudgment of a case or of specific issues in it is objectionable." The *Sunday Times* was then moved to claim that that decision of the Lords was a violation of Article 10 of the E.C.H.R. The European Court of Human Rights agreed:

"63 ... The speeches in the House of Lords emphasised above all the concern that the processes of the law may be brought into disrespect and the functions of the courts usurped either if the public is led to form an opinion on the subject-matter of litigation before adjudication by the courts or if the parties to litigation have to undergo 'trial by newspaper'. Such concern is in itself 'relevant' to the maintenance of the 'authority of the judiciary' as that expression is understood by the Court. . . If the issues arising in litigation are ventilated in such a way as to lead the public to form its own conclusion thereon in advance, it may lose its respect for and confidence in the courts. Again, it cannot be excluded that the public's becoming accustomed to the regular spectacle of pseudo-trials in the news media might in the long run have nefarious consequences for the acceptance of the courts as the proper forum for the settlement of legal disputes.

Nevertheless, the proposed *Sunday Times* article was couched in moderate terms and did not present just one side of the evidence or claim that there was only one possible result at which a court could arrive; although it analysed in detail evidence against Distillers, it also summarised arguments in their favour and closed with the words 'There appears to be no neat set of answers . . .' In the Court's opinion, the effect of the article, if published, would therefore have varied from reader to reader. Accordingly, even to the extent that the article might have led some readers to form an opinion on the negligence issue, this would not have had adverse consequences for the 'authority of the judiciary', especially since, as noted above, there had been a nationwide campaign in the meantime. . .

65. . . . There is general recognition of the fact that the courts cannot operate in a vacuum. Whilst they are the forum for the settlement of disputes, this does not mean that there can be no prior discussion of disputes elsewhere, be it in specialised journals, in the general press or amongst the public at large. Furthermore, whilst the mass media must not overstep the bounds imposed in the interests of the proper administration of justice, it is incumbent on them to impart information and ideas concerning matters that come before the courts just as in other areas of public interest. Not only do the media have the task of imparting such information and ideas: the public also has a right to receive them."

The test of contempt developed by the House of Lords was thus too wide.

13. The Contempt of Court Act 1981

The strict liability rule
1. In this Act 'the strict liability rule' means the rule of law whereby conduct may be treated as a contempt of court as tending to interfere with the course of justice in particular legal proceedings regardless of intent to do so.

Limitation of scope of strict liability
2.—(1) The strict liability rule applies only in relation to publications, and for this purpose 'publication' includes any speech, writing, broadcast or other communication in whatever form, which is addressed to the public at large or any section of the public.

(2) The strict liability rule applies only to a publication which creates a substantial risk that the course of justice in the proceedings in question will be seriously impeded or prejudiced.

(3) The strict liability rule applies to a publication only if the proceedings in question are active within the meaning of this section at the time of the publication.

(4) Schedule 1 applies for determining the times at which proceedings are to be treated as active within the meaning of this section.

*   *   *

SCHEDULE 1

TIMES WHEN PROCEEDINGS ARE ACTIVE FOR PURPOSES OF SECTION 2

Preliminary
1. In this Schedule 'criminal proceedings' means proceedings against a person in respect of an offence, not being appellate proceedings . . . and 'appellate proceedings' means proceedings on appeal from or for the review of the decision of a court in any proceedings.

2. Criminal, appellate and other proceedings are active within the meaning of

section 2 at times respectively prescribed by the following paragraphs of this Schedule; and in relation to proceedings in which more than one of the steps described in any of those paragraphs is taken, the reference in that paragraph is a reference to the first of those steps.

Criminal proceedings

3. Subject to the following provisions of this Schedule, criminal proceedings are active from the relevant initial step specified in paragraph 4 until concluded as described in paragraph 5.

4. The initial steps of criminal proceedings are:—
   (a) arrest without warrant;
   (b) ... the grant of a warrant for arrest;
   (c) the issue of a summons to appear, or in Scotland the grant of a warrant to cite;
   (d) the service of an indictment or other document specifying the charge;
   (e) except in Scotland, oral charge.

5. Criminal proceedings are concluded—
   (a) by acquittal or, as the case may be, by sentence;
   (b) by any other verdict, finding, order or decision which puts an end to the proceedings;
   (c) by discontinuance or by operation of law.

6. The reference in paragraph 5(a) to sentence includes any order or decision consequent on conviction or finding of guilt which disposes of the case, either absolutely or subject to future events. . .

7. Proceedings are discontinued within the meaning of paragraph 5(c) . . . in Scotland, if the proceedings are expressly abandoned by the prosecutor or are deserted *simpliciter*. . .

10. Without prejudice to paragraph 5(b) above, criminal proceedings against a person cease to be active—
   (a) if the accused is found to be under a disability such as to render him unfit to be tried or unfit to plead or, in Scotland, is found to be insane in bar of trial; or
   (b) ... where a transfer order ceases to have effect by virtue of section 73(1) of the Mental Health (Scotland) Act 1984,
but becomes active again if they are later resumed.

11. Criminal proceedings against a person which become active on the issue or the grant of a warrant for his arrest cease to be active at the end of the period of twelve months beginning with the date of the warrant unless he has been arrested within that period, but become active again if he is subsequently arrested.

Other proceedings at first instance

12. Proceedings other than criminal proceedings and appellate proceedings are active from the time when arrangements for the hearing are made or, if no such arrangements are previously made, from the time the hearing begins, until the proceedings are disposed of or discontinued or withdrawn. . .

14. In Scotland arrangements for the hearing of proceedings to which paragraph 12 applies are made within the meaning of that paragraph—
   (a) in the case of an ordinary action in the Court of Session or in the sheriff court, when the Record is closed;

(b) in the case of a motion or application,when it is enrolled or made;

(c) in any other case, when the date for a hearing is fixed or a hearing is allowed.

Appellate proceedings

15. Appellate proceedings are active from the time when they are commenced—

(a) by application for leave to appeal or apply for review, or by notice of such an application;

(b) by notice of appeal or of application for review;

(c) by other originating process,

until disposed of or abandoned, discontinued or withdrawn.

16. Where, in appellate proceedings relating to criminal proceedings, the court—

(a) remits the case to the court below; or

(b) orders a new trial or a *venire de novo*, or in Scotland grants authority to bring a new prosecution,

any further or new proceedings which result shall be treated as active from the conclusion of the appellate proceedings."

These provisions in fact introduce very little change to the substantive law of Scotland, which before 1981 had been governed by the common law. So far as strict liability is concerned, this was already the position (*Hall* v. *Associated Newspapers Ltd.*, 1978 S.L.T. 241). And it is to be noted that in retaining strict liability, the draftsman is faithful to the authors of the Phillimore Report who wrote:

"While the imposition of strict liability, especially in the field of press publication, might at first appear to be severe, it was not seriously criticised in the evidence submitted to us by witnesses speaking with experience of the press; and we are satisfied, subject to our recommendations later in the Report, that the administration of justice still requires the protection of that degree of strict liability which the law of contempt imposes, since the effect of the conduct may be to cause such serious harm to the administration of justice. No doubt there are occasions when a contempt may be committed inadvertently or where the person concerned is not fully aware of the significance of his action, but in such an event the degree of culpability or the lack of it in a particular case will undoubtedly be reflected in the penalty the court imposes."

So far as the test for contempt is concerned, the statute (s. 2(2)) is also very similar to the test fashioned by the common law. In *Atkins* v. *London Weekend Television Ltd.*, 1978 S.L.T. 76, the High Court addressed itself to "whether the contents of [a television] programme complained of were such as to give rise to a real risk of prejudice to the fair and impartial trial of the petitioner on the charges on which she stood indicted" (p. 78). However, the new test, though similar, may be stricter with "substantial" and "seriously" being crucial words of qualification. And so far as the time at which proceedings become active is concerned, it is true that this is a matter which in the past has caused difficulty in Scots law. In *Stirling* v. *Associated Newspapers Ltd.*, 1960 S.L.T. 5, Lord Justice-General Clyde expounded a very strict test when he said at p. 8:

". . . once a crime has been suspected and once the criminal authorities are investigating it, they and they alone have the duty of carrying out that investigation. If a newspaper arranges an interview with any person in any way involved in the suspected crime and then publishes the results of the interview, or an article based upon it, the newspaper is doing something which in all probability will interfere with the course of justice and hinder a fair trial."

These comments caused considerable anxiety amongst Scottish journalists, the law as expounded not only being very wide, but also uncertain as to the time when the law of contempt applied. However, Lord Clyde's remarks were subsequently disapproved of by a bench of five judges in *Hall* v. *Associated Newspapers Ltd.*, 1978 S.L.T. 241, where it was held that proceedings become active only from the moment of arrest or from the time of the granting of a warrant for arrest. In fact, then, the decision in *Hall* anticipated the 1981 Act. It is to be noted, however, that although consistent with *Hall*, the statutory provisions on this point depart from the Phillimore recommendation which was that in criminal proceedings, the case should become active from the time the suspected person is charged.

14. Atkins v. London Weekend Television Ltd.
1978 S.L.T. 76

On 13 November 1977 a "Weekend World" television broadcast contained a feature on brain death. The feature, which was a general review of the issues presented by patients who suffer severe brain damage, began with the following narrative:

"Tomorrow morning, Margaret 'Ginny' Atkins, an Edinburgh nurse, goes on trial. She's accused of assault, endangering the life of one of her patients. A Jury at the Sheriff's [*sic*] Court in the City will be told that Nurse Atkins tried twice to block the air supply to a thirteen-year-old girl in her care. The girl, Elizabeth Semple, was in the intensive-care unit of The Royal Edinburgh Infirmary. She was suffering from severe brain damage. Nurse Atkins will plead not guilty to the charges, but by the middle of the week the whole country will be talking about the issues raised in this Case. . ."

While this was being said, photographs of Margaret Atkins were shown. Was this programme calculated to prejudice and likely to prejudice the fair and impartial trial of Atkins? The following passage is from the opinion of the court:

"Counsel for the respondents with characteristic skill sought to persuade us that neither the feature as a whole nor any of its constituent parts created any such risk. Leaving aside the references to the petitioner the discussion was, he said, and we can readily accept this, quite unobjectionable in that it bore to be and was a serious debate upon a live question of immediate public concern. A reference to the impending trial of the petitioner and the nature of the charge against her could not by itself be an offence against the interests of justice for the charge and the fact that she was to be tried in Edinburgh on 14 November 1977 were public facts. We readily accept this also. The petitioner does not aver that the showing of her photograph was likely, by itself, to prejudice her in her defence and the feature as a whole involved no detailed discussion of the petitioner's case and it made no attempt to pre-judge her guilt or innocence. Indeed express mention was made of her plea of not guilty.

Even if there had been no reference made to the petitioner at all the feature might have had just the same effect upon the petitioner's trial. The complaint is, however, that the showing of photographs of the petitioner and the particular references to her in sound made all the difference and converted a discussion of what was already a matter of public interest and comment into an act of contempt. So far as the photographs were concerned, said the counsel for the respondents, there is no hard and fast rule that the publication of a photograph of an accused person will always constitute contempt. We have no difficulty in accepting this proposition and we accept, too, the further proposition that the publication of a photograph of an accused person will only constitute contempt where a question of identification has arisen or may arise and where the publication is calculated to prejudice the prospects of fair trial. . .

In our judgment there is not the slightest doubt that the references to the petitioner in the context of this particular feature as a whole were in the highest degree likely to prejudice the petitioner's prospects of a fair and impartial trial. We have seen and heard a videotape recording of the introduction of the programme and of the entire feature. For the purposes of considering the arguments of parties we have been supplied with, and we have had an opportunity of reading the transcript of the sound track. The feature was specifically concerned, and no doubt properly concerned to debate the serious issue on which medical opinion is divided, namely whether or not life support for certain patients who have suffered severe brain damage should, as matter of policy, be withdrawn. In course of that feature it was no doubt highly relevant and perfectly legitimate to refer to the two very recent cases, one in England and one in the United States, in which a decision to switch off the patient's breathing machine was deliberately taken. To introduce references to the . . . petitioner's trial on the indictment the very next day was, however, utterly indefensible and irresponsible for the references were made in such a way as to imply that this was another case of the same kind as those of Carol Wilkinson and Karen Quinlan and, it may be, the latest example of actings by a nurse towards a patient in implement of a view held by eminent medical men in Scotland that withdrawal of life support for certain victims of severe brain damage is desirable and morally justifiable. 'A Jury at the Sheriff's [sic] Court in the City will be told that Nurse Atkins tried twice to block the air supply to a thirteen-year-old girl in her care', said the commentator. Contrary to respondents' counsel's submission that this would be understood as no more than a reference to the allegations in the charges this sentence was, in our judgment, calculated to convey and likely to convey to the public mind in Scotland and to the minds of prospective jurors in Scotland that the evidence would be that the petitioner had committed the acts charged, and the sting is not removed by the bare mention of the fact that she 'will plead not guilty to the charges' because the commentator immediately added '*but* [the italicising is ours] by the middle of the week the whole country will be talking about the issues raised in this Case'. We accept from counsel for the respondents that the references to the petitioner were included for the sole purpose of giving topicality to the programme and, in short, we hold that this gratuitous introduction of the references to the petitioner, in the context of the feature as a whole and, in particular, in close company with the references to the Wilkinson and Quinlan cases, contained the clear insinuation that the real if not the only question which would arise out of the petitioner's trial would be whether she was medically and morally justified in committing the acts charged.

In fact the petitioner's plea of 'not guilty' necessarily raised the question of the identity of the person, if any, who attempted to block the child's air supply as well as the initial question whether any such acts as those charged were perpetrated at all by any person. It was therefore essential for the Crown to identify the petitioner as the perpetrator. In the whole circumstances the inclusion of the photographs but, more importantly, the verbal references to her in the context of the feature as a whole, were likely to be highly damaging to the prospects of a fair and impartial trial of the petitioner in Scotland. The Lord Advocate has informed us that in his opinion the conduct complained of on the part of those responsible for the feature 'The Living Dead' undoubtedly constituted a material interference with the due and proper administration of criminal justice in Scotland. We agree with him. Indeed, in our judgment, what was said and shown with reference to the petitioner in this feature was so prejudicial to the proper administration of justice in Scotland that we entertain the gravest doubt whether fair and impartial trial of the petitioner on the charges of assaulting Elizabeth Semple is now possible, however carefully the trial judge may direct the jury."

There are no reported Scots cases on this aspect of the law of contempt decided under the 1981 Act. Pre-1981 cases suggest, however, that the following conduct would amount to a breach of the strict liability rule:

(i) The publication of the photograph of an accused person on the ground that: "Identification may be a really substantial issue in the trial, and publication of such a photograph may gravely prejudice that trial by affecting the evidence of identification at the trial by witnesses who have already seen the photograph" (*Stirling* v. *Associated Newspapers Ltd.,* 1960 S.L.T. 5).

(ii) The publication of an article on the arrest of a person following the murder of a girl. The petition alleged that: "The said articles are narrated statements, purporting to have been given by the mother of the accused, by a business associate of the accused, and other persons, all of whom being

persons who may be required to give evidence in the trial of the petitioner...
The implication of the said statements, inter alia, is that a relationship of a
close nature existed between the petitioner and the [victim]" (*Stirling* v.
Associated Newspapers Ltd., supra).

15. The Contempt of Court Act 1981

"Defence of innocent publication or distribution
3.—(1) A person is not guilty of contempt of court under the strict liability rule
as the publisher of any matter to which that rule applies if at the time of the
publication (having taken all reasonable care) he does not know and has no reason
to suspect that relevant proceedings are active.

(2) A person is not guilty of contempt of court under the strict liability rule as
the distributor of a publication containing any such matter if at the time of
distribution (having taken all reasonable care) he does not know that it contains
such matter and has no reason to suspect that it is likely to do so.

(3) The burden of proof of any fact tending to establish a defence afforded by
this section to any person lies upon that person. . .

Contemporary reports of proceedings
4.—(1) Subject to this section a person is not guilty of contempt of court under
the strict liability rule in respect of a fair and accurate report of legal proceedings
held in public, published contemporaneously and in good faith.

(2) In any such proceedings the court may, where it appears to be necessary for
avoiding a substantial risk of prejudice to the administration of justice in those
proceedings, or in any other proceedings pending or imminent, order that the
publication of any report of the proceedings, or any part of the proceedings, be
postponed for such a period as the court thinks necessary for that purpose. . .

Discussion of public affairs
5. A publication made as or as part of a discussion in good faith of public affairs
or other matters of general public interest is not to be treated as a contempt of court
under the strict liability rule if the risk of impediment or prejudice to particular legal
proceedings is merely incidental to the discussion.

Savings
6. Nothing in the foregoing provisions of this Act—
(a) prejudices any defence available at common law to a charge of contempt
of court under the strict liability rule;
(b) implies that any publication is punishable as contempt of court under that
rule which would not be so punishable apart from those provisions;
(c) restricts liability for contempt of court in respect of conduct intended to
impede or prejudice the administration of justice."

These provisions allow for three circumstances in which the strict
liability rule will not apply. The first is the defence of innocent publication,
a defence which has existed in England and Wales since 1960, following

the enactment of the Administration of Justice Act 1960, s. 11, a measure which did not extend to Scotland. Although a Scots equivalent now exists, its limits should be appreciated. It is to be borne in mind that the offence is one of strict liability and that it will be no defence that the publisher honestly believed that the content of the publication did not constitute a contempt. In particular, the courts have held on several occasions that a conviction will lie even though the information was supplied by the police. See *MacAlister* v. *Associated Newspapers Ltd.*, 1954 S.L.T. 14, and *Hall* v. *Associated Newspapers Ltd., supra*. More recently, in *H. M. Advocate* v. *George Outram and Co. Ltd.*, 1980 S.L.T. (Notes) 13, the High Court struck the following warning:

"We have had occasion before to question the wisdom of the provision of such information by the police to the press at least at any time after a person to whom it relates has been arrested on criminal charges. However that may be there can surely be no lingering doubt that if information, even from police sources, about a person who has been charged with criminal offences and arrested, is such that if published it would constitute the offence labelled contempt of court, the source of the offending material cannot be relied upon in mitigation of the offence."

This applies with equal force to the new statutory régime. Section 3 only protects a publisher who does not know the proceedings are active: it offers no protection based on the content of the publication.

The second ground on which liability may be excluded is with regard to the contemporary reporting of judicial proceedings. Before the enactment of the 1981 Act, this defence was not recognised by statute. There was, however, authority for the view that it existed at common law. In *Stirling* v. *Associated Newspapers Ltd.*, 1960 S.L.T. 5, Lord Justice-General Clyde said that: "when a trial takes place, [the press is] free to publicise anything that is said or done by a Judge or a counsel, or a witness, or by the jury at that trial." The common law, and now the statute, would of course be subject to any statutory exceptions, one of which is the Judicial Proceedings (Regulation of Reports) Act 1926 which is dealt with in Chap. 4. The third situation in which the strict liability rule does not apply is with regard to the good faith discussion of public affairs. This provision (which like the previous two had been recommended by Phillimore) had also been anticipated by the common law in *Atkins* v. *London Weekend Television Ltd. (supra)*. In that case, however, the exclusion of strict liability for this reason did not succeed, partly because there was still a serious risk of prejudice to the chances of a fair trial. The source of the defence at common law is acknowledged to be *Ex p. Bread Manufacturers* (1937) S.R. (N.S.W.) 242 where Jordan C.J. said (at p. 249):

"... if in the course of ventilation, of a question of public concern matter is published which may prejudice a party on the conduct of a lawsuit it does not follow that a contempt has been committed. The case may be one in which as between competing matters of public interest the possibility of prejudice to a litigant may be required to yield to other and superior considerations. The discussion of public affairs and the denunciation of public abuses, actual or supposed, cannot be required to be suspended merely because the discussion or denunciation may, as an incidental but not intended by-product, cause a risk of prejudice to a person who happens to be a litigant at the time."

It is to be noted, however, that the defence has an older pedigree in Scotland. See *Cowie* v. *George Outram & Co. Ltd.*, 1912 S.C.(J.) 14. The leading case on section 5 follows.

16. Attorney-General v. English
[1983] A.C. 116

Dr Arthur, a well-known paediatrician, was charged with murdering a three-day old Down's Syndrome boy by giving him a drug which caused him to die of starvation. During the trial a by-election was held in North West Croydon, one of the candidates being Mrs Marilyn Carr who had been born without arms and who was standing as an independent pro-life candidate taking as a main plank in her campaign the stopping of the practice of killing newborn handicapped babies. During the campaign, and during the trial of Dr Arthur, the *Daily Mail* published an article by Mr Malcolm Muggeridge, who supported Mrs Carr. In his speech, Lord Diplock referred to the article in the following terms:

"The article complained of was directed exclusively to Mr Muggeridge's support of Mrs Carr's candidature in the by-election because of her support of the pro-life cause and in particular her opposition to deliberate failure to keep alive newly-born babies suffering from what are presently regarded as incurable physical or mental disabilities so severe as to deprive them of all possibility of their enjoying what a normal person would regard as a life that was worth living. For any human being to arrogate to himself the right to decide whether a human being was fit to be born or to go on living was regarded by Mr Muggeridge as contrary to Christian morality which regarded all human life as sacred. There was no mention in the article of Dr Arthur's trial.

The first part of the article described Mrs Carr herself and how she had succeeded in overcoming the terrible physical handicap with which she had been born and in carving out a useful career for herself. *'Today,'* he wrote, in a passage principally relied upon by the Attorney-General as amounting to contempt of court, *'the chances of such a baby surviving would be very small indeed. Someone would surely recommend letting her die of starvation, or otherwise disposing of her.'* The article then continued with a skilful piece of polemical journalism which concluded with the following passages derisive of those whose views he was condemning:

'Are human beings to be culled like livestock? No more sick or misshapen bodies, no more disturbed or twisted minds, no more hereditary idiots or mongoloid children. Babies not up to scratch to be destroyed, before or after birth, as would also the old beyond repair. *With the developing skills of modern medicine, the human race could be pruned and carefully tended until only the perfect blooms— the beauty queens, the Mensa I.Q.s, the athletes—remained.'*

The article then went on to contrast this with what the writer claimed to be the Christian view of the equal sanctity of all human life, whatever might be the individual human being's physical or mental qualities or deficiencies. As an example of a devotion to this view of Christian morality, he cited Mother Teresa of Calcutta."

The Divisional Court held that this was a contempt. The editor appealed.

LORD DIPLOCK: "There is, of course, no question that the article in the *Daily Mail* of which complaint is made by the Attorney-General was a 'publication' within the meaning of section 2(1). That being so, it appears to have been accepted in the Divisional Court by both parties that the onus of proving that the article satisfied the conditions stated in section 2(2) lay upon the Attorney-General and that, if he satisfied that onus, the onus lay upon the appellants to prove that it satisfied the conditions stated in section 5. For my part, I am unable to accept that this represents the effect of the relationship of section 5 to section 2(2). Section 5 does not take the form of a proviso or an exception to section 2(2). It stands on an equal footing with it. It does not set out exculpatory matter. Like section 2(2) it states what publications shall *not* amount to contempt of court despite their tendency to interfere with the course of justice in particular legal proceedings.

For the publication to constitute a contempt of court under the strict liability rule, it must be shown that the publication satisfies the criterion for which section 2(2) provides, *viz.* that it 'creates a substantial risk that the course of justice in the proceedings in question will be seriously impeded or prejudiced.' It is only if it falls within section 5 that anything more need be shown. So logically the first question always is: has the publication satisfied the criterion laid down by section 2(2).

My Lords, the first thing to be observed about this criterion is that the risk that has to be assessed is that which was created by the publication of the allegedly offending matter at the time when it was published. The public policy that underlies the strict liability rule in contempt of court is deterrence. Trial by newspaper or, as it should be more compendiously expressed today, trial by the media, is not to be permitted in this country. That the risk that was created by the publication when it was actually published does not ultimately affect the outcome of the proceedings is, as Lord Goddard C.J. said in *R.* v. *Evening Standard Co. Ltd.* [1954] 1 Q.B. 578, 582 'neither here nor there.' If there was a reasonable possibility that it might have done so if in the period subsequent to the publication the proceedings had not taken the course that in fact they did and Dr Arthur was acquitted, the offence was complete. The true course of justice must not at any stage be put at risk.

Next for consideration is the concatenation in the subsection of the adjective 'substantial' and the adverb 'seriously,' the former to describe the degree of risk, the latter to describe the degree of impediment or prejudice to the course of justice. 'Substantial' is hardly the most apt word to apply to 'risk' which is a noumenon. In combination I take the two words to be intended to exclude a risk that is only remote. With regard to the adverb 'seriously' a perusal of the cases cited in *Attorney-General* v. *Times Newspapers Ltd.* [1974] A.C. 273 discloses that the adjective 'serious' has from time to time been used as an alternative to 'real' to describe the degree of risk of interfering with the course of justice, but not the degree of interference itself. It is, however, an ordinary English word that is not intrinsically inapt when used to describe the extent of an impediment or prejudice to the cause of justice in particular legal proceedings, and I do not think that for the purposes of the instant appeal any attempt to paraphrase it is necessary or would be helpful. The subsection applies to all kinds of legal proceedings, not only criminal prosecutions before a jury. If, as in the instant case and probably in most other criminal trials upon indictment, it is the outcome of the trial or the need to discharge the jury without proceeding to a verdict that is put at risk, there can be no question that that which in the course of justice is put at risk is as serious as anything could be.

My Lords, that Mr Malcolm Muggeridge's article was capable of prejudicing the jury against Dr Arthur at the early stage of his trial when it was published, seems to me to be clear. It suggested that it was a common practice among paediatricians to do that which Dr Arthur was charged with having done, because they thought that it was justifiable in the interest of humanity even though it was against the law. At this stage of the trial the jury did not know what Dr Arthur's defence was going to be; and whether at that time the risk of the jury's being influenced by their recollection of the article when they came eventually to consider their verdict appeared to be more than a remote one, and was a matter which the judge before whom the trial was being conducted was in the best position to evaluate, even though his evaluation, although it should carry weight, would not be binding on the Divisional Court or on your Lordships. The judge thought at that stage of the trial that the risk was substantial, not remote. So, too, looking at the matter in retrospect, did the Divisional Court despite the fact that the risk had not turned into an actuality since Dr Arthur had by then been acquitted. For my part I am not prepared to dissent from this evaluation. I consider that the publication of the article on the third day of what was to prove a lengthy trial satisfied the criterion for which section 2(2) of the Act provides.

The article, however, fell also within the category dealt with in section 5. It was made, in undisputed good faith, as a discussion in itself of public affairs, *viz.* Mrs Carr's candidature as an independent pro-life candidate in the North West Croydon by-election for which the polling day was in one week's time. It was also part of a wider discussion on a matter of general public interest that had been proceeding intermittently over the last three months, upon the moral justification of mercy killing and in particular of allowing newly-born hopelessly handicapped babies to die. So it was for the Attorney-General to show that the risk of prejudice to the fair trial of Dr Arthur, which I agree was created by the publication of the article at the stage the trial had reached when it was published, was not 'merely incidental' to the discussion of the matter with which the article dealt.

My Lords, any article published at the time when Dr Arthur was being tried which asserted that it was a common practice among paediatricians to let severely physically or mentally handicapped newborn babies die of starvation or otherwise dispose of them would (as, in common with the trial judge and the Divisional Court, I have already accepted) involve a substantial risk of prejudicing his fair trial. But an article supporting Mrs Carr's candidature in the by-election as a pro-life candidate that contained no such assertion would depict her as tilting at imaginary windmills. One of the main planks of the policy for which she sought the suffrage of the electors was that these things did happen and ought to be stopped.

I have drawn attention to the passages principally relied upon by the Divisional Court as causing a risk of prejudice that was not 'merely incidental to the discussion.' The court described them as 'unnecessary' to the discussion and as 'accusations.' The test, however, is not whether an article could have been written as effectively without these passages or whether some other phraseology might have been substituted for them that could have reduced the risk of prejudicing Dr Arthur's fair trial; it is whether the risk created by the words actually chosen by the author was 'merely incidental to the discussion,' which I take to mean: no more than an incidental consequence of expounding its main theme. The Divisional Court also apparently regarded the passages complained of as disqualified from the immunity conferred by section 5 because they consisted of 'accusations' whereas the court considered, *ante*, p. 128 E-F, that 'discussion' was confined to 'the airing of views and the propounding and debating of principles and arguments.' I cannot accept this limited meaning of 'discussion' in the section. As already pointed out, in the absence of any accusation, believed to be true by Mrs Carr and Mr Muggeridge, that it was a common practice among some doctors to do what they are accused of doing in the passages complained of, the article would lose all its point whether as support for Mrs Carr's parliamentary candidature or as a contribution to the wider controversy as to the justifiability of mercy killing. The article would be emasculated into a mere contribution to a purely hypothetical problem appropriate, it may be, for debate between academic successors of the mediaeval schoolmen, but remote from all public affairs and devoid of any general public interest to readers of the *Daily Mail*.

My Lords, the article that is the subject of the instant case appears to me to be in nearly all respects the antithesis of the article which this House (*pace* a majority of the judges of the European Court of Human Rights) held to be a contempt of court in *Attorney-General* v. *Times Newspapers Ltd.* [1974] A.C. 273. There the whole subject of the article was the pending civil actions against Distillers Co. (Biochemicals) Ltd. arising out of their having placed upon the market the new drug thalidomide, and the whole purpose of it was to put pressure upon that company in the lawful conduct of their defence in those actions. In the instant case, in contrast, there is in the article no mention at all of Dr Arthur's trial. It may well be that many readers of the *Daily Mail* who saw the article and had read also the previous day's report of Dr Arthur's trial, and certainly if they were members of the jury at that trial, would think, 'that is the sort of thing that Dr Arthur is being tried for; it appears to be something that quite a lot of doctors do.' But the risk of their thinking that and allowing it to prejudice their minds in favour of finding him guilty on evidence that did not justify such a finding seems to me to be properly described in ordinary English language as 'merely incidental' to any meaningful discussion of Mrs Carr's election policy as a pro-life candidate in the by-election due to be held before Dr Arthur's trial was likely to be concluded, or to any meaningful discussion of the wider matters of general public interest involved in the current controversy as to the justification of mercy killing. To hold otherwise would have prevented Mrs Carr from putting forward and obtaining publicity for what was a main plank in her election programme and would have stifled all discussion in the press upon the wider controversy about mercy killing from the time that Dr Arthur was charged in the magistrates' court in February 1981 until the date of his acquittal at the beginning of November of that year; for those are the dates between which, under section 2(3) and Schedule 1, the legal proceedings against Dr Arthur would be 'active' and so attract the strict liability rule.

Such gagging of *bona fide* public discussion in the press of controversial matters of general public interest, merely because there are in existence contemporaneous legal proceedings in which some particular instance of those controversial matters may be in issue, is what section 5 of the Contempt of Court Act 1981 was in my view intended to prevent. I would allow this appeal."

Lords Elwyn-Jones, Keith of Kinkel, Scarman and Brandon of Oakbrook agreed.

On the question of penalties and remedies, there are two important developments in the modern history of Scots law in this area. First, until the watershed decision in *Stirling* v. *Associated Newspapers Ltd.*, 1960 S.L.T. 5 the practice appears to have been for the accused persons to come to court after prejudicial publicity for an order restraining any more such publicity. See, for example, *Smith* v. *John Ritchie & Co. Ltd.* (1892) 20 R.(J.) 52. The last reported case in which a restraining order of this kind was imposed is *MacAlister* v. *Associated Newspapers Ltd.*, 1954 S.L.T. 14. Since *Stirling* in 1960, however, a second phase began: the practice of the court has been to impose quasi-criminal sanctions. And here the courts had a wide discretion, for at common law there was no limit on the powers of the Court of Session or the High Court in the matter of penalty, nor was there any requirement that prison sentences should be for a fixed period. In practice the sentences imposed varied widely. In *Stirling* v. *Associated Newspapers Ltd.* the court refrained from imposing a penalty of imprisonment "with some hesitation." In *Atkins* v. *London Weekend Television Ltd.*, 1978 S.L.T. 76, the television company was fined £50,000, and fines of £5,000, £5,000 and £1,000 were imposed on the editor of the programme, the managing director of the company and the producer of the programme respectively. In *H. M. Advocate* v. *George Outram & Co. Ltd.*, 1980 S.L.T. (Notes) 13, the publishers were fined £20,000 and the editor £750. In *Hall* v. *Associated Newspapers Ltd.*, 1978 S.L.T. 241, the accused were admonished, with the Lord Justice-General (Emslie) saying:

"On the matter of penalty, we have, once more, little difficulty. From what has been said to us we accept that the newspaper had a system designed to avoid the publication of prejudicial material at a time when such publication might constitute contempt of court. We accept too that legal advice was taken, and we accept further, for reasons into which we need not go, that on this occasion the system performed imperfectly with the results which we have seen. That then is a factor which we take into account. The second factor which we take into account is that there has been tendered on behalf of the respondents, by counsel, an unreserved and unqualified apology and he has informed us, and we accept this, that there was no deliberate intention on the part of the respondents to interfere with the course of the administration of justice. The third factor, a factor which is perhaps special in this case, which we took into account, is that in the event the article cannot have had, in fact, any prejudicial affect upon the course which the proceedings ultimately took. Giving all due weight to these factors we are satisfied that a proper disposal of this case will be a sentence of admonition in respect of both respondents."

The discretion of the courts is now restricted by the Contempt of Court Act 1981, which provides by section 15:

"(1) In Scottish proceedings, when a person is committed to prison for contempt of court the committal shall (without prejudice to the power of the court to order his earlier discharge) be for a fixed term.

(2) The maximum penalty which may be imposed by way of imprisonment or fine for contempt of court in Scottish proceedings shall be two years' imprisonment or a fine or both, except that—

    (a) where the contempt is dealt with by the sheriff in the course of or in connection with proceedings other than criminal proceedings on indictment, such penalty shall not exceed three months' imprisonment or a fine of £500 or both; and

    (b) where the contempt is dealt with by the district court, such penalty shall not exceed sixty days' imprisonment or a fine of £200 or both."

It is to be noted that although in practice sentences would be for a fixed period, it was not unknown, even recently, for these to exceed two years. See *Cordiner, Petitioner* 1973 S.L.T. 125.

V. OFFICIAL INFORMATION

Perhaps the most politically controversial area of civil liberties law in recent years has concerned the struggle between the press and the government over the publication of sensitive information which the government would rather suppress, often because the information in question would lead to political embarrassment. Many of these struggles have led to legal proceedings. Thus we have had the disclosure by civil servants of the arrival of U.S. missiles at Greenham Common and of details concerning the sinking of the Argentine ship *General Belgrano* which the Government refused to give to the House of Commons. We have witnessed the systematic raiding of the BBC offices in Glasgow in connection with the proposed broadcasting of a programme about a satellite (the "Zircon" affair). And, more significantly still, we have witnessed the astonishing crusade against Mr Peter Wright who had the temerity to inform the public through his book *Spycatcher* of illegal activities perpetrated by the British security services. In a book of this size we cannot deal with all of these issues in the detail we would like. What follows is an account of some of the main developments.

1. IDENTIFYING THE SOURCE OF INFORMATION

17. Secretary of State for Defence v. Guardian
Newspapers Ltd.
[1985] 1 A.C. 359

A photocopy of a Ministry of Defence document classified as "secret" was delivered to *The Guardian*. The document contained information about the arrival of U.S. cruise missiles at Greenham Common, and its contents were published by the newspaper. The Crown claimed copyright in the document and sought an order for its immediate delivery. For its part the newspaper relied on section 10 of the Contempt of Court Act 1981 which provides:

"No court may require a person to disclose, nor is any person guilty of contempt of court for refusing to disclose, the source of information contained in a publication for which he is responsible, unless it be established to the satisfaction of the court that disclosure is necessary in the interests of justice or national security or for the prevention of disorder or crime."

At first instance Scott J. held that section 10 was not intended to interfere with proprietary interests and upheld the Crown's claim. The Court of Appeal upheld the decision, partly because the immediate return of the document was necessary in the interests of justice and national security. On appeal to the House of Lords:

LORD DIPLOCK:
"The interlocutory nature of the appeal
There is a further disadvantage, additional to its having caused a division of opinion between members of this House, which results from this case coming before this House upon what still remains an interlocutory appeal notwithstanding that the whole truth has come out at the trial of Miss Tisdall at the Central Criminal Court before Cantley J. on 23 March 1984. At the trial she pleaded guilty to an offence under section 2 of the Official Secrets Act 1911 by communicating to *The Guardian* two documents containing classified information, of which only one was the document that was published by that newspaper and was the subject of the interlocutory application for delivery up in which this appeal is brought. The disadvantage is that your Lordships, knowing the full facts, which since they were disclosed at a public trial held in open court and are thus within the public domain, have nevertheless to perform the difficult feat of mental gymnastics involved in dismissing from your minds the true and full facts as they are now known to be, and concentrating only upon that part of the primary facts that appeared in the evidence before the Court of Appeal, together with such further inferences of fact as may properly be drawn from them.

In carrying out this necessary exercise in mental gymnastics I have found it helpful to start by setting out the full facts as they are now known to be, using ordinary type for those facts known to the government at the time of the interlocutory proceedings and putting within square brackets such of those facts as are not expressly included in Mr Hastie-Smith's affidavit. Facts which at the date of the interlocutory proceedings were known only to Miss Tisdall or which are later in date than those proceedings are set out in italics.

The facts

On 20 October 1983, the Minister of Defence addressed to the Prime Minister a minute which bore the marking 'Secret' and which dealt with parliamentary and public statements to be made on 1st November about, and contemporaneously with, the delivery of Cruise Missiles to the Greenham Common R.A.F. base [which it was then intended should begin on that date]. Seven copies only of this minute were dispatched from [the private office of the Minister at] the Ministry of Defence; they were directed to the Home Secretary, the Foreign Secretary. the Lord President of the Council, the Lord Privy Seal, the Chief Whip and the Secretary of the Cabinet. [A separate minute by the Minister of Defence with, it may be inferred, no more extensive circulation to government offices, but dealing with contingency security arrangements for the arrival of the missiles was dispatched from the Ministry of Defence at the same time.] *On the next day Miss Tisdall, who was employed at the Foreign and Commonwealth Office as a clerk in the registry of the private office of the Secretary of State and, with three colleagues, had among her duties the operation of the photocopier, used this machine to make an extra copy of each of these minutes and took them away with her. After doing her best with a felt pen to render indecipherable the marginal markings on the documents which would enable them to be identified as the copies of the Defence Minister's two minutes that had been directed to the Foreign Secretary, she took them to the office of* The Guardian, *handed an envelope containing them to an attendant at the door and went away without disclosing her identity.*

Articles appearing in *The Guardian* between 22 and 25 October 1983 which were exhibited to the affidavit of the editor, made it clear that information in some form or another of the fact that it was the intention of the Governments of the United Kingdom and the U.S.A. that the date of arrival of the missiles would be 1 November had been leaked. [In consequence steps had to be taken, in conjunction with the Americans, to postpone the date from 1 to 13 November so as to prevent notice of the exact date of their arrival being disclosed sufficiently in advance to enable a mass demonstration to be organised to block by physical, even though not violent, means the arrival of the missiles at the Greenham Common base.] On 31 October *The Guardian* published in full the Defence Minister's minute of 20 October dealing with parliamentary and public statements about deliveries of Cruise Missiles to R.A.F. Greenham Common. *The editor did not publish either then or later the second and more sensitive minute dealing with contingent security arrangements, of which Miss Tisdall had also handed in a copy at his office. He caused it and any copies that might have been made of it in* The Guardian *office to be destroyed.*

[An enquiry was immediately undertaken of those persons in the Ministry of Defence and the recipient departments who had had access to the minute that had been published in *The Guardian*.] *Among them was Miss Tisdall who filled in a questionnaire in which she flatly denied having any responsibility for the leak, thus leaving (as Cantley J. stressed in passing sentence) under the shadow of suspicion those others not only in her own but also in other government departments to which copies of the minute had been sent.* [So the inquiry proved to have been fruitless by 11 November 1983.] On that date the Treasury Solicitor wrote to the editor of *The Guardian* requesting delivery up forthwith of the document published in its issue of 31 October 1983. Solicitors for *The Guardian* by letter of 17 November offered to return the document with the marginal markings excised lest they should disclose the identity of the newspaper's anonymous informant. This offer was refused and the writ claiming delivery up of the document was served on 22 November 1983. It was accompanied by notice of motion claiming, as interlocutory relief, immediate delivery up of the unmutilated document. This motion was dealt with in the manner that I have already stated. As a result the unmutilated document was handed over on 16 December 1983 to the Treasury Solicitor.

Examination of the document, on which the attempted erasure of the marginal markings had been ineffective, enabled it to be identified as a copy prepared upon the photocopying machine in the private office of the Secretary of State for Foreign and Commonwealth Affairs. This discovery reduced considerably the circle of those upon whom suspicion fell, and further investigation reduced to Miss Tisdall and her three colleagues whose duties included operating that photocopying machine. She persisted in her denials that she was the guilty party, pointing out as late as 6 January 1984 that it might be any of the other three; but after a weekend spent in consulting her parents she finally confessed on 9 January 1984.

The affidavit evidence

The relevant paragraphs in the affidavit of Mr Hastie-Smith, who describes himself as responsible for the security of records and other documents at the Ministry of Defence, that deal with the risk to national security are numbered 5 and 6. They read:

'5. Only seven copies of the said document were despatched from the Ministry of Defence. In addition to the copy sent to the Office of the Prime Minister, copies were directed to the Secretary of State for the Home Department, the Secretary of State for Foreign and Commonwealth Affairs, the Lord President of the Council, the Lord Privy Seal, the Chief Whip and Sir Robert Armstrong, the Secretary of the Cabinet.

'6. The fact that a document marked "Secret" addressed by the Secretary of State for Defence to the Prime Minister on 20 October 1983 which was concerned with a matter of great significance in relation to the defence of the United Kingdom and the North Atlantic Treaty Organisation had, by 31 October 1983, found its way into the possession of a national newspaper, is of the gravest importance to the continued maintenance of national security. It also represents a threat to the United Kingdom's relations with her allies, who cannot be expected to continue to entrust Her Majesty's Government with secret information which may be liable to unauthorised disclosure, even though its circulation is restricted to the innermost circles of government. Thus the identity of the person or persons who disclosed or assisted in the disclosure of the above mentioned document to the defendant must be established in order that national security should be preserved.'

My Lords, the significance of the classification 'secret' appearing on a document originating in a government office is a matter of public record of which your Lordships are, in my view, entitled to take judicial notice. It is to be found in the Statement on the Recommendations of the Security Commission (1982) (Cmnd. 8540) presented to Parliament by the Prime Minister in May 1982. It sets out in paragraphs 6 the definitions of the four classifications in use in the United Kingdom, as follows:

'TOP SECRET. Information and material the unauthorised disclosure of which would cause exceptionally grave damage to the nation. SECRET. Information and material the unauthorised disclosure of which would cause serious injury to the interests of the nation. CONFIDENTIAL. Information and material the unauthorised disclosure of which would be prejudicial to the interests of the nation. RESTRICTED. Information and material the unauthorised disclosure of which would be undesirable in the interests of the nation.'

None of these definitions uses the actual words 'national security' but documents which deal with weapons intended for the defence of the United Kingdom against potential hostile powers if the disclosure of their contents would cause serious injury to the interests of the nation clearly relate to 'national security' in the narrowest sense in which that term could be used.

It might, with advantage, have been spelled out expressly in Mr Hastie-Smith's affidavit that documents with a circulation limited as stated in paragraph 5 are (with the exception of the Chief Whip) dealt with in a private office of the minster concerned; and that civil servants employed in the private offices in those particular ministries at any rate, have access to many documents classified as 'Secret' or 'Top Secret', of which disclosure to any unauthorised person whether directly or by general publication in the press could do untold damage to national security. But the fact that civil servants who have access to a document that is classified as 'Secret' are likely to have access to others that are so classified is an inference which, in my view, any judge is entitled to draw as a matter of common sense even though he may not be aware of the details of the internal organisation of a government department.

It might, perhaps, also with advantage, have been stated expressly that the interval between 31 October when the minute classified as "Secret" was published in *The Guardian* and 11 November 1983 when the Treasury Solicitor requested the editor to deliver it up forthwith, was occupied by the government offices concerned in instituting and pursuing their own internal inquiries of those civil servants to whom access to copies of the secret minute had been available and that such 'in house' inquiries had not succeeded in identifying the culprit. But that such inquiries should have been undertaken without success, before recourse was had to tangling with the press upon what was currently so sensitive a matter as the identification of informants, with all the publicity that this was likely to entail, is another inference which any judge using his common sense alone without any special knowledge of civil service procedure would, in my view, be fully entitled to draw.

The first sentence of paragraph 6 refers to the subject-matter of the leaked document. There can be no question that the subject-matter, the deployment of nuclear missiles in the United Kingdom, is vitally concerned (and I use this adverb advisedly) with an aspect of national security which is likely to generate a considerable volume of documents recording 'Secret' or 'Top Secret' information, disclosure of which to a potential enemy power could do great harm to national security. Nor should the second sentence be brushed aside, since reliance for maintaining the national security of this country is placed upon close co-operation with our N.A.T.O. allies and if, unhappily, armed conflict should break out, upon interdependent action by us and them. Finally, the last sentence, although elliptically expressed, makes it, to my mind, clear that the risk to national security that the Government feared lay not in the publication of the particular document of which the delivery up was sought, but in the possibility—and in so potentially catastrophic a field as nuclear warfare I regard possibly as enough—that whoever leaked that document might leak in future other classified documents disclosure of which would have much more serious consequences on national security.

My Lords, the possibility elliptically referred to in the last sentence of paragraph 6, is an inference which common sense alone would justify any judge in drawing. We now know, as the Government did not at the time of the interlocutory proceedings, but the editor of *The Guardian* did, that this was no mere possibility; it was a reality.

Miss Tisdall had in fact already leaked another document, the second minute of 20 October 1983 dealing with contingency security arrangements, which must have been of considerably greater significance to national security, but which the editor of *The Guardian,* with a sense of responsibility that he has shown throughout this whole affair, not only refrained from publishing in his newspaper; he also arranged for it and all copies of it in the newspaper's possession to be destroyed.

My Lords, that is why after attempting to apply the necessary mental gymnastics, I feel compelled to range myself with those of you who, in agreement with all three members of the Court of Appeal, consider that the evidential material that was before that court at the interlocutory stage on 16 December 1983, was sufficient to establish that immediate delivery up of the document was necessary in the interests of national security.

My Lords, I am conscious that the foregoing excursus on the matter that divides us may have been disproportionately lengthy since, unlike the true construction of section 10, it does not raise any question of general importance but is peculiar to the instant case, where its importance is now limited to any effect that it might have on costs.

For the reasons I have given I would dismiss this appeal."

LORD FRASER OF TULLYBELTON: "My Lords, the origin and history of this appeal have been explained by my noble and learned friend, Lord Diplock, and I need not repeat what he has said. I respectfully agree with him on two matters which I mention briefly before coming to the critical question in the appeal. The first relates to the construction of the first part of section 10 of the Contempt of Court Act 1981 which provides that: 'No court may require a person to disclose, nor is any person guilty of contempt of court for refusing to disclose, the source of information contained in a publication for which he is responsible. . .' The application of that provision is, in my opinion, not limited to the case where a publisher of information is required in terms to disclose the source of information or to do something which *will* certainly disclose it, and refuses to do so. The provision extends also to a case such as the present, where the publisher is called upon, and refuses, to do something which may or may not lead to disclosure of the source.

Secondly, I am of opinion that the appellants are not precluded from relying on section 10 of the Act of 1981 by the mere fact that they are doing so in answer to a proprietary claim from the respondents for the delivery of their own property. The

Crown's proprietary right to the leaked document entitles the respondents to claim delivery of it under section 3(2)(*a*) of the Torts (Interference with Goods) Act 1977, but the publisher is still entitled to rely on section 10 of the Act of 1981 if he can. The property in question here is of negligible value, consisting as it does of four sheets of paper bearing a typewritten memorandum and some other marks. Neither the physical paper nor the matter typed or written on it has any substantial intrinsic value, and the sole reason why the respondents sought to have it returned to them was in order to examine the marginal marks in the hope that they would lead to identification of the source of the leak. I express no opinion in the question whether section 10 could be relied on by a publisher who might be in possession of property of substantial, or perhaps unique, value (such as an old master picture) the owner of which is seeking its return for its own sake. That would raise different issues.

Scott, J., having held (wrongly, as I think) that section 10 of the Act of 1981 was not applicable to limit the proprietary remedy sought by the respondents as owners of the property, did not have to decide how to deal with the matter if section 10 had applied. Nevertheless he went on to say that, if the question had arisen, he would have decided that he was not satisfied, as required by the latter part of section 10, that 'disclosure is necessary in the interests of justice or national security or for the prevention of disorder or crime.' It is quite clear that the only one of these grounds which is relevant here is national security. The judge explained his reasons for the view that he took. The question which is of importance lies in the guidance that may be given to courts which have to decide a similar question in future cases.

In considering the question now this House must do so on the information which was before the judge who had to decide the matter at the interlocutory stage. Since then of course much information has emerged; in particular the identity of the source of the leak has become known and she has been convicted and sentenced for her offence. All such later information must be excluded from our consideration, and I have endeavoured to prevent its influencing my mind.

Looking at the matter on the information which was before the judge at the interlocutory stage, the first obvious point is that the contents of the leaked documents are not, and were not then, of any military value at all. It revealed no secret information of military value, although it may have caused a little political embarrassment to the government. So much is rightly conceded on behalf of the respondents. Their case on national security, as developed in argument to the judge, rested on the fact that the leak took place at all. The occurrence of the leak, and the absence of any indication that the document had been stolen by an outsider, showed that there was some person in the government service, having access to the document, who was untrustworthy, and, although this particular leak might not have damaged national security, the danger was that, so long as the untrustworthy servant remained in office with access to secret documents, he or she was in a position to disclose information of real importance to national security. It was also said that the occurrence of the leak was a threat to the relations of the United Kingdom with friendly countries whose governments would not entrust Her Majesty's Government with secret information while there was a risk of it being leaked by an unknown source.

The only evidence in support of the Crown's case that was before the judge at the interlocutory stage was contained in an affidavit sworn by the principal establishment officer of the Ministry of Defence, with its appendices consisting of a copy of the leaked document and some correspondence between the parties' solicitors. The most material part of the affidavit was paragraph 6 which has already been quoted in full by my noble and learned friend, Lord Diplock, and which I do not repeat.

That paragraph provides the only foundation for the argument on behalf of the respondents to the effect that the continuance in office of the untrustworthy servant with access to secret documents was a threat to national security. But what is required in order to comply with the latter part of section 10 of the Act of 1981 is that the court must be 'satisfied' that disclosure of the source is 'necessary' in the interests of national security. The author of the affidavit does not seem to have had the terms of the section clearly in mind. He apparently did not appreciate that the final sentence of paragraph 6 which states that the identity of the person who disclosed the information must be established, is not by itself enough to satisfy the court that disclosure of that person's identity *by the publisher* of the information is necessary in the interests of national security. There may be other means of establishing it, and, unless special urgency is proved, the requirements of section 10 are not in my opinion met merely by showing that the easiest way of identifying the person is by calling upon the publisher of the information to disclose it. I have reached the opinion, in agreement with the judge, that the test of necessity was not satisfied by the information that was before him at the interlocutory stage. His own reason was expressed thus:

'. . . there is no real evidence as to the class of persons who had access to these documents; nor do I think it is a necessary inference that because some individual was prepared, in breach of his duty and reprehensibly, to leak to the press a document of the character here involved, national security requires that he be identified and got rid of.'

I agree. Before he could have been satisfied in the present case, the judge would in my view have reasonably required some information as to the approximate number of persons who might have had access to the document in course of his or her duties, and as to any efforts already made to find the guilty person without success. No doubt one might assume that some efforts had been made but in order to comply with the Act of 1981 the court requires evidence and not mere assumption. In some circumstances it might be urgent to find the guilty person immediately; if so, evidence of the reason for urgency would be required, and the court if satisfied that urgency was proved, might also be satisfied that it was necessary in the interests of national security to order immediate disclosure without waiting for other efforts to ascertain the identity of the source. The fact that a period of 12 days was allowed to elapse between publication of the document on 31 October 1983 and the writing of the letter dated 11 November 1983 from the Treasury Solicitor calling on the editor to deliver the document makes it impossible for the respondents to maintain that the present case was one of special urgency. They did not so maintain. Another matter on which evidence is noticeably lacking here is whether the classification of 'Secret' would be appropriate for a document which contains really significant military information, and, if not, whether a civil servant who had access to documents marked 'Secret' would necessarily have access also to documents bearing a higher security classification and containing significant military information.

My Lords, I have anxiously considered whether it is unreasonable to insist that further information on lines such as those I have indicated ought to have been made available to the judge. I have considered it all the more anxiously because my view involved differing from that of the Court of Appeal and of the majority of your Lordships. The difference between us is narrow but it is, in my view, important. I have concluded that, without more information than he had, the judge could not properly have been satisfied that disclosure was 'necessary.' The test of necessity is a strict one and its strictness ought not to be whittled away by reading section 10 of the Act of 1981 as if it said 'necessary or convenient' or 'necessary or expedient.' Parliament has used the word 'necessary' by itself, and it is not for this House in its judicial capacity to relax the standard fixed by Parliament, especially in a matter of this kind where there is a flavour of constitutional right of freedom of expression. Nor can the lack of evidence be made good by leaving the court to draw inferences which may or may not be justified. With the greatest respect to the judges in the Court of Appeal I consider that they gave insufficient weight to the test of necessity. Sir John Donaldson M.R. said [1984] Ch. 156, 165:

'The maintenance of national security requires that untrustworthy servants in a position to mishandle highly classified documents passing from the Secretary of State for Defence to other ministers shall be identified at the earliest possible moment and removed from their positions. This is blindingly obvious and would not become any less obvious at any trial.'

Griffiths L.J. said, at p. 168: 'The threat to national security lies in the fact that someone, *probably in a senior position* and with access to highly classified material, cannot be trusted.' (Emphasis added.) We now know that the person concerned was not in a senior position but in quite a junior one. I refer to the matter not in order to be wise after the event, but only to show the danger of relying on inference which may seem reasonable at the time but which may in fact be unsound.

The second point relied on by the respondents, and referred to in the second sentence of paragraph 6 of the affidavit, is that the leak represents a threat to the United Kingdom's relations with its allies. It is easy to see that this is a possibility, at least in theory, but I do not see how a court is in a position to judge the reality or the seriousness of the risk without some evidence. Here there was no evidence but merely a bare assertion in the affidavit. Again I consider that the judge was right in his view that he would not have been satisfied on this point if it had arisen for decision by him.

Finally, I must emphasise again that I have tried to consider the question that arises in this appeal only on the evidence that was before the judge. Subsequent events have shown that the untrustworthy servant in this case represented a serious security risk, and it is probable that, even when the matter was before the judge at the interlocutory stage, evidence could have been put before him on which he might have concluded that disclosure was necessary. That is uncertain and speculation about it is a fruitless exercise which is irrelevant to the question under consideration in this appeal. The practical conclusion is not that the judge ought to have been satisfied on the affidavit evidence that was before him of the necessity for a disclosure, but that the affidavit evidence ought to have been presented in sufficient detail to enable the judge to come to a decision upon proper evidence. I have little doubt that much of the evidence which would have been relevant, for instance as to the significance of the classification 'Secret' for documents, and as to the extent of the inquiries already made to ascertain the identity of the person responsible for the leak, was available and could have been presented if the necessity for it had been appreciated by those who drafted the affidavit. I hope that the result of this appeal will be that in any future case in which section 10 of the Act of 1981 is likely to be in issue, care will be taken to present to the court adequate evidence to the extent that it is available at the time.

I would allow the appeal."

Lords Roskill and Bridge of Harwich delivered speeches concurring with Lord Diplock. Lord Scarman delivered a speech concurring with Lord Fraser.

2. RESTRAINING PUBLICATION

18. Attorney-General v. Guardian Newspapers Ltd.
[1987] 3 All E.R. 316

A former member of British security services (Mr Peter Wright) proposed to publish (in Australia) his memoirs in a book called *Spycatcher*. In June 1986 both *The Guardian* and *The Observer* published an outline of the allegations contained in the book. On July 11, 1986, Millett J. granted injunctions against both newspapers restraining them from disclosing or obtaining any information obtained by Mr Wright. This was subject to a proviso that the newspapers could publish material disclosed in open court in legal proceedings being conducted in Australia. The Crown had taken action in Australia to prevent publication.

Between April 27 and July 14, 1987, a number of important developments occurred. First, extracts of the book were published in *The Independent*. Secondly, the *London Evening Standard* and the *London Daily News* published information drawn from the book. Thirdly, extracts were published in the *Washington Post* and the *Sunday Times*. And in addition to all of this the book went on sale in the United States and could easily be bought by British citizens.

The Guardian and *The Observer* applied to the courts to have the injunctions discharged. The same case dealt with an application by the Attorney-General to commit the *Sunday Times* for contempt. The newspapers succeeded before Sir Nicolas Browne-Wilkinson, but his decision was overturned by the Court of Appeal which reinstated the Millett injunction, with variations. This decision in turn was upheld by the House of Lords. Their Lordships, however, divided three to two, but the majority in refusing to discharge the Millett injunction varied its terms so that it was to operate even more restrictively. Now the newspapers were prohibited from publishing relevant material disclosed in open court.

LORD BRIDGE OF HARWICH: "... The basis of the claim for the Millett injunctions was to prevent disclosure of the *Spycatcher* allegations in breach of the life-long obligations of confidence which Mr Wright, as a former officer of the security service, owed to Her Majesty's government. So long as any of the *Spycatcher* allegations remained undisclosed, I should have been wholeheartedly in favour of maintaining the injunctions in the interests of national security for all the reasons so cogently deployed in the affidavit of Sir Robert Armstrong. But it is perfectly obvious and elementary that, once information is freely available to the general public, it is nonsensical to talk about preventing its 'disclosure'. Whether the *Spycatcher* allegations are true or false is beside the point. What is to the point is that they are now freely available to the public or, perhaps more accurately, to any member of the public who wants to read them. I deliberately refrain from using expressions such as 'the public domain" which may have technical overtones. The fact is that the intelligence and security services of any country in the world can buy the book *Spycatcher* and read what is in it. The fact is that any citizen of this country can buy the book in America and bring it home with him or order the book from America and receive a copy by post. Some enterprising small traders have apparently found it worth their while to import copies of the book and sell them by the roadside. It remains to be seen whether the Attorney-General will institute proceedings for contempt of court against any public library which imports copies of *Spycatcher* and makes it available to borrowers. Counsel for the Attorney-General had no instructions which enabled him to answer the question I asked about that.

If, as I have always thought, the interest of national security in protecting sensitive and classified information is to conceal it from those who might make improper use of it, it is manifestly now too late for the Millett injunctions to serve that interest. If the confidence of friendly countries in the ability of this country to protect its secrets has been undermined by the publication in the United States of America of *Spycatcher*, the maintenance of the Millett injunctions can do nothing to restore that confidence. So much, I believe, is obvious and incontrovertible.

I well understand the sense of indignation which all of us must feel that Mr Wright, to use the colloquialism, should have got away with it, worse still that he should make a profit from his breach of confidence. Perhaps his publishers come under the same condemnation. But the remedy for that wrong lies not in a futile injunction but in an action for an account of profits.

The legal basis for the Attorney-General's claim to enjoin the newspapers is that any third party who comes into possession of information knowing that it originated from a breach of confidence owes the same duty to the original confidant as that owed by the original confider. If this proposition is held to be of universal application, no matter how widely the original confidential information has been disseminated before reaching the third party, it would seem to me to lead to absurd and unacceptable consequences. But I am prepared to assume for present purposes that the Attorney-General is still in a position to assert a bare duty binding on the conscience of newspaper editors which is capable of surviving the publication of *Spycatcher* in America.

The key question in the case, to my mind, is whether there is any remaining interest of national security which the Millet injunctions are capable of protecting and, if so, whether it is of sufficient weight to justify the massive encroachment on freedom of speech which the continuance of the Millett injunctions in present circumstances necessarily involves.

There is no fresh evidence from Sir Robert Armstrong or anyone else who can speak for the security service about the security implications following the American publication of *Spycatcher*. Sir Robert's original affidavit was made in the radically different circumstances obtaining before that publication. So, in effect, the hapless counsel for the Attorney-General was left to make bricks without straw (which of course he did with his usual skill) in seeking to persuade your Lordships that, despite the free availability of the book *Spycatcher* itself and despite the citations from it and discussion of its contents which have been and will continue to be available in foreign newspapers freely circulating in this country, a blanket ban on any repetition, citation or discussion of its contents in the British press was necessary in the interests of national security. If I have understood the argument, stripped of rhetorical embellishment, it amounts to this. First, unless enjoined Mr Wright may make yet further disclosures about the security service not already contained in *Spycatcher*. This may be true, but is entirely beside the point. If the Attorney-General were prepared to modify the Millett injunctions so as to exclude from their ambit the *Spycatcher* allegations, in the same way that anything in Mr Chapman Pincher's book *Their Trade is Treachery* is excluded, there would be nothing left to argue about. What the newspapers seek is liberty to repeat and discuss the *Spycatcher* allegations: no more, no less. Second, counsel for the Attorney-General takes material from Sir Robert's affidavit out of the context in which it was made and seeks to rely on it for the proposition that the Millett injunctions should be maintained in their full rigour to deter other officers of the intelligence or security services from following Mr Wright's deplorable example. The suggestion must be, I take it, that a future Mr Wright contemplating going into exile and publishing his memoirs in the United States and who would not be deterred by the prospect of having to account to Her Majesty's government for his profits would nevertheless be deterred by the knowledge he would be denied by injunction any more than a limited access for his story to the general reading public in this country. This seems to me a rather fanciful suggestion, but if there is anything in it, now that the original aim of preventing disclosure of secret material can no longer be attained, the deterrent argument can only carry minimal weight.

What of the other side of the coin and the encroachment on freedom of speech? Having no written constitution, we have no equivalent in our law to the First Amendment to the Constitution of the United States of America. Some think that puts freedom of speech on too lofty a pedestal. Perhaps they are right. We have not adopted as part of our law the European convention on Human Rights (Convention for the Protection of Human Rights and Fundamental Freedoms (Rome, 4 November 1950; T.S. 71 (1953); Cmd, 8969)) to which this country is a signatory. Many think that we should. I have hitherto not been of that persuasion, in large part because I have had confidence in the capacity of the common law to safeguard the fundamental freedoms essential to a free society including the right to freedom of speech which is specifically safeguarded by art 10 of the convention. My confidence is seriously underminded by your Lordships' decision. All the judges in the courts below in this case have been concerned not to impose any unnecessary fetter on freedom of speech. I suspect that what the Court of Appeal would have liked to achieve, and perhaps set out to achieve by its compromise solution, was to inhibit the *Sunday Times* from continuing the serialisation of *Spycatcher,* but to leave the press at large at liberty to discuss and comment on the *Spycatcher* allegations. If there were a method of achieving these results which could be sustained in law, I can see much to be said for it on the merits. But I can see nothing whatever, either in law or on the merits, to be said for the maintenance of a total ban on discussion in the press of this country of matters of undoubted public interest and concern which the rest of the world now knows all about and can discuss freely. Still less can I approve your Lordships' decision to throw in for good measure a restriction on reporting court proceedings in Australia which the Attorney-General had never even asked for.

Freedom of speech is always the first casualty under a totalitarian régime. Such a régime cannot allow the free circulation of information and ideas among its citizens. Censorship is the indispensable tool to regulate what the public may and what they may not know. The present attempt to insulate the public in this country from information which is freely available elsewhere is a significant step down that very dangerous road. The maintenance of the ban, as more and more copies of the book *Spycatcher* enter this country and circulate here, will seem more and more ridiculous. If the government are determined to fight to maintain the ban to the end, they will face inevitable condemnation and humiliation by the European Court of Human Rights in Strasbourg. Long before that they will have been condemned at the bar of public opinion in the free world.

But there is another alternative. The government will surely want to reappraise the whole *Spycatcher* situation in the light of the views expressed in the courts below and in this House. I dare to hope that they will bring to that reappraisal qualities of vision and of statesmanship sufficient to recognise that their wafer-thin victory in this litigation has been gained at a price which no government committed to upholding the values of a free society can afford to pay.

I add a postscript to record that I have now had the opportunity to read first drafts of the opinions of my noble and learned friends Lord Templeman and Lord Ackner. I remain in profound disagreement with them."

LORD BRANDON OF OAKBROOK: "... I was a party to the majority decision of this House given on 30 July 1987 that the injunctions in issue should not be discharged but should be continued until trial. My reasons for being a party to that decision can be summarised in nine propositions as follows. (1) The action brought by the Attorney-General against the *Guardian* and the *Observer* has as its object the protection of an important public interest, namely the maintenance so far as possible of the secrecy of the British security service. (2) The injunctions in issue are interlocutory, that is to say temporary injunctions, having effect until the trial of the action only. (3) Before the publication of *Spycatcher* in America the Attorney-General had a strong arguable case for obtaining at trial final injunctions in terms similar to those of the temporary injunctions. (4) While the publication of *Spycatcher* in America has much weakened that case, it remains an arguable one. (5) The only way in which it can justly be decided whether the Attorney-General's case, being still arguable, should succeed or fail is by having the action tried. (6) On the hypothesis that the Attorney-General's claim, if tried, will succeed, the effect of discharging the temporary injunctions now will be to deprive him, summarily and without a trial, of all opportunity of achieving that success. (7) On the alternative hypothesis that the Attorney-General's claim, if tried, will fail, the effect of continuing the temporary injunctions until trial will be only to postpone, not to prevent, the exercise by the *Guardian* and the *Observer* of the rights to publish which it will in that event have been established that they have. (8) Having regard to (6) and (7) above, the discharge of the temporary injunctions now is capable of causing much greater injustice to the Attorney-General than the continuation of them until trial is capable of causing to the *Guardian* and the *Observer*. (9) Continuation of the injunctions until trial is therefore preferable to their discharge."

LORD TEMPLEMAN: ". . . The Secretary to the Cabinet, Sir Robert Armstrong, in an affidavit sworn in these proceedings, deposed as follows: '. . . the main function of the British Security Service is the defence of the realm as a whole, from external and internal dangers arising from attempts at espionage and sabotage, or from actions from person and organisations whether directed from within or without the United Kingdom, which may be judged to be subversive of the State.'

Mr Wright was employed by the British security service. On 1 September 1955 he signed a declaration that he understood the effect of s. 2 of the Official Secrets Act 1911, which was set out in the declaration and renders liable to prosecution any person in possession of information 'which he has obtained or to which he has had access owing to his position as a person who holds or who has held office under His Majesty . . . [and who] communicates the . . . information to any person, other than a person to whom he is authorised to communicate it, or a person to whom it is in the interests of the State his duty to communicate it. . .'

When Mr Wright left the security service he signed a further declaration, dated 30 January 1976, acknowledging, *inter alia*, that the provisions of the Official Secrets Acts applied to him after his appointment had ceased, that he was fully aware that serious consequences might follow any breach of the provisions of those Acts and that he understood 'that I am liable to be prosecuted if either in the United Kingdom or abroad I communicate, either orally or in writing, including publication in a speech, lecture, radio or television broadcast, or in the Press or in book form or otherwise, to any unauthorised person any information acquired by me as a result of my appointment (save such as has already officially been made public) unless I have previously obtained the official sanction in writing of the Department by which I was appointed.'

In addition to the obligations of secrecy expressly acknowledged by Mr Wright, he was also under an obligation arising out of his employment by the security service and enforceable in equity not to divulge any information which he obtained in the course of his employment. The obligation arises because of 'the broad principle of equity that he who has received information in confidence shall not take unfair advantage of it. He must not make use of it to the prejudice of him who gave it. . .' (See *Seager* v. *Copydex Ltd.* [1967] 2 All E.R. 415 at 417, [1976] 1 W.L.R. 923 at 931 *per* Lord Denning MR.) . . .

It follows that Mr Wright could not publish his memoirs as an employee of the security service without committing flagrant breaches of the duty of secrecy and confidentiality which he owed to the public in the national interest. No publisher or newspaper in this country may lawfully publish Mr Wright's memoirs or disclose information obtained by Mr Wright in the course of his service concerning any aspect of the work of the security service. Mr Wright, apart from making money out of his memoirs, protests that his memoirs will be helpful to the British public. The press and others consider that his memoirs will be helpful in achieving the objects of an inquiry into the working of the security service, and amendment of the Official Secrets Acts and the enactment of freedom of information legislation. But these objects are unlikely to be attained so long as the British press is prepared to publish confidential information relating to the British security service without investigation or corroboration and in disregard of orders of the court designed to preserve the security service from harm. . .

My Lords, this appeal involves a conflict between the right of the public to be protected by the security service and the right of the public to be supplied with full information by the press. This appeal therefore involves consideration of the European Convention on Human Rights to which the British government adheres. Article 10 of the convention is in these terms:

'1. Everyone has the right to freedom of expression. This right shall include freedom to hold opinions and to receive and impart information and ideas without interference by public authority and regardless of frontiers. . . 2. The exercise of these freedoms, since it carries with it duties and responsibilities, may be subject to such formalities, conditions, restrictions or penalties as are prescribed by law and are necessary in a democratic society, in the interests of national security, territorial integrity or public safety, for the prevention of disorder or crime, for the protection of health or morals, for the protection of the reputation or rights of others, for preventing the disclosure of information received in confidence, or for maintaining the authority and impartiality of the judiciary.' . . .

The question is therefore whether the interference with freedom of expression constituted by the Millett injunctions was, on 30 July 1987 when they were continued by this House, necessary in a democratic society in the interests of national security, for protecting the reputation or rights of others, for preventing the disclosure of information received in confidence or for maintaining the authority and impartiality of the judiciary having regard to the facts and circumstances prevailing on 30 July 1987 and in the light of the events which had happened. The continuance of the Millett injunctions appears to me to be necessary for all these purposes.

My Lords, in my opinion a democracy is entitled to take the view that a public servant who is employed in the security service must be restrained from making any disclosures concerning the security service and that similar restraints must be imposed on anybody who receives those disclosures knowing that they are confidential.

There are safeguards. No member of the secret service is immune from criminal prosecution or civil suit in respect of his actions. Instructions from superior officers are no defence. In addition, anyone, whether public servant, newspaper editor or journalist, who is aware that a crime has been committed or is dissatisfied with the activities of the secret service is free to report to the police in relation to crime and in other matters is free to report to the Prime Minister, who is charged with the responsibility of the security services, and to the Security Commission, which advises the Prime Minister. The security services are not above the law. In the present case there is not the slightest evidence that these safeguards have failed. Furthermore, there is nothing to prevent the press investigating all the allegations made by Mr Wright and reporting the results of their investigations to the public. It is only unlawful for the press to publish information unlawfully disclosed by Mr Wright and which may or may not be true.

In the terms of the convention there are three reasons why in the present case restraints are necessary to prevent the press publishing information by Mr Wright.

Any person who joins the security service accepts that he cannot defend himself or the security service against false accusations and cannot give any explanation for his actions or for the activities of the security service, without himself thereby endangering the secrecy of the security service, which is of paramount importance. Any person who joins the security service knows that no official defence or explanation can be given. He accepts that accusations may be made and circulated abroad and that rumours may reach individuals in this country. But he relies on the Attorney-General, acting in the public interest, to seek to prevent the mass circulation of accusations and attributions and insinuations in this country and to prevent so far as possible the revelation of security service activities. And he relies on the courts acting within their jurisdiction to prevent mass circulation of secret and confidential information in this country if the courts consider that such protection is necessary. The hundreds of pages of *Spycatcher* which embellish but cannot improve the general allegations already known to have been made by Mr Wright may include accusations, purported conversations, and unfair criticism which no individual member of the secret service can wish to be made the subject of sensational newspaper headlines or delivered up to the newspaper-reading public. So long as there are in this country only odd copies of *Spycatcher*, members of the security service are substantially free from harassment. But once mass circulation takes place in newspapers, and particularly once the *Sunday Times* publishes *Spycatcher* in serial form, then members of the security service will be liable to be harassed with accusations to which they cannot respond. The publication in this country of *Spycatcher* will thus cause grievous harm to individuals and deal a blow to the morale of the security service. The British public will lose confidence in the security service. Our friends will be dismayed and our enemies will rejoice at the failure of the British to protect the security service from calumny reported in the British press. Whatever may happen abroad it must be harmful to the security service and contrary to the public interest for Mr Wright to be allowed to attack the security service in this country by revealing or pretending to reveal information which he is forbidden to reveal by law and loyalty. There is a great difference between the power of the press operating through mass circulation and the power of Mr Wright confined to the export to this country of individual copies of *Spycatcher*.

I reject the argument that the law will appear ridiculous if it imposes a restriction on mass circulation when any individual member of the public may obtain a copy of *Spycatcher* from abroad. The court cannot exceed its territorial jurisdiction but the court can prevent the harm which will result from mass circulation within its own jurisdiction and can prevent Mr Wright and British newspapers from profiting from the unlawful conduct of Mr Wright. It is said that the same result could be achieved by an order on Mr Wright and the newspapers to account to the Attorney-General for any profits they will make from *Spycatcher*. The public interest does not lie in making profits but in preventing profits being made in this country from treachery to this country.

In my opinion, therefore, the injunctions are necessary in terms of the convention because harm will be caused to the security service if the press insist on disclosing to their readers not the general nature of Mr Wright's uncorroborated allegations but the mass circumstantial hearsay contained in *Spycatcher* relating to the security service and its activities.

The second reason which makes it necessary to continue restrictions on the press lies in the fact that if the injunctions are discharged in the present case an immutable precedent will have been created. If the injunctions are discharged it must follow that any disgruntled public servant or holder of secret or confidential information relating to the security service can achieve mass circulation in this country of damaging truths and falsehoods by the device of prior publications anywhere else abroad. Nothing will ever again be confidential save the identity of a source whom a newspaper wishes to conceal. If the Millett injunctions were discharged, Mr Wright could write to the *Washington Post* making a serious new allegation or bolstering up old allegations citing names and actions and purporting to give chapter and verse. Once the *Washington Post* had entertained an American audience with these revelations, then the products of Mr Wright's recollections and imaginations could be plastered across the British press. I reject the allegation that the press are being gagged or censored or submitted to Soviet discipline. The Millett injunctions were not imposed by the government: the injunctions were imposed and are being continued by independent and impartial judges because they consider that despite the importance of the right of freedom of expression it is necessary in the national interest to prevent the security service being harmed now and in the future. The imposition of restraints on the press in the exercise of a judicial discretion in conformity with the convention is an expression and not a negation of democracy in action.

There is a third and final reason why the restraints imposed in the present case satisfy the tests of the convention. All the newspaper reports between 27 April and 14 July 1987 were contrary to the object and purpose of the Millett injunctions. Those reports originated with Mr Wright and his publishers abroad and were intended to bring pressure on the English courts to allow *Spycatcher* to be published here. The Millet injunctions cannot now be discharged without surrendering to the press an untrammelled arbitrary and irresponsible power to evade an order of the court designed for the safety of the realm to protect the confidentiality of information obtained by a member of the secret service.

Finally, I must refer to one proviso to the Millett injunctions which was deleted by the order of your Lordships' House on 30 July. The proviso was in these terms: '(2) no breach of this Order shall be constituted by the disclosure or publication of any material disclosed in Open Court in the Supreme Court of New South Wales unless prohibited by the Judge there sitting or which, after the trial in action no. 4382 of 1985 is not prohibited from publication.'

When Millett J. made that proviso in the interests of the *Guardian* and the *Observer* it would not have occurred to him that other newspapers would subsequently publish extracts from *Spycatcher*. It is very likely that in the course of the proceedings in New South Wales long extracts from *Spycatcher* have been read in open court. The *Sunday Times* has demonstrated that it is prepared to go to any lengths to publish extracts from *Spycatcher*. The order of this House prohibiting, *inter alia,* the publication of extracts from *Spycatcher* in this country was made on Thursday, 30 July. It was quite possible that if the proviso had not been deleted then on Sunday, 2 August the *Sunday Times* would have published long extracts from *Spycatcher* explaining that these had been read in open court in New South Wales. Indeed, when deletion of the proviso was discussed, counsel for the *Sunday Times* very properly and prudently asked whether, if the proviso were deleted, the *Sunday Times* would be forbidden from publishing extracts from *Spycatcher* which had been read out in open court, and he was informed that such was the object and intent of the order proposed and made by this House.

At the conclusion of the hearing of this appeal I was satisfied that it was the duty of this House in its judicial capacity to stand firm in order to prevent harm to the security service, to preserve the right and duty of the court to uphold within the jurisdiction the secrecy of the security service when necessary and to ensure that the object and intent of orders made by the court are not flouted."

Lord Ackner delivered a speech concurring with Lords Brandon and Templeman. Lord Oliver delivered a speech concurring with Lord Bridge.

Lord Bridge's reference to public libraries' buying of *Spycatcher* was dealt with (so as to include them in the injunction) in (*A-G* v. *Observer Ltd.* [1988] All E.R. 385. As pointed out in the introduction to the previous case, a number of newspapers published extracts from *Spycatcher* or articles based on information gleaned from the book. Although these newspapers were not the subjects of the Millett injunction of July 11, 1986, the Attorney-General nonetheless brought criminal contempt proceedings against the newspapers alleging that the articles were intended or calculated to thwart injunctions. In *Attorney-General* v. *Newspaper Publishing plc* [1987] 3 All E.R. 276, a preliminary issue of law was tried, namely: "whether a publication made in the knowledge of an outstanding injunction against another party and which if made by that other party would be a breach thereof, constituted a criminal contempt of court on the footing that it assaulted or interfered with the process of justice in relation to that injunction." In reversing Sir Nicolas Browne-Wilkinson, the Court of Appeal responded in the affirmative, with Sir John Donaldson M.R. summarising his position at page 304 in the following terms:

"Although it has been necessary to explore this matter in considerable detail and depth, I can summarise the position very shortly. (1) Confidential information, whatever is nature (personal, financial, technical or security) has one essential common characteristic. It is *irremediably* damaged in its confidential character by every publication and the more widespread the publication, the greater the damage. (2) If a *prima facie* claim to confidentiality can be established, but this is opposed by a claim of a right to publish, whether on grounds of the public interest or otherwise, these opposing and wholly inconsistent claim must be evaluated and balanced the one against the other. (3) The public interest in ensuring that disputes are resolved justly and by due process of law may require a different balance to be struck at different stages. Thus, pending the trial of the action, the balance will normally come down in favour of preserving confidentiality, for the very obvious reason that, if this is not done and publication is permitted, there will be nothing left to have a trial about. (4) It is for the courts, and not for either of the opposing parties, to decide where, in the public interest, that balance lies. (5) Third parties (strangers to the action) who know that the court has made orders or accepted undertakings designed to protect the confidentiality of the information pending the trial, commit a serious offence against justice itself if they take action which will damage or destroy the confidentiality which the court is seeking to protect and so render the due process if law ineffectual. (6) If such third parties, having a legitimate interest in so doing, wish to contest the court's decision to protect the confidentiality of the information on any grounds, including in particular that they have special rights or interests of which account has not been taken, they should apply to the court which will hear them and make any modification of its orders which may be appropriate. ... Similarly they should apply to the court if they have doubts whether the action which they contemplate taking is lawful. (7) It is for the courts, and not for third parties, to decide whether, balancing competing public and private interests including those of the third parties, confidentiality should continue to be preserved at any particular time."

These decisions in the *Spycatcher* case concern only interlocutory injunctions. In the application for *permanent* injunction, the Court of Appeal decided that in view of the world-wide publicity given to the book, any damage was already done and refused to grant permanent injunctions. The House of Lords has not yet decided. In the meantime, another former intelligence officer, Anthony Cavendish, privately published and distributed 279 copies of a book *Inside Intelligence,* which he had been refused Government permission to publish. In A.-G. v. *Times Newspapers Ltd.* January 2, 1988 the Crown obtained an injunction which broke new ground as it applied not only against the respondents but also against "all persons having notice of" the injunction. In full knowledge of this injunction (which of course only applied in England) *The Scotsman* on January 5, 1988 published information falling within its scope. Thereupon the Lord Advocate sought interim interdict against the paper and its editor. This application sought to extend to Scotland the principle of an 'interdict' applying to all "having notice" of it. It was refused by the Lord Ordinary, and on reclaimer the Crown also sought a new basis for restraint, not as previously the harm done by disclosing the confidential information in question, but the harm caused by permitting *any* disclosure of confidential information even if innocuous.

19. Lord Advocate v. The Scotsman Publications Ltd. and Linklater
(April 9, 1988)

LORD JUSTICE-CLERK (ROSS): ..."The interdict which the Lord Advocate is seeking is in the following terms:

'To interdict the respondents or either of them or their agents, servants or anyone acting on their behalf or any person having notice of said interlocutor from disclosing or publishing or causing or permitting to be disclosed or published to any person all or any material or information obtained by Anthony Cavendish in the course of his employment with the British security and intelligence services or obtained by other officers of those services in the course of their employment with them and given by such officers to Anthony Cavendish being information concerning the British security and intelligence services or their activities or any other British security organisation or its activities provided that there shall not be prohibited publication of the following: (a) information contained in articles previously published by *The Sunday Times*; (b) information contained in the document entitled "Inside Intelligence," No. 27 of process, but only in so far as such information os not obscured to any extent by being lined through in the text; (c) information comprised in (i) fair and accurate reporting of proceedings in open court in the United Kingdom; (ii) fair and accurate reporting of proceedings in either House of Parliament whose publication is not prohibited by that House.'

The legal basis upon which interdict is sought is set forth in the first plea in law in the petition, which is in the following terms: 1. The petitioner being reasonably apprehensive that the respondents will publish, disclose and distribute confidential information to the prejudice of the Crown Interdict should be pronounced as prayed for.'

It was not disputed that the Crown would have been entitled to seek an interdict against Mr Cavendish based on the lifelong duty of confidentiality owed by him to the Crown. The question which arises in this process is as to the right of the Crown to seek interdict against a third party who has obtained information from Mr Cavendish's book.

It appears that at earlier hearings of these proceedings, it had not been entirely clear what the Crown''s position was in relation to the contents of the book. In his opinion of 23 February 1988 the Lord Ordinary points out that it is not averred by the Lord Advocate that publication of any of the information in the book, or any information in the possession of Mr Cavendish, would directly endanger national security. Before this court junior counsel for the Lord Advocate repeated that the Lord Advocate had never suggested that the contents of the book were a danger to national security; what was being contended was that national security would be endangered if the duty of confidentiality owed by ex-employees of the intelligence services was breached. This contention was further developed by senior counsel for the Lord Advocate. As the argument became further crystallised, a distinction was drawn between the case where national security was in danger by the disclosure of the contents of a book and what senior counsel referred to as 'the non-contents detriment case.' According to him, the present case was a non-content detriment case in respect that it was not the information in the book but the fact of publication by a former member of the security service which constituted the threat to national security.

It is not clear to me whether this distinction was explained as fully to the Lord Ordinary as it was to this court, but the greater part of the Lord Ordinary's opinion is concerned with the publication of confidential information, and thus appears to be directed to a case based on disclosure of the contents of the book.

. . . It appears to me that the Lord Ordinary was treating the case as one where the objection was being taken to the disclosure of the contents of the book, and that he was not directing his attention to a non-contents detriment case at all. . .

So far as I am concerned, it is the confusion between a contents case and a non-contents case which has bedevilled this reclaiming motion. In view of the fact that senior counsel for the Lord Advocate stated quite clearly that his case was a non-contents detriment case, a great deal of what the Lord Ordinary states in his opinion regarding the publication of information appears to me to be irrelevant. Having regard to the way in which the case was ultimately presented by senior counsel for the Lord Advocate, the only real issue in the reclaiming motion is a short and simple one. However, out of deference to the arguments which were deployed at the hearing of the reclaiming motion, and the views expressed by the Lord Ordinary in his Opinion, I propose to express my opinion upon these issues even though my observations will be no more than *obiter dicta*. Since they are *obiter dicta*, however, it is unnecessary to deal with these matters at a great length or in the detailed way in which counsel dealt with them in their submissions.

The Lord Ordinary in his opinion dated 23 February 1988 relied strongly upon the decision of Scott J. in . . . the *Spycatcher* case. Mr Cameron for the Lord Advocate submitted that the *Spycatcher* case was a non-contents detriment case. Although that feature may have been present in the case, I am of opinion that the *Spycatcher* case was much more than a non-contents detriment case. Scott J. at the outset of his judgment stated: 'The Attorney-General desires to prevent or restrict not only publication of this book but also publication of any comment on or report of its contents.'

Subsequently, in the course of his judgment he comments at length upon the contents of *Spycatcher*. Accordingly it is plain that the *Spycatcher* case raised the issue of the disclosure of the contents of the book. The *Spycatcher* case was accordingly a different case from the case which the Lord Advocate is seeking to make in the present petition. In the present case, I am of opinion that the Lord Ordinary was not justified in relying as strongly as he did upon the judgments of Scott J. and the Court of Appeal in the *Spycatcher* case. That he did rely heavily upon the *Spycatcher* case is plain. . .

Although assistance can no doubt be obtained from the *Spycatcher* case, it is important to bear in mind that it was a case where it was suggested that national security was endangered by the disclosure of the contents of the book.

Scott J. describes the case which was sought to be made to him as follows:

'National security requires an efficient M.I.5 and unless permanent injunctions are granted M.I.5 and its efficiency will be damaged in the following ways: the morale of loyal members of the service will suffer; other members of the service may be tempted to breach duty by publishing memoirs; publishers of illegal memoirs will be encouraged; media pressure on other members of the service to reply to allegations in *Spycatcher* will mount; security services in other countries will lose confidence in M.I.5; and potential informers will lose confidence in M.I.5. In short, the permanent injunctions are sought not in order to preserve the secret character of information that ought to be kept secret but in order to promote the efficiency and reputation of M.I.5.'

It must however be kept in mind that Scott J. was delivering his judgment against the background that by the end of October 1987 over 700,000 copies of the book had been published and sold in the United States of America, and a large number of copies of the book had found their way into this country. One estimate was that about 10,000 copies of the book were entering the United Kingdom every week.

The Lord Ordinary, in dealing with the fresh application for interim interdict, does not appear to have adopted the approach which is normally adopted in dealing with applications of this kind. He himself appreciated that it would be logical to deal first with the question of whether there were grounds for concluding that the respondents were under any duty to the petitioner. However, instead of considering that matter, he proceeded to dispose of the case upon another ground. The Lord Ordinary's reasons for refusing interim interdict appear to be that in his view the book had been sufficiently distributed to make it probable that any interested power was already familiar with its contents, with the result that it was impossible to see that there was any reasonable risk of further damage accruing which would be prevented by a grant if interim interdict.

In my opinion, however, the Lord Ordinary ought to have approached the matter in accordance with what is recognised to be the practice in the Scottish courts. . . [In] Scotland the proper approach would have been for the Lord Ordinary to consider whether the petitioners had made out a *prima facie* case; the issue would be whether there was a case to argue and a case to answer. If there was, then the next stage would be to consider the balance of convenience.

Before the Lord Ordinary the argument appeared to be that the petitioner's case depended upon a duty of confidence. The Lord Ordinary recognised that the Lord Advocate was founding upon considerations of public policy, but the Lord Ordinary concluded that: 'public policy considerations have become involved only so as to restrict the Crown's ability to enforce confidentiality when other public interests are involved.'

Before this court, however, counsel for the Lord Advocate put public policy at the forefront of his submissions. Counsel contended that considerations of public policy entitled the Lord Advocate to the remedy which he was seeking. They submitted that where as here a lifelong duty of confidentiality was owed to the Crown by Mr Cavendish, it was public policy which restricts anyone who aided or abetted Mr Cavendish and also any third party who received information from him in the knowledge that he was under such a lifelong obligation of confidentiality. No such argument appears to have been put forward in the *Spycatcher* case. . .

In my opinion, if the Lord Advocate had been in a position to say that the disclosure of information by the respondents would endanger national security, the court would, because of the considerations of public policy, have the power to stop such disclosure of publication. Indeed, I understood the respondents all to accept that the court would not be powerless to act in such an extreme situation. However, it is one thing to recognise a power in the court because of public policy to restrict the disclosure of the contents of a book; it is quite another thing to suggest that the court has power on the grounds of public policy to stop the mere publication of a book where it is accepted that the contents of that book present no danger to national security. The authorities to which we were referred on the matter of public policy were all English authorities, and there is no hint in them of considerations of public policy justifying the court in granting a remedy for what has been described in the present proceedings as a non-contents detriment case. So far as Scotland is concerned, I am not persuaded that public policy would entitle the court in Scotland to grant a remedy in such a non-contents detriment case. That being so, I need not say any more on the public policy aspect of the case.

Before the Lord Ordinary, the Lord Advocate's case was treated as being based upon breach of confidence. . . The question which arose was whether under Scots law a person coming into possession of confidential information, knowing it to be confidential, became subject to an obligation arising from conscience or good faith and not referable to contract or property. The Lord Ordinary observed that the conceptual basis of the English right did not fit easily into the framework of Scots law. . .

For my part I am of opinion that under the law of Scotland the person to whom the duty of confidence was owed would have a right to protect confidentiality against third parties who had received the information with the knowledge that it had originally been communicated in confidence. Although the law of confidence in relation to third parties is not fully developed, I am of opinion that there are sufficient dicta in Scottish cases to support the conclusion at which I have arrived.

A number of the reported cases were decided upon the view that a right of property or a right under contract was involved, but in my opinion, the dicta are wide enough to cover a situation where no right of property or contract is involved. The courts in Scotland administer an equitable as well as a common law jurisdiction. . .

In my opinion, there is ample justification for the conclusion that in this respect the laws of England and Scotland are to the same effect. Indeed I entirely agree with Lord McLaren when he observed that the laws on this subject could not well be different. Accordingly in so far as the Lord Ordinary upon this issue entertained some doubts, I find that I do not share his doubts.

As I have already observed, the Lord Ordinary arrived at his conclusion upon this case very largely upon the view that a third party recipient of confidential information is under no obligation to refrain from publishing unless the information has not already been published. On more than one occasion the Lord Ordinary appears to express the view that information ceases to be confidential once it has been published or become known. With these observations of the Lord Ordinary I do not agree. Confidential does not merely mean secret. In my opinion in this branch of the law the expression 'confidential' relates to information which is the subject of an obligation of confidence. That obligation of confidence does not come to an end merely because the information has become known to a third party. In other words, if information is disclosed in breach of confidence, that does not bring to an end the obligation of confidence. Were that not so, no action based on breach of confidence would ever lie. With all respect to the Lord Ordinary, I am of opinion that he has arrived at his erroneous view by attaching too much weight to the decision in the *Spycatcher* case. In the judgments of Scott J. and the Court of Appeal, it is clear that permanent injunction was refused largely because the book and its contents had been disseminated on a worldwide scale. Scott J. concluded that there was no 'obligation of conscience' on third parties, since the situation now was that virtually anyone who wanted a copy of the book could obtain it. Similar views were expressed by all the judges in the Court of Appeal. . .

I detect in the Lord Ordinary's opinion a failure to appreciate that whether publication has destroyed all secrecy and the obligation of confidence itself depends upon the extent of the publication. At no stage in his opinion does the Lord Ordinary deal adequately with the extent or degree of publication.

That it is a question of degree was recognised by Sir John Donaldson M.R. in the Court of Appeal. . .

There is all the difference in the world between a case such as *Spycatcher,* where about a million copies of the book had been published and distributed, and the present case where such publication as there had been was clearly limited. There is no question in the present case of the book having become generally available to the public. It has been disclosed only to a limited part of that public. According to the averment added by way of amendment, only 279 of the 500 copies were distributed. Although nothing has been said as to who received these 279 copies, on any view it is a limited part of the public only who have access to the book. Accordingly, if this had been a 'contents case,' I would have regarded the case as being more similar to the *Spycatcher* case at the stage of the interlocutory injunction than to the *Spycatcher* case at the stage of the application for permanent injunction. In these circumstances, if it had been a contents case, a strong case for interim interdict might have been made on the basis of preserving the *status quo*...

Two other matters should be mentioned. In both his opinions the Lord Ordinary refers to 'freedom of the press.' Before us, however, counsel for the respondents accepted that the press as such did not have any higher freedom than the freedom of speech which is generally enjoyed in this country. . .

In my opinion it is preferable to refer to freedom of speech rather than freedom of the press because referring to freedom of the press may suggest that the press have greater rights than the remainder of the general public enjoy in this country.

The second point is this. The Lord Ordinary refers in his opinion on many occasions to 'the balancing exercise' which the court requires to carry out. In particular he refers to the approach described by Lord Widgery C.J. in *Attorney-General* v. *Jonathan Cape Ltd.* [1976] Q.B. 752. In my opinion, however, in Scotland at the stage of interim interdict the balancing exercise to which the Lord Ordinary refers would only require to be carried out once it had been determined that the petitioners had made out a *prima facie* case and when regard was being had to the balance of convenience. For reasons which I shall explain presently, I have come to the conclusion that it is unnecessary in the present case to carry out a balancing exercise at all.

Having set forth these comments upon the opinion of the Lord Ordinary, I now turn to consider the merits of this reclaiming motion. Although I have been critical of the Lord Ordinary's approach in this case, it is only fair to say that he no doubt approached the matter in the light of the representations made to him by counsel. Whether or not the argument for the Lord Advocate before this court was different to the argument presented in the court below, it certainly appears that in this court the emphasis had changed. What was most important, however, was that counsel for the Lord Advocate made it absolutely clear that the case was being presented as a non-contents detriment case. It is as such that I now turn to consider the case for the Crown.

I share with counsel for the respondents some difficulty in understanding how this case can properly be treated as a non-contents case. . . [It] appears that the Crown are now agreeable to the publication of approximately two-thirds of the book, but that they are seeking to prohibit the publication of the remaining one-third. That would also suggest to me that the case was a contents case. If the argument were that the fact of publication would be harmful to national security, then logically one would expect the Crown to be seeking to prevent publication of the whole book. The fact that the Crown are now agreeable to the publication of about two-thirds of the book really makes their contention that this is a non-contents case barely tenable. Mr Cameron however was quite adamant that the Crown's position was that this was a non-contents case.

Treating this as a case based on breach of confidence, it is necessary to examine the Lord Advocate's averments to see whether he has set forth a *prima facie* case. In this connection I agree with the Lord Ordinary that the Lord Advocate like any other petitioner must set forth a case in his pleadings which is at least *prima facie* relevant. I also agree that there is no onus on the respondents to justify their publishing the contents of the book. The basis of the Lord Advocate's case is set out in statement 7 of the petition. It is there stated:

'Disclosure or publication of said material and information is prejudicial to the interests of the Crown. It is prejudicial to national security. It is prejudicial to said interests in the following respects: (a) the intelligence and security services of friendly foreign countries with which the British security and intelligence services are in liaison would be likely to lose confidence in their ability to protect classified information; (b) the British security and intelligence service depend upon the confidence and co-operation of other organisations and persons which confidence would be likely to suffer serious damage should Mr Cavendish reveal information of the nature described above; (c) there would be a risk that other persons who are or have been employed in the British security and intelligence services who have had access to similar information might seek to publish it; (d) there would be likely to be a serious adverse effect in the future on the morale and discipline of members of the British security and intelligence services if the disclosure of said information were allowed in breach of said duty of confidentiality; (e) in the absence of interdict pressure would be likely to be exerted by the media on other members or ex-members of the British security and intelligence services to give their views on matters referred to by Mr Cavendish; (f) detriment would be likely to flow from the publication of information about the methodology and personnel and organisation of the British security and intelligence services.'

Similar points were put forward in the *Spycatcher* case, but these required to be considered in the context of a case where there had been such a degree of publication that the information had ceased to be confidential.

In the present case the Lord Ordinary concluded that the considerations referred to in heads (a) to (e) did not appear to be relevant. He also appears to have concluded that head (f) was not supported by relevant averments. Although for different reasons from those which commended themselves to the Lord Ordinary, I am of opinion that the Lord Ordinary arrived at the correct conclusion on this critical issue. Bearing in mind that this is avowedly a non-contents case, I am of opinion that the Lord Advocate has failed to make out a *prima facie* case. Heads (a) to (f) might have been relevant if this had been a contents case. This is because heads (a) to (f) are all expressed as being referable to information, *i.e.* the contents of the book. But since this is a non-contents case, they are irrelevant. This can be seen clearly if each of the heads is examined separately.

So far as (a) is concerned it could not be contended that foreign security services would be likely to lose confidence in the ability of the British security and intelligence services to protect classified information unless it were being asserted that the book contained classified information. It is nowhere averred that there is classified information in the book, and in the context of a non-contents case this could not arise. So far as (b) is concerned the same comment can be made. The same is true of (c), since 'similar information' must be a reference back to classified information. The same is true of (d). So far as (e) is concerned what is said to be apprehended is that the media would exert pressure upon members or ex-members of the British security and intelligence services to give their views 'on matters referred to by Mr Cavendish.' This must be a reference to what is in the book, and cannot be material to a non-contents case.

What appears to lie behind (a) to (e) is that if Mr Cavendish is allowed to publish his memoirs there will be a loss of confidence in the British security and intelligence service and a risk of further disclosures. One can readily understand that once it is known that there has been disclosure by Mr Cavendish, these results will ensue. The trouble is that it is now known widely that Mr Cavendish has made these disclosures and accordingly the anticipated results must have occurred. That being so, there is no way in which the loss of confidence referred to and the reduction in morale can be averted by an order of the court. I would stress that in this context it is not the degree of publication which is important but the fact that there has been publication at all. As junior counsel for the first respondents put it: 'Once the leak occurs, the damage is done.' As soon as it becomes known that there has been disclosure or publication on the part of Mr Cavendish, the damaging consequences referred to in paragraphs (a) to (e) are inevitable. Paragraphs (a) to (e) might well have been convincing considerations if an interdict were being sought before any publication or disclosure by Mr Cavendish had taken place. However, since such publication and disclosure have taken place, granting interdict now would indeed be closing the proverbial stable door after the horse had bolted. I would only add, under reference to (c) and (d), that I doubt in any event whether the court would be justified in granting interdict if the purpose of the interdict was not to stop a wrong but was to deter others and to maintain morale. On this aspect I respectfully agree with what Lord Oliver said in the *Spycatcher* case ([1987] 1 W.L.R. at p. 1318).

So far as (f) is concerned it appears to me that this head would only be relevant in the context of a contents case. It clearly envisages publication of the contents of the book which might then enable the reader to learn something about the methodology, personnel and organisation of the British Security and Intelligence Services. But we know nothing about the contents of the book, and there is no suggestion that it contains information on these matters. In the context of a non-contents detriment case, I am of opinion that head (f) can have no proper relevance, and Mr Cameron appeared ultimately to recognise this.

It follows that in my opinion the Lord Ordinary was well-founded in declining to grant interim interdict in this case. On the issue of interim interdict one further matter should be mentioned. In *Toynar Ltd.* the court observed:

'Where matters of law are raised, it is neither necessary nor desirable for any concluded decision to be made upon them at the stage of considering the making of an interim order.'

In the present case however it was accepted by the Crown that at the stage of seeking permanent interdict they would be in no better position than they were now. The Crown did not suggest in this case that the position might be materially altered by any further adjustment of the pleadings, and accordingly, the Lord Ordinary was fully entitled to reach the conclusion that the particular heads upon which the Crown relied were indeed irrelevant. Likewise this court is entitled to arrive at the same conclusion. I recognise that a temporary injunction is in existence in England restraining disclosure and publication of material or information obtained by Mr Cavendish concerning the British security and intelligence services. It may be unfortunate for the Crown if they cannot obtain an interim interdict in similar terms in Scotland, but the Court in Scotland cannot grant an interim interdict when the Lord Advocate as petitioner has failed to make out a *prima facie* case on the pleadings.

I would only refer to two further matters. Towards the end of his opinion the Lord Ordinary dealt with the form of the interdict sought and the question of whether the interdict was worded too widely. I find myself in complete agreement with what the Lord Ordinary has said upon these two matters.

In *Attorney-General* v. *Newspaper Publishing plc* [1987] 3 All E.R. 276, Balcombe L.J. recognised that practical problems would arise if the injunction were not made binding on the world at large. Mr Cameron submitted that this was a problem which had arisen as a result of advances in modern technology. He submitted that if an order were to be made it should be made against the respondents 'or any person having notice of said interlocutor.' The Lord Ordinary regarded

Pattison v. *Fitzgerald* (1823) 2 S. 536 as authority for the proposition that such an order would be incompetent. In my opinion the Lord Ordinary was well-founded in reaching that conclusion. In my opinion, in Scots law there is no justification for the courts pronouncing an order of interdict against named respondents 'or any person having notice of said interlocutor.' I fully appreciate that if interim interdict were to be granted without the addition of these words, the position of the petitioner might be difficult in relation to persons other than the respondents who might then seek to disclose or publish the material in question. Whether or not the law of contempt would be adequate to deal with that situation is not a matter upon which it is necessary for me to express any concluded opinion. It is clear however that to pronounce an interim interdict against named respondents 'or any person having notice of said interlocutor' would conflict with the recognised practice and procedure in Scotland in relation to caveats. In my opinion the recognised practice and procedure in relation to caveats is a further reason for concluding that an interdict against 'any person having notice of said interlocutors' is not a form of interdict which the court in Scotland would be justified in pronouncing.

In the penultimate paragraph of his opinion the Lord Ordinary deals with the submission that the wording of the interdict was too wide in that it would prohibit the respondents from disclosing information in the possession of Mr Cavendish whether of not they had received that information from him. I agree with the Lord Ordinary that there is force in that objection and that if interim interdict were to be granted a limitation in the terms which the Lord Ordinary suggested would be required to be expressed in the order of the court.

In all the circumstances I would move your Lordships to refuse the reclaiming motion and to adhere to the interlocutor of the Lord Ordinary of 23 February 1988."

Lords Dunpark and McDonald delivered concurring opinions.

3. PUBLICATION AND THE CRIMINAL LAW

20. The Official Secrets Act 1911

"Wrongful communication etc. of information
2.—(1) If any person having in his possession or control any secret official code word, or pass word, or any sketch, plan, model, article, note, document, or information which relates to or is used in a prohibited place or anything in such a place or which has been made or obtained in contravention of this Act, or which has been entrusted in confidence to him by any person holding office under Her Majesty or which he has obtained or to which he has had access owing to his position as a person who holds or has held office under Her Majesty, or as a person who holds or has held a contract made on behalf of Her Majesty or as a person who is or has been employed under a person who holds or has held such an office or contract—

(*a*) communicates the code word, pass word, sketch, plan, model, note, document, or information to any person, other than a person to whom he is authorised to communicate it, or a person to whom it is in the interest of the State his duty to communicate it; or

(*aa*) uses the information in his possession for the benefit of any foreign Power or in any other manner prejudicial to the safety or interests of the State;

(*b*) retains the sketch, plan, model, article, note, or document in his possession or control when he has no right to retain it or when it is contrary to his duty to retain it, or fails to comply with all directions issued by lawful authority with regard to the return or disposal thereof; or

(*c*) fails to take reasonable care of, or so conducts himself as to endanger the safety of the sketch, plan, model, article, note, document, secret official code or pass word or information;

that person shall be guilty of a misdemeanour.

(1A) If any person having in his possession or control any sketch, plan, model, article, note, document, or information which relates to munitions of war, communicates it directly or indirectly to any foreign Power, or in any other manner prejudicial to the safety or interests of the State, that person shall be guilty of a misdemeanour.

(2) If any person receives any secret official code word, or pass word, or sketch, plan, model, article, note, document or information, knowing or having reasonable ground to believe, at the time when he receives it, that the code-word, pass-word, sketch, plan, model, article, note, document or information is communicated to him in contravention of this Act, he shall be guilty of a misdemeanour, unless he proves that the communication to him of the code word, pass word, sketch, plan, model, article, note, document, or information was contrary to his desire."

This section has been widely criticised. The main offence which it creates is the unauthorised communication of information (including documents) by a Crown servant. As a Departmental Committee (Franks, 1972) pointed out:

"The leading characteristic of this offence is its catch-all quality. It catches all official documents and information. It makes no distinctions of kind, and no distinctions of degree. All information which a Crown servant learns in the course of his duty is 'official' for the purposes of section 2, whatever its nature, whatever its importance, whatever its original source. A blanket is thrown over everything; nothing escapes. The section catches all Crown servants as well as official information. Again, it makes no distinctions according to the nature or importance of a Crown servant's duties. All are covered. Every Minister of the Crown, every civil servant, every member of the Armed Forces, every police officer, performs his duties subject to section 2."

The committee continued:

"Nevertheless governments regularly reveal a great deal of official information. These disclosures do not contravene section 2. A Crown servant who discloses official information commits an offence under the section only if the information is disclosed to someone 'other than a person to whom he is authorised to communicate it, or a person to whom it is in the interest of the State his duty to communicate it.' The Act does not explain the meaning of the quoted words. We found that they were commonly supposed, by persons outside the Government, to imply a fairly formal process of express authorisation. Actual practice within the Government rests heavily on a doctrine of implied authorisation, flowing from the nature of each Crown servant's job. In the words of the Home Office, 'the communication of official information is proper if such communication can be fairly regarded as part of the job of the officer concerned.' Ministers are, in effect, self-authorising. They decide for themselves what to reveal. Senior civil servants exercise a considerable degree of personal judgment in deciding what disclosures of official information they may properly make, and to whom. More junior civil servants, and those whose duties do not involve contact with members of the public, may have a very limited discretion, or none at all."

Section 2 is important because it restricts the circulation of information, by making it an offence to disclose and receive unauthorised information. Franks (1972) pointed out, however, that:

"Prosecutions have been few. Recently they have averaged about one a year. From 1945 to 1971 twenty-three prosecutions were brought, involving thirty-four defendants, of whom twenty-seven were convicted and six acquitted; in one case the charge was withdrawn. Nearly two-thirds of the defendants were Crown servants or former Crown servants, including a number of police and prison officers. Only two case since the war have involved professional journalists. Well over one-third of the twenty-three cases involved information relating to matters of defence, national security or intelligence. One-third concerned police or prison information. In three cases the information related to international affairs."

The effect of the section is not, however, to be judged by the number of unauthorised disclosures actually resulting in prosecution. A number of Government witnesses told the Franks Committee that "section 2 had a widespread deterrent effect in preventing improper disclosures by Crown servants." For their part, the news media said that "the section frequently deterred or prevented Crown servants from disclosing information of public interest which, in their view, should have been disclosed." The committee concluded that section 2 "is rarely activated in the courtroom, but is seen by many as having a pervasive influence on the work and the behaviour of hundreds of thousands of people." Although there have been many prosecutions under section 2, very few of the cases have been reported, despite the obscure drafting and difficulties in interpretation which the section raises.

(i) *R*. v. *Crisp* (1919) 83 J.P. 121. A civil servant passed on information containing particulars of contracts between the War Office and government contractors. Avery J. held that section 2 made it unlawful to pass on any information which an employee obtained by virtue of his employment under the Crown. It is not necessary for the purpose of securing a conviction that the information is secret.

(ii) *Lewis* v. *Cattle* [1938] 2 K.B. 454. A police force sent a circular to a number of other forces saying that a warrant had been issued for the arrest of a named individual. The *Daily Dispatch* published an article which was an almost verbatim account of the circular. The accused was a journalist who was charged under section 6 of the Official Secrets Act 1920 with failing to give to the respondent (a senior police officer) information on demand relating to an offence or suspected offence under the 1911 Act. The question which arose for decision was whether police officers in England and Wales hold office under Her Majesty for the purposes of section 2. It was held that they did: they are "required to take an oath of office and [their] primary duty is to preserve the King's peace" (p. 457).

(iii) *R. v. Fell* [1963] Crim.L.R. 207. The accused held a senior position at the Central Office of Information. Over a period of years she lent confidential information to an employee of a foreign embassy, explaining that her motive in so doing was to influence him in favour of British policies. She claimed that she had no intention of doing anything to prejudice the safety of the State. The Court of Criminal Appeal held that the offence is absolute and is committed whatever the document contains, whatever the motive, and whether or not the information is prejudicial to the State.

(iv) *Loat v. James* [1986] Crim.L.R. 744. The defendant was employed under a contract of employment with a county council. As such, he worked exclusively for the police, as a computer operator at a police station, under the supervision of the unit inspector (a police officer). He gave information to a burglar alarm company about roads and locations where burglaries had recently occurred, in return for money. He was charged on the grounds that (a) contrary to section 7 of the Official Secrets Act 1920 he did an act preparatory to the communication of information he had obtained as a person employed under a person who held office under Her Majesty to a person to whom he was not authorised to communicate that information; and (b) contrary to section 2(1) of the Official Secrets Act 1911 he communicated such information to such an unauthorised person. He was convicted by the magistrates and, on appeal, the Crown Court upheld his conviction. On further appeal, the Divisional Court upheld his conviction. The question was whether the appellant was "a person who was employed under" the unit inspector. The court rejected his argument that "employed under" meant "employed by" and accepted the prosecution submission that "employed" meant "worked" and "under" included instruction and control. In this case the accused worked under the instruction and control of the unit inspector (a police officer), from whom the county council expected him to take instruction as to the performance of his duties.

(v) Many of the important prosecutions under section 2 were never reported in the law reports. Details of some of these are to be found, however, in Aitken (1971) and Nicol (1979). Perhaps the most controversial prosecution in recent years is that involving Mr Clive Ponting (on which see further Ponting (1985)).

21. R. v. Ponting
[1985] Crim.L.R. 318

"The defendant was charged with an offence under section 2(1) of the Official Secrets Act 1911. On July 16, 1984 he sent to Mr Tam Dalyell, duly elected Member of Parliament for Linlithgow, two Ministry of Defence documents relating to Parliamentary inquiries about the sinking of the Argentine vessel, the *General Belgrano*, during the Falklands conflict. The first of these documents was a draft reply written by the defendant, in his capacity as head of the relevant Ministry of Defence department, to questions asked by Mr Dalyell to the Secretary of State which was never in fact sent by the Minister. The second was a minute by another Ministry of Defence department indicating that certain answers should be given to questions put by the Parliamentary Select Committee on Foreign Affairs concerning changes in the Rules of Engagement during the Falklands conflict. The first document was unclassified and the second was marked confidential.

It was conceded by the defence that the defendant had communicated this information to Mr Dalyell, that he had this information in his possession by virtue of his position as a civil servant, and that he had not been authorised to give this information to Mr Dalyell. The only live issue, therefore, was whether Mr Dalyell was a person to whom it was in the interest of the State the defendant's duty to communicate the information. During argument on the law by counsel, the judge commented that he was minded to direct the jury to convict, but he did not do so following submissions from the defence based on *D.P.P.* v. *Stonehouse* [1977] 3 W.L.R. 143 and a request from the prosecution that this should not be done.

Held (by McCowan J.): That this section of the Official Secrets Act is primarily concerned with the preservation of information which has been obtained by the communicator by virtue of his position as a servant of Her Majesty and that whether or not the document touched on national security was irrelevant. The judge also held that on a proper construction of section 2, there was no requirement of *mens rea* for this section further than an intention to commit the *actus reus*. The prosecution did not have to show that the defendant did not reasonably and honestly believe that the communication was in the interest of the State. He relied upon the judgement of Lord Parker C.J. in *R.* v. *Fell* [1983] Crim.L.R. 207 and upon Mars Jones J. in *R.* v. *Berry* and considered the speeches of the House of Lords in *Sweet* v. *Parsley* [1970] A.C. 132. The judge further held that the word duty in section 2(1) of the Official Secrets Act referred to an official duty imposed upon the communicator by virtue of his position as the duty arises out of the accused's office as a Crown servant. It must, therefore, indicate an official duty rather than a moral, contractual or civic duty. As to the meaning of the words 'in the interest of the State,' the learned judge preferred the views expressed in the speeches of Lord Devlin and Lord Pearce in *Chandler* v. *D.P.P.* [1964] A.C. 763, that the interests of the State meant what was in the interests of the State according to its recognised organs of government and the policies as expounded by the particular Government of the day. It was not, he held, for the jury to decide what the Government's policy should have been nor was it for them to enter into a political debate. In this case it was not in dispute that the policy of the Government was not to give the information which Mr Ponting communicated.

The defence had argued for a wider meaning of 'in the interest of the State,' namely in the interests of the country or the realm or in the national interest, and had been relied upon the speeches of Lord Reid and Lord Hodgson in *Chandler's* case and upon Lord Diplock's recent criticism of Lord Devlin's speech in *Chandler* (see *Council of Civil Service Unions* v. *Minister for the Civil Service* [1984] 3 W.L.R. 1174, 1193). The defence further argued that even if the learned judge directed the jury in accordance with the speeches of Lord Devlin and Lord Pearce, the policies of the government of the day had to be regarded as being subject to established constitutional conventions and rules one of which was that Ministers should always tell the truth to Parliament as was far as possible without harming national security. The defendant was acquitted."

But if *Ponting* was controversial, so too was the use of the Official Secrets Act 1911, s. 2 (and related measures) in the "Zircon" affair.

(vi) The "Zircon" affair. As part of a series of programmes on government secrecy, BBC Scotland made a programme in which it revealed the existence of "Zircon," a hitherto-unknown "spy-satellite," the funds for the construction of which had allegedly been taken from the Defence vote in breach of an undertaking by the government to reveal expenditure over a certain limit on particular projects to the House of Commons. Duncan Campbell, the journalist who researched the programme, claimed that he had access only to public information intelligently collated. However, a breach of section 2 of the Official Secrets Act 1911 was suspected and Special Branch obtained successive search warrants (the first two were adjudged defective: see Chap. 3 above) to seize evidence from the BBC studios. Copies of the film and much other BBC property was seized. A Parliamentary storm erupted. The Secretary of State for Scotland denied any Government involvement in the decision to make the search (109 H.C. Debs 691) and the matter was raised in Prime Minister's question time (110 H.C. Debs 806). Public showings of a copy of the film were arranged and well-attended, but when notice was given of intention to show the film in a House of Commons committee room, the Speaker ordered that it should not be shown, a ruling which led to a Report by the House of Commons Committee of Privileges (H.C. 365 (1986-87) and see Bradley (1987). To date no decision has been taken on whether to prosecute and the seized material is retained pending a decision.

22. Report of the Departmental Committee on Section 2 of the Official Secrets Act 1911
(Chairman: Lord Franks)
Cmnd. 5104 (1972)

"The need for change
88. The first part of our terms of reference was to review the operation of section 2. Part I of this Report has described what we found as a result of this review. We

found section 2 a mess. Its scope is enormously wide. Any law which impinges on the freedom of information in a democracy should be much more tightly drawn. A catch-all provision is saved from absurdity in operation only by the sparing exercise of the Attorney-General's discretion to prosecute. Yet the very width of this discretion, and the inevitably selective way in which it is exercised, give rise to considerable unease. The drafting and interpretation of the section are obscure. People are not sure what it means, or how it operates in practice, or what kinds of action involve real risk of prosecution under it.

89. A quite different issue arises from the taint of espionage which surrounds section 2. There is a widely held view that the Official Secrets Acts should be concerned only with spies and traitors. For the most part these Acts deal with espionage, the protection of defence establishments and matters of that kind. Section 2 stands out as a conspicuous exception. It deals with information of all kinds, and it catches people who have no thought of harming their country. Many consider it wrong that such a provision should appear side by side with the rest of the Official Secrets Acts.

90. These factors convinced us that change was essential, and we considered afresh what the law on this subject should be in the circumstances of the 1970s. An analysis of the existing situation and of the evidence shows that there are three broad possibilities. One is to retain a catch-all section. If this were done, a new section could be drafted in much clearer terms, removing some unsatisfactory features of the present section. The second possibility is simply to remove section 2, without replacement. The third is to repeal section 2 and to replace it by new provisions narrower in scope. The first major question facing us, once we had completed our review of the present situation and our examination of the evidence, was which of these three possibilities to recommend.

The case for retaining a catch-all

91. The main feature of section 2 is its catch-all quality. No government Department claimed in its evidence, however, that all the various kinds of official information with which it was concerned required the protection of . . . criminal sanctions. Indeed, it is not in dispute that a great deal of official information does not require such protection. This fact alone might be thought sufficient to undermine the case for a catch-all. The criminal law on this subject ought, if at all possible, to be confined to those kinds of official information for which the protection of criminal sanctions is really required. Sir Peter Rawlinson, the Attorney General, told us that his personal reaction to section 2, as a lawyer, was one of gross distaste, because it involved the criminal law in matters which the criminal law should not be involved in. This is a widely held viewpoint. Sir Peter went on to say that nevertheless, because of the great difficulties in the way of identifying and defining with certainty those kinds of official information which should be covered, and because the controls over prosecutions under section 2 exercised by Attorneys General ensured that in practice the section operated in a reasonable way, he thought it preferable on balance to retain a catch-all section, together with the Attorney's control over prosecutions, as the lesser of two evils.

92. Two main points were put to us by those who wished to rebut the *prima facie*

case for narrowing down section 2. The first argument is that the existence on the statute book of a provision of the criminal law which admittedly goes much wider than is strictly required should not be considered a serious evil in itself, without any regard to how this provision operates in practice. The second argument is that the case for reform depends upon the questionable assumption that it is possible to devise a satisfactory alternative, which would identify and define in a workable manner the kinds of official information requiring protection and would be free of fresh drawbacks. Those who take this view then point out, in positive support of the case for a catch-all, that section 2 has the merit of covering all the official information requiring the protection of the criminal law. This ensures that the section achieves its protective purpose. Some of the criticisms of the section, it is suggested, are based upon misunderstandings and others are exaggerated. The control exercised by the Attorney General means that the section operates quite satisfactorily in practice. It does not bear with undue harshness either upon Crown servants or upon others. Putting these negative and positive factors together, it is then argued that the balance of advantage may lie with the retention of a catch-all.

93. Arguments of this kind were put forward by several eminent witnesses as well as by a number of Government Departments. Mr James Callaghan summarised his viewpoint as 'different does not necessarily mean better', though he thought it worth consideration whether, while retaining section 2 in its present form, there should be a new defence that publication was in the public interest. Lord Brooke of Cumnor stressed the difficulties of devising a satisfactory alternative. He recalled that the Homicide Act 1957, which sought to find a half-way house between the retention and the abolition of capital punishment, had proved unsatisfactory and anomalous in practice,. He thought it likely that similar problems would arise in any attempt to find a half-way house in the law in official secrecy. Lord Parker thought the difficulties surrounding any satisfactory revision of the law so great that the preferred the *status quo,* with the possibility of some reinforcement of the arrangements for controlling prosecutions.

94. We gave all these arguments careful attention. We came to the conclusion, however, that the unsatisfactory features of the present situation, which we have set out in Part I of this Report, presented an overwhelming case for change. We did not find the formulation of alternative provisions impracticable.

The case for and against the removal of criminal sanctions
95. Those who advocate the removal of criminal sanctions agree that there is some official information which the Government should protect, and that the existence of criminal sanctions adds to the effectiveness of the protection. They put forward two main arguments for holding that section 2 should nevertheless be repealed without replacement. First, they point to a variety of defects in section 2, which we have described in Part I of this Report. We agree with the view that the only satisfactory treatment for a law suffering from many defects is to sweep it away entirely. This still leaves open the question whether or not section 2 should be replaced by new, narrower provisions free of such defects.

96. The second argument for removing criminal sanctions is of a more fundamental nature. It is that the use of the criminal law to restrict the publication

of matters of public interest is undesirable in principle, smacking of censorship, and something to be kept to an absolute minimum. According to this viewpoint, the use of criminal law to deal with spies and traitors, as in section 1, is legitimate. The use of a voluntary system of guidance to editors on matters affecting the defence of the nation, as in the 'D' Notice system, is legitimate. But these measures are thought to cover all that is of real importance to the nation. Over the rest of the field, it is suggested, the Government may properly protect by other means what it wishes to protect, but should not use the criminal law to deal with failures in its protective measures. Those expressing such views do not generally believe that the repeal of section 2 would in practice result in any significant increased risk of disclosures seriously damaging to the nation as a whole. The news media, they say, have a public function as well as the Government and would act responsibly by refraining from any seriously damaging disclosures of official information.

97. It seemed to us that this second argument rested upon a number of premises of doubtful validity and we discussed it closely with the representatives of organisations holding such views who came to see us. Reliance on voluntary restraint would be unsatisfactory for several reasons. There is a danger of confusing two different meanings of the word 'responsibility'—the duty to perform a particular function, and acting with common sense and restraint. The Government and the news media should both act responsibly, in this second sense, but their duties are distinct. The constitutional responsibilities of the Government and Parliament for protecting the nation cannot be abdicated on the basis that a failure to exercise them will be made good by the responsible behaviour of others. The same degree of responsible behaviour is not, in any event, shown by all those who may publish or communicate official information. Restraint in publication varies from one kind of publication to another. Any system which covered only one class of recipients of unauthorised disclosures—the news media—would be seriously incomplete. An effective system of protection must cover damaging disclosures to whomever they are made.

98. Most advocates of the removal of criminal sanctions, however, place their main reliance on the proposition that section 1 adequately covers all matters of importance to national security. We have described in Chapter 2 the effect of section 1 and its limitations. A conviction under section 1 requires proof that the defendant acted with a particular kind of bad intention, *i.e.* that he had a purpose prejudicial to the safety or interests of the State. Damage to the nation, however, is not caused by bad intentions alone. It is caused when certain kinds of official information get into the wrong hands. It makes no difference whether the information reached those hands as a result of espionage or of leakage. The damage to the nation is the same in either case. The intention of the person communicating the information is irrelevant, and in any case may be difficult to prove. It follows that, whether one takes a broad or a narrow view of the kinds of official information requiring the protection of the criminal law, section 1 does not provide full protection. Effective protection requires that the law should cover leakage of information, as well as espionage.

99. Some of those with whom we raised this point in discussion accepted that they might not have fully appreciated the limitations of section 1. They agreed that

it would be consistent with the grounds on which they advocated the removal of criminal sanctions if section 2 were replaced by limited new provisions covering leakage of information important to national security. A few witnesses maintained their view that section 1 was sufficient by itself. They argued that an intention to harm the nation was a proper criterion for the use of criminal sanctions to protect official information. If damage was caused by a person who did not intend it, then they thought it better that the country should suffer the consequences, however serious, rather than that those responsible for such leaks should be liable to punishment under the criminal law.

Replacement as the answer

100. Many witnesses advocated the replacement of section 2 by narrower provisions. The weight of the evidence points strongly in that direction. Our review of the present situation, the outcome of which is described in Part I of this Report, points with equal strength in that direction. Most of those who advocate the retention of a catch-all provision do so only because they see great difficulty in the way of formulating satisfactory narrower provisions. A number of those advocating the removal of section 2 without replacement accept that important matters of national security should be effectively protected by the criminal law. No convincing argument was put to us for the proposition that section 1 alone provides such protection. We have discussed in Chapter 1 the tension between openness and secrecy. A catch-all provision goes too far towards the protection of secrecy. Repeal of section 2 without replacement would go too far in reducing the protection of necessary secrecy. A proper balance between openness and secrecy requires a reformed law, in place of the present section. *Our first major proposal is that section 2 should be repealed, and replaced by narrower and more specific provisions."*

The Franks Committee proposed that section 2 should be replaced by a new statute, called the Official Information Act, which would apply only to official information which:

"a. is classified information relating to defence or internal security, or to foreign relations, or to the currency or to the reserves, the unauthorised disclosure of which would cause serious injury to the interests of the nation; *or*
b. is likely to assist criminal activities or to impede law enforcement; *or*
c. is a Cabinet document; *or*
d. has been entrusted to the Government by a private individual or concern."

Having identified the area of operation of any such Act, the Committee then proposed that it should be an offence under the Act:

"a. for a Crown servant to communicate information to which the Act applies, contrary to his official duty;
b. for a Government contractor or a person entrusted with official information in confidence to communicate information of one of the kinds [mentioned above], otherwise than for the purposes of the contract or for which it was entrusted;

c.   for any person to communicate information of one of the kinds [mentioned above], which he knows, or has reasonable ground to believe, has reached him as the result of a contravention of the Official Information Act;

d.   to communicate or use official information of any kind for purposes of private gain."

In so far as the prosecution of Crown servants is concerned, the Act would provide:

"a.   The prosecution should have to prove that the Crown servant had disclosed information to which the Official Information Act applies, contrary to his official duty.

b.   The Crown servant should have the defence that he believed, and had reasonable ground to believe, that he was not acting contrary to his official duty.

c.   The Crown servant should also have the defence that—

i.   in the case of classified information relating to defence or internal security, or foreign relations, or the currency or the reserves, he did not know, and had no reason to believe, that it was classified;

ii.   in the case of an offence of disclosing a Cabined document, or information covered by our proposals on the maintenance of law and order and the confidences of the citizen, he did not know, and had no reason to believe, that it was such a document, or was information of one of the kinds specified in proposals 10 and 12."

It is important to note that the mere receipt of official information would not be an offence. However,

"Where a person knows, or has reasonable ground to believe, that information in his possession has been communicated (whether or not directly to him) in contravention of the Official Information Act (other than the provisions relating to the confidences of the citizen and private gain) it should be an offence for him to communicate that information otherwise than in accordance with an authorisation given on behalf of the Crown. The prosecution should have to prove (a) that there had been a contravention of the Act by some other person, *and* (b) that the information in question was still covered by the Act at the time when the accused communicated it, *and* (c) that the accused knew that the information had at some earlier stage been communicated in contravention of the Act, or that he had reasonable ground to believe that this was the case. The accused should have the defence that he believed, and had reasonable ground to believe, that he had communicated the information in accordance with an authorisation given on behalf of the Crown to him, or given to some other person but in terms applicable to him. It should not be an offence to communicate information for the purpose of obtaining such an authorisation, or of delivering a document to a Crown servant or obtaining directions about its return or disposal."

Significant though they are, these recommendations have not been implemented, though the Franks Report has been an important document for the many groups arguing for reform of the largely discredited section 2 of the 1911 Act. It may be questioned, however, whether the Franks Report is satisfactory. First, it still protects by the threat of criminal sanctions a wide range of information to which the public has a legitimate claim to access. Secondly, and more importantly, it does not confer a right of access to any information. It would still be open to government to withhold any information they wished. It is true that the criminal law would not be as widely available to protect the information from disclosure. But, as the Franks Committee itself acknowledged, there are other ways whereby government can ensure confidentiality, including discrimination against, and the dismissal of civil servants. If the reform of section 2 is to have any practical effect so far as freedom of expression is concerned, it may have to be accompanied by a parallel provision which gives a right to information not protected by the Official Information Act.

CHAPTER 8

[In this Chapter the abbreviations CGSA and POA refer respectively to
the Civic Government (Scotland) Act 1982 and the Public Order Act
(1936 or 1986 as indicated)]

FREEDOM OF ASSEMBLY AND PUBLIC ORDER

IN this chapter we move from the freedom of expression to freedom of
assembly. In recent years this too has been controversial. Partly this has
been as a result of a high degree of public protest since the 1960s, much of
which has been accompanied by violence and disorder, sometimes because
of rather than despite a heavy police presence. Little work has been done
to explain why there should be a significant change in the level of public
protest in Britain. But perhaps there are three reasons. The first is social,
with growing social deprivation and social inequality being a factor
identified by Scarman (1981) as contributing to the riots in Brixton and
other inner-city areas in the early 1980s. The second is economic, with the
decline in the extraction and manufacturing industries leading to
unemployment and the dispossession of many working people of their
primary asset—their jobs. The threat to employment with the lack of any
real alternative opportunities for work may help to explain the degree of
passion with which many workers in the 1980s have protested to protect
their jobs, be they steelworkers, printers or coalminers. And the third factor
is perhaps political, in particular the breakdown of the post-war consensus
which made it difficult in the 1950s to draw any meaningful distinction on
major issues between the two principal political parties. The radicalisation
and polarisation of party politics has led effectively to the exclusion of
many people and many interests from the traditional political process. The
only means of access is now directly to the electorate.

But whatever the reasons for the growth in the level of public protest, it
is undeniable that it has met with a degree of impatience from the
established order. This is not to say that the freedom of assembly should be
unlimited. As Scarman (1975) wrote in his inquiry into the Red Lion
Square disorder:

"5. Amongst our fundamental human rights there are, without doubt, the rights of
peaceful assembly and public protest and the right to public order and tranquillity.
Civilised living collapses—it is obvious—if public protest becomes violent protest
or public order degenerates into the quietism imposed by successful oppression.
But the problem is more complex than a choice between two extremes—one, a right
to protest whenever and wherever you will and the other, a right to continuous calm
upon our streets unruffled by the noise and obstructive pressure of the protesting
procession. A balance has to be struck, a compromise found that will accommodate

365

the exercise of the right to protest within a framework of public order which enables ordinary citizens, who are not protesting, to go about their business and pleasure without obstruction or inconvenience. The fact that those who at any one time are concerned to secure the tranquillity of the streets are likely to be the majority must not lead us to deny the protesters their opportunity to march: the fact that the protesters are desperately sincere and are exercising a fundamental human right must not lead us to overlook the rights of the majority."

The need then is to maintain a balance between competing freedoms and competing claims. Yet a remarkable feature of Scots law (which it shares with English law) is that there is no formal legal protection of the freedom of assembly, despite the claim in the 1985 White Paper that: "The rights of peaceful protest and assembly are amongst our fundamental freedoms: they are numbered among the touchstones which distinguish a free society from a totalitarian one" (Home Office, (1985:2)). The position in Scots law is represented by Lord President Dunedin in *McAra* v. *Magistrates of Edinburgh,* 1913 S.C. 1059 where he said:

"As regards the common law, I wish most distinctly to state it as my opinion that the primary and overruling object for which streets exist is passage. The streets are public, but they are public for passage, and there is no such thing as a right in the public to hold meetings as such in the streets. . . What I mean is this: streets are for passage, and passage is paramount to everything else. That does not necessarily mean that anyone is doing an illegal act if he is not at the moment passing along. It is quite clear that citizens may meet in the streets and may stop and speak to each other. The whole thing is a question of degree and nothing else, and it is a question of degree which the Magistrates are the proper persons to consider in each case, and it is for them to take such measures as are necessary to preserve to the citizens in general that use which is paramount to all other uses of the streets. I say this because there is a good deal in the pursuer's pleadings about what he calls 'exercising his right to free speech in public places.' Now the right of free speech undoubtedly exists and the right of free speech is to promulgate your opinions by speech so long as you do not utter what is treasonable or libellous, or make yourself obnoxious to the statutes that deal with blasphemy and obscenity. But the right of free speech is a perfectly separate thing from the question of the place where that right is to be exercised. You may say what you like provided it is not obnoxious in the ways I have indicated, but that does not mean that you may say it anywhere."

So there is no right of assembly, whether conferred by statute or recognised by the common law. At best there is a freedom of assembly as recognised by Dicey (1908). That is to say, there is a freedom to assemble to the extent that it is not prohibited by law or to the extent that those who assemble do nothing which is unlawful. In practice, however, this does not leave very much freedom, for the reality is that the freedom to assemble is constrained by a large measure of statutory and common law restrictions. And as the level of public protest has increased, so has the area of freedom been restricted. Important statutory initiatives, including the Civic

Government (Scotland) Act 1982 and the Public Order Act 1986 have extended the powers of the public authorities, including the police. And major decisions of the courts, particularly in England (though not without implications for Scotland) have had a similar effect. But the important feature of the law is not just that the area of potential illegality is expanding. Also important is the nature of the regulation. In practice both statute and common law confer a remarkably wide discretion on the public authorities, including the police. As a result, we may parody Dicey (though accurately) and say that there is a freedom of assembly in Scotland, but only to the extent that it is permitted by the police. In fact the people of Scotland have no right or freedom as such. At best they may enjoy the exercise of police discretion in their favour.

I. A NEW STATUTORY FRAMEWORK

Freedom of assembly is an area where the law has moved very fast in recent years. Before 1982 the legal position governing this area was very confusing, with a number of legal régimes in operation. The position in the four major cities and in Greenock was governed by local Acts of Parliament which applied to each of them individually. As a result the powers of the authorities varied from city to city. So while Edinburgh had the authority to ban a particular march, Glasgow did not. Other towns in contrast were governed by the Burgh Police Act 1892, which gave some power to local authorities in the public order field. Finally, there was no direct statutory regulation of this kind for very small towns or for areas outside the towns (Finnie, (1981a)).

Apart from the fact that the law might thus be different between communities, it was often difficult to know precisely what was the law. In a remarkable passage the future Lord Cooper, then Lord Advocate, found himself unable to answer a question in Parliament on the existing power of Glasgow Corporation during the debates on the Public Order Bill in 1936:

"[T]he hon. Member will appreciate that it is an extraordinarily difficult thing—in fact, almost impossible—for anyone who is not the town clerk of a burgh to know exactly what the powers of that burgh are, and the information which I am giving to the House had to be collected with considerable effort without, obviously, applying to these burghs for information in relation to a topic which at that stage was confidential. To the best of my belief, however, Glasgow has no powers in relation to the proposed Measure comparable to those possessed by the other burghs. I may be wrong, and there may be powers tucked away in some corner, but I do not think there are."
(317 H.C. Debs. 1416).

The powers conferred by these statutes applied mainly to permit the local authorities to take various preventative measures to maintain the peace. Superimposed on this legislation were the additional powers conferred by the POA 1936. Section 3(1) authorised the chief officer of police to issue instructions as to the conduct of processions where he apprehended serious public disorder. And section 3(2) enabled the local authority, on the request of a chief officer of police, to issue an order banning all processions in the locality for a specified period.

The legal position was substantially reformed in 1982 by the CGSA, enacted following a review of civic government legislation (Scottish Office, (1976)). The law is now of universal application, though obviously there is room for manoeuvre in the manner of its application in different local authority areas. It is to be noted, however, that the 1982 Act is not a fully comprehensive code for the regulation of public assemblies. The review of public order legislation generally (Home Office, (1981), (1985)) has led to the repeal of the POA 1936, s. 3 and the introduction of new and more extensive powers for the agencies of the state. These apply, however, in a modified form to Scotland. The general position is that the CGSA deals exclusively with the regulatory powers of the local authorities, whereas the POA 1986 confers powers on the police.

II. PRIOR RESTRAINTS

As we have already suggested, there are certain circumstances where the public authorities and the police may prevent the freedom of assembly or where they may impose conditions in advance as to the exercise of the freedom. For this purpose it is convenient to distinguish between processions and meetings. The statutory powers to control are more extensive in the case of the former, though both have been the targets of legislation which has increased the power of the public authorities to regulate activity in advance.

A. PROCESSIONS

1. DUTY TO NOTIFY IN ADVANCE

Before the enactment of the CGSA, there was no general statutory duty on the organisers of a march or procession to give notice in advance to the public authorities. There were, however, obligations imposed by two of the local statutes. The Edinburgh Corporation Order Confirmation Act 1967 provided by s. 184 for example:

"(1) Any person intending to organise or conduct a street procession shall give notice thereof, of the route proposed to be taken, and of the date and time on and at which it is intended that such procession will take place, to the town clerk not less than seven days before the day proposed for such procession.

(2) Any person organising or conducting any street procession—

    (*a*)   without notice having been given in pursuance of the preceding subsection; or

    (*b*)   otherwise than in accordance with such notice (except where the proposals contained in such notice have been varied by an order under paragraph (*a*)(ii) of the succeeding subsection); shall be guilty of an offence...

    (4) This section shall not apply to a public or ceremonial procession regularly held."

Similar (though not identical) provision existed in Aberdeen. It was this measure which formed the basis of the new controls introduced by the CGSA (Scottish Office, 1976).

1. The Civic Government (Scotland) Act 1982

"Notification of processions

    62.—(1) A person proposing to hold a procession in public shall give written notice of that proposal in accordance with subsections (2) and (3) below (*a*) to the regional or islands council in whose area the procession is to be held, or if it is to be held in the areas of more than one such council, to each such council; and (*b*) to the chief constable.

    (2) Notice shall be given for the purposes of subsection (1) above by—

    (*a*)   its being posted to the main office of the regional or islands council and to the office of the chief constable so that in the normal course of post it might be expected to arrive not later than seven days before the date when the procession is to be held; or

    (*b*)   its being delivered by hand to those offices not later than seven days before that date.

    (3) The notice to be given under subsection (1) above shall specify—

    (*a*)   the date and time when the procession is to be held;

    (*b*)   its route;

    (*c*)   the number of persons likely to take part in it;

    (*d*)   the arrangements for its control being made by the person proposing to hold it; and

    (*e*)   the name and address of that person.

    (4) A regional or islands council may, on application in accordance with subsection (5) below by a person proposing to hold a procession in public in their area made to them within the period of seven days before the date when the procession is to be held, make an order dispensing with the requirements of subsection (2) above in relation to the time limits for the giving of notice of that proposal.

    (5) An application under subsection (4) above shall specify the matters mentioned in subsection (3) above and, where an order has been made under the said subsection (4), the application for it shall be treated as notice duly given for the purposes of subsection (1) above.

    (6) A regional or islands council may (whether upon application made to them or not) make an order exempting any person proposing to hold any procession in public being a procession specified in the order or one of a class of processions so

specified from the requirement under this section to give notice to the council of the proposal to hold that procession.

(7) This section does not apply in relation to processions commonly or customarily held; but a regional or islands council may, as respects their area, order that it shall apply to any such procession so held or any such class or procession so held as is specified in the order.

(8) An order under subsection (6) or (7) above may—

(a)   provide that its application in any case or class of cases is subject to such conditions as may be specified in the order;

(b)   classify processions by reference to any factor or factors whatsoever;

(c)   be varied or revoked by subsequent order made in like manner.

(9) The regional or islands council shall, before making an order under subsection (4) above or making, varying or revoking an order under subsection (6) or (7) above, consult the chief constable.

(10) The regional or islands council shall as soon as a notice under subsections (1) to (3) above, or an application under subsection (4), is received send a copy of that notice or application to the chief constable.

(11) The regional or islands council shall, as soon as possible after they make, vary or revoke an order under subsection (6) or (7) above, give public notice of that fact in a newspaper or newspapers circulating in their area.

(12) In this section and in sections 63 to 65 of this Act—

'procession in public' means a procession in a public place;

'chief constable' means, in relation to a regional or islands council, the chief constable of the police force for the area which comprises or includes the area of the council; and

'public place' has the same meaning as in Part II of the Public Order Act 1986."

The enactment of this measure attracted surprisingly little resistance in Parliament. The Opposition accepted the need for section 62, with Mr Donald Dewar conceding in Standing Committee that

"controlling processions needs police manpower, if only to ensure that there are not traffic accidents, traffic jams, foul-ups, snarl-ups, or malicious people causing trouble on the fringes. Given the size of that problem and that the measure is an intimation to allow effective regulation, I think that it would be wrong for us in any way to stand against the clause becoming part of the Bill."

(First Scottish Standing Committee, 18th sitting, June 24, 1982, col. 691). This is not to deny that some aspects of the section gave rise to difficulty. In the House of Lords concern was expressed that the duty to notify was a duty to notify the regional council rather than the district council: "It does not make sense that everything in relation to a small town in South Ayrshire has got to go way up to Glasgow" (428 H.L. Debs., 125 (Lord Ross of Marnock)). Indeed, it had been proposed by the Working Party on Civic Government in Scotland that the "regulating authority should be the district or islands council" (Scottish Office, (1976)). The Government, however, was persuaded otherwise by the Committee on Local Government in Scotland that the matter should be dealt with by the regional councils: "this is consistent with regional councils' responsibilities for police and the highways" (Stoddart, (1981:77)).

A second difficulty related to the fact that the clause as originally published appeared without what is now subsection (7) on its face. The concern of some members of both Houses was that the Act would thereby impose a duty to notify in the case of all processions, including customary and ceremonial processions. In the House of Lords examples were given of activities far removed from the mischief behind the Act, but which would nevertheless be caught by its terms. Thus reference was made to the Salvation Army, the Boy Scouts, Girl Guides and Boys' Brigade. In the words of Viscount Thurso: "They are not holding a procession in the customary way in which we understand the word 'procession,' but they are indeed probably holding a procession in a technical sense if they march from their headquarters to a church, or if they march down the street with their band playing and their banners flying" (428 H.L. Debs., 125-126). Lord Ross of Marnock gave examples of "local gala days, the processions of the children and the floats, and, in the Borders, the Common Riding processions" (*ibid.,* col. 127). The Government's view was that local authorities could make an exemption order under subsection (6) exempting such activity. This, however, did not satisfy the Opposition: "Local authorities being what they are, you could get a patchwork of different attitudes over the whole country and different administrative conditions laid down in respect of processions that would never have caused any trouble and which delight the people of Scotland" (*ibid.,* col. 128).

Subsection (7) was in fact designed principally to preserve the freedom of religious expression, with the Salvation Army particularly in mind. As a result of the amendment, which was carried despite initial government resistance (expressed in strong terms in the Lords), all such processions are now presumed excluded from the duty to notify, though it is open to the council to use its powers under the second limb of subsection (7) to impose a duty on the part of the organisation in question. The burden of apathy is thus now in favour of freedom to this limited extent. This is not to say that there was no substance in the Government's case. The Earl of Mansfield objected to the amendment on three grounds (though he later supported the amendment). First:

"As one of the objects of advance notice, coupled with powers to impose conditions in a march, is to help minimise the disruption which processions cause to the community, it would seem right, on the whole, not to have any exceptions at all, or, failing that, to draw any exemptions narrowly."
(*ibid,.* col. 132).

Second, he argued that it was now

"uncertain in particular cases whether any notice was required to be given, because it may not be clear whether a particular procession is one which is 'commonly or customarily held.' This could result in the organiser of a procession committing an offence by failing to give notice of a procession in the belief, which may prove to be mistaken, that his procession fitted the description of 'commonly or customarily held.' So this is a weakness . . . and it might adversely affect those whom it seeks to protect."

(*ibid.,* cols. 132-133).

Thirdly, the Minister saw no threat to religious freedom in the clause as originally introduced, since if local councillors displayed any religious intolerance, they would pay the electoral penalty. More credible was the argument that "we are treading on very dangerous ground so far as religious tolerance is concerned, because . . . the Orange Order could make some claim to be religious and that could cause problems too" (*ibid.,* col. 133). However, it would be open to a council to require the Orange Order to give notification of its Twelfth of July parades.

In its final form, then, section 62 creates five classes or potential classes of procession:

(a) processions commonly or customarily held. Section 62(7) *prima facie* exempts them from the need to be notified;

(b) processions commonly or customarily held in respect of which the regional council has disapplied the exemption (s. 62(7));

(c) processions with respect to which, because they are in response to current events or for some similar reason there is not time to give seven days' notice. The council *may* dispense with the notice of requirement in such cases (s. 62(4)), but the other matters specified in section 62(3) must still be notified;

(d) processions or classes of procession in relation to which generally, the regional council has given an exemption from the requirement to notify (s. 62(6)); and

(e) processions which do not fall into any of the preceding classes. In respect of these the full notification requirements apply.

As might be expected, there is enormous variation in the way in which councils have exercised the powers vested in them to exempt processions from notification requirements, ranging from no exemption in most regions to exemption of processions held by 238 named organisations in Strathclyde. Policy varies equally widely in the imposition of conditions and the acceptance of late applications. (For details, see Murdoch (1984).)

2. Forbidding and Regulating Processions

Before 1982 the power to prohibit and regulate processions was governed by three different measures. First, the POA 1936 empowered the chief officer of police to give directions imposing on both the organisers and the participants "such conditions as appear to him necessary for the preservation of public order." This power was exercisable only where the chief of police had "reasonable grounds for apprehending that the procession may occasion serious public disorder." The power to impose conditions did not include the power to ban a march altogether. Secondly, the local Acts generally contained powers exercisable by the magistrates. In Aberdeen, for example, the Aberdeen Corporation (General Powers) Order Confirmation Act 1938 provided by section 182(3):

"The magistrates may, if the conducting of any procession would or would be likely to cause or result in disorderly behaviour or a breach of the peace or any nuisance or annoyance or any obstruction to traffic, prohibit the conducting of such procession or may make an order prescribing a different route for such procession."

So, unlike the power of the police under section 3 of the POA 1936, the magistrates had a power to ban marches. The power was used in Aberdeen in 1981 to ban an Orange march, on the ground that it would be "composed of bands of imported religious zealots," would "outrage" many citizens, and would introduce for the first time to the city the "taint of religious bigotry" (*The Scotsman,* September 8, 1981). Similar powers existed in Edinburgh, though not in Glasgow or Dundee. The third source of power which permitted the prohibition and regulation of processions was a group of measures intended to be exercised with traffic considerations uppermost. One such measure was the Burgh Police (Scotland) Act 1892, s. 385, which enabled highway authorities to issue notices and orders

"(2) Diverting temporarily out of any street or streets, traffic of every kind, or such particular kinds of traffic as may be specified in any such order or notice: and the islands or district council may from time to time make bye-laws and issue notices and orders prohibiting or regulating public processions. And every breach of any such bye-law, notice, or order shall be deemed an offence against this Act, and every person committing such an offence shall be liable to a penalty not exceeding twenty-five pounds."

In *Loyal Orange Lodge No. 493 Hawick First Purple* v. *Roxburgh District Council,* 1981 S.L.T. 33, it was held by the Inner House that this measure could be invoked by a local authority to forbid a march on public order grounds. The position is now governed by the CGSA.

2. The Civic Government (Scotland) Act 1982

"63—(1) The regional or islands council may, after consulting the chief constable in respect of a procession notice of which has been given or falls to be treated as having been given in accordance with section 62(1) of this Act, make an order—

   (i)   prohibiting the holding of the procession; or

   (ii)   imposing conditions on the holding of it.

(1A) Where notice of a proposal to hold a procession has been given or falls to be treated as having been given in accordance with section 62(1) of this Act—

   (a)   if a regional or islands council have made an order under subsection (1) above they may at any time thereafter, after consulting the chief constable, vary or revoke the order and, where they revoke it, make any order which they were empowered to make under that subsection;

   (b)   If they have decided not to make an order they may at any time thereafter, after consulting the chief constable, make any order which they were empowered to make under that subsection.

(2) The conditions which may be imposed under subsection (1) or (1A) above on the holding of a procession may include conditions—

   (a)   as to the date, time and duration of the procession;

   (b)   as to the route to be taken by it;

   (c)   prohibiting its entry into any public place specified in the order.

(3) A regional or islands council shall—

   (a)   where notice of a proposal to hold a procession has been given or falls to be treated as having been given in accordance with section 62(1) of this Act, deliver at least 2 days before the date when, in terms of the notice, the procession is to be held, to the person who gave the notice—

   (i)   where they have made an order under subsection (1) or (1A) above, a copy of it and a written statement of the reason for it; or

   (ii)   where they decide not to make an order under subsection (1) above or to revoke an order already made under subsection (1) or (1A) above notification of that fact; and

   (iii)   where they have, under subsection (1A) above, varied such an order a copy of the order as varied and a written statement of the reasons for the variation, and

   (b)   where they have made an order under subsection (1) or (1A) above in relation to a proposal to hold a procession, make such arrangements as will ensure that persons who might take or are taking part in that procession are made aware of the fact the order has been made and, if the order has been varied under subsection (1A) above, that it has been so varied and of its effect; and

   (c)   where they have revoked an order made under subsection (1) or (1A) above in relation to a proposal to hold a procession, make such arrangements as will ensure that persons who might take or are taking part in that procession are made aware of the fact that the order has been revoked.

(4) The regional or islands council shall comply with subsection (3) above."

Section 63 confers important powers on local authorities. They may ban a procession, or they may impose conditions on the holding of it. The power to ban contrasts with the powers of local authorities in England and Wales under the POA 1986, s. 13. That measure, being based on section 3(2) of the POA 1936, does not permit the banning of individual marches or processions, but provides that a banning order shall apply to all such activity in the locality for a period of up to three months. A second important feature of the section 63 power is the remarkably wide discretion given to local authorities in the exercise of the power to ban or impose conditions. The banning power in England and Wales may be exercised only to prevent serious public disorder (POA 1986, s. 13(1)). And although the power to impose conditions has been extended, it is still nevertheless constrained by section 12 of the POA 1986 in the following way:

"12.—(1) This section applies if the senior police officer, having regard to the time or place at which and the circumstances in which any public procession is being held or is intended to be held and to its route or proposed route, reasonably believes that—

(a) it may result in serious public disorder, serious damage to property or serious disruption to the life of the community, or

(b) the purpose of the persons organising it is the intimidation of others with a view to compelling them not to do an act they have a right to do, or to do an act they have a right not to do.

(2) The senior police officer may give directions imposing on the persons organising or taking part in the procession any conditions which appear to him necessary to prevent such disorder, damage, disruption or intimidation, including conditions prescribing the route of the procession or prohibiting it from entering any public place specified in the directions."

In Scotland, in contrast, the public authorities appear empowered to ban or impose conditions for any reason. Conceivably this could include the fact that it would cost too much to police.

This point was raised in Standing Committee by Mr Donald Dewar for the Opposition, who pointed out that local authorities have been given a wide discretion, but that nowhere is a test specified, with the result that there is a danger of the authorities becoming censors or passing moral judgments on parades they did not like (First Scottish Standing Committee, 18th sitting, June 24, 1982, col. 691). In reply, the Solicitor General for Scotland pointed to three safeguards: first, the duty to intimate (s. 63 (3)); secondly, the duty to give reasons (s. 63(3)); and thirdly, the right of appeal to the sheriff in section 64, which provides as follows:

"The sheriff may uphold an appeal under this section only if he considers that the regional or islands council in arriving at their decision to make the order—

(a) erred in law;

(b) based their decision an any incorrect material fact;

(c) exercised their discretion in an unreasonable manner; or

(d) otherwise acted beyond their powers."

The introduction of this statutory right of appeal is an important innovation. There was no corresponding provision under the POA 1936, s. 3, nor is there such a right in England and Wales under the POA 1986. The only means of redress under these measures was or is judicial review. The

Government has pointed out that "the availability of judicial review as an effective remedy has been greatly extended, by the law and by the procedural reforms of recent years" (Home Office, (1985:28)). Nevertheless, a remedy by way of judicial review alone has been criticised because the courts have been reluctant to use their powers under this procedure (Thornton, (1985:52)). It is the case that the English courts appear to tread very warily in cases which seek to challenge the exercise of discretionary powers relating to public order.

Yet although the introduction of this statutory right is important, it should not be exaggerated. It is an appeal from the exercise of an unlimited discretion on very limited grounds. The limited nature of the appeal was stressed by the government in the House of Lords when the Earl of Mansfield said that it "is not some sort of rehearsing before a lawyer on the part of somebody who is dissatisfied with the determination of the matter by the local authority" (428 H.L. Debs. 143). In fact section 63(4) adds very little. This decision of the local authority would have been subject to judicial review on precisely the grounds specified in the subsection anyway. All the subsection does is to give statutory force to the grounds of judicial review and to provide that they are actionable before the sheriff. This is confirmed by the Secretary of State, who said that section 63(4)(c) "would not put the sheriff in the position of being the substitute local authority looking *de novo* at the circumstances and saying 'I would allow the march.' He would have to consider, because of this discretion, whether the decision was such that no reasonable local authority could have reached that view" (First Scottish Standing Committee, 18th sitting, June 24, 1982, col. 700). This stung Mr Donald Dewar to suggest that sheriffs "will not be keen to upset the discretion that has been exercised by the local authority" and to question whether the right of appeal is "as impressive and reassuring as might appear at first sight" (*ibid.*, 19th sitting, June 24, 1982, col. 704). This is not to deny that there will be cases where judicial accountability will be important. It does at least offer a check against the arbitrary and capricious use of power. An example given in Committee of where the right of appeal would be useful is "if a local authority were to say, following its own internal party political diktats, that there were to be no processions of any military character within its area, there would be a good chance that the sheriff would consider that that was an unreasonable exercise of discretion" (*ibid.*, col. 693, the Solicitor General for Scotland).

A second feature of the right of appeal is that it does not remove the strategic power of the public authorities. A ban or the imposition of a series of restrictions could have a serious chilling effect on a demonstration or procession if an appeal is to be conducted. Notice of appeal must be given within 14 days of the notice of the council received by the applicant. There is no provision in the Act for the speedy hearing of appeals. To a very large extent this may make irrelevant the potentially important provisions of section 64(6) and (7) which provide:

"(6) Subject to subsection (7) below, on an appeal under this section, the sheriff may

    (*a*) uphold the appeal and—
               (i) remit the case, with the reasons for his decision, to the regional or islands council for reconsideration of their decision, or
               (ii) if he considers that there is insufficient time for the case to be remitted under sub-paragraph (i) above vary the order which is the subject of the appeal or make any such order as the council were empowered to make under section 63(1) of this Act; or
    (*b*) dismiss the appeal,

and on remitting a case under paragraph (*a*)(i) above, the sheriff may—

    (i) specify a date by which the reconsideration by the council must take place;
    (ii) modify any procedural steps which otherwise would be required to be taken in relation to the matter by or under any enactment (including this Act).

(7) The sheriff shall not exercise any of his powers under subsection (6) above unless he is satisfied that all steps which in the circumstances were reasonable have been taken with a view to securing that notice of the appeal and an opportunity of being heard with respect to it have been given to the council whose order under section 63 of this Act is the subject of the appeal."

An appeal lies from the sheriff to the Court of Session (s. 64(8)). The 1982 Act is not, however, the only statutory basis for regulating the conduct of marches or processions.

3. The Public Order Act 1986

"*Imposing conditions on public processions*

12.—(1) This section applies if the senior police officer, having regard to the time or place at which and the circumstances in which any public procession is being held or is intended to be held and to its route or proposed route, reasonably believes that—

    (*a*) it may result in serious public disorder, serious damage to property or serious disruption to the life of the community, or
    (*b*) the purpose of the persons organising it is the intimidation of others with a view to compelling them not to do an act they have a right to do, or to do an act they have a right not to do.

(2) The senior police officer may give directions imposing on the persons organising or taking part in the procession or prohibiting it from entering any public place specified in the directions.

(3) In this section "the senior police officer" means—

    (*a*) in relation to a procession being held, or to a procession intended to be held in a case where persons are assembling with a view to taking part in it, the most senior in rank of the police officers present at the scene, and
    (*b*) in relation to a procession intended to be held in a case where paragraph (*a*) does not apply, the chief officer of police.

(4) A person who organises a public procession and knowingly fails to comply with a condition imposed under this section is guilty of an offence, but it is a defence for him to prove that the failure arose from circumstances beyond his control.

(5) A person who takes part in a public procession and knowingly fails to comply with a condition imposed under this section is guilty of an offence, but it is a defence for him to prove that the failure arose from circumstances beyond his control.

(6) A person who incites another to commit an offence under subsection (5) is guilty of an offence.

(7) A constable may arrest without warrant anyone he reasonably suspects is committing an offence under subsection (4), (5) or (6).

(8) A person guilty of an offence under subsection (4) is liable on summary conviction to imprisonment for a term not exceeding three months or a fine not exceeding level 4 on the standard scale or both.

(9) A person guilty of an offence under subsection (5) is liable on summary conviction to a fine not exceeding level 3 on the standard scale.

(10) A person guilty of an offence under subsection (6) is liable on summary conviction to imprisonment for a term not exceeding three months or a fine not exceeding level 4 on the standard scale or both, notwithstanding section 45(3) of the Magistrates' Courts Act 1980 (inciter liable to same penalty as incited).

(11) In Scotland this section applies only in relation to a procession being held, and to a procession intended to be held in a case where persons are assembling with a view to taking part in it."

This measure supplements the power of the local authorities under the 1982 Act. Section 12(11) does, however, impose an important limit on the power of the police in Scotland. Generally, conditions in advance should be imposed by local authorities (albeit in consultation with the police). But the government was of the view that this was insufficient, pointing out in the White Paper that "it seems desirable that the police should have clear statutory authority to issue directions for the control of a procession should this be seen to be necessary either immediately before the procession starts or when it is in progress" (Home Office, (1985:46)). The power of the police is not as wide as that of the local authorities, though it is much wider than that which existed under the POA 1936, s. 3(1). This enabled the police to issue directions only to prevent serious public disorder.

The police power to impose conditions overrides any decision of a local authority not to impose conditions under the 1982 Act and the police conditions take priority over any which the local authority may have issued. (s. 66, CGSA) The function of the new extended police powers was explained by the government in the White Paper (Home Office, (1985:27-28)) in the following terms:

"4.21. In proposing an extension of the police's power to impose conditions the Government has no intention of altering the present arrangements whereby the police negotiate agreements with the march organisers. The Government anticipates that in the great majority of cases the police will continue to proceed on the basis of informal agreements. But the Government does intend to alter the legal framework within which agreements are negotiated, by widening the circumstances in which the police will be empowered to impose conditions in default of agreement, or where they suspect that an agreement will not be kept. This means widening the present test of serious public disorder in section 3(1) by adding other criteria to it. The Green Paper suggested a reduction in the test for imposing conditions to one of public disorder. But there has been no evidence from the police that they have experienced difficulties in imposing conditions on marches where this was necessary *to prevent disorder*. The only change the Government would propose to the existing test is to make it clear that serious public disorder can include serious damage to property. But in addition the Government believes that greater flexibility can usefully be conferred by the introduction of two new tests.

4.22. The first test is one proposed by the Select Committee, who vividly described the degree of disruption which can be caused even by a procession of average size. Some degree of disruption must of course be accepted by the wider community; but it does not seem right that the police should have no power to re-route a procession in order to limit traffic congestion, or to prevent a bridge from being blocked, or to reduce the severe disruption sometimes suffered by pedestrians, business and commerce. The Committee therefore suggested an additional test which would enable the police to impose conditions on a procession in order to prevent serious disruption to the normal life of the community. The Government agrees that a new test of this kind is required, in order to prevent marches from causing unreasonable disruption to local residents, other users of the highway, and adjoining shops and businesses. An example of the circumstances in which the test might operate is provided by the policy of the Metropolitan Police in seeking to discourage demonstrators from using Oxford Street during business hours. A number of other police forces have given examples of marches being held through shopping centres on Saturdays or through city centres in the rush hour. At present the police have no legal powers should the organisers of a march be minded to defy police efforts to persuade them to change their plans. The proposed test would enable the police to re-route a march if they believed that it was likely to be seriously disruptive to the traffic, the shops or the shoppers.

4.23. Serious disruption can be caused by marches organised with the best of intentions. But the second new test proposed by the Government is directed at those who organise processions with more malicious intent. It would confer on the police a power to impose conditions in order to prevent the coercion of individuals. This is a libertarian safeguard designed to prevent demonstrations whose overt purpose is to persuade people, from being used as a cloak by those whose real purpose is to intimidate or coerce. Sometimes, however, their purpose is not even concealed: their literature proclaims their intention as being to 'stop' or 'smash' their opponents. (An example was provided last year in Manchester by the National Front, who when organising a counter-demonstration to a march by the Troops Out Movement described their purpose as being to 'stop this vermin . . . don't let them march').

4.24. On some such occasions the police will often need to impose conditions in order to prevent serious public disorder. Sometimes there is no clear risk of disorder because the target of the demonstration is a single individual, or a peaceful group who are unlikely to respond with violence. When the National Front march through Asian districts the reaction of the local community may be to board up their shops and businesses and to stay at home. It is on these occasions that the law needs to give the police powers to ensure that individuals are free to go about their business without fear of intimidation. Another example of marches whose purpose is to coerce is provided by animal rights protesters, who on occasion have marched on furriers' shops or food factories with the intention of preventing the employees from working. On other occasions a march may be coercive simply by reason of the number of marchers compared with its objective (for example, 1,000 people marching on the home of a local councillor, or an inquiry inspector). On such occasions there may not be a risk of public disorder, but the police may need to impose conditions on the march in order to protect the individual or individuals who are its target. In maintaining the balance between the freedom to demonstrate and the rights of the wider community the law must ensure that people are not so harassed by demonstrators that they are no longer free to come and go without fear of coercion or intimidation."

In view of the fact that they are imposed on the spot, and unlike the conditions imposed by the local authority, there is effectively no means of challenging the conditions imposed by the police. In England and Wales (where police powers are not subject to section 12(11)) the police may issue the instructions well in advance of the procession. In such circumstances judicial review would be available in theory, though perhaps not in practice. But although great reforms have taken place in judicial review in recent years, there is no way in which an organiser could get judicial review of conditions imposed by the police officer on the spot. The only control then is after the event. It is a criminal offence to fail to comply with a police instruction. Presumably, it would be open to someone arrested and charged to offer the defence that the conditions were unlawful because the police had no reasonable grounds to believe that there would be serious disruption, serious damage, or whatever. It is not clear, however, whether the courts would be anxious to challenge the exercise of the police officers' discretion, save in palpably absurd cases. Nor in a sense is this the point. The demonstration is killed by the conditions. Arrests may be made. Prosecutions may not be brought. Even if a prosecution is brought and fails, this hardly compensates the defence for the invasion of their liberties.

B.   MEETINGS AND ASSEMBLIES

We turn now from the question of prior restraints on marches and processions to the question of prior restraints on meetings and assemblies. The statutory position here contrasts sharply with that which applies to processions. In the first place, there is no general power to ban meetings or assemblies. The government considered but rejected the introduction of such a power:

"5.3.   A new power to ban static demonstrations would be a substantial limitation on the right of assembly and the right to demonstrate. The Government has been very concerned not to extend statutory controls over static demonstrations any further than is strictly necessary. Meetings and assemblies are a more important means of exercising freedom of speech than are marches: a power to ban them, even as a last resort, would be potentially a major infringement of freedom of speech

(especially at election time). It might also be difficult to enforce: and there was no strong request from the police for a power to ban. The Government has concluded that the new controls which it proposes over static demonstrations should not include a power to ban. The power to impose conditions should in most cases be sufficient to control those demonstrations which threaten to be disorderly, disruptive or intimidatory."
(Home Office, (1985:31-32))

There is, in addition, no general duty on the part of the organisers to notify the public authorities, whether it be the local council (as under the CGSA for processions), or the police (as under the CGSA as amended by the POA 1986, s. 12 for processions). Again the Government considered but rejected any such duty:

"5.4. The Government has been greatly assisted by advice from the police as to what powers they consider would be useful and practicable in relation to static demonstrations. Discussion of an advance notice requirement has made it clear that it would produce much unnecessary work for the police to little purpose. There is no legal definition of a static demonstration: an assembly covers the whole range of public gatherings, from political rallies to religious services and pop festivals to football matches. The Government has considered possible definitions based on the nature of an assembly, or its likely size; but it has not proved possible to devise a definition which restricts the category to those events of interest to the police. An advance notice requirement would therefore inundate the police with notifications of perfectly peaceful meetings. The administrative burden would far outweigh the information gain."
(Home Office, (1985))

It does not follow, however, that there is no power to impose prior restraints. First, restrictions may be imposed by local byelaws; and secondly the POA 1986, s. 14 extends new powers to the police.

1. Bye-Laws and Prior Restraint

The power to make bye-laws is one which has important implications for the holding of meetings and public assemblies. Bye-laws are a kind of delegated legislation, with the power to make them being vested in local authorities. The general bye-law making power is contained in the Local Government (Scotland) Act 1973 which provides by section 201:

"(1) A local authority may make byelaws for the good rule and government of the whole of any part of the region, islands area or district, as the case may be, and for the prevention and suppression of nuisances therein.
(2) The confirming authority in relation to byelaws made under this section shall be the Secretary of State.
(3) Byelaws shall not be made under this section for any purpose as respects any

area if provision for that purpose as respects that area is made by, or is or may be made under, any other enactment."

Section 201(2) provides that bye-laws must be "confirmed" by the Secretary of State. Before they are confirmed, however, they must be published and anyone aggrieved has a right to make representation to the confirming authority. Any objections must be considered by the Secretary of State, and if necessary a local inquiry must be held (s. 202(8)). Any such inquiry must be held by the sheriff, unless the Secretary of State otherwise directs. In addition to this general power to make bye-laws, there may also be specific power conferred by statute. For example, the Public Parks (Scotland) Act 1878 provides:

"3. From and after the passing of this Act any local authority may purchase or take on lease, lay out, plant, improve, and maintain lands for the purpose of being used as parks, public walks, or pleasure grounds, and may support or contribute to the support of parks, public walks, or pleasure grounds provided by any person whomsoever.
4. Any local authority may make byelaws for the regulation of any such parks, public walks, or pleasure grounds, and may by such byelaws provide for the removal from such parks, public walks, or pleasure grounds of any person infringing any such byelaw by any officer of the local authority or constable. . .
16. All byelaws made by a local authority under and for the purposes of this Act shall be signed by the clerk thereof; and any such byelaws may be altered or repealed by subsequent byelaws made pursuant to the provisions of this Act: Provided that no byelaws made under this Act by a local authority shall be of any effect if repugnant to the laws of Scotland or to the provisions of this Act."

Although made by popular elected bodies, the bye-law making power is not unlimited, and is constrained first by the *ultra vires* rule, and secondly by the requirement of reasonableness. As a result, bye-laws may be challenged at two points in the legal process. First, they may be questioned at the point of confirmation (see *Rothesay Town Council, Petitioners* (1898) 14 Sh.Ct.Rep. 189 and *Burgh of Dunblane, Petitioners,* 1947 S.L.T. (Sh.Ct) 27). Secondly, they can be challenged collaterally as a defence in criminal proceedings for breach of the bye-law, as in the following case.

4. Aldred v. Langmuir
1932 J.C. 22

"The following facts were admitted or proved:—'On Sunday, 5th July 1931, a large demonstration consisting of five to six thousand persons was observed by police officers approaching Glasgow Green, one of the public parks of the City of Glasgow. The officers followed the demonstrators, who entered the Green and proceeded as far as the Nelson Monument, where, from an improvised platform, the appellant, as well as the other accused, lectured to the crowd. The accused Andrew

Reilly acted as chairman, and each speaker spoke from five to fifteen minutes, the subject being "Free Speech" and the "Imprisonment of the Tramp Preachers." The meeting, which lasted from 3.15 p.m. until 5 p.m., was quite an orderly one, and during its progress a collection was taken by means of a hat. The name of each speaker was taken by the police officers, and all frankly admitted that they had not the written authority of the Corporation or the Director of Parks for the holding of said meeting as required by No. 20 of the bye-laws libelled. Neither the appellant nor any of the other accused, with the exception of the accused Daniel Lanaghan, had ever at any such time applied to the Corporation or the Director of Parks for such a written authority. An application by the accused Lanaghan to hold a meeting in the Green on 1st May last under the auspices of the Irish Labour League was refused by the Parks Committee of the Corporation. Lanaghan's object in going to the Green on 5th July 1931 was to protest against this refusal. Between the years 1916 and 1931 116 applications for permits to hold meetings in Glasgow Green have been made to the Corporation. Of that number, 94 were granted, and 22 refused. No permits have ever been issued by the Director of Parks personally. He has left that matter entirely in the hands of the Parks Committee of the Corporation. For some years prior to 1922 Bye-law No. 20 was not uniformly enforced, but since then it has been consistently applied."

The stipendiary magistrate found each of the accused guilty as libelled and imposed a fine on each of them. Aldred appealed to the High Court of Justiciary. One of the grounds of his appeal was that the bye-law under which he was convicted was *ultra vires*. The bye-law is reproduced in the opinion of the Lord Justice-General:

LORD JUSTICE-GENERAL (Clyde): "The power of the Corporation to regulate the public parks of the city is a power exercisable by bye-law, the power being conferred by section 37 of the Glasgow Public Parks Act, 1878, which is in the following terms:—'The Lord Provost, Magistrates, and Council may from time to time *make such bye-laws* as they shall think fit *for the good government and regulation of the said public parks,* gardens, and open spaces, and of the museums, galleries, and collections of natural history, science, and art, and other buildings, *and persons frequenting the same,* and of the superintendents, curators, rangers, park-keepers, and other officers or servants appointed and employed by them, and may impose such penalties for breaches of the bye-laws so to be made, not exceeding five pounds for each offence, as may be considered by them expedient, and from time to time, as they shall think fit, may repeal, alter, or re-enact any such bye-laws: Provided that such bye-laws shall not be repugnant to the law of Scotland, and shall be reduced into writing, and have affixed thereto the signatures of at least two of the magistrates of the city.' The bye-law which the appellant is said to have contravened is No. 20 of a set of bye-laws for the management and regulation of the public parks enacted by the Corporation, in virtue of the powers of the section just quoted, on 13th April 1916, and approved by the Sheriff of Lanarkshire on 20th June of the same year. It is in the following terms:—'No person shall, in any of the parks, sing, preach, lecture, or take part in any service, discussion, meeting, or demonstration, or hold any exhibition or public show, for any purpose whatsoever, or play any musical instrument, except with the written authority of the Corporation or the Superintendent, and then only on such places as may from time to time be by the Corporation or the Superintendent set apart by notice for such purposes.' The superintendent referred to is an officer of the Corporation in the parks department. It is not in dispute that Glasgow Green is one of the public parks of the city.

The attack upon the validity of Bye-law No. 20 rests on the principle of the decision pronounced in *McGregor* v. *Disselduff*. In that case the power of the magistrate to regulate the places and hours for bathing on or from the seashore of Dunoon was derived from a statute which authorised such regulation by bye-law. The bye-law enacted by the magistrates simply prohibited bathing on or from the seashore except at such places as might from time to time be appointed by the magistrates. It was held that a bye-law in these prohibitory terms was not one which regulated the places and hours of bathing, but merely reserved the power of regulation to the discretion of the magistrates as such discretion might be exercised from time to time. The power committed by the statute to the magistrates was a power exercisable by means of bye-laws, not a power of discretionary regulation. The bye-law was therefore held to be *ultra vires*.

If the power of regulation given to the Corporation by the Public Parks Act, 1878, had been no more than a power to regulate the use of the parks of the city for the purpose of lectures, meetings, and demonstrations, it is probable that the principle of the decision above referred to would have applied, to the effect of invalidating Bye-law No. 20. But the power conferred on the Corporation is much wider than that; it is a general power to regulate the public parks of the city and the persons resorting thereto. Broadly speaking, public parks are provided in the interests of the health of a city population—as the city's 'lungs,' to use a common expression—and for recreation from the crowded labours of an urban population. It is therefore that the power of regulation should include the prohibition of the use of the parks for purposes which are, or may be, inconsistent with, or detrimental or alien to, these general interests, or which may be harmful to the parks themselves. The Corporation's bye-laws contain many examples of prohibitory regulation of this kind besides Bye-law No. 20—Bye-law No. 9, for instance, which prohibits any person from bringing a dog into a public park except on leash; and also many examples of prohibitory regulations which are subject to exception by way of special permission,Bye-law No. 18, for instance, which prohibits picnics in a public park without special permission. All these bye-laws are, I think, plainly *intra vires* of a corporation empowered to regulate, by bye-law, the public parks under its administration and the public resorting thereto."

Lords Sands and Blackburn delivered concurring opinions. The fine imposed was reduced to a sum of 10 shillings.

2. POLICE POWERS TO REGULATE PUBLIC ASSEMBLIES

5. The Public Order Act 1986

"Imposing conditions on public assemblies
14.—(1) This section applies if the senior police officer, having regard to the time or place at which and the circumstances in which any public assembly is being

held or is intended to be held, reasonably believes that—

(a) it may result in serious public disorder, serious damage to property or serious disruption to the life of the community, or

(b) the purpose of the person organising it is the intimidation of others with a view to compelling them not to do an act they have a right to do, or to do an act they have a right not to do.

(2) The senior police officer may give directions imposing on the persons organising or taking part in the assembly any conditions which prescribe the place at which the assembly may be (or continue to be) held, its maximum duration, or the maximum number of persons who may constitute it, provided they are conditions which appear to the senior police officer necessary to prevent such disorder, damage, disruption or intimidation.

(3) In this section 'the senior police officer' means the chief officer of police (in relation to an assembly intended to be held) or the most senior in rank of police officers present at the scene (in relation to an assembly being held).

(4) A person who organises a public assembly and knowingly fails to comply with a condition imposed under this section is guilty of an offence, but it is a defence for him to prove that the failure arose from circumstances beyond his control.

(5) A person who takes part in a public assembly and knowingly fails to comply with a condition imposed under this section is guilty of an offence, but it is a defence for him to prove that the failure arose from circumstances beyond his control.

(6) A person who incites another to commit an offence under subsection (5) is guilty of an offence.

(7) A constable may arrest without warrant anyone he reasonably suspects is committing an offence under subsection (4), (5) or (6).

(8) A person guilty of an offence under subsection (4) is liable on summary conviction to imprisonment for a term not exceeding 3 months or a fine not exceeding level 4 on the standard scale or both.

(9) A person guilty of an offence under subsection (5) is liable on summary conviction to a fine not exceeding level 3 on the standard scale.

(10) A person guilty of an offence under subsection (6) is liable on summary conviction to imprisonment for a term not exceeding 3 months or a fine not exceeding level 4 on the standard scale or both, . . .

16. In this Part—

. . . 'public assembly' means an assembly of 20 or more persons in a public place which is wholly or partly open to the air;

'public place' means—

(a) any highway, or in Scotland any road within the meaning of the Roads (Scotland) Act 1984, and

(b) any place to which at the material time the public or any section of the public has access, on payment or otherwise, as of right or by virtue of express or implied permission;

'public procession' means a procession in a public place."

The conditions which may be imposed under section 14 are identical to those which may be imposed by the police officer on the spot under section 12 with regard to processions. Although there is no duty of advance notification, if the police are aware of an assembly which is imminent, they may impose conditions well in advance of the proposed day. Alternatively, conditions may be imposed on the spot. The conditions which may be imposed relate to numbers, location and duration. The background to section 14 was explained in the White Paper (Home Office: (1985)) in the following terms:

"5.7. It is right to give examples of how the Government anticipates that the new powers might operate in practice. The first test would enable the police to take preventative action to avoid serious public disorder. This might have proved useful on occasions in the past when marches have been banned and the organisers have announced their intention to hold a meeting instead. The National Front has on occasion staged a rally, after a march has been banned. The new power would not enable the police to ban the rally: but if they apprehended serious public disorder they would be able to insist that it was held in a less sensitive area. The power might also prove useful in relation to picketing which has resulted in outbreaks of serious public disorder: at Grunwick's or Warrington, for example, the police could have imposed conditions limiting the numbers of demonstrators, or moving the demonstration in support of the pickets further away from the factory. And the power could in suitable cases be used in relation to football matches: where the police apprehend serious public disorder in connection with a fixture they could where necessary impose conditions limiting the number of spectators.

5.8. As with marches, the test of serious public disorder will include serious damage to property. In most cases serious or widespread damage cannot be committed by demonstrators without engendering serious public disorder; but on occasion the clarification might prove useful in enabling the police to impose conditions on a demonstration where the main risk is damage to property (for example, animal rights protesters demonstrating outside an isolated laboratory or mink farm).

5.9. The second test is serious disruption to the life of the community. Static demonstrations may be thought in general to be less disruptive than marches, but on occasion they can deliberately or inadvertently result in serious disruption, and where this occurs it is right that the police should have power to take preventative action. An example of deliberate disruption is provided by the Stop The City demonstrations in 1983-84. These were intended to bring the City of London, and on one occasion Leeds, to a halt by a variety of disruptive activities. In the City of London the Commissioner had powers under the City of London Police Act 1839 to issue directions to his constables to keep order and to prevent any obstruction of the thoroughfares. No equivalent powers exist outside London. In such circumstances the police might on occasion find it helpful to be able to impose conditions limiting the numbers of demonstrators or indicating that certain areas would be out of bounds to them. In the diplomatic quarter of London residents have occasionally complained about the disruption caused by demonstrations outside neighbouring embassies: if the disruption was shown to be serious the police could limit the numbers or duration of a demonstration, or move it further away.

5.10. The third test is the coercion of individuals. The obvious example is picketing: where pickets deliberately try to obstruct the passage of those going to work, as they did at Grunwick's and during the miners' dispute, the police should be able to limit their numbers, or move them further away from the path of the workers. But examples can be given of other demonstrations which have attempted by force to obstruct the free movement of people or vehicles: in such cases it is right to give the police preventative powers to ensure that this does not happen. And examples of coercion go wider than deliberate obstruction: in the South Wales picketing case (*Thomas and others* v. *National Union of Mineworkers (South Wales Area)* Times Law Report 18 February 1985) the judge held that mass picketing which was not obstructive could nevertheless be intimidatory, especially outside someone's home.

5.11. It is not envisaged that the police will need formally to impose conditions at all frequently. But as with marches, their ability to do so will affect the legal framework within which negotiations with demonstration organisers are conducted. The police and the demonstrators will know that, in default of obtaining agreement about the ground rules, the police will be able to impose conditions if they apprehend that the demonstration will result in disorder, disruption or coercion. The organisers will have an incentive to negotiate; and the police will have to be reasonable, because if they impose conditions unreasonably, their decision will be open to challenge in the courts by judicial review."

It is important to stress that this power under section 14 may be utilised in advance of or at the time of the assembly. Unlike the CGSA, but like the other provisions of the POA 1986 there is no right of appeal against the conditions which the police may impose. At best there may be the possibility of judicial review, but the prospect of this does seem rather remote. If the police are late in imposing their conditions, it will be difficult to move quickly enough to persuade the court to intervene, and again the point has to be made that where police discretion is concerned the judges seem reluctant to second-guess the exercise of this power. Realistically, we are again left with ineffective safeguards against abuse, a situation which has aroused some concern. That concern was expressed by the N.C.C.L., albeit in rather exaggerated terms:

"11.5. The proposed tests for imposing conditions on static demonstrations are the same as for marches and processions: the reasonable apprehension of *serious disruption to the local community* or of *the coercion of individuals*. As we have argued above . . . these tests are unacceptably wide and vague. They involve the application of subjective judgment by the police, often in a political context. The exercise of police power in this way will provoke resentment and hostility. A test of disruption to the local community will become a test of convenience and a protest is never convenient to those against whom it is directed. A test of coercion of individuals is undoubtedly aimed at picketing. Every employer whose premises are picketed will call for the police to impose conditions by saying that the picket is disruptive and/or coercive to those seeking to enter the premises. The police will be obliged to act accordingly.

11.6. How will the police act? They will have no power to ban the static demonstration, but they will have the power to do the next best thing:
to impose conditions on the static demonstration in relation to *location, numbers*

and *duration*. In many circumstances the restrictions will be tantamount to a ban, a danger which the White Paper foresees, but fails to avoid. Parents protesting outside the Town Hall about inadequate child-care facilities could be removed to the local park, to what the White Paper calls a 'less sensitive area'. Pickets could be reduced to one in number. A proposed assembly at Greenham Common of 10,000 people could be restricted to 50 people for half an hour. The White Paper even suggests that the police should limit the numbers of spectators at football matches. These proposals undermine the necessary level of tolerance of the right of protest required in a free society. What price inconvenience? Will fireworks for a royal wedding, the carnival in Notting Hill, a 24-hour vigil outside South Africa House, a CND protest at Molesworth all fail the test?"
(Thornton, (1985:59-60))

Although there are no safeguards, there is nevertheless one crucial limitation. This is to be found in the definition of public place. The power to impose conditions applies only to public assemblies, which is defined to mean assemblies of 20 or more people in a public place which is wholly or partly open to the air. This has two consequences. First, the Act gives no power with regard to meetings held on private premises (such as those held in a university students union). Secondly, the Act applies only if the assembly consists of 20 or more people. As originally drafted the Bill applied to assemblies of three or more people. It may be questioned, however, whether this requirement as to numbers will be an effective limit on police powers under section 14. If the police anticipate that 20 or more people will assemble, can they issue instructions to the organisers that no more than six may assemble? Or if no conditions have been imposed and an assembly of 20 or more gather, could the police then insist that all but six people disperse? In this context it is important to note that a large crowd (standing silently) may in itself amount to intimidation (see *Thomas* v. *N.U.M. (South Wales Area)* [1985] 2 W.L.R. 1081). There is no reason in principle why such an instruction may not be issued. The power to issue instructions applies if 20 or more are anticipated, or if 20 or more attend. If as a result of these numbers the section is activated, then the police may impose conditions as to numbers which they deem necessary to prevent disorder, damage, disruption or intimidation. But what if less than 20 people assemble? Can the police issue conditions as to numbers, duration or location? The answer is not under section 14, but that they may in appropriate cases use common law powers which are probably as extensive as those conferred by the Public Order Act. This is a matter to which we return.

III. STATUTORY OFFENCES

In addition to the offences which may be committed under the provisions so far discussed, there is a range of other offences which may be committed by those who take part in assemblies of one form or another. The POA 1986 has introduced a number of new statutory offences for England and Wales, replacing some of the old common law crimes such as riot, unlawful assembly and rout. In addition, new offences of disorderly conduct and violent disorder have been introduced, replacing section 5 of the POA 1936 which prohibited offensive conduct conducive to breaches of the peace. Part I of the 1986 Act does not apply to Scotland, and indeed the government took the opportunity of repealing section 5 of the 1936 Act for both England and Wales and Scotland. The replacement provisions of the 1986 Act (which are wider) do not apply to Scotland, it being explained that: "Section 5 of the Public Order Act 1936 applies to Scotland . . . but is little used, because the offence which it defines is also covered by the common law offence of breach of the peace, as would be the offence which its proposed amendment would create. The Government, therefore, intends to take the opportunity to repeal section 5 so far as it extends to Scotland" (Home Office, 1985:45). We deal with common law offences in the following section (Section IV). In the rest of this section we deal with the principal statutory offences in Scots law. In presenting the material, we classify it according to:

A. The Location of the Assembly;
B. The Purposes of the Assembly; and
C. The Disruption of the Assembly.

We also deal with miscellaneous offences, particularly section 1 of the POA 1936, a measure which has survived the recent maelstrom of legislative change.

A.   THE LOCATION OF THE ASSEMBLY

6.   The Trespass (Scotland) Act 1865

"Interpretation
2. In this Act the following words shall have the meanings hereby assigned to them:
'Premises' shall mean and include any house, barn, stable, shed, loft, granary, outhouse, garden, stackyard, court, close, or inclosed space. . .

Parties lodging in premises or encamping on land, without permission or on turnpike or public road, guilty of an offence
3. Every person who lodges in any premises, or occupies or encamps on any land, being private property, without the consent and permission of the owner or legal occupier of such premises or land, and every person who encamps or lights a fire on or near any private road or enclosed or cultivated land, or in or near any plantation, without the consent and permission of the owner or legal occupier of such road, land, or plantation, or on or near any turnpike road, statute labour road, or other highway, shall be guilty of an offence punishable as herein-after provided."

This Act does not apply to processions, or at least to the overwhelming majority of them which take place on public streets; it is restricted to *private* land or buildings, though of course much land and many buildings owned by public authorities are "private" in this sense. As it applies to assemblies the major restriction is that it refers to "lodging" and "encamping," which imply some degree of duration. Clearly "protest camps" such as Greenham Common or Faslane would fall within the Act. "Sit-ins" or occupations may do so also (see *Galt* v. *Philp* [1984] I.R.L.R. 156, discussed later in this chapter). Whether a two-hour rally would do so seems much less likely. Where the Act *would* require the owner's permission the owner may be as arbitrary or politically-biased as he or she wishes. This may be acceptable if the owner is a private body, but wholly objectionable if the owner is a public body. Conceivably, though the matter has never been tested, general administrative law principles would prevent such a body from acting unreasonably (*Wheeler* v. *Leicester City Council* [1985] A.C. 1054).

7.   The Civic Government (Scotland) Act 1982

"Obstruction by pedestrians
  53. Any person who, being on foot in any public place—
  (a)   obstructs, along with another or others, the lawful passage of any other person and fails to desist on being require to do so by a constable in uniform, or
  (b)   wilfully obstructs the lawful passage of any other person
shall be guilty of an offence and liable, on summary conviction, to a fine not exceeding £50."

This is a potentially important power in the policing of public assemblies. Although the penalty on conviction is not high, the police are nevertheless entitled to arrest without a warrant, and they may do so to disperse a crown or to thin out a crowd. The crucial question is what amounts to obstruction? The corresponding provision in English law is contained in the Highways Act 1980, s. 137, which provides that it is an offence if a person "without lawful authority or excuse" (a qualification not found in the Scottish statute) "wilfully obstructs the passage along the highway." It has been commented that: "Cases under s. 137 and analogous statutory provisions have consistently taken the line that the obstruction of any part of the highway constitutes obstruction for these purposes, notwithstanding that there is room for persons to pass by, or that delay is minimal" (Bailey, Harris and Jones, (1985:133)). It has also been observed that "the amount and duration of an obstruction that [the police need] to establish in order to obtain a conviction are slight," with the result that "the police and the local authority have almost a *de facto* licensing power with regard to public meetings and even the distribution of leaflets in the streets" (de Smith, (1981:498)). The leading Scottish case suggests that these comments and observations are as appropriate here as they are in England and Wales.

8. Aldred v. Miller
1924 J.C. 117

This was a charge under the Glasgow (Police) Act 1866, s. 149(47) of which made liable to a penalty "Every person who occasions any kind of obstruction, nuisance, or annoyance in any road, street, court, or common stair, or obstructs or incommodes, hinders, or prevents the free passage along or through the same, or prejudices or annoys in any manner whatsoever any other person using the same."

It was alleged that Aldred caused an obstruction by standing in Hamilton Drive near Great Western Road, Glasgow, and lecturing in a loud voice, thereby causing a crowd of persons to assemble, with the result that the streets were wholly or to a large extent blocked up so as to obstruct, incommode, hinder, or prevent free passage along or through the streets. The accused was convicted by the magistrates, whereupon he brought a bill of suspension in which it was stated:

"'3. The *locus* libelled in the said complaint adjoins the Botanic Gardens, Glasgow, and is a favourite spot for the holding of open-air meetings for political and other purposes. The complainer had been, prior to the date libelled in said complaint, in the habit of addressing meetings at said *locus* on Sunday afternoons, and was doing so on Sunday, 10th February 1924, the date libelled. His said meetings were widely advertised, and were well known to the police. Said meetings were largely attended, and it was the duty of the police to regulate the crowd of people who attended the complainer's said meeting, and to see that the said people did not impede the passage of pedestrians or vehicular traffic at said *locus*.

4. Evidence was led on said 28th March 1924 in support of said complaint as follows:—Sergeant Thomas Ross, a police-sergeant, stated that he was on duty in Hamilton Drive on said date, and saw the complainer commence his lecture at 3.30 p.m. at said *locus,* and about 4 p.m. there would be nearly 300 persons present; that these persons blocked the east pavement, but the west pavement was not blocked at any time; that several motors came along and had to slow down, but were not held up, as the crowd made way for them to pass; that, after some time, a motor was brought to a standstill till a passage was made; that the driver of this motor complained to the witness, who spoke to the present complainer and asked the latter to stop lecturing; that the present complainer offered the witness his name and address, but said he was not going to give up his right to address a public meeting; and that there appeared to be no one in connexion with the meeting regulating the crowd. In cross-examination this witness stated (1) that he expected the complainer to keep the street clear, and (2) that he was not aware that it had been laid down in Glasgow that the police had to regulate the traffic. This witness was in general corroborated by Constable John Lyall. Mrs Eliza Gray, who was with her husband in the motor car said to have been brought to a standstill, stated that the said car had not been long held up, as the crowd made way for it. Mr Graeme Hunter stated that

he was not personally obstructed, but that he saw the meeting in progress, and saw the said delay to the motor car.

5. For the defence the following evidence was led:—Mr William Forbes stated that he was chairman at the said meeting; that he was going round about the crowd during the meeting; that people were standing at the side of the pavement; that neither pavement was blocked; that there was sufficient room for motors to pass; that the complainer at his meetings asked the crowd to keep a passage clear for traffic; that at the meeting in question he carried out his said custom, and made the said request of the crowd present. Mr Charles Dorran stated that he was selling literature at the said meeting; that he saw two or three motors slow down, but none stop. Mr William C. Stark stated that he was not a member of any political organisation; that he was present at the meeting in question; that the number of persons was smaller than the number attending meetings at the same place under the auspices of the Scottish Economic League and the Reconstruction Society; that he saw one or two cars slow down as they approached the meeting, but that motors usually slowed down near that point to take the corner.'. . .

The complainer pleaded, inter alia;—'(1) The complaint condescended on being irrelevant and not containing averments sufficient in law to constitute the offence libelled under the section of the Act therein described, the conviction and sentence complained of should be suspended, and the respondent ordered to repay the fine to the complainer, with expenses as craved. (2) The complainer having, at the time and place libelled in said complaint, conducted himself in an orderly manner in the exercise of his lawful right of addressing the lieges on his political views, the conviction and sentence complained of should be suspended, and the respondent ordered to repay the said fine to the complainer, with expenses as craved.' The case was heard before the High Court on 20th June 1924, when the complainer appeared in person and argued;—The evidence led for the prosecution pointed to an ordinary public meeting, which did not necessarily constitute an obstruction. It was held in a place where meetings were often held, and in such circumstances it was the duty of the police to do their best to keep the roadway clear, and this they did not do. There was no evidence that the complainer refused to co-operate in abating the obstruction. If there was any obstruction, it was of the most trifling character, and there was no evidence that it continued after the warning by the police. Accordingly, the conviction was not supported by evidence."

LORD JUSTICE-GENERAL (Clyde): "The complainer objected, and objects, to the relevancy of the complaint, but I do not think the objection is sound. The reasons adduced in argument in support of the objection appear to me to be vitiated by a fallacy which arises from the failure to distinguish between a private right and a public right. When a man exercises a private right, he is using that which is his own; and, because the right is his own, it is exclusive of the rights of others. But when a man exercises a public right he uses that which is not his own, but belongs to the community of which he is only a constituent unit. His participation in the benefits of the public right is not exclusive of, but must be so restricted as to be consistent with, the equal participation of the other constituent members of the public community to whom the right belongs. In short, the exercise of a public right is circumscribed on every hand by the duty (which arises out of the very nature of public rights) to respect the equal rights of the others to participate in them. Apart from questions regarding the special rights of frontagers, the right to use a public street, for any of the public purposes to which it is dedicated as such, is a public right, not a private one. Accordingly, if anybody does what the section on which the complaint was founded prohibits—if, that is to say, anybody causes an obstruction in a public street or hinders other members of the public in exercising the public right of free passage upon it—he selfishly engrosses the public right to himself, and his action is justly condemned.

The complaint is not against holding a public meeting; the complaint is that the accused caused an obstruction on a public street by holding a public meeting there. An obstruction to the exercise by members of the public of the public uses for which the streets exist—passage in particular—can certainly be created in that way: and an obstruction so caused is not any the less objectionable because the author of it is a person who advertises, or otherwise convenes, a public meeting in order that it may stand on the street and listen to his speeches. As I have already indicated, there is no such thing as a private right in any individual to make use of any public street for holding public meetings. If the thing is done at all, it must be done with due regard to the equal participation of all the members of the public in the various uses for which public streets are kept open.

I do not attempt to define the uses to which a public street, as such, is legally devoted. I have assumed in what I have said that the use for public meeting is not wholly excluded from the catalogue of legal public uses. But, assuming that it is such a use (like the use of part of the surface of a street as a stance for vehicles plying for hire), it must be conducted under the many and serious restrictions which are imposed by the necessity of avoiding interferences with other public uses. If those restrictions are not observed—and it is not always easy to observe them—the Magistrates have the duty of enforcing them. The section under which the present complaint was brought provides one of the means of enforcement. It must be remembered, as Lord Dunedin pointed out in *McAra* v. *Magistrates of Edinburgh*, 1913 S.C. 1059, that of all the public uses to which public streets are legally dedicated, that of free unrestricted passage is the most important.

It is impossible to say that there was no evidence in the case to support the conviction. There was clear evidence of obstruction. A large part of the street was blocked, and wheeled vehicles had to slow down in order to make a way through, or even to stop. It is no answer whatever, in the complainer's mouth, to say that the police ought to have come to his aid. The duty of the police is to vindicate public right, and not to facilitate abuse of the street by any individual for purposes of his own.

It seems to me that there is no ground of challenge of this conviction, and I propose that we should refuse the bill of suspension."

LORD SANDS: "I agree. I do not think that any question of the right to use a street as a place of public meeting arises in this case. There is no doubt that when meetings in such places are customary they are not interfered with. On the other hand, there is also no doubt that, if they cause an obstruction, they are an offence. The question whether an obstruction has been caused is one of fact; it is left to the local judge who tries the case. It may happen that he may take a view which another judge might not have taken. But we cannot interfere with his decision on a question of fact, whether or not we should have come to the same conclusion. But, on the facts stated in this particular case, I do not think there is any reason to doubt that the Judge was properly satisfied that there had been an obstruction. It may not have been a very grave or serious obstruction; but there was an obstruction, and he was entitled to convict.

Lord Cullen agreed.

B. THE PURPOSES OF THE ASSEMBLY

9. The Public Order Act 1986

"Words or gestures
19.—(1) A person who uses in a public place or at a public meeting words or gestures which are threatening, abusive or insulting is guilty of an offence if he intends hatred against a racial group in Great Britain to be stirred up, or such hatred is likely to be stirred up, by the use of the words or gestures.
(2) A person is guilty of an offence under this section only if he intends his words or gestures to be, or is aware that they may be, threatening, abusive or insulting."

This section has its origins in section 6 of the Race Relations Act 1965 which made it an offence, with intent to stir up hatred against any section of the public on grounds of colour, race, or ethnic or national origin, to use in a public place or at a public meeting threatening, abusive or insulting words which are likely to stir up such hatred. As originally enacted, section 6 was, however, widely criticised. Lord Scarman (1975:35) referred to it as "an embarrassment to the police. Hedged about with restrictions (proof of intent, requirement of the Attorney-General's consent) it is useless to a policeman on the street." The measure was repealed in 1976 and a new provision substituted in its place: this became section 5A of the POA 1936. This provided that it was an offence in a public place or at a public meeting to use words which are threatening, abusive or insulting where hatred is likely to be stirred up against any racial group. But this too was criticised as inadequate (Home Office, (1981:29-31)) with the Government expressing the view in the White Paper that section 5A "should be re-cast to penalise conduct which is either likely to stir up racial hatred or which is intended to do so" (Home Office, (1985:39)). This proposed change, which has been incorporated in section 19 of the 1986 Act, was welcomed by the N.C.C.L.:

"N.C.C.L. welcomes the moves to strengthen the law against stirring up racial hatred. It is right to penalise conduct which is *intended* to stir up racial hatred even though it may not be possible to prove that it is likely to do so. This arises where those confronted with the conduct either agree with it or are so implacably opposed to it that there is no chance of their being influenced by it. But for the present inadequacy of the law, two of the best known failed prosecutions would probably have been successful. The first case concerned the delivery of inflammatory material, a pamphlet entitled 'Blacks not wanted here', to Sidney Bidwell MP. The Court of Appeal decided that distribution of a pamphlet to the home of a Member

of Parliament was not publication to the public at large. The other case was the prosecution of John Kingsley Read, leader of the British Movement, who addressed his supporters, after an Asian youth was killed in Southall, with the words 'One down, a million to go.'"
(Thornton, 1985:41)

A second measure which deals with the purpose of the assembly is the Conspiracy and Protection of Property Act 1875, s. 7 (see Chapter 4). This provision applies mainly (though as we shall see not exclusively) to picketing. It has been applied mainly in the context of labour picketing, though there is no reason in principle why it could not be used to deal with consumer or other picketing if the ingredients of the offence are met. These are three in number: first that the action is done with a view to compel; secondly, that it is so done wrongfully and without legal authority; and thirdly, that the conduct takes one of the forms listed in 1 to 5. The main source of controversy caused by this section relates to item 4, that is to say watching and besetting. This means that picketing *per se* will be criminal if it is done wrongfully and without legal authority. So far as labour picketing is concerned, lawful authority has in fact been provided since 1875. The present authority is now to be found in the Trade Union and Labour Relations Act 1974, s. 15, as restricted by an amendment introduced by the Employment Act 1980, s. 16. As amended, section 15 now provides:

(1) It shall be lawful for a person in contemplation or furtherance of a trade dispute to attend—
    (*a*) at or near his own place of work, or
    (*b*) if he is an official of a trade union, at or near the place of work of a member of that union whom he is accompanying and whom he represents,
for the purpose only of peacefully obtaining or communicating information, or peacefully persuading any person to work or abstain from working.
(2) If a person works or normally works—
    (*a*) otherwise than at any one place, or
    (*b*) at a place the location of which is such that attendance there for a purpose mentioned in subsection (1) above is impracticable,
his place of work for the purposes of that subsection shall be any premises of his employer from which he works or from which his work is administered.
(3) In the case of a worker who is not in employment,
  Where—
    (*a*) his last employment was terminated in connection with a trade dispute, or
    (*b*) the termination of his employment was one of the circumstances giving rise to a trade dispute,
subsection (1) above shall in relation to that dispute have effect as if any reference to his place of work were a reference to his former place of work.
(4) A person who is an official of a trade union by virtue only of having been elected or appointed to be a representative of some of the members of the union shall be regarded for the purposes of subsection (1) above as representing only those

members; but otherwise an official of a trade union shall be regarded for those purposes as representing all its members."

But the question which arises is simply this: what is the status of picketing which is not labour picketing within the meaning of section 15, or is labour picketing outside the scope of the area of legality? Is the simple act of picketing (watching and besetting) wrongful? The issue is a controversial one, which has been considered on several occasions by the English courts. In *J. Lyons & Sons* v. *Wilkins* [1896] 1 Ch. 811 and [1899] 1 Ch. 255 there was a strike by the Society of Fancy Leather Workers at the premises of J. Lyons & Sons. A picket of two men was mounted to persuade workers not to work for the employer until the dispute was resolved. No violence, threats or intimidation were used. In an action for an injunction by the employer—based on section 7—it was argued for the union that the picketing must be independently actionable at common law, civilly or criminally; otherwise section 7 could not apply. This argument was rejected, however, with the court holding first that the use of the word "wrongful" in section 7 was superfluous, being only an indication of the phraseology to be used by the pleader. In other words the items in 1 to 5 were criminal; and secondly, it was argued that in any event watching and besetting is wrongful in the sense that it is an actionable tort (i.e. civil wrong), being a nuisance.

Some 10 years later, however, the matter was reconsidered by a differently-constituted Court of Appeal. In *Ward, Lock & Co.* v. *O.P.A.S.* (1906) 22 T.L.R. 327, a picket was set up with two aims. One was to induce men employed in printing works to join the union; and the second was to induce new members to join the strike which was being conducted. The aim of the strike was to force the employer to hire union-only labour. Again, there was no evidence of violence, threats or intimidation. This time, however, the court adopted a different construction. It was held that in order to constitute an offence, the acts listed in 1 to 5 must at least give rise to liability in reparation, thereby rejecting the view that the word "wrongfully" is superfluous. So to secure a conviction, the prosecution must show that the picketing was at least civilly actionable. The court then went on to hold, again in contrast to the *Lyons* case, that picketing is not *per se* a nuisance and that the tortious quality of the picketing would depend on the facts. In the case in question it was held that the peaceful picketing was not wrongful in this sense. So there is a direct conflict in these two decisions of the Court of Appeal. Later cases tend to favour *Ward, Lock,* which was endorsed in *Fowler* v. *Kibble* [1922] 1 Ch. 487 and, by Lord Denning, in *Hubbard* v. *Pitt* [1975] I.C.R. 308. It was also followed by Scott J. in the following case, though it has to be said that the learned judge also breathed new fire into the section by increasing the range of potential plaintiffs or pursuers, if his decision is followed in Scotland.

10. Thomas v. National Union of Mineworkers
(South Wales Area)
[1985] 2 W.L.R. 1081

The plaintiffs included miners who were known to have returned to work during the strike. In doing so, they were met by large gatherings of pickets and demonstrators, sometimes as many as 200-300. The crowds were kept back from the roads in to the collieries to allow the working miners to pass. Abuse was hurled at the men including "you scabby bastards," "you'll get your heads kicked in," and similar phrases which counsel for the defendants reassuringly claimed were merely "a little rough language," not likely to upset "a tough, self-reliant, down-to-earth miner." The plaintiffs nevertheless sought injunctions to restrain this picketing of their own places of work, and also of other sites which included collieries, power stations and steelworks.

SCOTT J.: "The working miners are entitled to use the highway for the purpose of entering and leaving their respective places of work. In the exercise of that right they are at present having to suffer the presence and behaviour of the pickets and demonstrators. The law has long recognised that unreasonable interference with the rights of others is actionable in tort. The law of nuisance is a classic example and was classically described by Lindley M.R. in *J Lyons & Sons* v. *Wilkins* [1899] Ch. 255 at p. 267. I have already cited the passage. It is, however, not every act of interference with the enjoyment by an individual of his property rights that will be actionable in nuisance. The law must strike a balance between conflicting rights and interests. The point is made in *Clark and Lindsell*, para, 23/01: 'A variety of different things may amount to a nuisance *in fact* but whether they are *actionable* as the *tort* of nuisance will depend upon a variety of considerations and a balance of conflicting interests.'

Nuisance is strictly concerned with, and may be regarded as confined to, activity which unduly interferes with the use or enjoyment of land or of easements. But there is no reason why the law should not protect on a similar basis the enjoyment of other rights. All citizens have the right to use the public highway. Suppose an individual were persistently to follow another in a public highway, making rude gestures or remarks in order to annoy or vex. If continuance of such conduct were threatened no one can doubt but that a civil court would, at the suit of the victim, restrain by an injunction the continuance of the conduct. The tort might be described as a species of private nuisance, namely unreasonable interference with the victim's rights to use the highway. But the label for the tort does not, in my view, matter.

In the present case, the working miners have the right to use the highway for the purpose of going to work. They are, in my judgment, entitled under the general law to exercise that right without unreasonable harassment by others. Unreasonable harassment of them in their exercise of that right would, in my judgment, be tortious.

A decision whether in this, or in any other similar case, the presence or conduct of pickets represents a tortious interference with the right of those who wish to go to work to do so without harassment must depend on the particular circumstances of the particular case. The balance to which I have earlier referred must be struck between the rights of those going to work and the rights of the pickets.

It was made clear in *Ward Lock & Co. Ltd.* v. *Operative Printers' Assistants' Society* (1906) 22 T.L.R. 327 that picketing was not, *per se,* a common law nuisance. The Court of Appeal was in that case considering the question from the point of view of the owner of the premises being picketed. The picketing was peaceful and *per* Vaughan Williams L.J. (at 329), 'there was no evidence that the comfort of the plaintiffs or the ordinary enjoyment of the Botolph Printing Works was seriously interfered with by the watching and besetting.' He held in effect, that there was no common law nuisance being committed.

Similarly, in the present case, the working miners cannot complain of picketing *per se* or of demonstrations *per se*. They can only complain of picketing or demonstrations which unreasonably harass them in their entry into and egress from their place of work.

From the comments I have already made earlier in this judgment it will be apparent that I think it plain from the evidence before me that the picketing at the colliery gates is of a nature and is carried out in a manner that represents an unreasonable harassment of the working miners. A daily congregation on average of 50 to 70 men hurling abuse and in circumstances that require a police presence and require the working miners to be conveyed in vehicles do not in my view leave any real room for argument. The working miners have the right to go to work. Neither they nor any other working man should be required, in order to exercise that right, to tolerate the situation I have described. Accordingly in my judgement the colliery gates picketing is tortious at the suit of the plaintiff or plaintiffs who work at the collieries in question. . .

The form of the injunctions is important and difficult. The injunctions must state the nature of the picketing which is to be restrained. The plaintiffs' rights are rights, in my view, not to be unreasonably harassed on their way to or from work. But an injunction cast in that form would be useless. It would beg practically every question raised by this application. The injunction must deal with the two aspects of the picketing that, in my view, have justified the plaintiffs' application for relief, namely the intimidatory quality of the picketing and the abuse and threats which accompany the picketing.

I have already expressed the view that given the temper of the local communities and the strong feelings that have plainly been raised by the return to work of some of the members of the union, sheer weight of sufficient numbers on the picket lines would be sufficient by itself to be intimidatory. It is, in my judgment, tortious for the South Wales branch by its lodges to organise or participate in picketing on an intimidatory scale. So the injunction must, in my view, restrain the union from organising or participating in picketing by more than some specified number of persons. What should that number be? Counsel for the first to seventh defendants pointed out that two or three might by their words and gestures intimidate, whereas a dozen might, by the calmness and reasonableness of their behaviour, not be intimidatory at all. I agree with that. Any number chosen is necessarily arbitrary. I am, however, given some statutory guidance.

Section 3 of the Employment Act 1980, provided, by subs. (1) for the Secretary of State to 'issue Codes of Practice containing such practical guidance as he thinks fit for the purpose of promoting the improvement of industrial relations.' The section provides for any such code to be preceded by consultation with ACAS, and, by subs. (4), to be approved by resolution of both Houses of Parliament. Subsection (8) provides:

'A failure on the part of any person to observe any provision of a Code of Practice issued under this section shall not of itself render him liable to any proceedings; but in any proceedings before a court or industrial tribunal or the Central Arbitration Committee—(a) any such Code shall be admissible in evidence, and (b) any provision of the Code which appears to the court, tribunal or committee to be relevant to any question arising in the proceedings shall be taken into account in determining that question.'

A code of practice has been issued by the Secretary of State under s. 3, and has been approved by both Houses of Parliament. It came into force on 17 December 1980 under the Employment Code of Practice (Picketing) Order 1980. Section E of the code is headed 'Limiting numbers of Pickets.' Paragraph 29 is in these terms:

'The main cause of violence and disorder on the picket line is excessive numbers. Wherever large numbers of people with strong feelings are involved there is a danger that the situation will get out of control and that those concerned will run the risk of arrest and prosecution.'

I need not read para. 30, but para. 31 is important:

'Large numbers on a picket line are also likely to give rise to fear and resentment amongst those seeking to cross that picket line, even where no criminal offence is committed. They exacerbate disputes and sour relations not only between management and employees but between the pickets and their fellow employees. Accordingly pickets and their organisers should ensure that in general the number of pickets does not exceed six at any entrance to a workplace. Frequently a smaller number would be appropriate.'

Paragraph 31 does not make it a criminal offence or tortious to have more than six persons on a picket line. Nor is less than six any guarantee of lawfulness. The paragraph simply provides a guide as to a sensible number for a picket line in order that the weight of numbers should not intimidate those who wish to go to work. I am directed by subs. (8) of s. 3 of the 1980 Act to take this guidance into account.

I do so and propose, therefore, to restrain the South Wales branch by its lodges, from organising picketing or demonstrations at colliery-gates by more than six persons. I should make it clear that there is, in my judgment, no legitimate distinction to be drawn between so-called pickets who are stationed close to the gates of the colliery and the rest, so-called demonstrators, who stand nearby.

I now come to the matter of verbal abuse and threats. The legitimate purpose of picketing is peaceful persuasion or the peaceful communication or obtaining of information. Threats of violence and intimidatory language are inconsistent with peaceful persuasion. Some use of insulting language may perhaps be consistent with peaceful persuasion, but nevertheless if carried to extremes and persisted in over a long period it would become, in my view, tortious. There is obviously a risk in a case such as this that pickets may use strong language. It is part of the defendant's case that on the South Wales picket lines strong language is almost bound to be used. But in order that picketing should remain peaceful picketing it is, in my judgment, the duty of those who organise the picketing to do their best to see that threats of violence are not offered by the pickets and that use of strong language does not get out of hand. If the number of pickets is kept down to six or thereabouts the problems about verbal abuse and threats may well become unimportant.

The evidence of the officers of the Abernant lodge, to which I have already referred, was that, as a matter of practice, they always advised pickets not to make threats to working miners. This is a practice which, it seems to me, ought to be adopted by all the lodges, and it should, in my view, be the responsibility of the South Wales branch to take such steps as are practicable to ensure that its lodges do so.

Accordingly I propose to grant an injunction in respect of each of the five collieries I have mentioned, restraining the union and its servants, agents and officers, including the officers of the lodge of the colliery in question, in these terms: from inciting, procuring, assisting, encouraging or organising members of the union or others, to congregate or assemble at or near the entrance to the colliery (a) otherwise than for the purpose of peacefully obtaining or communicating information or peacefully persuading any person to work or abstain from working, and (b) otherwise than in numbers not exceeding six."

It was once thought that section 7 was largely redundant. The section has, however, been revived in the 1980s. The decision in *Thomas* will clearly help that revival by extending its potential use. Scott J. comes close to saying that in certain circumstances a large attendance of pickets will *per se* give rise to liability in tort (reparation), is therefore wrongful, and therefore a violation of section 7. Parliament has also helped the revival of section 7. In the White Paper it was claimed:

"5.16. The section has been criticised as archaic; but the circumstances of the miners' dispute have shown how important it is to have an offence penalising conduct of this kind. The provision was used mainly in dealing with intimidation away from the picket line, in particular the besetting of people's homes. It was also used for offences on the picket line; but its effectiveness is hampered by the fact that it is not an arrestable offence, and by the maximum penalty being three months' imprisonment or a fine of £100. To enable the police to deal more effectively with criminal intimidation, the Government proposes that section 7 of the 1875 Act should be made an arrestable offence; and that the maximum penalty should be increased to six months' imprisonment or a fine of £2000."
(Home Office (1985)).

Parliament responded in the POA 1986, which amended the section to provide that suspects could be arrested without a warrant and by increasing the penalty. As suggested, the revival was due mainly to the miners' strike, with 643 charges in England and Wales (Wallington, (1985a: 130)), though with much fewer arrests and prosecutions in Scotland (only four) (*ibid.,* 151). Nevertheless, the revival of section 7 was led by the Scottish prosecution authorities. It was used during a strike of tax inspectors in *Elsey* v. *Smith* [1983] I.R.L.R. 292. Moreover, in 1984 a new use was found for the section in a very controversial incident which led to judicial criticism of the conduct of the police.

In *Galt* v. *Philp* [1984] I.R.L.R. 156 a dispute existed between medical laboratory scientific officers and medical consultants employed by Fife Health Board which was responsible for running hospital services in Fife, including the Victoria Hospital in Kirkcaldy. In the course of the dispute one of the medical laboratory scientific officers was suspended. In response, a sit-in in the laboratory was organised. The MLSOs refused entry to other hospital staff. Police officers, including the chief constable, were called and negotiations continued for some hours. Eventually, the police made a forced entry and arrested those inside, charging them under the Trespass (Scotland) Act 1865. For reasons which are not clear from the report, these charges were not proceeded with. A new charge was, however, brought under section 7(4) and one of the questions on an appeal from the sheriff (who refused to convict) to the High Court of Justiciary (which reversed the sheriff) was whether the section applied to sit-ins of this kind. The court held that it did. In view of the Lord Justice-General:

"The mischief to which s. 7, head 4, is directed is action designed to prevent persons from going into or coming out of a relevant place and it would be contrary to common sense to hold that control of access or egress from a position immediately outside the main door of a building is within the ambit of s. 7 whereas exercise of the same control from a position immediately on the inner side of the main door is not. What is libelled here is locking, barricading and otherwise securing the means of access to the Fife Area Laboratory and the laboratories and other rooms therein and on the evidence there was in my opinion besetting within the ordinary meaning of the word 'beset' both in the *Shorter Oxford English Dictionary* and in *Chambers' Dictionary.*"

Lord Cameron was more expansive:

"The evidence, so far as led, indicates that certain named persons were prevented from obtaining entry to the laboratory to which in performance of their contract of employment, they were entitled and required to have access at any time. Such action, if not warranted by legal authority, as this was not, would constitute a legal wrong and attract civil liability either by way of interdict or, if loss could be demonstrated, by action of damages. As to that I do not think there can be room for doubt: if that view of the circumstances disclosed be correct, as I think it is, then, should it amount to 'besetting' as is libelled in this complaint, the conduct of the respondents would be in contravention of s. 7 of the 1875 Act. The evidence so well and carefully narrated by the sheriff, (and it was not said that his narrative was in any way inaccurate), appears to me to demonstrate that access to the hospital laboratories was effectively blocked by the action of the respondents and therefore this could most properly be characterised as 'besetting.' The words of the statute used to describe the offence are: 'Watches or besets the house or other place. . . Where such other persons . . . works or carries on business. . . or the approach to such house or place.' The use of this language and of the alternative 'watches or besets' in my opinion is indicative that the offence is not limited to the maintenance of an external watch, nor does recourse to the *Oxford Dictionary* suggest that the word 'beset' is to receive so limited an interpretation. It would in any event be manifestly absurd, having regard to the evil which the statute seeks to suppress, so to construe the statute that the external watcher should be held guilty of an offence, but scatheless if he were to force his way in and occupy the house or place concerned, for precisely the same purpose and objective. In view of the fact that articles indicative of an occupation to be undertaken by a number of people and prolonged at least overnight, were recovered on the premises by the police, it appears to me that, in the absence of evidence pointing to the contrary, the sheriff would be entitled, if he accepted that evidence, to draw the inference of guilt in respect of all respondents remaining in the complaint."

C. THE DISRUPTION OF THE ASSEMBLY

11. The Public Meeting Act 1908

"Penalty on endeavour to break up public meeting
1.—(1) Any person who at a lawful public meeting acts in a disorderly manner for the purpose of preventing the transaction of the business for which the meeting was called together shall be guilty of an offence. . .

(2) Any person who incites others to commit an offence under this section shall be guilty of a like offence.

(3) If any constable reasonably suspects any person of committing an offence under the foregoing provisions of this section, he may if requested so to do by the chairman of the meeting require that person to declare to him immediately his name and address and, if that person refuses or fails so to declare his name and address or gives a false name and address he shall be guilty of an offence under this subsection and liable on summary conviction thereof to a fine not exceeding twenty five pounds, and if he refuses or fails so to declare his name and address or if the constable reasonably suspects him of giving a false name and address, the constable may without warrant arrest him."

This originated as a Private Member's Bill introduced to prevent the deliberate disruption of public meetings by the suffragettes (Home Office, 1985:7). The leading case is *Burden* v. *Rigler* [1911] 1 K.B. 337, where it was held that the Act also applies to lawful meetings held on the public highway. Subsection (3) was introduced by the POA 1936. The operation of this subsection requires co-operation between the organiser of a meeting and the police. It is quite clear, however, that the police would normally have a common law power to enter a meeting (public or private) to prevent a breach of the peace, with or without the permission of the organiser of the meeting. As a result the 1908 Act may be largely redundant.

12.   The Representation of the People Act 1983

"Disturbances at election meetings
"97.—(1) A person who at a lawful public meeting to which this section applies

acts, or incites others to act, in a disorderly manner for the purpose of preventing the transaction of the business for which the meeting was called together shall be guilty of an illegal practice.

(2) This section applies to—

(a) a political meeting held in any constituency between the date of the issue of a writ for the return of a member of Parliament for the constituency and the date at which a return to the writ is made;

(b) a meeting held with reference to a local government election in the electoral area for that election on, or within three weeks before, the day of the election.

(3) If a constable reasonably suspects any person of committing an offence under subsection (1) above, he may if requested so to do by the chairman of the meeting require that person to declare to him immediately his name and address and, if that person refuses or fails so to declare his name and address or gives a false name and address, he shall be liable on summary conviction to a fine not exceeding level 1 on the standard scale, and—

(a) if he refuses or fails so to declare his name and address or

(b) if the constable reasonably suspects him of giving a false name and address, the constable may without warrant arrest him."

Under the Representation of the People Act 1983, s. 95, candidates for parliamentary elections may use schoolrooms and other rooms maintained out of rates free of charge to promote their candidature. Candidates for local authority elections may use schoolrooms. Section 97 makes it an offence to disrupt such a meeting. The main problem in recent years, however, has not been disruption at meetings, but the provocative holding of meetings by the National Front in racially sensitive areas. The matter was considered at length by the Green Paper (Home Office, (1981:24-26)). The government has, however, decided to take no action (Home Office, (1985:36-37)), contending that "the response to the Green Paper has confirmed the difficulty of making any changes in this area" (ibid.:36). The White Paper addressed specifically two particular proposals. The first was whether a local authority in consultation with the police should be empowered to require a candidate to hold his or her meeting elsewhere in the constituency. This was rejected because it "would encroach upon the right of the candidate to convey his message to the electorate in the area of his choice; and it would involve the police and the public authorities in decisions bearing upon the political fortunes of particular candidates" (ibid.:36-37). The second proposal was that meetings held under section 95 should be genuinely open to the public and that candidates should not be permitted to hold closed meetings. The government thought that there would be considerable practical difficulty in implementing this proposal, which required that "a substantial proportion of seats at election meetings should be open to the public" (ibid.:37). It is to be noted that the N.C.C.L. has since responded by proposing that the phrase "public meeting," as used in section 95, should be defined to mean:

"any meeting held under the provisions of section 82 or section 83 of this Act and which any person may attend without restriction on entrance by ticket, invitation or otherwise, provided that a candidate or their agent may retain for the candidate's own purpose not more than one quarter of the seats available in the meeting room."

The N.C.C.L. explained that:

"This definition allows for the attendance, for example, of a local party's executive committee and other supporters. But above the proportion of a quarter of the seats available the meeting must be open to the public on a first come, first served basis. If any political party wishes to hold a meeting to show 'the widespread and national support a candidate enjoys,' it should hold a private meeting, at its own expense, to which the press can be invited."

D. OTHER OFFENCES

13. The Public Order Act 1936

"Prohibition of uniforms in connection with political objects
    1.—(1) Subject as hereinafter provided, any person who in any public place or at any public meeting wears uniform signifying his association with any political organisation or with the promotion of any political object shall be guilty of an offence:
    Provided that, if the chief officer of police is satisfied that the wearing of any such uniform aforesaid on any ceremonial, anniversary, or other special occasion will not be likely to involve risk of public disorder, he may, with the consent of a Secretary of State, by order permit the wearing of such uniform on that occasion either absolutely or subject to such conditions as may be specified in the order. . .
    9.—(1). . . 'Meeting' means a meeting held for the purpose of the discussion of matters of public interest or for the purpose of the expression of views on such matters. . .
    'Public meeting' includes any meeting in a public place and any meeting which the public or any section thereof are permitted to attend, whether on payment or otherwise;
    'Public place' includes any highway, or in Scotland any road within the meaning of the Roads (Scotland) Act 1984, and any other premises or place to which at the material time the public have or are permitted to have access, whether on payment or otherwise."

This section was introduced in response to the adoption of uniforms by a number of groups, but principally the Fascists, in the 1930s, their aim being, of course, to give themselves a paramilitary air, a feeling of strength and a more fear-inspiring presence. What was desired was to suppress this intimidating use of uniform without preventing such uses of uniform as that by the Boy Scouts. As Mr Clynes put it on Second Reading (317 H.C. Debs. 1369):

"We have no objection to the continued use of that innocent regalia associated with so many groups in this country. a ribbon, a sash, or some distinctive piece of pageantry has usually been used without complaint or even notice, and has been accepted as a gesture to some treasured memory or to some historical or worthy purpose. Shirts, jackets and jerseys are in themselves unimportant. The real point is what they signify and what they are intended to denote. A garb answering to a uniform and worn in what really is a military march and in a military manner and spirit brings into our political activities alien elements making for conflict and disorder."

The solution was the provision of a dispensing power to the chief constable and a deliberate avoidance of any definition of "uniform," leaving it as a matter of fact for local judges. A few prosecutions occurred in the 1930s establishing *inter alia* that a uniform need not be a complete livery and that a Fascist belt-buckle and armband were sufficient to constitute an offence (*R. v. Charnley* (1937) 81 Sol.J. 108; for other examples see Ivamy, (1949: 185-187)). The use of uniforms is not part of current street politics, although if the deliberate fostering of violence between defined groups can be considered itself to be a political end, certain current fashions would seem to be political uniforms (mods, skinheads, etc.). Instead the Act has found a new use against the I.R.A.

14. O'Moran v. D.P.P.; Whelan v. D.P.P.
[1975] 1 All E.R. 473

In one of these cases the accused was one of the bearers at the funeral of an I.R.A. prisoner. He was wearing a black roll-neck pullover, dark glasses and black beret. In the other case the accused was arrested for wearing a black beret, one of a number distributed at a Sinn Fein rally in London. They were charged with, and convicted of, an offence against s. 1(1) of the Public Order Act. On appeal:

LORD WIDGERY C.J.: "The question arises whether in those circumstances the magistrate acted within the law in finding that the charges were proved. I go back to the section itself which creates the offence. . .

The section, as will be remembered, refers to a person in a public place wearing uniform. 'Wearing,' in my judgment, implies some article of wearing apparel. I agree with the submission made in argument that one would not describe a badge pinned to the lapel as being a uniform worn for present purposes. In the present instance, however, the various items relied on, such as the beret, dark glasses, the pullovers and the other dark clothing, were clearly worn and therefore satisfy the first requirement of the section.

The next requirement is that that which was worn was a uniform, so one has to consider the meaning of that word. It seems to me that in deciding whether a person is wearing a uniform different considerations may apply according to whether he is alone or in company with others. If a man is seen walking down Whitehall wearing the uniform of a policeman or a soldier, it is unnecessary to prove that that is uniform of any sort because it is so universally recognised or known as being clothing worn by a member of the Metropolitan Police or the Army, as the case may be, that it is described as uniform on that account, and judges can take judicial notice of the fact that it is uniform in that sense.

If a man was seen walking down Whitehall wearing a black beret, that certainly would not be regarded as uniform unless evidence were called to show that that black beret, in conjunction with any other items appropriate to associate it, had been used and was recognised as the uniform of some body. . .

In this case of course the eight men in question were together. They were not seen in isolation. Where an article such as a beret is used in order to indicate that a group of men are together and in association, it seems to me that that article can be regarded as uniform without any proof that it has been previously used as such...

In this case of course the articles did go beyond the beret. They extended to the pullover, the dark glasses and the dark clothing, and I have no doubt at all in my own mind that those men wearing those clothes on that occasion were wearing uniform within the meaning of the Act.

Evidence has been called in this case from a police sergeant to the effect that the black beret was commonly used, or had been frequently used, by the members of the I.R.A., and I recognise that it is possible to prove that an article constitutes uniform by that means as well. But what I stress, first of all, is that it is not necessary to prove previous use of the article as uniform if it is clear from the activities of the accused on the day in question that they were adopting a similar style of dress in order to show their mutual association one with the other.

The next point, and perhaps the most difficult problem of all, is the requirement of the section that the uniform so worn shall signify the wearer's association with any political organisation. This can be done in my judgment in two ways. The first I have already referred to. It is open to the prosecution, if they have the evidence and wish to call it, to show that the particular article relied on as uniform has been used in the past as the uniform of a recognised association, and they can by that means, if the evidence is strong enough, and the court accepts it, prove that the black beret, or whatever it may be, is associated with a particular organisation. In my judgement it is not necessary for them to specify the particular organisation because in many instances the name of the organisation will be unknown or may have been recently changed. But if they can prove that the article in question has been associated with a political organisation capable of identification in some manner, then that would suffice for the purposes of the section.

Alternatively, in my judgment the significance of the uniform and its power to show the association of the wearer with a political organisation can be judged from the events to be seen on the occasion when the alleged uniform was worn. In other words it can be judged and proved without necessarily referring to the past history at all because in my judgment if a group of persons assemble together and wear a piece of uniform such as a black beret to indicate their association one with the other, and furthermore by their conduct indicate that that beret associates them with other activity of a political character, that is enough for the purposes of the section...

Turning finally to the questions which are submitted for the opinion of this court, the first one is:

'Was the dress worn capable of being a uniform and was the common denominator, the black beret, a uniform within the meaning of Section 1(1) of the Public Order Act of 1936?' I have already given sufficient reasons for my conclusion that it undoubtedly was.

The second question is:

'Is it necessary under this subsection for the prosecution to prove exactly which political organisation is concerned?' The answer is no. . .

In my judgment the appeals in the case headed by Seamus O'Moran are all to be dismissed.

The second case concerned again a number of appellants, each of whom was convicted of an offence under s. 1(1) of the Public Order Act 1936. . .

[His Lordship reviewed the facts.]

The appellants in question in the case which is before the court today were all wearing black berets. They were all involved in the march in some aspect or another. Several of them, though not all of them, carried flags or banners of the kind to which I have referred. . .

As I say, I would reserve the case of *de minimis* but apart from that I see no reason why a beret in itself, if worn in order to indicate association with a political body, should not be a uniform for present purposes. Accordingly in this case also I would dismiss all the appeals."

Melford Stevenson and Watkins JJ. concurred.

It is unlikely that section 1 would now need to be used to deal with the wearing of uniforms by Irish nationalist organisations. The Prevention of Terrorism (Temporary Provisions) Act 1984 provides:

"Any person who in a public place—
    (a)   wears any item of dress; or
    (b)   wears, carries or displays any article,
in such a way or in such circumstances as to arouse reasonable apprehension that he is a member or supporter of a proscribed organisation, shall be guilty of an offence, and shall be liable on summary conviction—
    (i)   to imprisonment for a term not exceeding six months; or
    (ii)   to a fine or an amount not exceeding level 5 on the standard scale.
or to both.
(2) A constable may arrest without warrant anyone whom he has reasonable grounds to suspect of being a person guilty of an offence under this section."

Both the I.R.A. and I.N.L.A. are proscribed organisations. Nevertheless, the Government took the view that section 1 of the Public Order Act 1936 should be retained, "in order to prevent the re-introduction of quasi-military methods of . . . display for political purposes" (Home Office, 1985:38).

IV. COMMON LAW OFFENCES

There are three major common law offences, sedition, mobbing and breach of the peace. In fact there has been no prosecution for sedition since the unfortunate Mr Guy Aldred, whom we have already met in this chapter, received a 12-month prison sentence because of his involvement in the publication of a community newspaper, *The Red Commune*, in 1922 (the case is not reported, but on subsidiary issues see 1922 J.C. 13), and this has led some to conclude that sedition is an obsolescent if not an obsolete offence. In view of the High Court's recent record in resurrecting old and inventing new offences to assist the Crown Office's moral crusades, this seems too sanguine a view.

A. SEDITION

The only reported cases on sedition are a group tried in the 1790s by Lord Justice-Clerk Braxfield of notorious memory and *Jas. Cumming, John Grant and Others* (1848) J. Shaw 17. These cases and others not appearing in the law reports were minutely examined and excoriated by Lord Cockburn (Cockburn (no date)). Of the trials before *Cumming and Grant*, Gordon (1978a) says: "Neither the political outlook which governed these trials nor Lord Braxfield's modes of expression would commend themselves at the present day, and the statements of the law made by the court at that time cannot be regarded as authoritative today." *Cumming and Grant* is thus, in effect, the sole authority. The case involved six judges and is reported at enormous length. Some of the accused had been convicted on a libel which argued that they had *intended* their words to produce "popular disaffection and resistance to lawful authority," but the jury had specifically found their language was not *intended* but was *calculated* (i.e. likely) to produce this effect (at p. 61). The major point, in other words, was the *mens rea* of the offence. In considering this point the Lord Justice-Clerk (Hope) also gave a *definition* of the offence.

15. James Cumming, John Grant and Others
(1848) J. Shaw 17

LORD JUSTICE-CLERK (Hope):—'The crime of sedition consists in wilfully, unlawfully, mischievously, and in violation of the party's allegiance, and in breach of the peace, and to the public danger, uttering language calculated to produce popular disaffection, disloyalty, resistance to lawful authority, or, in more aggravated cases, violence and insurrection. The party must be made out not to be exercising his right of free discussion for legitimate objects, but to be purposely, mischievously, without regard to his allegiance, and to the public danger, scattering burning firebrands, calculated to stimulate and excite such effects as I have mentioned—reckless of all consequences. As Mr Clark said in Palmer's case, 'He, whose speeches or writings have that tendency, is seditious, unless, in either case, the speaker or writer has a legal object in view.'

Now, in this case, I apprehend that the law does not look for or require, beside this illegal spirit, this general dole or legal malice, the additional and special element of the intention, or *purpose*, with reference to the precise *effects* which the words are *calculated* to produce. If such purpose is also proved, the case will be one of more deliberate, more dangerous, and more aggravated sedition. But very often the precise *effects* which the words are calculated to produce, are not at all what the party *intends*, and still more, not what he has brought his own mind up to, just because they point to immediate violence. The party guilty of sedition in uttering such language is often only playing the part of a field orator, hallooed on by shouts from an excited and turbulent crowd—often of the worst characters: He has to sustain his part as a leader; has to outbid in exaggeration and violence the man who spoke before him; has got so familiarized to violent and dangerous language that he does not think how they may affect others; has to secure a liberty for bold language, and often to secure pay for such achievements: He is aiming, perhaps, at being chosen as a delegate; thinks, perhaps, that by *intimidation* he may concuss and frighten others into an exaggerated notion of the numbers and power of those who venture to utter such language: He is reckless as to what he says; thinks and cares little about it, if it answers the object at the time; but all the while he may not desire or intend the precise effects which his words are calculated to produce—it may be of instant violence. Yet of sedition he is clearly guilty, if these reckless words are calculated to produce such results."

B. MOBBING AND RIOTING

The second common law offence of relevance is mobbing and rioting. It is possible to distinguish between "mobbing" as the behaviour of a group viewed as such, and "rioting" which is the behaviour of an individual (Alison (1823:509)), and one modern writer has suggested that there still lingers in Scots law a separate offence of "rioting" (Fleming (1984)). However, this view finds no general acceptance and the word "mobbing" and the full phrase are generally used interchangeably. There is no single authoritative definition of the offence, but a mid-nineteenth century one, which was recently approved by the High Court in *Hancock* v. *H.M. Advocate*, 1981 S.C.C.R. 32, is to be found in the following case.

16. John Robertson et al.
(1842) 1 Broun 152

The accused were charged with mobbing and rioting committed with intent to prevent a presbytery from performing its duty. The charge arose from the presentation of an unpopular person as minister of a parish and the intention of the appropriate presbytery to proceed to his induction. A crowd assembled and broke up the deliberations. The trial was very much concerned with conflicting evidence, but the Lord Justice-Clerk delivered an extensive charge to the jury on the law of mobbing and rioting.

LORD JUSTICE-CLERK (Hope): "I have to state to you, in point of law, that an illegal mob is any assemblage of people, acting together for a common and illegal purpose, effecting, or attempting to effect their purpose, either by violence or by demonstration of force or numbers, or by any species of intimidation, impediment, or obstruction, calculated to effect their object, and to impede, obstruct, and defeat others employed in discharge of duty. . .

It is not necessary that the purpose or object of the mob should have been previously concerted, or that they should be brought together and congregated with the view previously formed of effecting the object subsequently attempted. It is enough, that after they have been so assembled and brought together, finding their numbers, and ascertaining a common feeling, they then act in concert, and take up and resolve to effect a common purpose. There must, however, be a common purpose and object, for which they are combined and acting in concert, after they are congregated, and operating as such throughout the acts alleged to be acts of mobbing. That purpose or object must be unlawful. But then, such an unlawful purpose or object may consist in attempts to effect by violence and numbers, and not by legal measures, an object, the pursuit of which, in a lawful and peaceable manner, is lawful and laudable. . .

A charge of Mobbing and Rioting against a few of a great crowd, implies that only certain acts, and a certain share of what was going on, can be proved as to any individuals. But, when a jury is once satisfied of the existence of a common object, that parties were combined to effect, and were acting in union in order to effect, that common object, these acts of a whole body, done in furtherance, and to effect that object, and naturally arising out of the exertions of a mob to effect that common object, become necessarily, in the eye of the law, the acts of all who take part in the proceedings of the mob, who act along with them in any degree, and who aid, countenance, and support, even by presence, that object for which the mob are acting in concert. Presence in a mob, if such presence is in order to countenance what is done, will be a fact sufficient to establish a party's guilt of all that is done by the mob. . .

The *continued* presence of a party in a mob after its character has shewn itself, without any aid to those against whom the mob is directing its acts, may (I only say *may*) in common cases become very speedily accession to the mob; for such continued presence, especially by a person looked up to by the mob, and known to take a deep and keen interest in the object and feelings of the mob, though he may not declare his approbation of the acts of violence, gives them boldness, additional confidence, and, perhaps, a mistaken notion that they are encouraged by him; but, at all events, does give them, sanction and encouragement. . .

Any person present ought either to aid in quelling the disturbance, or at least instantly withdraw. If he continues in the heart of the scene without opposing himself, and, much more, if before or after, he is found in friendly communication with the mob, or even simply remains among them, then his continued presence constitutes accession, though the degree of his guilt may be greatly less than that of others. And this is justly so held, for he truly adds by his presence to the numbers of the mob, and to the apparent concert and union among them. . .

On the same general grounds, the law holds a party, who is shewn to be one of a mob, answerable for all the acts of Mobbing and Rioting committed by that mob, in prosecution and furtherance of their common object. . .

You cannot separate all the acts of a mob into distinct crimes, so that no one shall be guilty of mobbing, except in respect of his own individual acts of accession. He may be the ringleader, and yet not an act of violence, after the mob begins, may be proved against him individually. . .

I have reserved for my last remark, in point of law, a point of the utmost importance in this case, and by the application of which, I presume, your verdict will be much influenced. You will observe, that the duty which the Presbytery had to discharge, was one in which all the parishioners had an interest,—at which all were entitled to be present, none more so than those opposed to the settlement. They were all entitled to be present at and watch the proceedings. All parishioners and communicants are invited, as well as entitled in law, to be present. Hence the fact of being present, of being one of the crowd, nay, of remaining in the crowd, in itself, in this case, implies *by itself* no accession at all, in point of law, to the common and illegal purpose of the mob . . . if a person, entitled as a parishioner and communicant to be present throughout the whole scene, was perfectly quiet and peaceable during that scene,—never having been desired, even along with others, to leave the church,—his presence alone does not in this case make him responsible for the acts of the mob, or prove his secret concert with them. The fact that he was a ringleader or instigator, or otherwise a part of the mob, must be separately proved to your satisfaction, so as to shew that presence, apparently legal and peaceable, was yet in truth presence, in order to back, aid, countenance, support, and encourage the mob. . .

In the present case, the burden of giving this character to continued presence in the mob, is much more onerous than when a party has no legal interest or right in remaining to witness the whole proceedings which are going on."

The accused were acquitted.

From this it transpires that the effect of a finding of mobbing and rioting is that each individual is presumptively responsible for all the acts of the mob committed in furtherance of its common end. This extends criminal liability far beyond the normal rules of art and part guilt. The Scottish Law Commission (1984: Chap. 6) has pointed out that the exact extent of such liability is not clear. On the one hand a person can be considered guilty of being part of a mob which performed certain acts and the severity of those acts is relevant to sentence. On a more extreme view the accused is guilty of forming part of a mob and of each act which that mob commits as a separate offence. The consequence of the latter is that if, for example, a mob commits murder, the trial judge must sentence each guilty person to life imprisonment. The great extension of the rules of guilt by association is harder to justify if the latter view is adopted.

As to the elements of the offence, there are three: (i) a number of people, (ii) intimidation, and (iii) a common illegal purpose. The number of people required is not fixed. In *H.M. Advocate* v. *McAndrew* (unreported, see Scottish Law Commission (1984: para 2:8) the jury were directed that seven people would suffice. In *Sloan* v. *Macmillan,* 1922 J.C. 1 the court did not have to consider counsel's submission that five would be too few, but observed that it depends on "what these people do, the violence they show, the threats they use." As to intimidation, normally violence accompanies mobbing but this need not be so, although the threat of it probably is. Thus in *Sloan* (*supra*) the compliance of blacklegs during a strike was secured by a parade of strength, but no recourse to violence.

Most legal problems with mobbing are associated with the common illegal purpose. This illegal purpose is to be understood in the sense of immediate purpose. A crowd may lawfully assemble to urge a lawful end, but if its purpose is, or becomes, to effect that end by violence or intimidation then that is its immediate purpose and the crowd becomes a mob (*McDonald et al.* v. *Mackay* (1842) 1 Broun 435). An analysis of records of prosecutions for mobbing by the Scottish Law Commission (1984: Chap. III) shows that nowadays mobbing is almost entirely used to deal with gang fights and random street violence (see *Hancock* v. *H.M Advocate,* 1981 S.C.C.R. 32 following which the Scottish Law Commission understood that Crown Office policy had become not to charge mobbing unless the common purpose could be spelled out in the indictment, but the commission noted that no such policy had been adhered to.) Much of its memorandum is a consideration of whether it should become a statutory requirement to spell out such a purpose. Alternatively the offence could be abolished and replaced by a new statutory offence, or series of offences concerning public disorder. The Commission has not yet reported its definitive views.

C. BREACH OF THE PEACE

Breach of the peace, one of the most common offences committed and charged in Scotland, gives cause for concern in a variety of different ways. The first is the unrestricted scope of the conduct which can constitute the offence. In *Wilson* v. *Brown,* 1982 S.C.C.R. 49, it was said by Lord Dunpark:

"It is well settled that a test which may be applied in charges of breach of the peace is whether the proved conduct may reasonably be expected to cause any person to be alarmed, upset or annoyed or to provoke a disturbance of the peace. Positive evidence of actual harm, upset, annoyance or disturbance created by reprisal is not a prerequisite of conviction."

It is enough that the conduct of the accused "was likely to lead to a disturbance if allowed to continue" (p. 52). It is important to note, then, that conduct likely to cause (though not necessarily causing) alarm, upset or annoyance may constitute the offence. Indeed, in *Sinclair* v. *Annan,* 1980 S.L.T. (Notes) 55, the High Court approved a conviction for conduct which caused embarrassment. And remarkably in 1986 when a Caithness newspaper published an article on fire risks in churches under the title "Hellish worry of church fires," the local procurator fiscal wrote to the editor stating that in his view such a title amounted to a breach of the peace and that similar conduct in the future would lead to prosecution. Whether or not such a prosecution would succeed is to some extent immaterial. The affair highlights the extent to which breach of the peace has ceased to be a justifiable restriction on public disorder, having become concerned with enforcing standards of good taste and decorum.

A second important feature of the offence relates also to the requirement that the conduct must be reasonably expected to alarm, annoy or provoke third parties. It is one thing to convict people where the reaction to the accused is the reaction of a normal person. But it is something quite different to convict where the response is abnormal in the sense that that party is particularly sensitive to the conduct in question. This is the problem which, as we shall see, confronted the courts in *Deakin* v. *Milne* where members of the Salvation Army were found guilty of a breach of the peace for conducting an assembly opposed by a rival organisation, there being evidence of violence at earlier such assemblies. Yet the Salvation Army did not deliberately seek to provoke disorder and it is difficult to argue that any reasonable person would take exception to their parades, or be alarmed or upset by them. Nevertheless, on the facts the assembly was likely to provoke a disturbance, with the result that in principle the offence is committed, albeit that intolerable consequences are thereby produced. It is an open invitation to people who oppose the objects of a group holding a meeting or procession to resort to violence in order not only to disperse a particular meeting or procession, but also to provide a precedent, so that to organise or take part in a future march would constitute a breach of the peace. As we shall also see, the English court which decided *Beatty* v. *Gillbanks* (1882) 9 Q.B.D. 308 in a manner contrary to *Deakin* v. *Milne* did so partly for that reason.

A third important feature of breach of peace is a practical one. The criminal justice system is such that the offence confers a very wide discretion on the police in the policing of meetings, demonstrations and assemblies. It is to be noted that:

(1) The nature of the offence is such that fact and law merge almost imperceptibly. There is no appeal on question of fact, so there is often little point in undertaking the expense, delay and uncertainty of an appeal.

(2) In determining whether to convict, much will depend on facts and the surrounding circumstances. In practice the courts are likely to attach overriding importance to police evidence. After all, it is a matter of impression whether an accused person's conduct is vigorous protest, harassment of third parties, or abusive conduct likely to provoke serious violence. The officer on the spot will be better placed than the courts to interpret the events. Unfortunately, however, the fact that there is no need to produce evidence of the effect of the accused's conduct on others means that the only evidence of the offence will normally be the uncorroborated evidence of the police.

So in a sense the police define the scope of the offence and decide with virtual finality whether there has been an offence in any given situation (though *cf, Fisher* v. *Keane,* 1981 J.C. 50). In the following pages we consider how these wide powers enable the police to impose conditions on the conduct of a meeting or assembly; how they enable the police to disperse an assembly; and whether they enable the police to prevent an assembly from taking place at all. But before considering these matters, two preliminary points must be made. First, some of the authorities are drawn from English law and from Ireland. In most of the cases, the accused have been convicted under the Police Act 1964, s. 51(3) (or its predecessors). This provides that it is an offence to obstruct a police officer in the execution of his duty the Scottish equivalent being s. 41(1) of the Police (Scotland) Act 1967. For present purposes, failure to comply with an instruction from a police officer is not an offence under the statute (and its predecessors) unless the instruction was given by a police officer who apprehended a breach of the peace. So an apprehended breach of the peace is necessary for a successful prosecution under section 51(3). The English cases which follow relate to the question whether the police officer had reasonable grounds to apprehend a breach of the peace. For that reason they are of interest in Scotland. The second point which has to be made is that the power of the police to take steps to prevent a breach of the peace applies not only to meetings and assemblies held in public, but almost certainly also to those held in private. This tends to be confirmed by the following case:

17. Thomas v. Sawkins
[1935] 2 K.B. 249

Thomas was one of the convenors of a meeting called *inter alia* to urge the dismissal of the local chief constable. The public was invited to attend without payment. The police reasonably anticipated that breaches of the peace would occur at the meeting (though in fact none did occur). They insisted over Thomas's opposition upon entering and remaining in the hall. Thomas laid hands upon one constable to eject him but was restrained by another (Sawkins). He prosecuted for unlawful assault. The justices held that the police were lawfully on the premises and dismissed the information. On appeal:

LORD HEWART C.J.: "It is apparent that the conclusion of the justices in this case consisted of two parts. One part was a conclusion of fact that the respondent and the police officers who accompanied him believed that certain things might happen at the meeting which was then about to be held. There were ample materials on which the justices could come to that conclusion. The second part of the justices' finding is no less manifestly an expression of opinion. Finding the facts as they do, and drawing from those facts the inference which they draw, they go on to say that the officers were entitled to enter and to remain on the premises on which the meeting was being held.

Against that determination, it is said that it is an unheard of proposition of law, and that in the books no case is to be found which goes the length of deciding that, where an offence is expected to be committed, as distinct from the case of an offence being or having been committed, there is any right in the police to enter on private premises and to remain there against the will of those who, as hirers or otherwise, are for the time being in possession of the premises. When, however, I look at the passages which have been cited from Blackstone's *Commentaries,* and from the judgments in *Humphries* v. *Connor* and *O'Kelly* v. *Harvey.* . . I think that there is quite sufficient ground for the proposition that it is part of the preventative power, and, therefore, part of the preventative duty, of the police, in cases where there are such reasonable grounds of apprehension as the justices have found here, to enter and remain on private premises. It goes without saying that the powers and duties of the police are directed, not to the interests of the police, but to the protection and welfare of the public. . .

I think, therefore, that the justices were right and that this appeal should be dismissed."

AVORY J.: "I am of the same opinion. I think that it is very material in this particular case to observe that the meeting was described as a public meeting, that it was extensively advertised, and that the public were invited to attend. There can be no doubt that the police officers who attended the meeting were members of the public and were included in that sense in the invitation to attend. It is true that those who had hired the hall for the meeting might withdraw their invitation from any particular individual who was likely to commit a breach of the peace or some other offence, but it is quite a different proposition to say that they might withdraw the invitation from police officers who might be there for the express purpose of preventing a breach of the peace or the commission of an offence. . .

In my opinion, no express statutory authority is necessary where the police have reasonable grounds to apprehend a breach of the peace. . ."

Lawrence J. concurred.

Lord Hewart's judgment is wider than either of the other two judges', both of which decided the case on its particular facts and stressed the fact that the public generally was invited. Lord Hewart enthusiastically endorsed the wider general right of entry on private premises. Avory J. seems torn between this view and confining the case to its facts. On either interpretation this right of entry would seem to be justified only by the special requirements of public order and the courts' heavy predisposition in favour of it rather than private rights. It is not authority for a power of entry on suspicion of *any* offence, but since most offences are *also* breaches of the peace the decision could be so extended. In England and Wales police power of entry has now been placed on a secure statutory base by the Police and Criminal Evidence Act 1984. Section 17(5) of the Act provides that: "Subject to subsection (6) . . . all the rules of common law under which a constable has power to enter premises without a warrant are hereby abolished." However, section 17(6) provides that: "Nothing in subsection (5) above affects any power of entry to deal with or prevent a breach of the peace." It has been claimed that *Thomas* v. *Sawkins* is also the law in Scotland:

> "I am advised that under the existing [Scots] law the police are entitled to enter and remain in a hall during a meeting, if they are requested by the promoters to do so; also, if they have reason to believe that a breach of the law is being committed; or further, if they have reasonable grounds for apprehending that a breach of the law is about to be committed."

(Sir G. Collins, Secretary of State for Scotland, 312 H.C. Debs. 1807.)

1. THE POWER TO DISPERSE

One consequence of the discretion conferred on the police by breach of the peace is the power to disperse an assembly in order to prevent a breach of the peace from taking place. Very often the power of dispersal presents a choice as to which assembly to disperse, for often one gathering may attract a hostile audience intent on preventing an assembly from being held. Clearly the police would be empowered to disperse the hecklers or the counter-demonstrators in order to maintain the peace. An important question, however, is whether they may also disperse those who are being heckled. Is there a heckler's veto in Scots law? The classic decision in *Beatty* v. *Gillbanks* (1882) 9 Q.B.D. 308 suggests that there is no such veto in English law. Beatty was arrested after having assembled with more than 100 other people with a view to participating through Weston-super-Mare in a Salvation Army parade. In the past Salvation Army processions had attracted disorder from a rival organisation, the Skeleton Army. On this occasion, the magistrates had issued an order directing all persons to abstain from assembling to the disturbance of the public peace. The instruction was defied and Beatty was arrested. In the course of his judgment, Field J. said:

> "Now, without doubt, as a general rule it must be taken that every person intends what are the natural and necessary consequences of his own acts, and if in the present case it had been their intention, or if it had been the natural and necessary consequence of their acts, to produce the disturbance of the peace which occurred, then the appellants would have been responsible for it, and the magistrates would have been right in binding them over to keep the peace. But the evidence as set forth in the case shows that, so far from that being the case, the acts and conduct of the appellants caused nothing of the kind, but, on the contrary, that the disturbance that did take place was caused entirely by the unlawful and unjustifiable interference of the Skeleton Army, a body of persons opposed to the religious views of the appellants and the Salvation Army, and that but for the opposition and molestation

offered to the Salvationists by these other persons, no disturbance of any kind would have taken place. The appellants were guilty of no offence in their passing through the streets, and why should any other person interfere with or molest them? What right had they to do so? If they were doing anything unlawful it was for the magistrates and police, the appointed guardians of law and order, to imterpose. . .

Here the only terror that existed was caused by the unlawful resistance wilfully and designedly offered to the proceedings of the Salvation Army by an unlawful organisation outside and distinct from them, called the Skeleton Army. It was suggested by the respondent's counsel that, if these Salvation processions were allowed, similar opposition would be offered to them in future, and that similar disturbances would ensue. But I cannot believe that that will be so. I hope, and I cannot but think, that when the Skeleton Army, and all other persons who are opposed to the proceedings of the Salvation Army, come to learn, as they surely will learn, that they have no possible right to interfere with or in any way obstruct the Salvation Army in their lawful and peaceable processions, they will abstain from opposing or disturbing them. It is usual happily in this country for people to respect and obey the law when once declared and understood, and I have hope and have no doubt that it will be so in the present case. But, if it should not be so, there is no doubt that the magistrates and police, both at Weston-super-Mare and everywhere else, will understand their duty and not fail to do it efficiently, or hesitate, should the necessity arise, to deal with the Skeleton Army and other disturbers of the public peace as they did in the present instance with the appellants, for no one can doubt that the authorities are only anxious to do their duty and to prevent a disturbance of the public peace. The present decision of the justices, however, amounts to this, that a man may be punished for acting lawfully if he knows that his so doing may induce another man to act unlawfully—a proposition without any authority whatever to support it. Under these circumstances, the question put to us by the justices must be negatively answered, and the order appealed against be discharged."

A rather different conclusion was reached in the same year by a Scottish court faced with a similar problem also involving the Salvation Army.

18. Deakin v. Milne
(1882) 10 R. (J.) 22

At the time of this case the Salvation Army was in rivalry with the Skeleton Army to such an extent that almost any procession organised by the Salvation Army was likely by its mere existence to promote opposition by the Skeleton Army and consequent disorder. This happened on several occasions in Arbroath, the magistrates of which were stung to make a proclamation prohibiting these processions.

LORD JUSTICE-CLERK (Moncreiff): "In the opinion which I have formed in this case I do not desire to say anything that could for a moment be considered to reflect on the motives or objects of the persons whose conduct has here been brought in question. . . The question relates to the preservation of the order and peace of the burgh.

It appears that this class of persons called the Salvation Army, and another band who have a designation of their own, have been in the habit of making processions on Sunday forenoons to the great disturbance of the inhabitants, and also, as the prosecutor says and the magistrates have found, to the endangering of the public peace. The magistrates made various attempts to stop these proceedings, but, finding that the evil by no means diminished, they issued a proclamation on the 17th of March to prevent these disturbances. It appears to me that this was an exceedingly proper and discreet proceeding on the part of the magistrates, and that it was entirely within their power, not if these persons neither endangered the public peace nor annoyed the inhabitants, but if they were satisfied on reasonable grounds that what these people did had a tendency to these things. . . But notwithstanding this proclamation these persons did turn out, and there was a breach of the peace, and the result is that they are charged with a breach of the peace, or inciting to a breach of the peace, and, secondly, with a breach of the proclamation by the magistrates.

I am of the opinion that the proceedings of the magistrates were perfectly proper. There are many processions that may take place in the streets of a burgh which may attract a good deal of attention, but which the magistrates are quite entitled to permit. There are objects in which the inhabitants of the towns may take a legitimate interest, but the limit to that necessarily is that the assembling of persons, and the behaviour of persons when they so assemble, shall be within the law. But when it leads to breach of the peace, however good the intentions of the persons may be, the magistrates are entitled to interfere; and therefore I hold that the magistrates, having decided upon the facts, in the first place, that this procession and crowd had a tendency to cause, and did cause, a breach of the peace, came to a conclusion which they were entitled to reach. I am not here to say what the facts are. That is a matter for the magistrates alone. But I think it is impossible to say that they had not the means of reaching the conclusion they did on these facts. In the second place, I think that a breach of the proclamation which the magistrates were entitled to issue was a municipal offence. On the whole matter, therefore, I think that there is no ground whatever for the appeal."

Lords Young and Craighall delivered concurring opinions.

A similar position to that in *Deakin* v. *Milne* was adopted in the following year in Ireland. In *O'Kelly* v. *Harvey* (1883) 14 L.R. Ir. 105, justices of the peace for an area where a meeting pressing for reforms of land law was to be held apprehended that the meeting would lead to breach of the peace and, deciding that the dissolution of the meeting was the only means of preserving the peace, called upon those present to disperse. When they refused the defendant laid hands upon one participant, who thereupon sued for damages for assault. The judgment of the court was delivered by Law C., who said:

"The defence, however, positively states that the Defendant being a Justice of the Peace, and present, believed, and had reasonable grounds for believing, that the peace could not otherwise be preserved than by separating and dispersing the Plaintiff's land meeting; and justified his action on that ground. The question then seems to be reduced to this:—assuming the Plaintiff and others assembled with him to be doing nothing unlawful, but yet that there were reasonable grounds for the Defendant believing, as he did, that there would be a breach of the peace if they continued so assembled, and that there was no other way in which the breach of the peace could be avoided but by stopping and dispersing the Plaintiff's meeting— was the Defendant justified in taking the necessary steps to stop and disperse it? In my opinion he was so justified, under the peculiar circumstances stated in the defence, and which for the present must be taken as admitted to be there truly stated. Under such circumstances the Defendant was not to defer action until a breach of the peace had actually been committed. His paramount duty was to *preserve the peace unbroken,* and that, by whatever means were available for the purpose."

It is almost certainly also the case that the power of dispersal is not confined to Scotland and Ireland. Despite *Beatty* v. *Gillbanks* it is likely that English law would also recognise a power of dispersal, where a police officer could show that this was necessary in order to prevent a breach of the peace. This follows inexorably from *Duncan* v. *Jones* [1936] 1 K.B. 218, *Piddington* v. *Bates* [1961] 1 W.L.R. 162 and *Moss* v. *McLachlan* [1985] I.R.L.R. 76, which we discuss in the next section.

It is not to be assumed that because the police have the power to disperse an assembly to maintain the peace they will always do so. Sometimes they will disperse the counter demonstration, a step apparently encouraged by the dictum of O'Brien J. in *R.* v. *Justices of Londonderry* (1891) Ir. L.R. 440, who said that if "danger arises from the exercise of lawful rights resulting in a breach of the peace, the remedy is the presence of sufficient force to prevent that result, not the legal condemnation of those who exercise those rights." But the fact remains that the police have a discretion as to how to respond, and this they may exercise to permit or suppress the freedom of assembly. Their power of suppression was illustrated recently by *Alexander* v. *Smith,* 1984 S.L.T. 176, where the accused was charged with breach of peace. He was convicted and appealed by stated case, the justice finding the following facts admitted or proved:

"1. That the witnesses, Police Constables T. Taylor and N. Ward were on duty at McLeod Street on 8 January 1982; that a large crowd was making its way to Tynecastle Football Ground to watch a football match. 2. That the presence of the appellant at the locus was brought to the attention of said constables by some members of said crowd. That said members of the crowd shouted to the police officers as they passed, appeared to take exception to the appellant, told said police officers to get rid of him from the area and informed the said police officers that, if they took no action with regard to the appellant, there would be trouble. That the appellant was at that time attempting to sell *Bulldog,* a newspaper of the National Front political party. That the appellant was jumping up and down advertising said newspaper and was shouting things such as 'Get your *Bulldog* here, *Bulldog* 10 pence.' That the said police officers were concerned lest a more serious incident develop and were concerned for the safety of the appellant. That said members of the crowd, having intimated their attitude to the appellant to the said police officers, continued on to said football match. (The said police officers did not note the names and addresses of any of the persons referred to above and none was called as a witness by the respondent.) One of the said police officers, P.C. Taylor, gave evidence to the effect that the appellant had shouted at some members of the crowd and had called them 'nigger lovers.' This evidence was not spoken to by P.C. Ward. 3. That the appellant was shouting at the crowd and had called members of the public 'nigger lovers.' 4. That members of the crowd near the appellant seemed incensed by his attempts to sell the newspapers. That the appellant's hat was knocked off by a member of the crowd. 5. That the said police officers approached the appellant, asked him what he was selling, whereupon the appellant said 'You can't take them from me, it's not illegal to sell them.' That said police officers told the appellant to move on from the locus. That the appellant continued to try to sell said newspapers saying that he was doing nothing wrong and that it was lawful for him so to do (the newspapers were produced and identified by said police officers). 6. That said police officers then took said newspapers from the appellant, took hold of his arms and removed him from the locus. That the appellant then shouted at said police officers. That the appellant was protesting that he had done nothing unlawful."

The principal question for the High Court was whether the justice was entitled to convict. The court answered in the affirmative and, without delivering a formal opinion, refused the appeal. It is perhaps the case that the appellant could now be prosecuted under section 19 of the POA 1986. It is important to note, however, that the principle in *Alexander* v. *Smith* does not apply only where the "speaker" is doing something intrinsically unlawful. Examples of situations where the police might lawfully arrest the speaker include:

(1) The individual who displays the Irish tricolour in the presence of a crowd with a large element of Orangemen.

(2) The individual who sells anti-royalist material at a popular display of affection for a member of the Royal Family.

(3) The individual who wears C.N.D. material at a Remembrance Day ceremony or at an army display.

2. THE POWER TO IMPOSE CONDITIONS

The origin of the powers of the police to impose conditions on the conduct of a meeting or assembly is often traced back to the Irish case, *Humphries* v. *Connor* (1864) 17 Ir. C.L.R. 1, where the defendant, a police officer, was sued for assault, having removed an orange lily from the clothing of the plaintiff. The defendant took this step on the ground that it was necessary to prevent a breach of the peace. The court (by a majority) agreed. In accepting that this was a good defence to the action, O'Brien J. said:

"The defence states, that the defendant was Constabulary Inspector in the district in which the transaction occurred; and I need not say that it was his duty, as such, to preserve the public peace and prevent a breach of it. The defence also states in substance, that plaintiff's wearing the orange lily at that time was calculated and tended to provoke animosity among different classes of her Majesty's subjects; that several persons, who were provoked by it, followed the plaintiff, made a great disturbance, and threatened plaintiff with personal violence; that the defendant, in order to preserve the public peace and prevent a breach of it ... and to restore order, &c., requested plaintiff to remove the lily; that plaintiff refused to do so, and on the contrary continued to wear it, and thereby to excite and provoke those persons to inflict personal violence on her, and to cause such disturbance and threats. It further states, that it was likely the public peace would be broken ... in consequence of her continuing to wear the lily; and that in order to preserve the public peace ... the defendant *gently and quietly, and necessarily and unavoidably,* removed the lily from plaintiff, doing her no injury whatever, and thereby ... preserved the public peace, which would otherwise have been broken. Such is the substance of the defence... But assuming (as on the present demurrer we are bound to do) that the defence truly states and represents the facts, it appears from it that the act complained of—namely, the removal of the lily from plaintiff, gently and without doing her any injury whatever, was necessary for the purposes of restoring order and preserving the public peace ... that it had such an effect; and that but for it the public peace would have been broken."

It is to be noted, however, that in a powerful dissent Fitzgerald J. said:

"But the doubt which I have is, whether a constable is entitled to interfere with one who is not about to commit a breach of the peace, or to do, or join in any illegal act, but who is likely to be made an object of insult or injury by other persons who are about to break the Queen's peace. I would not have ventured to express my doubt except that very important consequences may result from the principle of the decision of my Brothers in this case.

I do not see where we are to draw the line. If a constable is at liberty to take a lily from one person, because the wearing of it is displeasing to others, who may make it an excuse for a breach of the peace, where are we to stop? It seems to me that we are making, not the law of the land, but the law of the mob supreme, and recognising in constables a power of interference with the rights of the Queen's subjects, which, if carried into effect to the full extent of the principle, might be accompanied by constitutional danger."

But despite these remarks, the case is clearly important. It is equally important, however, to note that the police officer's conduct was justified as a defence in civil proceedings. There is a qualitative difference between that and saying that it is an offence to fail to comply with a police officer's instruction, even where he or she apprehended a breach of the peace. That leap was, however, made by the Divisional Court in *Duncan* v. *Jones* [1936] 1 K.B. 218 where, following an address to a crowd by the appellant, a disturbance had taken place. A later meeting at the same place was announced, but a police officer tried to prevent any disorder by asking Mrs Duncan to conduct her address some yards down the street. She refused and was charged and convicted of obstructing a police officer in the execution of his duty. In dismissing her appeal, Lord Hewart C.J. said:

"There have been moments during the argument in this case when it appeared to be suggested that the court had to do with a grave case involving what is called the right of public meeting. I say 'called,' because English law does not recognise any special right of public meeting for political or other purposes. The right of assembly, as Professor Dicey puts it, is nothing more than a view taken by the court of the individual liberty of the subject. If I thought that the present case raised a question which has been held in suspense by more than one writer on constitutional law—namely, whether an assembly can properly be held to be unlawful merely because the holding of it is expected to give rise to a breach of the peace on the part of the persons opposed to those who are holding a meeting—I should wish to hear more argument before I expressed an opinion. This case, however, does not even touch that important question."

In a similar vein, Humphrey J. said:

"I regard this as a plain case. It has nothing to do with the law of unlawful assembly. No charge of that sort was even suggested against the appellant. The sole question raised by the case is whether the respondent, who was admittedly obstructed, was so obstructed when in the execution of his duty.

It does not require authority to emphasise the statement that it is the duty of a police officer to prevent apprehended breaches of the peace. Here it is found as a fact that the respondent reasonably apprehended a breach of the peace. It then, as is rightly expressed in the case, became his duty to prevent anything which in his view would cause that breach of the peace. While he was taking steps so to do he was wilfully obstructed by the appellant. I can conceive no clearer case within the statutes than that."

These cases suggest, then, that there is a common law power to regulate meetings and assemblies independently of the POA 1986, s. 14. The power is confirmed by the following case.

19. Piddington v. Bates
[1961] 1 W.L.R. 162

"The magistrate found the following facts: On June 26, 1959, there was in existence a trade dispute which involved a registered trade union of which the defendant was a member. On that day, at about 5.40 p.m., the prosecutor was on duty at Islington Police Station. As a result of a telephone message he sent a police constable to the premises of Free Press Ltd., Cross Street, London, N.1. There were two entrances to these premises, one in Cross Street which was six feet wide, and one in Fowler

Road at the back of the premises which was eleven feet wide. The full complement of staff at the premises was twenty-four and at the material time about eight of them were working there. There was nothing to show that the defendant knew either the full complement of staff or that about eight of them were there. After the arrival of the constable at the premises two vehicles drew up containing about eighteen men, most of whom were wearing picket badges. Two pickets stood outside the front door of the premises in Cross Street while some patrolled the street. Another police officer, in the presence of the constable, told the defendant that two pickets were enough for the front door. The prosecutor then went to the premises and found two pickets at the front door and four pickets at the back entrance in Fowler Road. The prosecutor spoke to the pickets at the back entrance and, as a result, two of them moved away. There were about ten or twelve persons in Fowler Road, most of whom were wearing picket badges, when the defendant approached and said: 'where is the rear entrance?' The prosecutor told the defendant three times that, in his view, two pickets at each entrance were sufficient. The defendant said: 'I'm going there and you can't stop me. I know my rights,' and 'I can stand by the gate if I want to' and finally 'I'm going to join them. If you don't want me to, you'd better arrest me.' The defendant then pushed gently past the prosecutor and was gently arrested.

There was no obstruction of the highway in the vicinity of the premises, nor any disorder, nor any violence threatened or offered by any of the pickets or other persons present. The prosecutor had arrived at his view that two pickets at each entrance were enough on the grounds that that number was sufficient for peaceful picketing in view of the number of persons who might then or later leave the premises, and that picketing by persons in excess of that number might lead to intimidation and a breach of the peace.

It was contended on behalf of the defendant, first, that when picketing was peaceful and no obstruction caused or violence threatened the prosecutor had no right in law to restrict the number of pickets on the doors to two and accordingly the defendant was not guilty of obstructing a constable in the execution of his duty; secondly, that two pickets on a door were insufficient to communicate with workers leaving or entering premises, as workers generally entered or left in some numbers at the same times, nor sufficient to communicate with lorry drivers and their mates who might be expected to deliver materials to or take products away from the factory premises; thirdly, that where a right of picketing was given by statute it was unlawful to interfere with that right unless there was a real and present indication that there might be obstruction or intimidation or a breach of the peace and that there was no such indication in this case; and, fourthly, that the restriction of the number of pickets to two was arbitrary and unlawful.

It was contended on behalf of the prosecutor, first, that the prosecutor had a duty to prevent breach of the peace; secondly, that in the circumstances the prosecutor had reasonable grounds for fearing that a breach of the peace might occur if more than two persons were allowed to picket at each of the entrances; and, thirdly, that in refusing to obey the directions of the prosecutor, and in beginning to act contrary to them, the defendant was obstructing the prosecutor in the execution of his duty.

The magistrate was of opinion that the prosecutor was acting in the execution of his duty in seeking to prevent the defendant from joining the two pickets at the back entrance to the premises and that the defendant, in refusing to comply with the prosecutor's direction and pushing past him, was obstructing him in the execution of that duty; and, accordingly, found the information proved.

The magistrate gave the following reasons, inter alia, for his decision:

(1) A police officer must always use his best endeavours to maintain the peace.

(2) Having regard to the whole of the evidence, the prosecutor was justified in anticipating the possibility of a breach of the peace unless steps were taken to prevent it, and it was his duty to decide what those steps should be. He must, of course, reach his decision impartially and in good faith and put it into effect without unnecessary force or provocation and there was no evidence that the prosecutor failed in, or exceeded, his duty in any of these respects.

(3) The provisions of the Trade Disputes Act did not render it unlawful for a police officer to limit the number of pickets if such limitation was necessary for maintaining the peace and therefore the fact that he did so did not alone and of itself divest a police officer of the status of 'acting in the execution of his duty.'

(4) Whether the limitation of pickets was necessary for the maintenance of the peace in any particular case and what number of pickets was consistent with ensuring the maintenance of peace must both be questions of fact and there was evidence from which the magistrate, in his view, could properly infer that the prosecutor was justified in limiting the pickets as he did. The defendant had called no evidence."

The defendant appealed.

LORD PARKER C.J.: "The court has been referred to a great number of cases, both Irish and English, dealing with the position when a police constable can be said to contemplate a breach of the peace and to take action to preserve it because, of course, the question here is whether the constables in question were acting in the course of the execution of their duty when they were obstructed. I find it unnecessary to refer to those cases. It seems to me that the law is reasonably plain. First, the mere statement by a constable that he did anticipate that there might be a breach of the peace is clearly not enough. There must exist proved facts from which a constable could reasonably anticipate such a breach. Secondly, it is not enough that his contemplation is that there is a remote possibility; there must be a real possibility of a breach of the peace. Accordingly, in every case, it becomes a question of whether, on the particular facts, it can be said that there were reasonable grounds on which a constable charged with this duty reasonably anticipated that a breach of the peace might occur. . .

The other point goes to an analysis of the evidence, from which it is said that no reasonable man could possibly anticipate a breach of the peace. It is pointed out that there was no obstruction in the street; that there was no actual intimidation; and that there were no threats or intimations of violence. It is said that there was really nothing save the fact that picketing was going on to suggest that a breach of the peace was a real possibility.

As I have said, every case must depend upon its exact facts, and the matter which influences me in this case is the matter of numbers. It is, I think, perfectly clear from the wording of the case, although it is not expressly so found, that the police knew in these small works there were only eight people working. They found two vehicles arriving, with 18 people milling about the street trying to form pickets at the doors. On that ground alone, coupled with the telephone calls which, I should have thought, intimated some sense of urgency and apprehension, the police were fully entitled to think as reasonable men that there was a real danger of something more than mere picketing to collect or impart information or peaceably to persuade. I think that in those circumstances the prosecutor had reasonable grounds for anticipating that a breach of the peace was a real possibility. It may be, and I think this is the real criticism, that it can be said: Well, to say that only two pickets should be allowed is purely arbitrary; why two? Why not three? Where do you draw the line? I think that a police officer charged with the duty of preserving the Queen's peace must be left to take such steps as on the evidence before him he thinks are proper. I am far from saying that there should be any rule that only two pickets should be allowed at any particular door. There, one gets into an arbitrary area, but so far as this case is concerned I cannot see that there was anything wrong in the action of the prosecutor.

Finally, I would like to say that all these matters are so much matters of degree that I would hesitate, except on the clearest evidence, to interfere with the findings of magistrates who have had the advantage of hearing the whole case and observing the witnesses. I am of opinion that the appeal of Piddington should be dismissed."

Taken together these three cases are crucially important. First, they establish the existence of a power of the police to impose conditions as to the numbers, location and conduct of a demonstration. This power exists independently of the powers contained in the POA 1986, s. 14, the terms of which are considered above. Secondly, the power is not constrained, as is the statute, by a requirement that the assembly must exceed 20 people. That is a point demonstrated forcefully by *Piddington* v. *Bates*. Thirdly, this common law based power is almost certainly applicable in any situation where the statute might also apply. Thus the four criteria in the statute authorising police officers to issue instructions (serious public disorder, serious damage to property, serious disruption to the life of the community, or intimidation) would almost certainly permit instructions to be issued at common law. In Scotland, at least, such factors would, in the view of the courts, give rise to a justifiable apprehension of a breach of the peace.

3. The Power to Prevent an Assembly?

It is evident from the foregoing that the police have a quite remarkable power to deal with assemblies, meetings and demonstrations. They may insist on being present; they may issue instructions as to location and numbers; and ultimately they may disperse. The final question is whether there is a common-law power on the part of the police to ban particular meetings and processions. This indeed would be a logical extension of the powers discussed so far, and it is unsurprising that the police should eventually claim to have just such a power. Thus, after the death of the I.R.A. hunger-striker Francis Hughes in May 1981 in Belfast, the most violent rioting in years hit the city. As a result the funeral cortège was not permitted to travel through the city.

"The decision was taken not under the Prevention of Terrorism Act or the Emergency Provisions Act, as claimed by the Republicans, but under common law which permitted the chief constable to take action to prevent any breach of the peace.

Police later explained that the decision was taken on the direction of the chief constable. 'The police believed that the provisional IRA had, in effect, taken over the arrangements for the conveyance of the body,' said a statement.

Had these arrangements been permitted to proceed there would have been a completely unacceptable and grave risk of breaches of the peace and a flouting of criminal law both in Belfast and en route to Bellaghy."

(*The Scotsman,* May 14, 1981.)

More recently, the police in England have "stopped and turned back National Front members outside Wakefield in January 1984, after they had been banned from marching in neighbouring towns" (Home Office, 1985:5). But it was during the miners' strike that this power came to prominence, when the police set up road blocks to prevent the movement of picketing miners.

The police road blocks had two purposes. The first was to prevent miners from leaving their own counties. This was true particularly of the road blocks set up at the Dartford Tunnel to prevent miners from leaving Kent on the way to picket lines in Nottinghamshire. The second purpose was to prevent miners from entering the vicinity of coalfields or other sites for picketing. This is true, for example, of the road blocks set up at the county boundary in Nottinghamshire and those set up to prevent miners from travelling to Hunterston where coal was being brought into the country from overseas. It is to be noted that the police operation led to thousands of people being turned away. Thus, the Chief Constable of Nottinghamshire estimated that 164,508 individuals, whom he described as presumed pickets, were prevented from entering the county in the first 27 weeks of the dispute. An inquiry into the policing of the dispute reported:

"We have received evidence from many people not connected with the dispute, and from miners travelling for purposes unconnected with the dispute, of police officers at road blocks requiring proof of identity and refusing under threat of arrest to allow people to pass; some non-miners have been arrested for obstructing the police in refusing to comply with instructions to turn back. Miners travelling to picket have reported variously being warned that they would be liable to arrest if they proceeded to a pit to picket, or told to turn back on pain of arrest for obstruction. Some have been arrested in these circumstances."

Not surprisingly, the practice was condemned:

"In many cases individuals have been inconvenienced or even prevented from making important journeys because the police did not accept their explanations. This smacks of the Soviet internal passport system or South African pass laws. There have moreover been reports of police officers at roadblocks causing gratuitous damage to pickets' cars. The balance between the liberties of working miners to travel to work and of striking miners to picket has been struck almost entirely in favour of the former, creating among the strikers an understandable impression that they were all assumed to be engaged on an enterprise of violence."

What then is the authority for this quite remarkable power? In England and Wales there was no statutory authority for the practice, though it is almost arguable that the Police and Criminal Evidence Act 1984 conferred such a power, but only from the commencement date, January 1, 1984. this involves a particularly generous construction of sections 4 and 116 of that Act. But even so there was and still is no statutory power authorising the practice in Scotland. So what about the common law? In the House of Commons the Attorney-General said:

"There is no doubt that if a constable reasonably comes to a conclusion that persons are travelling for the purpose of taking part in a picket in circumstances where there is likely to be a breach of the peace, he has the power at common law to call upon them not to continue their journey and to call upon drivers to take them no further. Any person who fails to comply with a police request in those circumstance will be committing the offence of obstructing a police officer in the course of his duty."
(56, H.C. Debs 279-280, 16 March 1984.)

Similarly, according to the Solicitor-General for Scotland:

"the police in Scotland have the authority—where they apprehend that there is the prospect of an offence—to ensure that that offence is not committed, whether it is a breach of the peace, obstruction of the highway or anything else ... they have power to precent the commission of offences, not being restricted simply to acting when an offence has already occurred."
(60, H.C. Debs 358-359, 14 May 1984.)

These views are endorsed by the following decision. Although it is true that it is a decision of the Divisional Court in England, under the Police Act 1964, s. 51(3), it is difficult to believe that a similar result would not be reached in Scotland.

20. Moss v. McLachlan
[1985] I.R.L.R. 76

SKINNER J.: "The judgement I am about to deliver is the judgment of the Court. This is an appeal by way of case stated by four appellants against decisions of the Justices of the Petty Sessional Division of Mansfield in the county of Nottingham. Each appellant was convicted in June of this year of wilfully obstructing a police officer in the execution of his duty on 25 April last contrary to s. 51(3) of the Police Act, 1964 as amended by the Criminal Law Act, 1977. ...

The facts were as follows. On the day in question, as a result of a trade dispute between the National Union of Mineworkers and the National Coal Board, a number of policemen were stationed at Junction 27 of the M1 at Annesley, in the county of Nottingham. The junction is between one-and-a-half and two miles from two collieries which are half a mile apart from one another and between four and five miles from two more collieries, also half a mile apart. The police had reason to believe that striking miners from outside the county were intending to demonstrate and form a mass picket at one or more of the four collieries near to the junction.

The object of the police was to stop cars carrying persons who appeared to be striking miners. Persons who satisfied them that they were not intent on a course of mass picketing were allowed to proceed. The object with the rest was to dissuade them, if possible, from taking part in any demonstration or mass picket and, if persuasion failed, to order them to turn back and prevent them from going further in the direction of the adjacent collieries.

Shortly after 10 a.m. some 25 or more cars arrived at the junction from the north carrying 60 to 80 men who, from their badges and the stickers on their cars, were clearly identifiable as striking miners. These cars were stopped and the occupants were addressed by Inspector Brammar, who was in charge of the police operation. He identified himself to the men and continued: 'I have reason to believe that you are all intent on going to the pits in this county to demonstrate. I have reason to fear a breach of the peace if you continue to the pits, and I am asking you all to turn back. I have a duty at common law to prevent a breach of the peace and the power at common law to act to prevent a breach of the peace. If you continue you will be obstructing an officer in the execution of his duty and therefore liable to arrest.'

The group of men discussed this advice among themselves and then returned to their vehicles and started to drive off. During the discussion the appellant Moss was heard to say: 'We're all agreed then lads. We won't follow the car round and we'll continue on to the pits.' The police had believed that they were going to accede to the request that had been made of them by going around the traffic island and returning north up the motorway. In the event the first car in the convoy driven by the appellant Moss drove right up to a contingent of Surrey officers who had just arrived at the scene and had formed themselves into three cordons, thereby blocking access to the A608 road. The other vehicles drew up close behind one another and eventually a second parallel line of vehicles drew up alongside the first. The exit from the motorway was eventually blocked. The occupants alighted.

They were advised by Inspector Brammar of the danger that the obstruction was causing and requested to remove their vehicles. There was however an impasse of some 35 or 40 minutes during which time the men seemed undecided as to what course of action to follow. During that period angry shouts from the men at passing National Coal Board vehicles and other comments by them made it plain that the police's suspicions that the men were intent on a mass demonstration or picket were justified. Further vehicles arrived during this interlude: the drivers of some were prevailed upon to return north, but others declined the advice.

Eventually the men advanced towards the Surrey officers who were blockading the road. Inspector Brammar shouted to them: 'I have every reason to fear a breach of the peace if you are allowed to continue. If you insist on going on then you are liable to arrest.' The miners' response made it clear that the majority were determined to continue, although one or two expressed reservations about the wisdom of doing so.

The first group to approach the cordon consisted of an estimated 15 men. Police Sergeant Crampton of the Surrey Constabulary gave a warning similar to Inspector Brammar's and added, 'Do you understand?' Several of the men replied 'Yes.' Police Sergeant Crampton continued: 'What do you intend to do—go on or go back?' Several indicated that they were going on, and endeavoured to push their way through the cordon. Those that did so were arrested.

In the upshot some 40 miners who insisted on going on towards the collieries and attempted to force their way through the cordon despite further warnings were arrested on the ground that if they proceeded the police feared a breach of the peace at one of the four collieries. The appellants were four of those arrested, charged, tried and convicted. They were each sentenced to be confined in the precincts of the court until the rising of the court and ordered to pay £30 towards the cost of the prosecution within 28 days of the end of the strike.

The appellants concede that they cannot challenge the magistrates' findings of wilful obstruction by them of the officers named in the charges. However they contend that the police orders to turn back and their subsequent refusal to allow them to pass were unlawful. In reality, they say, the police were restricting their right to freedom of movement. Though the police have a duty to ensure that the peace is kept, they had no power to take the steps they did in this case: their only power was to admonish. In these circumstances the police were not acting in the execution of their duty and the offence accordingly was not proved.

Subject to one submission by Mr Mansfield, to which I shall return later, the law on this subject is clear. If a constable apprehends, on reasonable grounds, that a breach of the peace may be committed, he is not only entitled but is under a duty to take reasonable steps to prevent that breach occurring.

The magistrates concluded that: 'The police honestly and on reasonable grounds feared that there would be a breach of the peace if there were a mass demonstration at whichever Nottinghamshire colliery the appellants and their colleagues chose to congregate.'

The appellants submit that there was no finding of fact by the magistrates to support that conclusion: there was no conduct from which any constable could reasonably have apprehended a breach of the peace. Mr Mansfield submits that the conduct in question must be conduct by the appellants themselves in the presence of the arresting officer, though he concedes that the latter is entitled to take into account the conduct of a group of which the appellants were members. He also contends that the fears must be specific. It is not enough, he says, to fear a breach of the peace at one or more of the collieries involved by some or all of the miners involved. The officer must be able to say which pit, which miners and when.

Mr Milmo replies that a police officer has to look at all the facts within his knowledge. He has the power to act if they raise in his mind a fear that the person or persons he is dealing with may cause a breach of the peace, even if he cannot precisely pinpoint when and where.

On this basis he relies on the magistrates' findings that: (a) there were four pits within five miles of the cordon; (b) over 25 cars carrying over 60 striking miners were involved in the attempt to break through the police cordon; (c) while waiting at the junction, angry shouts from the National Union of Mineworkers members at passing National Coal Board lorries and other comments by them made it plain that the police's suspicions that the men were intent on a mass demonstration or picket were justified; (d) the police suspicions that the gathering of a large picket would lead to a breach of the peace were based on their own experiences in the current and other trade disputes, on the knowledge gleaned from those experiences, from their colleagues and from the widespread public dissemination of the news that there had been severe disruptions of the peace, including many incidents of violence, at collieries within the Nottinghamshire coalfield area in the days and weeks of the dispute before 20.4.84. The officers however had no way of knowing which colliery it was the intention of the miners to picket.

The appellants say this is not enough. The police were not entitled to take into account the experiences of others of what they had heard or read on television or in the press. They could only prevent the men from proceeding if it was clear from the words and deeds of the man at the junction that a breach of the peace was intended.

In our judgement there was ample evidence before the magistrates to support their conclusion. That is enough to dispose of Mr Mansfield's argument that the magistrates here were dealing with action by the police to prevent the appellants from exercising their undoubted right to demonstrate peacefully in order to show support for and solidarity with fellow trade unionists.

On the magistrates' findings of fact anyone with knowledge of the current strike would realise that there was a substantial risk of an outbreak of violence. The mere presence of such a body of men at the junction in question in the context of the current situation in the Nottinghamshire coalfields would have been enough to justify the police in taking preventative action. In reaching their conclusion the police themselves are bound to take into account all they have heard and read and to exercise their judgment and common sense on that material as well as on the events which are taking place before their eyes.

The situation has to be assessed by the senior police officers present. Provided they honestly and reasonably form the opinion that there is a real risk of a breach of the peace in the sense that it is in close proximity both in place and time, then the conditions exist for reasonable preventive acting including, if necessary, the measures taken in this case.

The findings of fact by the magistrates therefore dispel any suggestions that (1) the belief of the officers present was other than honest or reasonable, or (2) that the steps taken were other than reasonable.

But, says Mr Mansfield, the police can only take preventive action if a breach of the peace is imminent and there was no such imminence here. In support of this proposition he relies on a passage in the judgment of Lord Justice Watkins in R. v. Howell [1981] 3 All E.R. 383 at p. 388: '. . . there is a power of arrest for breach of the peace where . . . (2) the arrestor reasonably believes that such a breach will be committed in the immediate future by the person arrested although he has not yet committed any breach. . .'

This passage must be read in the light of the judgment of Lord Parker, Chief Justice, in *Piddington* v. *Bates* [1960] 3 All E.R. 660 at p. 663, in which he says the police must anticipate 'a real, not a remote, possibility' of a breach of the peace before they are justified in taking preventive action.

We do not think that there is any conflict between the two approaches. The possibility of a breach of the peace must be real to justify any preventive action. The imminence or immediacy of the threat to the peace determines what action is reasonable. If the police feared that a convoy of cars travelling toward a working coal field bearing banners and broadcasting, by sight or sound, hostility or threats towards working miners might cause a violent episode, they would be justified in halting the convoy to enquire into its destination and purpose. If, on stopping the vehicles, the police were satisfied that there was a real possibility of the occupants causing a breach of the peace one-and-a-half miles away, a journey of less than five minutes by car, then in our judgment it would be their duty to prevent the convoy from proceeding further and they have the power to do so.

If and in so far as there may be any difference between the two approaches (and we do not believe there is), we respectfully prefer that of Lord Parker, Chief Justice, in *Piddington* v. *Bates*.

We also repeat the words of Lord Parker, Chief Justice, at p. 663 of that case: 'For my part, I think that a police officer charged with the duty of preserving the Queen's peace must be left to take such steps as, on the evidence before him, he thinks proper.'

For the reasons we have given, on the facts found by the magistrates, a breach of the peace was not only a real possibility but also, because of the proximity of the pits and the availability of cars, imminent, immediate and not remote. In our judgment the magistrates were correct in their reasoning and conclusions and we would dismiss these appeals.

The answers to the specific questions posed in the case are:

A. Yes.

B. Yes, it was sufficiently imminent to allow the police to take the steps actually taken in this case.

C. Yes.

D. Yes, on the basis amply supported by the evidence that the four appellants were members of a group which, it was feared, might cause a breach of the peace."

V. REFORM

The combined effect of the different restrictions and offences is that there is very little scope for freedom of assembly in Scots law. Two questions in particular are raised by the material presented so far. The first is the absence of any statutory right of public assembly, which means that those who participate in such activity are exposed to a wide range of statutory and common-law offences. The fact that they have no "right" to participate in activity of this kind means that they have no lawful excuse. The second feature of the present law is the extensive nature of the discretion which it vests in the public authorities.

(1) Local authorities (together with the police) have a wide discretion to ban a march or procession.

(2) Local authorities (together with the police) have a wide discretion to impose conditions on the conduct of a march or procession.

(3) The police have a discretionary power at common law to disperse an

assembly or to prevent it from taking place.

(4) The police have a statutory and common-law right to impose conditions on the conduct of a march, procession or assembly.

(5) The police have a wide discretion to arrest those who participate in a public assembly.

(6) The police have a discretion whether to charge or release an arrested person.

(7) If the police decide to charge, they have a discretion to decide which charge.

These two features of the present law are not unrelated. It is true that, in our view, the major problem at the present time is the second: that is to say the existence of an almost unregulated discretion in the hands of the public authorities and the police. In our view that discretion should be more closely and more carefully regulated and structured by law. This could be done in a number of ways.

(1) The freedom of public assembly should be recognised by statute as a legal right, subject to clearly defined exceptions.

(2) The discretion of the public authorities in the CGSA should be constrained by clear and precise criteria.

(3) The law in this area should be codified, so that there are no common-law offences. The statutory right would be displaced only by statutory limitations and not by common-law manoeuvring.

It is not suggested that these measures would eliminate all police discretion, nor indeed should that discretion be eliminated altogether. They would, however, significantly constrain that discretion, if only by creating a presumption of legality in favour of peaceful activity. The idea of a statutory right of assembly has not, however, won acceptance from the public authorities. In the Green Paper (Home Office, (1981:8-9)) the matter was considered in the following terms:

"24. There is frequent mention in public debate of the 'right to demonstrate.' In fact, our law does not in terms recognise a specific right to demonstrate. This is because the basic assumption in the law is that one is free to do whatever is not specifically prohibited by the law. So while there is in law no specific right to demonstrate, one is certainly free to do so, provided specific provisions of the law (e.g. those relevant to one's conduct while demonstrating) are not contravened.

25. It has been argued that this means that the right to demonstrate is inadequately protected, and that the balance of the law should be redressed by enshrining a statutory right to demonstrate in our law. In particular, it is sometimes said that the law gives undue prominence to the right of passage along the highway, and that it should also recognise a right to stand in the highway provided the rights of passage of others are not thereby infringed. A statutory right to demonstrate might help in this and other respects. Such a statutory right could not, however be absolute and would need to be subject to limitation in the interests of maintaining order. Countries with written constitutions which include protection for freedom of expression and assembly do not regard these rights as unfettered, and articles 10

and 11 of the European Convention on Human Rights, which affirm these rights, include a recognition that they may need to be restricted by law for, among other things, the prevention of disorder or crime and for the protection of the rights and freedom of others.

26. The inclusion in our law of a statutory right to demonstrate would be a novel and uncharted step. In modern times it has not been usual to introduce general rights into the law—as distinct from specific and precisely defined rights (such as rights of appeal and rights to inspect or receive information). The objections that have been made to a statutory right to demonstrate include broad philosophical as well as more practical points. It is argued that it is desirable to maintain the common law tradition under which the citizen has the freedom to do whatever is not prohibited by the law. In this way the boundaries of rights can be known to be as set by long established case law or approved by Parliament and are not open to extensive judicial redefinition. (The general issue of judicial involvement in the merits of decisions, e.g. to ban processions, to which the question of a right to demonstrate is related, is discussed later in this Green Paper.)

27. On the more practical level, it is argued that there would be difficulties in defining the precise boundaries of a right to demonstrate and that the existence of such a right, rather than simplifying the law, would greatly increase its complexity. This uncertainty might pose problems for the police in maintaining order, and increasing the scope for misunderstanding between police and public about what are the actual rights and duties of those who wish to demonstrate.

28. It is also argued that in practice the freedom to demonstrate is adequately recognised under existing law and needs no further protection. It is relevant that in paragraph 134(6) of the Red Lion Square report, Lord Scarman regarded the enactment of a positive right to demonstrate as unnecessary, except as part of any general codification of this branch of the law. 'the right,' he commented, 'of course exists, subject only to limits required by the need for good order and the passage of traffic'."

It may be that this analysis is unsatisfactory to the extent that it exaggerates the difficulties.

AUTHORITIES REFERRED TO IN THE TEXT

Alison, A. (1833): *Principles and Practice of the Criminal Law of Scotland* (vol. ii).

Angus, J. (1922): *Police Powers and Duties* (2nd ed.).

Annan, Lord (Chairman) (1977): *Report of the Committee on the Future of Broadcasting,* Cmnd. 6738.

Anon. (1979): "Interrogation and the Test of Fairness," 1979 S.L.T. (News) 189.

Bailey, S.H., Harris, D.J. and Jones, B.L. (1985): *Civil Liberties: Cases and Materials* (2nd ed.).

Black, R. (1987): "J.P.s, Sheriffs and Official Secrets," 32 J.L.S. 138.

Bradley, A.W. (1987): "Parliamentary Privilege, Zircon and National Security" [1987] P.L. 488.

Bradley, D. Walker, N., and Wilkie, R. (1986): *Managing the Police.*

Christie, D. (1977): "Manner of an Arrest," 1977 S.L.T. (News) 45.

Clive, E.M. (1982): *Husband and Wife* (2nd ed.).

Cockburn, Lord (no date): *Examination of the Trials for Sedition in Scotland* (2 vols.).

Colville, Lord (1987): *Review of the Operation of the Prevention of Terrorism (Temporary Provisions) Act 1984,* Cm. 264.

Commission for Racial Equality (1985): *Review of the Race Relations Act 1976: Proposals for Change.*

Creighton, W.B. (1979): *Working Women and the Law.*

Curran, J.H. and Carnie, J.K. (1986): *Detention or Voluntary Attendance: Police Use of Detention under Section 2, Criminal Justice (Scotland) Act 1980.*

Dicey, A.V. (1908): *Introduction to the study of the Law of the Constitution* (7th ed.).

Diplock, Lord (1981): *The Interception of Communications in Great Britain,* Cmnd. 8191.

Edwards J. (1978): *Positive Discrimination, Social Justice and Social Policy.*

Equal Opportunities Commission (1980): *Fifth Annual Report.*

Finnie, W. (1980): "Arrest," 1980 S.L.T. (News) 201.

Finnie, W. (1981): "Police Powers Falling Short of Arrest," 1987 S.L.T. (News) 173.

Finnie, W. (1981a): "The Burgh Police Acts," 26 J.L.S. 447.

Finnie, W. (1982): "Rights of Persons Detained under the Anti-Terrorist Legislation," 42 M.L.R. 215.

Finnie, W. (1982a): "Police Powers of Search in the Light of *Leckie* v. *Miln*," 1982 S.L.T. (News) 289.

Fleming, I.M. (1984): "Rioting Revived," 1985 S.L.T. (News) 36.

Franks, Lord (Chairman) (1972): *Report of a Departmental Committee on Section 2 of the Official Secrets Act 1911,* Cmnd. 5104.

Godwin, D. (1980): "Controversy," 1980 SCOLAG Bul. 87.

Gordon, G.H. (1978): "Admissibility of Answers to Police Questioning." in Glazebrook (ed.) *Reshaping the Criminal Law.*

Gordon, G.H. (1978a): *The Criminal Law of Scotland* (2nd ed.).

Gordon, G.H. (1981): *The Criminal Justice (Scotland) Act 1980.*

Grampian Police (1980): *Scottish Criminal Law, Police Duties and Procedure, Compiled by Grampian Police for the Scottish Police Service* (13th ed.).

Gray, J.W.R. (1966): "Admissibility of Evidence Illegally Obtained in Scotland," 11 J.R. 89.

Home Office (1981): *Review of the Public Order Act 1936 and Related Legislation,* Cmnd. 7891.

Home Office (1985): The Interception of Communications in the U.K., Cmnd. 9438.

Home Office (1985a): *Review of Public Order Law,* Cmnd. 9510.

Hume, D. (1844): *Commentaries on the Law of Scotland Respecting Crimes* (4th ed., by B.R. Bell).

Hutcheson (1806): *Treatise on the Office of Justice of the Peace, Constable etc.*

Ivamy, E.H.R. (1949): "The Right of Public Meeting" (1949) 2 C.L.P. 183.

Jellicoe (1983): *Review of the Operation of the Prevention of Terrorism (Temporary Provisions) Act 1976,* Cmnd. 8803.

J.T.C. (1969): "Evidence Obtained by Means Considered Irregular," 14 J.R. 55.

Kellas, J. (1984): The Scottish Political System (3rd ed.).

Kenneth, Brother (1965): "The Education (Scotland) Act 1918 in the making," 19 *Innes Review* 91.

Kilbrandon, Lord (Chairman) (1969): *Report of the Committee on the Marriage Law of Scotland,* Cmnd. 4011.

Labour Party Scottish Council (1972): *Report to the Scottish Annual Conference 1972 on Composite Resolution 14 at the 1971 Conference.*

Law Commission (1971): *Report on Polygamous Marriages,* Law Com. No. 42.

Law Commission (1981): *Working Paper No. 79: Offences against Religion and Public Worship.*

Leslie, R.D. (1972): "Polygamous Marriages and Bigamy," 1972 J.R. 113.

Lustgarten, L. (1978): "The New Meaning of Discrimination" [1978] P.L. 178.

Lyall, F. (1980): *Of Presbyters and Kings.*

Maher, G.: "Blasphemy," 1977 S.L.T. (News) 257.

Mill, J. (1944): *The Scottish Police.*

Millar (Chairman) (1972): *Report of a Committee on Moral and Religious Education in Scottish Schools.*

Murdoch, J.L. (1984): "The Civic Government Act and Processions," 1984 SCOLAG Bul.144.

Payne and Ford (1977): "Religion Class and Educational Policy," 9 *Scottish Educational Studies* 83.

Ponting, C. (1985): *The Right to Know: The Inside Story of the Belgrano Affair.*

Poulter, S. (1986): *English Law and Ethnic Minority Customs.*

Renton, R.W. and Brown, H.H. (1972): *Criminal Procedure According to the Law of Scotland* (4th ed. by G.H. Gordon).

Renton, R.W. and Brown, H.H. (1983): *Criminal Procedure According to the Law of Scotland* (5th ed. by G.H. Gordon).

Robilliard, St. J. A. (1984): *Religion and the Law; Religious Liberty in Modern English Law.*

Scarman, Lord (1981): *The Brixton Disorders of 10-12 April 1981,* Cmnd. 8427.

Scarman, Lord (1975): *The Red Lion Square Disorders of 15 June 1974.* Cmnd. 5919.

Scottish Education Department (1943): *Memorandum with Regard to the Provision made for Religious Instruction in the Schools of Scotland,* Cmd. 6426.

Scottish Home and Health Department (1985): *The Tape Recording of Police Interviews with Suspected Persons in Scotland.*

Scottish Law Commission Consultative Memorandum No. 60, *Mobbing and Rioting.*

Scottish Office (1976): *Report of the Working Party on Civic Government.*

Scottish Trades Union Congress (1974): *Annual Report for 1974.*

Taylor, Sir T. (1957): *"Church and State in Scotland"* 73 J.R. 121.

Thomson (Chairman) (1975): *2nd Report of the Committee on Criminal Procedure in Scotland,* Cmnd. 5218.

Thornton, P. (1985): *We Protest.*

Walker, C. (1986): *The Prevention of Terrorism in British Law.*

Wallington, P. (Chairman) (1985): *Civil Liberties and the Miners' Dispute, 1st Report of the Independent Inquiry.*

Wallington, P. (1985a): "Policing the Miners' Strike" (1985) 14 I.L.J. 145.

Williams, B. (Chairman) (1979): *Report of the Committee on Obscenity and Film Censorship,* Cmnd. 7772.

Younger (Chairman) (1972): *Report of the Committee on Privacy,* Cmnd. 5012.

INDEX